S0-ATD-150

General Motors Cars Automotive Repair Manual

Larry Warren
John H Haynes
Guild of Motoring Writers

Covered:

Chevrolet Cavalier, Pontiac J2000 & Sunbird
Buick Skynawk, Oldsmobile Firenza and
Cadillac Cimarron,
1982 through 1992

(12V10 – 766)

ABCDE
FGHIJ
KLMN
2

MEMBER

Haynes Publishing Group
Sparkford Nr Yeovil
Somerset BA22 7JJ England

Haynes North America, Inc
861 Lawrence Drive
Newbury Park
California 91320 USA

Acknowledgements

We are grateful for the help and cooperation of General Motors Corporation for their assistance with technical information, certain illustrations and vehicle photos, and the Champion Spark Plug Company supplied the illustrations of various spark plug conditions.

A book in the **Haynes Automotive Repair Manual Series**

Printed in the U.S.A.

ISBN 1 56392 028 X

Library of Congress Catalog Card Number 92-70522

While every attempt is made to ensure that the information in this manual is correct, no liability can be accepted by the authors or publishers for loss, damage or injury caused by any errors in, or omissions from, the information given.

Contents

1983 Chevrolet Cavalier Type 10

About this manual

Its purpose

The purpose of this manual is to help you get the best value from your vehicle. It can do so in several ways. It can help you decide what work must be done, even if you choose to have it done by a dealer service department or a repair shop; it provides information and procedures for routine maintenance and servicing; and it offers diagnostic and repair procedures to follow when trouble occurs.

It is hoped that you will use the manual to tackle the work yourself. For many simpler jobs, doing it yourself may be quicker than arranging an appointment to get the vehicle into a shop and making the trips to leave it and pick it up. More importantly, a lot of money can be saved by avoiding the expense the shop must pass on to you to cover its labor and overhead costs. An added benefit is the sense of satisfaction and accomplishment that you feel after having done the job yourself.

Using the manual

The manual is divided into Chapters. Each Chapter is divided into numbered Sections, which are headed in bold type between horizontal lines. Each Section consists of consecutively numbered paragraphs.

The two types of illustrations used (figures and photographs), are referenced by a number preceding their caption. Figure reference numbers denote Chapter and numerical sequence within the Chapter; (i.e. Fig. 3.4 means Chapter 3, figure number 4). Figure captions are followed by a Section number which ties the figure to a specific portion of the text. All photographs apply to the Chapter in which they appear and the reference number pinpoints the pertinent Section and paragraph; i.e., 3.2 means Section 3, paragraph 2.

Procedures, once described in the text, are not normally repeated. When it is necessary to refer to another Chapter, the reference will be given as Chapter and Section number i.e. Chapter 1/16). Cross references given without use of the word 'Chapter' apply to Sections and/or paragraphs in the same Chapter. For example, 'see Section 8' means in the same Chapter.

Reference to the left or right side of the vehicle is based on the assumption that one is sitting in the driver's seat, facing forward.

Even though extreme care has been taken during the preparation of this manual, neither the publisher nor the author can accept responsibility for any errors in, or omissions from, the information given.

Introduction to the General Motors J-car

These models are available in convertible, 2-door coupe or liftback, 4-door sedan and station wagon body styles and feature four coil suspension and front wheel drive.

The cross-mounted four-cylinder engine is equipped with fuel injection or a conventional carburetor, as well as turbocharging, depending on model. The engine drives the front wheels through a choice of either a 4-speed or 5-speed manual or a 3-speed automatic transaxle, by way of unequal length driveshafts. The rack and pinion steering gear is mounted behind the engine.

The brakes are disc at the front and drum-type at the rear, with vacuum servo assist as standard equipment

1984 Pontiac J2000 Sunbird convertible

1984 Cavalier 4-door sedan

General dimensions

Overall length . . . .   173 in
Overall width . . . .   66 in
Overall height . . . .   53 in
Wheelbase . . . .   101.2 in

Vehicle identification numbers

Modifications are a continuing and unpublicized process in vehicle manufacturing. Since spare parts manuals and lists are compiled on a numerical basis, the individual vehicle numbers are essential to correctly identify the component required.

Vehicle identification number (VIN)

This very important identification number is located on a plate attached to the top left corner of the dashboard and can easily be seen while looking through the windshield from the outside of the vehicle. The VIN also appears on the Vehicle Certificate of Title and Registration. It contains valuable information such as where and when the vehicle was manufactured, the model year and the body style.

Engine identification numbers

The ID number on the four-cylinder engine is found at the left front side of the engine, on the casting to the rear of the exhaust manifold.

Transaxle numbers

Transaxle ID numbers may be stamped in a variety of locations on pads on either side of the transaxle (refer to the accompanying illustration).

Alternator numbers

The alternator ID number is located on top of the drive end frame.

Starter numbers

The starter ID number is stamped on the outer case, toward the rear.

Battery numbers

The battery ID number is located on the cell cover segment on top of the battery.

Emissions Control Information label

The Emissions Control Information label is attached to the underside of the hood (photo).

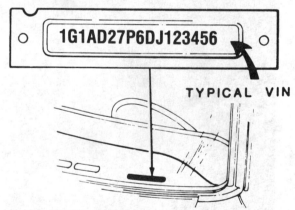

The Vehicle Identification Number (VIN) is located on the driver's side of the dashboard and is visible through the windshield

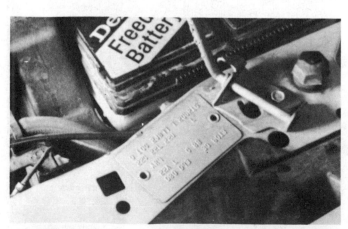

The body identification plate is located on the radiator support

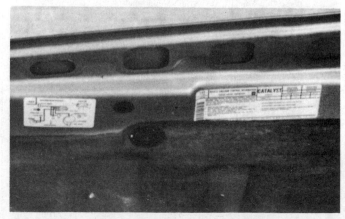

The Emissions Control Information label is attached to the inside of the hood

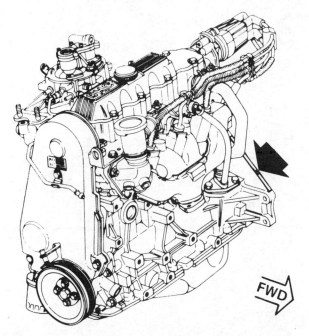

Location of the 1.8 liter OHC engine ID number (arrow)

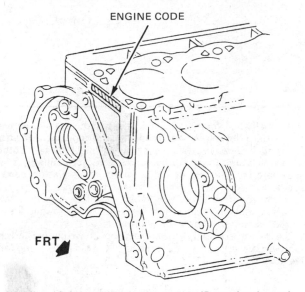

Location of the overhead valve engine ID number (arrow)

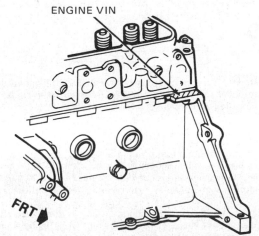

Overhead valve engine VIN number location (arrow)

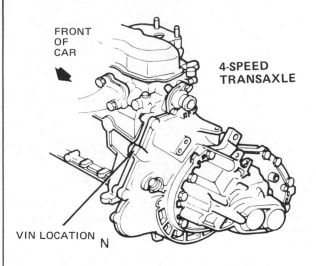

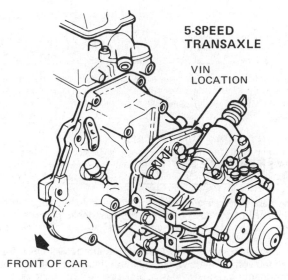

Manual transaxle ID number locations

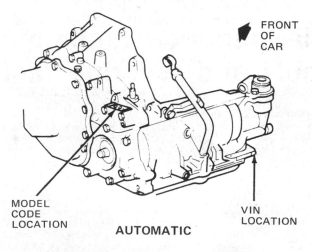

Location of the automatic transaxle ID numbers

Buying parts

Replacement parts are available from many sources, which generally fall into one of two categories – authorized dealer parts departments and independent retail auto parts stores. Our advice concerning these parts is as follows:

Retail auto parts stores: Good auto parts stores will stock frequently needed components which wear out relatively fast, such as clutch components, exhaust systems, brake parts, tune-up parts, etc. These stores often supply new or reconditioned parts on an exchange basis, which can save a considerable amount of money. Discount auto parts stores are often very good places to buy materials and parts needed for general vehicle maintenance such as oil, grease, filters, spark plugs, belts, touch-up paint, bulbs, etc. They also usually sell tools and general accessories, have convenient hours, charge lower prices and can often be found not far from home.

Authorized dealer parts department: This is the best source for parts which are unique to the vehicle and not generally available elsewhere (such as major engine parts, transmission parts, trim pieces, etc.).

Warranty information: If the vehicle is still covered under warranty, be sure that any replacement parts purchased – regardless of the source – do not invalidate the warranty!

To be sure of obtaining the correct parts, have engine and chassis numbers available and, if possible, take the old parts along for positive identification.

Maintenance techniques, tools and working facilities

Maintenance techniques

There are a number of techniques involved in maintenance and repair that will be referred to throughout this manual. Application of these techniques will enable the home mechanic to be more efficient, better organized and capable of performing the various tasks properly, which will ensure that the repair job is thorough and complete.

Fasteners

Fasteners are nuts, bolts, studs and screws used to hold two or more parts together. There are a few things to keep in mind when working with fasteners. Almost all of them use a locking device of some type, either a lock washer, locknut, locking tab or thread adhesive. All threaded fasteners should be clean and straight, with undamaged threads and undamaged corners on the hex head where the wrench fits. Develop the habit of replacing all damaged nuts and bolts with new ones. Special locknuts with nylon or fiber inserts can only be used once. If they are removed, they lose their locking ability and must be replaced with new ones.

Rusted nuts and bolts should be treated with a penetrating fluid to ease removal and prevent breakage. Some mechanics use turpentine in a spout-type oil can, which works quite well. After applying the rust penetrant, let it "work" for a few minutes before trying to loosen the nut or bolt. Badly rusted fasteners may have to be chiseled or sawed off or removed with a special nut breaker, available at tool stores.

If a bolt or stud breaks off in an assembly, it can be drilled and removed with a special tool commonly available for this purpose. Most automotive machine shops can perform this task, as well as other repair procedures (such as repair of threaded holes that have been stripped out).

Flat washers and lock washers, when removed from an assembly, should always be replaced exactly as removed. Replace any damaged washers with new ones. Always use a flat washer between a lock washer and any soft metal surface (such as aluminum), thin sheet metal or plastic.

Fastener sizes

For a number of reasons, automobile manufacturers are making wider and wider use of metric fasteners. Therefore, it is important to be able to tell the difference between standard (sometimes called U.S., English or SAE) and metric hardware, since they cannot be interchanged.

All bolts, whether standard or metric, are sized according to diameter, thread pitch and length. For example, a standard 1/2 — 13 x 1 bolt is 1/2 inch in diameter, has 13 threads per inch and is 1 inch long. An M12 — 1.75 x 25 metric bolt is 12 mm in diameter, has a thread pitch of 1.75 mm (the distance between threads) and is 25 mm long. The two bolts are nearly identical, and easily confused, but they are not interchangeable.

In addition to the differences in diameter, thread pitch and length, metric and standard bolts can also be distinguished by examining the bolt heads. To begin with, the distance across the flats on a standard bolt head is measured in inches, while the same dimension on a metric bolt is measured in millimeters (the same is true for nuts). As a result,

a standard wrench should not be used on a metric bolt and a metric wrench should not be used on a standard bolt. Also, most standard bolts have slashes radiating out from the center of the head to denote the grade or strength of the bolt (which is an indication of the amount of torque that can be applied to it). The greater the number of slashes, the greater the strength of the bolt (grades 0 through 5 are commonly used on automobiles). Metric bolts have a property class (grade) number, rather than a slash, molded into their heads to indicate bolt strength. In this case, the higher the number, the stronger the bolt (property class numbers 8.8, 9.8 and 10.9 are commonly used on automobiles).

Strength markings can also be used to distinguish standard hex nuts from metric hex nuts. Many standard nuts have dots stamped into one side, while metric nuts are marked with a number. The greater the number of dots, or the higher the number, the greater the strength of the nut.

Metric studs are also marked on their ends according to property class (grade). Larger studs are numbered (the same as metric bolts),

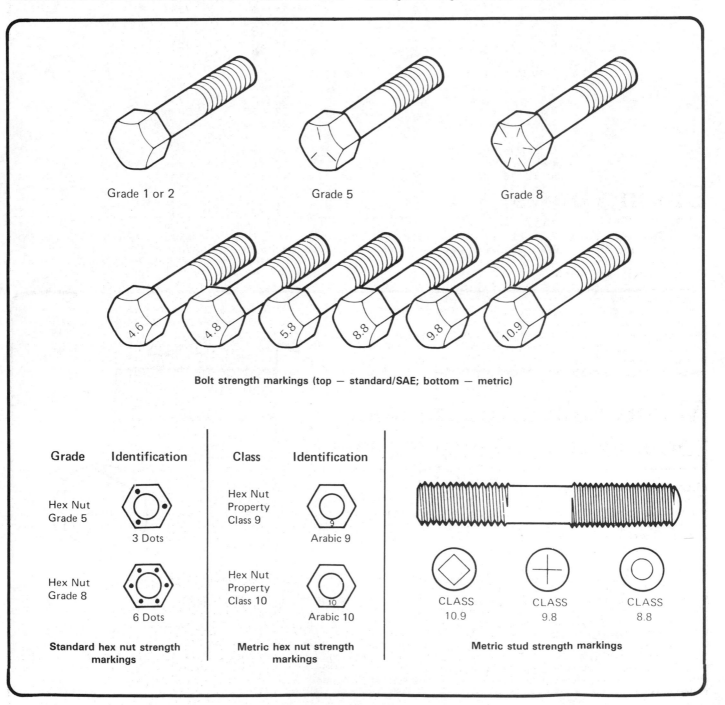

Grade 1 or 2   Grade 5   Grade 8

4.6   4.8   5.8   8.8   9.8   10.9

Bolt strength markings (top — standard/SAE; bottom — metric)

Grade	Identification
Hex Nut Grade 5	3 Dots
Hex Nut Grade 8	6 Dots

Standard hex nut strength markings

Class	Identification
Hex Nut Property Class 9	Arabic 9
Hex Nut Property Class 10	Arabic 10

Metric hex nut strength markings

CLASS 10.9   CLASS 9.8   CLASS 8.8

Metric stud strength markings

while smaller studs carry a geometric code to denote grade.

It should be noted that many fasteners, especially Grades 0 through 2, have no distinguishing marks on them. When such is the case, the only way to determine whether it is standard or metric is to measure the thread pitch or compare it to a known fastener of the same size.

Standard fasteners are often referred to as SAE, as opposed to metric. However, it should be noted that SAE technically refers to a non-metric *fine thread* fastener only. Coarse thread non-metric fasteners are referred to as USS sizes.

Since fasteners of the same size (both standard and metric) may have different strength ratings, be sure to reinstall any bolts, studs or nuts removed from your vehicle in their original locations. Also, when replacing a fastener with a new one, make sure that the new one has a strength rating equal to or greater than the original.

Tightening sequences and procedures

Most threaded fasteners should be tightened to a specific torque value (torque is a twisting force). Over-tightening the fastener can weaken it and cause it to break, while under-tightening can cause it to eventually come loose. Bolts, screws and studs, depending on the material they are made of and their thread diameters, have specific torque values (many of which are noted in the Specifications at the beginning of each Chapter). Be sure to follow the torque recommendations closely. For fasteners not assigned a specific torque, a general torque value chart is presented here as a guide. As was previously mentioned, the size and grade of a fastener determine the amount of torque that can safely be applied to it. The figures listed here are approximate for Grade 2 and Grade 3 fasteners (higher grades can tolerate higher torque values).

Metric thread sizes	Ft-lb	Nm
M-6	6 to 9	9 to 12
M-8	14 to 21	19 to 28
M-10	28 to 40	38 to 54
M-12	50 to 71	68 to 96
M-14	80 to 140	109 to 154

Pipe thread sizes		
1/8	5 to 8	7 to 10
1/4	12 to 18	17 to 24
3/8	22 to 33	30 to 44
1/2	25 to 35	34 to 47

U.S. thread sizes		
1/4 — 20	6 to 9	9 to 12
5/16 — 18	12 to 18	17 to 24
5/16 — 24	14 to 20	19 to 27
3/8 — 16	22 to 32	30 to 43
3/8 — 24	27 to 38	37 to 51
7/16 — 14	40 to 55	55 to 74
7/16 — 20	40 to 60	55 to 81
1/2 — 13	55 to 80	75 to 108

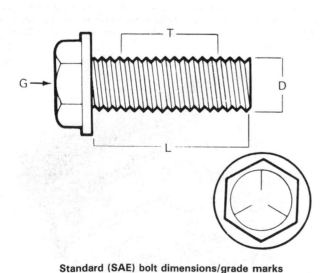

Standard (SAE) bolt dimensions/grade marks

G — Grade marks (bolt strength)
L — Length (in inches)
T — Thread pitch (number of threads per inch)
D — Nominal diameter (in inches)

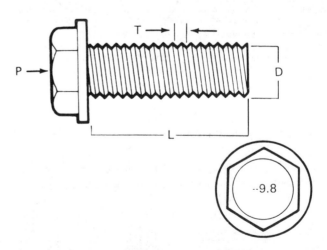

Metric bolt dimensions/grade marks

P — Property class (bolt strength)
L — Length (in millimeters)
T — Thread pitch (distance between threads; in millimeters)

Fasteners laid out in a pattern (i.e. cylinder head bolts, oil pan bolts, differential cover bolts, etc.) must be loosened or tightened in a sequence to avoid warping the component. This sequence will normally be shown in the appropriate Chapter. If a specific pattern is not given, the following procedures can be used to prevent warping. Initially, the bolts or nuts should be assembled finger-tight only. Next, they should be tightened one full turn each, in a crisscross or diagonal pattern. After each one has been tightened one full turn, return to the first one and tighten them all one-half turn, following the same pattern. Finally, tighten each of them one-quarter turn at a time until each fastener has been tightened to the proper torque. To loosen and remove the fasteners, the procedure would be reversed.

Component disassembly

Component disassembly should be done with care and purpose to help ensure that the parts go back together properly. Always keep track of the sequence in which parts are removed. Make note of special characteristics or marks on parts that can be installed more than one way (such as a grooved thrust washer on a shaft). It is a good idea to lay the disassembled parts out on a clean surface in the order that they were removed. It may also be helpful to make sketches or take instant photos of components before removal.

When removing fasteners from a component, keep track of their locations. Sometimes threading a bolt back in a part, or putting the washers and nut back on a stud, can prevent mix-ups later. If nuts and bolts cannot be returned to their original locations, they should be kept in a compartmented box or a series of small boxes. A cupcake or muffin tin is ideal for this purpose, since each cavity can hold the bolts and nuts from a particular area (i.e. oil pan bolts, valve cover bolts, engine mount bolts, etc.). A pan of this type is especially helpful when working on assemblies with very small parts, such as the carburetor, alternator, valve train or interior dash and trim pieces. The cavities can be marked with paint or tape to identify the contents.

Whenever wiring looms, harnesses or connectors are separated, it's a good idea to identify the two halves with numbered pieces of masking tape so they can be easily reconnected.

Gasket sealing surfaces

Throughout any vehicle, gaskets are used to seal the mating surfaces between two parts and keep lubricants, fluids, vacuum or pressure contained in an assembly.

Many times these gaskets are coated with a liquid or paste-type gasket sealing compound before assembly. Age, heat and pressure can sometimes cause the two parts to stick together so tightly that they are very difficult to separate. Often, the assembly can be loosened by striking it with a soft-faced hammer near the mating surfaces. A regular hammer can be used if a block of wood is placed between the hammer and the part. Do not hammer on cast parts or parts that could be easily damaged. With any particularly stubborn part, always recheck to make sure that every fastener has been removed.

Avoid using a screwdriver or bar to pry apart an assembly, as they can easily mar the gasket sealing surfaces of the parts (which must remain smooth). If prying is absolutely necessary, use an old broom handle, but keep in mind that extra clean-up will be necessary if the wood splinters.

After the parts are separated, the old gasket must be carefully scraped off and the gasket surfaces cleaned. Stubborn gasket material can be soaked with rust penetrant or treated with a special chemical to soften it so it can be easily scraped off. A scraper can be fashioned from a piece of copper tubing by flattening and sharpening one end. Copper is recommended because it is usually softer than the surfaces to be scraped, which reduces the chance of gouging the part. Some gaskets can be removed with a wire brush, but regardless of the method used, the mating surfaces must be left clean and smooth. If for some reason the gasket surface is gouged, then a gasket sealer thick enough to fill scratches will have to be used during reassembly of the components. For most applications, a non-drying (or semi-drying) gasket sealer should be used.

Hose removal tips

Caution: *If the vehicle is equipped with air conditioning, do not disconnect any of the A/C hoses without first having the system depressurized by a dealer service department or an air conditioning specialist.*

Hose removal precautions closely parallel gasket removal precautions. Avoid scratching or gouging the surface that the hose mates against or the connection may leak. This is especially true for radiator hoses. Because of various chemical reactions, the rubber in hoses can bond itself to the metal spigot that the hose fits over. To remove a hose, first loosen the hose clamps that secure it to the spigot. Then, with slip-joint pliers, grab the hose at the clamp and rotate it around the spigot. Work it back and forth until it is completely free, then pull it off. Silicone or other lubricants will ease removal if they can be applied between the hose and the outside of the spigot. Apply the same lubricant to the inside of the hose and the outside of the spigot to simplify installation.

As a last resort (and if the hose is to be replaced with a new one anyway), the rubber can be slit with a knife and the hose peeled from the spigot. If this must be done, be careful that the metal connection is not damaged.

If a hose clamp is broken or damaged, do not reuse it. Wire-type clamps usually weaken with age, so it is a good idea to replace them with screw-type clamps whenever a hose is removed.

Tools

A selection of good tools is a basic requirement for anyone who plans to maintain and repair his or her own vehicle. For the owner who has few tools, if any, the initial investment might seem high, but when compared to the spiraling costs of professional auto maintenance and repair, it is a wise one.

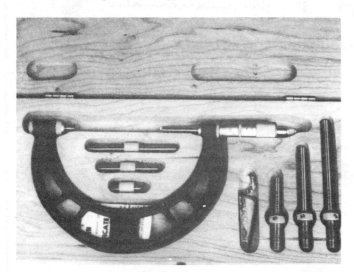

Micrometer set

Dial indicator set

Dial caliper

Hydraulic lifter removal tool

Universal-type puller

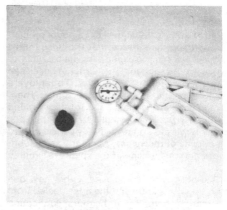

Hand-operated vacuum pump

Piston ring groove cleaning tool

Piston ring compressor

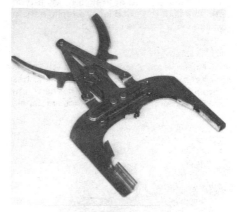

Piston ring removal/installation tool

Cylinder ridge reamer

Cylinder surfacing hone

Cylinder bore gauge

Brake shoe spring tool

Valve spring compressor

To help the owner decide which tools are needed to perform the tasks detailed in this manual, the following tool lists are offered: *Maintenance and minor repair, Repair and overhaul* and *Special*. The newcomer to practical mechanics should start off with the *Maintenance and minor repair tool kit*, which is adequate for the simpler jobs performed on a vehicle. Then, as confidence and experience grow, the owner can tackle more difficult tasks, buying additional tools as they are needed. Eventually the basic kit will be expanded into the *Repair and overhaul tool set*. Over a period of time, the experienced do-it-yourselfer will assemble a tool set complete enough for most repair and overhaul procedures and will add tools from the *Special* category when it is felt that the expense is justified by the frequency of use.

Maintenance and minor repair tool kit

The tools in this list should be considered the minimum required for performance of routine maintenance, servicing and minor repair work. We recommend the purchase of combination wrenches (box-end and open-end combined in one wrench); while more expensive than open-ended ones, they offer the advantages of both types of wrench.

> *Combination wrench set (1/4 in to 1 in or 6 mm to 19 mm)*
> *Adjustable wrench — 8 in*
> *Spark plug wrench (with rubber insert)*
> *Spark plug gap adjusting tool*
> *Feeler gauge set*
> *Brake bleeder wrench*
> *Standard screwdriver (5/16 in x 6 in)*
> *Phillips screwdriver (No. 2 x 6 in)*
> *Combination pliers — 6 in*
> *Hacksaw and assortment of blades*
> *Tire pressure gauge*
> *Grease gun*
> *Oil can*
> *Fine emery cloth*
> *Wire brush*
> *Battery post and cable cleaning tool*
> *Oil filter wrench*
> *Funnel (medium size)*
> *Safety goggles*
> *Jackstands (2)*
> *Drain pan*

Note: *If basic tune-ups are going to be part of routine maintenance, it will be necessary to purchase a good quality stroboscopic timing light and combination tachometer/dwell meter. Although they are included in the list of Special tools, it is mentioned here because they are absolutely necessary for tuning most vehicles properly.*

Repair and overhaul tool set

These tools are essential for anyone who plans to perform major repairs and are in addition to those in the *Maintenance and minor repair tool kit*. Included is a comprehensive set of sockets which, though expensive, are invaluable because of their versatility (especially when various extensions and drives are available). We recommend the 1/2-inch drive over the 3/8-inch drive. Although the larger drive is bulky and more expensive, it has the capacity of accepting a very wide range of large sockets (ideally, the mechanic would have a 3/8-inch drive set and a 1/2-inch drive set).

> *Socket set(s)*
> *Reversible ratchet*
> *Extension — 10 in*
> *Universal joint*
> *Torque wrench (same size drive as sockets)*
> *Ball peen hammer — 8 oz*
> *Soft-faced hammer (plastic/rubber)*
> *Standard screwdriver (1/4 in x 6 in)*
> *Standard screwdriver (stubby — 5/16 in)*
> *Phillips screwdriver (No. 3 x 8 in)*
> *Phillips screwdriver (stubby — No. 2)*
> *Pliers — vise grip*
> *Pliers — lineman's*
> *Pliers — needle nose*
> *Pliers — snap-ring (internal and external)*
> *Cold chisel — 1/2 in*
> *Scriber*
> *Scraper (made from flattened copper tubing)*
> *Center punch*
> *Pin punches (1/16, 1/8, 3/16 in)*
> *Steel rule/straightedge — 12 in*
> *Allen wrench set (1/8 to 3/8 in or 4 mm to 10 mm)*
> *A selection of files*
> *Wire brush (large)*
> *Jackstands (second set)*
> *Jack (scissor or hydraulic type)*

Note: *Another tool which is often useful is an electric drill motor (with a chuck capacity of 3/8-inch) and a set of good-quality drill bits.*

Special tools

The tools in this list include those which are not used regularly, are expensive to buy, or which need to be used in accordance with their manufacturer's instructions. Unless these tools will be used frequently, it is not very economical to purchase many of them. A consideration would be to split the cost and use between yourself and a friend or friends. In addition, most of these tools can be obtained from a tool rental shop on a temporary basis.

This list contains only those tools and instruments widely available to the public, and not those special tools produced by the vehicle manufacturer for distribution to dealer service departments. Occasionally, references to the manufacturer's special tools are included in the text of this manual. Generally, an alternative method of doing the job without the special tool is offered. However, sometimes there is no alternative to their use. Where this is the case, and the tool cannot be purchased or borrowed, the work should be turned over to the dealer service department or an automotive repair shop.

> *Valve spring compressor*
> *Piston ring groove cleaning tool*
> *Piston ring compressor*
> *Piston ring installation tool*
> *Cylinder compression gauge*
> *Cylinder ridge reamer*
> *Cylinder surfacing hone*
> *Cylinder bore gauge*
> *Micrometer(s) and/or dial calipers*
> *Hydraulic lifter removal tool*
> *Balljoint separator*
> *Universal-type puller*
> *Impact screwdriver*
> *Dial indicator set*
> *Stroboscopic timing light (inductive pick-up)*
> *Hand-operated vacuum/pressure pump*
> *Tachometer/dwell meter*
> *Universal electrical multimeter*
> *Cable hoist*
> *Brake spring removal and installation tools*
> *Floor jack*

Buying tools

For the do-it-yourselfer who is just starting to get involved in vehicle maintenance and repair, there are a number of options available when purchasing tools. If maintenance and minor repair is the extent of the work to be done, the purchase of individual tools is satisfactory. If, on the other hand, extensive work is planned, it would be a good idea to purchase a modest tool set from one of the large retail chain stores. A set can usually be bought at a substantial savings over the individual tool prices (and they often come with a tool box). As additional tools are needed, add-on sets, individual tools and a larger tool box can be purchased to expand the tool selection. Building a tool set gradually allows the cost of the tools to be spread over a longer period of time and gives the mechanic the freedom to choose only those tools that will actually be used.

Tool stores will often be the only source of some of the special tools that are needed, but regardless of where tools are bought, try to avoid cheap ones (especially when buying screwdrivers and sockets) because they won't last very long. The expense involved in replacing cheap tools will eventually be greater than the initial cost of quality tools.

Care and maintenance of tools

Good tools are expensive, so it makes sense to treat them with respect. Keep them clean and in usable condition and store them properly when not in use. Always wipe off any dirt, grease or metal chips before putting them away. Never leave tools lying around in the work area. Upon completion of a job, always check closely under the hood for tools that may have been left there (so they don't get lost during a test drive).

Some tools, such as screwdrivers, pliers, wrenches and sockets, can be hung on a panel mounted on the garage or workshop wall, while others should be kept in a tool box or tray. Measuring instruments, gauges, meters, etc. must be carefully stored where they cannot be damaged by weather or impact from other tools.

When tools are used with care and stored properly, they will last a very long time. Even with the best of care, tools will wear out if used frequently. When a tool is damaged or worn out, replace it; subsequent jobs will be safer and more enjoyable if you do.

Working facilities

Not to be overlooked when discussing tools is the workshop. If anything more than routine maintenance is to be carried out, some sort of suitable work area is essential.

It is understood, and appreciated, that many home mechanics do not have a good workshop or garage available and end up removing an engine or doing major repairs outside. It is recommended, however, that the overhaul or repair be completed under the cover of a roof.

A clean, flat workbench or table of comfortable working height is an absolute necessity. The workbench should be equipped with a vise that has a jaw opening of at least four inches.

As mentioned previously, some clean, dry storage space is also required for tools, as well as the lubricants, fluids, cleaning solvents, etc. which soon become necessary.

Sometimes waste oil and fluids, drained from the engine or cooling system during normal maintenance or repairs, present a disposal problem. To avoid pouring them on the ground or into a sewage system, simply pour the used fluids into large containers, seal them with caps and take them to an authorized disposal site or recycling center. Plastic jugs (such as old antifreeze containers) are ideal for this purpose.

Always keep a supply of old newspapers and clean rags available. Old towels are excellent for mopping up spills. Many mechanics use rolls of paper towels for most work because they are readily available and disposable. To help keep the area under the vehicle clean, a large cardboard box can be cut open and flattened to protect the garage or shop floor.

Whenever working over a painted surface (such as when leaning over a fender to service something under the hood), always cover it with an old blanket or bedspread to protect the finish. Vinyl covered pads, made especially for this purpose, are available at auto parts stores.

Booster battery (jump) starting

Certain precautions must be observed when using a booster battery to 'jump start' a vehicle.

a) Before connecting the booster battery, make sure that the ignition switch is in the Off position.
b) Turn off the lights, heater and other electrical loads.
c) The eyes should be shielded; safety goggles are a good idea.
d) Make sure the booster battery is the same voltage as the dead one in the vehicle.
e) The two vehicles must not touch each other.
f) Make sure the transmission is in Neutral (manual transmission) or Park (automatic transmission).

Connect the red jumper cable to the *positive* (+) terminals of each battery.

Connect one end of the black jumper cable to the *negative* (–) terminal of the booster battery. The other end of this cable should be connected to a good ground on the vehicle to be started, such as a bolt or bracket on the engine block. Use caution to ensure that the cables will not come into contact with the fan, drivebelts or other moving parts of the engine.

Start the engine using the booster battery, then, with the engine running at idle speed, disconnect the jumper cables in the reverse order of connection.

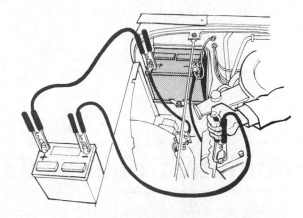

Booster battery cable connections (note that the negative cable is *NOT* attached to the negative terminal of the dead battery)

Jacking and towing

Jacking

The jack supplied with the vehicle should only be used for raising the vehicle when changing a tire or placing jackstands under the frame. **Caution:** *Never work under the vehicle or start the engine while this jack is being used as the only means of support.*

The vehicle should be on level ground with the wheels blocked and the transmission in Park (automatic) or Reverse (manual). Pry off the hub cap (if equipped) using the tapered end of the lug wrench. Loosen the wheel nuts one-half turn and leave them in place until the wheel is raised off the ground.

Place the jack under the side of the vehicle in the indicated position and place the jack lever in the 'up' position. Raise the jack until the jack head groove fits into the rocker flange notch. Operate the jack with a slow, smooth motion, using your hand or foot to pump the handle until the wheel is raised off the ground. Remove the wheel nuts, pull off the wheel and replace it with the spare. (If you have a stowaway spare, refer to the instructions accompanying the supplied inflator.)

With the beveled side in, replace the wheel nuts and tighten them until snug. Place the jack lever in the 'down' position and lower the vehicle. Remove the jack and tighten the nuts in a crisscross sequence by turning the wrench clockwise. Replace the hub cap (if equipped) by placing it into position and using the heel of your hand or a rubber mallet to seat it.

Towing

The vehicle can be towed with all four wheels on the ground, provided that speeds do not exceed 35 mph and the distance is not over 50 miles, otherwise transmission damage can result.

Towing equipment specifically designed for this purpose should be used and should be attached to the main structural members of the vehicle and not the bumper or brackets.

Safety is a major consideration when towing and all applicable state and local laws must be obeyed. A safety chain system must be used for all towing.

While towing, the parking brake should be released and the transmission should be in Neutral. The steering must be unlocked (ignition switch in the Off position). Remember that power steering and power brakes will not work with the engine off.

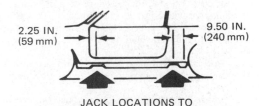

Location of the rocker panel flange notches used for jack placement (!eft side shown, right side similar)

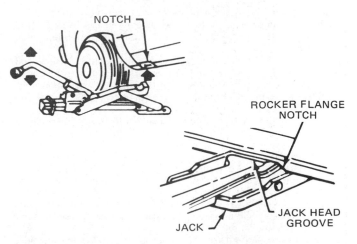

Placement and operation of the jack for tire changing (left) and details of matching the jack head groove-to-rocker panel flange notch (right)

Automotive chemicals and lubricants

A number of automotive chemicals and lubricants are available for use during vehicle maintenance and repair. They include a wide variety of products ranging from cleaning solvents and degreasers to lubricants and protective sprays for rubber, plastic and vinyl.

Contact point/spark plug cleaner is a solvent used to clean oily film and dirt from points, grime from electrical connectors and oil deposits from spark plugs. It is oil free and leaves no residue. It can also be used to remove gum and varnish from carburetor jets and other orifices.

Carburetor cleaner is similar to contact point/spark plug cleaner but it is a stronger solvent and may leave a slight oily residue. It is not recommended for cleaning electrical components or connections.

Brake system cleaner is used to remove grease or brake fluid from brake system components where clean surfaces are absolutely necessary and petroleum-based solvents cannot be used. It also leaves no residue.

Silicone-based lubricants are used to protect rubber parts such as hoses, weatherstripping and grommets, and are used as lubricants for hinges and locks.

Multi-purpose grease is an all-purpose lubricant used wherever grease is more practical than a liquid lubricant such as oil. Some multi-purpose grease is white and specially formulated to be more resistant to water than ordinary grease.

Bearing grease/wheel bearing grease is a heavy grease used where increased loads and friction are encountered (i.e. wheel bearings, universal joints, etc.).

High-temperature wheel bearing grease is designed to withstand the extreme temperatures encountered by wheel bearings in disc-brake equipped vehicles. It usually contains molybdenum disulfide, which is a 'dry' type lubricant.

Gear oil (sometimes called gear lube) is a specially designed oil used in differentials, manual transmissions and transfer cases, as well as other areas where high-friction, high-temperature lubrication is required. It is available in a number of viscosities (weights) for various applications.

Motor oil, of course, is the lubricant specially formulated for use in engines. It normally contains a wide variety of additives to prevent corrosion and reduce foaming and wear. Motor oil comes in various weights (viscosity ratings) of from 5 to 80. The recommended weight of the oil depends on the seasonal temperature and the demands on the engine. Light oil is used in cold climates and under light load conditions; heavy oil is used in hot climates and where high loads are encountered. Multi-viscosity oils are designed to have characteristics of both light and heavy oils and are available in a number of weights from 5W-20 to 20W-50.

Oil additives range from viscosity index improvers to slick chemical treatments that purportedly reduce friction. It should be noted that most oil manufacturers caution against using additives with their oils.

Gas additives perform several functions, depending on their chemical makeup. They usually contain solvents that help dissolve gum and varnish that build up on carburetor and intake parts. They also serve to break down carbon deposits that form on the inside surfaces of the combustion chambers. Some additives contain upper cylinder lubricants for valves and piston rings.

Brake fluid is a specially formulated hydraulic fluid that can withstand the heat and pressure encountered in brake systems. Care must be taken that this fluid does not come in contact with painted surfaces or plastics. An opened container should always be resealed to prevent contamination by water or dirt.

Undercoating is a petroleum-based, tar-like substance that is designed to protect metal surfaces on the underside of a vehicle from corrosion. It also acts as a sound-deadening agent by insulating the bottom of the vehicle.

Weatherstrip cement is used to bond weatherstripping around doors, windows and trunk lids. It is sometimes used to attach trim pieces as well.

Degreasers are heavy-duty solvents used to remove grease and grime that may accumulate on engine and chassis components. They can be sprayed or brushed on and, depending on the type, are rinsed off with either water or solvent.

Solvents are used alone or in combination with degreasers to clean parts and assemblies during repair and overhaul. The home mechanic should use only solvents that are non-flammable and that do not produce irritating fumes.

Gasket sealing compounds may be used in conjunction with gaskets, to improve their sealing capabilities, or alone, to seal metal-to-metal joints. Many gasket sealers can withstand extreme heat, some are impervious to gasoline and lubricants, while others are capable of filling and sealing large cavities. Depending on the intended use, gasket sealers either dry hard or stay relatively soft and pliable. They are usually applied by hand, with a brush, or are sprayed on the gasket sealing surfaces.

Thread cement is an adhesive locking compound that prevents threaded fasteners from loosening because of vibration. It is available in a variety of types for different applications.

Moisture dispersants are usually sprays that can be used to dry out electrical components such as the distributor, fuse block and wiring connectors. Some types can also be used as treatment for rubber and as a lubricant for hinges, cables and locks.

Waxes and polishes are used to help protect painted and plated surfaces from the weather. Different types of paint may require the use of different types of wax polish. Some polishes utilize a chemical or abrasive cleaner to help remove the top layer of oxidized (dull) paint on older vehicles. In recent years many non-wax polishes that contain a wide variety of chemicals such as polymers and silicones have been introduced. These non-wax polishes are usually easier to apply and last longer than conventional waxes and polishes.

Safety first!

Regardless of how enthusiastic you may be about getting on with the job at hand, take the time to ensure that your safety is not jeopardized. A moment's lack of attention can result in an accident, as can failure to observe certain simple safety precautions. The possibility of an accident will always exist, and the following points should not be considered a comprehensive list of all dangers. Rather, they are intended to make you aware of the risks and to encourage a safety conscious approach to all work you carry out on your vehicle.

Essential DOs and DON'Ts

DON'T rely on a jack when working under the vehicle. Always use approved jackstands to support the weight of the vehicle and place them under the recommended lift or support points.

DON'T attempt to loosen extremely tight fasteners (i.e. wheel lug nuts) while the vehicle is on a jack — it may fall.

DON'T start the engine without first making sure that the transmission is in Neutral (or Park where applicable) and the parking brake is set.

DON'T remove the radiator cap from a hot cooling system — let it cool or cover it with a cloth and release the pressure gradually.

DON'T attempt to drain the engine oil until you are sure it has cooled to the point that it will not burn you.

DON'T touch any part of the engine or exhaust system until it has cooled sufficiently to avoid burns.

DON'T siphon toxic liquids such as gasoline, antifreeze and brake fluid by mouth, or allow them to remain on your skin.

DON'T inhale brake lining dust — it is potentially hazardous (see *Asbestos* below)

DON'T allow spilled oil or grease to remain on the floor — wipe it up before someone slips on it.

DON'T use loose fitting wrenches or other tools which may slip and cause injury.

DON'T push on wrenches when loosening or tightening nuts or bolts. Always try to pull the wrench toward you. If the situation calls for pushing the wrench away, push with an open hand to avoid scraped knuckles if the wrench should slip.

DON'T attempt to lift a heavy component alone — get someone to help you.

DON'T rush or take unsafe shortcuts to finish a job.

DON'T allow children or animals in or around the vehicle while you are working on it.

DO wear eye protection when using power tools such as a drill, sander, bench grinder, etc. and when working under a vehicle.

DO keep loose clothing and long hair well out of the way of moving parts.

DO make sure that any hoist used has a safe working load rating adequate for the job.

DO get someone to check on you periodically when working alone on a vehicle.

DO carry out work in a logical sequence and make sure that everything is correctly assembled and tightened.

DO keep chemicals and fluids tightly capped and out of the reach of children and pets.

DO remember that your vehicle's safety affects that of yourself and others. If in doubt on any point, get professional advice.

Asbestos

Certain friction, insulating, sealing, and other products — such as brake linings, brake bands, clutch linings, torque converters, gaskets, etc. — contain asbestos. *Extreme care must be taken to avoid inhalation of dust from such products since it is hazardous to health.* If in doubt, assume that they *do* contain asbestos.

Fire

Remember at all times that gasoline is highly flammable. Never smoke or have any kind of open flame around when working on a vehicle. But the risk does not end there. A spark caused by an electrical short circuit, by two metal surfaces contacting each other, or even by static electricity built up in your body under certain conditions, can ignite gasoline vapors, which in a confined space are highly explosive. Do not, under any circumstances, use gasoline for cleaning parts. Use an approved safety solvent.

Always disconnect the battery ground (−) cable *at the battery* before working on any part of the fuel system or electrical system. Never risk spilling fuel on a hot engine or exhaust component.

It is strongly recommended that a fire extinguisher suitable for use on fuel and electrical fires be kept handy in the garage or workshop at all times. Never try to extinguish a fuel or electrical fire with water.

Fumes

Certain fumes are highly toxic and can quickly cause unconsciousness and even death if inhaled to any extent. Gasoline vapor falls into this category, as do the vapors from some cleaning solvents. Any draining or pouring of such volatile fluids should be done in a well ventilated area.

When using cleaning fluids and solvents, read the instructions on the container carefully. Never use materials from unmarked containers.

Never run the engine in an enclosed space, such as a garage. Exhaust fumes contain carbon monoxide, which is extremely poisonous. If you need to run the engine, always do so in the open air, or at least have the rear of the vehicle outside the work area.

If you are fortunate enough to have the use of an inspection pit, never drain or pour gasoline and never run the engine while the vehicle is over the pit. The fumes, being heavier than air, will concentrate in the pit with possibly lethal results.

The battery

Never create a spark or allow a bare light bulb near a battery. They normally give off a certain amount of hydrogen gas, which is highly explosive.

Always disconnect the battery ground (−) cable *at the battery* before working on the fuel or electrical systems.

If possible, loosen the filler caps or cover when charging the battery from an external source (this does not apply to sealed or maintenance-free batteries). Do not charge at an excessive rate or the battery may burst.

Take care when adding water to a non maintenance-free battery and when carrying a battery. The electrolyte, even when diluted, is very corrosive and should not be allowed to contact clothing or skin.

Always wear eye protection when cleaning the battery to prevent the caustic deposits from entering your eyes.

Household current

When using an electric power tool, inspection light, etc., which operates on household current, always make sure that the tool is correctly connected to its plug and that, where necessary, it is properly grounded. Do not use such items in damp conditions, and, again, do not create a spark or apply excessive heat in the vicinity of fuel or fuel vapor.

Secondary ignition system voltage

A severe electric shock can result from touching certain parts of the ignition system (such as the spark plug wires) when the engine is running or being cranked, particularly if components are damp or the insulation is defective. In the case of an electronic ignition system, the secondary system voltage is much higher and could prove fatal.

Troubleshooting

Contents

This section provides an easy-reference guide to the more common problems which may occur during the operation of your vehicle. These problems and possible causes are grouped under various components or systems i.e. Engine, Cooling system, etc., and also refer to the Chapter and/or Section which deals with the problem.

Remember that successful troubleshooting is not a mysterious 'black art' practiced only by professional mechanics; it's simply the result of a bit of knowledge combined with an intelligent, systematic approach to the problem. Always work by a process of elimination, starting with the simplest solution and working through to the most complex — and never overlook the obvious. Anyone can forget to fill the gas tank or leave the lights on overnight, so don't assume that you are above such oversights.

Finally, always get clear in your mind why a problem has occurred and take steps to ensure that it doesn't happen again. If the electrical system fails because of a poor connection, check all other connections in the system to make sure that they don't fail as well; if a particular fuse continues to blow, find out why — don't just go on replacing fuses. Remember, failure of a small component can often be indicative of potential failure or incorrect functioning of a more important component or system.

Engine

1 Engine will not rotate when attempting to start

1 Battery terminal connections loose or corroded. Check the cable terminals at the battery; tighten the cable or remove corrosion as necessary.
2 Battery discharged or faulty. If the cable connections are clean and tight on the battery posts, turn the key to the On position and switch on the headlights and/or windshield wipers. If they fail to function, the battery is discharged.
3 Automatic transmission not completely engaged in Park or clutch not completely depressed.
4 Broken, loose or disconnected wiring in the starting circuit. Inspect all wiring and connectors at the battery, starter solenoid and ignition switch.
5 Starter motor pinion jammed in flywheel ring gear. If manual transmission, place transmission in gear and rock the vehicle to manually turn the engine. Remove starter and inspect pinion and flywheel at earliest convenience.
6 Starter solenoid faulty (Chapter 5).
7 Starter motor faulty (Chapter 5).
8 Ignition switch faulty (Chapter 10).
9 Engine seized.
10 Hydrostatic lock, remove spark plugs and attempt to rotate.

2 Engine rotates but will not start

1 Fuel tank empty.
2 Battery discharged (engine rotates slowly). Check the operation of electrical components as described in previous Section.
3 Battery terminal connections loose or corroded. See previous Section.
4 Carburetor flooded and/or fuel level in carburetor incorrect. This will usually be accompanied by a strong fuel odor from under the hood. Wait a few minutes, depress the accelerator pedal all the way to the floor and attempt to start the engine.
5 Choke control inoperative (Chapter 1).
6 Fuel not reaching carburetor. With ignition switch in Off position, open hood, remove the top plate of air cleaner assembly and observe the top of the carburetor (manually move choke plate back if necessary). Have an assistant depress accelerator pedal and check that fuel spurts into carburetor. If not, check fuel filter (Chapter 1), fuel lines and fuel pump (Chapter 4).
7 Fuel injector or fuel pump faulty (fuel injected models) (Chapter 4).
8 Excessive moisture on, or damage to, ignition components (Chapter 5).
9 Worn, faulty or incorrectly gapped spark plugs (Chapter 1).
10 Broken, loose or disconnected wiring in the starting circuit (see previous Section).
11 Distributor loose, causing ignition timing to change. Turn the distributor as necessary to start the engine, then set ignition timing

as soon as possible (Chapter 1).
12 Broken, loose or disconnected wires at the ignition coil or faulty coil (Chapter 5).

3 Starter motor operates without rotating engine

1 Starter pinion sticking. Remove the starter (Chapter 5) and inspect.
2 Starter pinion or flywheel teeth worn or broken. Remove the cover at the rear of the engine and inspect.

4 Engine hard to start when cold

1 Battery discharged or low. Check as described in Section 1.
2 Choke control inoperative or out of adjustment (Chapter 4).
3 Carburetor flooded (see Section 2).
4 Fuel supply not reaching the carburetor (see Section 2).
5 Carburetor/fuel injection system in need of overhaul (Chapter 4).
6 Distributor rotor carbon tracked and/or mechanical advance mechanism rusted (Chapter 5).

5 Engine hard to start when hot

1 Choke sticking in the closed position (Chapter 1).
2 Carburetor flooded (see Section 2).
3 Air filter clogged (Chapter 1).
4 Fuel not reaching the carburetor (see Section 2).
5 Vapor lock.

6 Starter motor noisy or excessively rough in engagement

1 Pinion or flywheel gear teeth worn or broken. Remove the cover at the rear of the engine (if so equipped) and inspect.
2 Starter motor mounting bolts loose or missing.

7 Engine starts but stops immediately

1 Loose or faulty electrical connections at distributor, coil or alternator.
2 Insufficient fuel reaching the carburetor/fuel injector(s). Disconnect the fuel line at the carburetor/fuel injector(s) and remove the filter (Chapter 1). Place a container under the disconnected fuel line. Observe the flow of fuel from the line. If little or none at all, check for blockage in the lines and/or replace the fuel pump (Chapter 4).
3 Vacuum leak at the gasket surfaces of the intake manifold and/or carburetor/fuel injector unit(s). Make sure that all mounting bolts (nuts) are tightened securely and that all vacuum hoses connected to the carburetor/fuel injection unit(s) and manifold are positioned properly and in good condition.

8 Engine lopes while idling or idles erratically

1 Vacuum leakage. Check mounting bolts (nuts) at the carburetor/fuel injection unit and intake manifold for tightness. Make sure that all vacuum hoses are connected and in good condition. Use a stethoscope or a length of fuel hose held against your ear to listen for vacuum leaks while the engine is running. A hissing sound will be heard. A soapy water solution will also detect leaks. Check the carburetor/fuel injection unit and intake manifold gasket surfaces.
2 Leaking EGR valve or plugged PCV valve (see Chapters 1 and 6).
3 Air filter clogged (Chapter 1).
4 Fuel pump not delivering sufficient fuel to the carburetor/fuel injector (see Section 7).
5 Carburetor out of adjustment (Chapter 4).
6 Leaking head gasket. If this is suspected, take the vehicle to a repair shop or dealer where the engine can be pressure checked.
7 Timing chain and/or gears worn (Chapter 2).
8 Camshaft lobes worn (Chapter 2).

9 Engine misses at idle speed

1   Spark plugs worn or not gapped properly (Chapter 1).
2   Faulty spark plug wires (Chapter 1).
3   Choke not operating properly (Chapter 1)..
4   Lean air-fuel mixture.

10 Engine misses throughout driving speed range

1   Fuel filter clogged and/or impurities in the fuel system (Chapter 1). Also check fuel output at the carburetor/fuel injector (see Section 7).
2   Faulty or incorrectly gapped spark plugs (Chapter 1).
3   Incorrect ignition timing (Chapter 1).
4   Check for cracked distributor cap, disconnected distributor wires and damaged distributor components (Chapter 1).
5   Leaking spark plug wires (Chapter 1).
6   Faulty emissions system components (Chapter 6).
7   Low or uneven cylinder compression pressures. Remove spark plugs and test compression with gauge (Chapter 1).
8   Weak or faulty ignition system (Chapter 5).
9   Vacuum leaks at carburetor/fuel injection unit, intake manifold or vacuum hoses (see Section 8).

11 Engine stalls

1   Idle speed incorrect (Chapter 1).
2   Fuel filter clogged and/or water and impurities in the fuel system (Chapter 1).
3   Choke improperly adjusted or sticking (Chapter 1).
4   Distributor components damp or damaged (Chapter 5).
5   Faulty emissions system components (Chapter 6).
6   Faulty or incorrectly gapped spark plugs (Chapter 1). Also check spark plug wires (Chapter 1).
7   Vacuum leak at the carburetor/fuel injection unit, intake manifold or vacuum hoses. Check as described in Section 8.

12 Engine lacks power

1   Incorrect ignition timing (Chapter 1).
2   Excessive play in distributor shaft. At the same time, check for worn rotor, faulty distributor cap, wires, etc. (Chapters 1 and 5).
3   Faulty or incorrectly gapped spark plugs (Chapter 1).
4   Carburetor/fuel injection unit not adjusted properly or excessively worn (Chapter 4).
5   Faulty coil (Chapter 5).
6   Brakes binding (Chapter 1).
7   Automatic transmission fluid level incorrect (Chapter 1).
8   Clutch slipping (Chapter 8).
9   Fuel filter clogged and/or impurities in the fuel system (Chapter 1).
10 Emissions control system not functioning properly (Chapter 6).
11 Use of sub-standard fuel. Fill tank with proper octane fuel.
12 Low or uneven cylinder compression pressures. Test with compression tester, which will detect leaking valves and/or blown head gasket (Chapter 1).
13 Worn camshaft.

13 Engine backfires

1   Emissions system not functioning properly (Chapter 6).
2   Ignition timing incorrect (Chapter 1).
3   Faulty secondary ignition system (cracked spark plug insulator, faulty plug wires, distributor cap and/or rotor) (Chapters 1 and 5).
4   Carburetor/fuel injection in need of adjustment or worn excessively (Chapter 4).
5   Vacuum leak at carburetor/fuel injection unit, intake manifold or vacuum hoses. Check as described in Section 8.
6   Valve clearances incorrectly set, and/or valves sticking (Chapter 2).

14 Pinging or knocking engine sounds during acceleration or uphill

1   Incorrect grade of fuel. Fill tank with fuel of the proper octane rating.
2   Ignition timing incorrect (Chapter 1).
3   Carburetor/fuel injection unit in need of adjustment (Chapter 4).
4   Improper spark plugs. Check plug type against Emissions Control Information label located in engine compartment. Also check plugs and wires for damage (Chapter 1).
5   Worn or damaged distributor components (Chapter 5).
6   Faulty emissions system (Chapter 6).
7   Vacuum leak. Check as described in Section 8.
8   On 1982 models with a 1.8 liter engine, 2-barrel carburetor and cruise control , but no air conditioning, a General Motors dealer service bulletin concerning this problem has been issued. Take the vehicle to your dealer and inform him of the problem.

15 Oil leaks caused by excessive crankcase pressure (1982 models)

A General Motors dealer technical service bulletin concerning this problem has been issued. Take the vehicle to your dealer and inform him of the problem.

16 Engine 'diesels' (continues to run) after switching off

1   Idle speed too high (Chapter 1).
2   Electrical solenoid at side of carburetor not functioning properly (not all models, see Chapter 4).
3   Ignition timing incorrectly adjusted (Chapter 1).
4   Thermo-controlled air cleaner heat valve not operating properly (Chapter 1).
5   Excessive engine operating temperature. Probable causes of this are malfunctioning thermostat, clogged radiator, faulty water pump (Chapter 3).

Engine electrical system

17 Battery will not hold a charge

1   Alternator drivebelt defective or not adjusted properly (Chapter 1).
2   Electrolyte level low or battery discharged (Chapter 1).
3   Battery terminals loose or corroded (Chapter 1).
4   Alternator not charging properly (Chapter 5).
5   Loose, broken or faulty wiring in the charging circuit (Chapter 5).
6   Short in vehicle wiring causing a continual drain on battery.
7   Battery defective internally.

18 Ignition light fails to go out

1   Fault in alternator or charging circuit (Chapter 5).
2   Alternator drivebelt defective or not properly adjusted (Chapter 1).

19 Ignition light fails to come on when key is turned on

1   Warning light bulb defective (Chapter 10).
2   Alternator faulty (Chapter 5).
3   Fault in the printed circuit, dash wiring or bulb holder (Chapter 10).

20 'Check engine' light comes on

See Chapter 6.

Fuel system

21 Excessive fuel consumption

1 Dirty or clogged air filter element (Chapter 1).
2 Incorrectly set ignition timing (Chapter 1).
3 Choke sticking or improperly adjusted (Chapter 1).
4 Emissions system not functioning properly (not all vehicles, see Chapter 6).
5 Carburetor idle speed and/or mixture not adjusted properly (Chapter 1).
6 Fuel injection internal parts excessively worn or damaged (Chapter 4).
7 Low tire pressure or incorrect tire size (Chapter 1).

22 Fuel leakage and/or fuel odor

1 Leak in a fuel feed or vent line (Chapter 4).
2 Tank overfilled. Fill only to automatic shut-off.
3 Emissions system filter clogged (Chapter 1).
4 Vapor leaks from system lines (Chapter 4).
5 Carburetor/fuel injection internal parts excessively worn or out of adjustment (Chapter 4).

Engine cooling system

23 Overheating

1 Insufficient coolant in system (Chapter 1).
2 Water pump drivebelt defective or not adjusted properly (Chapter 1).
3 Radiator core blocked or radiator grille dirty and restricted (Chapter 3).
4 Thermostat faulty (Chapter 3).
5 Fan blades broken or cracked (Chapter 3).
6 Radiator cap not maintaining proper pressure. Have cap pressure tested by gas station or repair shop.
7 Ignition timing incorrect (Chapter 1).

24 Overcooling

1 Thermostat faulty (Chapter 3).
2 Inaccurate temperature gauge (Chapter 10)
3 Cooling fan stuck on.

25 External coolant leakage

1 Deteriorated or damaged hoses. Loosen clamps at hose connections (Chapter 1).
2 Water pump seals defective. If this is the case, water will drip from the 'weep' hole in the water pump body (Chapter 2).
3 Leakage from radiator core or header tank. This will require the radiator to be professionally repaired (see Chapter 3 for removal procedures).
4 Engine drain plugs or water jacket core plugs leaking (see Chapter 2).

26 Internal coolant leakage

Note: *Internal coolant leaks can usually be detected by examining the oil. Check the dipstick and inside of the rocker arm cover(s) for water deposits and an oil consistency like that of a milkshake.*

1 Leaking cylinder head gasket. Have the cooling system pressure-tested.
2 Cracked cylinder bore or cylinder head. Dismantle engine and inspect (Chapter 2).

27 Coolant loss

1 Too much coolant in system (Chapter 1).
2 Coolant boiling away due to overheating (see Section 16).
3 Internal or external leakage (see Sections 25 and 26).
4 Faulty radiator cap. Have the cap pressure-tested.

28 Poor coolant circulation

1 Inoperative water pump. A quick test is to pinch the top radiator hose closed with your hand while the engine is idling, then let it loose. You should feel the surge of coolant if the pump is working properly (Chapter 1).
2 Restriction in cooling system. Drain, flush and refill the system (Chapter 1). If necessary, remove the radiator (Chapter 3) and have it reverse-flushed.
3 Water pump drivebelt defective or not adjusted properly (Chapter 1).
4 Thermostat sticking (Chapter 3).

Clutch

29 Fails to release (pedal pressed to the floor — shift lever does not move freely in and out of Reverse)

1 Improper linkage free play adjustment (Chapter 8).
2 Clutch fork off ball stud. Look under the vehicle, on the left side of transmission.
3 Clutch plate warped or damaged (Chapter 8).

30 Clutch slips (engine speed increases with no increase in vehicle speed)

1 Linkage out of adjustment (Chapter 8).
2 Clutch plate oil soaked or lining worn. Remove clutch (Chapter 8) and inspect.
3 Clutch plate not seated. It may take 30 or 40 normal starts for a new one to seat.

31 Grabbing (chattering) as clutch is engaged

1 Oil on clutch plate lining. Remove (Chapter 8) and inspect. Correct any leakage source.
2 Worn or loose engine or transmission mounts. These units move slightly when clutch is released. Inspect mounts and bolts.
3 Worn splines on clutch plate hub. Remove clutch components (Chapter 8) and inspect.
4 Warped pressure plate or flywheel. Remove clutch components and inspect.

32 Squeal or rumble with clutch fully engaged (pedal released)

1 Improper adjustment; no free play (Chapter 1).
2 Release bearing binding on transmission bearing retainer. Remove clutch components (Chapter 8) and check bearing. Remove any burrs or nicks, clean and relubricate before reinstallation.
3 Weak linkage return spring. Replace the spring.

33 Squeal or rumble with clutch fully disengaged (pedal depressed)

1 Worn, defective or broken release bearing (Chapter 8).
2 Worn or broken pressure plate springs (or diaphragm fingers) (Chapter 8).

34 Clutch pedal stays on floor when disengaged

1   Bind in linkage or release bearing. Inspect linkage or remove clutch components as necessary.
2   Linkage springs being over-extended. Adjust linkage for proper free play. Make sure proper pedal stop (bumper) is installed.

Manual transaxle

35 Noisy in Neutral with engine running

1   Input shaft bearing worn.
2   Damaged main drive gear bearing.
3   Worn countershaft bearings.
4   Worn or damaged countershaft end play shims.

36 Noisy in all gears

1   Any of the above causes, and/or:
2   Insufficient lubricant (see checking procedures in Chapter 1).

37 Noisy in one particular gear

1   Worn, damaged or chipped gear teeth for that particular gear.
2   Worn or damaged synchronizer for that particular gear.

38 Slips out of high gear

1   Transmission loose on clutch housing (Chapter 7).
2   Shift rods interfering with engine mounts or clutch lever (Chapter 7).
3   Shift rods not working freely (Chapter 7).
4   Damaged mainshaft pilot bearing.
5   Dirt between transaxle case and engine or misalignment of transaxle (Chapter 7).
6   Worn or improperly adjusted linkage (Chapter 7).

39 Difficulty in engaging gears

1   Clutch not releasing completely (see clutch adjustment in Chapter 1).
2   Loose, damaged or out-of-adjustment shift linkage. Make a thorough inspection, replacing parts as necessary (Chapter 7).
3   On 1983 Cimarron models with a 5-speed transaxle only, a technical service bulletin concerning this problem has been issued. Take the vehicle to your dealer and inform him of the problem.

40 Oil leakage

1   Excessive amount of lubricant in transaxle (see Chapter 1 for correct checking procedures). Drain lubricant as required.
2   Side cover loose or gasket damaged.
3   Rear oil seal or speedometer oil seal in need of replacement (Chapter 7).

Automatic transaxle

Note: *Due to the complexity of the automatic transaxle, it is difficult for the home mechanic to properly diagnose and service this component. For problems other than the following, the vehicle should be taken to a dealer or reputable mechanic.*

41 General shift mechanism problems

1   Chapter 7 deals with checking and adjusting the shift linkage on automatic transaxles. Common problems which may be attributed to poorly adjusted linkage are:

Engine starting in gears other than Park or Neutral.
Indicator on shifter pointing to a gear other than the one actually being used.
Vehicle moves when in Park.
2   Refer to Chapter 7 to adjust the linkage.

42 Transaxle will not downshift with accelerator pedal pressed to the floor

Chapter 7 deals with adjusting the throttle valve (TV) cable to enable the transaxle to downshift properly.

43 Transaxle slips, shifts rough, is noisy or has no drive in forward or reverse gears

1   There are many probable causes for the above problems, but the home mechanic should be concerned with only one possibility — fluid level.
2   Before taking the vehicle to a repair shop, check the level and condition of the fluid as described in Chapter 1. Correct fluid level as necessary or change the fluid and filter if needed. If the problem persists, have a professional diagnose the probable cause.

44 Slipping 2nd to 3rd and/or no 3rd gear operation (1982 Cimarron models only)

A General Motors dealer technical service bulletin concerning this problem has been issued. Take the vehicle to your dealer and inform him of the problem.

45 Transaxle starts out in 2nd gear only (1982 models)

A General Motors dealer technical service bulletin concerning this problem has been issued. Take the vehicle to your dealer and inform him of the problem.

46 Foaming transaxle fluid (1982 models only)

A General Motors dealer technical service bulletin concerning this problem has been issued. Take the vehicle to your dealer and inform him of the problem.

47 Fluid leakage

1   Automatic transaxle fluid is a deep red color. Fluid leaks should not be confused with engine oil, which can easily be blown by air flow to the transaxle.
2   To pinpoint a leak, first remove all built-up dirt and grime from around the transaxle. Degreasing agents and/or steam cleaning will achieve this. With the underside clean, drive the vehicle at low speeds so air flow will not blow the leak far from its source. Raise the vehicle and determine where the leak is coming from. Common areas of leakage are:
   a) Pan: Tighten mounting bolts and/or replace pan gasket as necessary (see Chapters 1 and 7).
   b) Filler pipe: Replace the rubber seal where pipe enters transaxle case.
   c) Transaxle oil lines: Tighten connectors where lines enter transaxle case and/or replace lines.

48 Clicking noise in turns

1   Worn or damaged outboard joint. Check for cut or damaged seals. Repair as necessary (Chapter 8).

49 Knock or clunk when accelerating from a coast

1 Worn or damaged inboard joint. Check for cut or damaged seals. Repair as necessary Chapter 8).

50 Shudder or vibration during acceleration

1 Excessive joint angle. Have checked and correct as necessary (Chapter 8).
2 Worn or damaged inboard or outboard joints. Repair or replace as necessary (Chapter 8).
3 Sticking inboard joint assembly. Correct or replace as necessary (Chapter 8).

Rear axle

51 Noise

1 Road noise. No corrective procedures available.
2 Tire noise. Inspect tires and check pressures (Chapter 1).
3 Rear wheel bearings loose, worn or damaged (Chapter 11).

Brakes

Note: *Before assuming that a brake problem exists, make sure that the tires are in good condition and inflated properly (see Chapter 1), that the front end alignment is correct and that the vehicle is not loaded with weight in an unequal manner.*

52 Vehicle pulls to one side during braking

1 Defective, damaged or oil contaminated disc brake pads on one side. Inspect as described in Chapter 9.
2 Excessive wear of brake pad material or disc on one side. Inspect and correct as necessary.
3 Loose or disconnected front suspension components. Inspect and tighten all bolts to the specified torque (Chapter 11).
4 Defective caliper assembly. Remove caliper and inspect for stuck piston or other damage (Chapter 9).

53 Noise (high-pitched squeal without the brakes applied)

Disc brake pads worn out. The noise comes from the wear sensor rubbing against the disc (does not apply to all vehicles). Replace pads with new ones immediately (Chapter 9).

54 Excessive brake pedal travel

1 Partial brake system failure. Inspect entire system (Chapter 9) and correct as required.
2 Insufficient fluid in master cylinder. Check (Chapter 1), add fluid and bleed system if necessary (Chapter 9).
3 Rear brakes not adjusting properly. Make a series of starts and stops while the vehicle is in Reverse. If this does not correct the situation, remove drums and inspect self-adjusters (Chapter 9).

55 Brake pedal feels spongy when depressed

1 Air in hydraulic lines. Bleed the brake system (Chapter 9).
2 Faulty flexible hoses. Inspect all system hoses and lines. Replace parts as necessary.
3 Master cylinder mounting bolts/nuts loose.
4 Master cylinder defective (Chapter 9).

56 Excessive effort required to stop vehicle

1 Power brake booster not operating properly (Chapter 9).
2 Excessively worn linings or pads. Inspect and replace if necessary (Chapter 9).
3 One or more caliper pistons or wheel cylinders seized or sticking. Inspect and rebuild as required (Chapter 9).
4 Brake linings or pads contaminated with oil or grease. Inspect and replace as required (Chapter 9).
5 New pads or shoes installed and not yet seated. It will take a while for the new material to seat against the drum (or rotor).

57 Pedal travels to the floor with little resistance

Little or no fluid in the master cylinder reservoir caused by leaking wheel cylinder(s), leaking caliper piston(s), loose, damaged or disconnected brake lines. Inspect entire system and correct as necessary.

58 Brake pedal pulsates during brake application

1 Wheel bearings not adjusted properly or in need of replacement (Chapter 1).
2 Caliper not sliding properly due to improper installation or obstructions. Remove and inspect (Chapter 9).
3 Rotor defective. Remove the rotor (Chapter 9) and check for excessive lateral runout and parallelism. Have the rotor resurfaced or replace it with a new one.

59 Rattle in parking brake handle (1982 and 1983 Cavalier and Cimarron models only)

A General Motors dealer technical service bulletin concerning this problem has been issued. Take the vehicle to your dealer and inform him of the problem.

Suspension and steering systems

60 Vehicle pulls to one side

1 Tire pressures uneven (Chapter 1).
2 Defective tire (Chapter 1).
3 Excessive wear in suspension or steering components (Chapter 11).
4 Front end in need of alignment.
5 Front brakes dragging. Inspect brakes as described in Chapter 9.

61 Shimmy, shake or vibration

1 Tire or wheel out-of-balance or out-of-round. Have professionally balanced.
2 Loose, worn or out-of-adjustment wheel bearings (Chapters 1 and 8).
3 Shock absorbers and/or suspension components worn or damaged (Chapter 11).

62 Excessive pitching and/or rolling around corners or during braking

1 Defective shock absorbers. Replace as a set (Chapter 11).
2 Broken or weak springs and/or suspension components. Inspect as described in Chapter 11.

63 Excessively stiff steering

1 Lack of fluid in power steering fluid reservoir (Chapter 1).
2 Incorrect tire pressures (Chapter 1).
3 Lack of lubrication at steering joints (Chapter 1).
4 Front end out of alignment.
5 See also section titled *Lack of power assistance.*

64 Excessive play in steering

1 Loose front wheel bearings (Chapter 1).
2 Excessive wear in suspension or steering components (Chapter 11).
3 Steering gearbox out of adjustment (Chapter 11).

65 Lack of power assistance

1 Steering pump drivebelt faulty or not adjusted properly (Chapter 1).
2 Fluid level low (Chapter 1).
3 Hoses or lines restricted. Inspect and replace parts as necessary.
4 Air in power steering system. Bleed system (Chapter 11).

66 Excessive tire wear (not specific to one area)

1 Incorrect tire pressures (Chapter 1).
2 Tires out of balance. Have professionally balanced.

3 Wheels damaged. Inspect and replace as necessary.
4 Suspension or steering components excessively worn (Chapter 11).

67 Excessive tire wear on outside edge

1 Inflation pressures incorrect (Chapter 1).
2 Excessive speed in turns.
3 Front end alignment incorrect (excessive toe-in). Have professionally aligned.
4 Suspension arm bent or twisted (Chapter 11).

68 Excessive tire wear on inside edge

1 Inflation pressures incorrect (Chapter 1).
2 Front end alignment incorrect (toe-out). Have professionally aligned.
3 Loose or damaged steering components (Chapter 11).

69 Tire tread worn in one place

1 Tires out of balance.
2 Damaged or buckled wheel. Inspect and replace if necessary.
3 Defective tire (Chapter 1).

Chapter 1   Tune-up and routine maintenance

Refer to Chapter 13 for specifications related to 1985 and later models

Contents

Specifications

Recommended lubricants, fluids and capacities

Engine oil type	SG, SG/CD or SG/CE
Engine oil viscosity	
40° to 100° F (4° to 38° C)	SAE 30
20° to 100° F (-7° to 38° C)	SAE 20-20, 20-40, 20-50
10° to 100° F (-14' to 38° C)	SAE 15-40
0° to 100° F (-18° to 38° C)	SAE 10-30, 10-40
0° to 60° F (-18° to 17° C)	SAE 10
Below -20° to 60° F (below -30° to 17° C)	SAE 5-30
Below -20° to 20° F (below -30° to -7' C)	SAE 5-20
Engine oil capacity*	
OHC engine (early models)	3 qts
OHV engines (all, and later OHC engines)	4 qts
Cooling system capacity	
With air conditioning	
OHV engine	9.5 qts
OHC engine	7 qts
Without air conditioning	
OHV engine	9.75 qts
OHC engine	7.8 qts
Manual transaxle oil type	
4-speed	
1982 and 1983	Dexron II or equivalent ATF
1984	SAE 5W-30 SF engine oil
5-speed	
1982 through 1986	SAE 5W-30 SG engine oil
1987 on	Consult a dealer service department
Manual transaxle oil capacity	3 qts (except turbo — 4.1 pt)
Automatic transmission	
Fluid type	Dexron II or equivalent ATF
Fluid capacity (excluding converter)	4 qts
Power steering fluid type	GM 1050017 or equivalent
Windshield washer solvent	GM Optikleen or equivalent

* Plus additional oil for filter

Radiator cap opening pressure .... 15 psi
Thermostat rating .... 195-degrees F
Engine idle speed .... See emission control information label
Ignition system
  Distributor rotation
    OHC engines .... Counterclockwise (viewed from the distributor end of the engine)
    All others .... Clockwise
  Firing order 1-3-4-2
  Spark plug type and gap .... See emission control information label
  Ignition timing .... See emission control information label
Engine compression pressure .... 140 psi at 160 rpm

Torque specifications   **Ft-lbs**

Oil pan drain plug .... 15 to 20
Spark plugs .... 7 to 15
Carburetor/TBI mounting nuts/bolts
  Carburetor 9.6
  TBI .... 10 to 15
Distributor hold-down bolt
  OHV 20
  OHC 13
Automatic transaxle pan bolts 12
Brake caliper mounting bolts .... 21 to 25
Wheel lug nuts 100

1 Introduction and routine maintenance

This Chapter was designed to help the home mechanic maintain his (or her) vehicle for peak performance, economy, safety and long life.

On the following pages you will find a maintenance schedule, along with sections which deal specifically with each item on the schedule. Included are visual checks, adjustments and item replacements.

Servicing your vehicle, using the time/mileage maintenance schedule and the sequenced Sections, will give you a planned program of maintenance. Keep in mind that it is a full plan, and maintaining only a few items at the specified intervals will not give you the same results.

You will find as you service your vehicle that many of the procedures can, and should, be grouped together, due to the nature of the job at hand. Examples of this are as follows:

If the vehicle is fully raised for a chassis lubrication, for example, this is the ideal time for the following checks: exhaust system, suspension, steering and fuel system.

If the tires and wheels are removed, as during a routine tire rotation, go ahead and check the brakes and wheel bearings at the same time.

If you must borrow or rent a torque wrench, it is a good idea to service the spark plugs and check the carburetor or TBI mounting torque all in the same day to save time and money.

The first step of this, or any, maintenance plan is to prepare yourself before the actual work begins. Read through the appropriate Sections for all work that is to be performed before you begin. Gather together all the necessary parts and tools. If it appears that you could have a problem during a particular job, don't hesitate to seek advice from your local parts man or dealer service department.

Routine maintenance intervals

The following recommendations are given with the assumption that the vehicle owner will be doing the maintenance or service work (as opposed to having a dealer service department do the work). The following are factory maintence recommendations. However, subject to the preference of the individual owner, interested in keeping his or her vehicle in peak condition at all times and with the vehicle's ultimate resale in mind, many of these operations may be performed more often. We encourage such owner initiative.

When the vehicle is new it should be serviced initially by a factory authorized dealer service department to protect the factory warranty. In many cases the initial maintenance check is done at no cost to the owner.

Every 250 miles or weekly, whichever comes first

Check the engine oil level (Sec 4)

Check the engine coolant level (Sec 4)
Check the windshield washer fluid level (Sec 4)
Check the tires and tire pressures (Sec 3)
Check the automatic transaxle fluid level (Sec 4)

Every 3000 miles or 3 months, whichever comes first

Change the engine oil and oil filter (turbocharged models)

Every 5000 miles or 5 months, whichever comes first

Adjust the clutch pedal (Sec 24)

Every 6000 miles or 6 months, whichever comes first

Check the power steering fluid level (Sec 4)
Change the engine oil and oil filter (except turbocharged models) (Sec 16)
Lubricate the chassis components (Sec 10)
Check the cooling system (Sec 7)
Check and replace (if necessary) the underhood hoses (Sec 8)
Check the exhaust system (Sec 11)
Check the steering and suspension components (Sec 12)
Check and adjust (if necessary) the engine drivebelts (Sec 6)
Check the brake master cylinder fluid level (Sec 4)
Check the manual transaxle oil level (Sec 4)
Check the transaxle output shaft seals and drive axle boots (Sec 22)
Check the disc brake pads (Sec 13)
Check the brake system (Sec 13)
Check and service the battery (Sec 5)
Check and replace (if necessary) the windshield wiper blades (Sec 9)
Check the operation of the choke (at this interval, then every 12000 miles or 12 months, whichever comes first (Sec 14)

Every 12000 miles or 12 months, whichever comes first

Check the drum brake linings (Sec 13)
Check the parking brake (Sec 13)
Check and adjust (if necessary) the engine idle speed (Sec 15)
Rotate the tires (Sec 23)

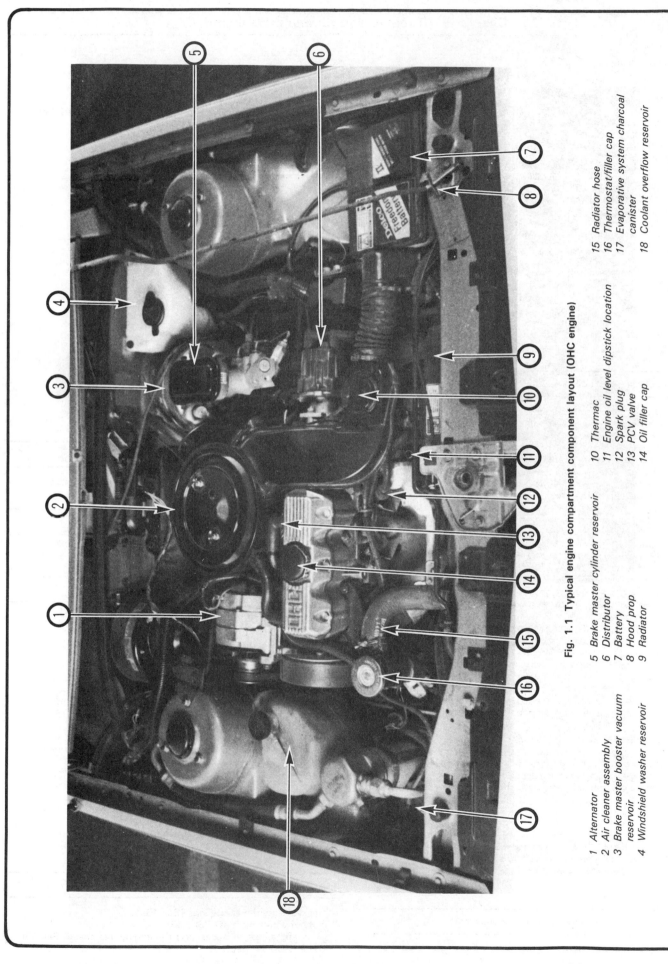

Fig. 1.1 Typical engine compartment component layout (OHC engine)

1 Alternator
2 Air cleaner assembly
3 Brake master booster vacuum reservoir
4 Windshield washer reservoir
5 Brake master cylinder reservoir
6 Distributor
7 Battery
8 Hood prop
9 Radiator
10 Thermac
11 Engine oil level dipstick location
12 Spark plug
13 PCV valve
14 Oil filler cap
15 Radiator hose
16 Thermostat/filler cap
17 Evaporative system charcoal canister
18 Coolant overflow reservoir

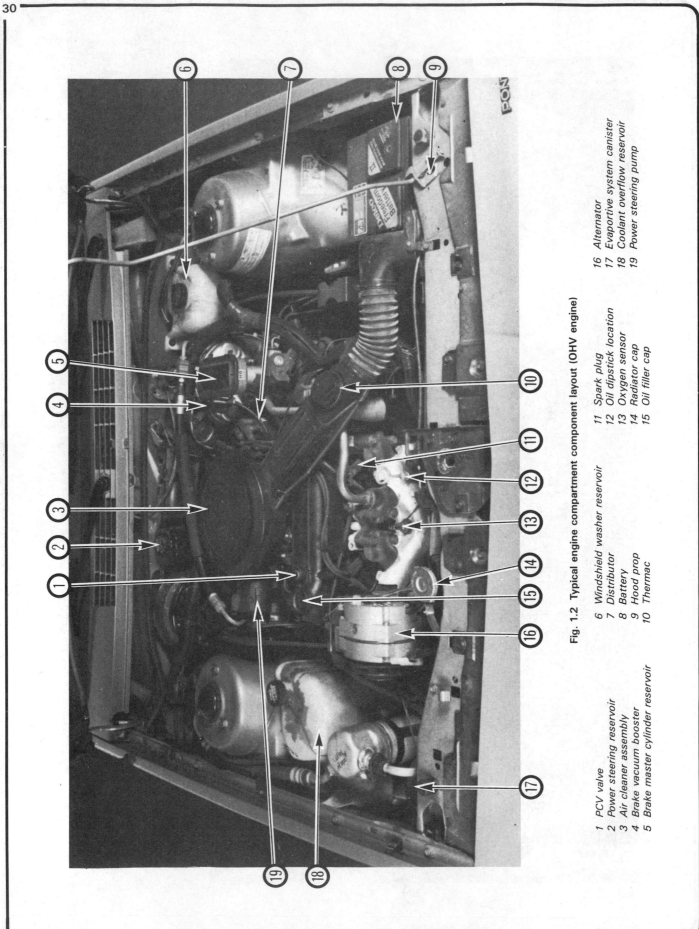

Fig. 1.2 Typical engine compartment component layout (OHV engine)

1 PCV valve	6 Windshield washer reservoir	11 Spark plug	16 Alternator
2 Power steering reservoir	7 Distributor	12 Oil dipstick location	17 Evaportive system canister
3 Air cleaner assembly	8 Battery	13 Oxygen sensor	18 Coolant overflow reservoir
4 Brake vacuum booster	9 Hood prop	14 Radiator cap	19 Power steering pump
5 Brake master cylinder reservoir	10 Thermac	15 Oil filler cap	

Fig. 1.3 Typical engine compartment underside component layout

1 Drivebelt
2 Air conditioning compressor
3 Oxygen sensor
4 Cooling fan
5 Brake hose
6 Disc brake caliper
7 Grease fitting
8 Manual transaxle oil drain plug
9 Transaxle case
10 Rack and pinion steering gear
11 CV joint
12 CV joint boot
13 Sway bar
14 Engine oil drain plug

1

Fig. 1.4 Typical vehicle rear underside component layout

1 Brake line   5 Shock absorber
2 Fuel tank   6 Muffler
3 Filler tube   7 Rear axle
4 Parking brake cable

Check the Thermo-controlled Air Cleaner (THERMAC) for proper operation (Sec 20)
Check the fuel system components (Sec 17)
Replace the fuel filter (Sec 18)
Check the operation of the EGR valve (Sec 32)
Check the throttle linkage (Sec 19)

Every 15000 miles or 15 months, whichever comes first

Change the automatic transaxle fluid and filter (if driven mainly in heavy city traffic, in hot climate regions, in hilly or mountainous areas, or for frequent trailer pulling (Sec 28)

Every 18000 miles or 18 months, whichever comes first

Check the tightness of the carburetor or TBI mounting bolts (Sec 21)
Drain, flush and refill the cooling system (Sec 26)

Every 24000 miles or 24 months, whichever comes first

Replace the oxygen sensor (if equipped) (Sec 30)
Check the EGR system (Sec 32)
Replace the PCV valve (Sec 31)
Replace the air filter and PCV filter (Sec 29)
Replace the spark plugs (Sec 35)
Replace the spark plug wires, distributor cap and rotor (Sec 36)
Check and adjust (if necessary) the ignition timing (Sec 34)
Check the EECS emissions system and replace the canister filter (Sec 33)
Check the engine compression (Sec 37)

Every 30000 miles or 30 months, whichever comes first

Change the automatic transaxle fluid and filter (Sec 28)

Every 48000 miles or 48 months, whichever comes first

Drain and refill the manual transaxle (Sec 25)

---

2 Tune-up sequence

The term 'tune-up' is loosely used for any general operation that puts the engine back in its proper running condition. A tune-up is not a specific operation, but rather a combination of individual operations, such as replacing the spark plugs, adjusting the idle speed, setting the ignition timing, etc.

If, from the time the vehicle is new, the routine maintenance schedule (Section 1) is followed closely and frequent checks are made of fluid levels and high wear items, as suggested throughout this manual, the engine will be kept in relatively good running condition and the need for additional tune-ups will be minimized.

More likely than not, however, there will be times when the engine is running poorly due to lack of regular maintenance. This is even more likely if a used vehicle (which has not received regular and frequent maintenance checks) is purchased. In such cases an engine tune-up will be needed outside of the regular routine maintenance intervals.

The following series of operations are those most often needed to bring a generally poor running engine back into a proper state of tune.

Minor tune-up

Clean, inspect and test battery (Sec 5)
Check all engine-related fluids (Sec 4)
Check engine compression (Sec 37)
Check and adjust drivebelts (Sec 6)

Replace spark plugs (Sec 35)
Inspect distributor cap and rotor (Sec 36)
Inspect spark plug and coil wires (Sec 36)
Check and adjust idle speed (Sec 15)
Check and adjust timing (Sec 34)
Check and adjust fuel/air mixture (see underhood VECI label)
Replace fuel filter (Sec 18)
Check PCV valve (Sec 31)
Check cooling system (Sec 7)

Major tune-up

(the above operations plus those listed below)
Check EGR system (Chapter 6)
Check ignition system (Chapter 5)
Check charging system (Chapter 5)
Check fuel system (Sec 17)

---

3 Tire and tire pressure checks

1   Periodically inspecting the tires may not only prevent you from being stranded with a flat tire, but can also give you clues as to possible problems with the steering and suspension systems before major damage occurs.

2   Proper tire inflation adds miles to the lifespan of the tires, allows the vehicle to achieve maximum miles per gallon figures and contributes to the overall quality of the ride.

3   When inspecting the tires, first check the tread wear. Irregularities in the tread pattern (cupping, flat spots, more wear on one side than the other) are indications of front end alignment and/or balance problems. If any of these conditions are noted, take the vehicle to a reputable repair shop to correct the problem.

4   Check the tread area for cuts and punctures. Many times a nail or tack will embed itself into the tire tread and yet the tire will hold air pressure for a short time. In most cases a repair shop or gas station can repair the punctured tire.

5   It is also important to check the sidewalls of the tires, both inside and outside. Check for deteriorated rubber, cuts, and punctures. Also inspect the inboard side of the tire for signs of brake fluid leakage, indicating that a thorough brake inspection is needed immediately.

6   Incorrect tire pressure cannot be determined merely by looking at the tire. This is especially true for radial tires. A tire pressure gauge must be used (photo). If you do not already have a reliable gauge it is a good idea to purchase one and keep it in the glovebox. Built-in pressure gauges at gas stations are often unreliable.

7   Always check tire inflation when the tires are cold. Cold, in this case, means the vehicle has not been driven more than one mile after sitting for three hours or more. It is normal for the pressure to increase four to eight pounds or more when the tires are hot.

8   Unscrew the valve cap protruding from the wheel or hubcap and

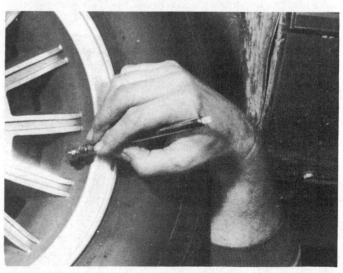

3.6 The use of an accurate tire pressure gauge is essential for long tire life

press the gauge firmly onto the valve stem. Observe the reading on the gauge and compare the figure to the recommended tire pressure listed on the tire placard. The tire placard is usually attached to the driver's door.

9   Check all tires and add air as necessary to bring them up to the recommended pressure levels. Do not forget the spare tire. Be sure to reinstall the valve caps (which will keep dirt and moisture out of the valve stem mechanism).

---

4   Fluid level checks

---

1   There are a number of components on a vehicle which rely on the use of fluids to perform their job. During normal operation of the vehicle these fluids are used up and must be replenished before damage occurs. See Recommended Lubricants and Fluids at the front of this Chapter for the specific fluid to be used when addition is required. When checking fluid levels it is important to have the vehicle on a level surface.

Engine oil
2   The engine oil level is checked with a dipstick, which is located at the side of the engine block. The dipstick travels through a tube and into the oil pan to the bottom of the engine.
3   The oil level should be checked before the vehicle has been driven, or about 15 minutes after the engine has been shut off. If the oil is checked immediately after driving the vehicle, some of the oil will remain in the upper engine components, producing an inaccurate reading on the dipstick.
4   Pull the dipstick from the tube (photo) and wipe all the oil from the end with a clean rag. Insert the clean dipstick all the way back into the oil pan and pull it out again. Observe the oil at the end of the dipstick (photo). At its highest point, the level should be between the Add and Full marks.
5   It takes approximately one quart of oil to raise the level from the Add mark to the Full mark on the dipstick. Do not allow the level to drop below the Add mark as engine damage due to oil starvation may occur. On the other hand, do not overfill the engine by adding oil above the Full mark, since it may result in oil-fouled spark plugs, oil leaks or oil seal failures.
6   Oil is added to the engine after removing a twist-off cap located on the rocker arm cover. The cap is marked 'Engine oil' or 'Oil.' An oil can spout or funnel will reduce spills as the oil is poured in.
7   Checking the oil level can also be an important preventative maintenance step. If you find the oil level dropping abnormally it is an indication of oil leakage or internal engine wear which should be corrected. If there are water droplets in the oil, or if it is milky looking, component failure is indicated and the engine should be checked immediately. The condition of the oil can also be checked along with the level. With the dipstick removed from the engine, take your thumb and index finger and wipe the oil up the dipstick, looking for small dirt or metal particles which will cling to the dipstick. This is an indication that the oil should be drained and fresh oil added (Section 16).

Engine coolant
8   All vehicles covered by this manual are equipped with a pressurized coolant recovery system, which makes coolant level checks very easy. A clear or white coolant reservoir, attached to the inner fender panel, is connected by a hose to the radiator cap. As the engine heats up during operation coolant is forced from the radiator, through the connecting tube, and into the reservoir. As the engine cools the coolant is automatically drawn back into the radiator to keep the level correct.
9   The coolant level should be checked when the engine is hot. Merely observe the level of fluid in the reservoir, which should be at or near the Full Hot mark on the side of the reservoir (photo). If the system is completely cool, also check the level in the radiator by removing the cap. Some models have the thermostat in a housing with a removable cap. On these models remove the cap and thermostat to check or add coolant to the radiator itself.
10 Caution: *Under no circumstances should the radiator cap, thermostat cap or the coolant recovery reservoir cap be removed when the system is hot. Escaping steam and scalding liquid can cause serious personal injury. In the case of the radiator or thermostat cap, wait until the system has cooled completely, then wrap a thick cloth around the cap and turn it to the first stop. If any steam escapes, wait until the system has cooled further, then remove the cap. The coolant recovery cap may be removed carefully after it is apparent that no further 'boiling' is occurring in the recovery tank.*
11   If only a small amount of coolant is required to bring the system up to the proper level, plain water can be used. However, to maintain the proper antifreeze/water mixture in the system, both should be mixed together to replenish a low level. High-quality antifreeze offering protection to -20 °F should be mixed with water in the proportion specified on the container. Do not allow antifreeze to come in contact with your skin or painted surfaces of the vehicle. Flush contacted areas immediately with plenty of water.
12   Coolant should be added to the reservoir until it reaches the Full Cold mark.
13   As the coolant level is checked, note the condition of the coolant. It should be relatively clear. If it is brown or a rust color, the system should be drained, flushed and refilled (Section 26).
14   If the cooling system requires repeated additions to maintain the proper level, have the radiator cap checked for proper sealing ability. Also check for leaks in the system (cracked hoses, loose hose connections, leaking gaskets, etc.).

Windshield washer fluid
15   Fluid for the windshield washer system is located in a plastic reservoir (photo). The level in the reservoir should be maintained at the Full mark, except during periods when freezing temperatures are expected, at which times the fluid level should be maintained no higher than 3/4 full to allow for expansion should the fluid freeze. The use of an additive such as Optikleen will help lower the freezing point of the fluid and will result in better cleaning of the windshield surface. Do not use antifreeze because it will cause damage to the vehicle's paint.
16   To help prevent icing in cold weather, warm the windshield with the defroster before using the washer.

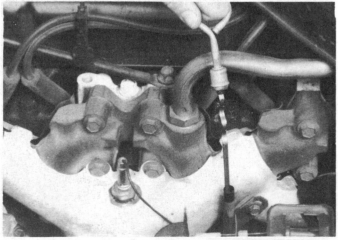

4.4A   After wiping off the engine oil dipstick, make sure it is reinserted all the way before withdrawing it for the oil level check

4.4B   The oil level should appear between the Add and Full marks. Do not overfill the crankcase

Battery electrolyte

17 All vehicles with which this manual is concerned are equipped with a 'Freedom' battery which is permanently sealed (except for vent holes) and has no filler caps (photo). Water does not have to be added to these batteries at any time.

Brake fluid

18 The master cylinder is mounted directly on the firewall (manual brake models) or on the front of the power booster unit (power brake models) in the engine compartment.

19 The master cylinder reservoir incorporates two windows, which allow checking the brake fluid level without removal of the reservoir cover. The level should be maintained at 1/4-inch below the lowest edge of each reservoir opening.

20 If a low level is indicated, be sure to wipe the top of the reservoir cover with a clean rag to prevent contamination of the brake system before lifting the cover.

21 When adding fluid, pour it carefully into the reservoir, taking care not to spill any onto surrounding painted surfaces. Be sure the specified fluid is used, since mixing different types of brake fluid can cause damage to the system. See Recommended Lubricants and Fluids or your owner's manual.

22 At this time the fluid and master cylinder can be inspected for contamination. Normally, the brake system will not need periodic draining and refilling, but if rust deposits, dirt particles or water droplets are seen in the fluid, the system should be dismantled, drained and refilled with fresh fluid.

23 After filling the reservoir to the proper level, make sure the lid is properly seated to prevent fluid leakage and/or system pressure loss.

24 The brake fluid in the master cylinder will drop slightly as the brake shoes or pads at each wheel wear down during normal operation. If the master cylinder requires repeated replenishing to keep it at the proper level, this is an indication of leakage in the brake system, which should be corrected immediately. Check all brake lines and connections, along with the wheel cylinders and booster (see Section 13 for more information).

25 If, upon checking the master cylinder fluid level, you discover one or both reservoirs empty or nearly empty, the brake system should be bled (Chapter 9).

Manual transaxle oil

26 A dipstick is used for checking the oil level in the manual transaxles used on these models.

1

4.9A The engine coolant level should appear near the Full Hot mark with the engine at normal operating temperature

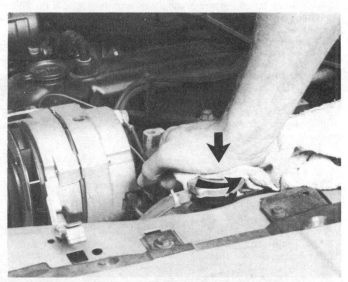

4.9B Never remove the radiator cap while the engine is hot. The cap is removed by pushing down and rotating (arrows)

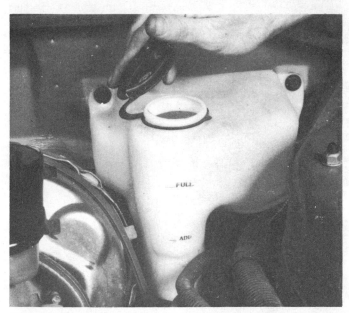

4.15 The windshield washer fluid level should be kept between the Full and Add marks

4.17 This type of battery never requires adding water, but normal maintenance should be performed

27 With the transaxle cold (cool to the touch) and the vehicle parked on a level surface, withdraw the dipstick from the filler tube (photo).

28 The oil level must be even with or slightly above the Full or Full Cold mark on the dipstick (photo).

29 If the level is low, add the specified fluid through the filler tube, using a funnel.

30 Insert the dipstick into the filler tube, making sure that it is seated securely.

Automatic transaxle fluid

31 The level of the automatic transaxle fluid should be carefully maintained. Low fluid level can lead to slipping or loss of drive, while overfilling can cause foaming and loss of fluid.

32 With the parking brake set, start the engine, then move the shift lever through all the gear ranges, ending in Park. The fluid level must be checked with the vehicle level and the engine running at idle. **Note:** *Incorrect fluid level readings will result if the vehicle has just been driven at high speeds for an extended period, in hot weather in city traffic, or if it's been pulling a trailer. If any of these conditions apply, wait until the fluid has cooled (about 30 minutes).*

33 Locate the dipstick at the rear of the engine compartment on the driver's side and pull it out of the filler tube.

34 Carefully touch the end of the dipstick to determine if the fluid is cool (about room temperature), warm, or hot (uncomfortable to the touch).

35 Wipe the fluid from the dipstick with a clean rag and push it back into the filler tube until the cap seats.

36 Pull the dipstick out again and note the fluid level.

37 If the fluid felt cool the level should be 1/8 to 3/8-inch below the Full Hot mark. The two dimples below the Full Hot mark indicate this range.

38 If the fluid felt warm, the level should be close to the Add mark (just above or below it).

39 If the fluid felt hot, the level should be near the Full mark.

40 Add just enough of the recommended fluid to fill the transmission to the proper level. It takes about one pint to raise the level from the Add mark to the Full mark with a hot transaxle, so add the fluid a little at a time and keep checking the level until it is correct.

41 The condition of the fluid should also be checked along with the level. If the fluid at the end of the dipstick is a dark reddish-brown color, or if the fluid has a burnt smell, the transaxle fluid should be changed. If you are in doubt about the condition of the fluid, purchase some new fluid and compare the two for color and smell.

Power steering fluid

42 Unlike manual steering, the power steering system relies on fluid which may, over a period of time, require replenishing.

43 The reservoir for the power steering pump is located on the right side of the firewall.

44 For the check the front wheels should be pointed straight ahead and the engine should be off.

45 Use a clean rag to wipe off the reservoir cap and the area around the cap. This will help prevent any foreign matter from entering the

4.27 The manual transaxle oil is checked with a dipstick

4.28 Follow the manual transaxle dipstick oil checking procedure and fluid type instructions on the dipstick

4.47A Make certain no foreign matter gets into the power steering fluid reservoir when the fluid level check is made

4.47B Checking the power steering fluid level is done with the engine at normal operating temperature. The level should be near the Full Hot mark

reservoir during the check.

46 Make sure the engine is at normal operating temperature.

47 Remove the dipstick (photo), wipe it off with a clean rag, reinsert it, then withdraw it and read the fluid level (photo). The level should be between the Add and Full Hot marks.

48 If additional fluid is required, pour the specified type directly into the reservoir, using a funnel to prevent spills.

49 If the reservoir requires frequent fluid additions, all power steering hoses, hose connections, the power steering pump and the rack and pinion assembly should be carefully checked for leaks.

5 Battery — check and maintenance

1 Tools and materials required for battery maintenance include eye and hand protection, baking soda, petroleum jelly, a battery cable puller and cable/terminal post cleaning tools (photo).

2 A sealed 'Freedom' battery is standard equipment on all vehicles with which this manual is concerned. Although this type of battery has many advantages over the older, capped cell type, and never requires the addition of water, it should nevertheless be routinely maintained according to the procedures which follow. **Warning:** *Hydrogen gas in small quantities is present in the area of the two small side vents on sealed batteries, so keep lighted tobacco and open flames or sparks away from them.*

5.1 Eye and hand protection, baking soda, petroleum jelly and tools required for battery maintenance

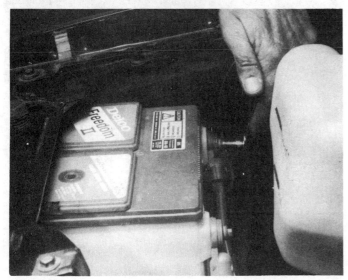

5.3 Unlike older model batteries, the cable terminals are on the side of 'Freedom' type batteries

3 The external condition of the battery should be monitored periodically for damage such as a cracked case or cover.

4 Check the tightness of the battery cable clamps to ensure good electrical connections and check the entire length of each cable for cracks and frayed conductors (photo).

5 If corrosion (visible as white, fluffy deposits) is evident, remove the cables from the terminals, clean them with a battery brush and reinstall the cables. Corrosion can be kept to a minimum by applying a layer of petroleum jelly or grease to the terminals and cable clamps after they are assembled.

6 Make sure that the rubber protector (if so equipped) over the positive terminal is not torn or missing. It should completely cover the terminal.

7 Check that the battery carrier is in good condition and that the hold-down clamp bolts are tight. If the battery is removed from the carrier, make sure that no parts remain in the bottom of the carrier when the battery is reinstalled (photo). When reinstalling the hold-down clamp bolts, do not overtighten them.

8 Corrosion on the hold-down components, battery case and surrounding areas may be removed with a solution of water and baking soda, but take care to prevent any solution from coming in contact with your eyes, skin or clothes. Protective gloves should be worn. Thoroughly wash all cleaned areas with plain water.

9 Any metal parts of the vehicle damaged by corrosion should be covered with a zinc-based primer, then painted after the affected areas have been cleaned and dried.

10 Further information on the battery, charging and jump-starting can be found in Chapter 5 and at the front of this manual.

6 Drivebelt — check and adjustment

1 The drivebelts, or V-belts as they are sometimes called, are located at the front of the engine and play an important role in the overall operation of the vehicle and its components. Due to their function and material make-up, the belts are prone to failure after a period of time and should be inspected and adjusted periodically to prevent major engine damage.

2 The number of belts used on a particular vehicle depends on the accessories installed. Drivebelts are used to turn the generator/alternator, power steering pump, water pump and air-conditioning compressor. Depending on the pulley arrangement, a single belt may be used to drive more than one of these components.

3 With the engine off, open the hood and locate the various belts at the front of the engine. Using your fingers (and a flashlight, if necessary), move along the belts checking for cracks and separation of the belt plies. Also check for fraying and glazing, which gives the belt a shiny appearance. Both sides of the belt should be inspected, which means you will have to twist the belt to check the underside.

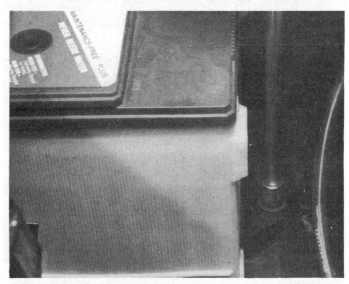

5.6 Use a socket and extension to reach the battery hold-down bolt

4   The tension of each belt is checked by pushing on the belt at a distance halfway between the pulleys. Push firmly with your thumb and see how much the belt moves down (deflects). A rule of thumb is that if the distance from pulley center-to-pulley center is between 7 and 11 inches, the belt should deflect 1/4-inch. If the belt is longer and travels between pulleys spaced 12 to 16 inches apart, the belt should deflect 1/2-inch.

5   If it is necessary to adjust the belt tension, either to make the belt tighter or looser, it is done by moving the belt-driven accessory on the bracket.

6   For each component there will be an adjustment or strap bolt and a pivot bolt. Both bolts must be loosened slightly to enable you to move the component.

7   After the two bolts have been loosened, move the component away from the engine (to tighten the belt) or toward the engine (to loosen the belt). Hold the accessory in position and check the belt tension. If it is correct, tighten the two bolts until just snug, then recheck the tension. If it is correct, tighten the bolts.

8   It will often be necessary to use some sort of pry bar to move the accessory while the belt is adjusted (photo). If this must be done to gain the proper leverage, be very careful not to damage the component being moved or the part being pried against.

---

7   Cooling system — check

---

1   Many major engine failures can be attributed to a faulty cooling system. If the vehicle is equipped with an automatic transmission, the cooling system also plays an important role in prolonging transmission life.

2   The cooling system should be checked with the engine cold. Do this before the vehicle is driven for the day or after it has been shut off for at least three hours.

3   Remove the radiator cap and thoroughly clean the cap (inside and out) with clean water. Also clean the filler neck on the radiator. All traces of corrosion should be removed. On some models the thermostat housing also has a cap. Refer to Chapter 3 for further information.

4   Carefully check the upper and lower radiator hoses along with the smaller diameter heater hoses. Inspect each hose along its entire length, replacing any hose which is cracked, swollen or shows signs of deterioration. Cracks may become more apparent if the hose is squeezed (photo).

5   Make sure that all hose connections are tight. A leak in the cooling system will usually show up as white or rust colored deposits on the areas adjoining the leak.

6   Use compressed air or a soft brush to remove bugs, leaves, etc.

from the front of the radiator or air-conditioning condenser. Be careful not to damage the delicate cooling fins or cut yourself on them.

7   Finally, have the cap and system pressure tested. If you do not have a pressure tester, most gas stations and repair shops will do this for a minimal charge.

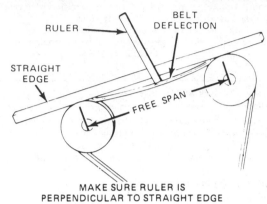

Fig. 1.5 Drivebelt tension can be checked with a straightedge and ruler (Sec 6)

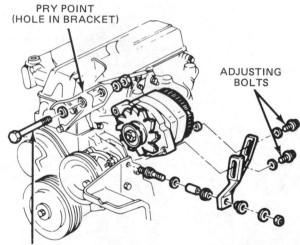

Fig. 1.6 Typical alternator drivebelt adjustment components (Sec 6)

6.8   A crowbar can be used to pry between the alternator housing and bracket to adjust the alternator drivebelt tension (be careful not to damage anything as this is done)

7.4   Although this radiator hose appears to be in good condition, it should be periodically checked for cracks (more easily revealed when squeezed)

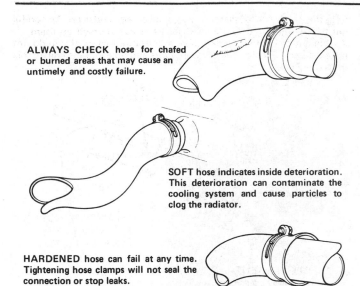

ALWAYS CHECK hose for chafed or burned areas that may cause an untimely and costly failure.

SOFT hose indicates inside deterioration. This deterioration can contaminate the cooling system and cause particles to clog the radiator.

HARDENED hose can fail at any time. Tightening hose clamps will not seal the connection or stop leaks.

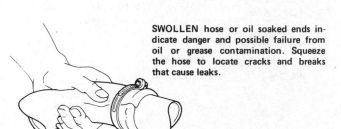

SWOLLEN hose or oil soaked ends indicate danger and possible failure from oil or grease contamination. Squeeze the hose to locate cracks and breaks that cause leaks.

Fig. 1.7 Simple checks can detect radiator hose defects (Sec 7)

8 Underhood hoses — check and replacement

Caution: *Replacement of air-conditioner hoses must be left to a dealer or air-conditioning specialist who can depressurize the system and perform the work safely.*

1   The high temperatures present under the hood can cause deterioration of the numerous rubber and plastic hoses.

2   Periodic inspection should be made for cracks, loose clamps and leaks because some of the hoses are part of the emissions control systems and can affect the engine's performance.

3   Remove the air cleaner, if necessary, and trace the entire length of each hose. Squeeze each hose to check for cracks and look for swelling, discoloration or leaks.

4   If the vehicle has considerable mileage or if one or more of the hoses is suspect, it is a good idea to replace all of the hoses at one time.

5   Measure the length and inside diameter of each hose and obtain and cut the replacement to size. Since original equipment hose clamps are often good for only one or two uses, it is a good idea to replace them with screw-type clamps.

6   Replace each hose one at a time to eliminate the possibility of confusion. Hoses attached to the heater and radiator contain coolant, so newspapers or rags should be kept handy to catch the spills when they are disconnected.

7   After installation, run the engine until it reaches operating temperature, shut it off and check for leaks. After the engine has cooled, retighten all of the screw-type clamps.

9 Windshield wiper blades — inspection and replacement

1   The windshield wiper and blade assembly should be inspected periodically for damage, loose components and cracked or worn blade elements.

2   Road film can build up on the wiper blades and affect their efficiency, so they should be washed regularly with a mild detergent solution.

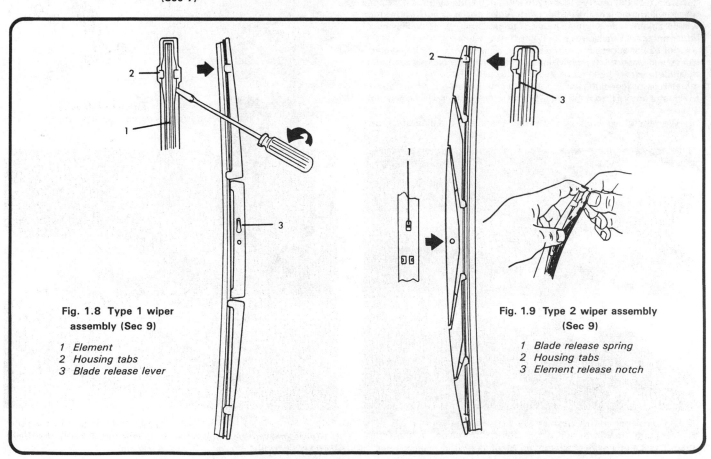

Fig. 1.8 Type 1 wiper assembly (Sec 9)

1 *Element*
2 *Housing tabs*
3 *Blade release lever*

Fig. 1.9 Type 2 wiper assembly (Sec 9)

1 *Blade release spring*
2 *Housing tabs*
3 *Element release notch*

3   The action of the wiping mechanism can loosen the bolts, nuts and fasteners, so they should be checked and tightened, as necessary, at the same time the wiper blades are checked.

4   If the wiper blade elements are cracked, worn or warped, they should be replaced with new ones.

5   Three types of wipers are used on these models.

6   Type 1 wipers are equipped with press-type release levers. Push the lever up or down and slide the old wiper blade assembly off the wiper arm pin (photo). Install the new blade by positioning it over the wiper arm pin and pressing on it until it snaps into place. The wiper blade element is locked in place at either end by a spring-loaded retainer and metal tabs. To remove the element, slide a screwdriver blade under the element near the tabs, rotate the screwdriver and slide the element up, out of the tabs. To install, slide the element into the retaining tabs, lining up the slot in the element with the tabs, and snap the element into place.

7   The Type 2 wiper is retained to the wiper arm by a release spring. To replace the element, bend the blade housing top down, pull the element up and twist it out when the housing tab and element release notch are lined up. Slide the element down until all of the tabs are removed through the notch.

8   The Type 3 wiper is removed from the wiper arm by inserting a screwdriver under the release spring. The element is retained by tabs on the blade housing. To disengage the tab, pull the housing back until the element can be pulled out of the assembly.

10   Chassis lubrication

1   A grease gun and a cartridge filled with the proper grease (see Recommended Lubricants and Fluids) are usually the only equipment necessary to lubricate the chassis components (photo). In some chassis locations, plugs may be installed rather than grease fittings, in which case grease fittings will have to be purchased and installed.

2   Refer to the accompanying illustration, which shows where the various grease fittings are located. Look under the vehicle to find these components and determine if grease fittings or solid plugs are installed. If there are plugs, remove them with a wrench and buy grease fittings, which will thread into the component. A GM dealer or auto parts store will be able to supply replacement fittings. Straight, as well as angled, fittings are available.

3   For easier access under the vehicle, raise it with a jack and place jackstands under the frame. Make sure the vehicle is securely supported by the stands.

4   Before proceeding, force a little of the grease out of the nozzle to remove any dirt from the end of the gun. Wipe the nozzle clean with a rag.

5   With the grease gun, plenty of clean rags and the diagram, crawl

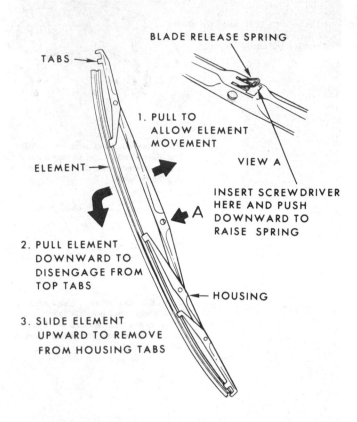

Fig. 1.10 Type 3 wiper assembly (Sec 9)

10.1   Tools required for chassis lubrication

1 Grease gun and flexible nozzle   3 Multi-purpose spray lubricant
2 Grease cartridge   4 Oil can

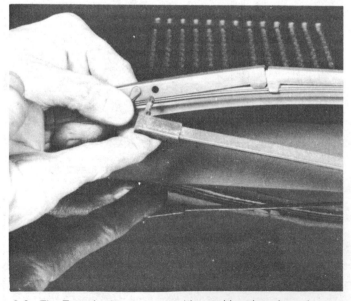

9.6   The Type 1 wiper is removed by pushing the release lever

10.6A The steering arm grease fitting can be reached through the wheel opening

10.6B The control arm balljoint grease fitting is accessible from under the vehicle

10.10 Multi-purpose grease is used to lubricate the hood latch mechanism

under the vehicle and begin lubricating the components.

6   Wipe the grease fitting nipple clean and push the nozzle firmly over the fitting nipple. Squeeze the trigger on the grease gun to force grease into the component (photos). **Note:** *The control arm balljoints (one for each front wheel) should be lubricated until the rubber reservoir is firm to the touch. Do not pump too much grease into these fittings as it could rupture the reservoir.* For all other suspension and steering fittings, continue pumping grease into the nipple until grease seeps out of the joint between the two components. If the grease seeps out around the grease gun nozzle, the nipple is clogged or the nozzle is not seated on the fitting nipple. Resecure the gun nozzle to the fitting and try again. If necessary, replace the fitting.

7   Wipe the excess grease from the components and the grease fitting. Follow the procedures for the remaining fittings.

8   While you are under the vehicle, clean and lubricate the parking brake cable, along with the cable guides and levers. This can be done by smearing some of the chassis grease onto the cable and its related parts with your fingers. Place a few drops of light engine oil on the transaxle shift linkage rods and swivels.

9   Lower the vehicle to the ground for the remaining body lubrication process.

10   Open the hood and smear a little chassis grease on the hood latch mechanism (photo). If the hood has an inside release, have an assistant pull the release knob from inside the vehicle as you lubricate the cable at the latch.

11   Lubricate all the hinges (door, hood, hatch) with a few drops of light engine oil to keep them in proper working order.

12   Finally, the key lock cylinders can be lubricated with spray-on graphite, which is available at auto parts stores.

11   Exhaust system — check

1   With the engine cold (at least three hours after the vehicle has been driven), check the complete exhaust system from its starting point at the engine to the end of the tailpipe. This should be done on a hoist where unrestricted access is available.

2   Check the pipes and connections for signs of leakage and/or corrosion, indicating a potential failure. Make sure that all brackets and hangers are in good condition and tight.

3   At the same time, inspect the underside of the body for holes, corrosion, open seams, etc. which may allow exhaust gases to enter the passenger compartment. Seal all body openings with silicone or body putty.

4   Rattles and other noises can often be traced to the exhaust system, especially the mounts and hangers. Try to move the pipes, muffler and catalytic converter (if so equipped). If the components can come in contact with the body or suspension parts, secure the exhaust system with new mounts.

5   This is also an ideal time to check the running condition of the engine by inspecting inside the very end of the tailpipe. The exhaust deposits here are an indication of engine state-of-tune. If the pipe is black and sooty or coated with white deposits, the engine is in need of a tune-up (including a thorough carburetor inspection and adjustment).

12   Suspension and steering — check

1   Whenever the front of the vehicle is raised for service it is a good idea to visually check the suspension and steering components for wear.

2   Indications of a fault in these systems are excessive play in the steering wheel before the front wheels react, excessive sway around corners, body movement over rough roads or binding at some point as the steering wheel is turned.

3   Before the vehicle is raised for inspection, test the shock absorbers by pushing down to rock the vehicle at each corner. If you push down and the vehicle does not come back to a level position within one or two bounces, the shocks/struts are worn and must be replaced. As this is done, check for squeaks and strange noises coming from the suspension components. Information on suspension components can be found in Chapter 11.

4   Raise the front end of the vehicle and support it firmly on jackstands

placed under the frame rails. Because of the work to be done, make sure the vehicle cannot fall from the stands.
5   Check the wheel bearings (see Section 27).
6   Crawl under the vehicle and check for loose bolts, broken or disconnected parts and deteriorated rubber bushings on all suspension and steering components. Look for grease or fluid leaking from around the steering rack and pinion boots. Check the power steering hoses and connections for leaks. Check the balljoints for wear.
7   Have an assistant turn the steering wheel from side-to-side and check the steering components for free movement, chafing and binding. If the steering does not react with the movement of the steering wheel, try to determine where the slack is located.

13   Brakes — check

Note: *For detailed photographs of the brake system refer to Chapter 9.*
1   The brakes should be inspected every time the wheels are removed or whenever a defect is suspected. Indications of a potential brake system defect are: the vehicle pulls to one side when the brake pedal is depressed; noises coming from the brakes when they are applied; excessive brake pedal travel; pulsating pedal; and leakage of fluid, usually seen on the inside of the tire or wheel.

Disc brakes
2   Both front disc brakes can be visually checked without removing any parts except the wheels.
3   Raise the vehicle and place it securely on jackstands. Remove the wheels (see Jacking and Towing at the front of the manual, if necessary).
4   The disc brake calipers, which contain the pads, are now visible. There is an outer pad and an inner pad in each caliper. All pads should be inspected.
5   The inner pads on the front wheels are equipped with a wear sensor. This is a small, bent piece of metal which is visible from the inboard side of the brake caliper. When the pads wear to the danger limit, the metal sensor rubs against the rotor and makes a screeching sound.
6   Check the pad thickness by looking at each end of the caliper and through the inspection hole in the caliper body (photo). If the wear sensor clip is very close to the rotor, or if the lining material is 1/16-inch or less in thickness, the pads should be replaced. Keep in mind that the lining material is riveted or bonded to a metal backing shoe, and the metal portion is not included in this measurement.
7   Since it will be difficult, if not impossible, to measure the exact thickness of the remaining lining material, remove the pads for further inspection or replacement if you are in doubt as to the quality of the pad.
8   Before installing the wheels check for leakage around the brake hose connections leading to the caliper and damage (cracking, splitting, etc.) to the brake hose. Replace the hose or fittings as necessary, referring to Chapter 9.
9   Check the condition of the rotor. Look for scoring, gouging and burnt spots. If these conditions exist, the hub/rotor assembly should be removed for servicing (Chapter 9).

Drum brakes
10   Using a scribe or chalk, mark the drum and hub so they can be reinstalled in the same positions.
11   Pull the brake drum off the axle and brake assembly. If this proves difficult, make sure the parking brake is released, then squirt some penetrating oil around the center hub area. Allow the oil to soak in and again try to pull the drum off. Then, if the drum cannot be pulled off, the brake shoes will have to be adjusted. In this case this is done by first removing the lanced knock-out in the backing plate with a hammer and chisel. With the lanced area punched in, pull the lever off the sprocket and then use a small screwdriver to turn the adjuster wheel, which will move the shoes away from the drum.
12   With the drum removed, carefully brush away any accumulations of dirt and dust. **Warning:** *Do not blow the dust out with compressed air. Make an effort not to inhale the dust because it contains asbestos and is harmful to your health.*
13   Note the thickness of the lining material on both the front and rear brake shoes. If the material has worn to within 1/16-inch of the recessed rivets or metal backing, the shoes should be replaced. If the linings look worn, but you are unable to determine their exact thickness, compare them with a new set at an auto parts store. The shoes should

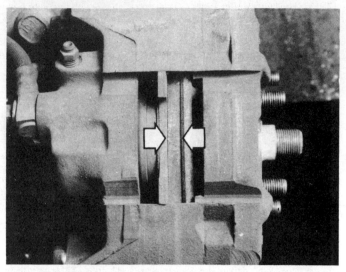

13.6   The amount of disc pad material (between the arrows) remaining can be checked by looking through the hole in the caliper

also be replaced if they are cracked, glazed (shiny surface) or contaminated with brake fluid.
14   Check to see that all the brake assembly springs are connected and in good condition.
15   Check the brake components for signs of fluid leakage. With your finger, carefully pry back the rubber cups on the wheel cylinder located at the top of the brake shoes. Any leakage is an indication that the wheel cylinders should be overhauled immediately (Chapter 9). Also check the hoses and connections for signs of leakage.
16   Wipe the inside of the drum with a clean rag and denatured alcohol. Again, be careful not to breathe the dangerous asbestos dust.
17   Check the inside of the drum for cracks, scores, deep scratches and hard spots, which will appear as small discolored areas (photo). If imperfections cannot be removed with fine emery cloth, the drum must be taken to a machine shop for resurfacing.
18   After the inspection process, if all parts are found to be in good condition, reinstall the brake drum (using a metal plug if the lanced knock-out was removed). Install the wheel and lower the vehicle to the ground.

Parking brake
19   The easiest way to check the operation of the parking brake is to park the vehicle on a steep hill with the parking brake set and the transmission in Neutral. If the parking brake cannot prevent the vehicle from rolling, it is in need of adjustment (see Chapter 9).

14   Carburetor choke — check

1   The choke only operates when the engine is cold, so this check should be performed before the engine has been started for the day.
2   Open the hood and remove the top plate of the air cleaner assembly. It is held in place by nuts or a wing nut. If any vacuum hoses must be disconnected, make sure you tag them to ensure reinstallation in their original positions. Place the top plate and nuts aside, out of the way of moving engine components.
3   Look at the top of the carburetor at the center of the air cleaner housing. You will notice a flat plate at the carburetor opening.
4   Have an assistant press the accelerator pedal to the floor. The plate should close completely. Start the engine while you observe the plate at the carburetor. **Caution:** *Do not position your face directly over the carburetor, because the engine could backfire and cause serious burns.* When the engine starts, the choke plate should open slightly.
5   Allow the engine to continue running at an idle speed. As the engine warms up to operating temperature the plate shold slowly open, allowing more air to enter through the top of the carburetor.
6   After a few minutes, the choke plate should be all the way open to the vertical position.

7   You will notice that engine speed corresponds with the plate opening. With the plate completely closed the engine should run at a fast idle. As the plate opens, the engine speed will decrease.
8   If a malfunction is detected during the above checks, refer to Chapter 4 for specific information related to adjusting and servicing choke components.

15 Engine idle speed — check and adjustment

1   The engine idle speed is adjustable on some models and should be checked at the scheduled maintenance interval.
2   On those vehicles with provisions for idle speed adjustment, the specifications for such adjustments are shown on the Vehicle Emissions Control Information label. However, the adjustments must be made using calibrated test equipment. The adjustments should therefore be made by a dealer or automotive repair facility.

16 Engine oil and filter change

1   Frequent oil changes may be the best form of preventative maintenance available to the home mechanic. When engine oil ages, it gets diluted and contaminated, which ultimately leads to premature engine wear.
2   Although some sources recommend oil filter changes every other oil change, we feel that the minimal cost of an oil filter and the relative ease with which it is installed dictate that a new filter be used whenever the oil is changed (photo).
3   The tools necessary for a normal oil and filter change are a wrench to fit the drain plug at the bottom of the oil pan, an oil filter wrench to remove the old filter, a container with at least a six-quart capacity to drain the old oil into and a funnel or oil can spout to help pour fresh oil into the engine (photo).
4   In addition, you should have plenty of clean rags and newspapers handy to mop up any spills. Access to the underside of the vehicle is greatly improved if the vehicle can be lifted on a hoist, driven onto ramps or supported by jackstands. **Warning:** *Do not work under a vehicle which is supported only a bumper, hydraulic or scissors-type jack.*
5   If this is your first oil change on the vehicle, it is recommended that you crawl underneath and familiarize yourself with the locations of the oil drain plug and the oil filter. The engine and exhaust components will be warm during the actual work, so it is a good idea to figure out any potential problems before the engine and accessories are hot.
6   Allow the engine to warm up to normal operating temperature. If the new oil or any tools are needed, use this warm-up time to gather everything necessary for the job. The correct type of oil to buy for your application can be found in Recommended Lubricants and Fluids near the front of this manual.
7   With the engine oil warm (warm engine oil will drain better and more built-up sludge will be removed with the oil), raise and support the vehicle. Make sure it is firmly supported. If jackstands are used, they should be placed toward the front of the frame rails which run the length of the vehicle.
8   Move all necessary tools, rags and newspapers under the vehicle. Position the drain pan under the drain plug. Keep in mind that the oil will initially flow from the pan with some force, so place the pan accordingly.
9   Being careful not to touch any of the hot exhaust components, use the wrench to remove the drain plug near the bottom of the oil pan. Depending on how hot the plug has become, you may want to wear gloves while unscrewing the plug the final few turns.
10 Allow the old oil to drain into the pan. It may be necessary to move the pan farther under the engine as the oil flow slows to a trickle.
11 After all the oil has drained, wipe off the drain plug with a clean rag. Small metal particles may cling to the plug and would immediately contaminate the new oil.
12 Clean the area around the drain plug opening and reinstall the plug. Tighten the plug securely with the wrench. If a torque wrench is available, use it to tighten the plug.
13 Move the drain pan into position under the oil filter.
14 Use the filter wrench to loosen the oil filter. Chain or metal band-type filter wrenches may distort the filter canister, but this is of no concern as the filter will be discarded.

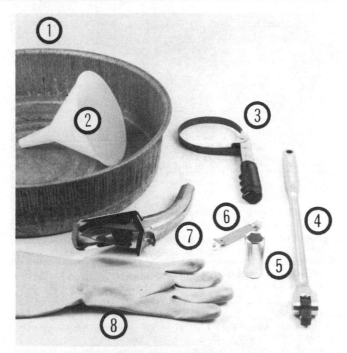

16.3   Typical oil change tools

1	Drain pan	5	Socket (6-point)
2	Funnel	6	Can opener
3	Filter wrench	7	Oil can spout
4	Breaker bar	8	Rubber gloves

16.14   A strap-type oil filter wrench works well in hard-to-reach locations

15 Sometimes the oil filter is on so tight it cannot be loosened, or it is positioned in an area which is inaccessible with a filter wrench. As a last resort, you can punch a metal bar or long screwdriver directly through the side of the canister and use it as a T-bar to turn the filter. If you do so, be prepared for oil to spurt out of the canister as it is punctured.
16 Completely unscrew the old filter. Be careful, it is full of oil. Empty the oil inside the filter into the drain pan.
17 Compare the old filter with the new one to make sure they are the same type.
18 Use a clean rag to remove all oil, dirt and sludge from the area where the oil filter mounts to the engine. Check the old filter to make sure the rubber gasket is not stuck to the engine mounting surface. If the gasket is stuck to the engine (use a flashlight if necessary), remove it.

16.22   Oil is added through a filler opening in the rocker arm cover

17.5   With today's sophisticated emissions systems it is essential that seals in the gas tank cap be checked regularly

19   Open one of the cans of new oil and fill the filter about half-full with fresh oil. Also, apply a light coat of oil to the rubber gasket of the filter.
20   Attach the filter to the engine, following the tightening directions printed on the filter canister or packing box. Most filter manufacturers recommend against using a filter wrench due to the possibility of over-tightening and damage to the seal.
21   Remove all tools, rags, etc. from under the vehicle, being careful not to spill the oil in the drain pan, then lower the vehicle.
22   Move to the engine compartment and locate the oil filler cap on the engine. In most cases there will be a screw-off cap on the rocker arm cover. The cap will most likely be labeled 'Engine Oil' or 'Oil' (photo).
23   If an oil can spout is used, push the spout into the top of the oil can and pour the fresh oil through the filler opening. A funnel may also be used.
24   Pour about three (3) quarts of fresh oil into the engine. Wait a few minutes to allow the oil to drain into the pan, then check the level on the oil dipstick (see Section 4 if necessary). If the oil level is at or near the lower Add mark, start the engine and allow the new oil to circulate.
25   Run the engine for only about a minute and then shut it off. Im-mediately look under the vehicle and check for leaks at the oil pan drain plug and around the oil filter. If either is leaking, tighten with a bit more force.
26   With the new oil circulated and the filter now completely full, recheck the level on the dipstick and add enough oil to bring the level to the Full mark on the dipstick.
27   During the first few trips after an oil change, make it a point to check frequently for leaks and proper oil level.
28   The old oil drained from the engine cannot be reused in its present state and should be disposed of. Oil reclamation centers, auto repair shops and gas stations will normally accept the oil, which can be refined and used again. After the oil has cooled it can be drained into a suitable container (capped plastic jugs, topped bottles, milk cartons, etc.) for transport to one of these disposal sites.

17   Fuel system — check

Warning: *There are certain precautions to take when inspecting or servicing the fuel system components. Work in a well-ventilated area and do not allow open flames (cigarettes, appliance pilot lights, etc.) to get near the work area. Mop up spills immediately and do not store fuel-soaked rags where they could ignite.*
1   If your vehicle is equipped with fuel injection (TBI), refer to the fuel injection pressure relief procedure (Chapter 4) before servicing any component of the fuel system.
2   The fuel system is under a small amount of pressure, so if any fuel lines are disconnected for servicing, be prepared to catch the fuel as it spurts out. Plug all disconnected fuel lines immediately after discon-

nection to prevent the tank from emptying itself.
3   The fuel system is most easily checked with the vehicle raised on a hoist so the components underneath the vehicle are readily visible and accessible.
4   If the smell of gasoline is noticed while driving or after the vehicle has been in the sun, the system should be thoroughly inspected immediately.
5   Remove the gas filler cap and check for damage, corrosion or a broken sealing imprint on the gasket (photo). Replace the cap with a new one, if necessary.
6   With the vehicle raised, inspect the gas tank and filler neck for punctures, cracks or other damage. The connection between the filler neck and the tank is especially critical. Sometimes a rubber filler neck will leak due to loose clamps or deteriorated rubber, problems a home mechanic can usually rectify. **Warning:** *Do not, under any cir-cumstances, try to repair a fuel tank yourself (except rubber com-ponents) unless you have had considerable experience. A welding torch or any open flame can easily cause the fuel vapors to explode if the proper precautions are not taken.*
7   Carefully check all rubber hoses and metal lines leading away from the fuel tank. Check for loose connections, deteriorated hoses, crimped lines or other damage. Follow the lines up to the front of the vehicle, carefully inspecting them all the way. Repair or replace damaged sec-tions as necessary.
8   If a fuel odor is still evident after the inspection, refer to Section 33.

18   Fuel filter — replacement

Carburetor equipped models
1   On these models, the fuel filter is located inside the fuel inlet nut at the carburetor. It is made of pleated paper and cannot be cleaned or reused.
2   The job should be done with the engine cold (after sitting at least three hours). The necessary tools include open-end wrenches to fit the fuel line nuts. Flare nut wrenches (which wrap around the nut) should be used if available. In addition, you will have to obtain the replacement filter (make sure it is for your specific vehicle and engine) and some clean rags.
3   Remove the air cleaner assembly. If vacuum hoses must be discon-nected, be sure to note their positions and/or tag them to ensure that they are reinstalled correctly.
4   Follow the fuel line from the fuel pump to the point where it enters the carburetor. The fuel pump is located low on the engine. In most cases the fuel line will be metal all the way from the fuel pump to the carburetor.
5   Place some rags under the fuel inlet fittings to catch spilled fuel as the fittings are disconnected.
6   With the proper size wrench, hold the fuel inlet nut immediately next to the carburetor body. Now loosen the nut fitting at the end of

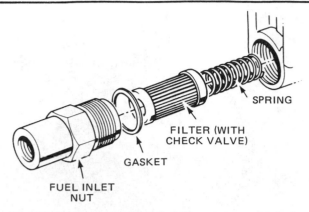

Fig. 1.11 Carburetor mounted fuel filter component layout (Sec 18)

Fig. 1.12 Engine mounted fuel filter used with TBI (Sec 18)

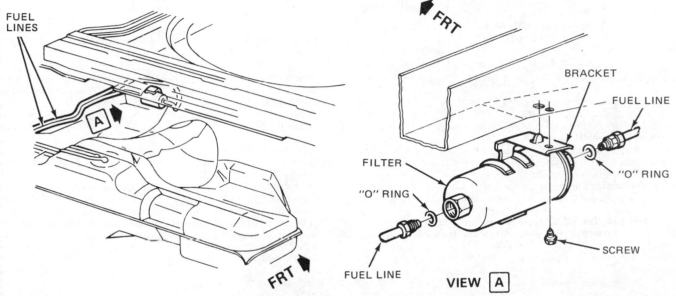

Fig. 1.13 Rear mounted fuel filter components (Sec 18)

the metal fuel line. A flare nut wrench on this fitting will help prevent slipping and possible damage. However, an open-end wrench should do the job. Make sure the fuel inlet nut next to the carburetor is held securely while the fuel line is disconnected.

7   After the fuel line is disconnected, move it aside for better access to the inlet filter nut. Do not crimp the fuel line.

8   Unscrew the fuel inlet nut, which was previously held steady. As this fitting is drawn away from the carburetor body, be careful not to lose the thin washer-type gasket on the nut or the spring, located behind the fuel filter. Also, pay close attention to how the filter is installed.

9   Compare the old filter with the new one to make sure they are the same length and design.

10   Reinstall the spring in the carburetor body.

11   Place the new filter in position (a gasket is usually supplied with the new filter) and tighten the nut. Make sure it is not cross-threaded. Tighten it securely (if a torque wrench is available, tighten the nut to 18 ft-lbs). Do not overtighten it, as the hole can strip easily, causing fuel leaks.

13   Hold the fuel inlet nut securely with a wrench while the fuel line is connected. Again, be careful not to cross-thread the connector. Tighten the fitting securely.

14   Plug the vacuum hose which leads to the air cleaner snorkel motor so the engine can be run.

15   Start the engine and check carefully for leaks. If the fuel line connector leaks, disconnect it, using the above procedures, and check for stripped or damaged threads. If the fuel line connector has stripped threads, remove the entire line and have a repair shop install a new fitting. If the threads look all right, purchase some thread sealing tape

and wrap the connector threads with it. Now reinstall and tighten it securely. Inlet repair kits are available at most auto parts stores to overcome leaking at the fuel inlet filter nut.

16   Reinstall the air cleaner assembly, connecting the hoses in their original positions.

Fuel-injected models

Caution: *Refer to the fuel injection pressure relief procedure in Chapter 4 before performing this procedure.*

17   Fuel-injected engines employ a stainless steel in-line fuel filter. The filter is located on the rear (firewall) side of the engine.

18   With the engine cold, place a container, newspapers or rags under the fuel filter.

19   Remove any bolts attaching the fuel filter bracket to the engine.

20   Using wrenches of the proper size, remove the line from the top of the filter.

21   Unclamp and remove the fuel line from the bottom of the filter and remove the filter.

22   Install the new filter by reversing the removal procedure. Do not overtighten the fitting at the top of the fuel filter. If a torque wrench is available, tighten the fitting to 18 ft-lbs.

23   On some models the fuel filter is located at the rear of the vehicle, adjacent to the fuel tank. Use wrenches to loosen the fuel line fittings until they can be removed from the filter. Unsnap the filter from the bracket. Snap the new filter securely into the bracket. Inspect the fuel line O-rings for damage and distortion, replacing them if necessary. Install the fuel lines and tighten the fittings securely, taking care not to cross-thread them.

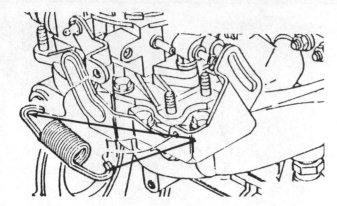

Fig. 1.14 Lubricate both ends of the OHC engine accelerator return spring (arrows) with multi-purpose grease (Sec 19)

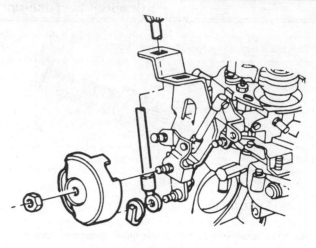

Fig. 1.15 Typical accelerator linkage-to-TBI connection and linkage protector (arrow) (Sec 19)

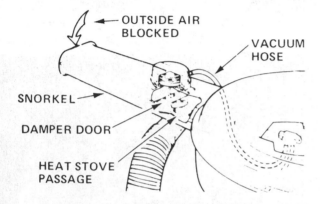

OUTSIDE AIR BLOCKED

VACUUM HOSE

SNORKEL

DAMPER DOOR

HEAT STOVE PASSAGE

Fig. 1.16 THERMAC assembly shown with the snorkel passage (damper door) closed (Sec 20)

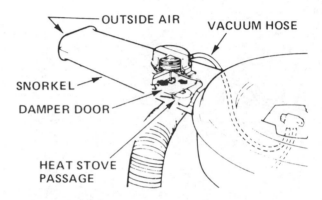

OUTSIDE AIR

VACUUM HOSE

SNORKEL

DAMPER DOOR

HEAT STOVE PASSAGE

Fig. 1.17 THERMAC assembly shown with the snorkel passage (damper door) open (Sec 20)

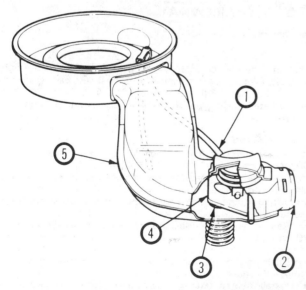

Fig. 1.18 THERMAC assembly (fuel injected-engine) shown with the snorkel closed (Sec 20)

1 Vacuum hose
2 Outside air passage (blocked)
3 Heat stove passage
4 Damper door
5 Snorkel

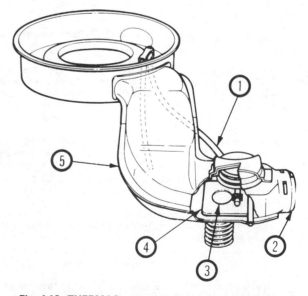

Fig. 1.19 THERMAC assembly (fuel injected-model engine) shown with the snorkel passage open (Sec 20)

1 Vacuum hose
2 Outside air passage (open)
3 Heat stove passage
4 Damper door
5 Snorkel

19   Throttle linkage — check

1   The throttle linkage is a cable type, and although there are no adjustments to the linkage itself, periodic maintenance is necessary to ensure proper operation.
2   Remove the air cleaner so the entire linkage is visible.
3   Check the entire length of the cable to make sure that it is not binding.
4   Check all the nylon bushings for wear, replacing them with new ones as necessary.
5   Lubricate the cable mechanisms with engine oil at the pivot points, but do not lubricate the cable itself.

20   Thermo-controlled Air Cleaner (THERMAC) — check

1   All engines are equipped with a thermostatically controlled air cleaner, which draws air to the carburetor from different locations, depending upon engine temperature.
2   This is a simple visual check. However, if access is limited, a small mirror may have to be used.
3   Open the hood and locate the damper door inside the air cleaner assembly. It will be located inside the long snorkel of the metal air cleaner housing. Make sure that the flexible air hose(s) are securely attached and undamaged.
4   If there is a flexible air duct attached to the end of the snorkel, leading to an area bnehind the grille, disconnect it at the snorkel. This will enable you to look through the end of the snorkel and see the damper.
5   The check should be done when the engine and outside air are cold. Start the engine and look through the snorkel at the damper, which should move to a closed position. With the damper closed, air cannot enter through the end of the snorkel, but instead enters the air cleaner through the flexible duct attached to the exhaust manifold and the heat stove passage.
6   As the engine warms up to operating temperature, the damper should open to allow air through the snorkel end. Depending upon ambient temperature, this may take 10 to 15 minutes. To speed up the check you can reconnect the snorkel air duct, drive the vehicle and then check to see if the damper is completely open.
7   If the thermo-controlled air cleaner is not operating properly see Chapter 6 for more information.

21   Carburetor/throttle body injection (TBI) mounting torque — check

1   The carburetor/TBI is attached to the top of the intake manifold by four nuts or bolts. These fasteners can sometimes work loose from vibration and temperature changes during normal engine operation and cause a vacuum leak.
2   To properly tighten the mounting nuts/bolts a torque wrench is necessary. If you do not own one they can usually be rented on a daily basis.
3   Remove the air cleaner assembly, tagging each hose to be disconnected with a piece of numbered tape to make reassembly easier.
4   Locate the mounting nuts/bolts at the base of the carburetor/TBI. Decide what special tools or adapters will be necessary, if any, to tighten the fasteners with a socket and the torque wrench.
5   Tighten the nuts/bolts to the specified torque. Do not overtighten them, as the threads could strip. On some models one of the TBI bolts is inaccessible and can only be tightened with a special tool. If a vacuum leak is suspected take the vehicle to your dealer to have the TBI torque checked.
6   If you suspect that a vacuum leak exists at the bottom of the carburetor/TBI, obtain a length of hose about the diameter of fuel hose. Start the engine and place one end of the hose next to your ear as you probe around the base of the carburetor with the other end. You will hear a hissing sound if a leak exists.
7   If, after the nuts/bolts are properly tightened, a vacuum leak still exists, the carburetor/TBI must be removed and a new gasket installed. See Chapter 4 for more information.
8   After tightening the fasteners reinstall the air cleaner and return all hoses to their original positions.

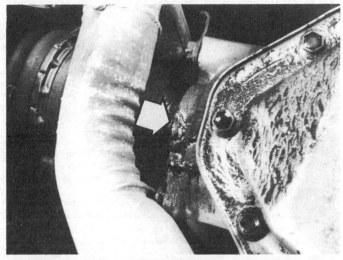

22.3   This transaxle is obviously leaking (arrow) at the output shaft seal

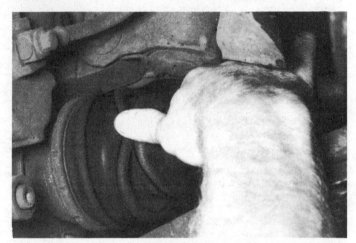

22.4   Check the driveaxle boot to make sure it is not cracked or loose

22   Transaxle output shaft seal and driveaxle boot — check

1   At the recommended intervals the transaxle output shaft seals and driveaxle boots should be inspected for leaks and damage.
2   Raise the front of the vehicle and support it securely on jackstands.
3   Check the transaxle output seals, located at the point where the driveaxles exit from the transaxle. It may be necessary to clean this area before inspection. If there is any oil leaking from either of the driveaxle/transaxle junctions, the output shaft seals must be replaced (photo).
4   The driveaxle boots are very important because they prevent dirt, water and other foreign material from entering and damaging the constant velocity (CV) joints. Inspect the condition of all four boots (two on each axle shaft). It is a good idea to wash the boots, using soap and water, as oil or grease will cause the boot material to deteriorate prematurely. If there are any tears or cracking in the boots, or there is any evidence of leaking lubricant, they must be replaced as described in Chapter 8. Also, check the tightness of the boot clamps. If they are loose and can't be tightened, the clamp must be replaced.

23   Tire rotation

1   The tires should be rotated at the specified intervals and whenever uneven wear is noticed. Since the vehicle will be raised and the tires removed anyway, this is a good time to check the brakes (Section 13)

and the wheel bearings (Section 27). Read over these Sections if this is to be done at the same time.

2   Refer to the accompanying illustration for the 'preferred' and 'optional' tire rotation patterns. Do not include 'Temporary Use Only' spare tires in the rotation sequence. The 'optional' X-rotation procedure is acceptable when required for more uniform tire wear.

3   Refer to the information in Jacking and Towing at the front of this manual for the proper procedures to follow when raising the vehicle and changing a tire. However, if the brakes are to be checked, do not apply the parking brake as stated. Make sure the tires are blocked to prevent the vehicle from rolling.

4   Preferably, the entire vehicle should be raised at the same time. This can be done on a hoist or by jacking up each corner and then lowering the vehicle onto jackstands placed under the frame rails. Always use four jackstands and make sure the vehicle is firmly supported.

5   After rotation, check and adjust the the tire pressures as necessary and be sure to check the lug nut tightness.

---

24   Clutch pedal — adjustment

1   At the specified interval the clutch pedal must be adjusted to maintain a constant tension on the clutch self-adjusting mechanism cable.

2   Grasp the pedal and pull it up to the rubber stop, then depress the pedal slowly (photo). **Note:** *Do not pull up on the pedal after it stops or the clutch linkage could be damaged.*

---

25   Manual transaxle — oil change

1   Raise the vehicle and support it securely on jackstands.

2   Move a drain pan, rags, newspapers and wrenches under the transaxle.

3   Remove the transaxle drain plug (photo) and allow the oil to drain into the pan.

4   After the oil has drained completely reinstall the plug and tighten it securely.

5   Remove the transaxle oil dipstick. Using a hand pump, syringe or funnel, fill the transaxle with the correct amount of the specified lubricant. Reinstall the dipstick.

6   Lower the vehicle. With the vehicle on a level surface, check the oil level as described in Section 4, adding more oil as necessary.

---

26   Cooling system — servicing (draining, flushing and refilling)

1   Periodically the cooling system should be drained, flushed and refilled to replenish the antifreeze mixture and prevent formation of rust and corrosion, which can impair the performance of the cooling system and ultimately cause engine damage.

2   At the same time the cooling system is serviced, all hoses and the

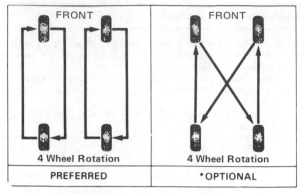

Do not include "Temporary Use Only" spare tire in rotation.

* The optional 'X' rotation pattern for radials is acceptable when required for more uniform tire wear.

Fig. 1.20 Tire rotation diagram (Sec 23)

radiator cap should be inspected and replaced if defective (see Section 7).

3   Since antifreeze is a corrosive and poisonous solution, be careful not to spill any of the coolant mixture on the vehicle's paint or your skin. If this happens, rinse immediately with plenty of clean water. Also, consult your local authorities about the dumping of antifreeze before draining the cooling system. In many areas reclamation centers have been set up to collect automobile oil and drained antifreeze/water mixtures, rather than allowing them to be added to the sewage system.

4   With the engine cold, remove the radiator cap. On models with the thermostat in a housing with a removable cap, remove the cap and the thermostat (Chapter 3).

5   Move a large container under the radiator to catch the coolant as it is drained.

6   Drain the radiator. Most models are equipped with a drain plug at the bottom. If this drain has excessive corrosion and cannot be turned easily, or if the radiator is not equipped with a drain, disconnect the lower radiator hose to allow the coolant to drain. Be careful that none of the solution is splashed on your skin or into your eyes.

7   If accessible, remove the engine coolant drain plug.

8   Disconnect the hose from the coolant reservoir and remove the reservoir. Flush it out with clean water.

9   Place a garden hose in the radiator filler neck and flush the system until the water runs clear at all drain points.

10   In severe cases of contamination or clogging of the radiator, remove

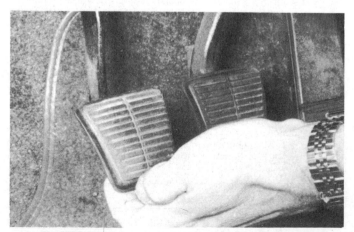

24.2   Pull the pedal back to the stop, then depress it slowly to adjust the free play

25.3   Manual transaxle drain plug location (arrow)

it (see Chapter 3) and reverse flush it. This involves simply inserting the hose in the bottom radiator outlet to allow the clear water to run against the normal flow, draining through the top. A radiator repair shop should be consulted if further cleaning or repair is necessary.

11 When the coolant is regularly drained and the system refilled with the correct antifreeze/water mixture, there should be no need to use chemical cleaners or descalers.

12 To refill the system, reconnect the radiator hoses and install the drain plugs securely in the engine. Special thread-sealing tape (available at auto parts stores) should be used on the drain plugs. Install the reservoir and the overflow hose, where applicable.

13 Fill the radiator to the base of the filler neck and then add more coolant to the reservoir until it reaches the mark. On models with a thermostat housing with a removable cap, install the radiator cap and fill the cooling system through the thermostat housing. Install the thermostat and cap.

14 Run the engine until normal operating temperature is reached and, with the engine idling, add coolant up to the Full Hot level. Install the radiator cap so that the arrows are in alignment with the overflow hose. Install the reservoir cap.

15 Always refill the system with a mixture of high quality antifreeze and water in the proportion called for on the antifreeze container or in your owner's manual. Chapter 3 also contains information on antifreeze mixtures.

16 Keep a close watch on the coolant level and the various cooling system hoses during the first few miles of driving. Tighten the hose clamps and/or add more coolant as necessary.

28.7 Begin the automatic transaxle pan removal by loosening the bolts at one end

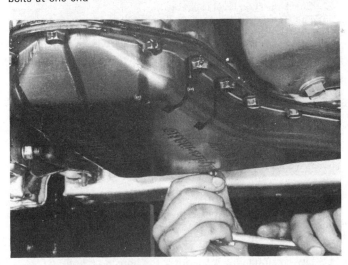

28.8 Work around the pan, loosening all of the bolts a little at a time

27 Wheel bearings — check and repack

1 In most cases the wheel bearings will not need servicing until the brake pads or shoes are replaced. However, these bearings should be checked whenever the vehicle is raised for any reason.

2 With the vehicle securely supported on jackstands, spin the wheels and check for noise, rolling resistance and free play. Next grab the top of the tire with one hand and the bottom of the tire with the other. Move the tire in-and-out. If it moves more than 0.005-inch, the bearings should be checked and replaced if necessary. Refer to Chapter 11 for the proper procedure.

28 Automatic transaxle — fluid change

1 At the specified time intervals the transaxle fluid should be changed and the filter replaced with a new one. The routine maintenance chart calls for an automatic transaxle fluid change once every 30,000 miles. This interval should be shortened to every 15,000 miles if the vehicle is normally driven under one or more of the following conditions: Heavy city traffic; where the outside temperature normally reaches 90° F. or higher; in very hilly or mountain areas; or if a trailer is frequently pulled.

2 Since there is no drain plug, the transaxle oil pan must be removed from the bottom of the transaxle to drain the fluid. Before beginning work, purchase the specified transmission fluid (see Recommended Fluids at the front of this Chapter) and a new filter. The necessary gaskets should be included with the filter. If not, purchase an oil pan gasket and a filter O-ring seal.

3 Other tools necessary for this job include jackstands to support the vehicle in a raised position, a wrench to remove the oil pan bolts, a standard screwdriver, a drain pan capable of holding at least 8 pints, newspapers and clean rags.

4 The fluid should be drained immediately after the vehicle has been driven. This will remove any built-up sediment better than if the fluid were cold. Because of this, it may be wise to wear protective gloves (fluid temperature can exceed 350°F in a hot transaxle).

5 After the vehicle has been driven to warm up the fluid, raise it and place it on the jackstands for access underneath.

6 Move the necessary equipment under the vehicle, being careful not to touch any of the hot exhaust components.

7 Place the drain pan under the transaxle oil pan and loosen, but do not remove, the bolts at one end of the pan (photo).

8 Moving around the pan, loosen all the bolts a little at a time. Be sure the drain pan is in position, as fluid will begin dripping out (photo). Continue in this manner until all of the bolts are removed, except for one at each of the corners..

9 While supporting the pan, remove the remaining bolts and lower the pan (photo). If necessary, use a screwdriver to break the gasket

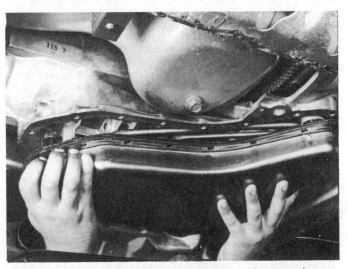

28.9 Separating the drain pan from the automatic transaxle

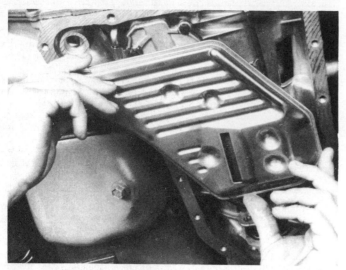

28.11   Removing the automatic transaxle filter

29.4   Removing the air filter element

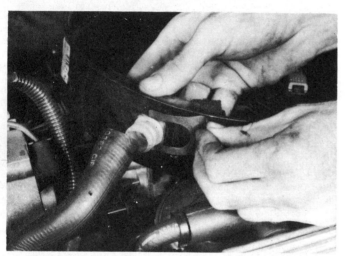

29.10A   Removing the PCV filter retaining clip from the air cleaner housing

29.10B   Removing the PCV filter

seal, but be careful not to damage the pan or transaxle gasket surfaces. Drain the remaining fluid into the drain pan. As this is done, check the fluid for metal particles, which may be an indication of internal failure.

10   Now visible on the bottom of the transaxle is the filter/strainer.

11   Remove the filter and O-ring seal (photo).

12   Thoroughly clean the transaxle oil pan with solvent. Check for metal filings or foreign material. Dry with compressed air if available. It is important that all remaining gasket material be removed from the oil pan mounting flange. Use a gasket scraper or putty knife for this.

13   Clean the filter mounting surface on the valve body. Again, this surface should be smooth and free of any leftover gasket material.

14   Install the new filter into position, complete with a new O-ring seal.

15   Install the new gasket into place on the pan, making sure all bolt holes line up. **Caution:** *Don't use any type of sealant on the gasket – install it dry.*

16   Lift the pan up to the bottom of the transaxle and install the mounting bolts. Tighten the bolts in a diagonal fashion, working around the pan. Using a torque wrench, tighten the bolts to the specified torque.

17   Lower the vehicle.

18   Open the hood and remove the transaxle fluid dipstick.

19   It is best to add a little fluid at a time, continually checking the level with the dipstick. Allow the fluid time to drain into the pan. Add four quarts of the specified fluid to the transaxle through the filler tube.

20   With the selector lever in Park, apply the parking brake and start the engine without depressing the accelerator pedal (if possible). Do

not race the engine at high speed; run at slow idle only.

21   With the engine still idling, check the level on the dipstick. Look under the vehicle for leaks around the transaxle oil pan mating surface.

22   Check the fluid level (Section 4).

23   Push the dipstick firmly back into its tube and drive the vehicle to reach normal operating temperature. Park the vehicle on a level surface and check the fluid level on the dipstick with the engine idling and the transaxle in Park. The level should now be at the Full Hot mark on the dipstick. If not, add more fluid to bring the level up to this point. Again, do not overfill.

---

29   Air filter and PCV filter – replacement

1   At the specified intervals the air filter and PCV filter should be replaced with new ones. A thorough program of preventative maintenance would call for the two filters to be inspected between changes.

Non-turbocharged models

2   The air filter is located inside the air cleaner housing on the top of the engine. The filter is generally replaced by removing the nuts at the top of the air cleaner assembly and lifting off the top plate.

3   While the top plate is off, be careful not to drop anything down into the carburetor.

4   Lift the air filter element out of the housing (photo).

5   To check the filter, hold it up to strong sunlight or place a flashlight or droplight on the inside of the filter. If you can see light coming

30.1   The oxygen sensor (arrow) threads into the exhaust manifold

30.4   Because the oxygen sensor is so crucial to engine performance, its condition provides a good clue to the engine and emissions system condition. This sensor's shield (arrow) was actually burned away by an excessively lean mixture

through the paper element, the filter is all right. Check all the way around the filter.
6   Wipe out the inside of the air cleaner housing with a clean rag.
7   Place the old filter (if in good condition) or the new filter (if the specified interval has elapsed) into the air cleaner housing. Make sure it seats properly in the bottom of the housing.
8   Connect any disconnected vacuum hoses to the top plate and reinstall the plate.
9   The PCV filter is also located inside the air cleaner housing. Remove the top plate and air filter as described previously, then locate the PCV filter on the side of the housing.
10   Remove the retaining clip from outside the housing, then remove the PCV filter (photos).
11   Install a new PCV filter, then reinstall the retaining clip, air filter, top plate and any hoses which were disconnected.

Turbocharged models
12   Raise the front of the vehicle and support it securely on jackstands.
13   Remove the retaining screws from the right side air dam to gain access to the close-out panel.
14   Remove the close-out panel.
15   Remove the air cleaner wing nut and lift out the filter element. Installation is the reverse of removal.
16   PCV filter replacement is the same as for non-turbocharged engines.

___

30   Oxygen sensor — replacement
___

Note: *Special care must be taken when handling the sensitive oxygen sensor.*
a)   The oxygen sensor has a permanently attached pigtail and connector, which should not be removed from the sensor. Damage or removal of the pigtail or connector can adversely affect sensor operation.
b)   Grease, dirt and other contaminants should be kept away from the electrical connector and the louvered end of the sensor.
c)   Do not use cleaning solvents of any kind on the oxygen sensor.
d)   Do not drop or roughly handle the sensor.
e)   The silicone boot must be installed in the correct position to prevent the boot from being melted and to allow the sensor to operate properly.
1   The sensor is located in the exhaust manifold or exhaust pipe and is accessible from under the vehicle (photo).
2   Since the oxygen sensor may be difficult to remove with the engine cold, begin by operating the engine until it has warmed to at least 120 °F (48 °C).

3   Disconnect the electrical wire from the oxygen sensor.
4   Note the position of the silicone boot and carefully back out the oxygen sensor from the exhaust manifold. Be advised that excessive force may damage the threads. Inspect the oxygen sensor for damage (photo).
5   A special anti-seize compound must be used on the threads of the oxygen sensor to aid in future removal. New or service sensors will have this compound already applied, but if for any reason an oxygen sensor is removed and then reinstalled, the threads must be coated before reinstallation.
6   Install the sensor and tighten it to 30 ft lbs.
7   Connect the electrical wire.

___

31   Positive Crankcase Ventilation (PCV) valve — checking and replacement
___

1   The PCV valve is located in the rocker arm cover. A hose connected to the valve runs to either the carburetor or TBI air cleaner.
2   When purchasing a replacement PCV valve make sure it is for your particular vehicle, model year and engine size.
3   Pull the valve (with hose attached) from the rocker arm cover.
4   Loosen the retaining clamp (if equipped) and pull the PCV valve

PCV VALVE

Fig. 1.21 The PCV valve is located in the rocker arm cover on OHV engines (Sec 31)

31.4A   Removing the PCV valve and adapter from the hose

from the end of the hose, noting its installed position and direction (photos).

5   Compare the old valve with the new one to make sure they are the same.

6   Push the valve into the end of the hose until it is seated and reinstall the clamp.

7   Inspect the rubber grommet for damage and replace it with a new one if faulty.

8   Push the PCV valve and hose securely into position.

9   More information on the PCV system can be found in Chapter 6.

32   Exhaust Gas Recirculation (EGR) valve — check

1   The EGR valve is located on the intake manifold, adjacent to the carburetor or TBI unit. Most of the time, when a problem develops in this emissions system, it is due to a stuck or corroded EGR valve.

2   With the engine cold to prevent burns, reach under the EGR valve and manually push on the diaphragm. Using moderate pressure, you should be able to press the diaphragm up and down within the housing (photo).

3   If the diaphragm does not move or moves only with much effort, replace the EGR valve with a new one. If in doubt about the quality of the valve, compare the free movement of your EGR valve with a new valve.

4   Refer to Chapter 6 for more information on the EGR system.

31.4B   Note the direction in which the PCV valve is installed in the adapter

32.2   The diaphragm, located under the EGR valve, should be checked for free movement

33.3   The EECS canister is located at the right front corner of the engine compartment

33.6   With the canister retaining bolts removed and the canister inverted, the filter is easily removed

33 Evaporative Emissions Control System (EECS) — filter replacement

1   The function of the Evaporative Emissions Control System is to draw fuel vapors from the tank and carburetor, store them in a charcoal canister and then burn them during normal engine operation.
2   The filter at the bottom of the charcoal canister should be replaced at the specified intervals. If, however, a fuel odor is detected, the canister, filter and system hoses should immediately be inspected.
3   To replace the filter, locate the canister at the front of the engine compartment. It will have between three and six hoses connected to the top (photo).
4   Mark the hoses with tape to simplify reinstallation, then disconnect them from the canister.
5   Remove the two bolts which secure the bottom of the canister to the body. On air conditioning equipped models it may be necessary to unbolt the drier for access to the canister.
6   Turn the canister upside-down and pull the old filter from the bottom of the canister (photo).
7   Push the new filter into the bottom of the canister, making sure it is seated all the way around.
8   Place the canister back into position and tighten the two mounting bolts. Connect the various hoses if disconnected.
9   The EECS is explained in more detail in Chapter 6.

34 Ignition timing — check and adjustment

Note: *It is imperative that the procedures included on the Vehicle Emissions Control Information label be followed when adjusting the ignition timing. The label will include all information concerning preliminary steps to be performed before adjusting the timing, as well as the timing specifications.*

1   The ignition timing is adjusted using the averaging method. This method is used to bring the timing of each cylinder into alignment with the base timing specification. These models feature a double notched crankshaft pulley with the notch for the number one cylinder scribed across all three edges of the the pulley. Another notch, scribed across only the center section of the pulley, is located 180 degrees away, as shown in the accompanying illustration. The coil wire, instead of the number one spark plug wire, is used to trigger the timing light. Because the trigger signal is picked up at the coil wire each spark firing causes a flash from the timing light. This makes the timing notch appear to 'jiggle,' since each firing is indicated and adjustment is accomplished by centering the total apparent notch width over the specified timing mark.
2   On electronic spark timing equipped models, disconnect the four terminal EST plug at the distributor so the engine will operate in the bypass timing mode.
3   Connect the timing light, following the manufacturer's instructions. Be very careful not to tangle the wires in moving engine parts.
4   Clamp the timing light inductive pickup around the high tension coil wire as shown in the accompanying illustration. Peel back the protective plastic on the wire when installing the timing light inductive pickup.
5   Loosen the distributor clamp nut sufficiently to allow the distributor to be rotated for adjustment.
6   Start the engine, aim the timing light at the timing tab and, if necessary, rotate the distributor to center the notch width over the specified mark. Remember that a slight 'jiggling' of the pulley notch is normal.
7   Shut the engine off and tighten the distributor clamp nut, taking care not to move the distributor.
8   Recheck the timing and repeat adjustment if necessary.
9   Plug in the EST connector, replace the plastic cover on the coil wire and remove the timing light. **Note:** *On some models it will be necessary to remove and replace the ECM '1' fuse to clear the trouble code memory.*

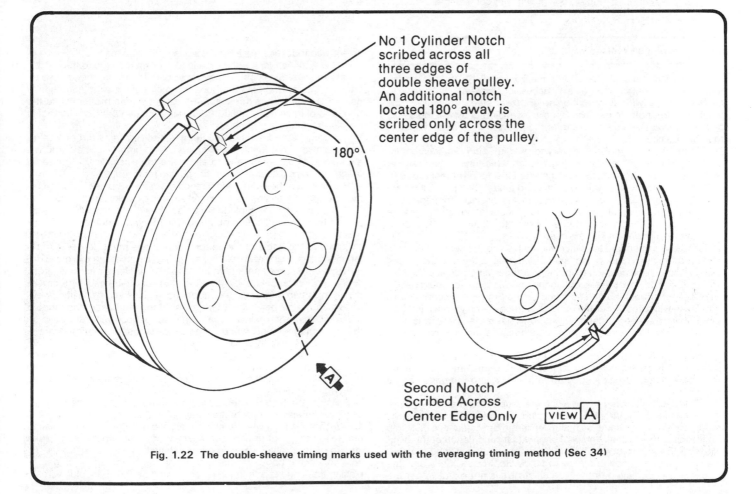

No 1 Cylinder Notch scribed across all three edges of double sheave pulley. An additional notch located 180° away is scribed only across the center edge of the pulley.

180°

Second Notch Scribed Across Center Edge Only   VIEW A

Fig. 1.22 The double-sheave timing marks used with the averaging timing method (Sec 34)

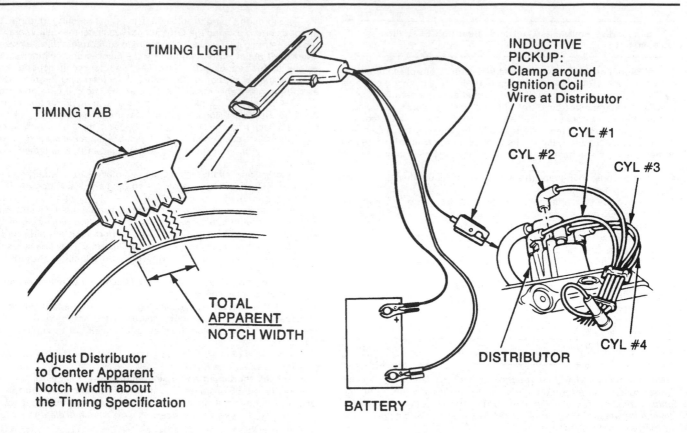

Fig. 1.23   Timing light connections used for engine timing using the averaging method (Sec 34)

35 Spark plugs - replacement

1   The spark plugs are located on the front (radiator) side of the engine. They may or may not be easily accessible for removal. If the vehicle is equipped with air conditioning or power steering, some of the plugs may be tricky to remove. Special extension or swivel tools may be necessary. Make a survey under the hood to determine if special tools will be needed.

2   In most cases, tools necessary for a spark plug replacement include a plug wrench or spark plug socket, which fits onto a ratchet wrench (this special socket will be insulated inside to protect the plug) and a wire-type feeler gauge to check and adjust the spark plug gap. Also, a special spark plug wire removal tool is available for separating the wires from the spark plugs. To simplify installation, obtain a piece of 3/16-inch inside diameter rubber hose, 8 to 12 inches in length, to use in starting the plugs into the head.

3   The best procedure to follow when replacing the spark plugs is to purchase the new spark plugs beforehand, adjust them to the proper gap, and then replace each plug one at a time. When buying the new spark plugs, it is important to obtain the correct plugs for your specific engine. This information can be found on the Emissions Control Information label located under the hood or in the owner's manual. If differences exist between these sources, purchase the spark plug type specified on the Emissions Control label because the information was printed for your specific engine.

4   With the new spark plugs at hand, allow the engine to cool completely before attempting plug removal. During this time, each of the new spark plugs can be inspected for defects and the gaps can be checked.

5   The gap is checked by inserting the proper thickness gauge between the electrodes at the tip of the plug. The gap between the electrodes should be the same as that given in the Specifications or on the Emissions Control label. The wire should just touch each of the electrodes. If the gap is incorrect, use the notched adjuster on the thickness gauge body to bend the curved side electrode slightly until the proper gap is achieved. If the side electrode is not exactly over the

center electrode, use the notched adjuster to align the two.

6   Cover the fenders of the vehicle to prevent damage to the paint.

7   With the engine cool, remove the spark plug wire from one spark plug. Do this by grabbing the boot at the end of the wire, not the wire itself. Sometimes it is necessary to use a twisting motion while the boot and plug wire are pulled free. Using a plug wire removal tool is the easiest and safest method.

8   If compressed air is available, use it to blow any dirt or foreign material away from the spark plug area. A common bicycle pump will also work. The idea here is to eliminate the possibility of material falling into the cylinder as the spark plug is removed.

9   Now place the spark plug wrench or socket over the plug and remove it from the engine by turning in a counterclockwise direction.

10   Compare the spark plug with those shown in the accompanying photos to get an indication of the overall running condition of the engine.

11   Due to the angle at which the spark plugs must be installed on most engines, installation will be simplified by inserting the plug wire terminal of the new spark plug into the 3/16-inch rubber hose, mentioned previously, before it is installed in the cylinder head. This procedure serves two purposes: the rubber hose gives you flexibility for establishing the proper angle of plug insertion in the head and, should the threads be improperly lined up, the rubber hose will merely slip on the spark plug terminal when it meets resistance, preventing damage to the cylinder head threads.

12   After installing the plug to the limit of the hose grip, tighten it with the socket. It is a good idea to use a torque wrench for this to ensure that the plug is seated correctly. The correct torque figure is included in the Specifications.

14   Before pushing the spark plug wire onto the end of the plug, inspect it following the procedures outlined in Section 36.

15   Attach the plug wire to the new spark plug, again using a twisting motion on the boot until it is firmly seated on the spark plug. Make sure the wire is routed away from the exhaust manifold.

16   Follow the above procedure for the remaining spark plugs, replacing them one at a time to prevent mixing up the spark plug wires.

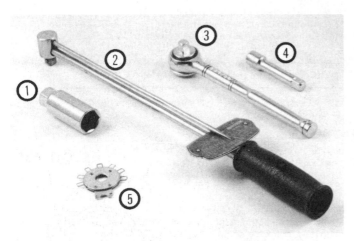

36.2 Tools required for spark plug replacement

   1 Spark plug socket   *4 Extension*
   2 Torque wrench   *5 Spark plug gap tool*
   3 Ratchet

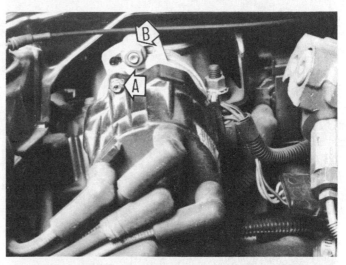

36.3 The screws retaining the distributor cap (A) should not be confused with the adjusting nut (B)

36.4 Inspect the distributor cap for cracks and carbon tracks and the contacts (arrow) for corrosion and damage

36.7 Check the distributor rotor contact (arrow) for wear and burn marks

36 Spark plug wires, distributor cap and rotor — check and replacement

1 Begin this procedure by making a visual check of the spark plug wires while the engine is running. In a darkened garage (make sure there is ventilation) start the engine and observe each plug wire. Be careful not to come into contact with any moving engine parts. If there is a break in the wire, you will see arcing or a small spark at the damaged area. If arcing is noticed, make a note to obtain new wires, then allow the engine to cool and check the distributor cap and rotor.

2 Disconnect the negative cable from the battery. At the distributor, disconnect the ECM connector and the coil wire.

3 Remove the distributor cap by removing the two retaining clamp screws (photo). Separate the cap from the distributor with the spark plug wires still attached.

4 Inspect the cap for cracks and other damage. Closely examine the contacts on the inside of the cap for excessive corrosion (photo). Slight scoring is normal. Deposits on the contacts may be removed with a small file.

5 If the inspection reveals damage to the cap, make a note to obtain a replacement for your particular engine, then examine the rotor.

6 The rotor is visible, with the cap removed, at the top of the distributor shaft. Remove the rotor by pulling it off the shaft.

7 Inspect the rotor for cracks and other damage. Carefully check the condition of the metal contact at the top of the rotor for excessive burning and pitting (photo).

8 If it is determined that a new rotor is required, make a note to that effect. If the rotor and cap are in good condition, reinstall them at this time. Be sure to apply a small dab of silicone lubricant to the contacts inside the cap before installing it.

9 If the cap must be replaced, do not reinstall it. Leave it off the distributor with the wires still connected.

10 If the spark plug wires are being replaced, now is the time to obtain a new set, along with a new cap and rotor as determined in the checks above. Purchase a wire set for your particular engine, pre-cut to the proper size, with the rubber boots already installed.

11 If the spark plug wires passed the check in Step 1, they should be checked further as follows.

12 Examine the wires one at a time to avoid mixing them up.

13 Disconnect the plug wire from the spark plug. A removal tool can be used for this, or you can grab the rubber boot, twist slightly and then pull the wire free. Do not pull on the wire itself, only on the rubber boot.

14 Inspect inside the boot for corrosion, which will look like a white crusty powder. Some models use a conductive white silicone lubricant, which should not be mistaken for corrosion.

15 Now push the wire and boot back onto the end of the spark plug.

37.4   Using a special gauge to check cylinder compression

It should be a tight fit on the plug end. If not, remove the wire and use pliers to carefully crimp the metal connector inside the wire boot until the fit is snug.

16   Now, using a clean rag, wipe the entire length of the wire. Remove all built-up dirt and grease. As this is done, check for burns, cracks and any other form of damage. Bend the wires in several places to ensure that the conductive wire inside has not hardened.

17   Next, the wires should be checked at the distributor cap in the same manner.

18   If the wires appear to be in good condition, make sure that they are secure at both ends. If the cap and rotor are also in good condition, the check is finished. Reconnect the wires at the distributor and at the battery.

19   If it was determined in Steps 12 through 17 that new wires are required, obtain them at this time, along with a new cap and rotor if so determined in the checks above.

20   Attach the rotor to the distributor.

21   If new wires are being installed, replace them one at a time. **Note:** *It is important to replace the wires one at a time, noting the routing as each wire is removed and installed, to maintain the correct firing order and to prevent short-circuiting.*

22   Attach the cap to the distributor, reconnecting all wires disconnected in Step 2, then reconnect the battery cable.

37 Compression check

1   A compression check will tell you what mechanical condition the engine is in. Specifically, it can tell you if the compression is down due to leakage caused by worn piston rings, defective valves and seats or a blown head gasket.

2   Begin by cleaning the area around the spark plugs before you remove them. This will keep dirt from falling into the cylinders while you are performing the compression test.

3   Disconnect the ignition switch feed wire at the distributor. This is the pink wire coming from the ignition coil. Block the throttle and choke valves open.

4   With the compression gauge in the number one cylinder's spark plug hole, crank the engine over at least four compression strokes and observe the gauge (the compression should build up quickly) (photo). Low compression on the first stroke, which does not build up during successive strokes, indicates leaking valves or a blown head gasket (a cracked head could also be the cause). Record the highest gauge reading obtained.

5   Repeat the procedure for the remaining cylinders and compare the results to the Specifications. Compression readings approximately 10-percent above or below the specified amount can be considered normal.

6   Pour a couple of teaspoons of engine oil (a squirt can works great for this) into each cylinder, through the spark plug hole, and repeat the test.

7   If the compression increases after after the oil is added, the piston rings are definitely worn. If the compression does not increase significantly, the leakage is occurring at the valves or head gasket. Leakage past the valves may be caused by burned valve seats or faces or warped, cracked or bent valves.

8   If two adjacent cylinders have equally low compression, there is a strong possibility that the head gasket between them is blown. The appearance of coolant in the combustion chambers or the crankcase would verify this condition.

9   If the compression is higher than normal, the combustion chambers are probably coated with carbon deposits. If that it the case, the cylinder head(s) should be removed and decarbonized.

10   If compression is way down or varies greatly between cylinders, it would be a good idea to have a leak-down test performed by a reputable automotive repair shop. This test will pinpoint exactly where the leakage is occurring and how severe it is.

CARBON DEPOSITS

Symptoms: Dry sooty deposits indicate a rich mixture or weak ignition. Causes misfiring, hard starting and hesitation.

Recommendation: Check for a clogged air cleaner, high float level, sticky choke and worn ignition points. Use a spark plug with a longer core nose for greater anti-fouling protection.

OIL DEPOSITS

Symptoms: Oily coating caused by poor oil control. Oil is leaking past worn valve guides or piston rings into the combustion chamber. Causes hard starting, misfiring and hesition.

Recommendation: Correct the mechanical condition with necessary repairs and install new plugs.

TOO HOT

Symptoms: Blistered, white insulator, eroded electrode and absence of deposits. Results in shortened plug life.

Recommendation: Check for the correct plug heat range, over-advanced ignition timing, lean fuel mixture, intake manifold vacuum leaks and sticking valves. Check the coolant level and make sure the radiator is not clogged.

PREIGNITION

Symptoms: Melted electrodes. Insulators are white, but may be dirty due to misfiring or flying debris in the combustion chamber. Can lead to engine damage.

Recommendation: Check for the correct plug heat range, over-advanced ignition timing, lean fuel mixture, clogged cooling system and lack of lubrication.

HIGH SPEED GLAZING

Symptoms: Insulator has yellowish, glazed appearance. Indicates that combustion chamber temperatures have risen suddenly during hard acceleration. Normal deposits melt to form a conductive coating. Causes misfiring at high speeds.

Recommendation: Install new plugs. Consider using a colder plug if driving habits warrant.

GAP BRIDGING

Symptoms: Combustion deposits lodge between the electrodes. Heavy deposits accumulate and bridge the electrode gap. The plug ceases to fire, resulting in a dead cylinder.

Recommendation: Locate the faulty plug and remove the deposits from between the electrodes.

NORMAL

Symptoms: Brown to grayish-tan color and slight electrode wear. Correct heat range for engine and operating conditions.

Recommendation: When new spark plugs are installed, replace with plugs of the same heat range.

ASH DEPOSITS

Symptoms: Light brown deposits encrusted on the side or center electrodes or both. Derived from oil and/or fuel additives. Excessive amounts may mask the spark, causing misfiring and hesitation during acceleration.

Recommendation: If excessive deposits accumulate over a short time or low mileage, install new valve guide seals to prevent seepage of oil into the combustion chambers. Also try changing gasoline brands.

1

WORN

Symptoms: Rounded electrodes with a small amount of deposits on the firing end. Normal color. Causes hard starting in damp or cold weather and poor fuel economy.

Recommendation: Replace with new plugs of the same heat range.

DETONATION

Symptoms: Insulators may be cracked or chipped. Improper gap setting techniques can also result in a fractured insulator tip. Can lead to piston damage.

Recommendation: Make sure the fuel anti-knock values meet engine requirements. Use care when setting the gaps on new plugs. Avoid lugging the engine.

SPLASHED DEPOSITS

Symptoms: After long periods of misfiring, deposits can loosen when normal combustion temperature is restored by an overdue tune-up. At high speeds, deposits flake off the piston and are thrown against the hot insulator, causing misfiring.

Recommendation: Replace the plugs with new ones or clean and reinstall the originals.

MECHANICAL DAMAGE

Symptoms: May be caused by a foreign object in the combustion chamber or the piston striking an incorrect reach (too long) plug. Causes a dead cylinder and could result in piston damage.

Recommendation: Remove the foreign object from the engine and/or install the correct reach plug.

Chapter 2 Part A
1.8 and 2.0 liter overhead valve (OHV) engine

Refer to Chapter 13 for specifications and information related to 1987 and later 2.0 liter engines

Contents

Specifications

Torque specifications	Ft-lbs
Alternator	
brace and pivot bolts	29 to 44
adjustment bolt	15 to 20
Air conditioner compressor	26 to 37
Air conditioner compressor bracket	26 to 37
Camshaft thrust plate bolts	4 to 14
Camshaft rear cover bolts	4 to 9
Camshaft sprocket bolts	66 to 88
Connecting rod cap bolts	34 to 43
Crankshaft pulley-to-hub bolts	29 to 44
Crankshaft pulley center bolt	66 to 88
Cylinder head bolts	65 to 75
EGR valve	13 to 27
Engine mounts	
front engine mount nut	25 to 35
lower engine mount nut	15 to 20
engine mount-to-frame	35 to 45
rear engine mount	36 to 44
Exhaust manifold bolts	20 to 30
Flywheel bolts	
automatic transaxle	45 to 59
manual transaxle	45 to 63
Intake manifold nuts/bolts	18 to 25
Main bearing cap bolts	63 to 77
Oil pan drain plug	30 to 38
Oil filter adapter	15 to 22
Oil filter connector	11 to 16
Oil pan	
to front cover	7 to 13
rear	11 to 18
stud	43 to 49
all others	4 to 14
Oil pump cover bolts	6 to 9
Oil pump mounting bolts	26 to 35
Rocker arm cover bolts	6 to 9
Rocker arm stud	43 to 49
Rocker nut	4 to 14

Spark plug	7 to 20
Starter motor	26 to 37
Thermostat adapter	13 to 18
Thermostat outlet	13 to 22
Timing chain cover bolts	7 to 13
Timing chain tensioner	13 to 18
Transaxle-to-engine	48 to 63
Water inlet	12 to 21
Water pump	12 to 21
Water pump pulley	15 to 20

Note: *Refer to Chapter 2, Part C, for additional specifications.*

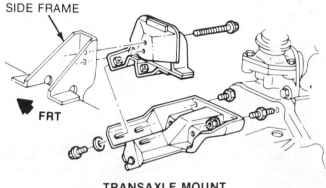

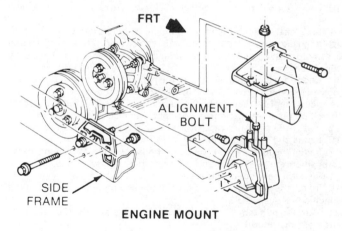

Fig. 2A.1 Front engine mount component layout (Sec 2)

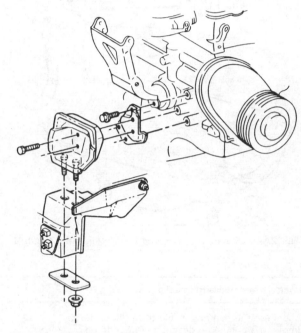

Fig. 2A.2 Rear engine mount component layout (Sec 2)

1 General information

The overhead valve (OHV) engine is made of cast iron with a removable cylinder head. The camshaft is located in the block and actuates the valves in the cylinder head via pushrods and rocker arms, hence the designation 'overhead valve'.

The forward Sections in this Part of Chapter 2 are devoted to 'in vehicle' repair procedures for the engine. The latter Sections in this part of Chapter 2 involve the removal and installation procedures for the engine. All information concerning engine block and cylinder head servicing can be found in Part C of this Chapter.

The repair procedures included in this part are based on the assumption that the engine is still installed in the vehicle. Therefore, if this information is being used during a complete engine overhaul, with the engine already out of the vehicle and on a stand, many of the steps included here will not apply.

The specifications included in this part of Chapter 2 apply only to the engine and procedures found here. For specifications regarding OHC engines see Part B. Part C of Chapter 2 contains the specifications necessary for engine block and cylinder head rebuilding.

2 Engine mounts — replacement with engine in vehicle

Removal
Front mount
1   Disconnect the negative cable from the battery.
2   Remove the nuts from the mount.
3   Raise the vehicle and support it securely on jackstands.
4   Support the weight of the engine with a jack.
5   Remove the inner fender shield.
6   Remove the bolts and lift the mount from the engine compartment. A large alignment bolt must be installed whenever the mount is removed to support the engine and prevent misalignment of the drive axles.
Rear mount
7   Disconnect the negative battery cable, raise the vehicle and support it on jackstands.
8   On manual transaxle models, remove the engine oil filter (Chapter 1).
9   Support the engine with a jack.
10   Remove the engine mount nuts, withdraw the bolts and remove the mount.

Installation
Front mount
11   Place the mount in position and insert new bolts.
12   Check the alignment bolt. If it is difficult to remove, loosen the transaxle adjustment bolts and adjust the transaxle position until the bolt can be removed easily.

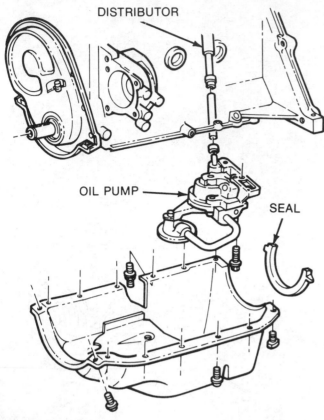

DISTRIBUTOR

OIL PUMP

SEAL

Fig. 2A.3 Oil pan and oil pump installation (Sec 3 and 4)

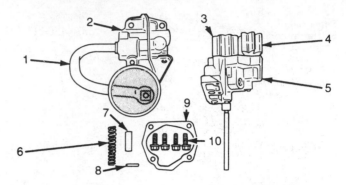

Fig. 2A.4 Oil pump components (Sec 4)

1 Pickup tube and screen	6 Pressure regulator spring
2 Pump cover	7 Pressure regulator valve
3 Drive gear and shaft	8 Retaining pin
4 Idler gear	9 Gasket
5 Pump body	10 Attaching bolts

6   Remove the pressure regulator valve retaining pin.
7   Remove the pressure regulator spring and valve.
8   If the pickup screen and pipe assembly must be replaced it is possible to remove the pipe and press the replacement in (with sealant). However, it is recommended that anyone without experience in this operation consult a GM dealer before proceeding.
9   Clean all parts with solvent. Allow to air dry or, if available, use compressed air.
10   Inspect the pump body and cover for cracks or signs of excessive wear.
11   Inspect the pump gears for damage or excessive wear.
12   If the pump gears or body are damaged or worn, the entire oil pump assembly must be replaced. The pump gears and body are not available separately.
13   Check the drive gear shaft and the pressure regulator valve for any looseness where they attach to the oil pump body.
14   Finally, before reassembling the oil pump, check to make sure that the oil pump shaft retainer is not split. Replace it if necessary.
15   Install the pressure regulator valve, spring and retaining pin.
16   Install the drive gear and shaft in the oil pump body.
17   Install the idler gear in the pump body. Use the alignment marks to position the gears just as they were before disassembly.
18   Install a new cover gasket.
19   Install the pump cover and tube brace and tighten the bolts to the specified torque.
20   Turn the pump drive shaft by hand to make sure the components are meshing smoothly.
21   Attach the pump and extension shaft with retainer to the rear main bearing cap. While aligning the pump with the two dowel pins at the bottom of the main bearing cap, align the top end of the hexagonal extension shaft with the lower end of the distributor drive gear.
22   Install the pump mounting bolts and tighten them to the specified torque.
23   Install the oil pan (refer to Section 3).

---

5   Intake manifold — removal and installation

1   Disconnect the negative battery cable from the battery.
2   Remove the air cleaner assembly, tagging each hose to be disconnected with a piece of numbered tape to simplify reinstallation.
3   Drain the coolant (refer to Chapter 1).
4   Tag and disconnect any electrical or vacuum lines which will interfere with manifold removal.
5   Remove the idler pulley and (if equipped) the AIR drivebelt.
6   Remove the power steering pump (if equipped) and lay it aside in an upright position.
7   Unbolt the AIR bracket from the manifold.
8   On models so equipped, remove the AIR through-bolt, the lower mounting bracket bolt and the power steering adjusting bracket.
9   Disconnect the throttle linkage and remove the carburetor or TBI unit (Chapter 4).

---

3   Oil pan — removal and installation

1   Disconnect the negative cable from the battery.
2   Remove the engine as described in Section 17.
3   Remove the oil pan mounting bolts and separate the oil pan from the engine.
4   Clean the oil pan and block sealing surfaces. Inspect the gasket sealing surfaces of the pan for distortion. Straighten them with a wood block and hammer if necessary.
5   Before installing the oil pan apply a thin coat of RTV-type sealant to both ends of the new rear oil pan seal. Do not let the sealant extend beyond the tabs of the seal. Install the seal securely into the rear main bearing cap.
6   Apply a uniform bead of RTV-type sealant (about 1/8-inch in diameter) to the oil pan side rails. The bead should run between the bolt holes and to the inside edge of each bolt hole. Do not apply sealant to the rear oil pan seal mating surface.
7   Apply a thin bead of RTV-type sealant to the timing cover mating surface on the oil pan. Make sure that the sealant meets the beads on the oil pan side rails.
8   Immediately attach the oil pan to the engine block, taking care not to smear the sealant.
9   Tighten the mounting bolts, working from the center of the pan out, to the specified torque.

---

4   Oil pump — removal, inspection and installation

1   Remove the oil pan (refer to Section 3).
2   Remove the oil screen bolt from the rear main bearing cap.
3   Remove the pump and extension shaft.
4   To disassemble the pump for inspection, first remove the cover attaching bolts and the cover. Mark the gear teeth so the gears can be reassembled with the same teeth indexing.
5   Remove the idler gear, drive gear and shaft from the pump body.

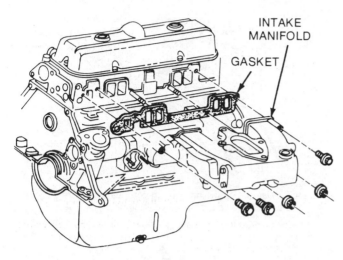

Fig. 2A.5 Intake manifold and related components (Sec 5)

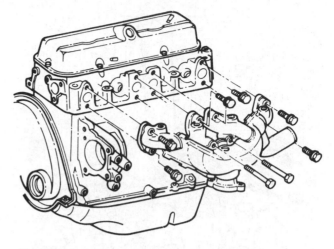

Fig. 2A.6 Exhaust manifold and related components (Sec 6)

2A

10 Remove the distributor.
11 Remove the mounting nuts and bolts from the intake manifold.
12 Separate the intake manifold and gasket from the engine. Scrape away all traces of gasket material from the intake manifold gasket mating surfaces.
13 Installation is the reverse of removal. Be sure to use a new gasket. Tighten the nuts/bolts to the specified torque, working in a criss-cross pattern from the center out.

6 Exhaust manifold — removal and installation

1   Disconnect the negative cable from the battery.
2   Disconnect the upper end of the exhaust pipe heat shield and position it forward.
3   Remove the engine oil dipstick and the air cleaner hot air duct-to-shroud screw.
4   Remove the hot air duct and hose, the dipstick tube bracket screw and, if so equipped, the air conditioner suction line bracket.
5   Unplug the oxygen sensor lead.
6   Loosen the alternator-to-support bolt and remove the two bracket-to-alternator bolts, taking care not to lose the spacer.
7   Remove the drivebelt and rotate the alternator up. Install the left bracket bolt loosely to act as a stop.
8   Remove the alternator brace from the cylinder head.
9   On AIR equipped models, remove the manifold-to-pipe hose and the AIR manifold-to-cylinder head bracket bolt.
10 On Pulsair equipped models, disconnect the Pulsair pipe.
11 Raise the vehicle, support it securely on jackstands and unbolt the exhaust pipe from the manifold. Lower the vehicle.
12 Remove the exhaust manifold-to-cylinder headbolts, lift the manifold off the exhaust pipe flange and remove the manifold from the engine.
13 Scrape all traces of gasket material from the exhaust manifold and cylinder head mating surfaces.
14 Clean all bolt and stud threads before installation. A wire brush can be used on the manifold mounting bolts, while a tap works well when cleaning the cylinder head bolt holes.
15 If a new manifold is being installed transfer all of the AIR components from the old manifold.
16 Installation is the reverse of removal. Be sure to use a new gasket and tighten all bolts to the specified torque.

7 Rocker arm cover — removal and installation

1   Remove the air cleaner assembly, tagging each hose to be disconnected with a piece of numbered tape to simplify installation.
2   Disconnect the throttle cable from the carburetor, making careful note of the exact locations of cable components and hardware to ensure correct reinstallation.

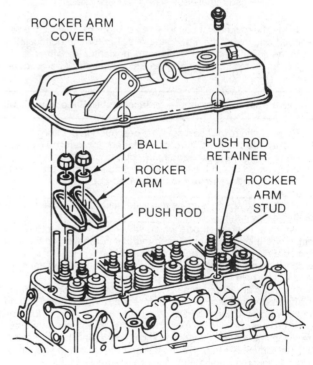

Fig. 2A.7 Valve train components (Sec 7 and 8)

3   Remove the PCV valve from the rocker arm cover.
4   Remove the spark plug wires from the spark plugs (refer to the removal technique described in Chapter 1), then remove the wires and retaining clips from the rocker arm cover. Be sure to label each wire before removal to ensure that all wires are reinstalled correctly.
5   Remove the distributor cap.
6   Disconnect the fuel vapor hoses from the harness pipes. Remove the retaining bolts from the harness pipes and remove the harness pipes.
7   Remove the rocker arm cover bolts.
8   Remove the rocker arm cover. **Note:** *If the cover sticks to the cylinder head, use a block of wood and a hammer to dislodge it. If the cover still will not come loose, pry on it carefully, but do not distort the sealing flange surface.*
9   Prior to installation of the cover, clean all dirt, oil and old gasket material from the sealing surfaces of the cover and cylinder head with a scraper and degreaser.
10 Apply a continuous 3/16-inch (5 mm) diameter bead of RTV-type sealant to the sealing flange of the cover. Be sure to apply the sealant inboard of the bolt holes.

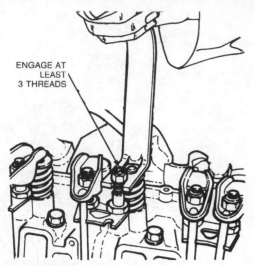

Fig. 2A.8   A special tool can be used to compress the valve springs and remove the spring keepers (Sec 8)

11   Place the rocker arm cover on the cylinder head while the sealant is still wet and install the mounting bolts. Tighten the bolts a little at a time to the specified torque. Work from the center to both ends.
12   Complete the installation by reversing the removal procedure.

8   Valve train components — replacement (cylinder head istalled)

1   Remove the rocker arm cover as described in Section 7.
2   If only the pushrod is to be replaced, loosen the rocker bolt enough to allow the rocker arm to be rotated away from the pushrod. Pull the pushrod out of the hole in the cylinder head. If the rocker arm is to be removed, remove the rocker bolt and pivot and lift off the rocker arm.
3   If the valve spring is to be removed, remove the spark plug from the affected cylinder.
4   There are two methods which will allow the valve to remain in place while the valve spring is removed. If you have access to compressed air, install an air hose adapter (GM part number J-23590) in the spark plug hole. When air pressure is applied to the adapter, the valves will be held in place by the pressure.
5   If you do not have access to compressed air, bring the piston of the affected cylinder to slightly before top dead center (TDC) on the compression stroke. Feed a long piece of 1/4-inch nylon cord in through the spark plug hole until it fills the combustion chamber. Be sure to leave the end of the cord hanging out of the spark plug hole so it can be removed easily. Rotate the crankshaft with a wrench (in the normal direction of rotation) until slight resistance is felt.
6   Install the rocker arm bolt (without the rocker arm).
7   Insert the slotted end of a valve spring compressing tool under the bolt head and compress the spring just enough to remove the spring keepers, then release the pressure on the tool.
8   Remove the retainer, cup shield, O-ring seal, spring, spring damper (if so equipped) and valve stem oil seal (if so equipped).
9   Inspection procedures for valve train components are covered in Section 10 and in Chapter 2, Part C.
10   Installation of the valve train components is the reverse of the removal procedure. Always use new valve stem oil seals whenever the spring keepers have been disturbed. Prior to installing the rocker arms, coat the bearing surfaces of the arms and rocker arm pivots with moly-based grease or engine assembly lube. Be sure to adjust the valve lash as detailed in Section 9

9   Valve lash — adjustment

1   Disconnect the cable from the negative battery terminal.
2   If the rocker arm cover is still on the engine, refer to Section 7 and remove it.
3   If the valve train components have been serviced just prior to this

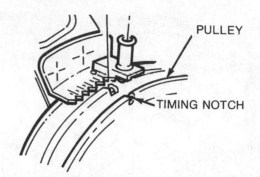

Fig. 2A.9   Use the crankshaft timing notches which are cut across the full width of the pulley when finding TDC (Sec 9)

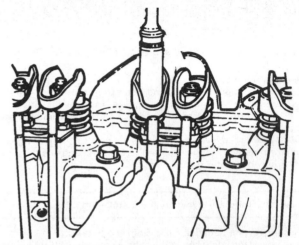

Fig. 2A.10   Adjusting the valve lash (Sec 9)

procedure, make sure that the components are completely reassembled.
4   Rotate the crankshaft until the number one piston is at top dead center (TDC) on the compression stroke. To make sure that you do not mix up the TDC positions of the number one and four pistons, check the position of the rotor in the distributor to see which terminal it is pointing at. Another method is to place your fingers on the number one rocker arms as the timing marks line up at the crankshaft pulley. If the rocker arms are not moving, the number one piston is at TDC. If they move as the timing marks line up, the number four piston is at TDC.
5   Back off the rocker arm nut until play is felt at the pushrod, then turn it back in just until all play is removed. This can be determined by rotating the pushrod while tightening the nut. When drag is felt at the pushrod, all lash has been removed. Now turn the nut in an additional 3/4-turn.
6   Adjust the number one and two cylinder intake valves and the number one and three cylinder exhaust valves with the crankshaft in this position, using the method just described.
7   Rotate the crankshaft until the number four piston is at TDC on the compression stroke and adjust the number three and four cylinder intake valves and the number two and four cylinder exhaust valves.
8   Refer to Section 7 and install the rocker arm cover.

10   Cylinder head — removal and installation

Removal
1   Remove the intake manifold as described in Section 5.
2   Remove the exhaust manifold as described in Section 6.
3   Remove the bolts that secure the alternator bracket to the cylinder head.
4   If so equipped, unbolt the air-conditioner compressor and swing it out of the way for clearance. **Caution:** *Do not disconnect any of the air-conditioning lines unless the system has been depressurized by a*

10.12 Removing the rocker arm nuts

10.13 Removing the pushrods

2A

10.18 Loosening the cylinder head mounting bolts

10.27 The cylinder head mounting bolts should be coated with sealant (arrows) as described in the text

dealer or repair shop, because personal injury may occur. Disconnection of the lines should not be necessary in this case.

5 Disconnect all electrical and vacuum lines from the cylinder head. Be sure to label the lines to simplify reinstallation.
6 Remove the upper radiator hose.
7 Remove the heater hoses.
8 Disconnect the spark plug wires and remove the spark plugs. Be sure to label the plug wires to simplify reinstallation.
9 Remove the distributor as described in Chapter 5.
10 Remove the rocker arm cover. To break the gasket seal it may be necessary to strike the cover with your hand or a rubber hammer. Do not pry between the sealing surfaces. Refer to Section 7 if necessary.
11 When disassembling the valve mechanisms, keep all of the components separate so they can be reinstalled in their original positions. A cardboard box or rack, numbered to correspond to the engine cylinders, can be used for this purpose.
12 Remove each of the rocker arm nuts and separate the rocker arms and pivots from the cylinder head (photo).
13 Remove the pushrods (photo).
14 Remove the air diverter valve from the mounting bracket.
15 Remove the AIR pump (if equipped) mounting bolts and remove the pump. Remove the upper AIR pump bracket.
16 Disconnect and plug the fuel line at the fuel pump.
17 Remove the ignition coil.
18 Loosen each of the cylinder head mounting bolts one turn at a time until they can be removed (photo). Note the length and position of each bolt to ensure correct reinstallation.
19 Lift the head off of the engine. If it is stuck to the engine block, do not attempt to pry it free, as you could damage the sealing surfaces. Instead, use a hammer and block of wood to tap the head and break the gasket seal. Place the head on a block of wood to prevent

damage to the gasket surface.
20 Remove the cylinder head gasket.
21 Refer to Chapter 2C for cylinder head disassembly and valve service procedures.

Installation
22 If a new cylinder head is being installed, transfer all external parts from the old cylinder head to the new one.
23 If not already done, thoroughly clean the gasket surfaces on the cylinder head and the engine block. Do not gouge or otherwise damage the gasket surfaces.
24 To get the proper torque readings, the threads of the head bolts must be clean. This also applies to the threaded holes in the engine block. Run a tap through the holes to ensure that they are clean.
25 Place the gasket in position over the engine block dowel pins.
26 Carefully lower the cylinder head onto the engine, over the dowel pins and the gasket.
27 Coat the threads of each cylinder head bolt and the point at which the head and the bolt meet with a sealing compound and install the bolts finger tight (photo). Do not tighten any of the bolts at this time.
28 Tighten each of the bolts a little at a time in the sequence shown in the accompanying illustration. Continue tightening in this sequence

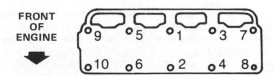

Fig. 2A.11 Cylinder head bolt tightening sequence (Sec 10)

until the proper torque reading is obtained. As a final check, work around the head in a front-to-rear sequence to make sure none of the bolts have been left out of the sequence.

29   The remaining installation steps are the reverse of removal.

11   Hydraulic lifters — removal, inspection and installation

1   A noisy valve lifter can be isolated when the engine is idling. Place a length of hose or tubing near the position of each valve while listening at the other end of the tube. Another method is to remove the rocker arm cover and, with the engine idling, place a finger on each of the valve spring retainers, one at a time. If a valve lifter is defective it will be evident from the shock felt at the retainer as the valve seats.

2   The most likely cause of a noisy valve lifter is a piece of dirt trapped between the plunger and the lifter body.

3   Remove the rocker arm cover as described in Section 7.

4   Remove the intake manifold as described in Section 5.

5   Loosen the rocker arm nut and rotate the rocker arm away from the pushrod.

6   Remove the pushrod.

7   To remove the lifter, a special hydraulic lifter removal tool should be used or a scribe can be positioned at the top of the lifter and used to force the lifter up and out of the bore. Do not use pliers or other tools on the outside of the lifter body, because they will damage the finished surface and render the lifter useless.

8   The lifters should be kept separate for reinstallation in their original positions.

9   To dismantle a valve lifter, hold the plunger down with a pushrod and then extract the retainer spring with a small screwdriver.

10   Remove the pushrod seat and the metering valve.

11   Remove the plunger, ball check valve and plunger spring. Remove the ball check valve and spring by prying them out with a small screwdriver.

12   Clean the lifter components with solvent and dry them with compressed air. Examine the internal components for wear and check the ball carefully for flat spots. **Note:** *Refer to Chapter 2, Part C, for additional lifter (and camshaft) inspection procedures.*

13   If the lifters are worn they must be replaced with new ones and the camshaft must be replaced as well (see Chapter 2, Part C). If the lifters are contaminated with dirt, they can be cleaned and reinstalled — they may operate normally.

14   Reassembly should be done in the following manner:

a)   Place the ball check valve on the small hole in the bottom of the plunger.

b)   Insert the ball check spring into the seat in the valve retainer and place the retainer over the ball so that the spring rests on the ball. Using a small screwdriver, carefully press the retainer into position in the plunger.

c)   Place the plunger spring over the ball retainer, invert the lifter body and slide it over the spring and plunger. Make sure the oil holes in the body and plunger line up.

d)   Fill the assembly with 10-weight oil. Place the metering valve and pushrod seat in position, press down on the seat and install the retainer spring.

15   When installing the lifters, make sure they are replaced in their original bores and coat them with moly-based grease or engine assembly lube.

16   The remaining installation steps are the reverse of removal.

12   Crankshaft pulley hub and front oil seal — removal and installation

1   Remove the cable from the negative battery terminal.

2   Loosen the accessory drivebelt tension adjusting bolts, as necessary, and remove the drivebelts. Tag each belt as it is removed to simplify reinstallation.

3   With the parking brake applied and the shifter in Park (automatic) or in gear (manual) to prevent the engine from turning over, remove the crank pulley bolt. A breaker bar will probably be necessary, since the bolt is very tight.

4   Mark the position of the pulley in relation to the hub (photo). Remove the bolts and separate the pulley from the hub.

5   Using a puller, remove the hub from the crankshaft (photo).

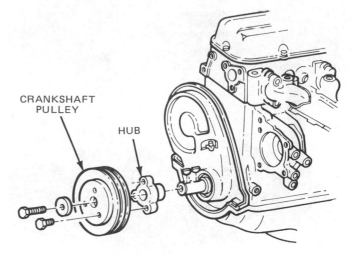

Fig. 2A.12 Crankshaft pulley and hub components (Sec 12)

CRANKSHAFT PULLEY

HUB

12.4   Always mark the position of the pulley prior to removal

12.5   Using a hub puller to remove the crankshaft hub

2A

12.9   Using the hub bolt to draw the hub into place

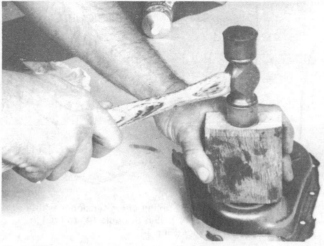

13.6   Using a block of wood to install the front oil seal squarely in the timing cover

6   Carefully pry the oil seal out of the front cover with a large screwdriver. Be careful not to distort the cover.
7   Install the new seal with the helical lip toward the rear of the engine. Drive the seal into place using a seal installation tool or a large socket. If there is enough room, a block of wood and hammer can also be used.
8   Apply a thin layer of clean multi-purpose grease to the seal contact surface of the hub.
9   Position the pulley hub on the crankshaft and slide it through the seal until it bottoms against the crankshaft gear. Note that the slot in the hub must be aligned with the Woodruff key in the end of the crankshaft. The hub-to-crankshaft bolt can also be used to press the hub into position (photo).
10   Install the crank pulley on the hub, noting the alignment marks made during removal. The pulley-to-hub bolts should be coated with Drylock 299, or equivalent, whenever they are removed and installed.
11   Tighten the hub-to-crankshaft and pulley-to-hub bolts to the specified torque.
12   The remaining installation steps are the reverse of removal. Tighten the drivebelts to the proper tension (refer to Chapter 1).

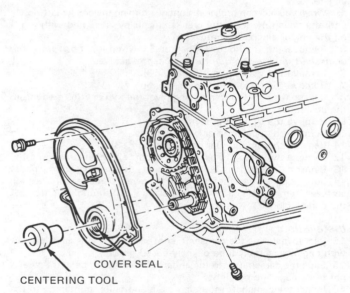

COVER SEAL

CENTERING TOOL

Fig. 2A.13   Timing chain cover components (Sec 13)

13   Timing gear cover — removal and installation

1   Remove the crankshaft pulley hub as described in Section 12.
2   Remove the oil pan-to-timing gear cover bolts.
3   Remove the cover-to-block bolts and remove the cover.
4   Using a scraper and degreaser, remove all dirt and old gasket material from the sealing surfaces of the timing gear cover, engine block and oil pan.
5   Replace the front oil seal by carefully prying it out of the timing gear cover with a large screwdriver. Do not distort the cover.
6   Install the new seal with the helical lip toward the inside of the cover. Drive the seal into place using a seal installation tool or a large socket and hammer. A block of wood will also work (photo).
7   Apply a thin (2 mm) bead of RTV-type sealant to the front sealing surface of the timing cover.
8   Apply a thin (3 mm) bead of RTV-type sealant to the oil pan surface of the timing cover.
9   Insert the hub through the cover seal and place the cover in position on the block as the hub slides onto the crankshaft.
10   Install the oil pan-to-cover bolts and partially tighten them.
11   Install the bolts that secure the cover to the block, then tighten all of the mounting bolts to the specified torque.
12   Complete the installation by reversing the removal procedure.

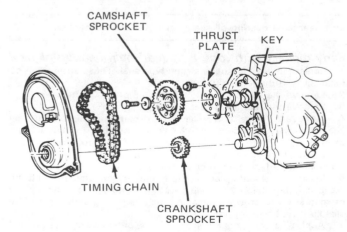

CAMSHAFT SPROCKET

THRUST PLATE   KEY

TIMING CHAIN

CRANKSHAFT SPROCKET

Fig. 2A.14   Timing chain and sprocket layout (Sec 14)

14   Timing chain and sprockets — inspection, removal and installation

1   Disconnect the cable from the negative battery terminal.

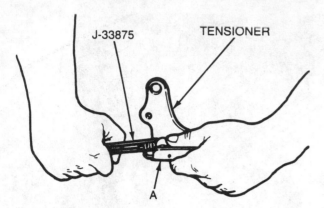

Fig. 2A.15 Compressing the timing chain tensioner with a special tool. Insert a pin or nail in the hole (A) to hold in place (Sec 14)

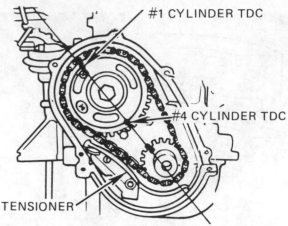

Fig. 2A.16 The timing sprocket marks in proper alignment (Sec 14)

2   Remove the crankshaft pulley hub (refer to Section 12).
3   Remove the timing cover (refer to Section 13).
4   Before removing the chain and sprockets, visually inspect the teeth on the sprockets for signs of wear and the chain for looseness. Also check the condition of the timing chain tensioner.
5   If either or both sprockets show any signs of wear (edges on the teeth of the camshaft sprocket not 'square,' bright or blue areas on the teeth of either sprocket, chipping, pitting, etc.), they should be replaced with new ones. Wear in these areas is very common.
6   Failure to replace a worn timing chain may result in erratic engine performance, loss of power and lowered gas mileage.
7   If any one component requires replacement, all related components, including the tensioners, should be replaced as well.
8   If it is determined that the timing components require replacement, proceed as follows.
9   Turn the engine over until the marks on the camshaft and crankshaft line up in a straight line. Do not attempt to remove either sprocket or the timing chain until this is done and do not turn the crankshaft or camshaft after the sprockets/chain are removed.
10 Remove the two camshaft sprocket retaining bolts and lift the camshaft sprocket and timing chain off the front of the engine. It may be necessary to tap the sprocket with a soft-faced hammer to dislodge it.
11 If it is necessary to remove the crankshaft sprocket, it can be withdrawn from the crankshaft with a puller.
12 Attach the crankshaft sprocket to the crankshaft using a bolt and washer from the puller set.
13 Lubricate the thrust (rear) surface of the camshaft sprocket with moly-based grease or engine assembly lube. Install the timing chain over the camshaft sprocket with slack in the chain hanging down over the crankshaft sprocket.
14 With the timing marks aligned, slip the chain over the crankshaft sprocket. Align the dowel in the camshaft with the dowel hole in the camshaft sprocket and install the sprocket on the camshaft. Draw the camshaft sprocket into place with the two retaining bolts. Do not hammer or attempt to drive the camshaft sprocket into place, as it could dislodge the welch plug at the rear of the engine.
15 With the chain and both sprockets in place, check again to ensure that the timing marks on the two sprockets are properly aligned. If not, remove the camshaft sprocket and move the camshaft until the marks align.
16 Lubricate the chain with engine oil and install the remaining components in the reverse order of removal. The timing chain tensioner spring must be comrpessed using a special tool such as GM No. J-33875 or equivalent, prior to installation. Insert a nail or cotter pin in the hole (A in the accompanying illustration) to hold the spring in place during installation. Remove the nail or pin after installation.

15   Camshaft — removal and installation

Removal
1   Remove the engine (Section 17) and mount it on a stand.
2   Remove the spark plugs.

3   Place your finger over the number one spark plug hole while turning the crankshaft with a wrench on the pulley bolt at the front of the engine.
4   When you feel compression, continue turning the crankshaft slowly until the timing mark on the crankshaft pulley is aligned with the 0 on the engine timing indicator.
5   Remove the distributor (Chapter 5). **Note:** *Do not rotate the crankshaft until the distributor has been reinstalled.*
6   Remove the water pump (Chapter 3).
7   Remove the rocker arm cover (Section 7).
8   Loosen the rocker arm nuts and pivot the rocker arms away from the pushrods.
9   Remove the fuel pump (Chapter 4).
10 Remove the pushrods and valve lifters.
11 Remove the timing gear cover (Section 13).
12 Remove the timing chain and camshaft sprocket (Section 14).
13 Remove the attaching bolts and remove the camshaft thrust plate.
14 Supporting the camshaft carefully to prevent damage to the bearing surfaces, remove the camshaft by pulling it out through the front of the engine block.

Installation
15 Prior to installing the camshaft, coat each of the lobes and journals with engine assembly lube or moly-based grease.
15 Slide the camshaft into the engine block. Again, be extra careful not to damage the bearings.
16 Install the camshaft mounting plate and bolts, tightening to the specified torque.
17 Complete the installation procedure by reversing the removal procedure, referring to the appropriate Sections and Chapters.

16   Rear main bearing oil seal — removal and installation

Early models with rope-type rear main bearing oil seal
1   Earlier models may have a rope-type seal. These seals must be replaced with the later type rubber seal.
2   Remove the oil pan (Section 3) and oil pump (Section 4).
3   Remove the rear main bearing cap.
4   Remove the upper and lower seal and clean any oil from the seal channel. It may be necessary to loosen the number 2, 3 and 4 main bearing cap bolts to aid in the installation of the upper seal.
5   Apply a very thin coat of sealant such as GM 1050026 to the outside diameter of the new rubber seal.
6   Insert the seal into place in the cylinder block while rotating the crankshaft, if necessary, to help the seal roll into position. Use a piece of shim stock to prevent damaging the seal during installation. The seal lip must be facing in.
7   Apply a very thin coat of sealant to the outer half of the new seal (outer diameter) and install it in the main bearing cap.
8   Place a strip of Plastigage on the rear main bearing or journal, install the main bearing cap and tighten the bolts to the specified torque.
9   Remove the cap and measure the Plastigage with the enclosed

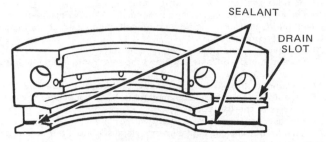

Fig. 2A.17 On 1982 and 1983 models, apply sealant to the areas marked (arrows) (Sec 16)

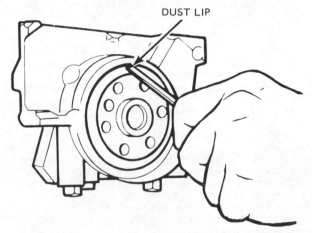

Fig. 2A.19 Prying out the thick rear main oil seal with a screwdriver (Sec 16)

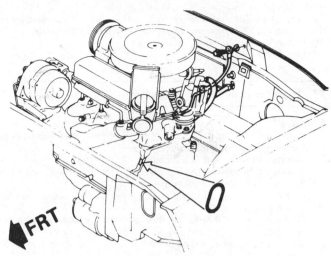

FRT

Fig. 2A.18 An oval mark on the engine at the location shown indicates that it is equipped with a thick rear main oil seal (Sec 16)

2A

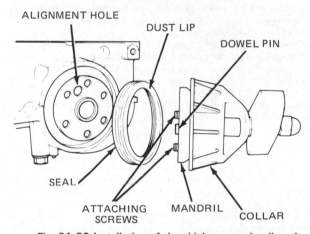

Fig. 2A.20 Installation of the thick rear main oil seal (Sec 16)

scale to make sure the clearance is within the specifications. Carefully clean all traces of Plastigage from the journal and bearing. Lightly lubricate the bearing with clean engine oil.

10 Apply a 1/32-inch wide bead of anaerobic sealant to the main bearing cap between the rear main seal end and the oil pan rear seal groove, as shown in the accompanying illustration. Make sure the sealant does not get on the rear main seal or in the drain slot.

11 Just before assembly apply a light coat of clean engine oil to the surface of the crankshaft which will contact the seal and install the main bearing cap. Tighten all bearing cap bolts to the specified torque.

12 Install the oil pump and pan.

Later models with one-piece rubber seals

13 These models use rear oil seals of two different thicknesses and design. They require two different replacement procedures as well as some special tools and techniques. Read through the procedures before attempting this procedure yourself, as you may want to leave seal replacement on these models to your dealer or a properly equipped shop. To determine whether your vehicle is equipped with a thick or thin rear main oil seal, refer to the accompanying illustration.

Thick rear main bearing oil seal

14 Remove the transaxle.

15 If equipped with a manual transaxle, remove the pressure plate and clutch disc.

16 Remove the flywheel mounting bolts and separate it from the crankshaft.

17 Using a screwdriver or pry bar, carefully remove the oil seal from the cylinder block. It is very important not to damage the crankshaft surface while prying with the tool.

18 Check the inner diameter of the seal mounting surface for nicks and scratches, carefully smoothing with a fine file if necessary.

19 A special tool is needed to install the replacement oil seal (GM no. J-34686). Slide the seal onto the mandril until the dust lip bottoms squarely against the collar of the tool.

20 Align the dowel pin of the tool with the dowel pin hole in the crankshaft and attach the tool to the crankshaft by hand-tightening the bolts.

21 Turn the tool handle until the collar bottoms against the case, seating the seal.

22 Loosen the tool handle and remove the bolts. Remove the tool.

23 Check the seal and make sure that it is seated squarely in the bore.

24 Install the flywheel and tighten the bolts to the specified torque.

25 If equipped with a manual transaxle, install the clutch disc and pressure plate.

26 Install the transaxle.

Thin rear main bearing oil seal

27 Remove the engine and mount it on an engine stand.

28 Remove the oil pan and oil pump.

29 Remove the front timing cover.

30 Remove the crankshaft (refer to Chapter 2C).

31 Remove the old oil seal and clean all traces of sealant from the main bearing cap, crankcase groove and crankshaft seal area.

32 Apply a thin bead (approximately 1 mm) of sealant such as GM no. 1052756 to the seal outside diameter. Place the seal tool on the rear of the crankshaft with the arrow pointing toward the rear of the engine, as shown in the accompanying illustration.

33 Place the crankshaft in position in the cylinder block with the tool in place.

34 Remove the tool.

35 Lubricate the crankshaft journals lightly with clean engine oil.

36 Seal the rear main bearing split line surface area with the sealant and install the main bearing cap.

37 Install the main bearings and caps and tighten the bolts to the specified torque.

38 Install the rod bearings and caps and oil pump, tightening the bolts

to the specified torque.
39 Align the crankshaft timing mark and install the cam sprocket and the timing chain, tightening the bolts to the specified torque.
40 Install the timing cover and oil pan.
41 Install the engine.

---

17 Engine — removal and installation

Removal

1   Disconnect the battery cables (negative first, then positive) and drain the cooling system (Chapter 1).
2   Remove the air cleaner assembly.
3   Remove the power steering pump (if equipped) and windshield washer reservoir and lay them aside.
4   On air conditioning equipped models, remove the relay bracket from the bulkhead connector.
5   Remove the bulkhead connector and unplug the harness connections.
6   On cruise control equipped models, remove the servo bracket and lay it aside.
7   Tag and disconnect the vacuum hoses and electrical wires.
8   Remove the master cylinder from the vacuum booster and lay it aside in an upright position.
9   Disconnect the heater hose from the hot water pipe on the engine.
10 Remove the cooling fan and horn assemblies.
11 Remove the throttle linkage.
12 Raise the vehicle and support it securely on jackstands.
13 Remove the air-conditioner brace (if equipped).
14 Remove the exhaust pipe shield and starter.
15 Disconnect the exhaust pipe from the manifold.
16 Remove the front wheels.
17 Disconnect the stabilizer bar from the lower control arms and the balljoints from the steering knuckle, then remove the driveaxles (Chapter 11).

18 Remove the transaxle strut (Chapter 7)
19 On air-conditioning equipped models, remove the inner fender shield, remove the air conditioner drivebelt, disconnect the wires and remove the compressor.
20 Remove the rear engine mount assembly.
21 On automatic transaxle equipped models, remove the engine oil filter.
22 Disconnect the speedometer cable and lower the vehicle.
23 On automatic transaxle equipped models, disconnect and plug the cooler lines at the transaxle.
24 Remove the front engine mount nuts.
25 On manual transaxle equipped models, disconnect the clutch cable at the transaxle.
26 On automatic transaxle equipped models, disconnect the detent cable.
27 Remove the transaxle mount and connect a hoist to the engine.
28 Lift the engine and transaxle assembly from the vehicle.

Installation

29 Install a suitable engine mount alignment bolt to insure proper drive axle alignment during installation.
30 Carefully lower the engine and transaxle assembly into position in the vehicle.
31 Install the transaxle mount bolts and the left front engine mount nuts.
32 Install all of the components removed or disconnected during engine removal.
33 If the engine mount alignment bolt is difficult to remove, loosen the transaxle mount adjusting bolts. Adjust the position of the mounts until the bolt can be removed easily, indicating that the driveline is in alignment, then tighten the adjusting bolts.
34 Adjust the drivebelt tension (Chapter 1).
35 Adjust the manual transaxle clutch cable or automatic transaxle detent cable (Chapter 8).
36 Check all fluid levels, adding as necessary (Chapter 1)

Chapter 2 Part B
1.8 liter overhead cam (OHC) engine

Refer to Chapter 13 for specifications and information related to 1985 and later 2.0/2.2 liter engines

Contents

2B

Specifications

Oil pump clearances
    idler gear-to-body . . . .   0.004 to 0.007 in
                                    (0.11 to 0.19 mm)
    drive gear-to-body . . . .   0.14 to 0.17 in
                                      (3.55 to 4.31 mm)
    gear-to-cover . . . .   0.001 to 0.003 in
                                      (0.02 to 0.08 mm)

Torque specifications	Ft-lbs
Camshaft carrier cover bolts	5
Camshaft carrier/cylinder head bolts (following procedure in text)	18.4
Camshaft sprocket retaining bolt	34
Camshaft thrust plate bolts	5.9
Crankshaft pulley-to-sprocket bolts	20
Crankshaft sprocket retaining bolt	115
Clutch pressure plate-to-flywheel bolts	50
Connecting rod cap bolts	39
Exhaust manifold bolts	16
Flywheel bolts	45
Intake manifold nuts	25
Main bearing cap bolts	57
Oil dipstick tube bolts	11
Oil pan drain plug	30
Oil pan bolts	5
Oil pump plug	15
Pickup tube-to-block bolts	5
Pickup tube-to-oil pump bolts	5
Timing belt front cover bolts	5
Timing belt rear cover bolts	19
Transaxle mount	40
Transaxle-to-engine	55
Water pump retaining bolts	19

Note: *Refer to Chapter 2, Part C, for additional specifications*

1 General information

The overhead cam (OHC) engine is made of cast iron with a removable aluminum head. The camshaft is located in the cylinder head and actuates the valves via rocker arms and hydraulic valve compensators.

The forward Sections in this Part of Chapter 2 are devoted to 'in vehicle' repair procedures for the OHC engine. The latter Sections involve the removal and installation procedures for the OHC engine. Information concerning engine block and cylinder head servicing can be found in Part C of this Chapter.

The repair procedures included in this part are based on the assumption that the engine is still installed in the vehicle. Therefore, if this information is being used during a complete engine overhaul, with the engine already out of the vehicle and on a stand, many of the steps included here will not apply.

The specifications included in this part of Chapter 2 apply only to the engine and procedures found here. For specifications regarding OHV engines, see Part A. Part C of Chapter 2 contains the specifications necessary for engine block and cylinder head rebuilding.

2   Camshaft cover — removal and installation

Removal

1   Remove the air cleaner assembly.
2   Remove the PVC valve and hose.
3   Remove the retaining bolts and separate the cover from the engine. It may be necessary to break the gasket seal by either tapping the cover with a soft-faced hammer or inserting a very thin-bladed scraper or screwdriver at the corner (photos).
4   Place clean rags in the camshaft gallery to keep foreign material from falling into the engine (photo).
5   Clean all traces of gasket material from the camshaft cover gasket mating surfaces. Be careful not to nick or gouge the soft aluminum (photo).

Installation

6   Place the cover and new gasket in position. Install the attaching bolts and tighten to the specified torque.
7   Install the air cleaner and PCV assemblies.

3   Timing belt front cover — removal and installation

1   Disconnect the negative cable from the battery.
2   Remove the coolant reservoir (Chapter 3) and disconnect the char-

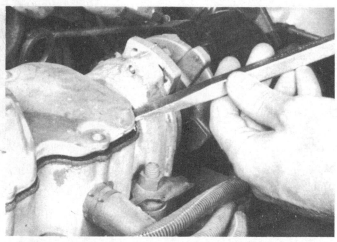

2.3   Breaking the camshaft cover gasket seal by tapping with a chisel and hammer

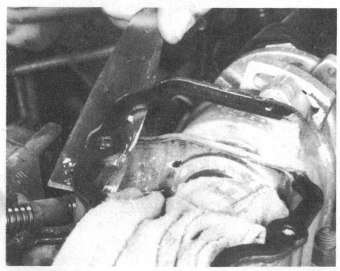

2.5   When removing the camshaft cover gasket with a scraper, be careful not to nick or gouge the soft aluminum surface of the head

coal canister purge line.
3   Remove the retaining clips and bolts and lift the cover from the engine.
4   Installation is the reverse of removal.

4   Timing belt rear cover — removal and installation

Removal

1   Remove the timing belt cover (Section 3) and timing belt (Section 5).
2   Remove the retaining bolts and separate the cover from the engine.

Installation

3   Place the cover in position and install the bolts. Tighten them to the specified torque.
4   Install the timing belt and front cover.

5   Timing belt — removal, installation and adjustment

Removal

1   Remove the timing belt front cover (Section 3).
2   Drain the coolant (Chapter 1).
3   On air conditioned models remove the compressor and drive belt. Move the compressor out of the way, taking care not to twist or damage the hoses.
4   Raise the vehicle and support it securely on jackstands.
5   Remove the right front wheel.

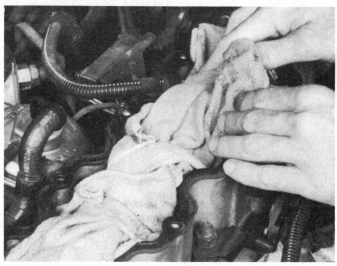

2.4   Rags placed in the camshaft gallery will keep foreign material out

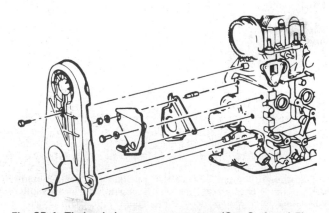

Fig. 2B.1   Timing belt cover components (Sec 3, 4 and 5)

6   Remove the inner splash panel bolts and detach the panel from the wheel well (photo).

7   Rotate the crankshaft until the mark on the pulley is aligned with the ten degree BTDC mark on the indicator scale and the camshaft sprocket mark lines up with the mark on the camshaft carrier (photos). If the belt broke while the engine was running, the camshaft and crankshaft will have to be turned separately to align the marks.

8   Remove the crankshaft bolts and pulley.

9   Remove the timing probe for access and loosen the water pump bolts.

10   Use a large screwdriver on the water pump to break the gasket loose (photo).

11   Grasp the water pump with locking pliers and release the tension from the belt (photo).

12   Slip the belt off of the pulleys. **Caution:** *Do not rotate the engine or sprockets while the timing belt is off or serious damage could result when the engine is started.*

Installation

13   Slip the new belt onto the sprockets, install the crankshaft pulley and make sure the crankshaft and camshaft marks are aligned.

Adjustment

14   Rotate the water pump to apply tension to the timing belt and tighten the water pump.

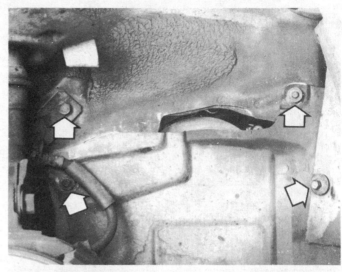

5.6   The inner fender splash panel retaining bolt locations (arrows)

2B

5.7A   The crankshaft pulley notch aligned with the 10 degree BTDC mark (arrows)

5.7B   The timing marks are easy-to-see grooves cast into the camshaft sprocket and carrier (arrows)

5.10   Pry out on the water pump to break the gasket loose

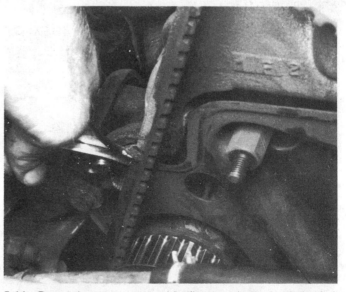

5.11   Rotate the water pump with pliers to release the timing belt tension

5.15   Using a ruler to check the timing belt deflection

6.4   Hold the camshaft with a large wrench at the flats provided and remove the sprocket bolt

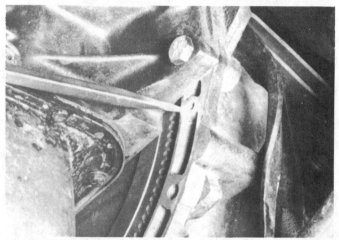

7.2   A screwdriver inserted in the flywheel starter gear teeth will lock the engine so the crankshaft pulley bolt can be loosened

15   Measure the deflection of the belt between the water pump and the camshaft pulley with a straightedge and a ruler. Adjust the belt tension until the deflection is 1/4-inch (photo).
16   Install the timing probe, timing belt front cover, inner splash panel and wheel and lower the vehicle.
17   Install any components which were removed from the engine and refill the cooling system.

---

6   Camshaft sprocket — removal and installation

Removal
1   Remove the timing belt front cover (Section 3).
2   Remove the timing belt (make sure the mark on the sprocket is aligned with one on the cover) (Section 5).
3   Remove the camshaft cover (Section 2).
4   Hold the camshaft with a wrench on the flats located between the lobes and remove the sprocket bolt (photo). The camshaft must not be allowed to turn.
5   Remove the sprocket and washer.

Installation
6   Place the sprocket in position on the camshaft and align the sprocket and cover marks.
7   Hold the camshaft with the wrench and install the washer and nut. Tighten the nut to the specified torque.
8   Install the timing belt, cover and any other components which were removed.

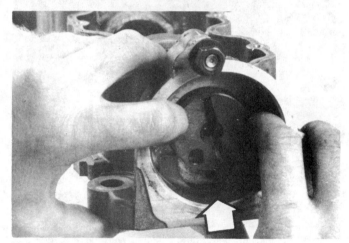

8.6   Push down on the ends of the retainer (arrow) to release it from the groove in the camshaft

---

7   Crankshaft sprocket — removal and installation

Removal
1   Remove the timing belt front cover (Section 3) and timing belt (Section 5).
2   Remove the flywheel cover and lock the flywheel in place with a screwdriver inserted between the teeth. The screwdriver must be wedged against the engine block and not the transaxle case (photo).
3   Remove the sprocket bolt, washer and sprocket.

Installation
4   Place the sprocket and washer on the crankshaft and install the bolt. Tighten the bolt to the specified torque.
5   Remove the screwdriver and install the flywheel cover.
6   Install the timing belt and front cover.

---

8   Camshaft — removal and installation

Removal
1   Remove the camshaft cover (Section 2).
2   Remove the rocker arm and valve lash compensator assemblies

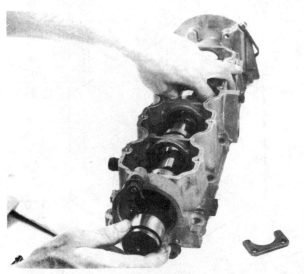

8.7 Carefully slide the camshaft out of the carrier

9.8 Check the camshaft retainer contact surface (arrow) for wear

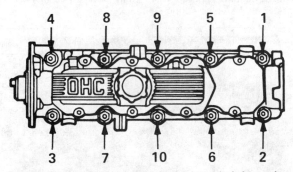

Fig. 2B.2 Camshaft carrier/cylinder head bolt loosening sequence (Sec 9 and 15)

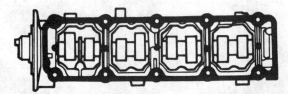

Fig. 2B.3 Camshaft carrier mating surface anaerobic sealer application diagram (Sec 9 and 15)

9.7 Inspect the camshaft carrier bearing surface (arrow) for scoring and wear

(Section 10).
3   Remove the front timing belt cover (Section 3), timing belt (Section 5) and camshaft sprocket (Section 6).
4   Remove the distributor (Chapter 5).
5   Remove the camshaft retainer Allen head mounting bolts.
6   Remove the retainer (photo).
7   Withdraw the camshaft from the carrier, taking care not to damage the lobes or bearing surfaces (photo).

Installation
8   Pry out the camshaft front oil seal and install a new one.
9   Insert the camshaft into the carrier, taking care not to damage the lobes, seal or bearing surfaces.
10 Install the retainer and bolts. Tighten the bolts to the specified torque.
11 Check the camshaft end play to make sure it is as specified.
12 Install the distributor, camshaft sprocket, timing belt and cover, rocker arm and valve lash compensators and camshaft cover.

9 Camshaft carrier — removal, inspection and installation

Note: *Whenever the camshaft carrier/cylinder head bolts are loosened or removed, the engine must be cold and the cylinder head gasket must be replaced with a new one (Section 15).*

Removal
1   Disconnect the PCV hose from the camshaft cover.
2   Remove the distributor (Chapter 5).
3   Remove the camshaft sprocket (Section 6).
4   Loosen the camshaft carrier/cylinder head bolts a little at a time in the sequence shown in the accompanying illustration. Remove the bolts and keep them in order, using a numbered box or piece of cardboard.
5   Separate the camshaft carrier assembly from the engine.

Inspection
6   Remove the camshaft and carrier oil seal (Section 8).
7   Measure the camshaft carrier bearing bores to make sure they are not out-of-round or worn beyond the specifications. Inspect the bearing surfaces for nicks, scoring and wear (photo).
8   Inspect the camshaft retainer surface for wear, scoring or damage. Replace it with a new one if necessary (photo).

Installation
9   Install a new carrier front oil seal and the camshaft (Section 8).
10 Install a new cylinder head gasket (Section 15).
11 Clean the mating surfaces of the camshaft carrier and the cylinder head and apply a thin (3 mm) bead of anaerobic sealer around the carrier mating surfaces, as shown in the accompanying illustration.
12 Place the camshaft carrier in position on the cylinder head and install the bolts. Tighten the bolts, following the procedure described in Section 15.

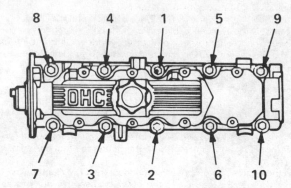

Fig. 2B.4 Camshaft carrier/cylinder head bolt tightening sequence (Sec 9 and 15)

13 Install the camshaft sprocket.
14 Install the distributor.
15 Connect the PCV hose to the camshaft cover.

10 Rocker arm and valve lash compensator — removal and installation

Removal

1 Disconnect the PCV valve hose from the camshaft cover.
2 Remove the camshaft cover.
3 Remove the camshaft carrier and camshaft assembly.
4 Remove the rocker arms and valve lash compensators and keep them in order in a numbered container (photos).

Installation

5 Install the valve lash compensators, followed by the rocker arms, in their original locations. Valve lash adjustment is not required on these models.
6 Install the camshaft carrier and cover and connect the PCV hose.

11 Crankshaft front oil seal — replacement

1 Drain the engine oil (Chapter 1).
2 Remove the crankshaft sprocket (Section 7).
3 Remove the pulley key and thrust washer from the crankshaft.
4 Pry the old oil seal out with a screwdriver, taking care not to damage the sealing surface (photo).

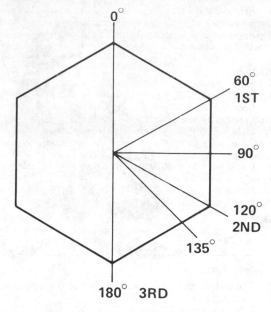

Fig. 2B.5 Camshaft carrier/cylinder head bolt tightening procedure diagram (Sec 9 and 15)

5 Apply a thin coat of RTV-type sealant around the outer diameter of the new seal.
6 Place the seal squarely in position in the bore.
7 Install the seal in the bore using a tool made up of a long metric coarse thread bolt, a proper diameter piece of pipe and washers (photos). Make sure the seal is seated completely in the bore.
8 Install the thrust washer, key and pulley.
9 Fill the engine with the proper amount of the specified oil.

12 Valves, springs and valve stem oil seals — removal and installation

Removal

1 Remove the camshaft carrier (Section 9) and cylinder head (Section 15).
2 Remove the rocker arms and valve lash compensators (Section 10).
3 Use a suitable special tool to compress the valve springs, one at a time, and remove the valve keepers. Release the compressor and remove the retainer, spring, valve stem oil seal and exhaust valve rotators or intake valve spring seat.

10.4A Lift the rocker arms off and keep them in order

10.4B The lash compensators can be removed with a magnet

4   Remove the valves one at a time and keep them in order in a numbered rack or piece of cardboard so they can be reinstalled in their original locations. Refer to Chapter 2, Part C for valve component inspection procedures.

Installation

5   Insert each valve into its original guide.
6   Install the intake valve spring seats and exhaust valve rotators.
7   Coat the first valve stem with clean engine oil then slide the supplied plastic sleeve onto the valve stem.
8   Slide the new valve stem oil seal over the valve stem, seat it over the valve guide using the plastic sleeve and then remove the sleeve. Repeat the procedure for the remaining valves.
9   Install the valve spring and retainers and use a valve spring compressor to install the keepers.
10   Install the valve lash compensators and rocker arms.
11   Install the camshaft carrier and cylinder head.

---

13   Intake manifold — removal and installation

Removal

1   Disconnect the negative cable from the battery and remove the air cleaner assembly.
2   Drain the coolant (Chapter 1).

3   Remove the alternator (Chapter 5).
4   Remove the power steering pump (if equipped).
5   Remove the throttle cable from the intake manifold bracket.
6   Disconnect the throttle and (if equipped) downshift and TV cables from the EFI assembly. To remove the cable from the bracket, pull up while using a screwdriver to push the snap in (photo).
7   Disconnect the vacuum brake hose from the fitting on the vacuum reservoir.
8   Disconnect and plug the fuel lines at the flex joints.
9   From below the engine compartment, remove the preheat water hose from the water pump and intake manifold.
10   Remove the 'S' hose from the inlet tube and water pump (photo).
11   Remove the starter motor (Chapter 5) and the four lower manifold retaining nuts.
12   In the engine compartment, disconnect the ECM electrical harness, remove the bracket and move the harness assembly out of the way for access to the lower manifold nuts.
13   Remove the five retaining nuts and separate the intake manifold from the engine.
14   Remove the gasket (photo).

Installation

15   Clean all traces of gasket and other foreign material from the manifold and cylinder head mating surfaces.
16   Install a new gasket, place the manifold in position on the studs and install the retaining nuts. Tighten the nuts to the specified torque.

2B

11.4   Removing the front oil seal with a screwdriver

11.7A   A tool for installing the front crankshaft oil seal can be made from pieces of pipe, washers and a bolt

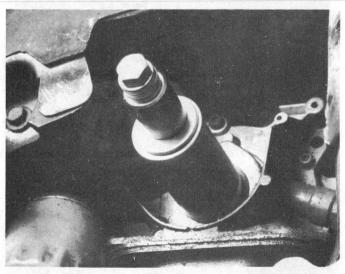
11.7B   Tighten the tool bolt slowly to push the seal squarely into position

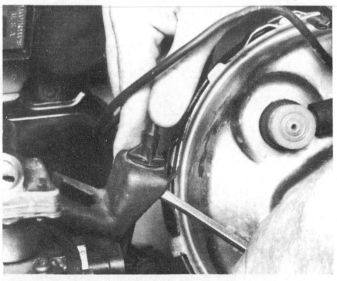
13.6   Disconnect the throttle cable from the bracket by pulling up while pushing in on the snap with a screwdriver

Work from the center of the manifold out, in a criss-cross pattern.

17 Install the components which were removed to gain access to the intake manifold.

14   Exhaust manifold — removal and installation

Removal

1 Disconnect the negative cable from the battery.

2 Remove the air cleaner assembly. Tag all hoses with pieces of tape to simplify reinstallation.

3 Disconnect the PCV vent hose from the camshaft cover.

4 Remove the upper radiator hose.

5 Disconnect the spark plug wires from the spark plugs. Label them if there is any possibility of installing them incorrectly.

6 Remove the dipstick tube and retaining nut.

7 Remove the exhaust manifold retaining nuts.

8 From under the engine compartment, unplug the oxygen sensor connector and remove the exhaust pipe-to-manifold nuts.

9 Separate the manifold from the engine.

Installation

10 Remove all traces of gasket material from the manifold and cylinder head with a gasket scraper. Take care not to nick or gouge the soft aluminum of the head.

11 Place the manifold in position, using a new gasket, and install the

retaining nuts. Tighten the nuts to the specified torque. Work from the center of the manifold out, in a criss-cross pattern.

12 Install the components which were removed for access and connect the battery cable.

15   Cylinder head — removal and installation

Note: *The engine must be cold whenever the camshaft carrier/cylinder head bolts are loosened or removed.*

Removal

1 Disconnect the negative cable from the battery and remove the air cleaner assembly.

2 Drain the cooling system, disconnect the upper radiator hose, unplug the connectors and remove the thermostat housing.

3 Remove the alternator and bracket.

4 Remove the power steering pump and bracket assembly (if equipped) and lay it to one side.

5 Remove the ignition coil.

6 Disconnect the spark plug wires and distributor cap and remove them as an assembly.

7 Disconnect the throttle cable from the intake manifold bracket.

8 Disconnect the throttle, downshift and TV cables from the EFI assembly.

9 Disconnect the ECM connectors from the EFI.

10 Remove the brake vacuum hose from the filter on the booster.

15.15 The cylinder head bolts will be easier to remove if penetrating oil is applied

15.16 Keep the cylinder head bolts in order in a marked piece of cardboard

15.19 Use a block of wood and a hammer to break the cylinder head gasket seal — don't strike the head directly with a metal hammer!

15.21 Removing the cylinder head gasket with a scraper

11 Remove the heater hose from the intake manifold fitting.
12 Disconnect the exhaust pipe from the exhaust manifold.
13 Disconnect the camshaft cover breather hose.
14 Remove the timing belt cover and timing belt.
15 Prior to removal, apply penetrating oil to the cylinder head bolts (photo).
16 Loosen the bolts a little at a time in the sequence given in the illustration shown in Section 9 until they can be removed. Place the bolts in a numbered piece of cardboard to keep them in order (photo).
17 Remove the rocker arm and valve lash compensator assemblies (Section 10).
18 Remove the camshaft carrier.
19 Break the gasket seal by tapping around the circumference of the cylinder head with a hammer and wood block (photo).
20 Separate the cylinder head from the engine.
21 Using a scraper, remove the gasket from the engine (photo).

Installation

22 Remove all traces of gasket material from the engine block and cylinder head. Make sure the cylinder head and block bolt threads are clean as this could affect torque readings during installation.
23 Place the new gasket and cylinder head in position, followed by the camshaft carrier.
24 Install the cylinder head bolts and tighten them to 18 ft-lb in the sequence shown in the accompanying illustration. Turn each bolt an additional 60 degrees, in sequence, three times, until each one has been rotated 180 degrees (1/2 turn), as shown in the accompanying diagram. After reinstalling all components which were removed, start the engine and run it until normal operating temperature is reached. Turn the engine off and tighten all of the head bolts, in sequence, an additional 30-to-50 degrees.

---

16 Oil pan — removal and installation

Removal

1 Disconnect the negative cable from the battery.
2 Loosen the lug nuts on the right front wheel.
3 Raise the front of the vehicle and support it securely on jackstands.
4 Remove the right front wheel.
5 Remove the right side splash shield.
6 Remove the air conditioner compressor lower bracket strut bolt and swing the strut out of the way.
7 Remove the flywheel dust cover, unbolt the exhaust pipe and disconnect it from the manifold.
8 Drain the engine oil (Chapter 1).
9 Remove the oil pan bolts and separate the oil pan from the engine. It may be necessary to use a rubber mallet to break the gasket seal.

Installation

10 Prior to installing the oil pan, remove all dirt and old gasket material from the sealing surfaces of the pan and engine block. Apply thread locking compound to the pan bolts.
11 Apply RTV-type sealant between the oil pan and oil pump gaskets, as shown in the accompanying illustration.
12 Place the oil pan and gasket in position and install the bolts. Tighten the bolts to the specified torque. Work from the center of the pan out, following a criss-cross pattern.
13 Install the drain plug and tighten it to the specified torque.
14 Connect the exhaust pipe and install the flywheel dust shield.
15 Install the air-conditioner compressor bracket, splash shield and right front wheel.
16 Lower the vehicle.
17 Fill the engine to the recommended level with the specified oil.
18 Connect the negative battery cable.
19 Start the engine and check for leaks at the oil pan-to-block junction.

---

17 Oil pump — removal and installation

Removal

1 Remove the crankshaft sprocket and timing belt covers.
2 Unplug the engine oil pressure switch harness from the switch.
3 Remove the oil pan and oil filter.
4 Unbolt and remove the pickup tube assembly.
5 Remove the six Allen head bolts and separate the oil pump from the engine.

Installation

6 Clean the oil pump mating surfaces to remove old gasket material and install a new gasket.
7 Place the pump and gasket in position and install the bolts. Tighten the bolts to the specified torque.
8 Using a new O-ring, install the pickup tube and support assembly. Tighten the bolts to the specified torque.
9 Install the oil pan.
10 Install a new oil filter and replace the oil pressure switch harness.
11 Install the timing belt covers and the crankshaft sprocket.

---

18 Oil pump — disassembly, inspection and reassembly

Disassembly

1 Remove the retaining screws and cover from the rear of the pump.
2 Remove the gears from the pump body. It may be necessary to turn the body over to remove the gears by allowing them to fall out.

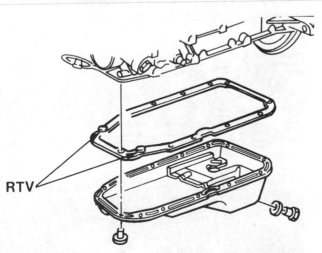

Fig. 2B.6 Apply RTV-type sealant between the oil pan and oil pump gaskets at the points indicated (Sec 16, 17 and 18)

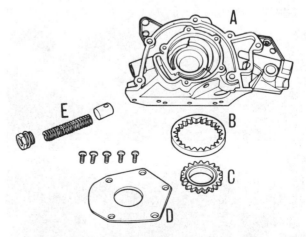

Fig. 2B.7 Oil pump component layout (Sec 18)

A Pump body   C Drive gear   E Valve plunger and
B Idler gear   D Cover   spring assembly

18.3   The oil pump will be easier to work on if mounted in a vise with padded jaws

18.6   Checking the outer gear-to-body clearance with a feeler gauge

18.8   The gear-to-cover clearance is checked by inserting a feeler gauge between the gear and a straightedge laid across the pump body at point A

3   Mount the pump body in a soft-jawed vise and remove the oil pressure sending unit, plug, pressure regulator valve, plunger and spring (photo).

Inspection

4   Wash the oil pump parts in solvent.
5   Inspect the components for wear, cracks or other damage.
6   Check the outer (idler) gear-to-body clearance (photo).
7   Check the inner (drive) gear-to-body clearance (photo).
8   Check the gear-to-cover clearance (photo).

Reassembly

9   Install the valve, plunger and spring assembly.
10   Coat the plug threads with a thread locking compound and tighten to the specified torque.
11   Install the gears, noting that the outer gear is identified by a mark. This mark must face the cover (photo).
12   Install the pump cover and tighten the screws securely.
13   Install the oil pressure sending unit.

19   Flywheel/driveplate and rear main bearing oil seal — removal and installation

Removal

1   Remove the engine (Section 21).

18.7   Checking the inner gear-to-body clearance

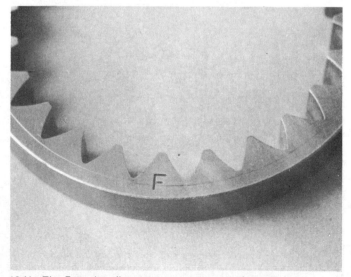

18.11   The F on the oil pump outer gear must face the cover

2   Remove the flywheel dust cover.
3   On automatic transaxle models, remove the torque converter retaining bolts.
4   Remove the bellhousing bolts and separate the transaxle and engine.
5   Remove the transaxle driveplate (automatic) or pressure plate, clutch disc and flywheel (manual).
6   Pry the old seal out very carefully with a screwdriver or similar tool (photo).

Installation

7   Carefully clean the sealing surfaces of the engine block and crankshaft. Inspect the crankshaft for nicks and scratches.

8   Coat the seal and engine contact surfaces with clean engine oil.
9   Insert the new seal squarely into position and tap it into place until it bottoms in the bore (photo).
10   Install the clutch (Chapter 8) and flywheel or driveplate and torque converter assemblies.
11   Connect the engine to the transaxle and install the flywheel dust cover.
12   Install the engine in the vehicle.

20   Engine mounts — replacement with engine in vehicle

1   If the rubber mounts have become hard, split or separated from

19.6   Prying the oil seal out with a screwdriver

19.9   Tap around the circumference of the oil seal with a hammer and a punch to seat it squarely in the bore

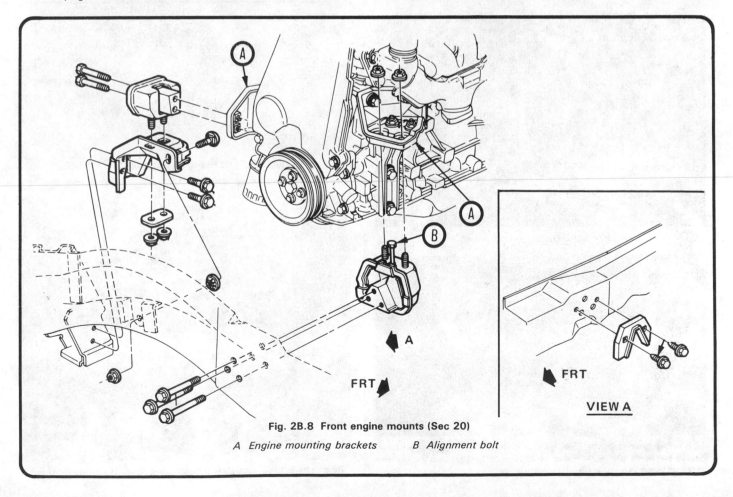

Fig. 2B.8 Front engine mounts (Sec 20)

A   Engine mounting brackets   *B   Alignment bolt*

the metal backing, they must be replaced. This operation may be carried out with the engine/transaxle still in the vehicle.

2   Disconnect the negative cable from the battery.
3   Raise the front of the vehicle and support it securely on jackstands.
4   Support the engine with a jack.

Front mounts

5   Remove the appropriate inner fender shield for access.
6   Remove the engine mount and bolts. Whenever the mount is removed a bolt must be inserted to keep the driveaxles properly aligned.
7   Place the new mount in position and install the bolts. If excessive effort is required to remove the alignment bolt, loosen the transaxle mount bolts and adjust the mount position until the bolt can be easily removed.
8   Remove the alignment bolt and tighten the mount bolts.

Rear mounts

9   On manual transaxle equipped models, remove the engine oil filter.
10   Remove the mount nuts and bolts and remove the mount.
11   Installation is the reverse of removal.

---

21   Engine — removal and installation

1   Remove the battery cables (negative first, then positive) and drain the cooling system (Chapter 1).
2   Remove the air cleaner assembly.
3   Loosen the retaining bolt, unplug the bulkhead harness connector and separate the engine connector from the body connector (photos).
4   Remove the two mounting screws, unplug the connector and lift the windshield washer reservoir out of the engine compartment.
5   Disconnect the electrical connector from the brake master cylinder (photo).
6   Disconnect the throttle cable and vacuum hoses from the EFI assembly.

7   Remove the power steering high pressure hose at the cut-off switch.
8   Disconnect the vacuum hoses from the MAP sensor and EVAP canister (photo).
9   Remove the starter motor (Chapter 5).
10   Remove the engine wiring harness bracket (photo).
11   Unplug the wiring harness connectors as necessary to allow removal of the engine and remove the harness.
12   Remove the upper and lower radiator hoses and thermostat housing.
13   On manual transaxle equipped models, disconnect the clutch cable and the shift cables, slide out the retaining clips and remove the cables from the transaxle (photo).
14   On automatic transaxle models, disconnect the shift cable.
15   Loosen the wheel lug nuts and raise the vehicle.
16   From underneath the vehicle, disconnect the speedometer cable.
17   Disconnect the exhaust pipe from the manifold.
18   Remove the exhaust pipe from the catalytic converter. If the pipe cannot be easily removed it may be necessary to disconnect the hangers and swing the entire exhaust system out of the way.
19   Disconnect the heater hoses from the heater core (photo).
20   Disconnect the fuel line flex hoses (photo).

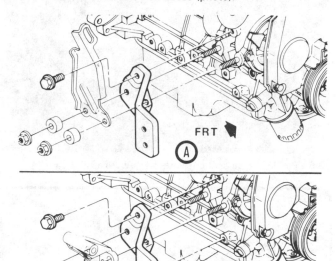

Fig. 2B.9 Rear engine mounts (Sec 20)

A Without power steering   B With power steering

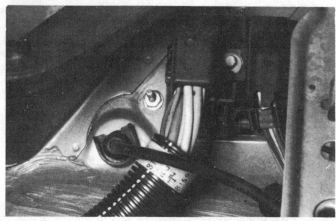

21.3A   Wiring harness bulkhead connector location

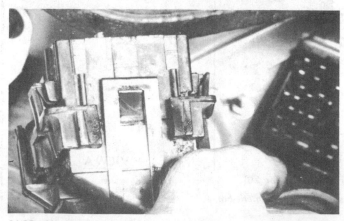

21.3B   Unplugging the harness connector

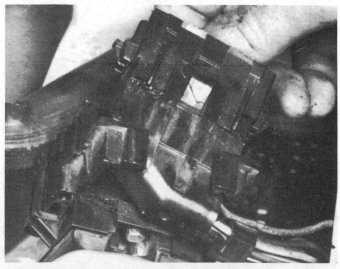

21.3C   Separating the engine connector from the body connector

2B

21.5   Brake master cylinder electrical connector

21.8   MAP sensor location (arrow)

21.10   Engine wiring harness bracket

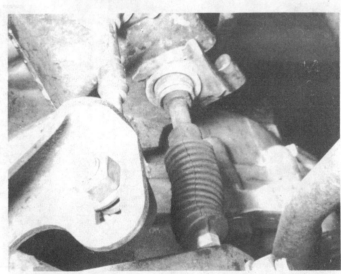

21.13   Manual transmission clutch (left) and shift cable connections

21.19   Heater hose-to-core connections (arrows)

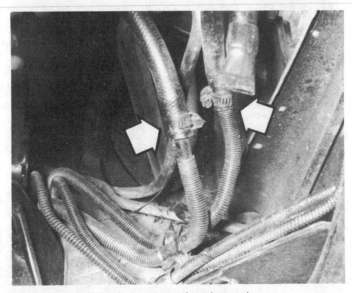

21.20   Fuel line flex hose connections (arrows)

21.23   Spoiler retaining bolts (arrows)

21.26   The air conditioner compressor can be held out of the way with a piece of wire

21.30   Transaxle mount-to-chassis nuts and bolt (arrows)

21   On automatic transaxle models, disconnect and plug the cooler lines at the flex hoses.
22   Remove the front wheels.
23   Remove the right side spoiler section and the inner fender splash panel (photo).
24   Remove the brake calipers, support them out of the way with wire and remove the rotors (Chapter 9).
25   Disconnect the tie rod ends at the steering arms (Chapter 11).
26   Remove the air conditioning compressor, swing it out of the way in the wheel well and support it with wire (photo).
27   Remove the six front suspension support bolts (Chapter 11).
28   Lower the vehicle.
29   Support the engine and transaxle assembly on wood blocks or a 4-wheel dolly.
30   Remove the transaxle mount-to-chassis attaching nuts and bolt (photo).
31   Remove the transaxle mount through-bolt.
32   Remove the three bolts attaching the engine mount to the cylinder block and then unbolt the mount and bracket from the chassis.
33   Remove the two engine support mount-to-body bolts located

21.35   The engine/transaxle unit must be removed by raising the vehicle

behind the right side inner axle CV joint.
34   Remove the upper strut-to-chassis mounting nuts (Chapter 11).
35   Slowly and carefully raise the vehicle, leaving the engine, transaxle and suspension resting on the blocks or 4-wheel dolly (photo).
36   Mark the location of the engine/transaxle/suspension assembly on the floor so that it can be replaced in the same position and the vehicle lowered over it during reinstallation.
37   The assembly can now be moved out from under the vehicle and the engine separated from the transaxle.
38   Installation is the reverse of removal, taking care to lower the vehicle very slowly onto the engine/transaxle/suspension assembly and making sure the bolts are aligned. As the vehicle is lowered, have two assistants guide the upper struts into position and support the drive-axles so the CV joints don't become disengaged.

Chapter 2 Part C
General engine overhaul procedures

Refer to Chapter 13 for specifications and information related to 1985 and later models

Contents

2C

Specifications

OHV engine
Cylinder numbers (front-to-rear)	1–2–3–4
Firing order	1–3–4–2

Valves and related components

Valve face angle....................................	45°
Valve seat angle...................................	46°
Stem to guide clearance	
Intake	0.0011 to 0.0026 in (0.028 to 0.066 mm)
Exhaust.......................................	0.0014 to 0.003 in (0.035 to 0.078 mm)
Valve seat width	
Intake	0.049 to 0.059 in (1.25 to 1.50mm)
Exhaust.......................................	0.063 to 0.075 in (1.60 to 1.90 mm)
Valve spring installed height	1.60 in (40.6 mm)
Valve spring pressure and length (intake and exhaust)	
Valve closed	73 to 81 lbs at 1.6 in
Valve open	176 to 188 lbs at 1.33 in

Crankshaft and connecting rods

Crankshaft end play	0.002 to 0.008 in (0.05 to 0.21 mm)
Connecting rod end play (side clearance)	0.004 to 0.015 in (0.10 to 0.38 mm)
Main bearing journal diameter	
Nos. 1 through 4.............................	2.4945 to 2.4954 in (63.36 to 63.384 mm)
No. 5	2.4937 to 2.4946 in (63.34 to 63.364 mm)
Main bearing clearance	
1982 and 1984	
Nos. 1 through 4.........................	0.0006 to 0.0019 in (0.015 to 0.047 mm)
No. 5	0.0014 to 0.0027 in (0.101 to 0.068 mm)
1983	
Nos. 1 through 4.........................	0.001 to 0.0022 in (0.026 to 0.058 mm)
No. 5	0.0018 to 0.003 in (0.046 to 0.078 mm)
Connecting rod journal diameter	1.9983 to 1.9994 in (50.758 to 50.784 mm)
Connecting rod bearing clearance	0.001 to 0.0031 in (0.025 to 0.079 mm)
Crankshaft journal taper/out of round limit	0.0002 in (0.005 mm)

Engine block

Cylinder bore diameter	3.50 in (89 mm)
Out of round limit	0.001 in (0.02 mm)
Taper limit	0.001 in (0.02 mm)
Piston-to-bore clearance	.0007 to .0017 (.018 to .043 mm)

Pistons and rings

Compression ring side clearance	0.001 to 0.003 in (0.03 to 0.07 mm)
Oil ring side clearance	0.008 in (0.20 mm)
Compression ring end gap	0.010 to 0.020 in (0.25 to 0.50 mm)
Oil ring end gap	0.020 to 0.060 in (0.5 to 1.5 mm)

Camshaft

Lobe lift (intake and exhaust)	0.26 in (6.67 mm)
Bearing journal diameter	1.867 to 1.869 in (47.44 to 47.49 mm)
Bearing oil clearance...............................	0.001 to 0.004in (0.026 to 0.101 mm)

Torque specifications

	Ft-lbs
Alternator mounting bolts and nuts	40 to 60
Alternator pivot bolt	29 to 44
Air conditioning compressor mounting bolts	26 to 67
Camshaft thrust plate bolts	4 to 14
Camshaft sprocket bolt	66 to 88
Camshaft rear cover bolts	4 to 5
Connecting rod cap bolts	34 to 43
Crankshaft pulley-to-hub bolts	29 to 44
Crankshaft center bolt	66 to 89
Cylinder head bolts	65 to 75
EGR valve bolts	13 to 27
Engine mount	
Front mount nuts	25 to 35
Front lower mount nuts	15 to 20
Mount-to-frame bolts	35 to 45
Exhaust manifold bolts	20 to 30
Flywheel/flexplate	
Automatic transmission flexplate bolts	45 to 59
Manual transmission flywheel bolts	45 to 63
Intake manifold nuts and bolts	18 to 25
Main bearing cap bolts	63 to 77
Oil drain plug	30 to 38
Oil filter	10 to 13
Oil filter adapter	15 to 22
Oil filter connector nut	11 to 16
Oil pan-to-front cover bolts	7 to 13
Oil pan-to-rear cover bolts	11 to 18
Oil pan stud	5 to 7
Oil pump mounting bolts	26 to 38
Oil pump cover bolts	6 to 9
Rocker arm cover bolts	4 to 9
Rocker arm nuts	4 to 14
Spark plugs	7 to 20
Starter motor block bolts	26 to 37
Thermostat adapter bolts	13 to 18
Thermostat outlet bolts	13 to 22
Timing chain cover bolts	13 to 13
Timing chain tensioner bolt	13 to 18
Water inlet bolts	12 to 21
Water pump bolts	12 to 21
Water pump pulley bolts	15 to 20

OHC engine
Valves and related components

Valve face angle	46°
Valve seat angle	45°
Seat run out limit	0.0002 in (0.005 mm)
Stem-to-guide clearance	
Intake	0.0006 to 0.0016 in (0.015 to 0.042 mm)
Exhaust	0.0012 to 0.0024 in (0.030 to 0.060 mm)

Valve seat width
    Intake . . . . 0.051 to 0.055 in
    (1.30 to 1.40 mm)
    Exhaust . . . . 0.067 to 0.071 in
    (1.70 to 1.80 mm)

Crankshaft and connecting rods
Crankshaft end play . . . . 0.0118 to 0.0027 in
    (0.299 to 0.068 mm)
Connecting rod end play (side clearance) . . . . 0.0027 to 0.0095 in
    (0.0704 to 0.242 mm)
Main bearing journal diameter
    Coded brown . . . . 2.2830 to 2.2832 in
    (57.9885 to 57.9950 mm)
    Coded green . . . . 2.2827 to 2.283 in
    (57.9820 to 57.9885 mm)
Main bearing oil clearance . . . . 0.0006 to 0.0016 in
    (0.015 to 0.041 mm)
Connecting rod bearing journal diameter . . . . 1.9278 to 1.9286 in
    (48.971 to 48.987 mm)
Connecting rod bearing oil clearance . . . . 0.0007 to 0.0024 in
    (0.019 to 0.063 mm)
Crankshaft journal taper/out-of-round limits . . . . 0.0002 in (0.005 mm)

Engine block
Cylinder bore diameter . . . . 3.336 to 3.342 in
    (84.75 to 84.90 mm)
Out-of-round limit . . . . 0.005 in (0.127 mm)

Taper limit (thrust side) . . . . 0.005 in (0.127 mm)
Piston-to-bore clearance . . . . 0.00808 in (0.205 mm)
Piston ring-to-groove clearance
    Top . . . . 0.002 to 0.003 in
    (0.051 to 0.076 mm)
    2nd . . . . 0.001 to 0.0024 in
    (0.03 to 0.062 mm)
End gap (all) . . . . 0.001 to 0.002 in
    (0.030 to 0.050 mm)
Piston pin clearance . . . . 0.00019 to 0.00004 in
    (0.005 to 0.0011 mm)

Camshaft
Lobe lift (intake and exhaust) . . . . 0.2409 in (6.12 mm)
Bearing journal diameter
    No. 1 . . . . 1.672 to 1.6714 in
    (42.470 to 42.455 mm)
    No. 2 . . . . 1.6816 to 1.6812 in
    (42.720 to 42.705 mm)
    No. 3 . . . . 1.6917 to 1.6911 in
    (42.970 to 42.955 mm)
    No. 4 . . . . 1.7015 to 1.7009 in
    (43.220 to 43.205 mm)
    No. 5 . . . . 1.7114 to 1.7108 in
    (43.470 to 43.455 mm)
Bearing oil clearance . . . . 0.0008 in (0.020 mm)

Oil pump clearances
    Idler gear-to-body . . . . 0.004 to 0.007 in
    (0.11 to 0.19 mm)
    Drive gear-to-body . . . . 0.14 to 0.17 in
    (3.55 to 4.31 mm)
    Gear-to-cover . . . . 0.001 to 0.003 in
    (0.025 to 0.076 mm)
Cylinder numbers (front-to-rear) 1–2–3–4
Firing order 1–3–4–2

Torque specifications   **Ft-lbs**
Camshaft carrier cover bolts 5
Camshaft carrier/cylinder head bolts (following
    procedure in text) 18.4
Camshaft sprocket retaining bolt 34
Camshaft thrust plate bolts 5.9
Crankshaft pulley-to-sprocket bolts 20
Crankshaft sprocket retaining bolt 115
Clutch pressure plate-to-flywheel bolts 50

2C

1   General information

Included in this portion of Chapter 2 are the general overhaul procedures for the cylinder head and internal engine components. The information ranges from advice concerning preparation for an overhaul and the purchase of replacement parts to detailed, step-by-step procedures covering removal and installation of internal engine components and the inspection of parts.

The following Sections have been written based on the assumption that the engine has been removed from the vehicle. For information concerning in-vehicle engine repair, as well as removal and installation of the external components necessary for the overhaul, see Part A or B of Chapter 2 (depending on engine type) and Section 2 of this Part. The specifications included here in Part C are only those necessary for the inspection and overhaul procedures which follow. Refer to Part A or B for additional specifications related to the various engines covered in this manual.

2   Repair operations possible with the engine in the vehicle

Many major repair operations can be accomplished without removing the engine from the vehicle.

It is a very good idea to clean the engine compartment and the exterior of the engine with some type of pressure washer before any work is begun. A clean engine will make the job easier and will prevent the possibility of getting dirt into internal areas of the engine.

Remove the hood (Chapter 12) and cover the fenders to provide as much working room as possible and to prevent damage to the painted surfaces.

If oil or coolant leaks develop, indicating a need for gasket or seal replacement, the repairs can generally be made with the engine in the vehicle. The oil pan gasket, the cylinder head gasket, intake and exhaust manifold gaskets, timing cover gaskets and the front crankshaft oil seal are accessible with the engine in place.

Exterior engine components, such as the water pump, the starter motor, the alternator, the distributor, the fuel pump and the carburetor or TBI, as well as the intake and exhaust manifolds, are quite easily removed for repair with the engine in place.

Since the cylinder head can be removed without pulling the engine, valve component servicing can also be accomplished with the engine in the vehicle.

Replacement of, repairs to or inspection of the timing sprockets and chain or belt and the oil pump are all possible with the engine in place. In extreme cases caused by a lack of necessary equipment, repair or replacement of piston rings, pistons, connecting rods and rod bearings and reconditioning of the cylinder bores is possible with the engine in the vehicle. However, this practice is not recommended because of the cleaning and preparation work that must be done to the components involved.

Detailed removal, inspection, repair and installation procedures for the above mentioned components can be found in the appropriate Part of Chapter 2 or the other Chapters in this manual.

3   Engine overhaul — general information

It is not always easy to determine when, or if, an engine should be completely overhauled, as a number of factors must be considered.

High mileage is not necessarily an indication that an overhaul is needed, while low mileage, on the other hand, does not preclude the need for an overhaul. Frequency of servicing is probably the single most important consideration. An engine that has had regular (and frequent) oil and filter changes, as well as other required maintenance, will most likely give many thousands of miles of reliable service. Conversely, a neglected engine may require an overhaul very early in its life.

Excessive oil consumption is an indication that piston rings and/or valve guides are in need of attention (make sure that oil leaks are not responsible before deciding that the rings and guides are bad). Have a cylinder compression or leak-down test performed by an experienced tune-up mechanic to determine for certain the extent of the work required.

If the engine is making obvious knocking or rumbling noises, the connecting rod and/or main bearings are probably at fault. Check the oil pressure with a gauge (installed in place of the oil pressure sending unit) and compare it to the Specifications. If it is extremely low, the bearings and/or oil pump are probably worn out.

Loss of power, rough running, excessive valve train noise and high fuel consumption rates may also point to the need for an overhaul (especially if they are all present at the same time). If a complete tune-up does not remedy the situation, major mechanical work is the only solution.

An engine overhaul generally involves restoring the internal parts to the specifications of a new engine. During an overhaul, the piston rings are replaced and the cylinder walls are reconditioned (rebored and/or honed). If a rebore is done, then new pistons are also required. The main and connecting rod bearings are replaced with new ones and, if necessary, the crankshaft may be reground to restore the journals. Generally, the valves are serviced as well, since they are usually in less-than-perfect condition at this point. While the engine is being overhauled other components, such as the carburetor, distributor, starter and alternator can be rebuilt as well. The end result should be a like-new engine that will give as many trouble-free miles as the original.

Before beginning the engine overhaul, read through the entire procedure to familiarize yourself with the scope and requirements of the job. Overhauling an engine is not that difficult, but it is time consuming. Plan on the vehicle being tied up for a minimum of two weeks, especially if parts must be taken to an automotive machine shop for repair or reconditioning. Check on availability of parts and make sure that any necessary special tools and equipment are obtained in advance. Most work can be done with typical shop hand tools, although a number of precision measuring tools are required for inspecting parts to determine if they must be replaced. Often a reputable automotive machine shop will handle the inspection of parts and offer advice concerning reconditioning and replacement. **Note:** *Always wait until the engine has been completely disassembled and all components, especially the engine block, have been inspected before deciding what service and repair operations must be performed by an automotive machine shop.* Since the block's condition will be the major factor to consider when determining whether to overhaul the original engine or buy a rebuilt one, never purchase parts or have machine work done on other components until the block has been thoroughly inspected. As a general rule, time is the primary cost of an overhaul, so it does not pay to install worn or sub-standard parts.

As a final note, to ensure maximum life and minimum trouble from a rebuilt engine, everything must be assembled with care in a spotlessly clean environment.

4 Engine rebuilding alternatives

The do-it-yourselfer is faced with a number of options when performing an engine overhaul. The decision to replace the engine block, piston/connecting rod assemblies and crankshaft depends on a number of factors, with the number one consideration being the condition of the block. Other considerations are cost, access to machine shop facilities, parts availability, time required to complete the project and experience.

Some of the rebuilding alternatives include:

Individual parts — If the inspection procedures reveal that the engine block and most engine components are in reusable condition, purchasing individual parts may be the most economical alternative. The block, crankshaft and piston/connecting rod assemblies should all be inspected carefully. Even if the block shows little wear, the cylinder bores should receive a finish hone; a job for an automotive machine shop.

Master kit (crankshaft kit) — This rebuild package usually consists of a reground crankshaft and a matched set of pistons and connecting rods. The pistons will already be installed on the connecting rods. Piston rings and the necessary bearings may or may not be included in the kit. These kits are commonly available for standard cylinder bores, as well as for engine blocks which have been bored to a regular oversize.

Short block — A short block consists of an engine block with a crankshaft and piston/connecting rod assemblies already installed. All new bearings are incorporated and all clearances will be correct. Depending on where the short block is purchased, a guarantee may be included. The existing camshaft, valve train components, cylinder head and external parts can be bolted to the short block with little or no machine shop work necessary.

Long block — A long block consists of a short block plus an oil pump, oil pan, cylinder head, rocker arm cover, camshaft and valve train components, timing sprockets and chain or belt and timing chain or belt cover. All components are installed with new bearings, seals and gaskets incorporated throughout. The installation of manifolds and external parts is all that is necessary. Some form of guarantee is usually included with the purchase.

Give careful thought to which alternative is best for you and discuss the situation with local automotive machine shops, auto parts dealers or dealership partsmen before ordering or purchasing replacement parts.

5 Engine removal — methods and precautions

If it has been decided that an engine must be removed for overhaul or major repair work, certain preliminary steps should be taken. Locating a suitable work area is extremely important. A shop is, of course, the most desirable place to work. Adequate work space, along with storage space for the vehicle, is very important. If a shop or garage is not available, at the very least a flat, level, clean work surface made of concrete or asphalt is required.

Cleaning the engine compartment and engine prior to removal will help keep tools clean and organized.

An engine hoist or A-frame will also be necessary. Make sure that the equipment is rated in excess of the combined weight of the engine and its accessories. Safety is of primary importance, considering the potential hazards involved in lifting the engine out of the vehicle.

If the engine is being removed by a novice, a helper should be available. Advice and aid from someone more experienced would also be helpful. There are many instances when one person cannot simultaneously perform all of the operations required when lifting the engine out of the vehicle.

Plan the operation ahead of time. Arrange for or obtain all of the tools and equipment you will need prior to beginning the job. Some of the equipment necessary to perform engine removal and in-

stallation safely and with relative ease are (in addition to an engine hoist) a heavy duty floor jack, complete sets of wrenches and sockets as described in the front of this manual, wooden blocks and plenty of rags and cleaning solvent for mopping up the inevitable spills. If the hoist is to be rented, make sure that you arrange for it in advance and perform beforehand all of the operations possible without it. This will save you money and time.

Plan for the vehicle to be out of use for a considerable amount of time. A machine shop will be required to perform some of the work which the do-it-yourselfer cannot accomplish due to a lack of special equipment. These shops often have a busy schedule, so it would be wise to consult them before removing the engine in order to accurately estimate the amount of time required to rebuild or repair components that may need work.

Always use extreme caution when removing and installing the engine. Serious injury can result from careless actions. Plan ahead. Take your time and a job of this nature, although major, can be accomplished successfully.

6 Engine overhaul disassembly sequence

1 It is much easier to disassemble and work on the engine if it is mounted on a portable engine stand. These stands can often be rented for a reasonable fee from an equipment rental yard. Before the engine is mounted on a stand, the flywheel/driveplate should be removed from the engine (refer to Chapter 8).
2 If a stand is not available, it is possible to disassemble the engine with it blocked up on a sturdy workbench or on the floor. Be extra careful not to tip or drop the engine when working without a stand.
3 If you are going to obtain a rebuilt engine, all external components must come off first in order to be transferred to the replacement engine (just as they will if you are doing a complete engine overhaul yourself). These include:

    Alternator and brackets
    Emissions control components
    Distributor, spark plug wires and spark plugs
    Thermostat and housing cover
    Water pump
    Carburetor/fuel injection components
    Intake/exhaust manifolds
    Oil filter
    Fuel pump
    Engine mounts
    Flywheel/driveplate

Note: *When removing the external components from the engine, pay close attention to details that may be helpful or important during installation. Note the installed position of gaskets, seals, spacers, pins, washers, bolts and other small items.*

4 If you are obtaining a short block (which consists of the engine block, crankshaft, pistons and connecting rods all assembled), then the cylinder head, oil pan and oil pump will have to be removed also. See Engine rebuilding alternatives for additional information regarding the different possibilities to be considered.
5 If you are planning a complete overhaul, the engine must be disassembled and the internal components removed in the following order:

    Rocker arm or camshaft cover
    Cylinder head and pushrods
    Valve lifters
    Timing chain/belt cover
    Timing chain/sprockets or belt
    Camshaft
    Oil pan
    Oil pump
    Piston/connecting rod assemblies
    Crankshaft

6 Before beginning the disassembly and overhaul procedures, make sure the following items are available:

    Common hand tools
    Small cardboard boxes or plastic bags for storing parts
    Gasket scraper
    Ridge reamer
    Vibration damper puller
    Micrometers

2C

7.3   Use a valve spring compressor to compress the spring then remove the keepers from the valve stem (OHV engine shown)

Small hole gauges
Telescoping gauges
Dial indicator set
Valve spring compressor
Cylinder surfacing hone
Piston ring groove cleaning tool
Electric drill motor
Tap and die set
Wire brushes
Cleaning solvent

7   Cylinder head — disassembly

Note: *New and rebuilt cylinder heads are commonly available for most engines at dealerships and auto parts stores. Due to the fact that some specialized tools are necessary for the disassembly and inspection procedures, and replacement parts may not be readily available, it may be more practical and economical for the home mechanic to purchase a replacement head rather than taking the time to disassemble, inspect and recondition the original head.*

1   Cylinder head disassembly involves removal and disassembly of the intake and exhaust valves and their related components. If they are still in place, remove the nuts or bolts and pivot balls, then separate the rocker arms from the cylinder head. Label the parts or store them separately so they can be reinstalled in their original locations.
2   Before the valves are removed, arrange to label and store them, along with their related components, so they can be kept separate and reinstalled in the same valve guides they are removed from. Also, on OHV engines, measure the valve spring installed height (for each valve) and compare it to the Specifications. If it is greater than specified, the valve seats and valve faces need attention.
3   Compress the valve spring on the first valve with a spring compressor and remove the keepers (photo). Carefully release the valve spring compressor and remove the retainer, the shield (if so equipped), the springs, the valve guide seal and/or O-ring seal, the spring seat and the valve from the head. If the valve binds in the guide (won't pull through), push it back into the head and deburr the area around the keeper groove with a fine file or whetstone.
4   Repeat the procedure for the remaining valves. Remember to keep together all the parts for each valve so they can be reinstalled in the same locations.
5   Once the valves have been removed and safely stored, the head should be thoroughly cleaned and inspected. If a complete engine overhaul is being done, finish the engine disassembly procedures before beginning the cylinder head cleaning and inspection process.

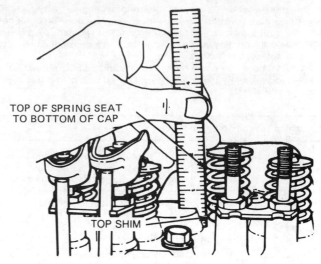

Fig. 2C.1 Measuring the valve spring installed height (OHV engines only) (Sec 7)

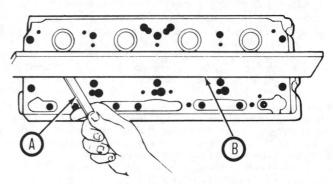

Fig. 2C.2 Checking the cylinder head gasket mating surface for warpage by using a feeler gauge (A) and ruler (B) (Sec 8)

8   Cylinder head — cleaning and inspection

1   Thorough cleaning of the cylinder head and related valve train components, followed by a detailed inspection, will enable you to decide how much valve service work must be done during the engine overhaul.

Cleaning
2   Scrape away all traces of old gasket material and sealing compound from the head gasket, intake manifold and exhaust manifold sealing surfaces. On OHC engines work slowly and do not nick or gouge the soft aluminum of the head and intake manifold.
3   Remove any built-up scale around the coolant passages.
4   Run a stiff wire brush through the oil holes to remove any deposits that may have formed in them.
5   It is a good idea to run an appropriate size tap into each of the threaded holes to remove any corrosion and thread sealant that may be present. If compressed air is available, use it to clear the holes of debris produced by this operation.
6   Clean the exhaust and intake manifold stud threads in a similar manner with an appropriate size die. Clean the rocker arm pivot bolt or stud threads with a wire brush.
7   Clean the cylinder head with solvent and dry it thoroughly. Compressed air will speed the drying process and ensure that all holes and recessed areas are clean. **Note:** *Decarbonizing chemicals are available and may prove very useful when cleaning cylinder heads and valve train components. They are very caustic and should be used with caution. Be sure to follow the instructions on the container.*
8   Clean the rocker arms, pivot balls and pushrods with solvent and dry them thoroughly. Compressed air will speed the drying process and can be used to clean out the oil passages.

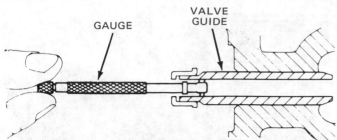

Fig. 2C.3 Use a small hole gauge to determine the inside diameter of the valve guides (the gauge is then measured with a micrometer)(Sec 8)

Fig. 2C.4 A dial indicator can also be used to determine the valve stem-to-guide clearance (Sec 8)

9   Clean all the valve springs, keepers, retainers, shields and spring seats with solvent and dry them thoroughly. Do the components from one valve at a time to avoid mixing up the parts.

10   Scrape off any heavy deposits that may have formed on the valves, then use a motorized wire brush to remove deposits from the valve heads and stems. Again, make sure the valves do not get mixed up.

Inspection

Cylinder head

11   Inspect the head very carefully for cracks, evidence of coolant leakage or other damage. If cracks are found, a new cylinder head should be obtained.

12   Using a straightedge and feeler gauge, check the head gasket mating surface for warpage. If the warpage exceeds 0.006-inch over the length of the head, it can be resurfaced at an automotive machine shop.

13   Examine the valve seats in each of the combustion chambers. If they are pitted, cracked or burned, the head will require valve service that is beyond the scope of the home mechanic.

14   Measure the inside diameters of the valve guides (at both ends and the center of each guide) with a small hole gauge and a 0-to-1-inch micrometer. Record the measurements for future reference. These measurements, along with the valve stem diameter measurements, will enable you to compute the valve stem-to-guide clearances. These clearances, when compared to the Specifications, will be one factor that will determine the extent of valve service work required. The guides are measured at the ends and at the center to determine if they are worn in a bell-mouth pattern (more wear at the ends). If they are, guide reconditioning or replacement is necessary. As an alternative, use a dial indicator to measure the lateral movement of each valve stem with the valve in the guide and approximately 1/16-inch off the seat (see the accompanying illustration).

15   On OHC engines inspect the camshaft bearing bores for wear, galling, gouges or discoloration, indicating overheating.

Rocker arm components

16   Check the rocker arm faces (that contact the pushrod ends and valve stems) for pits, wear and rough spots. Check the pivot contact areas as well.

17   Inspect the pushrod ends for scuffing and excessive wear. Roll the pushrod on a flat surface, such as a piece of glass, to determine if it is bent.

18   Any damaged or excessively worn parts must be replaced with new ones.

Valves

19   Carefully inspect each valve face for cracks, pits and burned spots. Check the valve stem and neck for cracks. Rotate the valve and check for any obvious indication that it is bent. Check the end of the stem for pits and excessive wear. The presence of any of these conditions indicates the need for valve service by a properly equipped professional.

20   Measure the valve stem diameter (photo). **Note:** *The exhaust valves used in the OHV engine have tapered stems and are approximately 0.001-inch larger at the tip end than at the head end.* By subtracting the stem diameter from the corresponding valve guide diameter, the valve stem-to-guide clearance is obtained. Compare the results to the Specifications. If the stem-to-guide clearance is greater than specified, the guides will have to be reconditioned and new valves may have to be installed, depending on the condition of the old valves.

Valve components

21   Check each valve spring for wear (on the ends) and pits. Measure the free length (photo) and compare it to the Specifications. Any springs that are shorter than specified have sagged and should not be reused. Stand the spring on a flat surface and check it for squareness (photo).

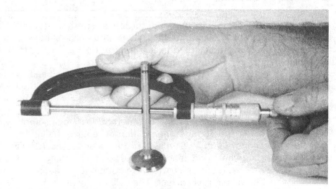

8.20   Measure the valve stem diameter at three points

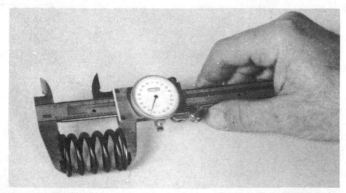

8.21A   Measure the free length of each valve spring with a dial or vernier caliper

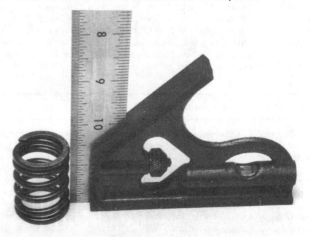

8.21B   Check each valve spring for squareness

2C

11.2 A special tool is required to remove the ridge at the top of each cylinder bore (do it before removing the piston)

11.6 Checking the connecting rod side play with a feeler gauge

22 Check the spring retainers and keepers for obvious wear and cracks. Any questionable parts should be replaced with new ones, as extensive damage will occur in the event of failure during engine operation.

23 If the inspection process indicates that the valve components are in generally poor condition and worn beyond the limits specified, which is usually the case in an engine that is being overhauled, reassemble the valves in the cylinder head and refer to Section 9 for valve servicing recommendations.

24 If the inspection turns up no excessively worn parts, and if the valve faces and seats are in good condition, the valve train components can be reinstalled in the cylinder head without major servicing. Refer to the appropriate Section for cylinder head reassembly procedures.

9 Valves — servicing

1   Because of the complex nature of the job and the special tools and equipment needed, servicing of the valves, the valve seats and the valve guides (commonly known as a 'valve job') is best left to a professional.

2   The home mechanic can remove and disassemble the head, do the initial cleaning and inspection, then reassemble and deliver the head to a dealer service department or a reputable automotive machine shop for the actual valve servicing.

3   The dealer service department, or automotive machine shop, will remove the valves and springs, recondition or replace the valves and valve seats, recondition the valve guides, check and replace the valve springs, spring retainers and keepers (as necessary), replace the valve seals with new ones, reassemble the valve components and make sure the installed spring height is correct. The cylinder head gasket surface will also be resurfaced if it is warped.

4   After the valve job has been performed by a professional, the head will be in like-new condition. When the head is returned, be sure to clean it again, very thoroughly (before installation on the engine), to remove any metal particles and abrasive grit that may still be present from the valve service or head resurfacing operations. Use compressed air, if available, to blow out all the oil holes and passages.

10 Cylinder head — reassembly

1   Regardless of whether or not the head was sent to an automotive repair shop for valve servicing, make sure it is clean before beginning reassembly.

2   If the head was sent out for valve servicing, the valves and related components will already be in place. Begin the reassembly procedure with Step 8 for OHV engines and Step 10 for OHC engines.

OHV engine

3   Install new seals on each of the valve guides. Using a hammer and an appropriate size deep socket, gently tap each seal into place until

it is properly seated on the guide. Do not twist or cock the seals during installation or they will not seal properly on the valve stems.

4   Install the valves (taking care not to damage the new valve stem oil seals), drop the valve spring shim(s) around the valve guide boss and set the valve spring, cap and retainer in place.

5   Compress the spring with a valve compressor tool and install the valve locks. Release the compressor tool, making sure the locks are seated properly in the valve stem upper groove. If necessary, grease can be used to hold the locks in place while the compressor tool is released.

7   Double-check the installed valve spring height. If it was correct before reassembly it should still be within the specified limits. If it is not, install an additional valve spring seat shims (available from your dealer) to bring the height to within the specified limit.

8   Install the rocker arms and tighten the nuts to the specified torque. Be sure to lubricate the ball pivots with moly-based grease or engine assembly lube.

OHC engine

9   Remove the valves, one at a time, from their numbered container, insert them in the cylinder head, and install new seals as described in Chapter 2B, Section 12.

10 Install the valve springs, caps, retainers and locks, using a spring compressor.

11 Install the rocker arm and valve lash compensator assemblies and camshaft carrier referring to the appropriate Sections of Chapter 2B.

11 Piston/connecting rod assembly — removal

1   Prior to removal of the piston/connecting rod assemblies, the engine should be positioned upright.

2   Using a ridge reamer, completely remove the ridge at the top of each cylinder (follow the manufacturer's instructions provided with the ridge reaming tool) (photo). Failure to remove the ridge before attempting to remove the piston/connecting rod assemblies will result in piston breakage.

3   After all of the cylinder wear ridges have been removed, turn the engine upside-down.

4   Before the connecting rods are removed, check the end play as follows. Mount a dial indicator with its stem in line with the crankshaft and touching the side of the number one connecting rod cap.

5   Push the connecting rod backward, as far as possible, and zero the dial indicator. Next, push the connecting rod all the way to the front and check the reading on the dial indicator. The distance that it moves is the end play. If the end play exceeds the service limit, a new connecting rod will be required. Repeat the procedure for the remaining connecting rods.

6   An alternative method is to slip feeler gauges between the connecting rod and the crankshaft throw until the play is removed (photo). The end play is then equal to the thickness of the feeler gauge(s).

11.8 To prevent damage to the crankshaft journals and cylinder walls, slip sections of hose over the rod bolts before removing the pistons

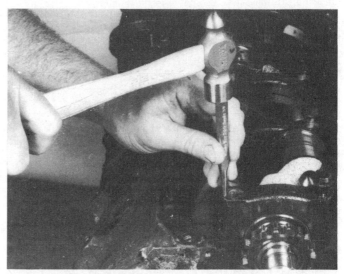

12.4 Mark the bearing caps with a center punch before removing them

2C

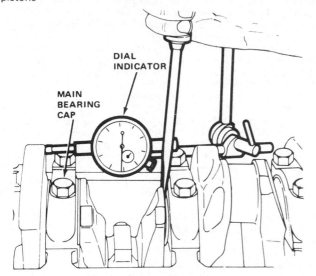

Fig. 2C.5 Checking crankshaft end play with a dial indicator (Sec 12)

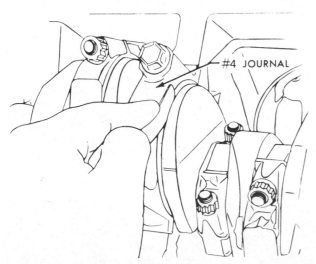

Fig. 2C.6 On OHV engines, the crankshaft end play can be checked with a feeler gauge inserted between the front of the number four journal and the thrust surface of the bearing (Sec 12)

7   Check the connecting rods and connecting rod caps for identification marks. If they are not plainly marked, identify each rod and cap, using a small punch to make the appropriate number of indentations to indicate the cylinders they are associated with.
8   Loosen each of the connecting rod cap nuts approximately 1/2 turn each. Remove the number one connecting rod cap and bearing insert. Do not drop the bearing insert out of the cap. Slip a short length of plastic or rubber hose over each connecting rod cap bolt to protect the crankshaft journal and cylinder wall when the piston is removed (photo) and push the connecting rod/piston assembly out through the top of the engine. Use a wooden tool to push on the upper bearing insert in the connecting rod. If resistance is felt, double-check to make sure that all of the ridge was removed from the cylinder.
9   Repeat the procedure for the remaining cylinders. After removal, reassemble the connecting rod caps and bearing inserts in their respective connecting rods and install the cap nuts finger tight. Leaving the old bearing inserts in place until reassembly will help prevent the connecting rod bearing surfaces from being accidentally nicked or gouged.

12   Crankshaft — removal

1   Before the crankshaft is removed, check the end play as follows. Mount a dial indicator with the stem in line with the crankshaft and just touching one of the crank throws (see accompanying illustration).
2   Push the crankshaft all the way to the rear and zero the dial indicator. Next, pry the crankshaft to the front as far as possible and check the reading on the dial indicator. The distance that it moves is the end play. If it is greater than specified, check the crankshaft thrust surfaces for wear. If no wear is apparent, new main bearings should correct the end play.
3   If a dial indicator is not available, feeler gauges can be used. Gently pry or push the crankshaft all the way to the front of the engine. Slip feeler gauges between the crankshaft and the front face of the thrust main bearing to determine the clearance (which is equivalent to crankshaft end play).
4   Loosen each of the main bearing cap bolts 1/4-turn at a time, until they can be removed by hand. Check the main bearing caps to see if they are marked as to their locations. They are usually numbered consecutively (beginning with 1) from the front of the engine to the rear. If they are not, mark them with number stamping dies or a center punch (photo). Most main bearing caps have a cast-in arrow, which points to the front of the engine.
5   Gently tap the caps with a soft-faced hammer, then separate them from the engine block. If necessary, use the main bearing cap bolts as levers to remove the caps. Try not to drop the bearing insert if it comes out with the cap.
6   On OHC engines, the rear main bearing cap is recessed into the cylinder block. Rock the cap back and forth while pulling up on the

crankshaft to remove it, as shown in the illustration.

7   Carefully lift the crankshaft out of the engine. It is a good idea to have an assistant available, since the crankshaft is quite heavy. With the bearing inserts in place in the engine block and in the main bearing caps, return the caps to their respective locations on the engine block and tighten the bolts finger tight.

13 Engine block — cleaning

1   Remove the soft plugs from the engine block. To do this, knock the plugs into the block (using a hammer and punch), then grasp them with large pliers and pull them back through the holes (photo).

2   Using a gasket scraper, remove all traces of gasket material from the engine block. Be very careful not to nick or gouge the gasket sealing surfaces.

3   Remove the main bearing caps and separate the bearing inserts from the caps and the engine block. Tag the bearings according to which cylinder they removed from (and whether they were in the cap or the block) and set them aside.

4   Using a hex wrench of the appropriate size, remove the threaded oil gallery plugs from the front and back of the block.

5   If the engine is extremely dirty it should be taken to an automotive machine shop to be steam cleaned or hot tanked. Any bearings left

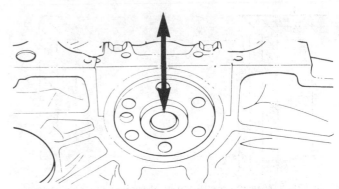

Fig. 2C.7 Because the OHC engine rear main bearing cap extends some distance into the block, to remove it rock it back and forth while pulling upwards (Sec 12)

in the block (such as the camshaft bearings) will be damaged by the cleaning process, so plan on having new ones installed while the block is at the machine shop.

6   After the block is returned, clean all oil holes and oil galleries one more time (brushes for cleaning oil holes and galleries are available at most auto parts stores). Flush the passages with warm water until the water runs clear, dry the block thoroughly and wipe all machined surfaces with a light, rust-preventative oil. If you have access to compressed air, use it to speed the drying process and to blow out all the oil holes and galleries.

7   If the block is not extremely dirty or sludged up, you can do an adequate cleaning job with warm soapy water and a stiff brush. Take plenty of time and do a thorough job. Regardless of the cleaning method used, be very sure to thoroughly clean all oil holes and galleries, dry the block completely and coat all machined surfaces with light oil.

8   The threaded holes in the block must be clean to ensure accurate torque readings during reassembly. Run the proper size tap into each of the holes to remove any rust, corrosion, thread sealant or sludge and to restore any damaged threads. If possible, use compressed air to clear the holes of debris produced by this operation. Now is a good time to thoroughly clean the threads on the head bolts and the main bearing cap bolts as well.

9   Reinstall the main bearing caps and tighten the bolts finger tight.

10   After coating the sealing surfaces of the new soft plugs with a good quality gasket sealer, install them in the engine block (photo). Make sure they are driven in straight and seated properly or leakage could result. Special tools are available for this purpose, but equally good results can be obtained using a large socket (with an outside diameter that will just slip into the soft plug) and a hammer.

11   If the engine is not going to be reassembled right away, cover it with a large plastic trash bag to keep it clean.

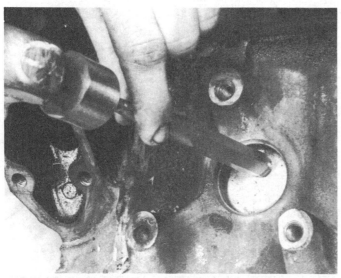

13.1A   A hammer and large punch can be used to drive the soft plugs into the block

13.1B   Using pliers to remove a soft plug from the block

13.10   A large socket on an extension can be used to force the new soft plugs into their bores

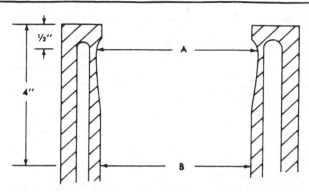

Fig. 2C.8 Measure the diameter of each cylinder just under the wear ridge (A), at the center (B) and at the bottom (C) (Sec 14)

14 Engine block — inspection

1   Thoroughly clean the engine block as described in Section 13 and double-check to make sure that the ridge at the top of each cylinder has been completely removed.
2   Visually check the block for cracks, rust and corrosion. Look for stripped threads in the threaded holes. It is also a good idea to have

the block checked for hidden cracks by an automotive machine shop that has the special equipment to do this type of work. If defects are found, have the block repaired, if possible, or replaced.
3   Check the cylinder bores for scuffing and scoring.
4   Using the appropriate precision measuring tools, measure each cylinder's diameter at the top (just under the ridge), center and bottom of the cylinder bore, parallel to the crankshaft axis (photos). Next, measure each cylinder's diameter at the same three locations across the crankshaft axis. Compare the results to the Specifications. If the cylinder walls are badly scuffed or scored, or if they are out-of-round or tapered beyond the limits given in the Specifications, have the engine block rebored and honed at an automotive machine shop. If a rebore is done, oversize pistons and rings will be required.
5   If the cylinders are in reasonably good condition and not worn to the outside of the limits, and if the piston-to-cylinder clearances can be maintained properly, then they do not have to be rebored; honing is all that is necessary.
6   Before honing the cylinders, install the main bearing caps (without the bearings) and tighten the bolts to the specified torque.
7   To perform the honing operation you will need the proper size flexible hone (with fine stones), plenty of light oil or honing oil, some rags and an electric drill motor. Mount the hone in the drill motor, compress the stones and slip the hone into the first cylinder (photo). Lubricate the cylinder thoroughly, turn on the drill and move the hone up and down in the cylinder at a pace which will produce a fine cross-hatch pattern on the cylinder walls (with the cross-hatch lines intersecting at approximately a 60° angle). Be sure to use plenty of lubricant and do not take off any more material than is absolutely necessary to pro-

2C

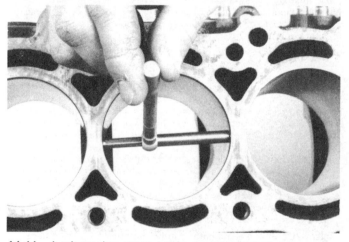

14.4A   A telescoping gauge can be used to determine the cylinder bore diameter

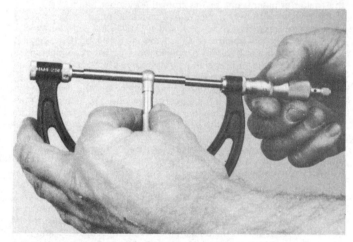

14.4B   The gauge is then measured with a micrometer to determine the bore size

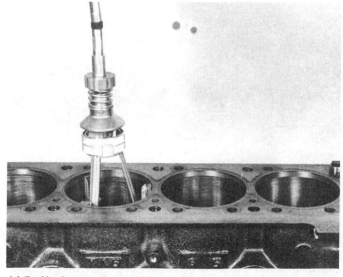

14.7   Honing a cylinder with a surfacing stone

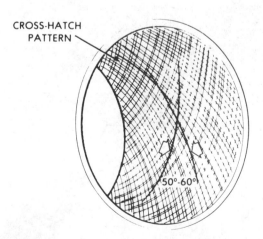

Fig. 2C.9 The cylinder hone should leave a cross-hatch pattern with the lines intersecting at approximately a 60 degree angle (Sec 14)

duce the desired finish. Do not withdraw the hone from the cylinder while it is running. Instead, shut off the drill and continue moving the hone up and down in the cylinder until it comes to a complete stop, then compress the stones and withdraw the hone. Wipe the oil out of the cylinder and repeat the procedure on the remaining cylinders. Remember, do not remove too much material from the cylinder wall. If you do not have the tools or do not desire to perform the honing operation, most automotive machine shops will do it for a reasonable fee.

8   After the honing job is complete, chamfer the top edges of the cylinder bores with a small file so the rings will not catch when the pistons are installed.

9   The entire engine block must be thoroughly washed again with warm, soapy water to remove all traces of the abrasive grit produced during the honing operation. Be sure to run a brush through all oil holes and galleries and flush them with running water. After rinsing, dry the block and apply a coat of light rust preventative oil to all machined surfaces. Wrap the block in a plastic trash bag to keep it clean and set it aside until reassembly.

---

15   Camshaft, lifters, lash compensators and bearings — inspection and bearing replacement

---

Camshaft

1   The most critical camshaft inspection procedure is lobe lift measurement, which must be done before the engine is disassembled.

2   Remove the rocker arm cover, then remove the nuts and separate the rocker arms and ball pivots from the cylinder head.

3   Beginning with the number one (1) cylinder, mount a dial indicator with the stem resting on the end of, and directly in line with, the exhaust valve pushrod (OHV engine) or directly on the cam lobe (OHC engine).

4   Rotate the crankshaft very slowly in the direction of normal running rotation until the lifter or dial indicator stem is on the heel of the cam lobe. At this point the pushrod will be at its lowest position.

5   Zero the dial indicator, then very slowly rotate the crankshaft in the direction of rotation until the pushrod or lobe is at its highest position. Note and record the reading on the dial indicator, then compare it to the lobe lift specifications. Repeat the procedure for each of the remaining valves.

7   If the lobe lift measurements are not as specified, a new camshaft should be installed.

8   After the camshaft has been removed from the engine, cleaned with solvent and dried, inspect the bearing journals for uneven wear, pitting or evidence of seizure. If the journals are damaged, the bearing inserts in the block or bores in the carrier are probably damaged as well. Both the camshaft and bearings will have to be replaced with new ones. Measure the inside diameter of each camshaft bearing and record the results (take two measurements, 90° apart, at each bearing).

9   Measure the bearing journals with a micrometer (photo) to determine if they are excessively worn or out-of-round. If they are more than 0.001-inch out-of-round, the camshaft should be replaced with a new one. Subtract the bearing journal diameter(s) from the corresponding bearing inside diameter measurement to obtain the clearance. If it is excessive, new bearings must be installed.

10   Check the camshaft lobes for heat discoloration, score marks, chipped areas, pitting or uneven wear. If the lobes are in good condition and if the lobe lift measurements (Steps 1 through 7) are as specified, the camshaft can be reused.

Lifters or valve lash compensators

11   Clean the lifters or valve lash compensators with solvent and dry them thoroughly without mixing them up.

12   Check each lifter or compensator wall, pushrod seat and foot for scuffing, score marks or uneven wear. Each lifter foot (the surface that rides on the cam lobe) must be slightly convex — if they are concave (photo), the lifters and camshaft must be replaced with new ones. If the lifter walls are damaged or worn (which is not very likely), inspect the lifter bores in the engine block as well. If the pushrod seats are worn, check the pushrod ends.

13   If new lifters or valve lash compensators are being installed, a new camshaft must also be installed. If a new camshaft is installed, then use new lifters or compensators as well. Never install used lifters or compensators unless the original camshaft is used and the lifters or compensators can be installed in their original locations.

Bearing replacement

14   Camshaft bearing replacement on OHV engines requires special tools and expertise that place it outside the scope of the do-it-yourselfer. Take the block to an automotive machine shop to ensure that the job is done correctly.

Fig. 2C.10   A dial indicator can be mounted as shown here to check the camshaft lobe lift (OHV engine) (Sec 15)

15.9   The camshaft journal diameter is subtracted from the bearing inside diameter to obtain the clearance, which must be as specified

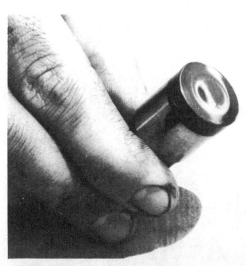

15.12   If the bottom of any lifter is worn concave, scratched or galled, it should be replaced with a new one

15 OHC engines do not have bearings, as the camshaft rides in the camshaft bores themselves. Consequently, the camshaft carrier must be replaced with a new one if the bores are worn or damaged.

---

16   Piston/connecting rod assembly — inspection

1   Before the inspection process can be carried out, the piston/connecting rod assemblies must be cleaned and the original piston rings removed from the pistons. **Note:** *Always use new piston rings when the engine is reassembled.*
2   Using a piston ring installation tool, carefully remove the rings from the pistons. Do not nick or gouge the pistons in the process.
3   Scrape all traces of carbon from the top (or crown) of the piston. A hand-held wire brush or a piece of fine emery cloth can be used once the majority of the deposits have been scraped away. Do not, under any circumstances, use a wire brush mounted in a drill motor to remove deposits from the pistons. The piston material is soft and will be eroded away by the wire brush.
4   Use a piston ring groove cleaning tool to remove any carbon deposits from the ring grooves. If a tool is not available, a piece broken off the old ring will do the job. Be very careful to remove only the carbon deposits. Do not remove any metal and do not nick or scratch the sides of the ring grooves (photo).
5   Once the deposits have been removed, clean the piston/rod assemblies with solvent and dry them thoroughly. Make sure that the oil hole in the big end of the connecting rod and the oil return holes in the back sides of the ring grooves are clear.
6   If the pistons are not damaged or worn excessively, and if the engine block is not rebored, new pistons will not be necessary. Normal

piston wear appears as even vertical wear on the piston thrust surfaces and slight looseness of the top ring in its groove. New piston rings, on the other hand, should always be used when an engine is rebuilt.
7   Carefully inspect each piston for cracks around the skirt, at the pin bosses and at the ring lands.
8   Look for scoring and scuffing on the thrust faces of the skirt, holes in the piston crown and burned areas at the edge of the crown. If the skirt is scored or scuffed, the engine may have been suffering from overheating and/or abnormal combustion, which caused excessively high operating temperatures. The cooling and lubrication systems should be checked thoroughly. A hole in the piston crown is an indication that abnormal combustion (preignition) was occurring. Burned areas at the edge of the piston crown are usually evidence of spark knock (detonation). If any of the above problems exist, the causes must be corrected or the damage will occur again.
9   Corrosion of the piston (evidenced by pitting) indicates that coolant is leaking into the combustion chamber and/or the crankcase. Again, the cause must be corrected or the problem may persist in the rebuilt engine.
10   Measure the piston ring side clearance by laying a new piston ring in each ring groove and slipping a feeler gauge in between the ring and the edge of the ring groove (photo). Check the clearance at three or four locations around each groove. Be sure to use the correct ring for each groove; they are different. If the side clearance is greater than specified, new pistons and/or rings will have to be used.
11   Check the piston-to-bore clearance by measuring the bore (see Section 14) and the piston diameter. Make sure that the pistons and bores are correctly matched. Measure the piston across the skirt, as shown in the accompanying illustrations. Subtract the piston diameter from the bore diameter to obtain the clearance. If it is greater than specified, the block will have to be rebored and new pistons and rings installed.

2C

16.4   Cleaning the piston ring grooves with a piston ring groove cleaning tool

16.10   Checking the piston ring side clearance with a feeler gauge

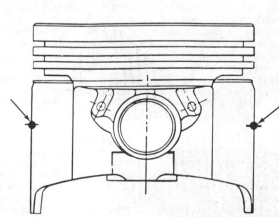

Fig. 2C.11 Measure OHV pistons at the points shown (Sec 16)

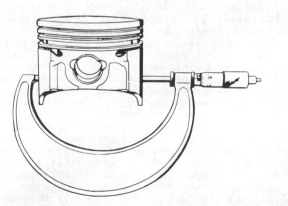

Fig. 2C.12 Measure the piston in line with the pin center at the bottom of the skirt on OHC engines (Sec 16)

Check the piston-to-rod clearance by twisting the piston and rod in opposite directions. Any noticeable play indicates that there is excessive wear, which must be corrected. The piston/connecting rod assemblies should be taken to an automotive machine shop to have new piston pins installed and the pistons and connecting rods rebored.

12 If the pistons must be removed from the connecting rods, such as when new pistons must be installed, or if the piston pins have too much play in them, they should be taken to an automotive machine shop. While they are there have the connecting rods checked for bend and twist, as automotive machine shops have special equipment for this purpose. Unless new pistons or connecting rods must be installed, do not disassemble the pistons from the connecting rods.

13 Check the connecting rods for cracks and other damage. Temporarily remove the rod caps, lift out the old bearing inserts, wipe the rod and cap bearing surfaces clean and inspect them for nicks, gouges or scratches. After checking the rods, replace the old bearings, slip the caps into place and tighten the nuts finger tight.

17 Crankshaft — inspection

1 Clean the crankshaft with solvent and dry it thoroughly. Be sure to clean the oil holes with a stiff brush and flush them with solvent. Check the main and connecting rod bearing journals for uneven wear, scoring, pitting or cracks. Check the remainder of the crankshaft for cracks and damage.

2 Using an appropriate size micromoeter, measure the diameter of the main and connecting rod journals (photo) and compare the results to the Specifications. By measuring the diameter at a number of points around the journal's circumference, you will be able to determine whether or not the journal is out of round. Take the measurement at each end of the journal, near the crank counterweights, to determine whether the journal is tapered.

3 If the crankshaft journals are damaged, tapered, out of round or worn beyond the limits given in the Specifications, have the crankshaft reground by a reputable automotive machine shop. Be sure to use the correct undersize bearing inserts if the crankshaft is reconditioned.

4 Refer to Section 18 and examine the main and rod bearing inserts.

18 Main and connecting rod bearings — inspection

1 Even though the main and connecting rod bearings should be replaced with new ones during the engine overhaul, the old bearings should be retained for close examination, as they may reveal valuable information about the condition of the engine.

2 Bearing failure occurs mainly because of lack of lubrication, the presence of dirt or other foreign particles, overloading the engine and corrosion. Regardless of the cause of bearing failure, it must be corrected before the engine is reassembled to prevent it from happening again.

3 When examining the bearings, remove them from the engine block, the main bearing caps, the connecting rods and the rod caps and lay them out on a clean surface in the same general position as their location in the engine. This will enable you to match any noted bearing problems with the corresponding crankshaft journal.

4 Dirt and other foreign particles get into the engine in a variety of ways. If may be left in the engine during assembly, or it may pass through filters or breathers. It may get into the oil, and from there into the bearings. Metal chips from machining operations and normal engine wear are often present. Abrasives are sometimes left in engine components after reconditioning, especially when parts are not thoroughly cleaned using the proper cleaning methods. Whatever the source, these foreign objects often end up embedded in the soft bearing material and are easily recognized. Large particles will not embed in the bearing and will score or gouge the bearing and shaft. The best prevention for this cause of bearing failure is to clean all parts thoroughly and keep everything spotlessly clean during engine assembly. Frequent and regular engine oil and filter changes are also recommended.

5 Lack of lubrication (or lubrication breakdown) has a number of interrelated causes. Excessive heat (which thins the oil), overloading (which squeezes the oil from the bearing face) and oil leakage or throw-off (from excessive bearing clearances, worn oil pump or high engine speeds) all contribute to lubrication breakdown. Blocked oil passages,

17.2 Measure the diameter of each crankshaft journal at several points to detect taper or an out-of-round condition

which usually are the result of misaligned oil holes in a bearing shell, will also oil-starve a bearing and destroy it. When lack of lubrication is the cause of bearing failure, the bearing material is wiped or extruded from the steel backing of the bearing. Temperatures may increase to the point where the steel backing turns blue from overheating.

6 Driving habits can have a definite effect on bearing life.

Full-throttle, low-speed operation (or 'lugging' the engine) puts very high loads on bearings, which tends to squeeze out the oil film. These loads cause the bearings to flex, which produces fine cracks in the bearing face (fatigue failure). Eventually the bearing material will loosen in pieces and tear away from the steel backing.

Short-trip driving leads to corrosion of bearings because insufficient engine heat is produced to drive off the condensed water and corrosive gases. These products collect in the engine oil, forming acid and sludge. As the oil is carried to the engine bearings, the acid attacks and corrodes the bearing material.

Incorrect bearing installation during engine assembly will lead to bearing failure as well. Tight-fitting bearings leave insufficient bearing oil clearance and will result in oil starvation. Dirt or foreign particles trapped behind a bearing insert result in high spots on the bearing which lead to failure.

19 Piston rings — installation

1 Before installing the new piston rings, the ring end gaps must be checked. It is assumed that the piston ring side clearance has been checked and verified correct (Section 16).

2 Lay out the piston/connecting rod assemblies and the new ring sets so the ring sets will be matched with the same piston and cylinder during the end gap measurement and engine assembly.

3 Insert the top (number one) ring into the first cylinder and square it up with the cylinder walls by pushing it in with the top of the piston (photo). The ring should be near the bottom of the cylinder at the lower limit of ring travel. To measure the end gap, slip a feeler gauge between the ends of the ring (photo). Compare the measurement to the Specifications.

4 If the gap is larger or smaller than specified, double-check to make sure that you have the correct rings before proceeding.

5 If the gap is too small, it must be enlarged or the ring ends may come in contact with each other during engine operation, which can cause serious damage to the engine. The end gap can be increased by filing the ring ends very carefully with a fine file. Mount the file in a vise equipped with soft jaws, slip the ring over the file with the ends contacting the file face and slowly move the ring to remove material from the ends. When performing this operation, file only from the outside in.

6 Excess end gap is not critical unless it is greater than 0.040-inch

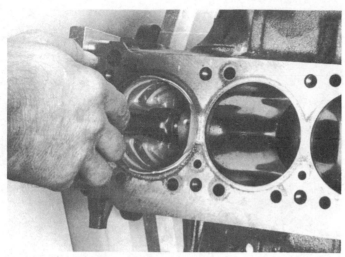

19.3A Use the piston to square up the ring in the cylinder prior to checking ring end gap

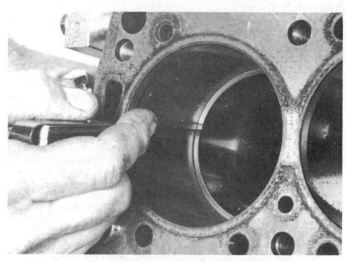

19.3B Measure the ring end gap with a feeler gauge

2C

19.9A Installing the spacer/expander in the oil control ring groove

19.9B Do not use a piston ring tool when installing oil ring side rails

(1 mm). Again, double-check to make sure you have the correct rings for your engine.

7　Repeat the procedure for each ring that will be installed in the first cylinder and for each ring in the remaining cylinders. Remember to keep rings, pistons and cylinders matched up.

8　Once the ring end gaps have been checked/corrected, the rings can be installed on the pistons.

9　The oil control ring (lowest one on the piston) is installed first. It is composed of three separate components. Slip the spacer/expander into the groove (photo), then install the upper side rail. Do not use a piston ring installation tool on the oil ring side rails, as they may be damaged. Instead, place one end of the side rail into the groove between the spacer/expander and the ring land, hold it firmly in place and slide a finger around the piston while pushing the rail into the groove (photo). Next, install the lower side rail in the same manner.

10　After the three oil ring components have been installed, check to make sure that both the upper and lower side rails can be turned smoothly in the ring groove.

11　The number two (middle) ring is installed next. It should be stamped with a mark so it can be readily distinguished from the top ring. **Note:** *Always follow the instructions printed on the ring package or box — different manufacturers may require different approaches.* Do not mix up the top and middle rings, as they have different cross sections.

12　Use a piston ring installation tool and make sure that the identification mark is facing the top of the piston, then slip the ring into the middle groove on the piston (photo). Do not expand the ring any more than

19.12 Installing the compression rings with a special tool — the mark (arrow) must face up

is necessary to slide it over the piston.

13 Finally, install the number one (top) ring in the same manner. Make sure the identifying mark is facing up.

14 Repeat the procedure for the remaining pistons and rings. Be careful not to confuse the number one and number two rings.

20 Crankshaft — installation and main bearing oil clearance check

1   Crankshaft installation is generally one of the first steps in engine reassembly; it is assumed at this point that the engine block and crankshaft have been cleaned, inspected and repaired or reconditioned. **Note:** *Because of the variety of rear main bear oil seals used on OHV engines, refer to Chapter 2, Part A, Section 16 to determine if it is necessary to install the oil seal before proceeding.*

2   Position the engine with the bottom facing up.

3   Remove the main bearing cap bolts and lift out the caps. Lay them out in the proper order to help ensure that they are installed correctly.

4   If they are still in place, remove the old bearing inserts from the block and the main bearing caps. Wipe the main bearing surfaces of the block and caps with a clean, lint-free cloth (they must be kept spotlessly clean).

5   Clean the back sides of the new main bearing inserts and lay one bearing half in each main bearing saddle in the block. Lay the other bearing half from each bearing set in the corresponding main bearing cap. Make sure the tab on the bearing insert fits into the recess in the block or cap. Also, the oil holes in the block and cap must line up with the oil holes in the bearing insert. Do not hammer the bearing into place and do not nick or gouge the bearing faces. No lubrication should be used at this time.

6   The flanged thust bearing must be installed in the number four (4) cap and saddle on OHV engines and the number three (3) cap and saddle on OHC engines.

7   Clean the faces of the bearings in the block and the crankshaft main bearing journals with a clean, lint-free cloth. Check or clean the oil holes in the crankshaft, as any dirt here can go only one way — straight through the new bearings.

8   Once you are certain that the crankshaft is clean, carefully lay it in position (an assistant would be very helpful here) in the main bearings.

9   Before the crankshaft can be permanently installed, the main bearing oil clearance must be checked.

10 Trim several pieces of the appropriate size of Plastigage (so they are slightly shorter than the width of the main bearings) and place one piece on each crankshaft main bearing journal, parallel with the journal axis. Do not lay them across the oil holes.

11 Clean the faces of the bearings in the caps and install the caps in their respective positions (do not mix them up) with the arrows pointing toward the front of the engine. Do not disturb the Plastigage.

12 Starting with the center main and working out toward the ends, tighten the main bearing cap bolts, in three steps, to the specified torque. Do not rotate the crankshaft at any time during this operation.

13 Remove the bolts and carefully lift off the main bearing caps. Keep them in order. Do not disturb the Plastigage or rotate the crankshaft. If any of the main bsearing caps are difficult to remove, tap them gently from side-to-side with a soft-faced hammer to loosen them.

14 Compare the width of the crushed Plastigage on each journal to the scale printed on the Plastigage container (photo) to obtain the main bearing oil clearance. Check the Specifications to make sure it is correct.

15 If the clearance is not correct, double-check to make sure you have the right size bearing inserts. Also, make sure that no dirt or oil was between the bearing inserts and the main bearing caps or the block when the clearance was measured.

16 Carefully scrape all traces of the Plastigage material off the main bearing journals and/or the bearing faces. Do not nick or scratch the bearing faces.

17 Carefully lift the crankshaft out of the engine. Clean the bearing faces in the block, then apply a thin, uniform layer of clean, high-quality moly-based grease or engine assembly lube to each of the bearing surfaces. Be sure to coat the thrust flange faces as well as the journal face of the thrust bearing.

18 Lubricate the rear main bearing oil seal (where it contacts the crankshaft) with moly-based grease or engine assembly lube on the appropriate OHV engine (See Chapter 2, Part A, Section 16). Note that on OHC engines and some OHV engines the oil seal is installed after

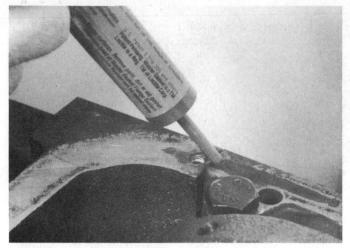

20.20 Filling the OHC rear main bearing cap groove with sealant using the special sealing kit

the crankshaft is in place.

19 If you are working on an OHV engine, refer to Chapter 2A, Section 16 and apply anaerobic-type gasket sealant to the rear main bearing cap or block as described there. Make sure the crankshaft journals are clean, then lay the crankshaft back in place in the block. Clean the faces of the bearings in the caps, then apply a thin, uniform layer of clean, moly-based grease to each of the bearing faces. Install the caps in their respective positions with the arrows or tops of the number 1 on the caps pointing toward the front of the engine. Install the bolts.

20 On OHC engines, fill the rear bearing cap side grooves with sealing compound using GM seal kit number GM 3997597 (photo).

21 On OHV engines, tighten all except the number four main bearing cap bolts to the specified torque. Tighten the number four cap bolts to 10 to 12 ft-lbs. Tap the end of the crankshaft, first rearward, then forward, using a lead faced hammer, to line up the rear main bearing and crankshaft thrust surfaces. Retighten all main bearing cap bolts to the specified torque.

22 On OHC engines, slightly tighten the main bearing cap bolts and tap the rear of the crankshaft with a plastic hammer. Tighten the bolts to the specified torque.

23 On all models, rotate the crankshaft a number of times by hand and check for any obvious binding.

24 Check the crankshaft end play with a feeler gauge or a dial indicator as described in Section 12.

25 Install the rear main bearing oil seal on OHC engines (Chapter 2, Part B, Section 19) or appropriate OHV engines (Chapter 2, Part A, Section 16).

21 Piston/connecting rod assembly — installation and bearing oil clearance check

1   Before installing the piston/connecting rod assemblies the cylinder walls must be perfectly clean, the top edge of each cylinder must be chamfered, and the crankshaft must be in place.

2   Remove the connecting rod cap from the end of the number one connecting rod. Remove the old bearing inserts and wipe the bearing surfaces of the connecting rod and cap with a clean, lint-free cloth (they must be kept spotlessly clean).

3   Clean the back side of the new upper bearing half, then lay it in place in the connecting rod. Make sure that the tab on the bearing fits into the recess in the rod. Do not hammer the bearing insert into place and be very careful not to nick or gouge the bearing face. Do not lubricate the bearing at this time.

4   Clean the back side of the other bearing insert and install it in the rod cap. Again, make sure the tab on the bearing fits into the recess in the cap, and do not apply any lubricant. It is critically important that the mating surfaces of the bearing and connecting rod are perfectly clean and oil-free when they are assembled.

5   Position the piston ring gaps as shown in the accompanying illustra-

ENGINE LEFT - ENGINE FRONT - ENGINE RIGHT

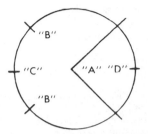

"A" OIL RING SPACER GAP
(Tang in hole or slot within arc)

"B" OIL RING RAIL GAPS

"C" 2nd COMPRESSION RING GAP

"D" TOP COMPRESSION RING GAP

Fig. 2C.13 Before installing the pistons, position the ring end gaps as shown (Sec 21)

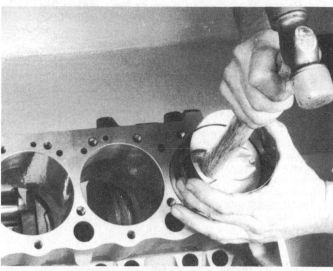

21.10 If resistance is encountered when tapping the piston/connecting rod assembly into the block, stop immediately and make sure the rings are fully compressed

2C

21.12 Position the Plastigage strip on the bearing journal, parallel to the journal axis

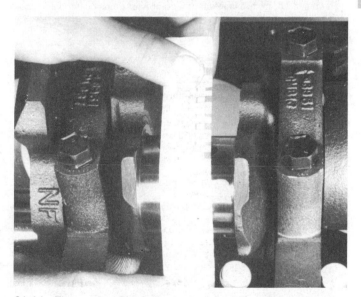

21.14 The crushed Plastigage is compared to the scale printed on the container to obtain the bearing clearance

tions, then slip a section of plastic or rubber hose over the connecting rod cap bolts.

6   Lubricate the piston and rings with clean engine oil and attach a piston ring compressor to the piston. Leave the skirt protruding about 1/4-inch to guide the piston into the cylinder. The rings must be compressed as far as possible.

7   Rotate the crankshaft until the number one connecting rod journal is as far from the number one cylinder as possible (bottom dead center), and apply a uniform coat of engine oil to the cylinder walls.

8   With the notch on top of the piston facing to the front of the engine, gently place the piston/connecting rod assembly into the number one cylinder bore and rest the bottom edge of the ring compressor on the engine block. Tap the top edge of the ring compressor to make sure it is contacting the block around its entire circumference. **Note:** *On OHV engines, the bearing tab recess in the rod must be opposite the camshaft.*

9   Clean the number one connecting rod journal on the crankshaft and the bearing faces in the rod.

10   Carefully tap on the top of the piston with the end of a wooden hammer handle (photo) while guiding the end of the connecting rod into place on the crankshaft journal. The piston rings may try to pop out of the ring compressor just before entering the cylinder bore, so

keep some downward pressure on the ring compressor. Work slowly, and if any resistance is felt as the piston enters the cylinder, stop immediately. Find out what is hanging up and fix it before proceeding. Do not, for any reason, force the piston into the cylinder, as you will break a ring and/or the piston.

11   Once the piston/connecting rod assembly is installed, the connecting rod bearing oil clearance must be checked before the rod cap is permanently bolted in place.

12   Cut a piece of the the appropriate size Plastigage slightly shorter than the width of the connecting rod bearing and lay it in place on the number one connecting rod journal, parallel with the journal axis (it must not cross the oil hole in the journal) (photo).

13   Clean the connecting rod cap bearing face, remove the protective hoses from the connecting rod bolts and gently install the rod cap in place. Make sure the mating mark on the cap is on the same side as the mark on the connecting rod. Install the nuts and tighten them to the specified torque, working up to it in three steps. Do not rotate the crankshaft at any time during this operation.

14   Remove the rod cap, being very careful not to disturb the Plastigage. Compare the width of the crushed Plastigage to the scale printed on the Plastigage container to obtain the oil clearance (photo). Compare it to the Specifications to make sure the clearance is correct.

If the clearance is not correct, double-check to make sure that you have the correct size bearing inserts. Also, recheck the crankshaft connecting rod journal diameter and make sure that no dirt or oil was between the bearing inserts and the connecting rod or cap when the clearance was measured.

15   Carefully scrape all traces of the Plastigage material off the rod journal and/or bearing face (be very careful not to scratch the bearing — use your fingernail or a piece of hardwood). Make sure the bearing faces are perfectly clean, then apply a uniform layer of clean, high quality moly-based grease or engine assembly lube to both of them. You will have to push the piston into the cylinder to expose the face of the bearing insert in the connecting rod; be sure to slip the protective hoses over the rod bolts first.

16   Slide the connecting rod back into place on the journal, remove the protective hoses from the rod cap bolts, install the rod cap and tighten the nuts to the specified torque. Again, work up to the torque in three steps.

17   Repeat the entire procedure for the remaining piston/connecting rod assemblies. Keep the back sides of the bearing inserts and the inside of the connecting rod and cap perfectly clean when assembling them. Make sure you have the correct piston for the cylinder and that the notch on the piston faces to the front of the engine when the piston is installed. Remember, use plenty of oil to lubricate the piston before installing the ring compressor. Also, when installing the rod caps for the final time, be sure to lubricate the bearing faces adequately.

18   After all the piston/connecting rod assemblies have been properly installed, rotate the crankshaft a number of times by hand and check for any obvious binding.

19   As a final step, the connecting rod end play must be checked. Refer to Section 11 for this procedure. Compare the measured end play to the Specifications to make sure it is correct.

22   Engine overhaul — reassembly sequence

1   Before beginning engine reassembly, make sure you have all the necessary new parts, gaskets and seals as well as the following items on hand:

Common hand tools
A 1/2-inch drive torque wrench
Piston ring installation tool
Piston ring compressor
Short lengths of rubber or plastic hose to fit over connecting rod
   bolts
Plastigage
Feeler gauges
A fine-tooth file
New engine oil
Engine assembly lube or moly-based grease
RTV-type gasket sealant
Anaerobic-type gasket sealant
Thread locking compound

2   In order to save time and avoid problems, engine reassembly must be done in the following order.

Rear main oil seal (some OHV engines)
Crankshaft and main bearings
Piston rings

Piston/connecting rod assemblies
Oil pump
Oil pan
Camshaft
Timing chain/sprockets or gears
Timing chain/gear cover
Valve lifters/valve lash compensators
Cylinder head and pushrods
Intake and exhaust manifolds
Oil filter
Rocker arm/camshaft cover
Fuel pump
Water pump
Rear main oil seal (OHC and some OHV engines)
Flywheel/driveplate
Carburetor/fuel injection components
Thermostat and housing cover
Distributor, spark plug wires and spark plugs
Emissions control components
Alternator

23   Initial start-up and break-in after overhaul

1   Once the engine has been properly installed in the vehicle, double-check the engine oil and coolant levels.

2   With the spark plugs out of the engine and the coil high-tension lead grounded to the engine block, crank the engine over until oil pressure registers on the gauge (if so equipped) or until the oil light goes off.

3   Install the spark plugs, hook up the plug wires and the coil high tension lead.

4   Make sure the carburetor choke plate is closed, then start the engine. It may take a few moments for the gasoline to reach the carburetor, but the engine should start without a great deal of effort.

5   As soon as the engine starts it should be set at a fast idle (to ensure proper oil circulation) and allowed to warm up to normal operating temperature. While the engine is warming up, make a thorough check for oil and coolant leaks.

6   Shut the engine off and recheck the engine oil and coolant levels. Restart the engine and check the ignition timing and the engine idle speed (refer to Chapter 1). Make any necessary adjustments.

7   Drive the vehicle to an area with minimum traffic, accelerate at full throttle from 30 to 50 mph, then allow the vehicle to slow to 30 mph with the throttle closed. Repeat the procedure 10 or 12 times. This will load the piston rings and cause them to seat properly against the cylinder walls. Check again for oil and coolant leaks.

8   Drive the vehicle gently for the first 500 miles (no sustained high speeds) and keep a constant check on the oil level. It is not unusual for an engine to use oil during the break-in period.

9   At approximately 500 to 600 miles, change the oil and filter, retorque the cylinder head bolts and recheck the valve clearances (if applicable).

10   For the next few hundred miles, drive the vehicle normally. Do not either pamper it or abuse it.

11   After 2000 miles, change the oil and filter again and consider the engine fully broken in.

Chapter 3
Cooling, heating and air conditioning systems

Contents

3

Specifications

Radiator cap pressure	15 psi
Thermostat rating	195 deg. F
Coolant capacity	See Chapter 1

Torque specifications	Ft-lbs
Fan-to-motor bolts	7
Water pump bolts	
OHV engine	13 to 18
OHC engine	19
OHV engine thermostat housing bolts	13 to 22

1 General information

The cooling system consists of a crossflow radiator, an engine driven water pump and thermostat-controlled coolant flow.

The fan is driven by an electric motor which is mounted in the radiator shroud and is activated by a temperature switch. **Caution:** *The fan can start even when the engine is Off as long as the ignition switch is On. The battery negative cable should be disconnected whenever you are working in the vicinity of the fan.*

The water pump is mounted on the front of the engine. On OHV engines, the pump is driven by a belt from the crankshaft pulley. On OHC engines, the water pump is turned by the timing belt and acts as the tensioner for this belt.

The heater utilizes the heat produced by the engine, which is absorbed by the coolant, to warm the vehicle interior. It is manually controlled by the driver or passenger.

Air conditioning is available as an option on these vehicles. The air conditioning system is located in the engine compartment and the compressor is driven by the crankshaft pulley by way of a drive belt.

2 Antifreeze — general information

Caution: *Do not allow antifreeze to come in contact with your skin or painted surfaces of the vehicle. Flush contacted areas immediately with plenty of water. Antifreeze can be fatal to children and pets. They like it because it is sweet. Just a few licks can cause death. Wipe up garage floor and drip pan coolant spills immediately. Keep antifreeze*

containers covered and repair leaks in your cooling system immediately.

The cooling system should be filled with a water/ethylene glycol based antifreeze solution, which will prevent freezing down to at least -20°F. It also provides protection against corrosion and increases the coolant boiling point.

The cooling system should be drained, flushed and refilled at least every other year (see Chapter 1). The use of antifreeze solutions for periods of longer than two years is likely to cause damage and encourage the formation of rust and scale in the system.

Before adding antifreeze to the system, check all hose connections and retorque the cylinder head bolts, because antifreeze tends to search out and leak through very minute openings.

The exact mixture of antifreeze-to-water which you should use depends on the relative weather conditions. The mixture should contain at least 50 percent antifreeze, but should never contain more than 70 percent antifreeze.

3 Thermostat — replacement

Caution: *The engine must be completely cool before beginning this procedure. Also, when working in the vicinity of the electric fan, disconnect the negative battery cable from the battery to prevent the fan from coming on accidentally.*

OHV engine

1 Refer to the Cautions in Sections 1 and 2.
2 Disconnect the cable from the negative battery terminal (if not done previously).

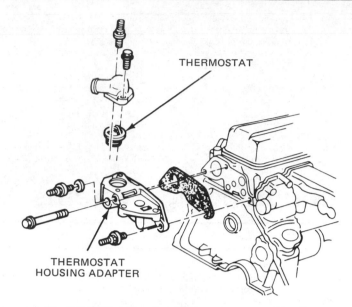

Fig. 3.1 OHV engine thermostat components (Sec 3)

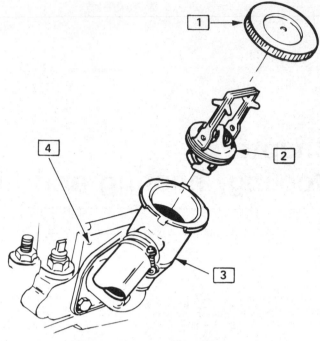

Fig. 3.2 OHC engine thermostat housing components
(Sec 3)

1 Cap   3 Housing
2 Thermostat   4 Cylinder head

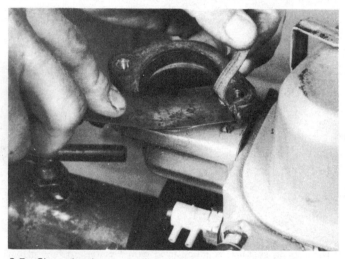

3.7 Clean the thermostat housing with a scraper. Not all models use a gasket

3   Drain the cooling system until the level is below the thermostat by opening the petcock at the bottom right side of the radiator. Close the petcock when enough coolant has drained.
4   Remove the upper radiator hose from the water outlet housing.
5   Remove the two housing bolts and separate the housing from the engine.
6   Remove the thermostat from the thermostat housing.
7   Before installing the thermostat, clean the gasket sealing surfaces on the water outlet and thermostat housing (photo).
8   Apply a 1/8-inch bead of RTV-type sealant to the sealing surface on the engine and place the thermostat in the housing. Install the water outlet and tighten the water outlet bolts to the specified torque (photo).
9   Install the upper radiator hose.
10 Fill the cooling system with the proper antifreeze/water mixture (refer to Chapter 1).

3.8 When installing the thermostat, make sure the power element (arrow) is pointed down as shown

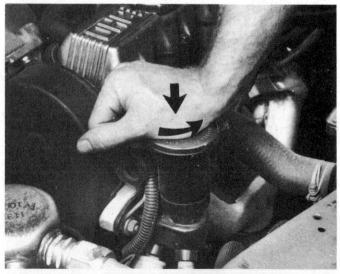

3.15 Push down while rotating (arrows) to remove the thermostat cap

3.16A With the cap removed, the thermostat handle (arrow) is visible

3.16B Removing the thermostat

3.17 Whenever the thermostat is removed, make sure the O-ring (arrow) is not damaged

11 Reconnect the battery cable and start the engine.
12 Run the engine with the radiator cap removed until the upper radiator hose is hot (thermostat open).
13 With the engine idling, add coolant to the radiator until the level reaches the bottom of the filler neck.
14 Install the radiator cap, making sure the arrows on the cap line up with the radiator overflow tube.

OHC engine
15 Remove the thermostat housing cap by pushing it down and rotating in a counterclockwise direction (photo).
16 Grasp the handle and pull the thermostat from the housing (photos).
17 If the old thermostat is to be reinstalled, inspect the rubber O-ring for cuts or damage (photo).
18 To install, insert the thermostat fully into the housing until it is seated and install the cap.

---

4 Thermostat — check

1 The best way to check the operation of the thermostat is with it removed from the engine. In most cases, if the thermostat is suspect, it is more economical to simply buy and install a replacement thermostat, as they are not very costly.
2 To check the thermostat, first remove it as described in Section 3.
3 Inspect the thermostat for excessive corrosion and damage. Replace it with a new one if either of these conditions is noted.
4 Place the thermostat in hot water (25 degrees above the temperature stamped on the thermostat). The water temperature should be approximately 220 degrees. When submerged in the water (which should be agitated thoroughly), the valve should open all the way.
5 Next, remove the thermostat, using a piece of bent wire, and place it in water which is 10 degrees below the temperature on the thermostat, or about 185 degrees. At this temperature, the thermostat valve should close completely.
6 Reinstall the thermostat if it operates properly. If it does not, purchase a new thermostat of the same temperature rating.

---

5 Radiator — removal, servicing and installation

Caution: *The engine must be completely cool before beginning this procedure. Also, when working in the vicinity of the electric fan, disconnect the negative (-) battery cable from the battery to prevent the fan from coming on accidentally.*
1 Refer to the Caution in Section 2.
2 Disconnect the cable from the negative (-) battery terminal (if not done previously).
3 Drain the radiator (refer to Chapter 1, if necessary).
4 On some models, it may be necessary to remove that portion of the air cleaner assembly which is adjacent to the radiator.

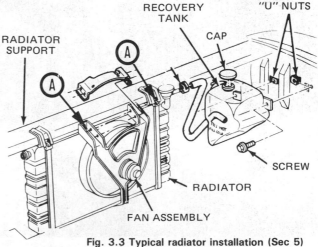

Fig. 3.3 Typical radiator installation (Sec 5)
A Retaining clamp bolts

5   Remove the radiator hoses from the radiator, disconnect the coolant recovery hose and, on automatic transaxle models, disconnect and plug the cooler lines.

6   Remove the fan and shroud assembly (Section 6).

7   Remove the radiator clamp bolts.

8   Lean the top of the radiator rearward, then slide the radiator toward the right and lift it from the engine compartment.

9   Carefully examine the radiator for evidence of leaks or damage. It is recommended that any necessary repairs be performed by a reputable radiator repair shop.

10   With the radiator removed, brush accumulations of insects and leaves from the fins and examine and replace, if necessary, any hoses or clamps which have deteriorated.

11   The radiator can be flushed as described in Chapter 1.

12   Replace the radiator cap with a new one of the same rating, or if the cap is comparatively new, have it tested by a service station.

13   If you are installing a new radiator, transfer the fittings from the old unit to the new one.

14   Installation is the reverse of removal. When setting the radiator in the chassis, make sure that it seats securely in the lower rubber mounting pads (photos).

15   After installing the radiator, refill it with the proper coolant mixture (refer to Chapter 1), then start the engine and check for leaks.

5.14A   Inspect the lower radiator mount (arrow) for damage prior to installation

5.14B   The radiator should be securely inserted into the radiator mount (arrow)

6   Fan — removal and installation

Caution: *The engine must be completely cool before beginning this procedure. Also, when working in the vicinity of the electric fan, disconnect the negative (-) battery cable from the battery to prevent the fan from coming on accidentally.*

1   Remove the fan frame-to-radiator bolts.

2   Lift the retaining tabs and unplug the fan connector (photo).

3   Lift the fan assembly from the engine compartment.

4   To install, plug in the electrical connector, place the fan assembly in position and install the retaining bolts.

5   Connect the negative (-) battery cable and check for proper operation as the engine warms up to operating temperature.

7   Water pump — check

1   A failure in the water pump can cause overheating and serious engine damage (the pump will not circulate coolant through the engine).

2   There are three ways to check the operation of the water pump while it is still installed on the engine. If the pump is defective, it should be replaced with a new or rebuilt unit.

3   With the engine at normal operating temperature, squeeze the upper radiator hose. If the water pump is working properly, a pressure surge will be felt as the hose is released.

4   Water pumps are equipped with 'weep' or vent holes. If a pump seal failure occurs, small amounts of coolant will leak from the weep holes. In most cases it will be necessary to use a flashlight from under the vehicle to see evidence of leakage from this point on the pump body.

5   If the water pump shaft bearings fail, there may be a squealing sound emitted from the front of the engine while it is running. Shaft wear can be felt if the water pump pulley is forced up and down. Do not mistake drivebelt slippage (which also causes a squealing sound) for water pump failure.

8   Water pump — removal and installation

Caution: *The engine must be completely cool before beginning this procedure. Also, when working in the vicinity of the electric fan, disconnect the negative (-) battery cable from the battery to prevent the fan from coming on accidentally.*

1   Refer to the Caution in Section 2.

2   Drain the cooling system (refer to Chapter 1, if necessary).

3   Remove the accessory drivebelts, alternator, air conditioning compressor or other components which could interfere with removal.

4   On OHC engines, remove the timing belt front cover, timing belt

6.2   Electric fan connector (arrow)

and rear cover (Chapter 2).

5   On all models, disconnect the hoses, remove the retaining bolts and lift the water pump from the engine (photo).

6   If installing a new or rebuilt pump, transfer the pulley from the old unit to the new one.

7   On OHC engines, remove the O-ring from the water pump, inspect the seating surface of the groove for nicks, corrosion or damage and the O-ring for cuts (photos). Replace the O-ring with a new one if there is any doubt as to its sealing ability. Lubricate the groove with moly-based grease and install the O-ring.

8   Make sure the sealing surfaces are clean of any foreign material.

9   On OHV engines, place a 1/8-inch bead of RTV-type sealant on the pump sealing surface. While the sealant is still wet, install the pump, tighten the mounting bolts to the specified torque and connect the water hoses.

10   On OHC engines, place the water pump in position with the adjusting tab up, install the mounting bolts finger tight and connect the water hoses. Install the timing belt rear cover, followed by the timing belt. Adjust the timing belt tension as described in Chapter 2, tighten the water pump mounting bolts to the specified torque and install the timing belt cover.

11   Install the drivebelts, alternator and other components which were removed for access.

12   Refill the cooling system with a 50/50 solution of water and the specified coolant (Chapter 1).

13   Connect the battery negative (-) cable, start the engine and run it until normal operating temperature is reached, then check for leaks.

9   Coolant temperature sending unit — check and replacement

1   The coolant temperature indicator system is composed of a light or temperature gauge mounted in the instrument panel and a coolant temperature sending unit located at the corner of the cylinder head.

2   **Caution:** *Since battery cables must be connected for some of the diagnostic steps, be especially careful to stay clear of the electric fan blades, which can come on at any time.*

3   If overheating occurs, check the coolant level in the system and then make sure that the wiring between the light or gauge and the sending unit is secure.

4   When the ignition switch is turned On and the starter motor is turning, the indicator light should be on (overheated engine indication). If the light is not on, the bulb may be burned out, the ignition switch may be faulty or the circuit may be open.

5   As soon as the engine starts, the light should go out and remain out unless the engine overheats. Failure of the light to go out may be due to grounded wiring between the light and the sending unit, a defective sending unit or a faulty ignition switch. Check the coolant to make sure it is of the proper type, as plain water has too low a boiling point

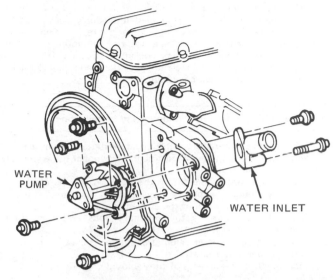

Fig. 3.4 OHV engine water pump installation (Sec 8)

3

8.5   OHC engine water pump retaining bolts (arrows)

8.7A   Inspect the OHC engine O-ring groove (arrow) for nicks or damage

8.7B   Check the OHC engine water pump cavity (arrow) for damage and corrosion

to activate the sending unit.

6   If the sending unit is to be replaced, it is simply unscrewed from the cylinder head or thermostat housing and a replacement installed (photo). Make sure that the engine is cool before removing the defective sending unit. There will be some coolant loss as the unit is removed, so be prepared to catch the coolant in a bucket and to check the level after the replacement has been installed.

10   Heater blower motor — removal and installation

1   Disconnect the cable from the negative battery terminal.
2   Working in the engine compartment, disconnect the wires at the blower motor and resistor.
3   Remove the water shield from the right side of the cowl.
4   On some models it may be necessary to disconnect the radio capacitor to allow removal of the blower motor.
5   Remove the blower motor mounting bolts and separate the motor/cage assembly from the case.
6   While holding the cage, remove the cage retaining nut and slide the cage off the motor shaft.
7   Installation is the reverse of the removal procedure.

9.6   The coolant temperature sending units (arrows) are located in the thermostat housing on OHC engines

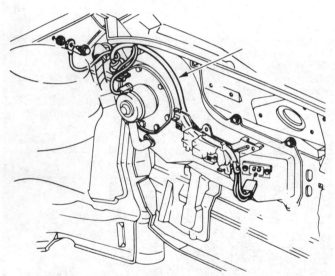

Fig. 3.5 Heater blower motor location (arrow) (Sec 10)

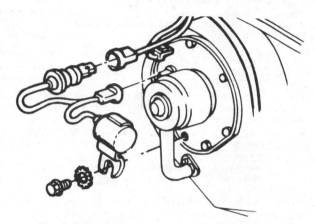

Fig. 3.6 Blower motor resistor installation (Sec 10)

11   Air conditioning system — servicing

Caution: *The air conditioning system is under high pressure. Do not disassemble any portion of the system (hoses, compressor, line fittings, etc.) without having the system depressurized by a dealer or competent repair facility.*

1   Regularly inspect the condenser fins (located ahead of the radiator) and brush away leaves and bugs.
2   Clean the evaporator drain tubes.
3   Check the condition of the system hoses. If there is any sign of deterioration or hardening, have them replaced by a dealer or competent repair facility.
4   At the recommended intervals, check and adjust the compressor drivebelt as described in Chapter 1.
5   Because of the special tools, equipment and skills required to service air conditioning systems, and the differences between the various systems that may be installed on vehicles, major air conditioning servicing procedures cannot be covered in this manual.

Chapter 4 Part A Fuel and exhaust systems

Refer to Chapter 13 for specifications and information related to 1985 and later models

Contents

4A

Specifications

Carburetor specifications

Float adjustment	5/16 in (7.65 mm)
Fast idle cam (choke rod) adjustment	24°
Primary vacuum break adjustment	20°
Air valve rod link adjustment	1°
Secondary vacuum break adjustment	0.157 in (3.98 mm)
Unloader adjustment	35°
Air valve spring adjustment	1/2 turn

Torque specifications **Ft-lbs**

Carburetor retaining bolts	17 to 20
Carburetor stud......................................	2 to 3
Exhaust pipe-to-manifold nuts	15 to 22
Early Fuel Evaporation (EFE) heater nuts	4 to 12
Intermediate exhaust pipe-to-bracket	15 to 25
Idle Air Control (IAC) assembly-to-throttle body	13
Muffler exhaust pipe clamp	7 to 14
Throttle Body Injection (TBI) fuel return line	17
TBI throttle body attaching screws	17
TBI-to-manifold	24
Fuel meter body screws	3
Fuel feed and return nuts	21
Fuel meter cover screws	2.2
Fuel pump retaining nuts (carbureted engines)	15 to 22

---

1 General information

The fuel system consists of a rear mounted fuel tank, a mechanically operated fuel pump (carburetor-equipped engines) or an electrically operated fuel pump (fuel-injected engines), a carburetor or fuel injection assembly and an air cleaner.

Some models are also equipped with a turbocharger. Information on the turbocharger can be found in Part B of this Chapter.

The exhaust system includes a catalytic converter, muffler, related emissions equipment and associated pipes and hardware.

2 Fuel pump — check

Warning: *Gasoline is extremely flammable, so extra precautions must be taken when working on any part of the fuel system. Do not smoke or allow open flames or bare light bulbs near the work area. Also, do not work in a garage if a natural gas-type appliance with a pilot light is present.*

1 On carburetor-equipped engines the fuel pump is located on the back (firewall) side of the engine.

2 The fuel pump for fuel-injected models is located in the fuel tank.

3   Both types of fuel pumps are sealed and no repairs are possible. However, on carburetor-equipped models, the fuel pump can be inspected and tested on the vehicle as follows:

4   Make sure that there is fuel in the fuel tank.

5   With the engine running, check for leaks at all gasoline line connections between the fuel tank and the carburetor. Tighten any loose connections. Inspect all hoses for flat spots or kinks which could restrict fuel flow. Air leaks or restrictions on the suction side of the fuel pump will greatly affect pump output.

6   Check for leaks at the fuel pump diaphragm flange.

7   Disconnect the high energy ignition (HEI) connector at the distributor, then disconnect the fuel inlet line from the carburetor and place it in a metal container.

8   Crank the engine a few revolutions and make sure that well-defined spurts of fuel are ejected from the open end of the line. If not, the fuel line is clogged or the fuel pump is defective.

9   Disconnect the fuel line at both ends and blow through it with compressed air. If the fuel line is not clogged, replace the fuel pump with a new one.

3   Fuel pump (carbureted models) — removal and installation

Warning: *Gasoline is extremely flammable, so extra precautions must be taken when working on any part of the fuel system. Do not smoke or allow open flames or bare light bulbs near the work area. Also, do not work in a garage if a natural gas-type appliance with a pilot light is present.*

1   Disconnect the cable from the negative battery terminal.

2   Remove the fuel inlet and outlet lines. Use two wrenches to prevent damage to the pump and connections (photo).

3   Remove the fuel pump mounting bolts, the pump and the gasket.

4   Install the pump using a new gasket. Use gasket sealant on the screw threads.

5   Connect the fuel lines, start the engine and check for leaks.

4   Fuel line — repair and replacement

Warning: *Gasoline is extremely flammable, so extra precautions must be taken when working on any part of the fuel system. Do not smoke or allow open flames or bare light bulbs near the work area. Also, do not work in a garage if a natural gas-type appliance with a pilot light is present.*

Note: *Before starting this procedure on fuel-injected models, the fuel system pressure must be relieved as outlined in Section 10.*

1   If a section of metal fuel line must be replaced, only brazed, seamless steel tubing should be used, since copper or aluminum does not have enough durability to withstand normal operating vibrations.

2   If only one section of a metal fuel line is damaged, it can be cut out and replaced with a piece of rubber hose. Be sure to use only reinforced fuel resistant hose, identified by the word 'Fluroelastomer' on the hose. The inside diameter of the hose should match the outside diameter of the metal line. The rubber hose should be cut four inches longer than the section it's replacing, so there are two inches of overlap between the rubber and metal line at either end of the section. Hose clamps should be used to secure both ends of the repaired section.

3   If a section of metal line longer than six inches is being removed, use a combination of metal tubing and rubber hose so the hose lengths will be no longer than ten inches.

4   Never use rubber hose within four inches of any part of the exhaust system or within ten inches of the catalytic converter.

5   When replacing clamps, make sure the replacement clamp is identical to the one being replaced, as different clamps are used depending on location.

5   Fuel tank — removal and installation

Warning: *Gasoline is extremely flammable, so extra precautions must be taken when working on any part of the fuel system. Do not smoke or allow open flames or bare light bulbs near the work area. Also, do not work in a garage if a natural gas-type appliance with a pilot light is present. While performing any work on the fuel tank it is advisable*

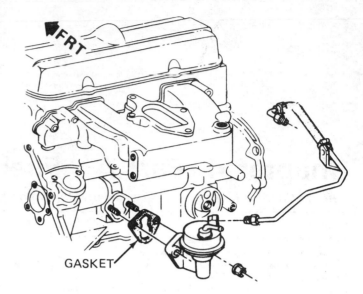

Fig. 4A.1 Fuel pump installation details (Sec 3)

to have a CO-2 fire extinguisher on hand and to wear safety glasses.

Note: *Before starting this procedure on fuel-injected models, the fuel system pressure must be relieved as outlined in Section 10.*

1   Raise the rear of the car and support it on jackstands.

2   Remove the cable from the negative battery terminal.

3   Disconnect the fuel feed line at the pump.

4   Drain all fuel from the tank into a clean container. Since there are no drain plugs on the tank, siphon the fuel through the filler neck or drain the fuel through the fuel line running to the carburetor or fuel injection unit. Do not start the siphoning process with your mouth because serious personal injury could result.

5   Disconnect the fuel pressure and fuel return hoses at the point where the rubber lines connect with the rigid steel lines.

6   Remove the ground wire screw.

7   Disconnect the fuel fill and vapor return lines.

8   Remove the heat shield located between the exhaust pipe and the forward end of the fuel tank.

9   Disconnect the fuel gauge wire (fuel gauge/fuel pump wire on fuel-injected models). **Note:** *The wiring harness on the fuel pump/gauge sending assembly is an integral, permanent part of the sending assembly. Do not pry up on the cover connector. Make the disconnection at the body wiring harness.*

10   While the tank is supported by an assistant or a floor jack, remove the two rear support strap bolts.

11   Lower and remove the tank.

12   **Caution:** *Never perform any repair work involving heat or flame on the tank until it has been purged of gas and vapors. All repair work should be performed by a professional (see the following Section).*

13   Before reinstalling the tank make sure that all traces of dirt and corrosion are cleaned from it. A coat of rust-preventative paint is recommended. If the tank is rusted internally, however, it should be replaced with a new one.

14   Installation is the reverse of the removal procedure.

6   Fuel tank — repair

1   Any repairs to the fuel tank or filler neck should be carried out by a professional who has experience in this critical and potentially dangerous work. Even after cleaning and flushing of the fuel system, explosive fumes can remain and ignite during repair of the tank.

2   If the fuel tank is removed from the vehicle, it should not be placed in an area where sparks or open flames could ignite the fumes coming out of the tank. Be especially careful inside garages where a natural gas-type appliance is located, because the pilot light could cause an explosion.

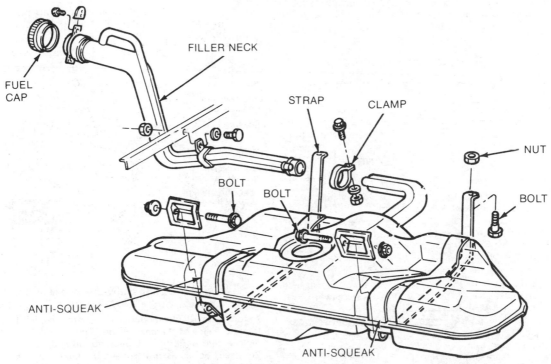

Fig. 4A.2 Fuel tank installation details (Sec 5)

4A

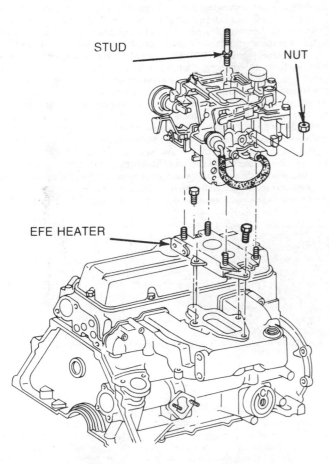

Fig. 4A.3 Carburetor installation details (Sec 7)

7 Carburetor — removal and installation

Warning: *Gasoline is extremely flammable, so extra precautions must be taken when working on any part of the fuel system. Do not smoke or allow open flames or bare light bulbs near the work area. Also, do not work in a garage if a natural gas type appliance with a pilot light is present.*

1   Remove the cable from the negative battery terminal.
2   Remove the air cleaner.
3   Disconnect the fuel and vacuum lines from the carburetor, noting their locations.
4   Disconnect the accelerator linkage and cruise control linkage (if so equipped).
5   Disconnect the throttle linkage and downshift cable (automatic transaxle).
6   Remove all hoses and wires, making very careful note of how they are attached. Tags or coded pieces of tape will help.
7   Remove the carburetor mounting nuts and/or bolts and separate the carburetor from the manifold.
8   Remove the gasket and/or Early Fuel Evaporation (EFE) insulator.
9   Installation is the reverse of the removal procedure, but the following points should be noted:
   a) By filling the carburetor bowl with fuel, the initial start-up will be easier and less drain on the battery.
   b) New gaskets should be used.
   c) Idle speed and mixture settings should be checked and, if necessary, adjusted.

8 Carburetor (E2SE) — overhaul

Note: *Carburetor overhaul is an involved procedure that requires some experience. The home mechanic without much experience should have the overhaul done by a dealer service department or repair shop. Because of running production changes, some details of the unit overhauled here may not exactly match those of your carburetor, although the home mechanic with previous experience should be able to detect the differences and modify the procedure.*

Disassembly

1   Before disassembling the carburetor, purchase a carburetor rebuild

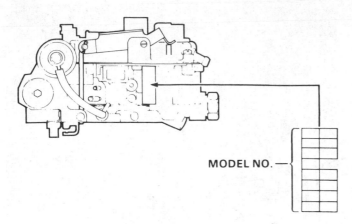

Fig. 4A.4 Location of the carburetor identification tag
(Sec 8)

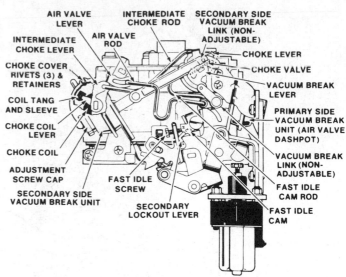

Fig. 4A.5 E2SE carburetor choke system (Sec 8)

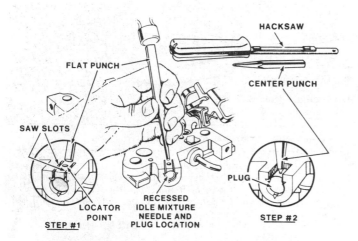

Fig. 4A.6 Carburetor idle mixture needle removal details
(Sec 8)

kit for your particular model (the model number will be found on a metal tag at the side of the carburetor). This kit will have all the necessary replacement parts for the overhaul procedure.

2   It will be necessary to have a relatively large, clean workbench to lay out all of the parts as they are removed. Many of the parts are very small and can be lost easily if the work space is cluttered.

3   Carburetor disassembly is illustrated in the following step-by-step photo sequence to make the operation as easy as possible. Work slowly through the procedure, and if at any point you feel the reassembly of a certain component may prove confusing, stop and make a rough sketch or apply identification marks. The time to think about reassembling the carburetor is when it is being taken apart. The disassembly photo sequence begins with photo 8.3/1.

4   The final step in disassembly involves the idle mixture needle. It is recessed in the throttle body and sealed with a hardened steel plug. The plug should not be removed unless the needle requires replacement or normal cleaning procedures fail to clean the idle mixture passages. If the idle mixture needle must be removed, refer to the accompanying illustration and proceed as follows:

5   Secure the throttle body in a vise so it is inverted with the manifold side up. Use blocks of wood to cushion the throttle body.

6   Locate the idle mixture needle and plug. It should be marked by an indented locator point on the underside of the throttle body. Using a hacksaw, make two parallel cuts in the throttle body on either side

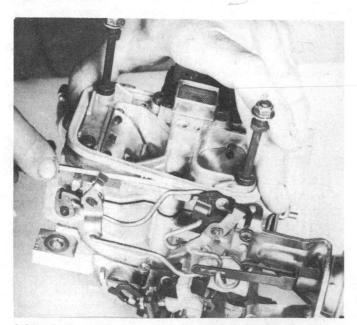

8.3/1   Remove the gasket from the top of the air horn

8.3/2   Remove the fuel inlet nut, fuel filter and spring

8.3/3   Remove the pump lever attaching screw

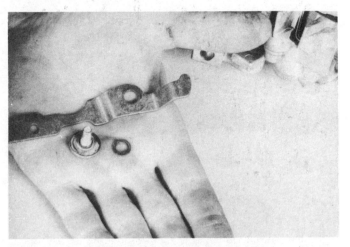

8.3/4   Disconnect the pump rod from the pump lever and remove the pump lever

8.3/5   Disconnect the primary vacuum break diaphragm hose from the throttle body

8.3/6   Remove the screws that retain the idle speed solenoid/vacuum break diaphragm bracket

4A

8.3/7   Lift off the idle speed solenoid/vacuum break diaphragm assembly and disconnect the air valve link from the vacuum break plunger (repeat this step for the secondary vacuum break assembly, disconnecting the link from the slot in the choke lever)

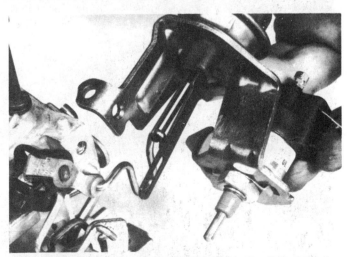

8.3/8   Disconnect the vacuum break and air valve links from the levers (**Note:** *It is not necessary to disconnect the links from the vacuum break plungers unless either of the rods or vacuum break units are being replaced*)

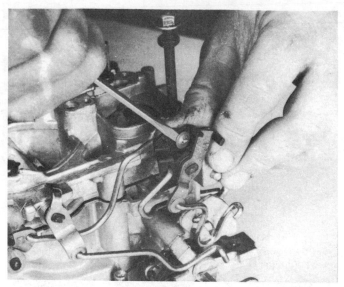

8.3/9 Pry off the clip that retains the intermediate choke link to the choke lever and separate the link from the lever

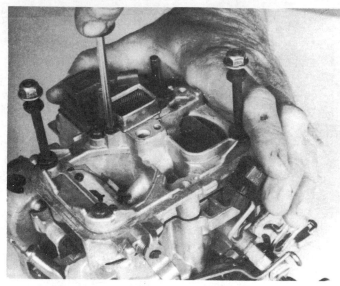

8.3/10   Remove the screws that retain the vent/screen assembly to the air horn and lift off the assembly

8.3/11   Remove the screws that retain the mixture control solenoid and, using a slight twisting motion, lift the solenoid out of the air horn

8.3/12   Remove the screws securing the air horn to the float bowl, noting their various lengths and positions to simplify installation

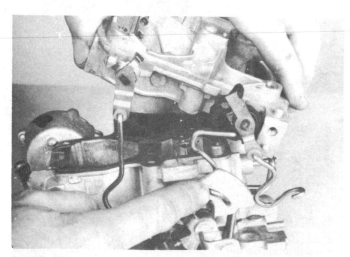

8.3/13   Rotate the fast idle cam up, lift off the air horn and disconnect the fast idle cam link from the fast idle cam

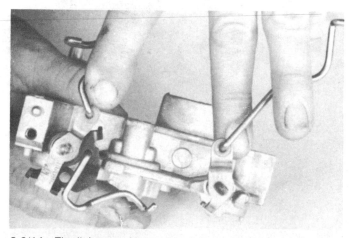

8.3/14   The links attached to the air horn need not be removed unless their replacement or removal is required to service other components

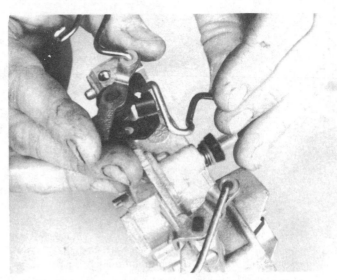

8.3/15   Disengage the fast idle cam link from the choke lever and save the bushing for reassembly

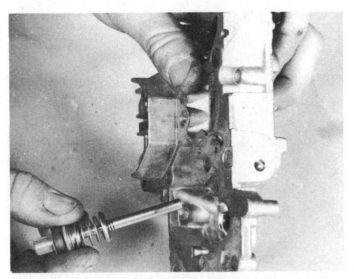

8.3/16   Remove the pump plunger from the air horn or the pump well in the float bowl (**Note:** *For throttle position sensor (TPS) equipped carburetors, refer to the exploded-view drawing at this time and remove the TPS*)

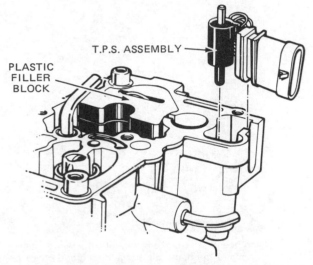

Fig. 4A.7 To remove the TPS, push up from the bottom of the electrical connector and remove the TPS and connector assembly from the float bowl; also remove the spring from the bottom of the float bowl (Sec 8)

T.P.S. ASSEMBLY

PLASTIC FILLER BLOCK

4A

8.3/17   Compress the pump plunger spring and separate the spring retainer clip and spring from the piston

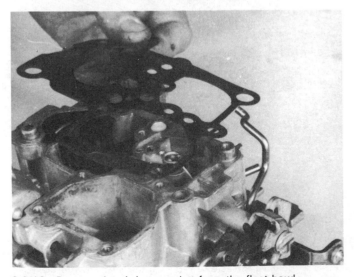

8.3/18   Remove the air horn gasket from the float bowl

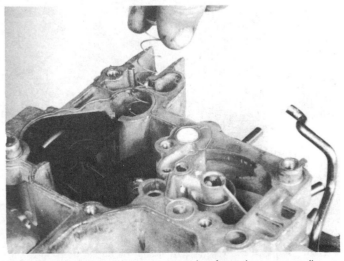

8.3/19   Remove the pump return spring from the pump well

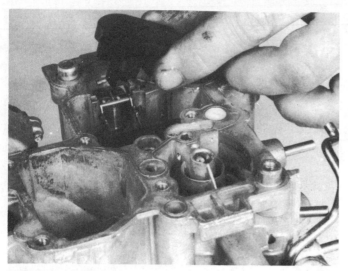

8.3/20   Remove the plastic filler block that covers the float valve

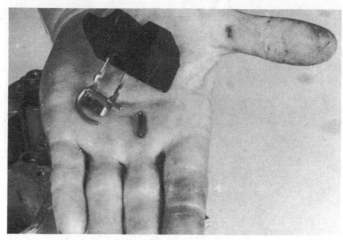

8.3/21   Remove the float and lever assembly, float valve and stabilizing spring (if used) by pulling up on the hinge pin

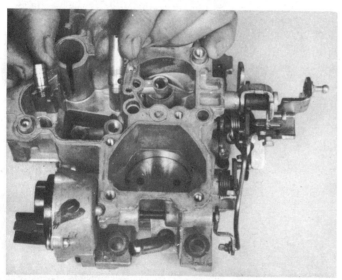

8.3/22   Remove the float valve seat and gasket (left) and extended metering jet (right) from the float bowl

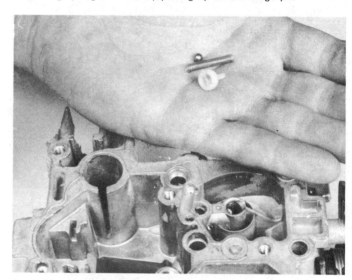

8.3/23   Using needle nosed pliers, pull out the white plastic retainer and remove the pump discharge spring and check ball (do not pry on the retainer to remove it)

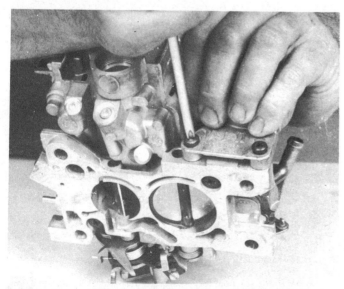

8.3/24   Remove the screws that retain the choke housing to the throttle body

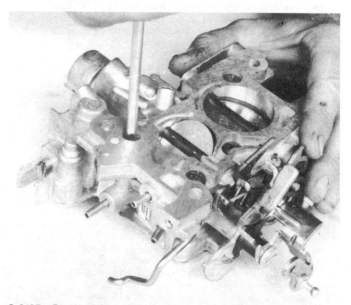

8.3/25   Remove the screws retaining the float bowl to the throttle body

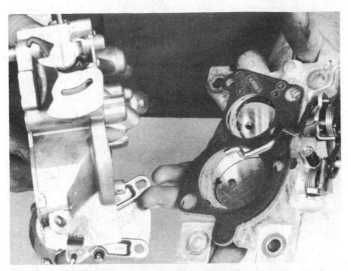

8.3/26   Separate the float bowl from the throttle body

8.3/27 Carefully file the heads off the pop rivets retaining the choke cover to the choke housing, remove the cover and tap out the remainder of the rivets

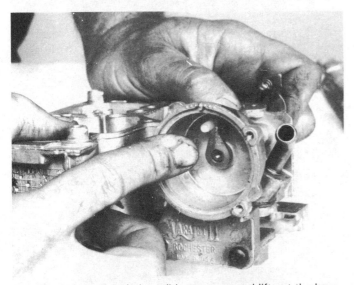

8.3/28   Remove the choke coil lever screw and lift out the lever

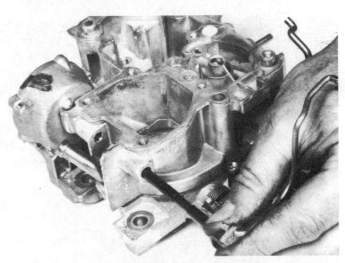

8.3/29   Remove the intermediate shaft and lever assembly by sliding it out of the lever side of the float bowl (**Note:** *For further procedures, refer to Step 4 in the text*)

4A

of the locator mark. The cuts should be deep enough to touch the steel plug, but should not extend more than 1/8-inch beyond the locator point.

7   Position a flat punch at a point near the ends of the saw marks. Holding it at a 45° angle, drive it into the throttle body until the casting breaks away, exposing the steel plug.

8   Use a center punch to make an indentation in the steel plug. Holding it at a 45° angle, drive the plug from the throttle body casting. **Note:** *If the plug breaks apart, be sure to remove all of the pieces.*

9   Use a 3/16-inch deep socket to remove the idle mixture needle and spring from the throttle body.

Cleaning and inspection

10   Clean the air horn, float bowl, throttle body and related components with clean solvent and blow them out with compressed air. A can of compressed air can be used if an air compressor is not available. Do not use a piece of wire for cleaning the jets and passages.

11   The idle speed solenoid, mixture control solenoid, Throttle Position Sensor, electric choke, pump plunger, diaphragm, plastic filler block and other electrical, rubber and plastic parts should not be immersed in carburetor cleaner because they will harden, swell or distort.

12   Make sure all fuel passages, jets and other metering components are free of burrs and dirt.

13   Inspect the upper and lower surfaces of the air horn, float bowl and throttle body for damage. Be sure all material has been removed.

14   Inspect all lever holes and plastic bushings for excessive wear and an out-of-round condition and replace them if necessary.

15   Inspect the float valve and seat for dirt, deep wear grooves or scoring and replace it if necessary.

16   Inspect the float valve pull clip for proper installation and adjust it if necessary.

17   Inspect the float, float arms and hinge pin for distortion or binding and correct or replace as necessary.

18   Inspect the rubber cup on the pump plunger for excessive wear or cracks.

19   Check the choke valve and linkage for excessive wear, binding or distortion and correct or replace as necessary.

20   Inspect the choke vacuum diaphragm for leaks and replace if necessary.

21   Check the choke valve for freedom of movement.

22   Check the mixture control solenoid in the following manner:

   a)   Connect one end of a jumper wire to either end of the solenoid connector and the other end to the positive terminal of the battery.

   b)   Connect another jumper wire between the other terminal of the solenoid connector and the negative terminal of the battery.

   c)   Remove the rubber seal and retainer from the end of the solenoid stem and attach a hand vacuum pump to the stem (photo).

   d)   With the solenoid fully energized (lean position), apply at least 25 in-Hg of vacuum and time the leak-down rate from 20 to 15 in-Hg. The leak-down rate should not exceed 5 in-Hg in five seconds. If leakage exceeds that amount, replace the solenoid.

e) To check if the solenoid is sticking in the down position, again apply about 25 in-Hg of vacuum to it, then disconnect the jumper lead to the battery and watch the pump gauge reading. It should fall to zero in less than one second.

Reassembly

23 Before reassembling the carburetor, compare all old and new gaskets back-to-back to make sure they match perfectly. Check especially that all the necessary holes are present and in the proper positions in the new gaskets.

24 If the idle mixture needle and spring have been removed, reinstall them by lightly seating the needle, then back it off three turns. This will provide a preliminary idle mixture adjustment. Final idle mixture adjustment must be made on the vehicle. Proper adjustment must be done using special emission sensing equipment, making it impractical for the home mechanic. To have the mixture settings checked or readjusted, take your vehicle to a GM dealer or other qualified mechanic with the proper equipment.

25 Install a new gasket on the bottom of the float bowl (photo).

26 Mount the throttle body on the float bowl so it is properly installed over the locating dowels on the bowl (photo), reinstall the screws and

tighten them evenly and securely (photo). Be sure that the steps on the fast idle cam face toward the fast idle screw on the throttle lever when installed.

27 Inspect the linkage to make sure that the lockout tang properly engages in the slot of the secondary lockout lever and that the linkage moves freely without binding (photo).

28 Attach the choke housing to the throttle body, making sure the locating lug on the rear of the housing sits in the recess in the float bowl (photos).

29 Install the intermediate choke shaft and lever assembly in the float bowl by pushing it through from the throttle lever side.

30 Position the intermediate choke lever in the Up position and install the thermostatic coil lever on the end sticking into the choke housing. The coil lever is properly aligned when the coil pick-up tang is in the 12 o'clock position (photo). Install the screw in the end of the intermediate shaft to secure the coil lever.

31 Three self-tapping screws supplied in the overhaul kit are used in place of the original pop rivets to secure the choke cover and coil assembly to the choke housing. Thread the screws into the housing, making sure they start easily and are properly aligned (photo), then remove them.

32 Place the fast idle screw on the highest step of the fast idle cam, then install the choke cover on the housing, aligning the notch in the cover with the raised casting projection on the housing cover flange

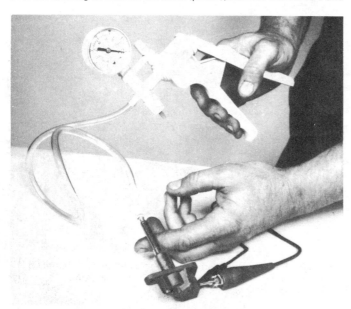

8.22 Attaching a hand vacuum pump to the end of the mixture control solenoid

8.25 Installing the gasket on the bottom of the float bowl

8.26A Mounting the throttle body on the float bowl

8.26B Installing the throttle body-to-float attaching screws

8.27   Checking the engagement of the lockout tang in the secondary lockout lever

8.28A   Attaching the choke housing to the throttle body

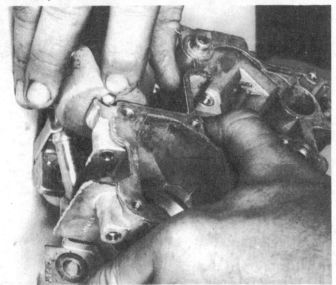

8.28B   The lug at the rear of the choke housing should sit in the bowl recess

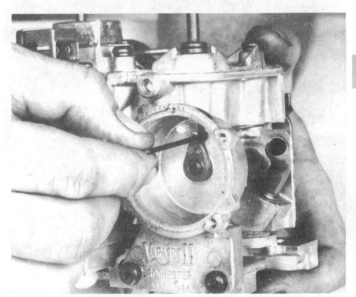

8.30   Install the thermostatic coil lever so it is in the 12 o'clock position when the intermediate choke lever is facing up

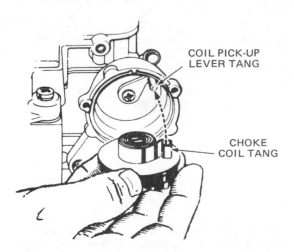

COIL PICK-UP
LEVER TANG

CHOKE
COIL TANG

Fig. 4A.8   Details of the choke housing assembly (Sec 8)

8.31   The choke cover is reinstalled with the self-tapping screws supplied in the overhaul kit

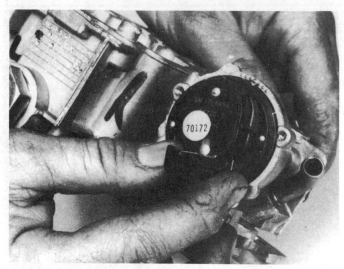

8.32   Be sure the notch in the choke cover is aligned with the raised casting projection on the housing cover flange

8.35   Installing the main metering jet

8.36   Installing the float valve seat assembly

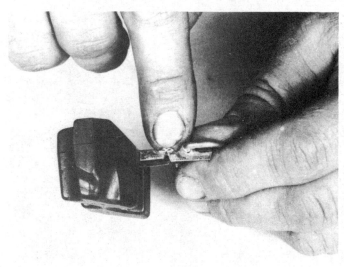

8.37   Prior to installation, bend the float arm up slightly at the point shown

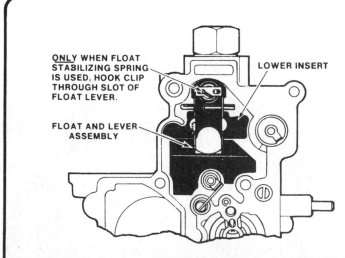

ONLY WHEN FLOAT STABILIZING SPRING IS USED, HOOK CLIP THROUGH SLOT OF FLOAT LEVER.

LOWER INSERT

FLOAT AND LEVER ASSEMBLY

Fig. 4A.9   Correct installation of the pull clip on stabilizing spring-equipped carburetor floats (Sec 8)

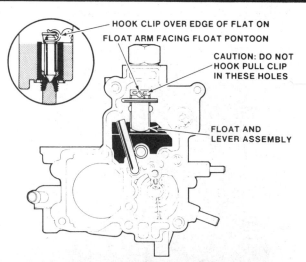

HOOK CLIP OVER EDGE OF FLAT ON FLOAT ARM FACING FLOAT PONTOON

CAUTION: DO NOT HOOK PULL CLIP IN THESE HOLES

FLOAT AND LEVER ASSEMBLY

Fig. 4A.10   Correct installation of the pull clip on carburetor floats not equipped with a stabilizer spring Sec 8)

(photo). When installing the cover, be sure the coil pick-up tang engages the inside choke lever. **Note:** *The thermostatic coil tang is formed so that it will completely encircle the coil pick-up lever. Make sure the lever is inside of the tang when installing the cover (refer to the accompanying illustration).*

33   With the choke cover in place, install the self-tapping screws and tighten them securely.

34   Install the pump discharge check ball and spring in the passage next to the float chamber, then place a new plastic retainer in the hole so that the end engages the spring. Tap it lightly into place until the retainer top is flush with the bowl surface.

35   Install the main metering jet in the bottom of the float chamber (photo).

36   Install the float valve seat assembly and gasket (photo).

37   To make float level adjustments easier, bend the float arm up slightly at the notch before installing the float (photo).

38   Install the float valve onto the float arm by sliding the lever under the pull clip. The correct installation of the pull clip is shown in the accompanying illustrations. Install the float pin in the float lever (photo). Install the float assembly by aligning the valve and seat and the float retaining pin and locating channels in the float bowl.

39   To adjust the float level, hold the float pin firmly in place, push down on the float arm at the outer end, against the top of the float valve, and see if the top of the float is the specified distance from the float bowl surface (photo). Bend the float arm as necessary to achieve the proper measurement by pushing down on the pontoon. See the Specifications for the proper float measurement for your vehicle. Check the float level visually following adjustment.

40   Install the plastic filler block over the float valve so that it is flush with the float bowl surface (photo).

41   If the carburetor is equipped with a Throttle Position Sensor, install

the TPS return spring in the bottom of the well in the float bowl. Install the TPS and connector assembly by aligning the groove in the electrical connector with the slot in the float bowl. When properly installed, the assembly should sit below the float bowl surface.

42   Install a new air horn gasket on the float bowl (photo).

43   Install the pump return spring in the pump well (photo).

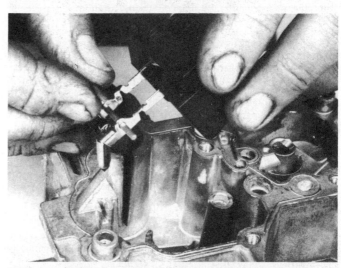

8.38   Installing the float retaining pin in the float lever

8.40   Installing the plastic float block

8.39   Measuring the float level

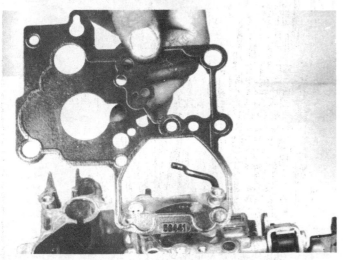

8.42   Installing a new air horn gasket on the float bowl

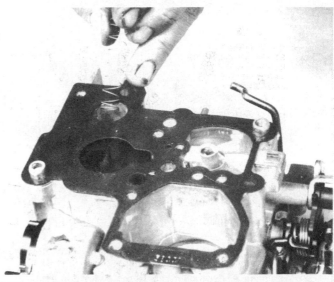

8.43   Installing the pump return spring in the pump well

4A

44 Reassemble the pump plunger assembly, lubricate the plunger cap with a thin coat of engine oil and install the pump plunger in the pump well (photo).

45 If used, remove the old pump plunger seal and retainer and the old TPS plunger seal and retainer from the air horn. Install new seals and retainers in both locations and lightly stake both seal retainers in three places other than the original staking locations.

46 Install the fast idle cam rod in the lower hole of the choke lever.

47 If so equipped, apply a light coat of silicone grease or engine oil to the TPS plunger and push it through the seal in the air horn so that about one-half of the plunger extends above the seal.

48 Before installing the air horn, apply a light coat of silicone grease or engine oil to the pump plunger stem to aid in slipping it through the seal in the air horn.

49 Rotate the fast idle cam to the Up position so it can be engaged with the lower end of the fast idle cam rod (photo). While holding down on the pump plunger assembly, carefully lower the air horn onto the float bowl and guide the pump plunger stem through the seal.

50 Install the air horn retaining screws and washers, making sure the different length screws are inserted into their respective holes, then tighten them in the sequence illustrated.

51 Install a new seal in the recess of the float bowl and attach the hot idle compensator valve, if so equipped.

52 Slide a new rubber seal onto the end of the mixture control solenoid stem until it is up against the boss on the stem (photo).

53 Using a 3/16-inch socket and a hammer (photo), drive the retainer over the mixture control solenoid stem just far enough to retain the

rubber seal, while leaving a slight clearance between them for seal expansion.

54 Apply a light coat of engine oil to the rubber seal and, using a new gasket, install the mixture control solenoid in the air horn. Use a slight twisting motion while installing the solenoid to help the rubber seal slip into the recess.

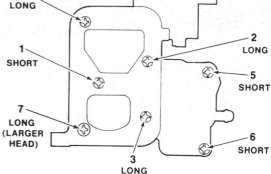

Fig. 4A.11 Recommended carburetor air horn screw tightening sequence (Sec 8)

8.44   Installing the pump plunger in the pump well

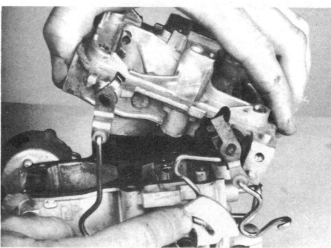

8.49   Engage the fast idle cam link in the fast idle cam prior to installation of the air horn

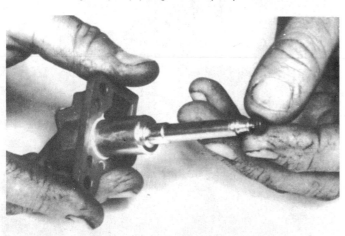

8.52   Attaching a new rubber seal to the end of the mixture control solenoid

8.53   Using a hammer and hollow tool to tap the seal retainer onto the mixture control solenoid stem

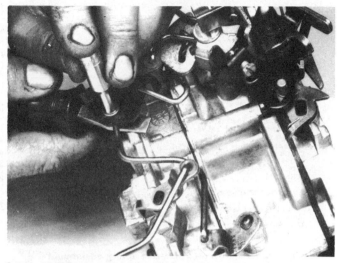

8.56 Attaching a retaining clip to the intermediate choke rod to secure it to the choke lever

55 Install the vent/screen assembly on the air horn.

56 Install a plastic bushing in the hole in the choke lever, with the small end facing out, then, with the intermediate choke lever at the 12 o'clock position, install the intermediate choke rod in the bushing. Install a new retaining clip on the end of the rod. Use a broad flat-blade screwdriver and a 3/16-inch socket, as shown in the photo. Make sure the clip is not seated too tightly against the bushing and that the linkage moves freely.

57 Reattach the primary and secondary vacuum break links and install the vacuum break and idle speed solenoid assemblies (photo).

58 Engage the pump rod with the pump rod lever (photo). Install a new retaining clip on the pump rod and install the pump lever on the air horn with the washer between the lever and the air horn (photo).

59 Reconnect the vacuum break hoses.

60 Install the fuel filter with the hole facing toward the inlet nut.

61 Place a new gasket on the inlet nut and install and tighten it securely. Take care not to overtighten the nut, as it could damage the gasket, leading to a fuel leak.

62 Install a new gasket on the top of the air horn (photo).

63 Check that all linkage hook-ups have been made and that they do not bind.

64 For external linkage adjustment procedures, refer to the accompanying illustrations.

8.57 Installing the idle speed solenoid/vacuum break diaphragm assembly

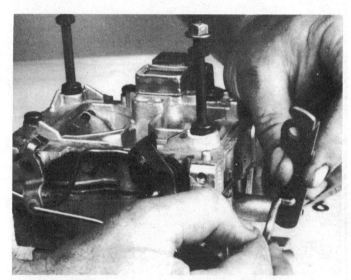

8.58A Engaging the pump with the pump rod lever

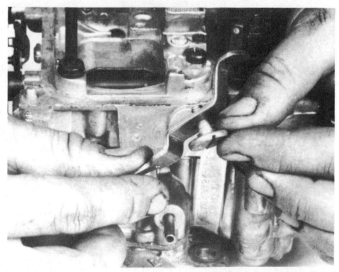

8.58B Inserting the pump rod mounting screw through the pump rod prior to installation

8.62 Installing a new gasket on top of the air horn

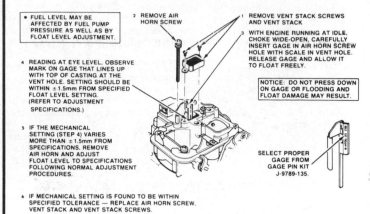

- FUEL LEVEL MAY BE AFFECTED BY FUEL PUMP PRESSURE AS WELL AS BY FLOAT LEVEL ADJUSTMENT.

2 REMOVE AIR HORN SCREW

1 REMOVE VENT STACK SCREWS AND VENT STACK

3 WITH ENGINE RUNNING AT IDLE, CHOKE WIDE-OPEN, CAREFULLY INSERT GAGE IN AIR HORN SCREW HOLE WITH SCALE IN VENT HOLE. RELEASE GAGE AND ALLOW IT TO FLOAT FREELY.

4 READING AT EYE LEVEL, OBSERVE MARK ON GAGE THAT LINES UP WITH TOP OF CASTING AT THE VENT HOLE. SETTING SHOULD BE WITHIN ±1.5mm FROM SPECIFIED FLOAT LEVEL SETTING. (REFER TO ADJUSTMENT SPECIFICATIONS.)

5 IF THE MECHANICAL SETTING (STEP 4) VARIES MORE THAN ±1.5mm FROM SPECIFICATIONS, REMOVE AIR HORN AND ADJUST FLOAT LEVEL TO SPECIFICATIONS FOLLOWING NORMAL ADJUSTMENT PROCEDURES.

6 IF MECHANICAL SETTING IS FOUND TO BE WITHIN SPECIFIED TOLERANCE — REPLACE AIR HORN SCREW. VENT STACK AND VENT STACK SCREWS.

NOTICE: DO NOT PRESS DOWN ON GAGE OR FLOODING AND FLOAT DAMAGE MAY RESULT.

SELECT PROPER GAGE FROM GAGE PIN KIT J-9789-135.

Fig. 4A.12 Carburetor external float check procedure (Sec 8)

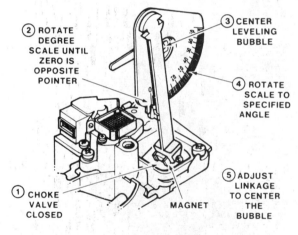

1 IF NECESSARY, REMOVE INTERMEDIATE CHOKE ROD, TO GAIN ACCESS TO LOCK SCREW.

2 LOOSEN LOCK SCREW USING 3/32" (2.381mm) HEX WRENCH.

3 TURN TENSION-ADJUSTING SCREW CLOCKWISE UNTIL AIR VALVE OPENS SLIGHTLY. TURN ADJUSTING SCREW COUNTER-CLOCKWISE UNTIL AIR VALVE JUST CLOSES. CONTINUE COUNTER-CLOCKWISE SPECIFIED NUMBER OF TURNS.

4 TIGHTEN LOCK SCREW.

5 APPLY LITHIUM BASE GREASE TO LUBRICATE PIN AND SPRING CONTACT AREA.

Fig. 4A.13 Carburetor air valve spring adjustment procedure (Sec 8)

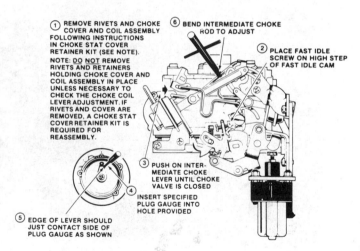

1 REMOVE RIVETS AND CHOKE COVER AND COIL ASSEMBLY FOLLOWING INSTRUCTIONS IN CHOKE STAT COVER RETAINER KIT (SEE NOTE). NOTE: DO NOT REMOVE RIVETS AND RETAINERS HOLDING CHOKE COVER AND COIL ASSEMBLY IN PLACE UNLESS NECESSARY TO CHECK THE CHOKE COIL LEVER ADJUSTMENT. IF RIVETS AND COVER ARE REMOVED, A CHOKE STAT COVER RETAINER KIT IS REQUIRED FOR REASSEMBLY.

6 BEND INTERMEDIATE CHOKE ROD TO ADJUST

2 PLACE FAST IDLE SCREW ON HIGH STEP OF FAST IDLE CAM

3 PUSH ON INTERMEDIATE CHOKE LEVER UNTIL CHOKE VALVE IS CLOSED

4 INSERT SPECIFIED PLUG GAUGE INTO HOLE PROVIDED

5 EDGE OF LEVER SHOULD JUST CONTACT SIDE OF PLUG GAUGE AS SHOWN

Fig. 4A.14 Carburetor choke coil lever adjustment (typical) (Sec 8)

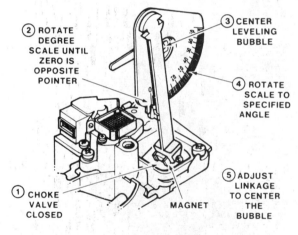

2 ROTATE DEGREE SCALE UNTIL ZERO IS OPPOSITE POINTER

3 CENTER LEVELING BUBBLE

4 ROTATE SCALE TO SPECIFIED ANGLE

5 ADJUST LINKAGE TO CENTER THE BUBBLE

1 CHOKE VALVE CLOSED

MAGNET

Fig. 4A.15 Measuring the choke valve angle using an angle gauge (Sec 8)

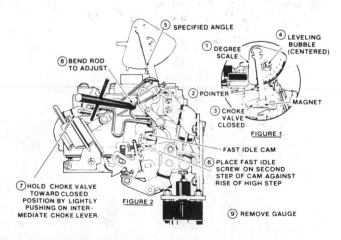

5 SPECIFIED ANGLE

8 BEND ROD TO ADJUST

1 DEGREE SCALE

4 LEVELING BUBBLE (CENTERED)

2 POINTER

3 CHOKE VALVE CLOSED

MAGNET

FIGURE 1

FAST IDLE CAM

6 PLACE FAST IDLE SCREW ON SECOND STEP OF CAM AGAINST RISE OF HIGH STEP

7 HOLD CHOKE VALVE TOWARD CLOSED POSITION BY LIGHTLY PUSHING ON INTERMEDIATE CHOKE LEVER.

FIGURE 2

9 REMOVE GAUGE

Fig. 4A.16 Choke rod fast idle cam adjustment (Sec 8)

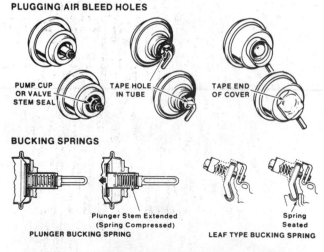

PLUGGING AIR BLEED HOLES

PUMP CUP OR VALVE STEM SEAL

TAPE HOLE IN TUBE

TAPE END OF COVER

BUCKING SPRINGS

Plunger Stem Extended (Spring Compressed)

PLUNGER BUCKING SPRING

Spring Seated

LEAF TYPE BUCKING SPRING

Fig. 4A.17 Carburetor vacuum break adjustment details (Sec 8)

NOTE: PRIOR TO ADJUSTMENT, REMOVE VACUUM BREAK FROM CARBURETOR. PLACE BRACKET IN VICE AND, USING SAFETY PRECAUTIONS, GRIND OFF ADJUSTMENT SCREW CAP. REINSTALL VACUUM BREAK.

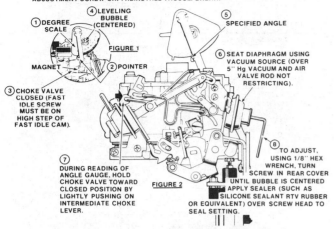

① DEGREE SCALE

④ LEVELING BUBBLE (CENTERED)

FIGURE 1

MAGNET

② POINTER

③ CHOKE VALVE CLOSED (FAST IDLE SCREW MUST BE ON HIGH STEP OF FAST IDLE CAM).

⑤ SPECIFIED ANGLE

⑥ SEAT DIAPHRAGM USING VACUUM SOURCE (OVER 5" Hg VACUUM AND AIR VALVE ROD NOT RESTRICTING).

⑦ DURING READING OF ANGLE GAUGE, HOLD CHOKE VALVE TOWARD CLOSED POSITION BY LIGHTLY PUSHING ON INTERMEDIATE CHOKE LEVER.

FIGURE 2

⑧ TO ADJUST, USING 1/8" HEX WRENCH, TURN SCREW IN REAR COVER UNTIL BUBBLE IS CENTERED APPLY SEALER (SUCH AS SILICONE SEALANT RTV RUBBER OR EQUIVALENT) OVER SCREW HEAD TO SEAL SETTING.

Fig. 4A.18 Primary vacuum break adjustment procedure (models with dual vacuum break units (Sec 8)

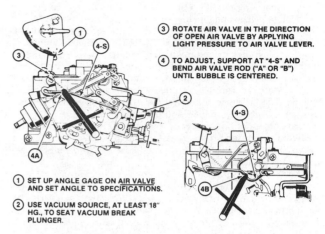

③ ROTATE AIR VALVE IN THE DIRECTION OF OPEN AIR VALVE BY APPLYING LIGHT PRESSURE TO AIR VALVE LEVER.

④ TO ADJUST, SUPPORT AT "4-S" AND BEND AIR VALVE ROD ("A" OR "B") UNTIL BUBBLE IS CENTERED.

① SET UP ANGLE GAGE ON AIR VALVE AND SET ANGLE TO SPECIFICATIONS.

② USE VACUUM SOURCE, AT LEAST 18" HG., TO SEAT VACUUM BREAK PLUNGER.

Fig. 4A.19 Air valve link adjustment (Sec 8)

① HOLD CHOKE VALVE WIDE OPEN BY PUSHING COUNTER-CLOCKWISE ON INTERMEDIATE CHOKE LEVER.

④ IF NECESSARY TO ADJUST, BEND LOCKOUT LEVER TANG CONTACTING FAST IDLE CAM.

③ GAUGE CLEARANCE - DIMENSION SHOULD BE AS SPECIFIED.

② OPEN THROTTLE LEVER UNTIL END OF SECONDARY ACTUATING LEVER IS OPPOSITE TOE OF LOCKOUT LEVER.

Fig. 4A.20 Secondary vacuum break adjustment (Sec 8)

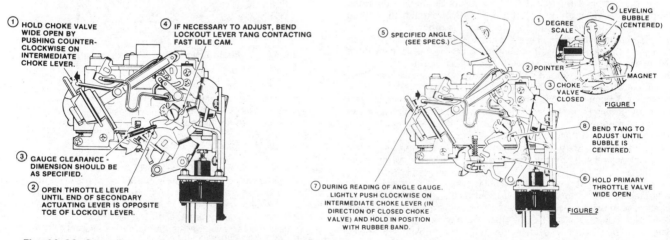

⑤ SPECIFIED ANGLE (SEE SPECS.)

① DEGREE SCALE

④ LEVELING BUBBLE (CENTERED)

② POINTER

③ CHOKE VALVE CLOSED

MAGNET

FIGURE 1

⑧ BEND TANG TO ADJUST UNTIL BUBBLE IS CENTERED.

⑥ HOLD PRIMARY THROTTLE VALVE WIDE OPEN

FIGURE 2

⑦ DURING READING OF ANGLE GAUGE. LIGHTLY PUSH CLOCKWISE ON INTERMEDIATE CHOKE LEVER (IN DIRECTION OF CLOSED CHOKE VALVE) AND HOLD IN POSITION WITH RUBBER BAND.

Fig. 4A.21 Carburetor unloader adjustment procedure (Sec 8)

4A

① PREPARE VEHICLE FOR ADJUSTMENTS - SEE EMISSION LABLE ON VEHICLE. PLACE TRANSMISSION IN PARK/NEUTRAL.

② PLACE FAST IDLE SCREW ON HIGHEST STEP OF FAST IDLE CAM.

③ TURN FAST IDLE SCREW IN OR OUT TO OBTAIN SPECIFIED FAST IDLE R.P.M.

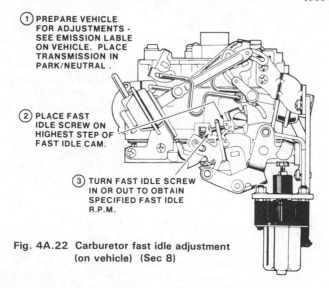

Fig. 4A.22 Carburetor fast idle adjustment (on vehicle) (Sec 8)

9   Electronic Fuel Injection (EFI) system — general information

All later models employ EFI in place of the conventional carburetor-fed intake system. The specific fuel injection units used are the Models 300 and 500 Throttle Body Injection (TBI). Turbocharged models are equipped with port fuel injection. Fuel injection provides optimum mixture ratios at all stages of combustion. Combined with its immediate response characteristics, EFI permits the engine to run on the leanest possible air/fuel mixture, which greatly reduces exhaust gas emissions.

The EFI system is controlled directly by the vehicle's Electronic Control Module (ECM), which automatically adjusts the air/fuel mixture in accordance with engine load and performance.

The main component of the EFI system is the Throttle Body Injector (TBI), which is mounted on the intake manifold just like a carburetor. The TBI is made up of two major assemblies: the throttle body and the fuel metering assembly.

The throttle body contains a single throttle valve, controlled by the accelerator pedal, much like a carburetor. Attached to the exterior of the body are the throttle position sensor (TPS), which sends throttle position information to the ECM, and the idle air control assembly (IAC), which is used by the ECM to maintain a constant idle speed during normal engine operation.

The fuel metering assembly contains the fuel pressure regulator and the single fuel injector. The regulator dampens the pulsations of the fuel pump and maintains a steady pressure at the injector. The fuel injector is controlled by the ECM through an electrically operated solenoid. The amount of fuel injected into the intake manifold is varied by the length of time the injector plunger is held open.

The ECM controlling the EFI system has a learning capability for certain performance conditions. If the battery is disconnected, part of the ECM memory is erased, which makes it necessary to reteach the computer. This is done by thoroughly warming up the engine and operating the vehicle at part throttle, stop and go and idle.

No mechanical fuel pump is employed in this system. Rather, an electric pump, located in the fuel tank, is used. When the ignition is turned on, the fuel pump relay immediately supplies current to the fuel pump. If the engine doesn't start after two seconds, the fuel pump will automatically shut off to avoid flooding. If the fuel pump relay fails, the fuel pump will still operate after about four pounds of oil pressure has built up.

The throttle stop screw, used to regulate the minimum idle speed, is adjusted at the factory and sealed with a plug to discourage unnecessary readjustment. For this reason, this adjustment, if necessary, should be left to a dealer or other qualified mechanic.

The complexity of the EFI system prevents many problems from being accurately diagnosed by the home mechanic. Therefore, if a problem should develop in the system, take the vehicle to a dealer to locate the fault.

Caution: *Prior to any operation in which a fuel line will be disconnected, the high pressure in the system must first be relieved as described in Section 10. Also, disconnect the negative battery cable to eliminate the possibility of sparks occurring when fuel vapors are present.*

10   Fuel injection pressure relief procedure

Caution: *To reduce the risk of fire and personal injury, relieve the pressure in the fuel system before servicing any fuel injection components.*
1   Remove the fuel pump fuse from the fuse block located in the passenger compartment under the left side of the dash.
2   Start the engine and let it run until lack of fuel causes it to stop.
3   Engage the starter again for about three seconds to ensure that all pressure has been relieved.
4   Turn the ignition off and disconnect the negative cable from the battery.
5   After servicing the fuel system, reinstall the fuel pump fuse and reconnect the battery cable.

11   Fuel pump (fuel injected models) — removal and installation

Note: *Before starting this procedure, the fuel system pressure must*

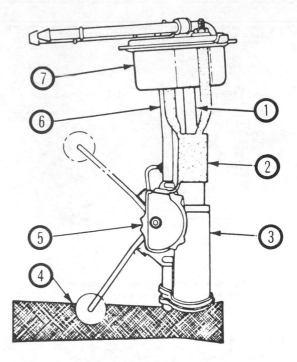

Fig. 4A.23 Fuel meter/pump assembly component layout (Sec 11)

1 Fuel tube	*4 Filter strainer*
2 Rubber coupler and	*5 Fuel level sender*
* sound isolator*	*6 Return tube*
3 Electric fuel pump	*7 Vapor separator*

be relieved as outlined in Section 10.
1   On fuel injected models, the electric fuel pump is an integral part of the fuel gauge tank unit, but it may be replaced separately after the fuel gauge/fuel pump assembly has been removed from the fuel tank.
2   Remove the fuel tank (refer to Section 5).
3   Unbolt and remove the fuel pump/gauge assembly from the fuel tank.
4   Installation is the reverse of the removal procedure.
5   When the installation is complete, carefully check all lines, hoses and fittings for leaks.

12   Idle Air Control (IAC) assembly — removal and installation

1   Relieve the pressure in the fuel system (refer to Section 10).
2   Disconnect the cable from the negative battery terminal.
3   Remove the air cleaner.
4   Disconnect the wire from the IAC assembly.
5   Use a wrench to unscrew the assembly from the throttle body injection unit.
6   Before installing the IAC, measure the distance between the end of the motor assembly housing and the tip of the conical valve. The valve should be extended from the housing no more than 1.125-inch (28.6 mm) or damage may occur to the motor when it is installed. If the distance is excessive, first determine if the assembly is a Type 1 (with a collar at the end of the motor) or Type 2 (without a collar). The pintle on a Type 1 assembly can be retracted simply by pushing on the end of the cone until it's in position. For a Type 2, push the pintle in and attempt to turn it clockwise. If it turns, continue turning until it is properly set. If it will not turn, exert firm hand pressure to retract it. **Note:** *If the pintle was turned, be sure the spring is in its original position with the straight portion of the spring end aligned with the flat surface under the pintle head.*
7   Installation of the IAC assembly is the reverse of removal. Be sure to install the gasket with the assembly.

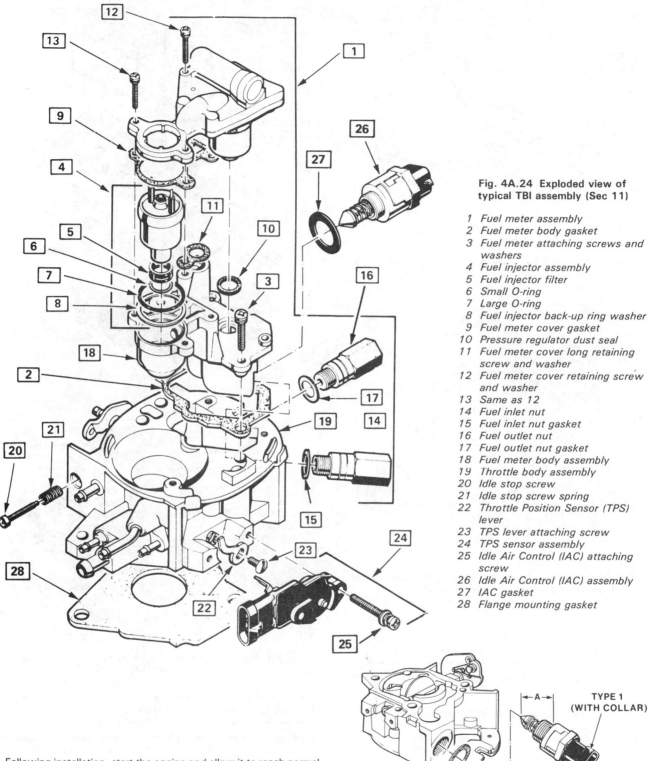

Fig. 4A.24 Exploded view of typical TBI assembly (Sec 11)

1 Fuel meter assembly
2 Fuel meter body gasket
3 Fuel meter attaching screws and washers
4 Fuel injector assembly
5 Fuel injector filter
6 Small O-ring
7 Large O-ring
8 Fuel injector back-up ring washer
9 Fuel meter cover gasket
10 Pressure regulator dust seal
11 Fuel meter cover long retaining screw and washer
12 Fuel meter cover retaining screw and washer
13 Same as 12
14 Fuel inlet nut
15 Fuel inlet nut gasket
16 Fuel outlet nut
17 Fuel outlet nut gasket
18 Fuel meter body assembly
19 Throttle body assembly
20 Idle stop screw
21 Idle stop screw spring
22 Throttle Position Sensor (TPS) lever
23 TPS lever attaching screw
24 TPS sensor assembly
25 Idle Air Control (IAC) attaching screw
26 Idle Air Control (IAC) assembly
27 IAC gasket
28 Flange mounting gasket

4A

8 Following installation, start the engine and allow it to reach normal operating temperature. On manual transmission-equipped vehicles, the idle speed will automatically be controlled when operating temperature is reached. On automatic transmission-equipped vehicles, the assembly will begin controlling idle speed when the engine is at operating temperature and the transmission is shifted into Drive.

9 If the idle speed is abnormally high and does not regulate back to normal after a few moments, operate the vehicle at a speed of 45 mph (72 kph). At that speed the ECM will command the IAC pintle to extend fully to the mating seat in the throttle body and allow the ECM to establish an accurate reference with respect to the pintle position. Proper idle regulation will result.

Fig. 4A.25 Idle Air Control assembly identification (refer to text for dimension A specifications) (Sec 12)

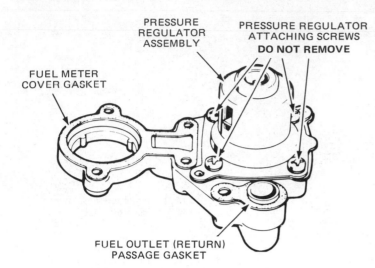

Fig. 4A.26 Bottom view of the fuel meter body, showing the fuel pressure regulator (Sec 13)

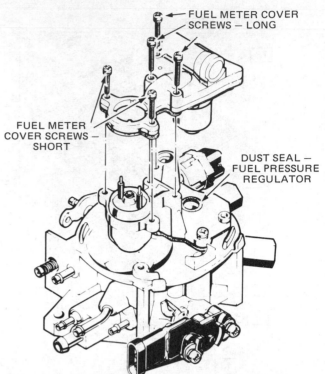

Fig. 4A.27 Fuel meter cover-to-fuel meter body screw locations (Sec 13)

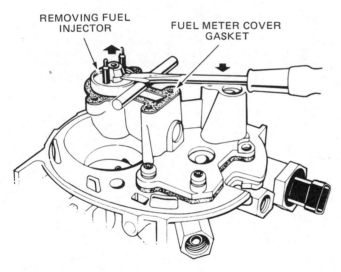

Fig. 4A.28 Correct procedure for removing the fuel injector assembly from the fuel meter body (Sec 14)

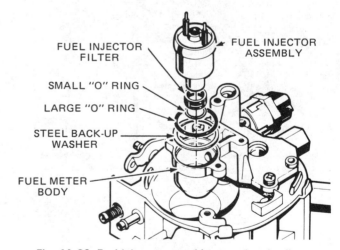

Fig. 4A.29 Fuel injector assembly mounting details (Sec 14)

13 Fuel pressure regulator — removal and installation

1   Relieve the pressure in the fuel system (refer to Section 10).
2   Remove the cable from the negative battery terminal.
3   Remove the air cleaner assembly.
4   Disconnect the wire from the injector by squeezing the two tabs on the connector and pulling straight up.
5   The fuel meter cover assembly, including the fuel pressure regulator, is serviced only as a complete unit; if either the regulator or cover requires replacement, the entire assembly must be replaced.
Caution: *The fuel pressure regulator is enclosed in the fuel meter cover. It is under heavy spring tension and the four screws securing the pressure regulator to the fuel meter cover should not be removed, as personal injury could result.*
6   Remove the five fuel meter cover mounting screws and separate the cover from the body. Note the positions of the two shorter screws, because they must be replaced in the same positions.
7   Do not immerse the fuel meter cover in solvent or cleaner, as it will damage the pressure regulator diaphragm and gaskets.
8   Installation is the reverse of the removal procedure. Be sure to use new gaskets and a new regulator dust seal.

14 Injector — removal and installation

1   Relieve the pressure in the fuel system (refer to Section 10).
2   Remove the cable from the negative battery terminal.
3   Remove the fuel meter cover as described in Section 13.
4   With the fuel meter cover gasket still in place to prevent damage to the casting, place a screwdriver shank atop the gasket to serve as a fulcrum and carefully pry the injector from the fuel meter body with another screwdriver, as shown in the accompanying illustration.
5   Do not push the injector out from underneath, as this could damage the injector tip.
6   Do not immerse the injector in solvent or carburetor cleaner. If it is defective, the injector must be replaced as a unit.
7   Check and clean the fuel filter on the base of the injector. To remove the filter, carefully rotate it back-and-forth to pull it off. The filter is installed by pushing it into the injector until it is seated.

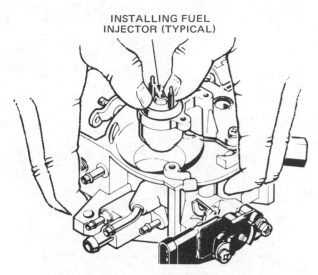

Fig. 4A.30 Correct procedure for attaching the fuel injector assembly to the fuel meter body (Sec 14)

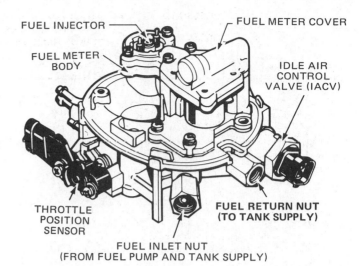

Fig. 4A.31 Throttle Body Injector assembly (Sec 15)

8   Whenever the injector is removed, new O-rings should be installed. Remove the large O-ring and steel backup washer from the injector cavity, then remove the small O-ring from the bottom of the cavity.
9   Lubricate a new small O-ring with lithium grease and push it over the nozzle end of the injector so it is seated against the fuel filter.
10 Install the steel backup ring washer in the injector cavity. Lubricate the large O-ring with lithium grease and install it in the cavity, directly above the washer. When properly installed, the O-ring is flush with the fuel meter body surface. **Note:** *Do not attempt to reverse this procedure by installing the backup washer and O-ring after the injector is located in the cavity, as this will prevent proper seating of the O-ring.*
11 Use a pushing and twisting motion to install the injector into the cavity. Be sure it is fully seated and that the raised lug in the injector base is aligned with the notch in the fuel meter body.
12 The remainder of the installation is the reverse of removal.

---

15   Throttle Body Injection (TBI) assembly — removal and installation

1   Relieve the pressure in the fuel system (refer to Section 10).
2   Remove the cable from the negative battery terminal.
3   Remove the air cleaner.
4   Disconnect the wires leading to the Idle Air Control (IAC), throttle position sensor and injector included in the TBI assembly.
5   Disconnect the throttle linkage and return spring from the TBI.
6   If so equipped, disconnect the cruise control linkage from the TBI.
7   Use tape to label the installed locations of all vacuum hoses leading to the TBI, then disconnect them.
8   Disconnect the fuel lines from the TBI.
9   Remove the three TBI mounting bolts and lift it off, along with the gasket.
10 Prior to installing the TBI, be sure the intake manifold mating surface is clean and that all old gasket material has been scraped off.
11 Using a new gasket, place the TBI into position on the intake manifold. Connect the fuel lines to the assembly. **Note:** *Be sure the fuel line O-rings are not nicked, cut or damaged before connecting the lines.*
12 Install the TBI mounting bolts and tighten them to the specified torque.
13 The remainder of the installation procedure is the reverse of removal.
14 Following installation, start the engine and check for fuel leaks.

---

16   Throttle Body Injection (TBI) assembly — overhaul

Note: *The following procedures cover the complete disassembly,*

cleaning, inspection and reassembly of the TBI assembly after it has been removed from the engine. Refer to the illustrations throughout this Chapter for location and identification of parts. In many cases, service and repair of individual TBI systems may be completed without removing the TBI unit from the engine. If such service is indicated, refer to the appropriate Section in this Chapter.
1   The TBI assembly must be supported on a fixture to prevent damage to the throttle valve.

Disassembly
2   Refer to the appropriate Steps in Section 13 and remove the fuel meter cover.
3   Refer to the appropriate Steps in Section 14 and remove the fuel injector assembly.
4   If not previously done, remove the air cleaner stud.
5   Remove the fuel inlet and outlet nuts and gaskets from the fuel meter body.
6   Remove the three screws and washers retaining the fuel meter body to the throttle body assembly and separate them.
7   Remove the fuel meter body insulator gasket.
8   Invert the throttle body and place it on a clean, level surface.
9   Remove the two Throttle Position Sensor (TPS) retaining screws and separate the TPS from the throttle body.
10 Remove the Idle Air Control (IAC) valve and gasket from the throttle body and discard the gasket.
11 Further disassembly of the throttle body is not required for cleaning and inspection purposes. The throttle valve retaining screws are welded in place and should not be removed. If defective, the throttle body must be replaced as a unit.

Cleaning and inspection
12 Clean all metal parts in a cold immersion-type cleaner and blow them dry. **Note:** *The TPS, IAC assembly, fuel meter cover (with the fuel pressure regulator), fuel injector, fuel injector filter and all diaphragms and other rubber parts should not be immersed in cleaner, as it will cause swelling, hardening and distortion. Clean these parts by hand with clean shop rags. Make sure all air and fuel passages are clear; however, any thread locking compound on the IAC mounting threads should be allowed to remain.*

Reassembly
13 Refer to the appropriate Steps in Section 12, check the pintle position in the IAC and install the IAC in the throttle body.
14 Place the throttle body assembly on the holding fixture to avoid damage to the throttle valve.
15 Install a new fuel meter body insulator gasket on the throttle body. Make sure the cutout portions of the gasket match the openings in the throttle body.

4A

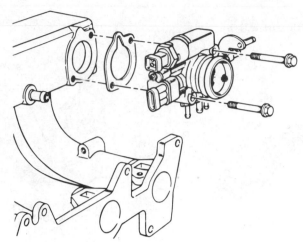

Fig. 4A.32 Port fuel injection throttle body (Sec 17)

16 Attach the fuel meter body to the throttle body.

17   Apply thread locking compound, supplied in the service kit, to the threads on the three fuel meter body mounting screws. If locking compound is not provided, Threadlock Adhesive 262 or its equivalent may be substituted. Do not use a compound of higher strength than recommended, as it may promote screwhead breakage or prevent removal of the screws when service is again required.

18 Install the fuel meter body mounting screws and lock washers and tighten the screws to the specified torque.

19 Install the fuel feed and return nuts (with new gaskets) in the fuel meter body and tighten them to the specified torque.

20 Refer to the appropriate Steps in Section 14 and reassemble and install the injector in the injector cavity in the fuel meter body.

21 Refer to the appropriate Steps in Section 13 and install the fuel meter cover.

22 With the throttle valve in the closed idle position, install the TPS on the throttle body assembly, making sure the TPS pick-up lever is located above the tang on the throttle actuator lever.

23 Install two new screws, retainers and lock washers to secure the TPS to the throttle body. Use thread locking compound on the screw threads.

17   Port fuel injection system — general information

Turbocharged models use port fuel injection in place of the Throttle Body Injection (TBI).

The port fuel injection system consists of an air intake manifold, throttle body, injectors, fuel rail, electric fuel pump and attendant plumbing. Air is drawn through the air cleaner and throttle body and then into the manifold. The throttle body contains an integral Idle Air Control unit (IAC) to control engine idle speed and Throttle Position Sensor (TPS), both of which are controlled by the Electronic Control Module. The air passes into the cylinders, where fuel from the fuel rail is injected above the intake valves. The fuel constantly circulates through the fuel rail while the engine is running, which removes vapors and keeps it cool while maintaining a constant pressure at the injectors of 36 psi.

The operation of the fuel injection system is controlled by the ECM so that it works in conjunction with the rest of the vehicle functions to provide improved driveability and emissions control. Because it meters the fuel precisely, engines equipped with port fuel injection do not require several of the commonly used emissions systems, including THERMAC, EFE, barosensor, AIR and dual-bed catalytic converter.

Due to the complexity of the electronic controls and the special tools required to check and service this system, diagnosis and repair must be left to a GM dealer service department or a reputable repair shop.

18   Exhaust system components -- removal and installation

Caution: *The vehicle's exhaust system generates very high*

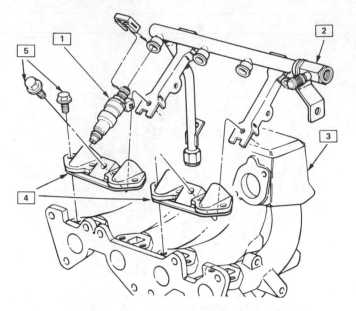

Fig. 4A.33 Port fuel injection fuel rail components (Sec 17)

1 Injector assembly   *4 Injector housing*
2 Fuel rail   *5 Retaining bolt*
3 Intake manifold

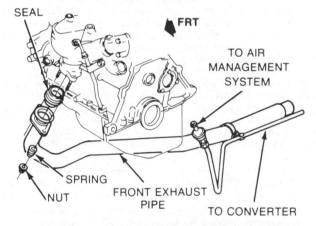

Fig. 4A.34 Exhaust pipe-to-manifold connection (Sec 18)

temperatures and should be allowed to cool down completely before any of the components are touched. Be especially careful around the catalytic converter, where the highest temperatures are generated.

Due to the high temperatures and exposed locations of the exhaust system components, rust and corrosion can 'freeze' parts together. Liquid penetrating oils are available to help loosen frozen fasteners. However, in some cases it may be necessary to cut the pieces apart with a hacksaw or cutting torch. The latter method should be employed only by persons experienced in this work.

1   Raise the vehicle and support it securely on jackstands.

Front exhaust pipe

2   Remove the bolts securing the exhaust pipe to the exhaust manifold.

3   Remove the clamp securing the exhaust pipe to the catalytic converter.

4   Separate the exhaust pipe from the exhaust manifold and the catalytic converter.

5   Installation is the reverse of the removal procedure. Be sure to install new gaskets, nuts and bolts.

Catalytic converter

Caution: *Make sure the catalytic converter has been allowed sufficient time to cool before attempting removal.*

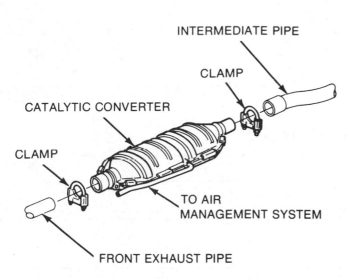

Fig. 4A.35 Catalytic converter installation details (Sec 18)

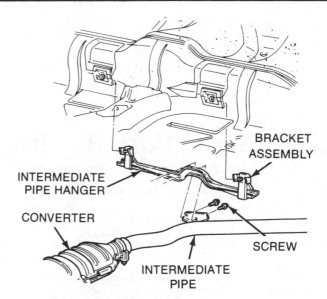

Fig. 4A.36 Intermediate pipe installation (Sec 18)

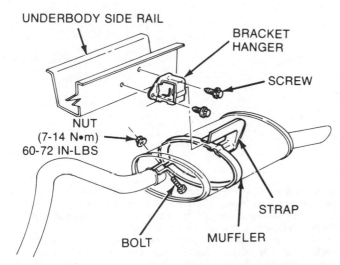

Fig. 4A.37 Muffler installation (Sec 18)

6   Remove the converter-to-front exhaust pipe clamp.
7   Remove the air management pipe-to-converter clamp.
8   Remove the bolts securing the rear of the converter to the converter/intermediate pipe and remove the converter.
9   Installation is the reverse of the removal procedure. Be sure to use new gaskets, nuts and bolts.

Intermediate exhaust pipe
10 Remove the clamp securing the intermediate pipe to the muffler/tailpipe assembly.
11 Remove the bolts securing the intermediate pipe to the intermediate pipe/converter bracket and remove the intermediate pipe.
12 Installation is the reverse of the removal procedure. Be sure to use new gaskets, nuts and bolts.

Muffler and tailpipe
13 The tailpipe is actually part of the muffler assembly.
14 Remove the bolts and nuts which connect the muffler to the intermediate exhaust pipe.
15 Remove the muffler/tailpipe assembly rear hanger bolts and separate the muffler/tailpipe assembly from the vehicle.
16 Installation is the reverse of the removal procedure. Be sure to use new nuts and bolts.

4A

Chapter 4 Part B   Turbocharger

Contents

Specifications

Torque specifications	Ft-lbs
Exhaust manifold	16
Exhaust pipe-to-elbow	18
Intake manifold	18
Oil feed pipe-to-turbo	12
Oil feed pipe union	12
Oil feed pipe-to-block	12
Oil drain hose	35
Turbocharger throttle body	18
Turbocharger-to-exhaust manifold	18
Turbocharger outlet elbow-to-turbocharger	18
Turbocharger support bracket	
Lower bolt	37
Retaining nut	18

1   General information

The turbocharger system increases power by using an exhaust gas-driven turbine to pressurize the fuel/air mixture as it enters the combustion chamber. The amount of boost (intake manifold pressure) is controlled by the wastegate (exhaust bypass valve). This is operated by a spring-loaded actuator assembly which controls the maximum boost level by allowing some of the exhaust gas to bypass the turbine. The wastegate solenoid is controlled by the Electronic Control Module (ECM).

2   Turbocharger — checking

1   While a comparatively simple design, the turbocharger is a precision device which can be severely damaged by an interrupted oil supply or loose or damaged ducting.
2   Due to the special techniques and equipment required, any checking or diagnosis of suspected problems should be left to your dealer. The home mechanic can, however, check the connections and linkages for security, damage or obvious faults.
3   Because each turbocharger has its own distinctive sound, a change in the noise level can be a sign of potential problems.
4   A high-pitched or whistling sound is a symptom of an inlet air or exhaust gas leak. Another sign of a loose duct or an exhaust leak is low engine power or black exhaust smoke. Check the air ducting between the air cleaner and the turbocharger and the cross-over duct between the turbocharger and the intake system for loose connections.
5   If an unusual sound issues from the vicinity of the turbine, the ducting can be removed and the turbine wheel inspected. **Caution:** *All checks must be made with the engine off and cool to the touch and the turbocharger stopped or personal injury could result. Operating the*

turbocharger without all the ducts and filters installed is also dangerous and can result in damage to the turbine wheel blades.
6   Check the operation of the turbine wheel to make sure it turns freely. If it does not, this could be a sign that the cooling oil has sludged or coked from overheating. Push inward on the shaft wheels and check for binding. The wheels should rotate freely with no binding or rubbing on the housing.
7   Inspect the exhaust manifold for cracks and loose connections.
8   Because the turbine wheel rotates at speeds up to 140,000 rpm, severe damage can result from the interruption or contamination of the oil supply to the turbine bearings. Check for leaks in the oil inlet line or obstructions in the oil drain line, as this can cause severe oil loss through the turbocharger seals. Burned oil on the turbine housing is a sign of this. **Note:** *Any time a major engine bearing such as a main, connecting rod or camshaft bearing is replaced, the turbocharger should be flushed with clean oil.*

3   Turbocharger assembly — removal and installation

Note: *The engine oil and filter should be changed as part of the procedure whenever the turbocharger is replaced.*

Removal
1   Disconnect the battery negative cable, raise the vehicle and support it securely on jackstands.
2   Remove the lower cooling fan retaining screw and disconnect the exhaust pipe from the manifold.
3   Remove the rear bolt on the air conditioner support bracket (if equipped) and loosen the remaining bolts.
4   Remove the rear turbocharger-to-engine support bracket bolt.
5   Disconnect the oil drain hose at the turbocharger.
6   Lower the vehicle.

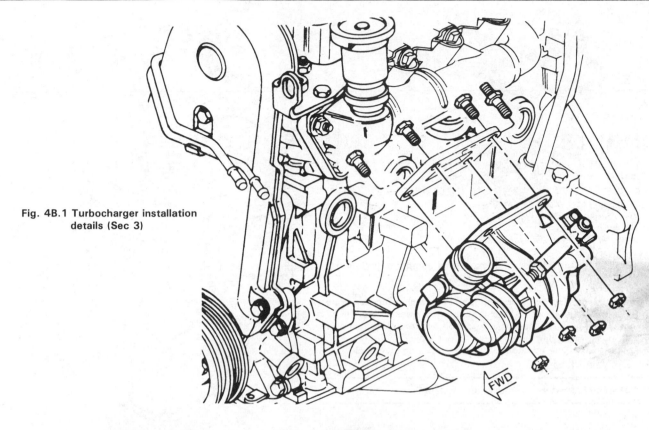

Fig. 4B.1 Turbocharger installation details (Sec 3)

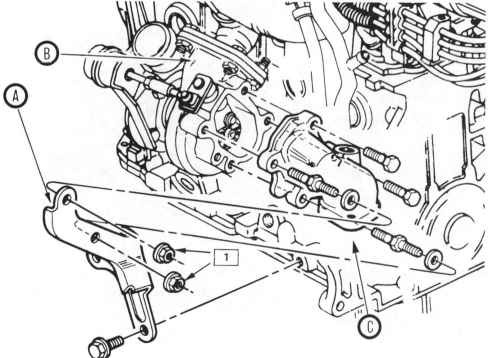

Fig. 4B.2 Turbocharger outlet and support bracket assembly details (Sec 3)

A Support
B Turbocharger assembly
C Outlet elbow

4B

7   Disconnect the coolant recovery pipe and move it out of the way.
8   Remove the induction tube, cooling fan (Chapter 3) and oxygen sensor.
9   Disconnect the oil feed pipe at the union.
10 Disconnect the air intake duct and vacuum hose at the wastegate actuator.
11 Unbolt and remove the turbocharger and exhaust manifold as an assembly.

12 Remove the oil feed pipe, exhaust elbow, support bracket, actuator assembly and turbocharger from the exhaust manifold.

Installation

13 Clean the contact surfaces and install the exhaust manifold and turbocharger assembly (Section 5).
14 Install the oil feed lines, oxygen sensor, air intake duct and actuator vacuum hose.

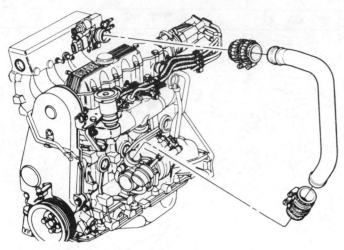

Fig. 4B.3 Turbocharger induction tube components (Sec 3)

15 Install the cooling fan, induction tube and coolant recovery pipe.
16 Raise the vehicle and support it securely on jackstands.
17 Install the rear turbocharger support bolt, air conditioner support, oil drain hose, lower fan screw and exhaust pipe.
18 Lower the vehicle and connect the battery negative cable.

---

4   Wastegate actuator — removal and installation

Removal
1 Disconnect the battery negative cable.
2 Remove the induction tube.
3 Remove the actuator rod-to-wastegate clip and disconnect the vacuum hose.
4 Remove the retaining screws and lift the actuator assembly from the turbocharger.

Installation
5 Place the actuator assembly in position and install the retaining screws.
6 Connect the vacuum hose and install the rod clip and induction tube.
7 Connect the battery negative cable.

---

5   Exhaust manifold — removal and installation

Removal
1 Disconnect the battery negative cable.
2 Disconnect the turbocharger induction tube.
3 Remove the spark plug wires.
4 Unbolt and remove the turbocharger assembly.
5 Remove the retaining nuts and lift the exhaust manifold from the engine.

Installation
6 Carefully clean the mating surfaces of the manifold and cylinder head, removing all traces of gasket material.
7 Place the exhaust manifold and a new gasket in position and install the retaining nuts, tightening them in the sequence shown in the accompanying illustration.
8 Install the turbocharger.
9 Install the spark plug wires and the turbocharger induction tube.
10 Connect the battery negative cable.

---

6   Intake manifold — removal and installation

Removal
1 Disconnect the battery negative cable.

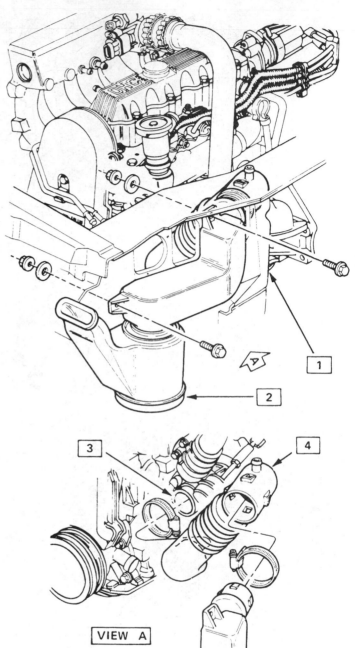

Fig. 4B.4 Air cleaner and intake duct assembly (Sec 3)

1 Engine compartment front panel   *3 Turbocharger*
2 Air cleaner assembly   *4 Air inlet duct*

2 Remove the induction tube and hoses.
3 Disconnect the wiring and vacuum hose from the throttle body.
4 Disconnect the wiring from the MAP sensor (see Chapter 6) and the wastegate.
5 Disconnect PCV hose.
6 Disconnect the throttle cable and (if equipped) cruise control cable.
7 Disconnect the ignition coil and fuel injection wiring.
8 Remove the rear alternator bracket-to-alternator bolt.
9 Remove the power steering adjusting bracket and alternator front adjusting bracket.
10 Disconnect the fuel lines at the fuel rail inlet and the regulator outlet.
11 Remove the retaining nuts and washers and lift the manifold and gasket from the engine.

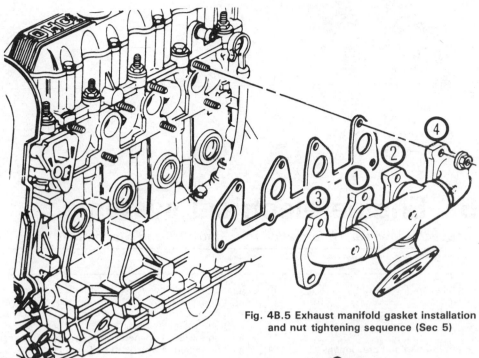

Fig. 4B.5 Exhaust manifold gasket installation
and nut tightening sequence (Sec 5)

Installation

12 Clean the mating surfaces of the manifold and cylinder head, removing all traces of gasket material.

13 Install the manifold and gasket, tightening the nuts to the specified torque.

14 Connect the fuel lines.

15 Install the power steering and alternator adjusting brackets. The rear power steering adjusting bracket must be installed last and the bolt torque sequence described in Chapter 11 must be followed.

16 Connect the wiring to the fuel injectors, ignition coil, MAP sensor, throttle body and wastegate.

17 Connect the throttle and cruise control cables.

18 Connect the vacuum and PCV hoses.

19 Install the induction tube and hoses.

20 Connect the negative battery cable.

4B

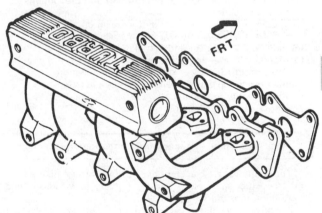

Fig. 4B.6 Intake manifold and gasket installation (Sec 6)

Chapter 5 Engine electrical systems

Refer to Chapter 13 for specifications and information related to 1985 and later models

Contents

1 Ignition system — general information and precautions

The ignition system is composed of the battery, distributor, coil, ignition switch, spark plugs and the primary (low tension) and secondary (high tension) wiring circuits.

A high energy ignition (HEI) distributor is used on all vehicles. Some vehicles use a coil mounted integrally with the distributor, while others use a separately mounted coil.

The HEI works in conjunction with the Electronic Spark Timing (EST) system and uses a magnetic pickup assembly located inside the distributor, which contains a permanent magnet, a pole piece with internal teeth and a pickup coil, in place of the traditional ignition point assembly.

All ignition timing changes in the HEI-ESC distributor are accomplished by an Electronic Control Module (ECM), which monitors data from various engine sensors, computes the desired spark timing and signals the distributor to change the timing accordingly. The Electronic Spark Control (ESC) used on some engines retards the spark advance when detonation occurs. This retard mode is held for approximately 20 seconds, after which the spark control will revert to the ESC.

There are three basic components involved in the ESC system. The sensor, the controller and the distributor. The ESC sensor detects the presence (or absence) and intensity of detonation through vibrations in the engine and sends the data to the controller. The ESC controller changes the sensor signal into a command signal to the distributor, which then adjusts the spark timing accordingly.

The distributor is modified to respond to the controller signal. This command is delayed when detonation occurs, thus providing the level of retard required. The degree of retard is based on the detonation.

The secondary (spark plug) wire used with the HEI system is a carbon-impregnated cord conductor encased in an 8 mm (5/16-inch) diameter rubber jacket with an outer silicone jacket. This type of wire will withstand very high temperatures and still provide insulation for the HEI's high voltage. For more information refer to Chapter 1.

Note: *Because of the very high voltage generated by the HEI system,*

extreme care should be taken whenever an operation involving ignition components is performed. This not only includes the distributor, coil, control module and spark plug wires, but related items that are connected to the system as well (such as the plug connections, tachometer, and testing equipment). Consequently, before any work is performed, the ignition should be turned off and the negative battery cable disconnected.

2 Battery — removal and installation

1   The battery is located at the front of the engine compartment. It is held in place by a hold-down clamp near the bottom of the battery case.
2   Hydrogen gas is produced by the battery, so keep open flames and lighted cigarettes away from it at all times.
3   Always keep the battery in an upright position. Spilled electrolyte should be rinsed off immediately with large quantities of water. Always wear eye protection when working around a battery.
4   Always disconnect the negative (-) battery cable first, followed by the positive (+) cable.
5   After the cables are disconnected from the battery, remove the hold-down clamp.
6   Carefully lift the battery out of the engine compartment.
7   Installation is the reverse of removal. The cable bolts should be tight, but do not overtighten them as damage to the battery case could occur. The battery conntections and cable ends should be cleaned prior to connection (see Chapter 1).

3 Battery — emergency jump starting

Refer to the Booster battery (jump) starting procedure at the front of this manual.

4 Battery cables — check and replacement

1   Periodically inspect the entire length of each battery cable for damage, cracked or burned insulation and corrosion. Poor battery cable connections can cause starting problems and decreased engine performance.

2   Check the cable-to-terminal connections at the ends of the cables for cracks, loose wire strands and corrosion. The presence of white, fluffy deposits under the insulation at the cable terminal connection is a sign the cable is corroded and should be replaced.

3   If only the positive cable is to be replaced, be sure to disconnect the negative cable from the battery first.

4   Disconnect and remove the cable(s) from the vehicle. Make sure the replacement cable(s) is the same length and diameter.

5   Clean the threads of the starter or ground connection with a wire brush to remove rust and corrosion. Apply a light coat of petroleum jelly to the threads to ease installation and prevent future corrosion. Inspect the connections frequently to make sure they are clean and tight.

6   Attach the cable(s) to the starter or ground connection and tighten the mounting nut(s) securely.

7   Before connecting the new cable(s) to the battery, make sure they reach the terminals without having to be stretched.

8   Connect the positive cable first, followed by the negative cable. Tighten the bolts and apply a thin coat of petroleum jelly to the terminal and cable connection.

5 Ignition system — check

Caution: *Because of the very high voltage generated by the HEI system, extreme care should be taken whenever an operation is performed involving ignition components. This not only includes the distributor, coil, control module and spark plug wires, but related items that are connected to the system as well, such as the plug connections, tachometer and any test equipment. Consequently, before any work is performed, the ignition should be turned off or the battery ground cable disconnected.*

1   If the engine turns over but will not start, remove the spark plug wire from a spark plug and, using an insulated tool, hold the wire about 1/4-inch from a good ground and have an assistant crank the engine. **Note:** *A special tool, ST-125, is available for making the above test. It is available from your dealer and auto parts stores.*

2   If there is no spark, check another wire in the same manner. A few sparks, then no spark, should be considered as no spark.

3   If there is good spark, check the spark plugs (refer to Chapter 1) and/or the fuel system (refer to Chapter 4).

4   If there is a weak spark or no spark, unplug the coil lead from the distributor, hold it about 1/4-inch from a good ground and check for spark as described above.

5   If there is no spark, have the system checked by a dealer or repair shop.

6   If there is a spark, check the distributor cap and/or rotor (refer to Chapter 1).

7   Further checks of the HEI ignition system must be done by a dealer or repair shop.

6 Distributor (OHV engine) — removal and installation

Removal

1   Disconnect the negative cable from the battery and remove the air cleaner. Disconnect the ignition switch/battery feed wire (BAT) and the tachometer lead (TACH), if so equipped, from the distributor cap.

2   Release the coil connectors from the cap. Depress the locking tabs by hand; do not use a screwdriver or other tool. It may be necessary to remove the air pipe and rear engine lift bracket for access.

3   Turn the two distributor cap locking latches counterclockwise, remove the cap and position it out of the way.

4   Disconnect the four-terminal ECM wiring harness connector from the distributor.

5   If necessary for clearance (on distributor caps with secondary wiring harness attached to the cap), release the wiring harness latches

and remove the wiring harness retainer. Note that the spark plug wire numbers are indicated on the retainer.

6   Remove the distributor hold-down clamp bolt and the hold-down clamp.

7   Make matching marks on the base of the distributor and the engine block to insure that you will be able to put the distributor back in the same position.

8   Make a mark on the distributor housing to show the direction the rotor is pointing. Lift the distributor slowly. As you lift it the rotor will turn slightly. When it stops turning make another mark on the distributor body to show where it is pointing when the gear on the distributor is disengaged. This is the position the rotor should be in when you begin reinstallation.

9   Remove the distributor. Avoid turning the crankshaft with the distributor removed, as this will change the timing position of rotor and require retiming the engine.

Installation if the crankshaft was not turned after distributor removal

10   Position the rotor in the exact location (second mark on the housing) it was in when the distributor was removed.

11   Lower the distributor into the engine. To mesh the gears at the bottom of the distributor it may be necessary to turn the rotor slightly.

12   With the base of the distributor seated against the engine block turn the distributor housing to align the marks made on the distributor base and the engine block.

13   With the distributor all the way down and the marks aligned the rotor should point to the first mark made on the distributor housing.

14   Place the hold-down clamp in position and loosely install the hold-down bolt.

15   Reconnect the ignition wiring harness.

16   Install the distributor cap. If the secondary wiring harness was removed from the cap, reinstall it.

17   Reconnect the coil connector.

18   With the distributor in its original position, tighten the hold-down bolt and check the ignition timing (Chapter 1).

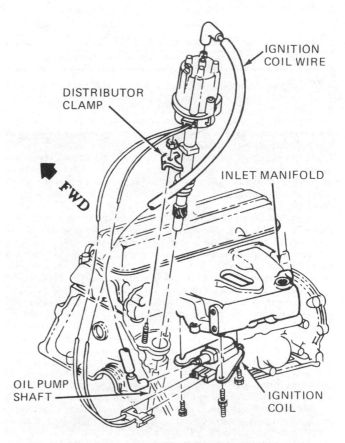

Fig. 5.1 OHV engine distributor and ignition coil installation details (Sec 6)

*Installation if the crankshaft was turned
after distributor removal*

19 Remove the number one spark plug.
20 Place your finger over the spark plug hole while turning the crankshaft with a wrench on the pulley bolt at the front of the engine.
21 When you feel compression continue turning the crankshaft slowly until the timing mark on the crankshaft pulley is aligned with the 0 on the engine timing indicator.
22 Position the rotor between the number one and three spark plug terminals on the cap.
23 Complete the installation by referring to Steps 11 through 18.

---

7 Distributor (OHC engine) — removal and installation

Removal

1   Disconnect the battery negative cable.
2   Remove the air cleaner assembly.
3   Remove the distributor cap.
4   Connect the battery negative cable temporarily so the engine can be rotated with the starter until the distributor rotor points straight up (photo).
5   Scribe a line across the distributor body and base for reference during installation (photo).
6   Unplug the electrical connectors from the ignition coil and the distributor.
7   Remove the two retaining nuts and lift the distributor from the engine.

Installation

8   Place the distributor in position, align the drive tabs with the slot in the camshaft and insert, lining up the marks made during removal. Install the retaining nuts and tighten them securely.
9   Plug in the electrical connectors and install the distributor cap.
10 Install the air cleaner assembly.
11 Connect the battery negative cable.

---

8 Ignition pickup coil (OHV engine) — replacement

1   Remove the distributor from the engine as previously described (Section 6).
2   Remove the two rotor mounting screws and remove the rotor.
3   Disconnect the pickup coil leads from the module.

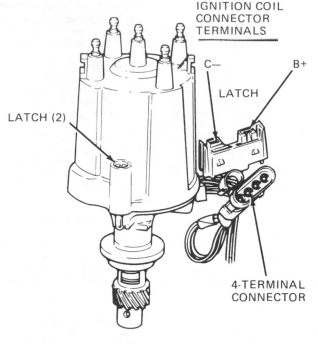

Fig. 5.2 OHV engine distributor and electrical connector details (Sec 6)

4   Mark the distributor gear and shaft so they can be reassembled in the same position.
5   Carefully mount the distributor in a soft-jawed vice and, using a hammer and punch, remove the roll pin from the distributor shaft and gear.
6   Remove the gear and washers from the shaft.
7   Carefully pull the shaft out through the top of the distributor.
8   Remove the 'C' washer retaining ring at the center of the distributor and remove the pickup coil.
9   Installation is the reverse of the removal procedure.

7.4 The distributor rotor must be pointed straight up (in the direction of the arrow) prior to removal

7.5 A line scribed across the distributor and block (arrow) will make installation easier

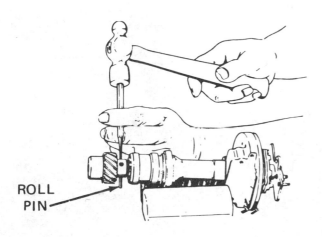

Fig. 5.3 Removing the roll pin from the distributor shaft (Sec 8)

ROLL PIN

9 Ignition pick-up coil (OHC engine) — check and replacement

Check

1 Remove the distributor cap and unplug the pick-up coil connector (photo).
2 Check the coil resistance with an ohmmeter. The meter should read between 500 and 1500 ohms (photo).

Replacement

3 Remove the distributor from the engine (Section 6).
4 Mount the distributor drive tang securely in a vise. Mark the tang and shaft so they can be reassembled in the same position.
5 Use a hammer and suitable size punch to drive out retaining pin. Have an assistant hold the distributor, as the shaft is spring loaded.
6 Remove the shaft, spring and washers from the distributor body.
7 Remove the pole piece and pick-up coil from the body.
8 Install the new pick-up coil.
9 Install the pole piece with the screws snug.
10 Lubricate the shaft with light oil and insert it into the body.
11 Assemble the shaft tensioner assembly (photo).
12 Depress the spring and rotate the retainer counterclockwise to lock it (photo).

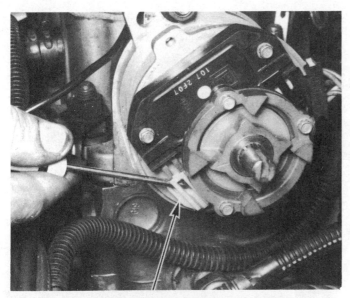

9.1 Use a small screwdriver to release the clip (arrow) so the pick-up coil connector can be unplugged

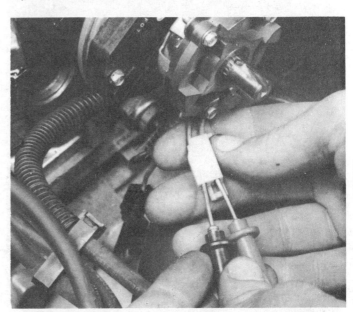

9.2 Checking the pick-up coil resistance

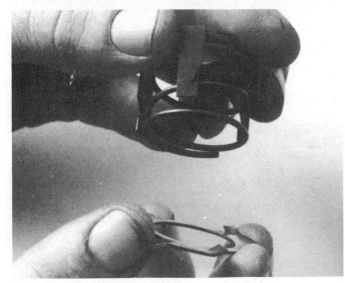

9.11 Proper assembly of the tensioner assembly

9.12 With the spring depressed, rotate the retainer counterclockwise into position until it is locked as shown

9.13   The tensioner assembly installed in the distributor body

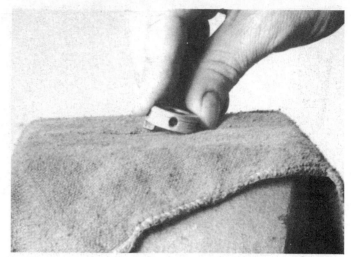

9.15   Place the drive tang securely in a vise, using a cloth to protect the surface

9.16   Lower the distributor into the drive tang, aligning the shaft slot with the tang pin hole (arrow)

9.18   Proper installation of the retaining spring (arrow)

13   Install the tensioner spring assembly into the body (photo).
14   Lightly oil the washer and install it over the spring assembly.
15   Mount the drive tang in the vise (photo).
16   Align the marks made during disassembly and lower the distributor over the drive tang with the slot aligned with the pin hole (photo).
17   Insert the pin and drive it into place until the ends are flush with the shaft.
18   Install the retaining spring over the drive tang (photo).
19   Position the pole piece so that it does not make contact when the rotor is turned and tighten the screws securely.

10   Ignition module (OHV engine) — removal and replacement

1   Remove the distributor (Section 6).
2   Remove the pick-up coil assembly (Section 8).
3   On distributors with an internal capacitor, remove the module mounting screws and the capacitor mounting screw, then separate the module, capacitor and harness assembly from the distributor base and disconnect the wiring harness from the module.
4   On distributors without an internal capacitor, disconnect the wiring harness from the module, remove the two mounting screws and remove

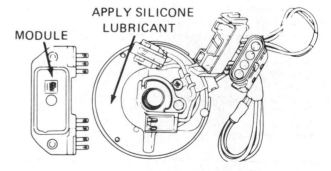

APPLY SILICONE LUBRICANT

MODULE

Fig. 5.4 A coat of silicone lubricant must be applied under the ignition module to provide a good electrical contact (Sec 10 and 11)

the module.
5   Installation is the reverse of the removal procedure. Before installing the module apply silicone lubricant to the housing on which the module mounts.

11.2   Ignition module retaining screw locations (arrows)

11.3   Using small screwdriver (arrow) to remove the module connector

13.4   Insert the ohmmeter probe into the module positive terminal (arrow) to check for voltage

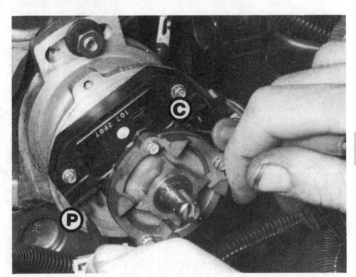

13.9   With a test light connected at the 'P' terminal, check the voltage with the meter probe at the 'C' terminal

5

11   Ignition module (OHC engine) — replacement

1   Remove the distributor cap.
2   Remove the module retaining screws (photo).
3   Rotate the module clear of the distributor. Unplug the connectors and remove the module (photo).
4   Coat the back of the module with silicone grease.
5   Plug in the electrical connector, rotate it into position and install the retaining screws, tightening them securely.
6   Install the distributor cap.

12   Ignition coil — removal and installation

1   Disconnect the battery negative cable.
2   Remove the air cleaner assembly.
3   On some models it will be necessary to remove the fuel filter bracket and fuel pump to gain access to the coil.
4   Unplug the coil electrical connectors.
5   Remove the retaining bolts and lift the coil from the engine.
6   Installation is the reverse of removal.

13   Ignition module — testing

1   Disconnect the tachometer (if so equipped) at the distributor.
2   Check for a spark at the coil and spark plug wires (Section 5).
3   If there is no spark, remove the distributor cap. Remove the ignition module from the distributor but leave the connector plugged in.
4   With the ignition switch turned On, check for voltage at the module positive terminal (photo).
5   If the reading is less than ten volts, there is a fault in the wire between the module positive (+) terminal and the ignition coil positive connector or the ignition coil and primary circuit-to-ignition switch.
6   If the reading is ten volts or more, check the 'C' terminal on the module as shown in the accompanying illustration.
7   If the reading is less than one volt, there is an open or grounded lead in the distributor-to-coil 'C' terminal connection or ignition coil or an open primary circuit in the coil itself.
8   If the reading is one to ten volts, replace the module with a new one and check for a spark (Section 5). If there is a spark the module was faulty and the system is now operating properly. If there is no spark, there is a fault in the ignition coil.
9   If the reading in Step 4 is ten volts or more, unplug the pickup coil connector from the module. Check the 'C' terminal voltage with the

13.11   As the test light (1) is removed, check for a spark at the coil wire (2)

ignition switch On and watch the voltage reading as a test light is momentarily (five seconds or less) connected between the battery positive (+) terminal and the module 'P' terminal (photo).
10 If there is no drop in voltage, check the module ground and, if it is good, replace the module with a new one.
11 If the voltage drops, check for spark at the coil wire as the test light is removed from the module terminal. If there is no spark, the module is faulty and should be replaced with a new one. If there is a spark, the pick-up coil or connections are faulty or not grounded (photo).

14 Charging system — general information and precautions

The charging system is made up of the alternator, voltage regulator and battery. These components work together to supply electrical power for the engine ignition, lights, radio, etc.
The alternator is turned by a drivebelt at the front of the engine. When the engine is operating, voltage is generated by the internal components of the alternator to be sent to the battery for storage.
The purpose of the voltage regulator is to limit the alternator voltage to a preset value. This prevents power surges, circuit overloads, etc., during peak voltage output. On all models with which this manual is concerned, the voltage regulator is contained within the alternator housing.
The charging system does not ordinarily require periodic maintenance. The drivebelts, electrical wiring and connections should, however, be inspected at the intervals suggested in Chapter 1.
Take extreme care when making circuit connections to a vehicle equipped with an alternator and note the following. When making connections to the alternator from a battery, always match correct polarity. Before using arc welding equipment to repair any part of the vehicle, disconnect the wires from the alternator and the battery terminal. Never start the engine with a battery charger connected. Always disconnect both battery leads before using a battery charger.

15 Charging system — check

1   If a malfunction occurs in the charging circuit, do not immediately assume that the alternator is causing the problem. First check the following items:
  a) The battery cables where they connect to the battery (make sure the connections are clean and tight).
  b) The battery electrolyte specific gravity (if it is low, charge the battery).
  c) Check the external alternator wiring and connections (they must be in good condition).

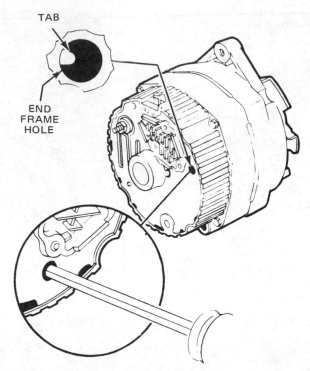

Fig. 5.5 Location of the test hole in the rear of the alternator (inset shows the grounding procedure) (Sec 15)

  d) Check the drivebelt condition and tension (see Chapter 1).
  e) Check the alternator mount bolts for tightness.
  f) Run the engine and check the alternator for abnormal noise.
2   Using a voltmeter, check the battery voltage with the engine off. It should be approximately 12 volts.
3   Start the engine and check the battery voltage again. It should now be approximately 14 to 15 volts. If it does not rise when the engine is started, or if it exceeds 15 volts, proceed to Step 4.
4   Locate the test hole in the back of the alternator and ground the tab that is located inside the hole by inserting a screwdriver blade into the hole and touching the tab and the case at the same time. **Note:** *Do not run the engine with the tab grounded any longer than necessary to obtain a voltmeter reading. The alternator, if it is charging, is running unregulated at this point. This condition may overload the electrical system and cause damage to the components.*
5   The reading on the voltmeter should be 15 volts or higher with the tab grounded in the test hole.
6   If the voltmeter indicates low battery voltage, the alternator is faulty and should be replaced with a new one (refer to Section 16).
7   If the voltage reading is 15 volts or higher and a no-charge condition is present, the regulator or field circuit is the problem. Remove the alternator and have it checked further by an auto electric shop.

16 Alternator — removal and installation

Removal
1   Disconnect the battery negative cable.
2   Unplug the two terminal plug and battery leads from the back of the alternator.
3   Loosen the adjusting bolts and remove the drive belt.
4   Remove the through-bolt and nut and the adjusting bolt. Lift the alternator from the engine.
5   Installation is the reverse of removal.

Installation
6   Place the alternator in position and install the through-bolt and nut. Install the adjusting bolt.
7   Install the drivebelt and adjust the tension (Chapter 1).
8   Plug in the alternator connectors.
9   Connect the battery negative cable.

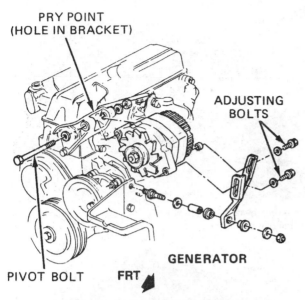

PRY POINT
(HOLE IN BRACKET)

ADJUSTING
BOLTS

PIVOT BOLT   FRT

GENERATOR

**Fig. 5.6 Details of a typical OHV engine alternator
installation (Sec 16)**

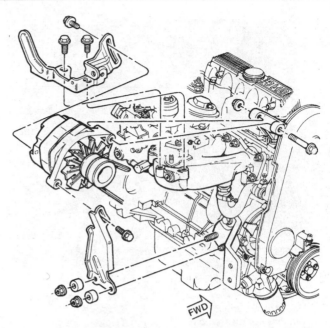

FWD

Fig. 5.7 Typical OHC engine alternator installation details (Sec 16)

17.2 Mark the drive end frame and rectifier end frame assemblies with
a scribe or paint before separating the two halves

17 Alternator brushes - replacement

Note: *The following procedure applies only to SI type alternators. CS
types have riveted housings and cannot be disassembled.*

1   Remove the alternator from the vehicle (Section 15).
2   Scribe or paint marks on the front and rear end frame housings of
the alternator to facilitate reassembly (photo).
3   Remove the four through-bolts holding the front and rear end
frames together, then separate the drive end frame from the rectifier
end frame (photos)
4   Remove the bolts holding the stator to the rear end frame and
separate the stator from the end frame (photo).
5   Remove the nuts attaching the diode trio to the rectifier bridge
and remove the trio (photo).
6   Remove the screws attaching the resistor (not used on all models) and regulator to the end frame and remove the regulator (photo).
7   Remove the brushes from the regulator by slipping the brush retainer off the regulator (photo).
8   Remove the springs from the brush holder.
9   Installation is the reverse of the removal procedure, noting the following:
10   When installing the brushes in the brush holder, install the brush
closest to the end frame first. Slip the paper clip through the rear of
the end frame to hold the brush, then insert the second brush and

17.3a With the through bolts removed, carefully separate the drive
end frame and the rectifier end frame

push the paper clip in to hold both brushes while reassembly is completed (photo). The paper clip should not be removed until the front
and rear end frames have been bolted together.

18 Starting system - general information

The function of the starting system is to crank the engine. This
system is composed of a starting motor, solenoid and battery. The
battery supplies the electrical energy to the solenoid, which then com-
pletes the circuit to the starting motor, which does the actual work of
cranking the engine.
The solenoid and starting motor are mounted together at the
lower right side of the engine. No periodic lubrication or maintenance
is required.
The electrical circuitry of the vehicle is arranged so that the
starter motor can only be operated when the clutch pedal is depressed (manual transmission) or the transmission selector lever is in
Park or Neutral (automatic transmission).
Never operate the starter motor for more than 30 seconds at a
time without pausing to allow it to cool for at least two minutes. Excessive cranking can cause overheating, which can seriously damage the
starter.

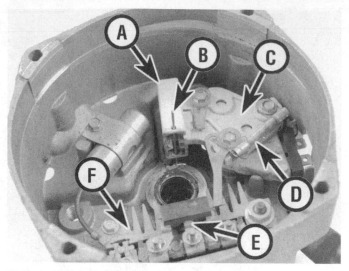

17.3b Inside a typical SI alternator

A   Brush holder
B   Paper clip retaining
    brushes (for reassembly)
C   Regulator
D   Resistor (not all models)
E   Diode trio
F   Rectifier bridge

17.5 Remove the nuts attaching the diode trio to the rectifier bridge and remove the trio

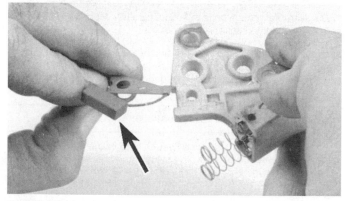

17.7 Slip the brush retainer off the regulator and remove the brushes (arrow)

19 Starter motor - testing in vehicle

1   If the starter motor does not turn at all when the switch is operated, make sure that the shift lever is in Neutral or Park (automatic transmission) or that the clutch pedal is depressed (manual transmission).

2   Make sure that the battery is charged and that all cables, both at

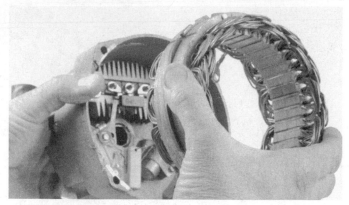

17.4 After removing the bolts holding the stator assembly to the end frame, remove the stator

17.6 After removing the screws that attach the regulator and the resistor (if equipped) to the end frame, remove the regulator

17.10 To hold the brushes in place during disassembly and reassembly, insert a paper clip through the hole in the end frame nearest to the rotor shaft

the battery and starter solenoid terminals, are secure.

3   If the motor spins but the engine is not being cranked, then the overrunning clutch in the starter motor is slipping and the motor must be removed from the engine and disassembled.

4   If, when the switch is actuated, the starter motor does not operate at all but the solenoid clicks, then the problem is in the main solenoid contacts or the starter motor itself.

5   If the solenoid plunger cannot be heard when the switch is actuated, the solenoid itself is defective or the solenoid circuit is open.

6   To check out the solenoid, connect a jumper lead between the battery (+) and the S terminal on the solenoid. If the starter motor now operates, the solenoid is OK and the problem is in the ignition switch, neutral start switch or in the wiring.

7   If the starter motor still does not operate, remove the starter/solenoid assembly for disassembly, testing and repair.

8   If the starter motor cranks the engine at an abnormally slow speed,

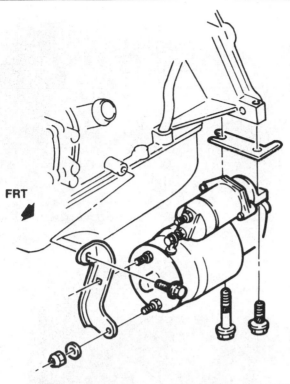

Fig. 5.8 OHV engine starter motor installation (Sec 20)

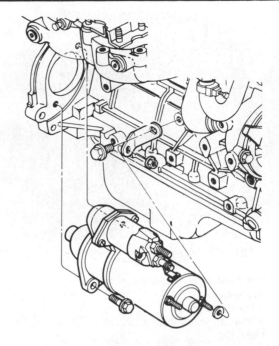

Fig. 5.9 OHC engine starter motor installation details (Sec 21)

first make sure that the battery is charged and that all terminal connections are tight. If the engine is partially seized, or has the wrong viscosity oil in it, it will crank slowly also.

9   Run the engine until normal operating temperature is reached, then disconnect the coil wire from the distributor cap and ground it on the engine.

10 Connect a voltmeter positive lead to the starter motor terminal of the solenoid and then connect the negative lead to ground.

11 Actuate the ignition switch and take the voltmeter readings as soon as a steady figure is indicated. Do not allow the starter motor to turn for more than 30 seconds at a time. A reading of 9 volts or more, with the starter motor turning at normal cranking speed, is normal. If the reading is 9 volts or more but the cranking speed is slow, the motor is faulty. If the reading is less than 9 volts and the cranking speed is slow, the solenoid contacts are probably burned (refer to Section 22).

20 Starter motor (OHV engine) — removal and installation

1   Disconnect the negative battery cable.
2   Raise the front of the vehicle and support it securely on jackstands.
3   From under the vehicle, disconnect the solenoid wires and battery cable from the starter motor.
4   Remove the support bracket.
5   Remove the retaining bolts and lower the starter motor from the engine.
6   Installation is the reverse of the removal procedure. Make sure that any removed shims are reinstalled.

21 Starter motor (OHC engine) — removal and installation

1   Disconnect the battery negative cable.
2   Remove the air cleaner assembly.
3   Disconnect the fuel lines and fuel filter bracket and remove the ignition coil from the engine block.
4   Remove the upper starter motor retaining bolt.
5   Raise the vehicle and support it securely on jackstands.
6   From under the vehicle, disconnect the battery cable from the starter motor.

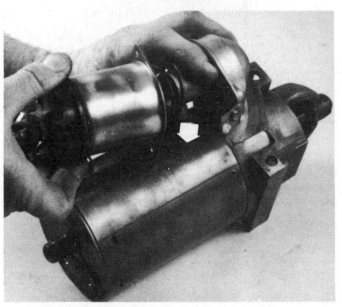

22.3   Withdrawing the solenoid assembly while turning it clockwise (arrow)

7   Disconnect the speedometer cable and remove the rear starter motor brace.
8   Remove the lower starter motor-to-engine bolt.
9   Remove the solenoid cover and disconnect the wires.
10 Separate the starter motor from the engine.
11 Installation is the reverse of the removal procedure.

22 Starter solenoid — removal and installation

1   After removing the starter as described in Section 21 disconnect the strap from the solenoid MOTOR terminal.
2   Remove the two screws which secure the solenoid housing to the starter end frame.
3   Twist the solenoid in a clockwise direction to disengage the flange from the starter body (photo).

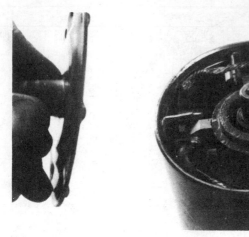

23.4   Removing the end frame from the field frame housing

4   Remove the nuts and washers from the solenoid terminals and then unscrew the two solenoid end cover retaining screws and washers and pull off the end cover.
5   Unscrew the nut from the battery terminal on the end cover and remove the terminal.
6   Remove the resistor bypass terminal and contact.
7   Remove the MOTOR connector strap terminal and solder a new terminal in position.
8   Install a new battery terminal. Install the bypass terminal and contact.
9   Install the end cover and the remaining terminal nuts.
10   To install first make sure the return spring is in position on the plunger, then insert the solenoid body into the starter housing and turn the solenoid counterclockwise to engage the flange.
11   Install the two solenoid screws and connect the MOTOR strap.

23   Starter motor brushes — replacement

1   Remove the starter and solenoid assembly from the vehicle as described in Section 20 or 21.
2   Remove the solenoid from the starter housing (refer to Section 22).
3   Remove the starter motor through bolts after marking the relationship of the commutator end frame to the field frame housing to simplify reassembly.
4   Remove the end frame from the field frame housing (photo).
5   Mark the relationship of the field frame housing to the drive end housing. Pull the field frame housing away from the drive end housing and over the armature.
6   Unbolt the brushes and brush supports from the brush holders in the field frame housing (photo).
7   To install new brushes, attach the brushes to the brush supports,

23.6   Unbolting the brush and brush support from the brush holder

23.8   Installing the field frame over the armature (note the position of the brushes on the armature collar)

making sure they are flush with the bottom of the supports, and bolt the brushes/supports to the brush holders.
8   Install the field frame over the armature, with the brushes resting on the first step of the armature collar at this point (photo).
9   Make sure the field frame is properly aligned with the drive end housing, then push the brushes off the collar and into place on the armature.
10   The remaining installation steps are the reverse of those for removal.

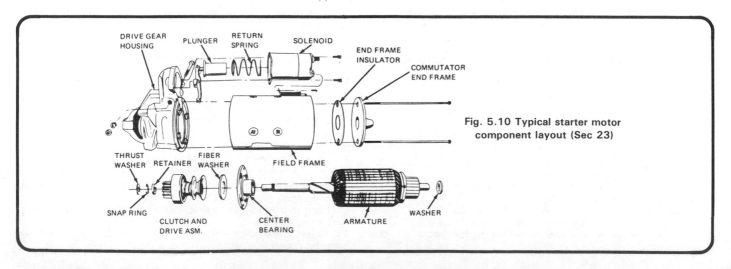

Fig. 5.10 Typical starter motor component layout (Sec 23)

DRIVE GEAR HOUSING
PLUNGER
RETURN SPRING
SOLENOID
END FRAME INSULATOR
COMMUTATOR END FRAME
THRUST WASHER
RETAINER
FIBER WASHER
FIELD FRAME
SNAP RING
CLUTCH AND DRIVE ASM.
CENTER BEARING
ARMATURE
WASHER

Chapter 6 Emissions control systems

Refer to Chapter 13 for information related to 1985 and later models

Contents

Specifications

Torque specifications	Ft-lbs
EGR valve	10 to 20
EFE heater relay	3
AIR pump pulley	24
AIR pump through-bolt	23
Oxygen sensor	30

1 General information

To prevent pollution of the atmosphere from burned and evaporating gases, a number of emissions control systems are incorporated on the vehicles covered by this manual. The combination of systems used depends on the year in which the vehicle was manufactured, the locality to which it was originally delivered and the engine type. The major systems incorporated on the vehicles with which this manual is concerned include the:

Air Injection Reactor (AIR)
Fuel Control System
Electronic Spark Timing (EST)
Early Fuel Evaporation (EFE)
Exhaust Gas Recirculation (EGR)
Evaporative Emissions Control (EECS)
Transmission Converter Clutch (TCC)
Positive Crankcase Ventilation (PCV)
Thermostatic Air Cleaner (THERMAC)
All of these systems are linked, directly or indirectly, to the Com-

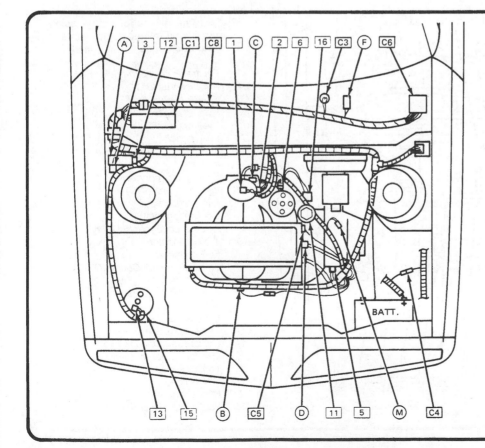

Fig. 6.1 Typical locations of emission system and related components (OHV TBI engine)

Cl *Electronic Control Module (ECM)*
C2 *ALDL connector*
C3 *'Check engine' light*
C4 *System power*
C5 *System ground*
C6 *Fuse panel*
C8 *Computer control electrical harness*
1 *Throttle body injection*
2 *Idle air control*
3 *Fuel pump relay*
5 *Transmission converter clutch connection*
6 *Electronic spark timing connector*
11 *EGR valve*
12 *EGR solenoid valve*
13 *Canister purge solenoid valve*
15 *Vapor canister*
16 *PULSAIR control*
A *Manifold pressure sensor*
B *Exhaust gas sensor*
C *Throttle position sensor*
D *Coolant sensor*
F *Vehicle speed sensor*
M *Fuel pump test connector*

6

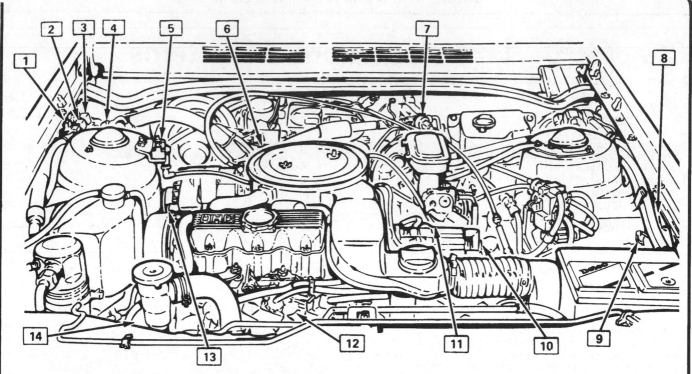

Fig. 6.2 Typical locations of emission system and related components (OHC engine)

1 Air conditioner control relay
2 Air conditioner constant run relay
3 Fuel pump relay
4 Air conditioner cycling pressure switch
5 MAP sensor

6 Blower motor relay (on cowl)
7 Power steering cutout switch
8 Fan control relay
9 ECM pigtail connector on positive battery cable
10 TCC connector

11 EST four terminal electrical harness from distributor
12 Oxygen sensor (in exhaust manifold)
13 Oil pressure switch
14 Coolant sensor (in thermostat housing)

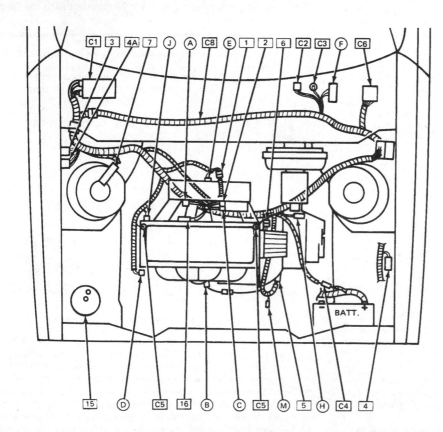

Fig. 6.3 Typical locations of emission system and related components (turbocharged OHC engine)

Cl Electronic control module (ECM)
C2 ALDL connector
C3 'Check engine' light
C4 System power
C5 System ground
C6 Fuse panel
C8 Computer control electrical harness
1   Fuel injector connector
2   Idle air control (IAC) valve
3   Fuel pump relay
4   Cooling fan relay
4A Air conditioner control relay
5   TCC connector
6   EST connector
7   Electronic Spark Control (ESC)
15 Vapor canister
16 Turbocharger wastegate solenoid
A   Manifold pressure sensor
B   Exhaust gas sensor
C   Throttle position sensor
D   Coolant sensor connector
E   Manifold air temperature sensor
F   Vehicle speed sensor
H   P/N switch
J   Knock sensor
M   Fuel pump test connector

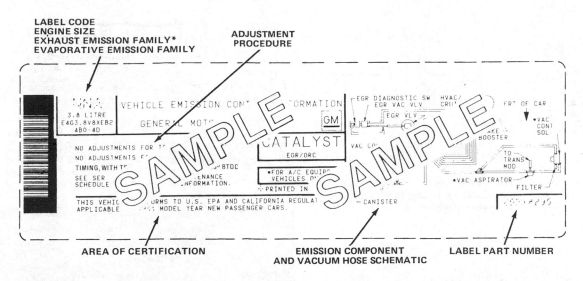

LABEL CODE
ENGINE SIZE
EXHAUST EMISSION FAMILY*
EVAPORATIVE EMISSION FAMILY

ADJUSTMENT PROCEDURE

AREA OF CERTIFICATION

EMISSION COMPONENT
AND VACUUM HOSE SCHEMATIC

LABEL PART NUMBER

Fig. 6.4 A Vehicle Emissions Control Information label will be found in the engine compartment of all vehicles (Sec 1)

puter Command Control System (CCCS).

The Sections in this Chapter include general descriptions, checking procedures (where possible) and component replacement procedures (where applicable) for each of the systems listed above.

Before assuming that an emissions control system is malfunctioning, check the fuel and ignition systems carefully. In some cases special tools and equipment, as well as specialized training, are required to accurately diagnose the causes of a rough running or difficult to start engine. If checking and servicing become too difficult, or if a procedure is beyond the scope of the home mechanic, consult your dealer service department. This does not necessarily mean, however, that the emissions control systems are particularly difficult to maintain and repair. You can quickly and easily perform many checks and do most (if not all) of the regular maintenance at home with common tune-up and hand tools. **Note:** *The most frequent cause of emissions system problems is simply a loose or broken vacuum hose or wiring connection. Therefore, always check the hose and wiring connections first.*

Pay close attention to any special precautions outlined in this Chapter. It should be noted that the illustrations of the various systems may not exactly match the system installed on your particular vehicle due to changes made by the manufacturer during production or from year to year.

A Vehicle Emissions Control Information label is located in the engine compartment of all vehicles with which this manual is concerned. This label contains important emissions specifications and setting procedures, as well as a vacuum hose schematic with emissions components identified. When servicing the engine or emissions systems, the VECI label in your particular vehicle should always be checked for up-to-date information.

2   Computer Command Control System (CCCS)

General description

This electronically controlled emissions system is linked with as many as nine other related emissions systems. It consists mainly of sensors (as many as 15) and an Electronic Control Module (ECM). Completing the system are various engine components which respond to commands from the ECM.

In many ways, this system can be compared to the central nervous system in the human body. The sensors (nerves) constantly gather information and send this data to the ECM (brain), which processes the data and, if necessary, sends out a command for some type of vehicle (body) change.

Here's a specific example of how one portion of this system operates. An oxygen sensor, mounted in the exhaust manifold and protruding into

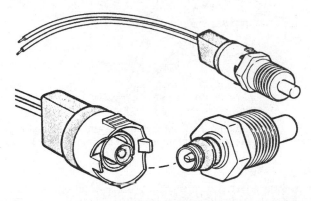

Fig. 6.5 The engine coolant sensor (right), shown with its ECM harness, is located in a coolant passage (Sec 2)

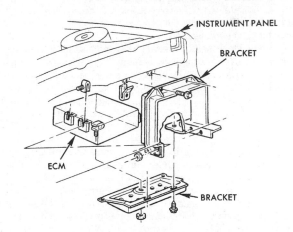

INSTRUMENT PANEL

BRACKET

ECM

BRACKET

Fig. 6.6 Typical ECM installation (Sec 2)

the exhaust gas stream, constantly monitors the oxygen content of the exhaust gas as it travels through the exhaust pipe. If the percentage of oxygen in the exhaust gas is incorrect, an electrical signal is sent to the ECM. The ECM takes this information, processes it and then sends a command to the carburetor Mixture Control (M/C) solenoid, telling it to change the fuel/air mixture. To be effective, all this happens in a fraction of a second, and it goes on continuously while the engine is running. The end result is a fuel/air ratio which is constantly kept at a predetermined "exact" proportion, regardless of driving conditions.

6

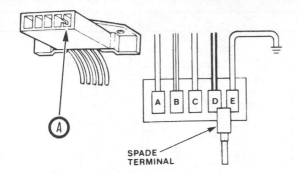

Fig. 6.7a On 1982 models, the ECM test terminal is marked by a notch on the connector (A) and can be grounded with a spade terminal or a paper clip (Sec 2)

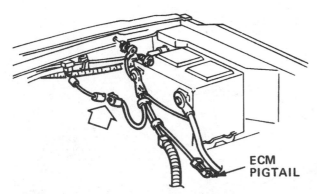

Fig. 6.8 Disconnecting the ECM pigtail wire at the connector (arrow) will clear the memory of intermittent trouble codes (Sec 2)

Testing

One might think that a system which uses exotic electrical sensors and is controlled by an on-board computer would be difficult to diagnose. This is not necessarily the case.

The Computer Command Control System has a built-in diagnostic system which indicates a problem by flashing a *CHECK ENGINE* light on the instrument panel. When this light comes on during normal vehicle operation, a fault has been detected.

Perhaps more importantly, the exact cause of this fault is determined and automatically stored in the ECM memory. Thus, troubleshooting this system is easily accomplished by you or a dealer mechanic.

To extract this information from the ECM memory, you must use a short jumper wire to ground a *TEST* terminal. This terminal is part of a wiring connector located just behind the dashboard, next to the steering column. A small, rectangular plate is used to cover the connector and must be pried out of place to provide access to the terminals.

With the connector exposed to view, push one end of the jumper wire into the *TEST* terminal and the other end into the GROUND terminal. **Note:** *Do not start the engine with the TEST terminal grounded.*

Turn the ignition to the On position – not the Start position. The *CHECK ENGINE* light should flash *Trouble Code 12*, indicating that the diagnostic system is working. Code 12 will consist of one flash, followed by a short pause, and then two flashes in quick succession. After a longer pause, the code will repeat itself two more times.

If no other codes have been stored, Code 12 will continue to repeat itself until the jumper wire is disconnected. If additional Trouble Codes have been stored, they will follow Code 12. Again, each Trouble Code will flash three times before moving on.

The ECM can also be checked for stored codes on carbureted models with the engine running. Completely remove the jumper wire from the *TEST* and *GROUND* terminals, start the engine, and then plug the jumper wire back in. With the engine running, all stored Trouble Codes will flash. However, Code 12 will flash only if there is a fault in the distributor reference circuit.

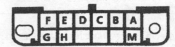

Fig. 6.7b On 1983 and later models, connect a jumper wire between terminals A and B of the connector (Sec 2)

A   Ground
B   Test terminal
C   AIR (if used)
D   Service Engine Soon light

E   Serial data (special tool required – do not use)
F   TCC (if used)
G   Fuel pump (if used)
M   Serial data (if used)

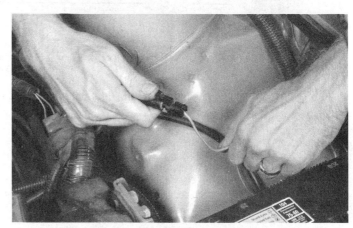

2.1   Unplugging the ECM harness pigtail

Once the code(s) have been noted, use the Trouble Code Identification information which follows to locate the source of the fault. **Note:** *Whenever the positive battery cable is disconnected, all stored Trouble Codes in the EMC are erased. Be aware of this before you disconnect the battery for servicing or replacement of electrical components, engine removal, etc.*

It should be noted that the self-diagnosis feature built into this system does not detect all possible faults. If you suspect a problem with the Computer Command Control System, but a *CHECK ENGINE* light has not come on, have your local dealer perform a *System Performance Check*.

Furthermore, when diagnosing an engine performance, fuel economy or exhaust emissions problem (which is not accompanied by a *CHECK ENGINE* light) do not automatically assume the fault lies in this system. Perform all standard troubleshooting procedures, as indicated elsewhere in this manual, before turning to the Computer Command Control System.

Finally, since this is an electronic system, you should have a basic knowledge of automotive electronics before attempting any diagnosis. Damage to the ECM, Programmable Read Only Memory Calibration Unit (PROM) or related components can easily occur if care is not exercised.

Trouble Code Identification

Following is a list of the typical Trouble Codes which may be encountered while diagnosing the Computer Command Control System. Also included are simplified troubleshooting procedures. If the problem persists after these checks have been made, the vehicle must be diagnosed by a professional mechanic who can use specialized diagnostic tools and advanced troubleshooting methods to check the system. Procedures marked with an asterisk (*) indicate component replacements which may *not* cure the problem in all cases. For this reason, you may want to seek professional advice before purchasing replacement parts.

To clear the Trouble Code(s) from the ECM memory, unplug the ECM electrical pigtail at the positive (+) battery cable.

Disconnecting the power to the ECM to clear the memory can be an important diagnostic tool, especially on intermittent problems. On later models it is a simple matter to unplug the ECM harness positive battery cable pigtail for ten seconds to clear all the stored Trouble Codes (photo).

	Trouble Code	Circuit or system	Probable cause
12	(one flash, pause, two flashes)	No reference pulses to ECM	This code should flash whenever the 'Test' terminal is grounded with the ignition On and the engine not running. If additional Trouble Codes are stored (indicating a problem), they will appear after this code has flashed three times With the engine running, the appearance of this code indicates that no references from the distributor are reaching the ECM Carefully check the four-terminal EST connector at the distributor
13	(one flash, pause, three flashes)	Oxygen sensor circuit	Check for a sticking or misadjusted throttle position sensor Check the wiring and connectors from the oxygen sensor Replace oxygen sensor (see Chapter 1)
14	(one flash, pause, four flashes)	Coolant sensor circuit	**Note:** *If the engine is experiencing overheating problems (as indicated by high temperature gauge readings or the 'hot' light coming on), rectify by referring to Chapters 1 and 3 before continuing* Check all wiring and connectors from the coolant sensor *Replace coolant sensor (located at the front of the engine block
15	(one flash, pause, five flashes)	Coolant sensor circuit	See above, plus: Check the wiring connections at the ECM
21	(two flashes, pause, one flash)	TPS circuit	Check for sticking or misadjusted TPS plunger Check all wiring and connections at the TPS and at the ECM *Adjust or replace TPS (see Chapter 4)
22	(two flashes, pause, two flashes)	TPS circuit	Check TPS adjustment (Chapter 4) Check ECM connector *Replace TPS (Chapter 4)
23	(two flashes, pause, three flashes)	M/C solenoid circuit	Check the electrical connections at the M/C solenoid (see Chapter 4). If OK, clear the ECM memory and recheck for code(s) after driving the vehicle Check wiring connections at the ECM Check wiring from M/C solenoid (Chapter 4)
24	(two flashes, pause, four flashes)	Vehicle Speed Sensor (VSS) circuit	**Note:** *A fault in this circuit should be indicated only while the vehicle is in motion. Disregard code 24 if set when drive wheels are not turning* Check connections at the ECM Check the TPS setting (Chapter 4)
32	(three flashes, pause, two flashes)	Baro sensor circuit	Check for a short between sensor terminals B and C or the wires leading to these terminals Check the wire leading to ECM terminal 1 Check the ECM connections Check the wires leading to ECM terminals 21 and 22 *Replace Baro sensor (located in the engine compartment, attached to the firewall)

6

Trouble code	Circuit or system	Probable cause
33 (three flashes, pause, three flashes)	MAP sensor	Check vacuum hose(s) from MAP sensor Check electrical connections at ECM *Replace MAP sensor
34 (three flashes, pause, four flashes)	Vacuum sensor circuit	Check the wiring leading to terminals 20, 21 and 22 of the ECM Check the connections at the ECM Check the vacuum sensor wiring and connections *Replace vacuum sensor (located in the engine compartment)
41 (four flashes, pause, one flash)	No distributor signals	Check all wires and connections at the distributor and ECM Check distributor pickup coil connections (Chapter 5) Check vacuum sensor circuit (see above)
42 (four flashes, pause, two flashes)	Bypass or EST problem	**Note:** *If the vehicle will not start and run, check the wire leading to ECM terminal 12* **Note:** *An improper HEI module can cause this Trouble Code.* Check the EST wire leading to the HEI module E terminal Check all distributor wires Check the wire leading from EST terminal A to ECM terminal 12 and the wire from EST terminal C to ECM terminal 11 Check all ECM connections *Replace HEI module
43 (four flashes, pause, three flashes)	Electronic Spark Control (ESC)	Check wire leading to ECM terminal L Check the wiring connector at the ESC controller and at the ECM Check wire from knock sensor to ESC controller; if necessary, reroute it away from other wires such as spark plug, etc.
44 (four flashes, pause, four flashes)	Lean exhaust	*On carburetor-equipped vehicles:* Check for a sticking M/C solenoid (Chapter 4) Check ECM wiring connections, particularly terminals 14 and 9 Check for vacuum leakage at carburetor base gasket, vacuum hoses or intake manifold gasket Check for air leakage at air management system-to-exhaust ports and at decel valve *Replace oxygen sensor *On fuel-injected vehicles:* Check ECM wiring connections Check for incorrect fuel pressure Check for water in the fuel *Replace oxygen sensor
45 (four flashes, pause, five flashes)	Rich exhaust	*On carburetor-equipped vehicles:* Check for a sticking M/C solenoid (Chapter 4) Check wiring at M/C solenoid connector Check the evaporative charcoal canister and its components for the presence of fuel (Chapters 1, 6) *Replace oxygen sensor

Trouble code	Circuit or system	Probable cause
45 (Continued)		*On fuel-injected models:* Check ECM wiring connections Check fuel pressure (Chapter 4) Check injectors for leakage (Chapter 4) Check for intermittent bursts of fuel from the injectors at idle, in- dicating a faulty TPS
51 (five flashes, pause, one flash) **52** (five flashes, pause, two flashes)	PROM problem	The PROM is located inside the ECM and is very delicate and easily broken. All diagnostic pro- cedures should be done by a dealer mechanic
54 (five flashes, pause, four flashes)	M/C solenoid	Check all M/C solenoid (carburetor-equipped vehicles) and ECM wires and connections *Replace the M/C solenoid (see Chapter 4)
55 (five flashes, pause, five flashes)	Oxygen sensor circuit	Check for corrosion on the ECM connectors and terminals Make sure that the four-terminal EST wiring harness is not too close to electrical signals such as spark plug wires, distributor housing, alternator, etc. Check the wiring of the various sensors *Replace the oxygen sensor

3 Fuel Control System

General description

1   The function of this system is to control the flow of fuel through the carburetor idle and main metering circuits. The major components of the system are the mixture control (M/C) solenoid and the oxygen sensor.

2   The M/C solenoid changes the fuel/air mixture by allowing more or less fuel to flow through the carburetor. The M/C solenoid, located in the carburetor air horn, is in turn controlled by the Electronic Control Module (ECM), which provides a ground for the solenoid. When the solenoid is energized, the fuel flow through the carburetor is reduced providing a leaner mixture. When the ECM removes the ground path, the solenoid de-energizes and allows more fuel flow.

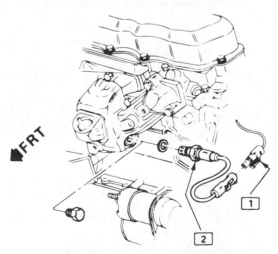

**Fig. 6.9 Detail of a typical oxygen sensor installation
(OHV engine shown) (Sec 3)**

1   *TBI harness connector*   2   *Oxygen sensor*

3   The ECM determines the proper fuel mixture required by monitoring a signal sent by the oxygen sensor, located in the exhaust stream. When the mixture is lean, the oxygen sensor voltage is low and the ECM commands a richer mixture. Conversely, when the mixture is rich, the oxygen sensor voltage is higher and the ECM commands a leaner mixture.

Checking

Oxygen sensor

4   Make sure that the oxygen sensor has been replaced at the proper maintenance interval (refer to Chapter 1).

5   The proper operation of the sensor depends on the four conditions which follow:

6   *Electrical conditions:* The low voltages and low currents generated by the sensor depend upon good, clean connections which should be checked whenever a malfunction of the sensor is suspected or indicated.

7   *Outside air supply:* The sensor is designed to allow air circulation to the internal portion of the sensor. Whenever the sensor is removed and installed or replaced, make sure the air passages are not restricted.

8   *Proper operating temperature:* The ECM will not react to the sensor signal until the sensor reaches approximately 600°F (315°C). This factor must be taken into consideration when evaluating the performance of the sensor.

9   *Non-leaded fuel:* The use of non-leaded fuel is essential for proper operation of the sensor. Make sure the fuel you are using is of this type.

10   In addition to observing the above conditions, special care must be taken whenever the sensor is handled, as directed in Chapter 1. Violation of any of these cautionary procedures may lead to sensor failure. **Note:** *Do not attempt to measure the voltage output of the oxygen sensor, because the current drain from a conventional voltmeter would be enough to permanently damage the sensor. For the same reason, never hook up test leads, jumpers or other electrical connections.*

Mixture control solenoid

11   Check the wiring connectors and wires leading to the mixture control solenoid for looseness, fraying and other damage. Repair or replace any damaged wiring as necessary.

12   Check the mixture control solenoid for apparent physical damage. Replace it if damage is found.

6

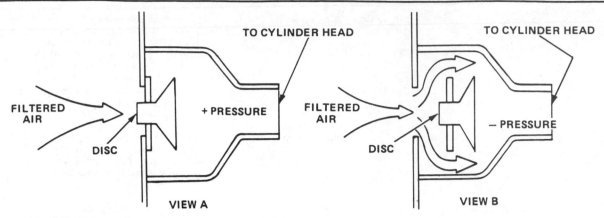

Fig. 6.10 With positive pressure present in the PULSAIR valve (left), the valve disc remains closed and no air enters the valve; when a vacuum is present in the valve (right), the disc opens and air mixes with the exhaust gases (Sec 5)

Component replacement

Oxygen sensor
13 To replace the sensor, refer to Chapter 1.

Mixture control solenoid
14 For E2SE carburetors, refer to Chapter 4.

4 Electronic Spark Timing (EST)

1 Electronic Spark Timing is used on all engines with which this manual is concerned. The EST distributor contains no vacuum or centrifugal advance, depending on commands from the ECM instead. The ECM receives a reference pulse from the distributor, indicating both engine rpm and crankshaft position, determines the proper spark advance for the engine operating conditions and sends an EST pulse to the distributor.
2 Under normal operating conditions, the ECM will always control the spark advance; however, under certain conditions, such as cranking or setting base timing, the distributor can operate independently of ECM control. This condition is called *bypass* and is determined by the bypass lead from the ECM to the distributor. When the bypass lead is over two volts, the ECM will control the spark; however, disconnecting the four-terminal EST connector, or grounding the bypass lead, will cause the engine to operate in the bypass mode.
3 For further information (and checking and component replacement procedures) regarding the EST distributor, refer to Chapter 5.

5 Air Injection Reactor (AIR/PULSAIR) system

General description
Note: *If your engine is equipped with an air pump, your concern in this Section will be with the AIR system. If no air pump is present, refer to the procedures involving the PULSAIR system.*

AIR system
1 The AIR system helps reduce hydrocarbons and carbon monoxide levels in the exhaust by injecting air into the exhaust ports of each cylinder during cold engine operation, or directly into the catalytic converter during normal operation. It also helps the catalytic converter reach proper operating temperature quickly during warm-up.
2 The AIR system uses an air pump to force the air into the exhaust stream. An air management valve, controlled by the vehicle's electronic control module (ECM) directs the air to the correct location, depending on engine temperature and driving conditions. During certain situations, such as deceleration, the air is diverted to the air cleaner to prevent backfiring from too much oxygen in the exhaust stream. One-way check valves are also used in the AIR system's air lines to prevent exhaust gases from being forced back through the system.
3 The following components are utilized in the AIR system: an engine driven air pump; air control, air switching and divert management valves; air flow and control hoses; check valves; and a dual bed catalytic converter.

PULSAIR system
4 This system performs some of the same functions as the AIR system, but utilizes exhaust pressure pulses to draw air into the exhaust system. Fresh air that is filtered by the air cleaner, to avoid the build-up of dirt on the check valve seat, is supplied to the system on a command from the ECM. The air cleaner also serves as a muffler to reduce noise in the system.
5 Components utilized in the system include the PULSAIR valve and external tubes and hoses.
6 The PULSAIR system's operation begins with the engine's firing, creating a pulsating flow of exhaust gases which are of positive or negative pressure. The pressure or vacuum is transmitted through the external tubes to the PULSAIR valve, which reacts as follows:
7 If the pressure is positive, the disc in the valve is forced to the closed position and no exhaust gas is allowed to flow past the valve and into the air supply.
8 If there is negative pressure (vacuum) present in the exhaust system at the valve, the disc will open, allowing fresh air to mix with the exhaust gases.
9 The disc, due to the inertia of the system, ceases to follow the pressure pulsations at high engine rpm. At this point the disc remains closed, preventing any further flow of fresh air.

Checking
AIR system
10 Because of the complexity of this system it is difficult for the home mechanic to make a proper diagnosis. If the system is suspected of not operating properly, individual components can be checked.
11 Begin any inspection by carefully checking all hoses, vacuum lines and wires. Be sure they are in good condition and that all connections are tight and clean. Also make sure that the pump drivebelt is in good condition and properly adjusted.
12 To check the pump allow the engine to reach normal operating temperature and run it at about 1500 rpm. Locate the hose running from the air pump and squeeze it to feel the pulsations (photo). Have an assistant increase the engine speed and check for a parallel increase in air flow. If this is observed as described, the pump is functioning properly. If it is not operating in this manner, a faulty pump is indicated.
13 The check valve can be inspected by first removing it from the air line. Attempt to blow through it from both directions. Air should only pass through it in the direction of normal air flow. If it is either stuck open or stuck closed the valve should be replaced.
14 To check the air management valve disconnect the vacuum signal line at the valve (photo). With the engine running see if vacuum is present in the line. If not, the line is clogged.
15 To check the deceleration valve plug the air cleaner vacuum source. With the engine running at the specified idle speed remove the small deceleration valve signal hose from the manifold vacuum source, then reconnect the signal hose and listen for air flow through the ventilation pipe and into the deceleration valve.
There should also be a noticeable engine speed drop when the signal hose is reconnected. If the air flow does not continue for at least one second, or the engine speed does not drop noticeably, check the deceleration valve hoses for restrictions and leaks. If no restrictions or leaks are found replace the deceleration valve.

Fig. 6.11 Details of a typical AIR pump installation (Sec 5)

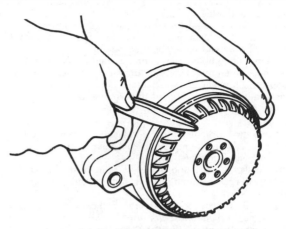

Fig. 6.12 Removing the AIR pump filter (remove as shown — do not insert any tool behind the filter, as damage to the pump may occur) (Sec 5)

PULSAIR system

16 A simple, functional test of this system can be performed with the engine running. Disconnect the rubber hose from the air valve and hold your hand over the valve's inlet hole. With the engine idling there should be a steady stream of air being sucked into the valve. Have an assistant apply throttle, and as the engine gains speed, see if the suction increases. If this does not occur, the lines are leaking or restricted or the check valves are sticking. Also make sure that air is not being blown out of the air valve, as this is also an indication that the check valves are sticking open. Service or replace the components as necessary. If other PULSAIR problems are suspected, have a dealer or repair shop diagnose the problems, as they might relate to the ECM/Computer Command Control System.

Component replacement (AIR system)

Drivebelt
17 Loosen the pump mounting bolt and the pump adjustment bracket bolt.
18 Move the pump inboard until the belt can be removed.
19 Install the new belt and adjust it (refer to Chapter 1).

AIR pump pulley and filter
20 Compress the drivebelt to keep the pulley from turning and loosen the pulley bolts.
21 Remove the drivebelt as described above.
22 Remove the mounting bolts and lift off the pulley.
23 If the fan-like filter must be removed, grasp it firmly with needle-nose pliers, as shown in the accompanying illustration, and pull it from the pump. **Note:** *Do not insert a screwdriver between the filter and pump housing as the edge of the housing could be damaged. The filter will usually be distorted when pulled off. Be sure no fragments fall into the air intake hose.*
24 The new filter is installed by placing it in position on the pump, placing the pulley over it and tightening the pulley bolts evenly to draw the filter into the pump. Do not attempt to install a filter by pressing or hammering it into place. **Note:** *It is normal for the new filter to have an interference fit with the pump housing and, upon initial operation, it may squeal until worn in.*
25 Install the drivebelt and, while compressing the belt, tighten the pulley bolts to the specified torque.
26 Adjust the drivebelt tension.

Hoses and tubes
27 To replace any tube or hose always note how it is routed first, either with a sketch or with numbered pieces of tape.
28 Remove the defective hose or tube and replace it with a new one of the same material and size and tighten all connections.

Check valve
29 Disconnect the pump outlet hose at the check valve.
30 Remove the check valve from the pipe assembly, making sure not to bend or twist the assembly.
31 Install a new valve after making sure that it is a duplicate of the part removed, then tighten all connections.

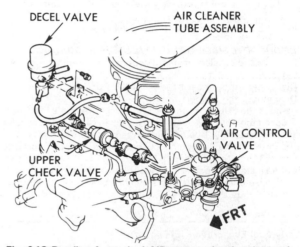

Fig. 6.13 Details of a typical AIR system deceleration and check valve installation (Sec 5)

6

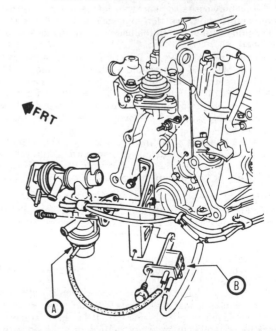

Fig. 6.14 Details of a typical AIR management valve installation (Sec 5)

A AIR management valve   B Control solenoid

Air management valve

32 Disconnect the negative battery cable at the battery.
33 Disconnect the vacuum signal line from the valve. Also disconnect the air hoses and wiring connectors.
34 If the mounting bolts are retained by tabbed lock washers, bend the tabs back, then remove the mounting bolts and lift the valve off the adaptor or bracket.
35 Installation is the reverse of the removal procedure. Be sure to use a new gasket when installing the valve.

Air pump

36 Remove the air management valve and adapter, if so equipped.
37 If the pulley must be removed from the pump it should be done prior to removing the drivebelt.
38 If the pulley is not being removed, remove the drivebelt.
39 Remove the pump mounting bolts and separate the pump from the engine.
40 Installation is the reverse of the removal procedure. **Note:** *Do not tighten the pump mounting bolts until all components are installed.*
41 Following installation adjust the drivebelt tension as described in Chapter 1.

Deceleration valve

42 Disconnect the vacuum hoses from the valve.
43 Remove the screws retaining the valve to the engine bracket (if present) and remove the valve.
44 Install a new valve and reconnect all hoses.

Component replacement (PULSAIR system)

45 Remove the air cleaner and disconnect the negative cable from the battery.
46 Disconnect the rubber hose from the PULSAIR valve.
47 Disconnect the support bracket.
48 Remove the PULSAIR solenoid and bracket from the PULSAIR unit.
49 Loosen the nuts that secure the air tubes to the cylinder head and remove the assembly. Due to the high temperature at this area, these connections may be difficult to loosen. Penetrating oil applied to the threads of the nuts may help.
50 Before installing, apply a light coat of oil to the ends of the air tubes and anti-seize compound to the threads of the attaching nuts.
51 Installation is the reverse of the removal procedure.

---

6 Early Fuel Evaporation (EFE) system

General description

1 This unit provides rapid heat to the intake air supply on carbureted and some throttle body injection engines by means of a ceramic heater grid. The grid is integral with the base gasket and located under the primary bore.
2 The components involved in the EFE's operation include the heater grid, a relay, electrical wires and connectors and the ECM.
3 The EFE heater unit is controlled by the vehicle's Electronic Control Module (ECM) through a relay. The ECM senses the coolant temperature level and applies voltage to the heater unit only when the engine temperature is below a predetermined level. At normal operating temperatures the heater unit is off.
4 If the EFE heater is not coming on poor cold engine performance will be experienced. If the heater unit is not shutting off when the engine is warmed up the engine will run as if it is out of tune (due to the constant flow of hot air through the carburetor or TBI).

Checking

5 If the EFE system is suspected of malfunctioning while the engine is cold, first check all electrical wires and connectors to be sure they are clean, tight and in good condition.
6 With the ignition switch in the On position, use a circuit tester or voltmeter to check that current is reaching the relay. If not, there is a problem in the wiring leading to the relay, in the ECM's thermo switch or the ECM itself.
7 With the engine cold and the ignition switch On, disconnect the heater unit wiring connector and use a circuit tester or voltmeter to see if current is reaching the heater unit. If so, use a continuity tester to check for continuity in the wiring connector attached to the heater unit. If continuity exists, the system is operating correctly in the cold engine mode.
8 If current is not reaching the heater unit, but is reaching the relay,

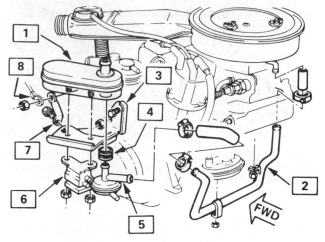

Fig. 6.15 Typical PULSAIR component layout (Sec 5)

1 *Valve assembly*	5 *Valve*
2 *Pipe*	6 *Actuator*
3 *Bracket*	7 *Brace*
4 *Grommet*	8 *Ground strap*

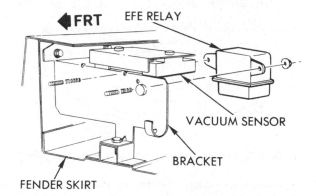

Fig. 6.16 EFE relay installation details (carbureted engine) (Sec 6)

replace the relay.
9 To check that the system turns off at normal engine operating temperature, first allow the engine to warm up thoroughly. With the engine idling, disconnect the heater unit wiring connector and use a circuit tester or voltmeter to check for current at the heater unit.
10 If current is reaching the heater unit a faulty ECM is indicated.
11 For confirmation of the ECM's condition, refer to Section 2 or have the system checked by a dealer or automotive repair shop.

TBI engines

12 Unplug the electrical connector from the EFE heater switch and connect a 12 volt test lamp across the the connector terminals.
13 If the lamp lights with the ignition switch On and the engine off, the EFE heater is operating properly.
14 If the test lamp does not light, plug in the connector and, with the engine temperature below 140 degrees, measure the voltage across the EFE heater. This is accomplished by inserting the voltmeter probes into the rear of the connector body, noting that the black wire is negative. The voltage should be between 11 and 13 volts.
15 If the reading is not between 11 and 13 volts, check the voltage at the black wire to ground connection. The voltage reading must be zero and if it is not, the ground (black) wire circuit is open and must be repaired.
16 If the ground wire reading is zero, check the voltage to ground at each of the heater switch terminals to make sure they are all between 11 and 13 volts. If any of the terminal readings are low or zero, while the others are normal, check the connector terminals for damage. If the terminals are in good condition and making proper contact, replace the heater switch with a new one.

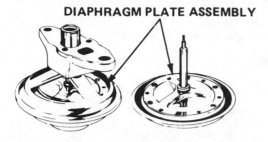

DIAPHRAGM PLATE ASSEMBLY

Fig. 6.17 Different types of EGR valves are identified by
their diaphragm plate assembly designs (be sure to obtain a
valve of the identical type when replacing it) (Sec 7)

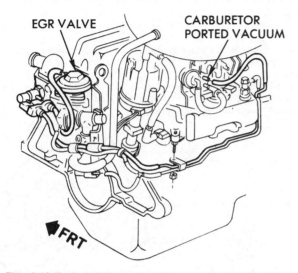

EGR VALVE   CARBURETOR
                 PORTED VACUUM

FRT

Fig. 6.19 Typical OHV engine EGR valve installation (Sec 7)

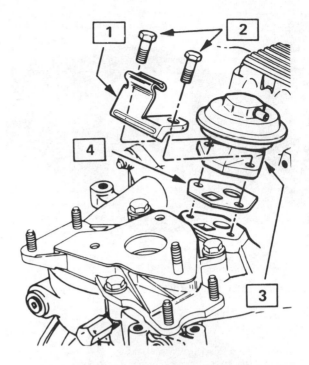

Fig. 6.18 Details of a typical OHC engine EGR valve
installation (Sec 7)

1 Bracket   3 EGR valve assembly
2 Bolts   4 Gasket

17 If the reading is not 11 to 13 volts at both of the switch terminals, there is a fault in the wiring circuit between heater switch and ignition switch.

18 Start the engine, allow it to warm up to normal operating temperature and check the voltage across the EFE heater terminals to make sure it is zero. If the voltage reading is not zero, replace the temperature switch with a new one.

Component replacement — carbureted engines

Heater relay
19 Disconnect the battery negative cable.
20 Remove the relay bracket from the fender skirt.
21 Unplug the electrical connectors, remove the retaining bolts and lift the relay from the vehicle.
22 Installation is the reverse of removal.

Heater
23 Remove the air cleaner and disconnect all electrical, vacuum and fuel connections from the carburetor.
24 Unplug the EFE heater electrical connector.
25 Remove the carburetor (Chapter 4).
26 Remove the EFE isolator assembly.
27 Installation is the reverse of removal.

Component replacement — TBI engines

Heater
28 Release the fuel system pressure (Chapter 1).
29 Remove the air cleaner assembly.
30 Disconnect the electrical, vacuum and fuel connections from the throttle body.
31 Unplug the EFE heater electrical connector.
32 Remove the throttle body assembly (Chapter 4).
33 Remove the heater insulator assembly.
34 Installation is the reverse of removal.

7 Exhaust Gas Recirculation (EGR) system

General description
1 An EGR system is used on all engines with which this manual is concerned. The system meters exhaust gases into the engine induction system through passages cast into the intake manifold. From there the exhaust gases pass into the fuel/air mixture for the purpose of lowering combustion temperatures, thereby reducing the amount of oxides of nitrogen (NOX) formed.
2 The amount of exhaust gas admitted is regulated by a vacuum or backpressure controlled (EGR) valve in response to engine operating conditions. The EGR valve, in turn, is under the control of the CCCS/ECM.
3 Common engine problems associated with the EGR system are rough idling or stalling at idle, rough engine performance during light throttle application and stalling during deceleration.

Checking
4 Refer to Chapter 1 for EGR valve checking procedures.
5 If the EGR valve appears to be in proper operating condition, carefully check all hoses connected to the valve for breaks, leaks or kinks. Replace or repair the valve/hoses as necessary.
6 Due to the interrelationship of the EGR system and the ECM, further checks of the system should be made by referring to Section 2 or having the system checked by a dealer or repair shop.

Component replacement
EGR valve
7 Disconnect the vacuum hose at the EGR valve. On OHC engines it will be necessary to remove the Throttle Body Injection Unit (Chapter 4) and alternator for access.
8 Remove the nuts or bolts which secure the valve to the intake manifold or adapter.
9 Lift the EGR valve from the engine.
10 Clean the mounting surfaces of the EGR valve. Remove all traces of gasket material.

6

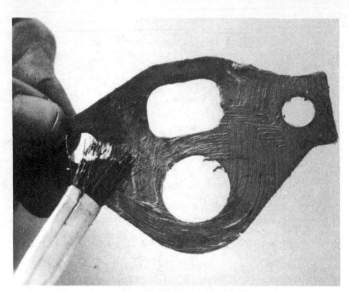

7.11   Coating the EGR gasket with lithium-based grease

11 Place the new EGR valve, with a new lithium-based grease coated gasket, on the intake manifold or adapter and tighten the attaching nuts or bolts (photo).
12 Connect the vacuum signal hose.

Cleaning

EGR valve
13 Inspect the valve pintle for deposits.
14 Depress the valve diaphragm and check for deposits around the valve seating area (photo).
15 Hold the valve securely and tap lightly on the round pintle with a plastic hammer, using a light snapping action, to remove any deposits from the valve seat. Make sure to empty any loose particles from the valve. Depress the valve diaphragm again and inspect the valve seating area, repeating the cleaning operation as necessary.
16 Use a wire brush to carefully clean deposits from the pintle.
17   Remove any deposits from the valve outlet using a screwdriver.

EGR passages
18 With the EGR valve removed, inspect the passages for excessive deposits.
19 It is a good idea to place a rag securely in the passage opening to keep debris from entering. Clean the passages by hand, using a drill bit (photo).
20 If the TBI spacer EGR channel used on OHC engines is removed, reinstall it using gasket sealant and apply a 1/16 inch bead of RTV-type sealant around the edge (photo).

7.14   Depress the EGR valve diaphragm and inspect the full length of the pintle (arrow) and the seat at its base for deposits

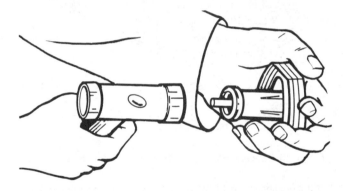

Fig. 6.20 Deposits can be removed from the EGR pintle seating area by tapping the end of the pintle lightly with a plastic hammer (Sec 7)

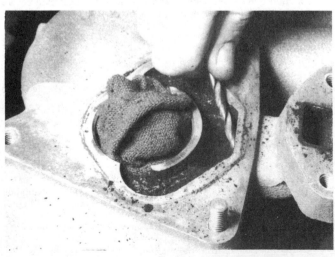

7.19   With a rag in the passage opening, the EGR cavity can be scraped clean of deposits using a drill bit

7.20   If the OHC engine TBI spacer EGR channel becomes detached, it can be reinstalled using a bead of sealant around the circumference (arrows)

8 Evaporative Emissions Control System (EECS)

General description

1   This system is designed to trap and store fuel that evaporates from the carburetor and fuel tank which would normally enter the atmosphere and contribute to hydrocarbon (HC) emissions.

2   The system consists of a charcoal-filled canister and lines running to and from the canister. These lines include a vent line from the gas tank, a vent line from the carburetor float bowl or injection unit, an idle purge line into the vehicle's induction system and a vacuum line to the manifold. In addition, there is a purge valve in the canister. The CCCS/ECM controls the vacuum to the purge valve with an electrically operated solenoid. The fuel tank cap is also an integral part of the system.

3   An indication that the system is not operating properly is a strong fuel odor.

Checking

4   Maintenance and replacement of the charcoal canister filter is covered in Chapter 1.

5   Check all lines in and out of the canister for kinks, leaks and breaks along their entire lengths. Repair or replace as necessary.

6   Check the gasket in the gas cap for signs of drying, cracking or breaks. Replace the gas cap with a new one if defects are found.

7   Due to its interrelationship with the CCCS/ECM, other system checks should be made by referring to Section 2 or having the system checked by a dealer or repair shop.

Component replacement

8   Replacement of the canister filter is covered in Chapter 1.

9   When replacing any line running to or from the canister, make sure the replacement line is a duplicate of the one you are replacing. These lines are often color-coded to denote their particular usage.

9 Positive Crankcase Ventilation (PCV) system

General description

1   The positive crankcase ventilation system reduced hydrocarbon emissions by circulating fresh air through the crankcase to pick up blow by gasses, ,which are rerouted through the carburetor to be burned in the engine.

2   The main components of this system are vacuum hoses and a PCV valve, which regulates the flow of gasses according to engine speed and manifold vacuum.

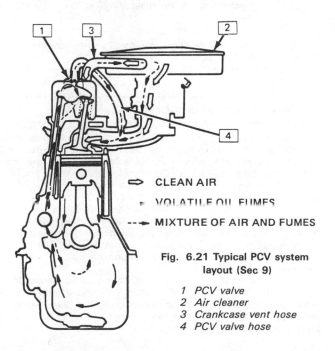

➡ **CLEAN AIR**

▸ **VOLATILE OIL FUMES**

--▸ **MIXTURE OF AIR AND FUMES**

Fig. 6.21 Typical PCV system layout (Sec 9)

1 PCV valve
2 Air cleaner
3 Crankcase vent hose
4 PCV valve hose

Checking

3   The PCV system can be checked quickly and easily for proper operation. The system should be checked regularly, as carbon and gunk deposited by the blow-by gasses will eventually clog the PCV valve and/or system hoses. When the flow of the PCV system is reduced or stopped, common symptoms are rough idling or reduced engine speed at idle.

4   To check for proper vacuum in the system, remove the top plate of the air cleaner and locate the small PCV filter on the inside of the air cleaner housing.

5   Disconnect the hose leading to this filter. Be careful not to break the molded fitting on the filter.

6   With the engine idling, place your thumb lightly over the end of the hose. You should feel a slight pull or vacuum. The suction may be heard as your thumb is released. This will indicate that air is being drawn all the way through the system. If a vacuum is felt, the system is functioning properly. Check that the filter inside the air cleaner housing is not clogged or dirty. If in doubt, replace the filter with a new one, an inexpensive safeguard (refer to Chapter 1).

7   If there is very little vacuum or none at all at the end of the hose, the system is clogged and must be inspected further.

8   Shut off the engine and locate the PCV valve. Carefully pull it from its rubber grommet. Shake it and listen for a clicking sound. That is the rattle of the valve's check ball. If the valve does not click freely, replace it with a new one.

9   Now start the engine and run it at idle speed with the PCV valve removed. Place your thumb over the end of the valve and feel for suction. This should be a relatively strong vacuum which will be felt immediately.

10   If little or no vacuum is felt at the PCV valve, turn off the engine and disconnect the vacuum hose from the other end of the valve. Run the engine at idle speed and check for vacuum at the end of the hose just disconnected. No vacuum at this point indicates that the vacuum hose or inlet fitting at the engine is plugged. If it is the hose which is blocked replace it with a new one or remove it from the engine and blow it out sufficiently with compressed air. A clogged passage at the carburetor or manifold requires that the component be removed and thoroughly cleaned to remove carbon build-up. A strong vacuum felt going into the PCV valve, but little or no vacuum coming out of the valve, indicates a failure of the PCV valve requiring replacement with a new one.

11   When purchasing a new PCV valve, make sure it is the correct one for your engine. An incorrect PCV valve may pull too little or too much vacuum, possibly leading to engine damage.

Component replacement

12   The replacement procedures for both the PCV valve and filter are covered in Chapter 1.

10 Thermostatic Air Cleaner (THERMAC)

General description

1   The thermostatic air cleaner (THERMAC) system is provided to improve engine efficiency and reduce hydrocarbon emissions during the initial warm-up period by maintaining a controlled air temperature at the carburetor. This temperature control of the incoming air allows leaner carburetor and choke calibrations.

2   The system uses a damper assembly, located in the snorkel of the air cleaner housing, to control the ratio of cold and warm air directed into the carburetor. This damper is controlled by a vacuum motor which is, in turn, modulated by a temperature sensor in the air cleaner. On some engines a check valve is used in the sensor, which delays the opening of the damper flap when the engine is cold and the vacuum signal is low.

3   It is during the first few miles of driving (depending on outside temperature) that this system has its greatest effect on engine performance and emissions output. When the engine is cold, the damper flap blocks off the air cleaner inlet snorkel, allowing only warm air from around the exhaust manifold to enter the carburetor. Gradually, as the engine warms up, the flap opens the snorkel passage, increasing the amount of cold air allowed in. Once the engine reaches normal operating temperature, the flap opens completely, allowing only cold, fresh air to enter.

4   Because of this cold-engine-only function, it is important to

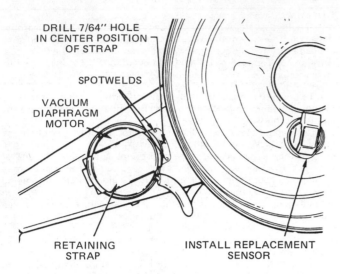

DRILL 7/64" HOLE
IN CENTER POSITION
OF STRAP

SPOTWELDS

VACUUM
DIAPHRAGM
MOTOR

RETAINING
STRAP

INSTALL REPLACEMENT
SENSOR

**Fig. 6.22 Typical carbureted engine THERMAC vacuum
motor replacement (Sec 10)**

periodically check this system to prevent poor engine performance.
If the air cleaner valve sticks in the 'no heat' position, the engine will
run poorly, stall and waste gas until it has warmed up on its own. A
valve sticking in the 'heat' position causes the engine to run as if it
is out of tune due to the constant flow of hot air to the carburetor.

Checking

5   Refer to Chapter 1 for maintenance and checking procedures for
this system. If problems were encountered in the system's performance
while performing the routine maintenance checks, refer to the procedures which follow.
6   If the damper door did not close off snorkel air when the cold engine
was first started, disconnect the vacuum hose at the snorkel vacuum
motor and place your thumb over the hose end, checking for vacuum.
If there is vacuum going to the motor, check that the damper door and
link are not frozen or binding within the air cleaner snorkel. Replace
the vacuum motor if the hose routing is correct and the damper door
moves freely.
7   If there was no vacuum going to the motor in the above test, check
the hoses for cracks, crimps and proper connection. If the hoses are
clear and in good condition, replace the temperature sensor inside the
air cleaner housing.

Component replacement

Air cleaner vacuum motor
8   Remove the air cleaner assembly from the engine and disconnect
the vacuum hose from the motor.
9   Drill out the two spot welds which secure the vacuum motor retaining strap to the snorkel tube.
10   Remove the motor attaching strap.
11   Lift up the motor, cocking it to one side to unhook the motor linkage
at the control damper assembly.
12   To install, drill a 7/64-inch hole in the snorkel tube at the center
of the retaining strap.
13   Insert the vacuum motor linkage into the control damper assembly.
14   Using the sheet metal screw supplied with the motor service kit,
attach the motor and retaining strap to the snorkel. Make sure the sheet
metal screw does not interfere with the operation of the damper door.
Shorten the screw if necessary.
15   Connect the vacuum hose to the motor and install the air cleaner
assembly.

Air cleaner temperature sensor
16   Remove the air cleaner from the engine and disconnect the vacuum
hoses at the sensor.
17   Carefully note the position of the sensor. The new sensor must
be installed in exactly the same position.
18   Pry up the tabs on the sensor retaining clip and remove the sensor and clip from the air cleaner.
19   Install the new sensor with a new gasket in the same position as

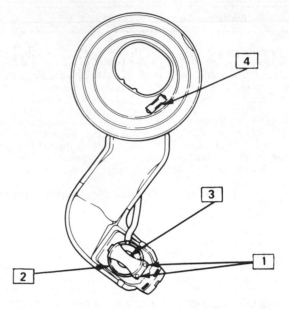

**Fig. 6.23 Components involved in removing the THERMAC
vacuum motor on a typical fuel-injected vehicle (Sec 10)**

1 *Spot welds*   3 *Retaining strap*
2 *Motor assembly*   4 *Sensor*

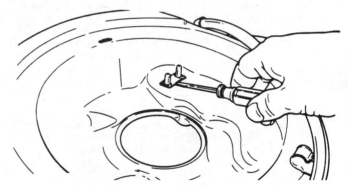

**Fig. 6.24 Carefully note the position of the sensor before
removing the retaining clip (Sec 10)**

the old one.
20   Press the retaining clip onto the sensor. Do not damage the control mechanism in the center of the sensor.
21   Connect the vacuum hoses and attach the air cleaner to the engine.

---

11   Transmission Converter Clutch (TCC)

1   Toward optimizing the efficiency of the emissions control
network, the ECM controls an electrical solenoid mounted in the
automatic transmission of vehicles so equipped. When the vehicle
reaches a specified speed, the ECM energizes the solenoid and allows
the torque converter to mechanically couple the engine to the transmission, under which conditions emissions are at their minimum. However,
because of other operating condition demands (deceleration, passing,
idle, etc.), the transmission must also function in its normal, fluid-
coupled mode. When such latter conditions exist, the solenoid de-
energizes, returning the transmission to fluid coupling. The transmission also returns to fluid-coupling operation whenever the brake pedal
is depressed.
2   Due to the requirement of special diagnostic equipment for the
testing of this system, and the possible requirement for dismantling
of the automatic transmission to replace components of this system,
checking and replacing of the components should be handled by a
dealer or automotive repair shop.

Chapter 7 Part A   Manual transaxle

Contents

Specifications

Torque specifications	Ft-lbs
Clutch cover housing bolts	10
Shift control retaining nuts	20
Strut bracket-to-transaxle bolts	35
Strut bracket mounting stud nut	30
Strut bolts	30
Suspension support bolts	75
Transaxle ground cable stud nut	30
Transaxle-to-engine bolts	55
Transaxle mount-to-engine bolts	40
Transaxle mount-to-side frame	
bolts	40
nuts	23
Transaxle mount through-bolt	95 to 118

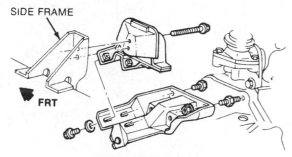

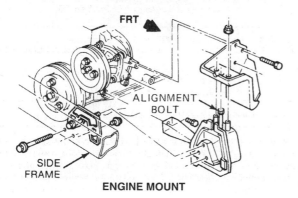

**Fig. 7A.1   Transaxle and engine mount installation details
(Sec 2 and 7)**

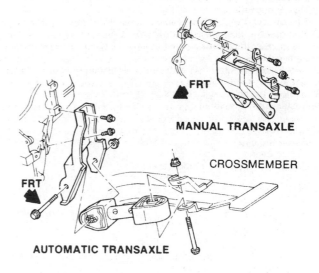

**Fig. 7A.2 Typical transaxle engine mount strut component layout
(Sec 2 and 7)**

---

1   General information

The manual transaxle combines the transmission and differential assemblies into one compact unit. These models are equipped with either four or five speed transaxles, which are very similar in design.

Shifting is accomplished by a floor-mounted shifter, which is connected to the transaxle shift levers by cable assemblies.

2   Transaxle mounts — check and replacement

Caution: *A suitable size (1/4 X 4-inch) alignment bolt or punch must be inserted in the right front engine mount whenever a transmission mount is removed to prevent damage to the driveaxle CV joints.*

Checking

1   Watch the mount as an assistant pulls up and pushes down on the transaxle. If the rubber separates from the plate or the case moves up but not down, indicating the mount is bottomed out, replace the mount with a new one.

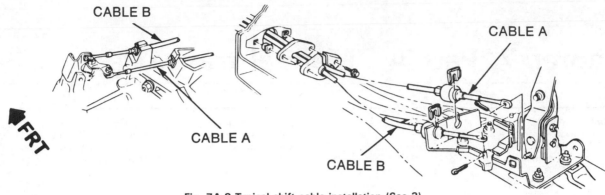

Fig. 7A.3 Typical shift cable installation (Sec 3)

Replacement

2   Disconnect the battery negative cable.
3   Support the transaxle with a jack.
4   Remove the transaxle mount through-bolt.
5   Remove the retaining bolts and remove the mount.
6   Place the new mount in position and install the mount-to-side frame bolts.
7   Install the through-bolt and tighten the nut to the specified torque.
8   Loosen the two nuts at the top of the mount and lower the jack supporting the transaxle so the weight will center the mount. Tighten the nuts to the specified torque.
9   Remove the alignment bolt and connect the battery negative cable.

3   Transaxle shift cables — removal and installation

Removal

1   Disconnect the battery negative cable.
2   Disconnect the retaining clips and cables at the transaxle.
3   Remove the console and shift boot (Chapter 12).
4   Disconnect the cables and remove the shift control lever assembly (Section 5).
5   Remove the left front sill plate and pull the carpet back sufficiently to gain access to the cables.
6   Remove the shift cable cover screws from the floor pan and remove the cables from the vehicle.

Installation

7   Route the cables into position and install the cable cover and attaching screws.
8   Place the carpet in position and install the sill plate.
9   From under the vehicle, route the cables to the transaxle.
10   In the engine compartment, connect the cables and retainers to the transaxle levers.
11   In the passenger compartment, connect the cables to the shift lever and install the console and shifter boot.
12   Adjust the shift linkage (Section 5 or 6).
13   Connect the battery negative cable.

4   Shift control lever — removal and installation

Removal

1   Disconnect the battery negative cable.
2   In the engine compartment, loosen the shift cables at the transaxle levers.
3   Remove the console and shifter boot.
4   Disconnect the cables from the control lever.
5   Unbolt and remove the control lever.

Installation

6   Place the control lever in position and install the attaching nuts, tightening them to the specified torque.
7   Connect the cables to the control assembly and follow the adjustment procedure in Section 5 or 6.
8   Install the console and shifter boot.

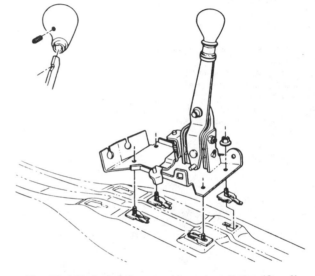

Fig. 7A.4 Typical shift control lever installation (Sec 4)

9   Adjust the shift linkage (Section 5 or 6).
10   Connect the battery negative cable.

5   Transaxle shift linkage (4-speed) — adjustment

1   Disconnect the battery negative cable.
2   Place the transaxle in first gear.
3   Referring to the accompanying illustration, loosen the cable attaching nuts (E) at the transaxle levers (D and F).
4   Remove the console trim plate, slide the shifter boot up the handle and remove the console.
5   With the shifter pulled to the left and held against the stop (first gear position), insert a yoke clip or suitable shim so that it is snug enough to hold the lever as shown in View D.
6   Insert a 5/32 inch or No. 22 drill bit into the alignment hole at the side of the shifter assembly as shown in View C.
7   Install a yoke clip or suitable shim between the tower and carrier as shown in view D.
8   To remove any lash from the transaxle, rotate lever D in the direction of the arrow while tightening nut E (View B).
9   Remove the drill bit or yoke clip from the shifter assembly and install the shifter boot and retainer.
10   Lubricate the moving parts of the shift mechanism with white lithium base grease using a suitable stiff-bristled brush.
11   Connect the battery negative cable and road test the vehicle to check the shifting operation. It may be necessary to repeat the adjustment procedure to completely remove looseness or misalignment from the linkage.

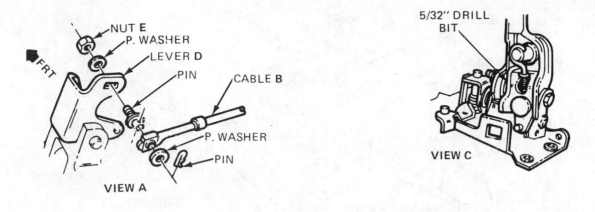

NUT **E**
P. WASHER
LEVER **D**
PIN
CABLE **B**
FRT
P. WASHER
PIN

VIEW A

5/32" DRILL BIT

VIEW C

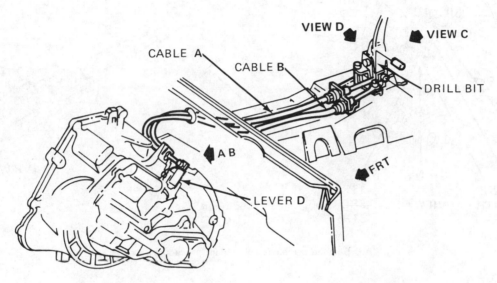

VIEW D
VIEW C
CABLE **A**
CABLE **B**
DRILL BIT
A B
FRT
LEVER **D**

7A

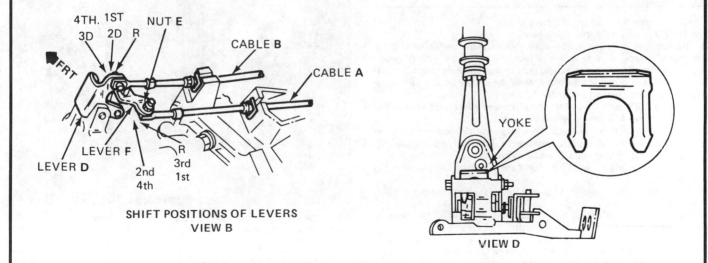

4TH. 1ST
3D 2D R
NUT **E**
CABLE **B**
CABLE **A**
FRT
LEVER **F**
LEVER **D**
2nd
4th
R
3rd
1st

SHIFT POSITIONS OF LEVERS
VIEW B

YOKE

VIEW D

Fig. 7A.5 4-speed transaxle adjustment procedure (Sec 5)

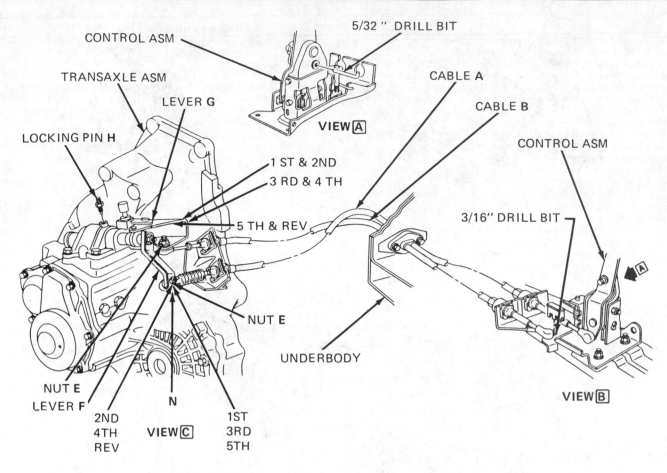

Fig. 7A.6 5-speed transaxle adjustment procedure (Sec 6)

6 Transaxle shift linkage (5-speed) — adjustment

1   Disconnect the battery negative cable.
2   Shift the transaxle into third gear.
3   Referring to the accompanying illustration, remove the locking pin and install it tapered side down to lock the transaxle in third gear.
4   Loosen the shift cable attaching nuts at the transaxle levers G and F.
5   Remove the console trim plate, slide the shifter boot up the lever and remove the console (Chapter 12).
6   Insert a 5/32-inch drill bit into the alignment hole next to the shifter assembly (View A in the illustration).
7   Refer to View B in the illustration, align the slot in the shift lever with the slot in the shifter plate and insert a 3/16-inch drill bit (photo).
8   Tighten nuts E at levers G and F (View C).
9   Remove the drill bit used for alignment and install the locking pin with the tapered side up.
10 Install the console, shifter boot and trim plate and connect the battery negative cable.
11 Lubricate the shift mechanism moving parts with white lithium-base grease using a stiff-bristled brush.
12 Road test the vehicle and check the shifting operation. It may be necessary to repeat the adjustment procedure to eliminate all looseness or misalignment from the shift mechanism.

7 Transaxle — removal and installation

Removal

1   Disconnect the battery negative cable.
2   Raise the vehicle to provide sufficient clearance for lowering the transaxle and support it securely on jackstands.

6.7   The shift mechanism is held in alignment during adjustment by inserting a drill bit (arrow) as shown

3   Support the engine weight with a suitable lifting device. Alternately, a jack under the engine can be used, although this must be placed in a position where it won't affect access while working underneath.
4   Insert a suitable size alignment bolt (1/4 x 4-inches) or pin into the right front engine mount to prevent damage to the driveaxle CV joints or boots caused by driveline misalignment when the transaxle mount is removed (see Fig. 7A.1).
5   Remove the transaxle mount attachment bolts.
6   Disconnect the shift cables and clutch linkage.

7   Disconnect the ground cables and the back-up light connector from the transaxle.
8   On 4-speed models, remove the heater hose clamp at the transaxle mount bracket and remove the horn assembly.
9   If so equipped, remove the air management valve attaching bolts to provide clearance to the right upper transaxle-to-engine bolt.
10   Drain the transaxle lubricant into a suitable container.
11   Remove the left front wheel and the inner splash shield.
12   Remove the transaxle strut and strut bracket from the transaxle.
13   Remove the clutch housing cover.
14   Disconnect the speedometer cable from the transaxle.
15   Disconnect the stabilizer bar from the control arm.
16   Disconnect the inner CV joints from the transaxle (Chapter 8).
17   Remove the brake caliper, hang it out of the way using a piece of wire, and remove the brake disc (Chapter 9).
18   Place a jack under the left front suspension assembly. **Caution:** *Care must be taken not to overextend the CV joints and boots whenever the suspension is disconnected.*
19   Remove the six suspension support attaching bolts and lower the support, suspension and driveaxle from the vehicle as an assembly.
20   Remove the transaxle-to-engine mounting bolts.
21   Slide the transaxle away from the engine until it is clear and then lower it from the vehicle.

Installation

22   Raise the transaxle into position and carefully guide the right-hand driveaxle into the bore.
23   With the transaxle in position, install two four-inch long bolts with the same threads as the mounting bolts in the top transaxle-to-engine bolt holes to use as guide pins when drawing the transaxle into place. Insert the input shaft and slide the transaxle toward the engine. If it does not move easily, have an assistant turn the engine over using a socket on the front pulley bolt as the transaxle is moved into position.
24   Install the transaxle-to-engine mounting bolts, tightening to the specified torque.
25   Install the transaxle mount, bracket and bolts.
26   Install the left hand driveaxle into its bore and seat both driveaxles (Chapter 8).
27   Place the suspension support in position and install the attaching bolts, tightening to the specified torque.
28   Install the brake disc and caliper.
29   Connect the sway bar to the suspension support and control arm.
30   Connect the speedometer cable.
31   Install the clutch housing cover.
32   Install the strut bracket and strut assembly, tightening to the specified torque.
33   Install the inner splash shield and the wheel and lower the vehicle.
34   Install the air management valve attaching bolts (if so equipped).
35   Connect the ground cables and back-up light connector to the transaxle.
36   Install the transaxle mount bracket and connect the clutch cable to the release lever and the bracket.
37   Install the transaxle mount to the side frame.
38   Tighten the mount-to-transaxle bracket bolts to the specified torque at this time. Before tightening the bolts, check the alignment bolt or pin in the engine mount to make sure excessive effort is not required to remove it. If there is, re-align the drive train. Remove the bolt.
39   Install the hose clamp and install the horn.
40   Remove the engine supports or jack, connect the negative battery cable and refill the transaxle with the specified fluid.
41   Adjust the shift linkage cables (Section 5 or 6).

7A

Chapter 7 Part B Automatic transaxle

Contents

Specifications

Torque specifications	Ft-lbs
Shifter assembly retaining nuts	18
Shifter cover screws	12 in-lb
Shifter cable bracket-to-transaxle bolt	18
Shifter cable-to-transaxle lever pin nut	15
Shifter lever-to-transaxle nut	20
Strut mount through-bolt	31
Transaxle-to-engine bolts	55
Throttle valve cable-to-transaxle bolt	9

1 General information

Due to the complexity of the clutches and the hydraulic control system, and because of the special tools and expertise required to perform an automatic transaxle overhaul, it should not be undertaken by the home mechanic. Therefore, the procedures in this Chapter are limited to general diagnosis, routine maintenance and adjustment and transaxle removal and installation.

If the transaxle requires major repair work, it should be left to a dealer service department or a reputable automotive or transmission repair shop. You can, however, remove and install the transaxle yourself and save the expense, even if the repair work is done by a transmission specialist.

Adjustments that the home mechanic may perform include those involving the throttle valve cable, the shift linkage and the neutral safety switch.

2 Diagnosis — general

Automatic transaxle malfunctions may be caused by four general conditions: poor engine performance, improper adjustments, hydraulic malfunctions and mechanical malfunctions. Diagnosis of these problems should always begin with a check of the easily repaired items: fluid level and condition, shift linkage adjustment and throttle linkage adjustment.

Next, perform a road test to determine if the problem has been corrected or if more diagnosis is necessary. If the problem persists after the preliminary tests and corrections are completed, additional diagnosis should be done by a dealer service department or a reputable automotive or transmission repair shop.

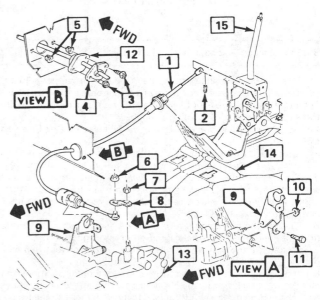

Fig. 7B.1 Details of the components involved in shift linkage adjustment (Sec 3)

1 Cable	8 Transaxle shift lever
2 Retaining pin	9 Cable bracket
3 Screws	10 Bracket retaining nut
4 Cover	11 Bracket bolt
5 Nut	12 Cable grommet assembly
6 Shift cable pin nut	13 Transaxle
7 Transaxle shift lever	14 Floor pan
pin nut	15 Shifter assembly

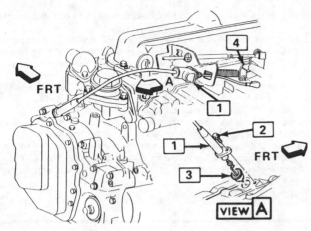

Fig. 7B.2 Details of the TV cable installation (Sec 4)

1 Cable assembly   3 Seal
2 Retaining bolt   4 Cable actuating lever

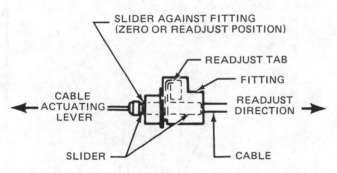

Fig. 7B.4 Details of components involved with TV cable adjustment (Sec 4)

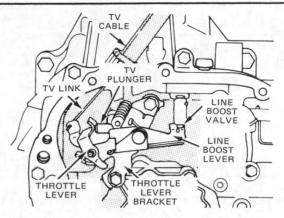

Fig. 7B.3 Details of the TV cable connection in the transaxle (Sec 4)

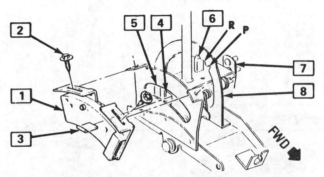

Fig. 7B.5 Details of the components involved in adjusting the Neutral safety and back-up light switch (Sec 5)

1 Switch assembly   5 Tang slot
2 Screw   6 Neutral notch
3 Carrier tang   7 Shifter
4 Tang hole   8 Detent plate

3   Shift linkage — check and adjustment

1   The manual shift linkage must be maintained in proper adjustment so that the shifter detents always correspond with the transaxle detents. If the linkage is not kept in adjustment, an internal leak in the transaxle could result, causing slippage.
2   Apply the parking brake and block the wheels to prevent the vehicle from rolling.
3   Loosen the nut retaining the shift cable to the transaxle shift lever.
4   Place the console shift lever (inside the vehicle) in Neutral.
5   Place the transaxle lever in the Neutral position. This is accomplished by rotating the lever clockwise from the Park position, through Park and Reverse and into Neutral, or counterclockwise through 1, 2 and Drive into Neutral.
6   Tighten the attaching nut to the specified torque. The shift lever must be held out of the Park position during tightening.
7   Make sure the engine will start in the Park and Neutral positions only.
8   If the engine can be started in any of the drive positions (as indicated by the shifter inside the vehicle), repeat the steps above or have the vehicle examined by a dealer to avoid damage to the transaxle.

4   Throttle valve (TV) cable — description and adjustment

1   The throttle valve cable controls the transaxle line pressure and consequently the shift feel and timing, as well as the part throttle and detent downshifts.
2   The TV cable is attached to the link at the throttle lever and bracket at the transaxle and to the throttle lever on the carburetor or TBI on the engine.

3   Whenever the TV cable has been disconnected from the carburetor/TBI unit, it must be adjusted after installation.
4   The freeness of the TV cable can be checked by pulling the upper end of the cable. The cable should travel a short distance with light resistance, due to the small return spring. Pull the cable farther out to move the lever into contact with the plunger, thus compressing the heavier TV spring. When released, the cable should return to the closed position, verifying that the cable in the housing, TV lever and bracket and the TV plunger in its bushing are moving freely.
5   The engine must be off during adjustment.
6   If not previously done, remove the air cleaner, labeling all hoses as they are removed to simplify installation.
7   Depress and hold down the metal readjusting tab at the engine end of the TV cable.
8   While holding the tab down, move the slider until it stops against the fitting.
9   Release the readjustment tab.
10 Rotate the throttle lever to the maximum travel stop position. The cable will ratchet through the slider and automatically readjust itself.
11 Road test the vehicle. If delayed or only full-throttle shifts still occur, have the vehicle checked by a dealer.

5   Neutral safety and back-up light switch — adjustment

1   Remove the shift indicator plate.
2   Place the transaxle shifter lever in Neutral.
3   Loosen, but do not remove, the screws retaining the switch assembly to the shifter assembly.
4   Rotate the switch assembly so that the service adjustment hole on the switch is aligned with the carrier tang hole.
5   Insert a 3/32-inch gauge pin (a drill bit will work fine) through the

service adjustment hole to a depth of 19/32-inch.
6   Tighten the switch assembly retaining screws.
7   Remove the gauge pin.
8   Install the shift indicator plate.

6   Transaxle — removal and installation

Removal

1   Disconnect the battery negative cable.
2   Insert a 1/4 X 2-inch bolt into the right front engine mount to maintain mount alignment during the transaxle removal.
3   Remove the air cleaner assembly, tagging all hoses for ease of installation. Disconnect the TV cable at the carburetor or TBI.
4   Remove the TV cable-to-transaxle bolt, pull up on the cable cover

until the cable is visible, then disconnect the cable from the transaxle rod.
5   Disconnect the vacuum hoses at the TVS switch (if equipped).
6   On TCC equipped models, disconnect the connector at the transaxle and the coolant sensor connector at the water outlet.
7   Remove the horn assembly.
8   Attach a suitable lifting device to the engine and raise the engine sufficiently to remove the weight from the engine mounts.
9   Remove the top transaxle mount and bracket assembly.
10   Remove the air management valve (if equipped) attaching bolts for access to the upper right transaxle-to-engine bolts.
11   Remove the top transaxle-to-engine mounting bolts and loosen, but do not remove, the transaxle-to-engine bolt near the starter.
12   With the steering column unlocked, raise the vehicle and support it securely on jackstands.
13   Remove the left front wheel.

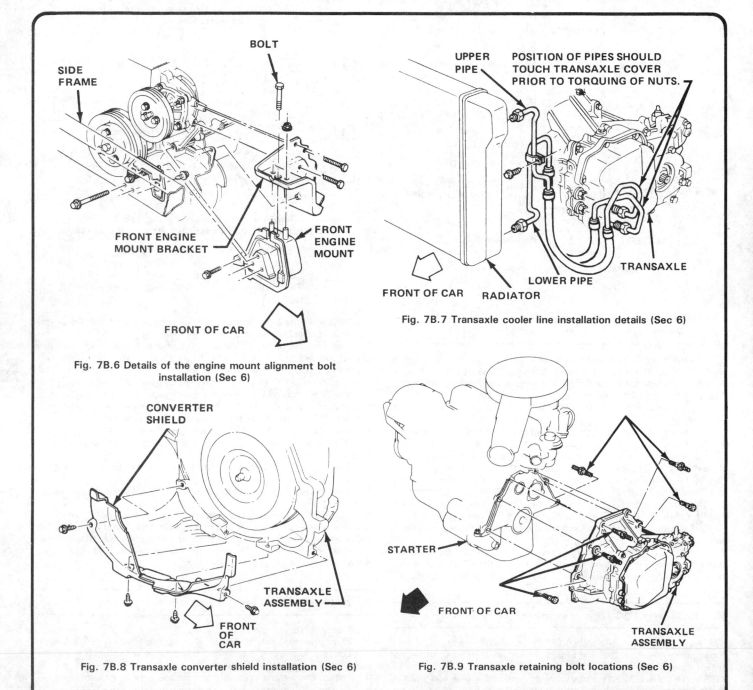

Fig. 7B.6 Details of the engine mount alignment bolt installation (Sec 6)

Fig. 7B.7 Transaxle cooler line installation details (Sec 6)

Fig. 7B.8 Transaxle converter shield installation (Sec 6)

Fig. 7B.9 Transaxle retaining bolt locations (Sec 6)

14 Remove the lower left balljoint cotter pin and nut, then separate the balljoint (Chapter 11).

15 Disconnect the stabilizer bar at the lower control arm.

16 Remove the six bolts attaching the left suspension support assembly.

17 Disconnect the left driveaxle (Chapter 8) and plug the transaxle bore.

18 Remove the control cable bracket-to-transaxle nut, followed by the engine-to-transaxle stud.

19 Disconnect the speedometer cable from the transaxle.

20 Disconnect the transaxle strut at the transaxle.

21 Remove torque converter shield.

22 Mark the relative position of the torque converter and flex plate and remove the retaining bolts.

23 Disconnect and plug the transaxle cooler lines.

24 On air conditioning equipped models, remove the compressor brace attachment bolt from the right side of the transaxle.

25 Support the transaxle with a jack and remove the remaining transaxle-to-engine bolts.

26 Remove the transaxle from the engine by sliding it toward the left side of the vehicle. The right drive axle will come out of the transaxle bore at this point and must be supported.

Installation

27 Installation is the reverse of removal, with attention paid to the following points:

    a) Guide the right hand axle into the transaxle at the time of installation as it cannot be inserted later.

    b) Follow the front suspension support assembly bolt tightening sequence described in Chapter 11.

    c) The suspension alignment should be checked by a dealer or suitably equipped shop.

    d) Adjust the TV cable (Section 4).

    e) Check the transaxle fluid level (Chapter 1).

7B

Chapter 8 Clutch and driveaxles

Contents

Specifications

Torque specifications	Ft-lbs
Clutch release lever bolt	20
Clutch pedal-to-mounting bracket bolt	25
Clutch pedal-to-locking pawl bolt	3.7
Clutch pressure plate-to-flywheel bolt	15
Flywheel bolt	50
Neutral start switch screw	2.2

1 Clutch — general information

All manual transaxle-equipped vehicles use a single dry plate, diaphragm spring-type clutch. Operation is through a foot pedal, incorporating a self-adjusting mechanism, cable, fork lever, clutch shaft and fork assembly and a release bearing.

The adjusting mechanism is integral to the pedal and bracket assembly and has a fixed length cable. The cable position can be changed by adjusting the position of the detent relative to the clutch pedal. By lifting the pedal up against the rubber stop (Chapter 1), the pawl is then forced against a metal stop, which rotates it out of mesh with the detent teeth. This allows the cable to play out until the detent spring load is balanced against the load applied by the clutch release bearing, thereby adjusting for wear of the clutch plate face material.

2 Clutch operation — checking

1   Before performing any operations on the clutch, several checks can be made to determine if there is actually a fault in the clutch itself.
2   With the engine running and the brake applied, hold the clutch pedal approximately 1/2-inch from the floor mat surface and shift through the gears several times. If the shifts are smooth, the clutch is releasing properly. If it is not the clutch is not releasing fully and the linkage should be checked.
3   Inspect the clutch pedal bushings for wear or binding.
4   Observe the clutch fork lever travel at the transaxle while an assistant depresses the pedal fully. The end of the fork should travel between 1.5 and 1.7 inches.
5   If the fork travel is not within specification, check the adjusting mechanism by depressing the clutch pedal and watching the pawl to make sure it engages firmly with the detent teeth.

3 Clutch release lever — removal and installation

Removal
1   Support the clutch pedal upward against the bumper stop to release the pawl.
2   Disconnect the clutch cable from the release lever at the transaxle, taking care not to let it snap rearward, which could damage the adjusting mechanism.
3   Remove the attaching bolt and lift the lever from the clutch fork shaft.

Installation
4   Place the release lever in position on the fork shaft and install the bolt and washers, tightening them to the specified torque.
5   Attach the clutch cable to the release lever.
6   Check the clutch operation by lifting the pedal up to allow the mechanism to adjust the cable length, then depress it slowly several times to mesh the pawl with the detent teeth.

4 Clutch pedal — removal and installation

Removal
1   Perform the operations described in Steps 1 and 2 of Section 3.
2   Remove the under-dash hush panel and detach the Neutral start switch from the pedal and bracket.
3   Disconnect the clutch cable from the tangs of the detent, lift the pawl away and slide the cable between the detent and pawl.
4   Remove the pivot bolt and remove the spring, pawl and spacer from the pedal assembly.
5   Remove the detent spacer, bushings, spring and pawl.
6   Clean the parts and inspect them for wear or damage. Replace both the pawl and detent if the teeth on either is damaged or worn.

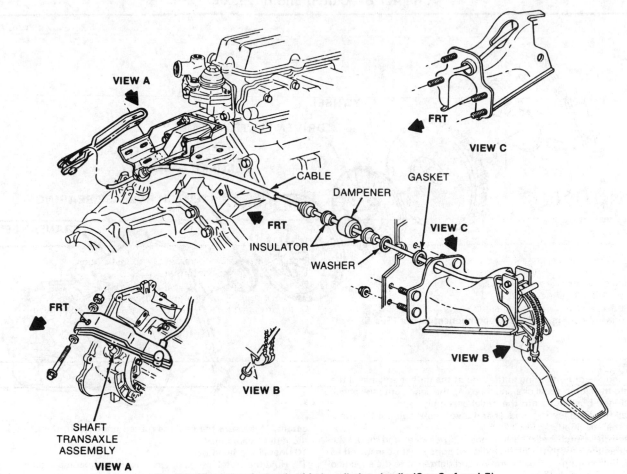

VIEW A

VIEW C

FRT

CABLE

DAMPENER

GASKET

VIEW C

FRT

INSULATOR

WASHER

VIEW B

VIEW B

FRT

SHAFT
TRANSAXLE
ASSEMBLY

VIEW A

Fig. 8.1 Clutch bracket and cable installation details (Sec 3, 4 and 5)

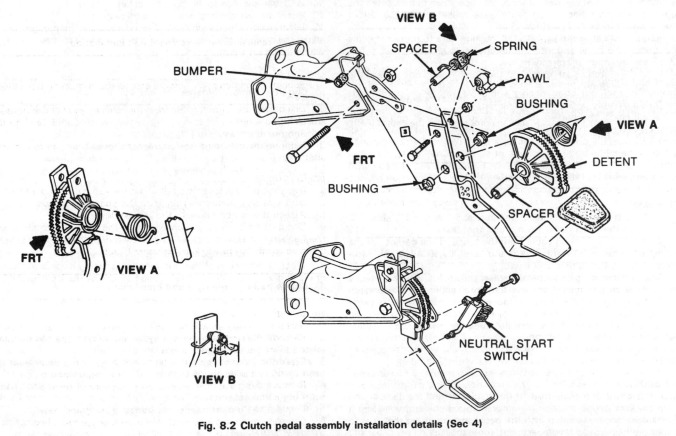

VIEW B

SPACER

SPRING

PAWL

BUMPER

BUSHING

VIEW A

FRT

BUSHING

DETENT

SPACER

FRT

VIEW A

VIEW B

NEUTRAL START
SWITCH

Fig. 8.2 Clutch pedal assembly installation details (Sec 4)

8

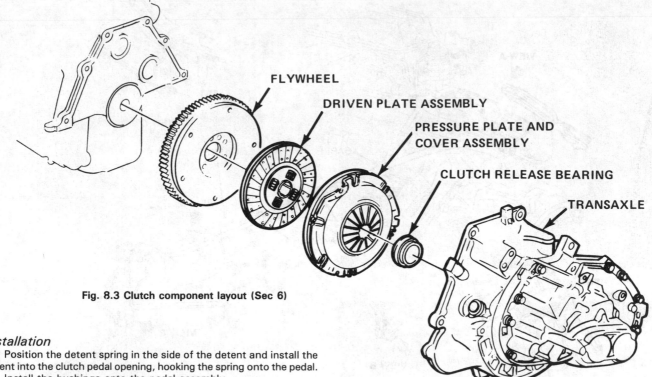

Fig. 8.3 Clutch component layout (Sec 6)

Installation

7   Position the detent spring in the side of the detent and install the detent into the clutch pedal opening, hooking the spring onto the pedal.
8   Install the bushings onto the pedal assembly.
9   Install the pawl, spring, spacer and pivot mounting bolt, tightening it to the specified torque.
10   Attach the clutch pedal to the mounting bracket and install the pivot bolt and nut. Both the pivot and pawl bolts must be installed as shown in the accompanying illustration and tightened to the specified torque.
11   Check the pawl and detent for proper operation to make sure the pawl disengages when pulled to its upper position and the detent rotates freely in both directions.
12   Attach the cable end to the pawl, making sure to route the cable underneath the pawl and into the detent cable groove.
13   Install the neutral start switch.
14   Hold the clutch pedal up against the bumper stop and release the pawl from the detent.
15   Check the clutch pedal mechanism for proper operation and adjust the cable length by lifting the pedal (Chapter 1). Depress the pedal slowly several times so the pawl meshes properly with the detent teeth.
16   Install the hush panel.

5   Clutch cable — removal and installation

Removal

1   Perform the operations described in Steps 1 and 2 of Section 3.
2   Remove the hush panel from under the dash.
3   Disconnect the clutch cable from the tangs of the detent, lift the locking pawl away from the detent and carefully slide the cable forward between the detent and pawl.
4   Remove the windshield washer reservoir.
5   In the engine compartment, pull the clutch cable out to disengage it from the clutch pedal mounting bracket. Be prepared to retrieve the insulators, dampener and washers, which may separate during removal.
6   Disconnect the cable from the mounting bracket on the transaxle and remove it from the vehicle.
7   Inspect the cable and replace if it is frayed, worn, damaged or kinked.

Installation

8   Connect the cable into both of the insulators and the damper and washers. Lubricating the rear insulator with a small amount of light oil will ease the installation into the pedal mounting bracket.
9   Inside the passenger compartment, route the liner on the cable into the rubber isolator on the pedal bracket. Attach the cable end to the

detent. Make sure the cable is routed underneath the pawl and into the detent cable groove.
10   Install the hush panel.
11   Hold the clutch pedal upward against the bumper stop to release the pawl from the detent. Install the other end of the cable into the release lever and transaxle mount bracket.
12   Install the windshield washer reservoir.
13   Lift the clutch pedal up several times to allow the mechanism to adjust the cable length, then depress it several times to mesh the pawl with the detent teeth.

6   Clutch — removal, inspection and installation

Removal

1   Remove the transaxle (Chapter 7A).
2   If the clutch is to be reinstalled, mark the pressure plate-to-flywheel relationship so that it can be installed in the same position.
3   Loosen the clutch pressure plate retaining bolts evenly, one turn at a time, in a criss-cross pattern so as not to warp the cover.
4   Remove the pressure plate and clutch disc assemblies.
5   Handle the disc carefully, taking care not to touch the lining surface, and set it aside.

Inspection

6   Inspect the clutch release bearing for damage or wear (Section 7).
7   Clean the dust out of the clutch housing, using a vacuum cleaner or clean cloth. Do not use compressed air as the dust can endanger your health if inhaled.
8   Inspect the friction surfaces of the clutch disc and flywheel for signs of uneven contact, indicating improper mounting or damaged clutch springs. Also check the surfaces for burned areas, grooves, cracks or other signs of wear. It may be necessary to remove a badly grooved flywheel and have it machined to restore the surface. Light glazing of the flywheel surface can be removed with fine sandpaper. Inspect the clutch lining for contamination by oil, grease or any other substance and replace the disc with a new one if contamination is present. Slide the disc onto the input shaft temporarily to make sure the fit is snug and the splines are not burred or worn.

Installation

9   Place the clutch disc in position on the flywheel, centering it with

6.11 Clutch retaining bolts (arrows)

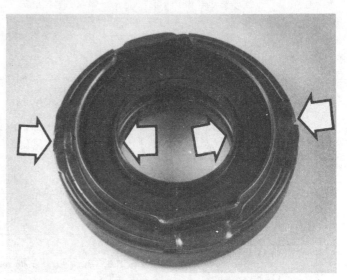

7.3 Inspect the inner and outer contact surfaces of the clutch release bearing for damage at the areas shown (arrows)

7.4A A brush makes it easier to lubricate the clutch fork ends

7.4B After packing it with grease, lubricate the inner contact surface of the clutch release bearing

an alignment tool. The disc spring offset and the stamped 'Flywheel Side' letters must face the flywheel.

10 With the clutch disc held in place by the alignment tool, place the pressure plate assembly in position and align it with any marks made prior to removal.

11 Install the bolts and tighten them in a criss-cross pattern, one or two turns at a time, until they are tightened to the specified torque (photo).

12 Install the clutch release bearing (Section 7).

13 Remove the alignment tool and install the transaxle.

7 Clutch release bearing — removal and installation

Removal

1 Remove the transaxle (Chapter 7A).

2 Remove the clutch release bearing from the clutch fork.

3 Hold the center of the bearing and spin the outer portion. If the bearing doesn't turn smoothly or if it is noisy, replace it with a new one. Wipe the bearing with a clean rag and inspect it for damage, wear or cracks (photo).

Installation

4 Lubricate the clutch fork ends where they contact the bearing lightly with white lithium-base grease. Pack the inner diameter of the bearing with this grease also, as shown in the accompanying illustration and photos.

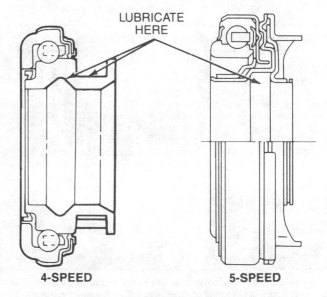

LUBRICATE HERE

4-SPEED   5-SPEED

Fig. 8.4 Clutch release bearing lubrication (Sec 7)

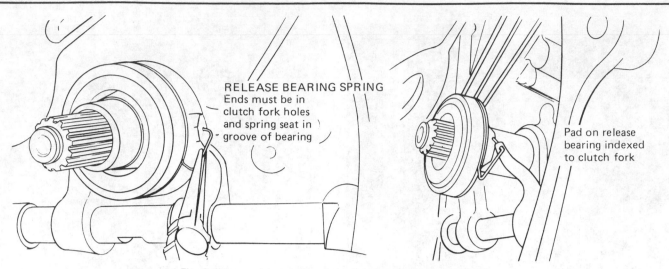

RELEASE BEARING SPRING
Ends must be in
clutch fork holes
and spring seat in
groove of bearing

Pad on release
bearing indexed
to clutch fork

Fig. 8.5 5-speed transaxle release bearing installation (Sec 7)

5   Install the release bearing on the transaxle retainer so that both of the fork tangs fit into the outer diameter of the bearing groove. On 5-speed transaxles, make sure the bearing pads are securely located in the fork ends with the pads indexed and the spring ends seated in the bearing groove as shown in the accompanying illustration.
6   Install the transaxle, making sure that the clutch lever does not move toward the flywheel until the transaxle is bolted to the engine.
7   Check the clutch operation, adjust the clutch cable and depress the pedal slowly several times to mesh the pawl with the detent teeth.

8   Driveaxles — general information

Power is transmitted from the transaxle to the front wheels by two driveaxles, which consist of splined solid axles with constant velocity (CV) joints at each end. The CV joints are protected by rubber boots.
The boots should be inspected periodically (Chapter 1) for damage, leaking lubricant or cuts. The inner boots have very small breather holes, which may leak a small amount of lubricant under some circumstances, such as when the joint is compressed during removal. This is normal.
Damaged CV joint boots must be replaced immediately or the joints can be damaged. The outer boots can be replaced with the driveaxles in the vehicle using an aftermarket boot kit featuring split boots (Section 11).
The most common symptom of worn or damaged CV joints besides lubricant leakage is a clicking noise in turns, a 'clunk' when accelerating from a coasting condition or vibration at highway speeds.

9   Driveaxles — removal and installation

Removal
1   Remove the driveaxle hub nut.
2   Raise the front of the vehicle, support it securely on jackstands and remove the front wheel.
3   Remove the brake caliper and disc and support the caliper out of the way with a piece of wire (Chapter 9).
4   Remove the bolts attaching the steering knuckle to the strut.
5   Disconnect the knuckle assembly from the strut bracket.
6   Carefully pry the inner end of the axle from the transaxle, using a suitable pry bar and tapping with a hammer (photo).
7   Disengage the driveaxle from the hub by using a suitable puller tool (photo).
8   Support the Constant Velocity (CV) joints and remove the driveaxle from the vehicle.

Installation
9   Raise the driveaxle into position while supporting the CV joints and insert the splined ends into the hub and transaxle. Place the steering knuckle in position in the strut bracket and install the bolts (Chapter 11).
10 Install the brake disc and caliper.
11 Install the hub nut.
12 Lock the disc so that it cannot turn, using a screwdriver or punch inserted through the caliper into a disc cooling vane, and tighten the hub nut (Chapter 11).

9.6   After inserting the pry bar, tap on the bar with a hammer at the point shown (arrow) to disengage the driveaxle from the transaxle

9.7   Removing the hub with a puller

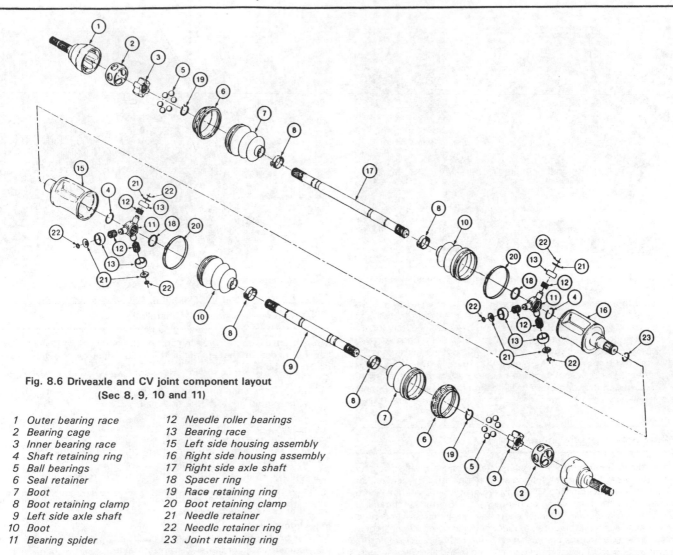

**Fig. 8.6 Driveaxle and CV joint component layout
(Sec 8, 9, 10 and 11)**

1	Outer bearing race	12	Needle roller bearings
2	Bearing cage	13	Bearing race
3	Inner bearing race	15	Left side housing assembly
4	Shaft retaining ring	16	Right side housing assembly
5	Ball bearings	17	Right side axle shaft
6	Seal retainer	18	Spacer ring
7	Boot	19	Race retaining ring
8	Boot retaining clamp	20	Boot retaining clamp
9	Left side axle shaft	21	Needle retainer
10	Boot	22	Needle retainer ring
11	Bearing spider	23	Joint retaining ring

13 Seat the driveaxle into the transaxle by inserting a screwdriver into the groove in the CV joint and tapping it into position with a hammer (photo).
14 Grasp the CV housing (not the driveaxle) and pull outwards to make sure that the axle has seated securely in the transaxle.
15 Install the wheel and lower the vehicle.

10 Driveaxle boot — replacement (driveaxle removed)

1 Remove the driveaxle (Section 9)
2 Place the driveaxle in a vise.
Outer boot
3 Carefully remove the seal retainer by driving it off the hub with

8

9.13 Insert a screwdriver as shown and tap on the end with a hammer to install the driveaxle into the transaxle

10.3 Use a hammer and punch to disengage the seal retainer, working completely around the outer circumference

10.4   Cutting the boot retainer band

10.5   After removing the snap-ring, the joint assembly can be removed

10.12   Tap the boot retainer evenly into place with a hammer and punch

a punch and a hammer, working around the outer circumference. Take care not to deform the retainer as this would destroy its ability to seal properly (photo).

4   Cut off the band retaining the boot to the shaft (photo).
5   Remove the snap-ring and slide the joint assembly off (photo).
6   Slide the old boot off the driveaxle.
7   Clean the old grease from the joint.
8   Repack the CV joint with half the grease supplied with the new boot and put the remaining half in the boot.
9   Slide the retainer and boot into position on the driveaxle.
10   Install the joint and snap-ring.
11   Seat the inner end of the boot in the seal groove and install the retaining clamp.
12   Install the seal retainer securely in place by tapping evenly around the outer circumference with a hammer and punch (photo).

Inner boot
13   Cut off the boot seal retaining clamps.
14   Remove the joint housing from the axle.
15   Use tape or a cloth wrapped around the spider bearing assembly

10.21   The spider bearing recess (arrow) must face away from the inner end of the driveaxle as shown

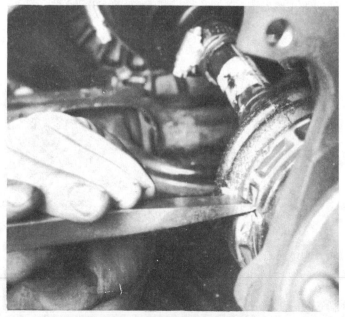

11.4   Cut off the old boot retainer with a chisel

11.8A   On split-type aftermarket boots, it is very important to apply the adhesive fluid evenly (A) and to make sure the boot mounting surface (B) is clean and free of grease

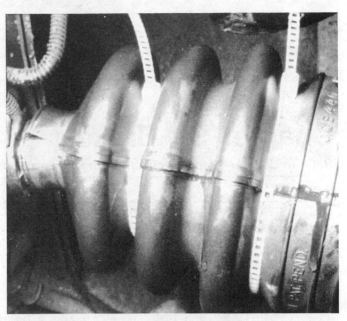

11.8B   Plastic tie straps can be used to hold the boot in place while the adhesive fluid 'welds' the boot together

to retain the bearings during removal and installation.
16   Remove the assembly from the axle.
17   Slide the boot off the axle.
18   Clean old grease from the housing and spider assembly.
19   Pack the housing with half the grease furnished with the new boot and place the remainder in the boot.
20   Slide the boot onto the axle.
21   Install the spider bearing with the recess in the counterbore facing away from the inner end of the driveaxle (photo).
22   Install the housing.
23   Seat the boot in the housing and axle seal grooves and install the retaining clamps.

11   Outer driveaxle boot — replacement (driveaxle installed)

1   The outer boot can be replaced with the axle installed, using an aftermarket boot replacement kit. These boots are split so they can be installed with the driveaxle in place.
2   Raise the vehicle, support it securely on jackstands and remove the front wheel. Raise the suspension arm with a jack so that the axle shaft is level, to ease installation of the replacement boot.
3   Remove the brake caliper and rotor and wire the caliper out of the way.
4   Using a suitable punch and a hammer, drive the boot retainer off the joint housing (photo).
5   Remove the remaining boot retaining strap.
6   Cut the old boot and remove it.
7   Inspect the CV joint to determine if the damaged boot has allowed the grease to become contaminated with dirt or water. If it has, wipe out the old grease and apply new grease from the replacement boot kit, working it in with your fingers. **Note:** *The following steps describe a typical installation. Follow the specific instructions included with the replacement boot kit.*
8   Place the new boot in position over the axle. Typically these kits use a special fluid which, when applied to the sealing grooves, 'welds' the boot into one piece. The retaining straps are installed to hold it in place until the sealant has set (photos).
9   Install the boot in the sealing grooves on the driveaxle shaft and joint and securely install the retaining straps, following the kit instructions.

8

Chapter 9 Brakes

Refer to Chapter 13 for specifications and information related to 1985 and later models

Contents

Specifications

Disc brakes

Rotor thickness after resurfacing (minimum)	0.830 in
Discard thickness	0.815 in
Disc runout (maximum)	0.005 in
Disc thickness variation (maximum)	0.0005 in
Caliper piston bore	2.244 in

Rear drum brakes

Drum diameter	
standard	7.88 in
service limit	7.90 in
discard diameter	7.93 in
Drum taper (maximum)	0.003 in
Out-of-round (maximum)	0.002 in

Torque specifications

	Ft-lbs
Brake pedal-to-bracket	25
Brake booster-to-pedal bracket	20
Brake booster-to-firewall	22 to 33
Caliper mounting bolts	21 to 25
Caliper fluid inlet fitting	18 to 30
Caliper bleeder screw	9 to 16
Failure switch-to-master cylinder	2 to 4
Master cylinder-to-booster	16
Master cylinder tube nuts	11 to 14
Proportioner valve-to-master cylinder	18 to 30
Parking brake lever-to-body	13
Parking brake front cable nut	24
Switch piston-to-master cylinder	2 to 4
Wheel cylinder bleeder screw	3 to 6
Wheel cylinder inlet tube nut	11 to 14
Wheel lug nuts	100

1 General information

All vehicles covered by this manual are equipped with hydraulically operated front and rear brake systems. All front brake systems are disc type, while the rear brakes are drum type.

All brakes are self-adjusting. The front disc brakes automatically compensate for pad wear, while the rear drum brakes incorporate a mechanism which automatically adjusts the brakes whenever they are applied with the vehicle is moving backwards.

The hydraulic system consists of separate front and rear circuits. The master cylinder has separate reservoirs for the two circuits, and in the event of a leak or failure in one hydraulic circuit, the other circuit will remain operative. A visual warning of circuit failure, air in the system, or other pressure differential conditions in the brake system is given by a warning light. The light is activated by a failure warning switch in the master cylinder.

The parking brake mechanically operates the rear brakes only. It is activated by a pull-handle in the center console between the front seats.

The power brake booster, located in the engine compartment on the

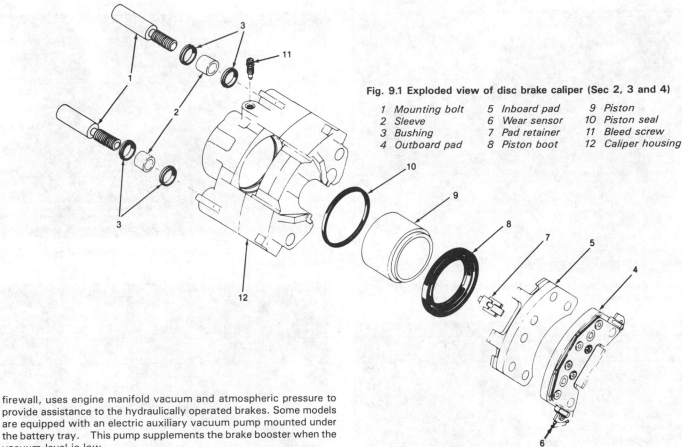

Fig. 9.1 Exploded view of disc brake caliper (Sec 2, 3 and 4)

1	Mounting bolt	5 Inboard pad	9 Piston
2	Sleeve	6 Wear sensor	10 Piston seal
3	Bushing	7 Pad retainer	11 Bleed screw
4	Outboard pad	8 Piston boot	12 Caliper housing

firewall, uses engine manifold vacuum and atmospheric pressure to provide assistance to the hydraulically operated brakes. Some models are equipped with an electric auxiliary vacuum pump mounted under the battery tray. This pump supplements the brake booster when the vacuum level is low.

After completing any operation involving the disassembly of any part of the brake system, always test drive the vehicle to check for proper braking performance before resuming normal driving. Test the brakes while driving on a clean, dry, flat surface. Conditions other than these can lead to inaccurate test results. Test the brakes at various speeds with both light and heavy pedal pressure. The vehicle should stop evenly without pulling to one side or the other. Avoid locking the brakes since this slides the tires and diminishes braking efficiency and control.

Tires, vehicle load and front end alignment are factors which also affect braking performance.

Torque values given in the Specifications section are for dry, unlubricated fasteners.

2   Disc brake pads — replacement

Note: *Disc brake pads should be replaced on both wheels at the same time.*

1   Whenever you are working on the brake system, be aware that asbestos dust is present and be careful not to inhale any of it as this could be harmful to your health.
2   Remove the brake caliper as described in Section 3.
3   Refer to the accompanying photographs and perform the procedure illustrated. Start with photograph 2.3/1.

2.3/1   Remove the inner pad by snapping it out of the piston in the direction shown (arrow)

2.3/2   Remove the outboard pad by bending the tabs (arrow) straight out with channel-lock pliers

2.3/3 Snap the inner pad retainer spring into the new pad in the direction shown (arrow)

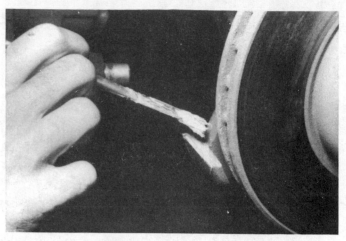

2.3/4 Lubricate the lower steering knuckle contact surface lightly with white lithium-base grease

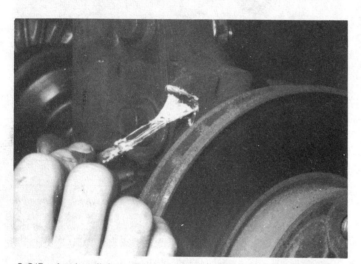

2.3/5 Apply a light coat of white lithium-base grease to the upper steering knuckle-to-caliper contact surface

2.3/6 Place the pads in position and snap the inner pad into place in the piston (arrow)

2.3/7 After installing the caliper, insert a large screwdriver between the outer pad flange and the disc hat to seat the pad, then bend the tabs over using a hammer

3 Disc brake caliper — removal and installation

Removal

1 Remove the cover from the brake fluid reservoir and siphon off two-thirds of the fluid into a container and discard it.
2 Raise the front of the vehicle, support it securely on jackstands and remove the front wheel(s).
3 Reinstall two lug nuts (flat side against the disc) to hold the disc rotor in place.
4 Bottom the piston in the caliper bore. This is accomplished by pushing on the caliper, although it may be necessary to carefully use a C-clamp or a flat pry bar (photo).
5 If the caliper is to be removed from the vehicle, remove the brake line hose inlet fitting bolt and disconnect the fitting.
6 Remove the two mounting bolts and lift the caliper from the vehicle. If the caliper is not to be removed from the vehicle, hang it out of the way with a piece of wire so the brake hose will not be damaged.

Installation

7 Inspect the mounting bolts and bushings and caliper contact surfaces for damage or excessive corrosion, replacing any unserviceable components with new ones (photo). Lubricate new bushings with silicone grease before installation.

3.4A Compress the caliper piston with a large C-clamp

3.4B A large screwdriver or similar tool can also be used to compress the caliper piston

3.7 Inspect the caliper bolts and bushings (A) for damage and the contact surfaces (B) for excessive corrosion

3.8 Carefully peel back the edge of the piston boot and check for corrosion and leaking fluid

8 Check the piston seal for damage or leaking fluid (photo).
9 Place the caliper in position over the rotor and mounting bracket, install the bolts and tighten to the specified torque.
10 Check to make sure the clearance between the caliper and the bracket stops at the points shown in the accompanying illustration is between 0.005 and 0.012 in.
11 Connect the inlet fitting (if removed) and install the retaining bolt. It will be necessary to bleed the brakes if the fitting was disconnected (Section 12).
12 Install the wheel(s) and lower the vehicle.

4 Disc brake caliper — overhaul

1 Purchase a caliper overhaul kit, which will contain all of the necessary replacement parts for this procedure.
2 Disconnect the caliper from the caliper bracket and remove the pads from the caliper as described in Sections 2 and 3. In this operation, the inlet brake line should be removed from the caliper.
3 Use clean rags to pad the inside of the caliper. If you have access to compressed air, place an air nozzle in the caliper inlet hole and slowly apply air pressure until the piston is forced out of the bore (photo).
Caution: *Do not use your fingers to try to catch the piston as serious injury could result.* If you do not have access to compressed air, hold the caliper with the inlet hole up and carefully bang the caliper down

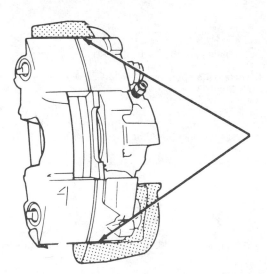

Fig. 9.2 Measure the clearance between the caliper and bracket stops at the points indicated (Sec 3)

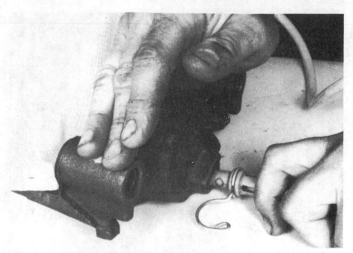

4.3   With the caliper padded to catch the piston, use compressed air to force the piston out of its bore. Make sure your hands or fingers are not between the piston and caliper

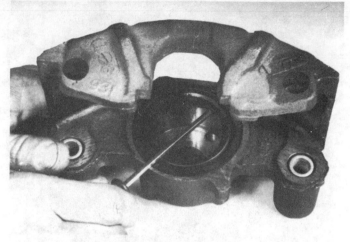

4.5   Carefully pry the dust boot out of the housing, taking care not to scratch the bore surface

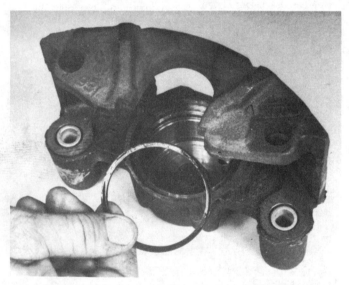

4.6   The piston seal, removed from the caliper bore

4.8   Remove the bleeder screw from the caliper housing

on a block of wood to force the piston out. As a last resort, temporarily reinstall the brake line on the caliper and have an assistant gently depress the brake pedal. The fluid pressure will force the piston out of the caliper.

4   Inspect the piston for scoring, nicks, corrosion and worn or damaged chrome plating. Replace if necessary.

5   Remove the dust boot by prying it out with a screwdriver. Be careful not to scratch the housing (photo).

6   Remove the piston seal from the groove with a wood or plastic dowel. Do not use a metal tool here, as it could damage the bore (photo).

7   Inspect the caliper bore for nicks, scoring, corrosion or wear. Light corrosion can be removed with crocus cloth. If crocus cloth will not clean up the bore the caliper housing must be replaced.

8   Remove the bleeder screw (photo).

9   Clean the piston, housing bore and bleeder screw with denatured alcohol. Do not use gasoline or mineral-based solvent.

10 Lubricate the bore and the new piston seal with clean brake fluid and install the seal in its groove. Be sure the seal is not twisted.

11 Install the new dust boot into the groove of the piston as shown in the accompanying illustration.

12 Insert the piston into the bore and press it down, working it through the seal until it bottoms.

13 Seat the new dust boot in the caliper bore (photo).

14 Install the bleeder screw.

15 Apply multi-purpose lithium grease to all surfaces where the caliper assembly meets the caliper bracket.

16 Complete the operation by following the procedures described in Sections 2 and 3.

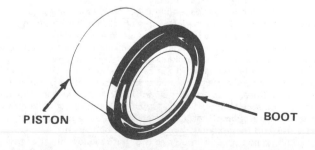

Fig. 9.3   Proper installation of the dust boot on the disc brake piston (Sec 4)

4.13   Seat the new dust boot squarely in the caliper bore

5.6   Check the disc pad surface runout with a dial indicator

5.7   Use a micrometer to check the disc brake rotor thickness

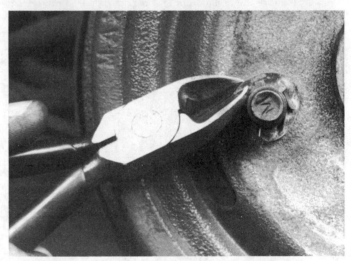

6.5/1   Remove and discard the brake drum retaining clip

5   Disc brake rotor — inspection, removal and installation

1   Raise the front of the vehicle and support it securely on jack-stands.
2   Remove the appropriate wheel.
3   Reinstall two wheel lugs (flat side against the rotor) to hold the rotor in place during inspection.
4   Remove the caliper assembly (Section 3) and hang it out of the way on a piece of wire to avoid damage to the brake hose.
5   Inspect the rotor surfaces. Light scoring or grooving is normal, but deep grooves or severe erosion is not. If pulsating has been noticed during application of the brakes, suspect disc runout.
6   Attach a dial indicator to the caliper mounting bracket, turn the rotor and note the amount of runout. Check both inboard and outboard surfaces (photo). If the runout is more than the maximum allowable, the rotor must be removed from the vehicle and taken to an automotive shop for resurfacing. Runout can sometimes be reduced by removing the rotor and reindexing it by one or two bolt holes.
7   Using a micrometer, measure the thickness of the rotor (photo). If it is less than the minimum specified, replace the rotor with a new one. Also measure the rotor thickness at several points to determine variations in the surface. Any variation over 0.0005-inch may cause pedal pulsations during brake application. If this condition exists and

the disc thickness is not below the minimum, the rotor can be removed and taken to an automotive machine shop for resurfacing.
8   The rotor is removed by simply lifting it off the wheel studs.

6   Drum brake shoes — inspection and replacement

1   Whenever working on the brake system, be aware that asbestos dust is present. It has been proven to be harmful to your health, so be careful not to inhale it.
2   Raise the vehicle and support it securely on jackstands.
3   Release the parking brake handle.
4   Remove the wheel. **Note:** *All four rear shoes should be replaced at the same time, but to avoid mixing up parts, work on only one brake assembly at a time.*
5   Refer to the accompanying photographs and perform the brake shoe inspection and, if necessary, the replacement procedure. Start with photo 6.5/1. If the brake drum cannot be easily pulled off the axle and shoe assembly, make sure that the parking brake is completely released, then squirt some penetrating oil around the center hub area. Allow the oil to soak in and try to pull the drum off. If the drum still cannot be pulled off, the brake shoes will have to be retracted. This is accomplished by first removing the lanced cutout in the brake drum

9

6.5/2 Remove the brake drum (if it cannot be pulled off, refer to text)

6.5/3 Remove the return springs using brake spring pliers

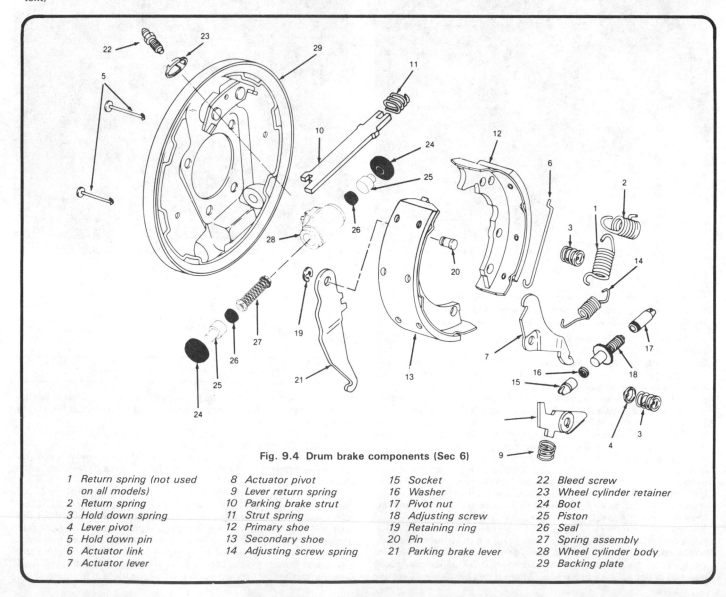

Fig. 9.4 Drum brake components (Sec 6)

1 Return spring (not used on all models)	8 Actuator pivot	15 Socket	22 Bleed screw
2 Return spring	9 Lever return spring	16 Washer	23 Wheel cylinder retainer
3 Hold down spring	10 Parking brake strut	17 Pivot nut	24 Boot
4 Lever pivot	11 Strut spring	18 Adjusting screw	25 Piston
5 Hold down pin	12 Primary shoe	19 Retaining ring	26 Seal
6 Actuator link	13 Secondary shoe	20 Pin	27 Spring assembly
7 Actuator lever	14 Adjusting screw spring	21 Parking brake lever	28 Wheel cylinder body
			29 Backing plate

6.5/4 Remove the hold down springs and pins by pushing in with pliers and turning (arrows)

6.5/5 Lift up on the actuator lever and remove the actuating link from the anchor pin pivot (arrow)

6.5/6 Remove the actuator lever, pivot and return spring

6.5/7 Spread the shoes apart and remove the parking brake strut

6.5/8 With the shoe assembly spread to clear the hub flange, lift it from the backing plate

6.5/9 Disconnect the parking brake lever from the cable in the direction shown (arrow) and remove the shoe assembly from the vehicle

9

6.5/10   Remove the adjusting screw (A) and spring (B) from the shoe assembly, making sure to note the direction in which they are installed

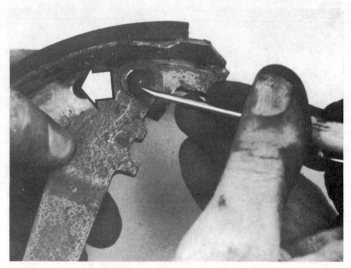

6.5/11   Remove the parking brake lever by prying the C-clip off in the direction shown (arrow)

6.5/12   Lubricate the contact surfaces of the backing plate with white lithium-base grease

6.5/13   Lubricate the adjuster screw with white lithium-base grease prior to installation

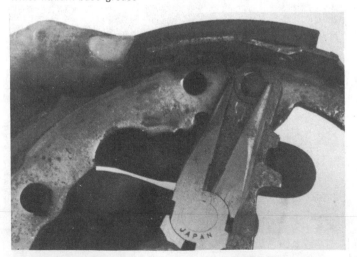

6.5/14   Install the parking brake lever on the new brake shoe by pressing the C-clip into place with needle-nose pliers

6.5/15   Connect the parking brake lever to the cable

6.5/16   Spread the brake assembly apart sufficiently to clear the hub flange and raise it into position

6.5/17   Install the parking brake strut

6.5/18   Make sure the parking brake strut is positioned in the shoes properly (arrows)

6.5/19   Install the actuator pivot, lever and return spring

6.5/20   Install the actuating link (A) to the actuator lever (B) and install the hold down spring assemblies (C)

6.5/21   Install the return springs

9

6.5/22 Center the brake shoe assembly so the drum will slide over it

6.5/23 If the drum will not fit over the shoes, back the adjuster off by turning the star wheel

6.5/24 The drum has a maximum permissible diameter cast into it which must not be exceeded when removing scoring or other imperfections in the friction surface

7.4 Plugging the brake line using a piece of hose with a bolt screwed into the end

7.5 Method of removing the retaining clip using two awls (cylinder has been removed from the vehicle for illustration purposes)

7.12 A suitable size wood block will hold the wheel cylinder in position during installation

with a hammer and chisel. With the cutout removed, pull the lever off the adjusting screw wheel with one small screwdriver while turning the adjusting wheel with another small screwdriver, moving the shoes away from the drum. The drum may now be pulled off.

6   Before reinstalling the drum it should be checked for cracks, score marks, deep scratches or hard spots, which will appear as small discolored areas. If the hard spots cannot be removed with a fine emery cloth and/or if any of the other conditions listed above exist, the drum must be taken to an automotive machine shop to have it turned. If the drum will not 'clean up' before the maximum drum diameter is reached in the machining operation, the drum will have to be replaced with a new one. **Note:** *The maximum diameter is cast into the each brake drum.*

7   Install the brake drum. It will not be necessary to install a wheel stud lock washer.

8   Mount the wheel, install the wheel lugs and tighten to the specified torque, then lower the vehicle.

9   Make a number of forward and reverse stops to adjust the brakes until a satisfactory pedal action is obtained.

---

7   Drum brake wheel cylinder — removal, overhaul and installation

Removal

1   Raise the rear of the vehicle and support it securely on jackstands.
2   Remove the brake shoe assembly (Section 6).
3   Carefully clean all dirt and foreign material from around the wheel cylinder.
4   Disconnect and plug the brake fluid inlet tube.
4   Remove the wheel cylinder retainer by using a screwdriver to release the clips (photo).
5   Remove the wheel cylinder from the brake backing plate and place it on a clean workbench.
6   Remove the bleeder valve, seals, pistons, boots and spring assembly from the cylinder body.
7   Clean the wheel cylinder with brake fluid, denatured alcohol or brake system cleaner. Do not, under any circumstances, use petroleum-based solvents to clean brake parts.
8   Use compressed air to remove excess fluid from the wheel cylinder and to blow out the passages.
9   Check the cylinder bore for corrosion or scoring. Crocus cloth may be used to remove light corrosion and stains, but the cylinder must be replaced with a new one if the defects cannot be removed easily, or if the bore is scored.
10   Lubricate the new seals with brake fluid.
11   Assemble the brake cylinder, making sure the boots are properly seated.

Installation

12   Place the wheel cylinder in position and use a wooden block wedged against the axle flange to hold it in place (photo).
13   Install the retainer over the wheel cylinder using a 1-1/8 inch 12 point socket to press it into place.
14   Connect the brake tube and install brake shoe assembly.

---

8   Master cylinder — removal, overhaul and installation

1   A master cylinder overhaul kit should be purchased before beginning this procedure. The kit will include all the replacement parts necessary for the overhaul procedure. The rubber replacement parts, particularly the seals, are the key to fluid control within the master cylinder. Therefore it is very important that they be installed securely and facing in the proper direction. Be careful during the rebuild procedure that no grease or mineral-based solvents come in contact with the rubber parts.

2   Completely cover the front fender and cowling area of the vehicle, as brake fluid can ruin painted surfaces if it is spilled.

3   Disconnect the electrical lead from the brake failure warning switch (photo).

4   Disconnect the brake line fittings (photo). Rags or newspapers should be placed under the master cylinder to soak up the fluid that will drain out.

8.3   Disconnect the brake warning switch electrical lead

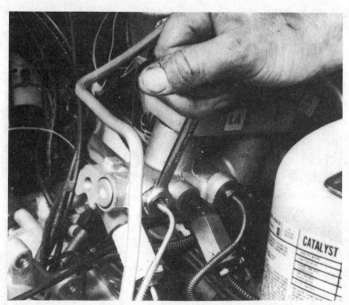

8.4   Disconnect the brake line connections from the master cylinder

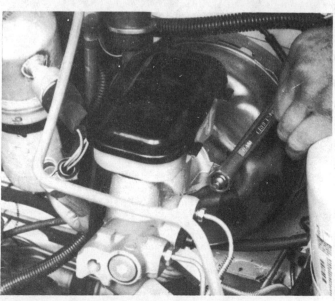

8.6   Remove the master cylinder mounting nuts

9

5   On vehicles with manual (non-power assisted) brakes the master cylinder pushrod must be disconnected from the pedal inside the vehicle.

6   Remove the two master cylinder mounting nuts (photo).

7   Remove the master cylinder from the vehicle and drain any remaining fluid from it.

8   Remove the brake failure warning switch (photo).

9   Remove the two proportioner valves (photo). Make a note of their respective positions in the master cylinder body, as the two valves are different.

10 At this point it would be advantageous for further disassembly to place the master cylinder in a vise. Two blocks of wood (photo) should be used to hold the cylinder. Remember that the body is made of aluminum and should not be overstressed.

11 With an Allen wrench remove the switch piston plug (photo).

12 Remove the switch piston assembly (photo). Slight tapping of the cylinder on a block of wood may be necessary to dislodge the switch piston assembly from the bore.

13 Remove the primary piston retaining ring by depressing the piston and prying out the retaining ring (photo).

14 Remove the primary piston assembly (photo).

15 Remove the secondary piston assembly (photo).

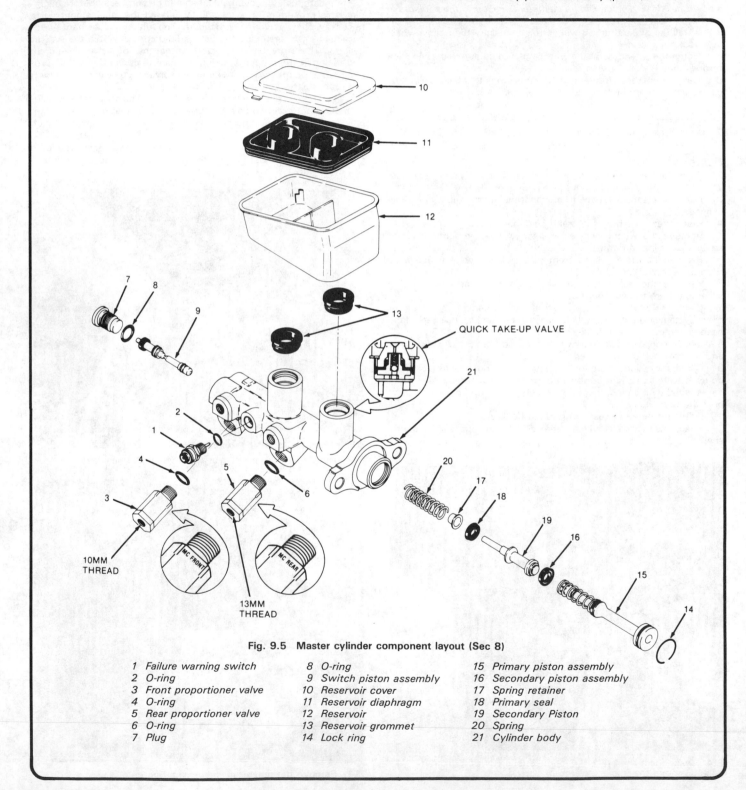

Fig. 9.5 Master cylinder component layout (Sec 8)

1 Failure warning switch	8 O-ring	15 Primary piston assembly
2 O-ring	9 Switch piston assembly	16 Secondary piston assembly
3 Front proportioner valve	10 Reservoir cover	17 Spring retainer
4 O-ring	11 Reservoir diaphragm	18 Primary seal
5 Rear proportioner valve	12 Reservoir	19 Secondary Piston
6 O-ring	13 Reservoir grommet	20 Spring
7 Plug	14 Lock ring	21 Cylinder body

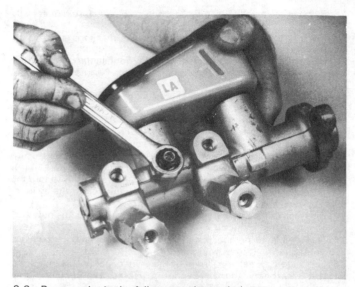

8.8 Remove the brake failure warning switch

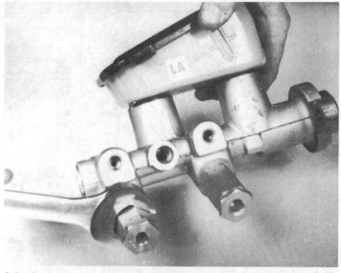

8.9 Remove the proportioner valves

8.11 Remove the switch piston plug

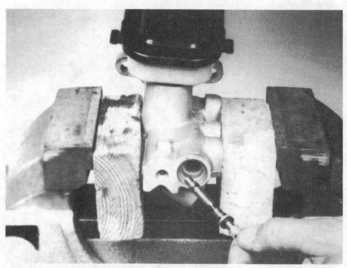

8.12 Remove the switch piston assembly

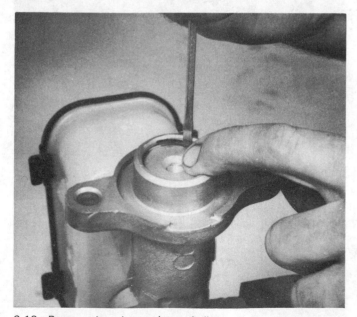

8.13 Remove the primary piston circlip

8.14 Remove the primary piston assembly

9

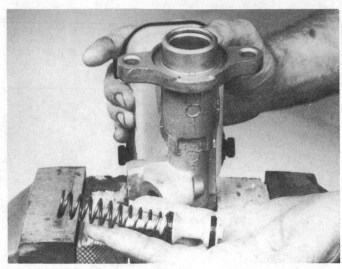

8.15   Remove the secondary piston assembly

16   Remove the plastic reservoir by prying it out of the cylinder body (photo).
17   Remove the quick take-up valve retaining ring (photo).
18   Remove the quick take-up valve.
19   Clean all parts in denatured alcohol. Do not use gasoline or other petroleum-based solvents, as these contain contaminents which soften and ruin the rubber seals.
20   Inspect the cylinder bore for scoring, excessive roughness, nicks or corrosion. Slight corrosion or scratches can be taken out with crocus cloth, but always rinse the bore with clean brake fluid before attempting this. Never use crocus cloth on a dry bore. If the imperfections cannot be eliminated with crocus cloth, the cylinder should be replaced.
21   Remove the old seals from the secondary piston assembly and install the new seals so the cups face in the directions shown (photo).
22   Lubricate the bore with clean brake fluid and insert the spring, the spring retainer and the secondary piston assembly into the cylinder bore (photo).
23   Disassemble the primary piston assembly and install the new seal so the cup faces in the direction shown (photo).
24   Reassemble the primary piston assembly by following the sequence shown in photos 8.24a through 8.24e.
25   Lubricate the seal and O-ring of the primary piston assembly and insert it into the cylinder bore (photo). Depress the primary piston assembly and install the primary piston retaining ring.

8.16   Pry the plastic reservoir from the cylinder body

8.18   The quick take-up valve and retaining ring

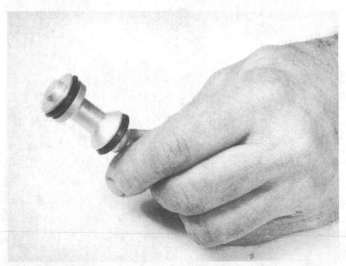

8.21   The secondary piston seals must be installed with the lips facing outwards, as shown

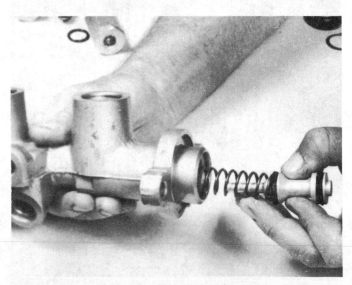

8.22   Install the secondary piston assembly

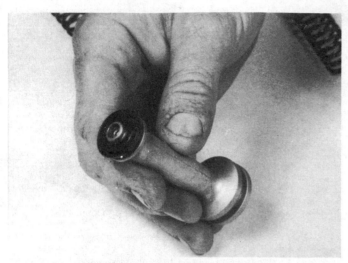

8.23 The primary piston seal must be installed with the lip facing away from the piston

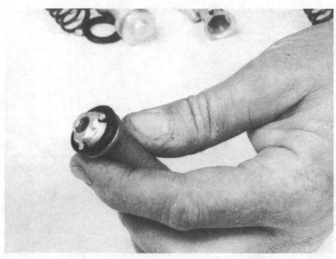

8.24a Install the seal guard over the seal

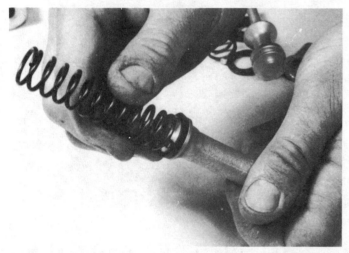

8.24b Place the primary piston spring into position

8.24c Insert the spring retainer into the spring

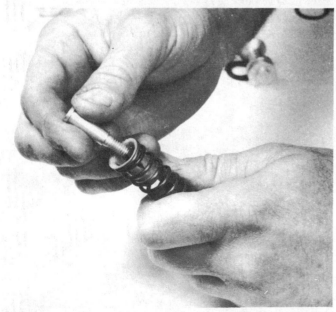

8.24d Insert the spring retaining bolt through the retainer and spring and thread it into the piston

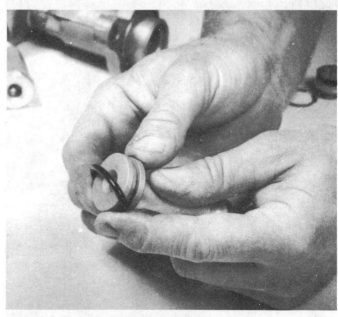

8.24e Install the O-ring on the piston

9

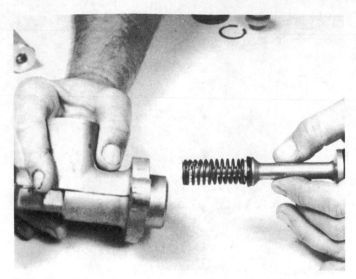

8.25   Install the primary piston assembly into the body

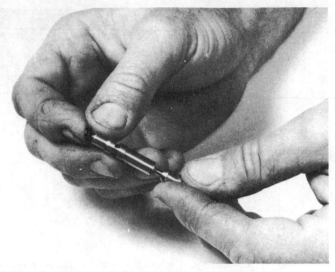

8.26a   Install the small O-ring on the switch piston

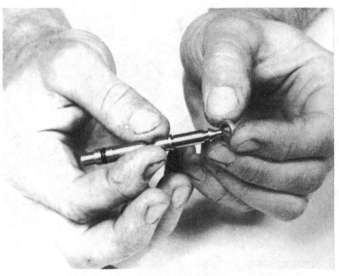

8.26b   Install the metal retainer on the switch piston

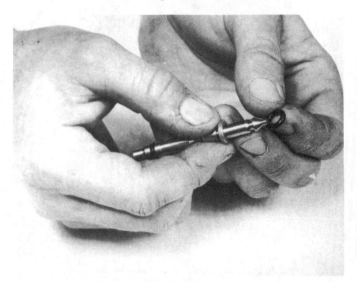

8.26c   Install the large O-ring on the switch piston

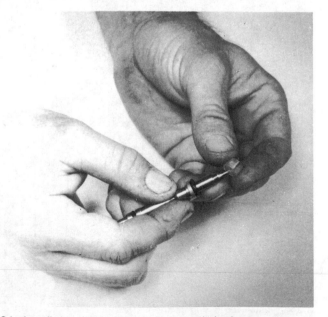

8.26d   Install the plastic retainer on the switch piston

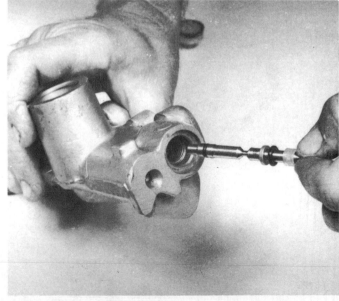

8.27   Install the switch piston assembly in the cylinder body

26 Disassemble the switch piston assembly and install new O-rings and retainers as shown in photos 8.26a through 8.26d.

27 Install the switch piston assembly into the cylinder as shown in photo 8.27.

28 Install a new O-ring on the switch piston plug, thread it into the cylinder and tighten it to the specified torque (photo).

29 Install new O-rings on the proportioner valves and insert them into the cylinder, tightening them to the specified torque (photo).

30 Install a new O-ring on the failure warning switch and install it in the cylinder, tightening it to the specified torque (photo).

31 Insert the quick take-up valve into the cylinder body as shown (photo).

32 Install the quick take-up valve retaining ring into its groove in the cylinder body (photo).

33 Press new reservoir grommets into the cylinder body as shown. Be sure they are seated properly (photo).

34 Place the reservoir top down on a flat, hard surface, as shown, and press the cylinder body onto it, using a rocking motion (photo).

35 Place the cylinder over the mounting studs and install the nuts. Tighten them to the specified torque.

36 On a manual brake system, reconnect the master cylinder pushrod to the brake pedal.

37 Connect the four brake line fittings to the master cylinder.

38 Connect the electrical lead to the failure warning switch.

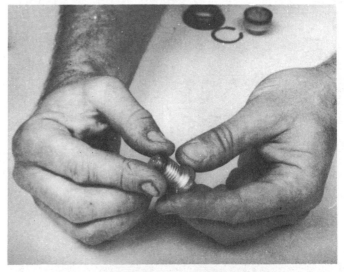

8.28 Install the new O-ring on the switch piston plug

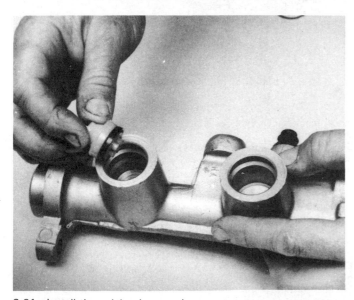

8.29 Install the new O-rings on the proportioner valves

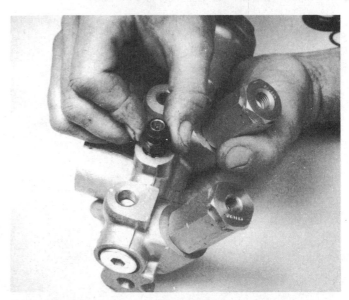

8.30 Install the failure warning switch

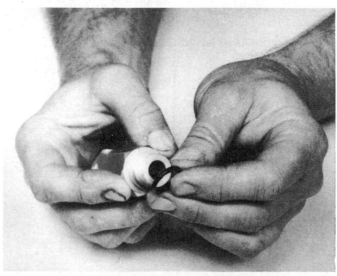

8.31 Install the quick take-up valve

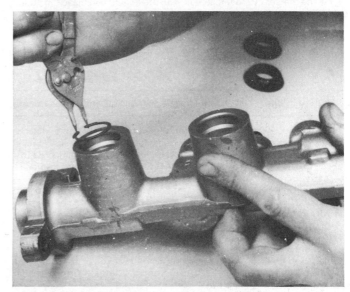

8.32 Install the quick take-up valve retaining ring

9

8.33   Install new reservoir grommets into the body

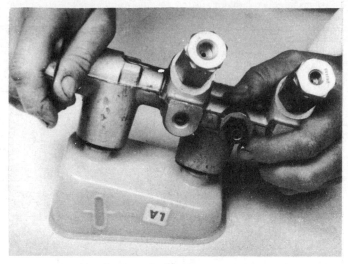

8.34   Press the cylinder body onto the reservoir

8.40   Install the reservoir diaphragm in the cover

39 Fill the master cylinder reservoir with brake fluid and bleed the entire brake system as described in Section 12.
40 Install the reservoir diaphragm in the reservoir cover (photo) and install the cover on the reservoir.
41   Test drive the vehicle and check for proper braking performance and leaks.

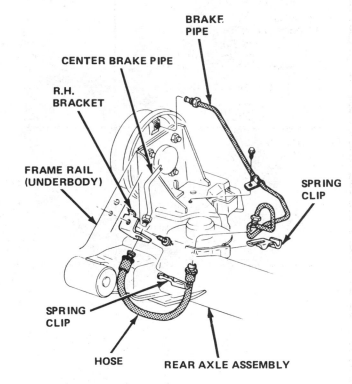

Fig. 9.6   Details of the rear brake hose installation (Sec 9)

9   Hydraulic brake hoses and lines — inspection and replacement

1   About every six months, with the vehicle raised and placed securely on jackstands, the flexible hoses which connect the steel brake lines with the front and rear brake assemblies should be inspected for cracks, chafing of the outer cover, leaks, blisters or other damage. These are important and vulnerable parts of the brake system and inspection should be complete. A light and mirror will prove helpful for a thorough check. If a hose exhibits any of the above conditions, replace it with a new one as follows:

Front brake hose
2   Using a back-up wrench, disconnect the brake line from the hose fitting, being careful not to bend the frame bracket or brake line.
3   Use pliers to remove the U-clip from the female fitting at the bracket, then remove the hose from the bracket.
4   At the caliper end of the hose, remove the bolt from the fitting

block, then remove the hose and the copper gaskets on either side of the fitting block.
5   When installing the hose, always use new copper gaskets on either side of the fitting block and lubricate all bolt threads with clean brake fluid before installing them.
6   With the fitting flange engaged with the caliper locating ledge, attach the hose to the caliper and tighten it to the specified torque.
7   Without twisting the hose, install the female fitting in the hose bracket (it will fit the bracket in only one position).
8   Install the U-clip retaining the female fitting to the frame bracket.
9   Using a back-up wrench, attach the brake line to the hose fitting.
10 When the brake hose installation is complete there should be no kinks in the hose. Also, make sure the hose does not contact any part of the suspension. Check this by turning the wheels to the extreme left and right positions. If the hose makes contact, remove the hose and correct the installation as necessary.

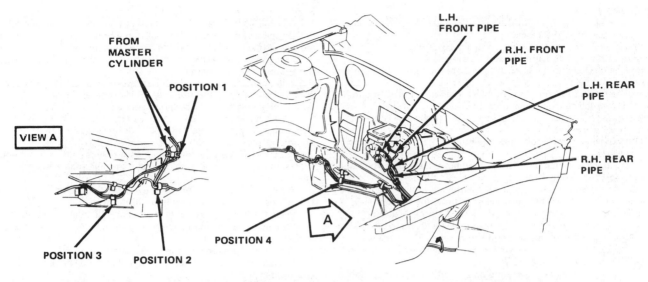

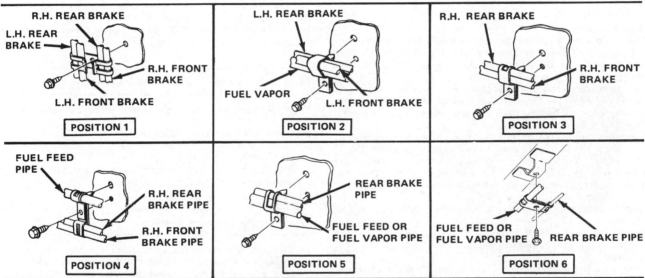

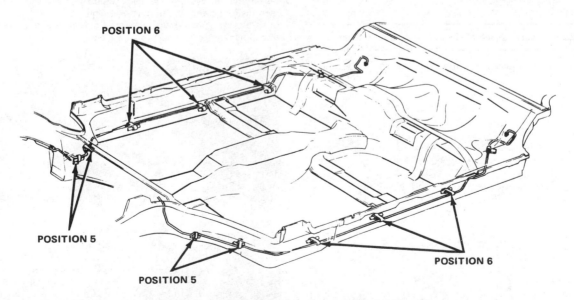

Fig. 9.7 Details of the brake hose and layout (Sec 9)

9

Rear brake hose

11 Locate the junction block at the rear axle and disconnect the two steel brake lines from the block.
12 Using a back-up wrench, remove the hose at the female fitting, being careful not to bend the bracket or steel lines.
13 Remove the U-clip with pliers and separate the female fitting from the bracket.
14 Note the position of the junction block carefully so that it can be reinstalled in precisely the same position.
15 Remove the bolt attaching the junction block to the axle and remove the hose from the block.
16 When installing, thread both steel line fittings into the junction block at the rear axle.
17 Bolt the junction block to the axle, then tighten the block bolt and steel lines to the specified torque.
18 Without twisting the hose, install the female end of the hose in the frame bracket (it will fit the bracket in only one position).
19 Install the U-clip retaining the female end to the bracket.
20 Using a back-up wrench, attach the steel line fitting to the female fitting. Again, be careful not to bend the bracket or steel line.
21 Check that the hose installation did not loosen the frame bracket. Retorque the bracket if necessary.
22 Fill the master cylinder reservoirs and bleed the system (refer to Section 12).

Steel brake lines

23 When it becomes necessary to replace steel lines, use only double wall steel tubing. Never substitute copper tubing because copper is subject to fatigue cracking and corrosion. The outside diameter of the tubing is used for sizing.
24 Auto parts stores and brake supply houses carry various lengths of prefabricated brake line. Depending on the type of tubing used, these sections can either be bent by hand into the desired shape or can be bent in a tubing bender.
25 If prefabricated lengths are not available, obtain the recommended steel tubing and fittings to match the line to be replaced. Determine the correct length by measuring the old brake line, and cut the new tubing to length, leaving about 1/2-inch extra for flaring the ends.
26 Install the fittings onto the cut tubing and flare the ends using an ISO flaring tool.
27 Using a tubing bender, bend the tubing to match the shape of the old brake line.
28 Tube flaring and bending can usually be performed by a local auto parts store if the proper equipment mentioned in Steps 26 and 27 is not available.
29 When installing the brake line, leave at least 3/4-inch clearance between the line and any moving parts.

10 Power brake booster assembly — removal and installation

1 The power brake booster assembly is located in the engine compartment on the driver's side firewall. The brake master cylinder is attached to the front of it.
2 Remove the brake master cylinder as described in Section 8.
3 Disconnect the vacuum hose from the booster assembly by loosening the clamp and removing the hose from the metal nipple.
4 Move to the inside of the vehicle and disconnect the pushrod from the top of the brake pedal.
5 Still inside the vehicle, remove the four nuts which secure the booster assembly to the firewall. These nuts are in a square pattern around the pushrod previously disconnected.
6 Move back to the engine compartment and pull the booster assembly away from the firewall until the studs clear. Remove the assembly from the engine compartment (photo).
7 Because overhauling the booster assembly is a difficult job requiring special tools, it is advisable to purchase a rebuilt assembly as a replacement unit.
8 Apply silicone sealer to the firewall where the booster assembly fits against it. This will provide an air-tight seal.
9 Place the booster assembly in position and push the studs through the firewall. Move to the inside of the vehicle and secure it with the four nuts and washers.
10 Attach the pushrod to the brake pedal.
11 Connect the vacuum hose to the nipple on the shell of the assembly and tighten the clamp.
12 Install the brake master cylinder as described in Section 8.
13 Bleed the brake system as described in Section 12.
14 Check for proper operation of the power brakes with the engine running.

11 Vacuum pump — removal and installation

1 Raise the front of the vehicle and support it securely on jackstands.
2 Remove the left side splash shield.
3 Disconnect the vacuum hoses and electrical connector from the vacuum pump.
4 Remove the retaining nuts and lower the pump from the vehicle.
5 Installation is the reverse of removal.

12 Hydraulic system — bleeding

1 Bleeding the hydraulic system is necessary to remove air whenever it has been introduced into the brake system.
2 It may be necessary to bleed the system at all four brakes if air has entered the system due to low fluid level, or if the brake lines have been disconnected at the master cylinder.
3 If a brake line was disconnected only at a wheel, then only that wheel cylinder (or caliper) must be bled.

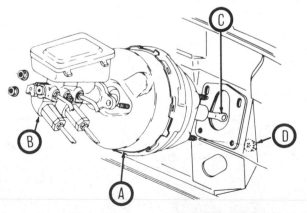

Fig. 9.8 Brake booster installation details (Sec 10)

A Booster   C Pushrod
B Master cylinder   D Retaining nut

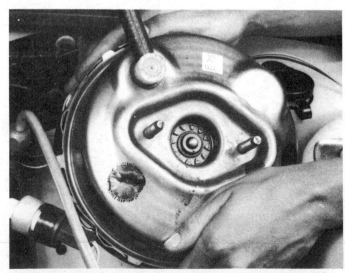

10.6 Remove the power brake booster from the engine compartment

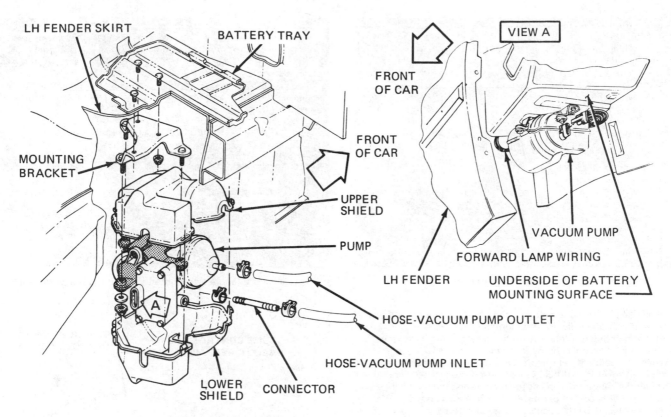

Fig. 9.9 Details of the auxiliary vacuum pump installation (Sec 11)

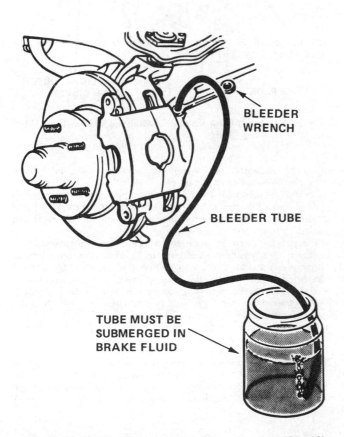

Fig. 9.10 Details of the brake bleeding procedure (Sec 12)

4   If a brake line is disconnected at a fitting located between the master cylinder and any of the brakes, that part of the system served by the disconnected line must be bled.

5   If the master cylinder is known to have, or is suspected of having air in the bore, the master cylinder must be bled before any wheel cylinder (or caliper) is bled. Follow Steps 6 through 15 to bleed the master cylinder while it is installed on the vehicle.

6   Remove the vacuum reserve from the brake power booster by applying the brake several times with the engine off.

7   Remove the master cylinder reservoir cover and fill the reservoirs with brake fluid. Keep checking the fluid level often during the bleeding operation, adding fluid as necessary to keep the reservoirs full. Reinstall the cover.

8   Disconnect the forward brake line connection at the master cylinder.

9   Allow brake fluid to fill the master cylinder bore until it begins to flow from the forward line connector port (have a container and shop rags handy to catch and clean up spilled fluid).

10   Reconnect the forward brake line to the master cylinder.

11   Have an assistant depress the brake pedal very slowly (one time only) and hold it down.

12   Loosen the forward brake line at the master cylinder to purge the air from the bore, retighten the connection, then have the brake pedal released slowly.

13   Wait 15 seconds (important).

14   Repeat the sequence, including the 15 second wait, until all air is removed from the bore.

15   After the forward port has been completely purged of air, bleed the rear port in the same manner.

16   To bleed the individual wheel cylinders or calipers, first refer to Steps 6 and 7.

17   Have an assistant on hand, as well as a supply of new brake fluid, an empty clear plastic container, a length of 3/16-inch plastic, rubber or vinyl tubing to fit over the bleeder valve and a wrench to open and close the bleeder valve. The vehicle may have to be raised and placed on jackstands for clearance.

18   Beginning at the right rear wheel, loosen the bleeder valve slightly, then tighten it to a point where it is snug but can still be loosened quickly and easily.

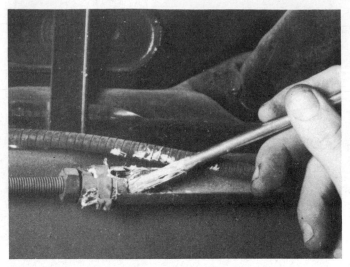

13.3　Lubricate the parking brake equalizer nut

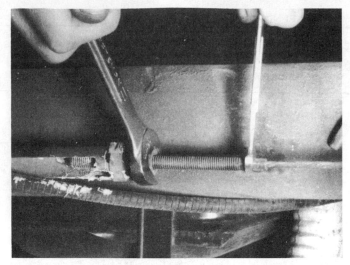

13.4　Use two wrenches to tighten the parking brake adjusting nut

19　Place one end of the tubing over the bleeder valve and submerge the other end in brake fluid in the container.
20　Have the assistant pump the brakes a few times to get pressure in the system, then hold the pedal firmly depressed.
21　While the pedal is held depressed, open the bleeder valve just enough to allow a flow of fluid to leave the valve. Watch for air bubbles to exit the submerged end of the tube. When the fluid flow slows after a couple of seconds, close the valve again and have your assistant release the pedal. If the pedal is released before the valve is closed again, air can be drawn back into the system.
22　Repeat Steps 20 and 21 until no more air is seen leaving the tube, then tighten the bleeder valve and proceed to the left rear wheel, the right front wheel and the left front wheel, in that order, and perform the same procedure (photos). Be sure to check the fluid in the master cylinder reservoir frequently.
23　Never use old brake fluid because it attracts moisture which will deteriorate the brake system components.
24　Refill the master cylinder with fluid at the end of the operation.
25　If any difficulty is experienced in bleeding the hydraulic system, or if an assistant is not available, a pressure bleeding kit is a worthwhile investment. If connected in accordance with the instructions, each bleeder valve can be opened in turn to allow the fluid to be pressure ejected until it is clear of air bubbles without the need to replenish the master cylinder reservoir during the process.

13　Parking brake — adjustment

1　Pull up exactly five clicks on the parking brake handle.
2　Raise the vehicle and support it securely on jackstands.
3　Before adjusting, make sure the equalizer nut groove is lubricated liberally with multi-purpose lithium-base grease (photo).
4　Tighten the adjusting nut until the right rear wheel can just be turned backward with two hands, but locks when forward motion is attempted (photo).
5　Release the parking brake lever and check to make sure the rear wheels turn freely in both directions with no drag.
6　Lower the vehicle.

14　Stop light switch — removal, installation and adjustment

1　The switch is located on a flange or bracket protruding from the brake pedal support. Two types are used, with the cruise control

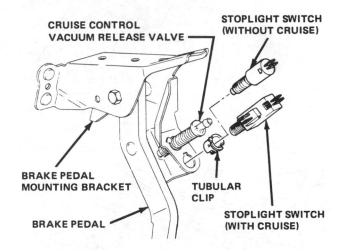

Fig. 9.11 Details of the stoplight switch installation (Sec 14)

equipped model switch incorporating a vacuum release valve. Procedures are the same for both types.
2　With the brake pedal in the fully released position, the plunger on the body of the switch should be completely pressed in. When the pedal is pushed in, the plunger releases and sends electrical current to the stop lights at the rear of the vehicle.
3　If the stop lights are inoperative and it has been determined that the bulbs are not burned out, push the stop light switch into the tubular clip, noting that audible clicks can be heard as the threaded portion of the switch is pushed through the clip toward the brake pedal.
4　Pull the brake pedal all the way to the rear against the pedal stop until no further clicks can be heard. This will seat the switch in the tubular clip and provide the correct adjustment.
5　Release the brake pedal and repeat Step 4 to ensure that no further clicks can be heard.
6　Make sure that the stop lights are working.
7　If the lights are not working, disconnect the electrical connectors at the stop light switch and remove the switch from the clip.
8　Install a new switch and adjust it by performing Steps 3 through 6, making sure the electrical connectors are hooked up.

Chapter 10 Chassis electrical system

Refer to Chapter 13 for information related to 1985 and later models

Contents

Specifications

Bulb application	Type
Headlight	
Dual — high and low beam	4652
Dual — high beam (ex. hlgn.)	4651
Dual — halogen high beam	H46561
Front park and turn signal	1157NA
Front side marker	194
Underhood light	94
Dome light	561
Dome light with reading light	562
Reading light	90
Courtesy light	906
Instrument cluster illumination	
Standard	194
Gauges	168
Clock, heater control, brake, 'check engine', 'fasten belt',	
choke, radio dial and ash tray lights	168
Radio dial	194
Tail, stop and turn signal	1157
Rear turn signal	1157A
Rear side marker	1157
License plate light	194
Back-up light	1156

1 General information

The electrical system is a 12-volt, negative ground type. Power for the lights and all electrical accessories is supplied by a lead/acid-type battery, which is charged by the alternator.

This chapter covers repair and service procedures for the various electrical components not associated with the engine. Information on the battery, alternator, distributor and starter motor can be found in Chapter 5.

It should be noted that whenever portions of the electrical system are worked on, the negative cable should be disconnected at the battery to prevent electrical shorts and/or fires. During circuit testing, of course, the battery will have to remain connected to determine system electrical continuity.

10

2   Electrical troubleshooting — general information

A typical electrical circuit consists of an electrical component, any switches, relays, motors, etc. related to that component and the wiring and connectors that connect the component to both the battery and the chassis. To aid in locating a problem in any electrical circuit, wiring diagrams for each model are included at the end of this manual.

Before tackling any troublesome electrical circuit, first study the appropriate diagrams to get a complete understanding of what makes up that individual circuit. Trouble spots, for instance, can often be narrowed down by noting if other components related to that circuit are operating properly or not. If several components or circuits fail at one time, chances are the problem lies in the fuse or ground connection, as several circuits often are routed through the same fuse and ground connections.

Electrical problems often stem from simple causes, such as loose or corroded connections, a blown fuse or melted fusible link. Prior to any electrical troubleshooting, always visually check the condition of the fuse, wires and connections in the problem circuit.

If testing instruments are going to be utilized, use the diagrams to plan ahead of time where you will make the necessary connections in order to accurately pinpoint the trouble spot.

The basic tools needed for electrical troubleshooting include a circuit tester or voltmeter (a 12-volt bulb with a set of test leads can also be used), a continuity tester (which includes a bulb, battery and set of test leads) and a jumper wire, preferably with a circuit breaker incorporated, which can be used to bypass electrical components.

Voltage checks should be performed if a circuit is not functioning properly. Connect one lead of a circuit tester to either the negative battery terminal or a known good ground. Connect the other lead to a connector in the circuit being tested, preferably nearest to the battery or fuse. If the bulb of the tester goes on, voltage is reaching that point (which means the part of the circuit between that connector and the battery is problem free). Continue checking along the entire circuit in the same fashion. When you reach a point where no voltage is present, the problem lies between there and the last good test point. Most of the time the problem is due to a loose connection. Keep in mind that some circuits receive voltage only when the ignition key is in the Accessory or Run position.

A method of finding shorts in a circuit is to remove the fuse and connect a test light or voltmeter in its place. With the component being energized by that circuit shut off, there should be no load in the circuit. Move the wiring harness from side-to-side while watching the test light. If the bulb goes on, there is a short to ground somewhere in that area, probably where insulation has rubbed off of a wire. The same test can be performed on other components of the circuit, including the switch.

A ground check should be done to see if a component is grounded properly. Disconnect the battery and connect one lead of a self-powered test light, such as a continuity tester, to a known good ground. Connect the other lead to the wire or ground connection being tested. If the bulb goes on, the ground is good. If the bulb does not go on, the ground is not good.

A continuity check is performed to see if a circuit, section of circuit or individual component is passing electricity properly. Disconnect the battery and connect one lead of a self-powered test light to the battery side of the circuit. Connect the other lead of the test light to a good ground. If the bulb goes on, there is continuity, which means the circuit is passing electricity properly. Switches can be checked in the same way.

Remember that all electrical circuits are composed of electricity running from the battery, through the wires, switches, relays, etc. to the electrical component (light bulb, motor, etc.). From there it is run to the body or frame (ground) where it is passed back to the battery. Any electrical problem is an interruption in the flow of electricity to and from the battery.

3   Fuses — general information

The electrical circuits of the vehicle are protected by a combination of fuses, circuit breakers and fusible links. The fuse block is located on the underside of the instrument panel adjacent to the hood release

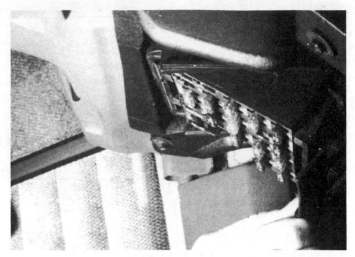

3.1   The fuses are accessible after swinging the fuse block down

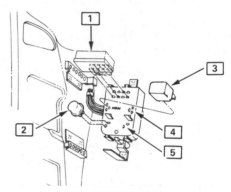

CONVENIENCE CENTER

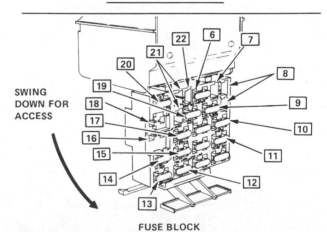

SWING
DOWN FOR
ACCESS

FUSE BLOCK

Fig. 10.1 The fuse block and convenience center are located under the left side of the instrument panel (Sec 3, 5 and 6)

1	Buzzer assembly	13	Choke heater fuse
2	Hazard flasher	14	Heater and air conditioner fuse
3	Horn relay	15	Tail light fuse
4	Choke heater relay	16	Power window circuit breaker receptacle
5	Not used	17	Courtesy light and cigar lighter fuse
6	Wiper fuse		
7	Light fuse receptacle	18	Power accessory circuit breaker receptacle
8	Ignition fuse receptacle		
9	Instrument light fuse	19	Radio fuse
10	Gauges fuse	20	ECM fuse
11	Turn signal and back-up light fuse	21	Battery circuit breaker
12	Stop light fuse	22	Accessory circuit breaker

handle. The fuses are accessible after pulling the fuse block down (photo).

Each of the fuses is designed to protect a specific circuit, and the various circuits are identified on the fuse panel.

ATC fuses are employed in the fuse block. These compact fuses, with blade terminal design, allow fingertip removal and replacement.

If an electrical component has failed, your first check should be the fuse. A fuse which has 'blown' is easily identified by inspecting the element inside the plastic body. Also, the blade terminal tips are exposed in the fuse body, allowing for continuity checks.

It is important that the correct fuse be installed. The different electrical circuits need varying amounts of protection, indicated by the amperage rating molded in bold, color-coded numbers on the fuse body.

At no time should the fuse be bypassed with pieces of metal or foil. Serious damage to the electrical system could result.

If the replacement fuse immediately fails, do not replace it again until the cause of the problem is isolated and corrected. In most cases, this will be a short circuit in the wiring caused by a broken or deteriorated wire.

4 Fusible links — general information

In addition to fuses, the wiring is protected by fusible links. These links are used in circuits which are not ordinarily fused, such as the ignition circuit.

Although the fusible links appear to be a heavier gauge than the wire they are protecting, the appearance is due to the thick insulation. All fusible links are four wire gauges smaller than the wire they are designed to protect.

The location of the fusible links on your particular vehicle may be determined by referring to the wiring diagrams at the end of this manual.

The fusible links cannot be repaired, but a new link of the same size wire can be put in its place. The procedure is as follows:

a) Disconnect the battery ground cable.
b) Disconnect the fusible link from the starter solenoid.
c) Cut the damaged fusible link out of the wiring just behind the connector.
d) Strip the insulation approximately 1/2-inch.
e) Position the connector on the new fusible link and crimp it into place.
f) Use rosin core solder at each end of the new link to obtain a good solder joint.
g) Use plenty of electrical tape around the soldered joint. No wires should be exposed.
h) Connect the fusible link at the starter solenoid. Connect the battery ground cable. Test the circuit for proper operation.

5 Circuit breakers — general information

A circuit breaker is used to protect the headlight wiring and is located in the light switch. An electrical overload in the system will cause the lights to go on and off, or in some cases to remain off. If this happens, check the entire headlight circuit immediately. Once the overload condition is corrected, the circuit breaker will function normally.

Circuit breakers are also used with accessories such as power windows, power door locks and the rear window defogger.

The circuit breakers in your particular vehicle may be found by referring to the wiring diagrams at the end of this manual.

6 Turn signal and hazard flashers — check and replacement

1 Small canister-shaped flasher units are incorporated into the electrical circuits for the turn signal and hazard warning lights.
2 When the units are functioning properly, an audible click can be heard with the circuit in operation. If the turn signals fail on one side only and the flasher unit cannot be heard, a faulty bulb is indicated.
3 If the turn signal fails on both sides, the problem many be due to a blown fuse, faulty flasher unit or switch, or a broken or loose connection. If the fuse has blown, check the wiring for a short before installing a new fuse.
4 The hazard warning lights are checked as described in Paragraph 3 above.
5 The hazard warning flasher is located in the convenience center adjacent to the fuse block under the left side of the dash.
6 The turn signal flasher is mounted on the right side of the steering column and is retained by a spring clip.
7 When replacing either of the flasher units, be sure to buy a replacement of the same capacity. Compare the new flasher to the old one before installing it.

7 Steering column switches — removal and installation

Turn signal switch

1 Disconnect the negative battery cable from the battery.
2 Remove the steering wheel (Chapter 11).
3 Pry the lock ring cover off with two screwdrivers (photo).
4 Buy or make a yoke-type tool to push the lock ring in enough to allow removal of the ring retainer with two screwdrivers (photo).
5 Release the tool and remove the lock ring.
6 Remove the retaining screw and remove the turn signal actuator lever.

10

7.3 Insert two small screwdrivers behind the cover plate and pry it off

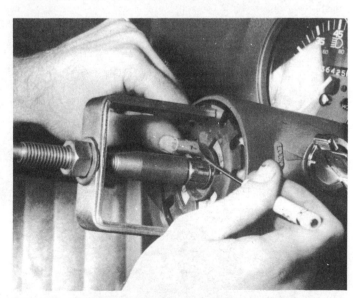

7.4 After compressing the locking ring with a tool, the split retaining ring can be removed with two screwdrivers

7.7a   Turn signal retaining screws
A   Actuating lever   B   Switch assembly

7.7b   Removing the hazard switch button

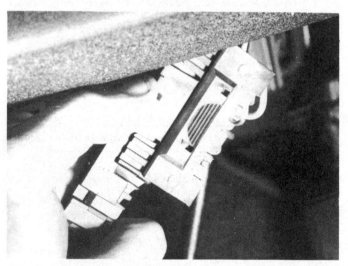

7.9   Unplug the turn signal switch connector under the dash

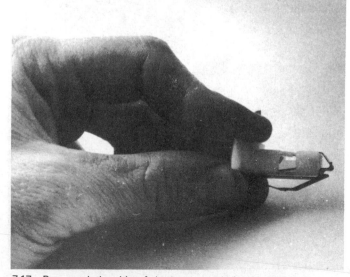

7.17   Proper relationship of the buzzer switch components

7.11   Attach a piece of wire to the harness (arrow) before removing it to make reinstallation easier

7   Remove the three retaining screws and the hazard switch button (photos).
8   Remove the trim panel from beneath the steering column to gain access to the turn signal switch harness.
9   Unplug the switch connector (photo).
10   Remove the steering column retaining bracket bolts and lower the bracket.
11   Remove the switch assembly and harness, carefully guiding the harness and connector out of the column. To simplify reassembly, tie a string or fasten a thin wire to the harness connector to use in pulling the connector back into the narrow confines of the steering column (photo).
12   Installation is the reverse of removal.

Ignition lock cylinder
13   Follow Steps 1 through 9 and pull the turn signal switch up enough to provide access to the ignition lock cylinder.
14   With the keys in the On position, remove the ignition warning buzzer switch contacts with needle-nose pliers.
15   Remove the lock cylinder retaining screw.
16   Withdraw the lock cylinder from the steering column.
17   Installation is the reverse of removal, paying attention to the following points:
  a) Assemble the ignition warning buzzer contacts before inserting them (photo).
  b) When installing the turn signal actuator arm, make sure it is securely engaged in the lever mechanism before tightening the screw.

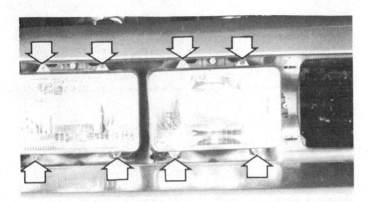

8.3 Remove only the four headlight retaining screws (arrows), not the adjustment screws

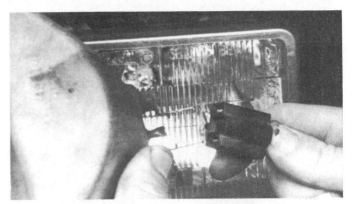

8.4 Support the headlight while unplugging the connector

Fig. 10.2 Headlight adjustment screw locations (Sec 9)

VERTICAL AIM SCREWS

HORIZONTAL AIM SCREWS

8 Headlight — removal and installation

Removal
1 When replacing the headlight, do not turn the spring-loaded adjusting screws or the headlight aim will be changed.
2 Remove the special Torx-type headlight bezel retaining screws and the decorative bezel.
3 Remove the four retaining screws which secure the retaining ring and withdraw the ring (photo). Support the light as this is done.
4 Pull the light away, unplug the connector and remove the light from the vehicle (photo).

Installation
5 Position the new unit close enough to connect the wires. Make sure the numbers molded into the lens are at the top.
6 Install the retaining ring and mounting screws.
7 Install the bezel and check for proper operation. If the adjusting screws were not turned, the headlight should not require adjustment.

9 Headlights — adjustment

1 Any adjustments made by the home mechanic that affect the aim of the headlights should be considered temporary only. After adjustment, always have the beams readjusted by a facility with the proper aligning equipment as soon as possible. In some states these facilities must be state-authorized. Check with your local motor vehicle department concerning the laws in your area.
2 Adjustment screws are provided at the front of each headlight to alter the beam horizontally (side screw) and vertically (top screw). When making adjustments, be careful not to scratch the paint on the body.

10 Bulb replacement

Front end
Parking, turn signal and side marker lights
1 The front parking, turn signal and side marker light bulbs can be replaced from inside the engine compartment after removing the four screws and detaching the fascia panel. The side marker bulb is located between the front end panel and radiator support. Turn the bulbs to remove them from the housings.

Interior
Courtesy lights
2 The lower courtesy light bulbs are replaced by grasping and pulling them directly out of the socket (photo).
Dome light
3 On some models screws retain the dome light lens; on others, grasp the lens to remove it (photo). Remove the bulb by pulling it straight down.

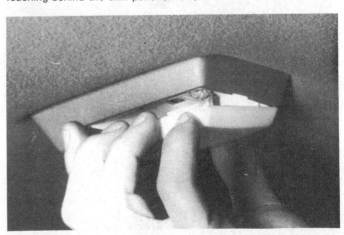

10.2 The lower courtesy light bulbs are accessible by reaching behind the trim panel (arrow)

10.3 On most models the dome light lens is simply unsnapped from the housing

10

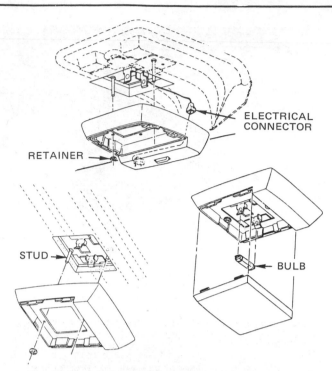

Fig. 10.3 Typical dome light bulb installation (Sec 10)

Instrument panel lights
4   Most instrument panel bulbs can be replaced after removal of the instrument cluster (Section 15). If a bulb is located in a recess and cannot be grasped with the fingers, push a piece of tubing, such as vacuum hose, over the bulb and pull straight out to remove it.

Ash tray
5   Remove the ash tray and the console cover (Chapter 12) for access to the bulb.

Glove box
6   Open the glove box, remove the striker assembly and remove the bulb.

Heater and air conditioner control
7   Remove the right side trim cover and the screws retaining the control to the instrument panel.
8   Pull the control out enough to gain access to the bulb socket and remove it. Remove the bulb from the socket.

Radio dial
9   Remove the radio (Section 11).
10   Remove the top cover from the radio, grasp the bulb and pull it straight out.

Console
11   Remove the console cover retaining screws and pull the cover up enough to gain access to the bulb socket. Twist the socket counterclockwise to remove it, then remove the bulb.

Courtesy light
12   The rear compartment courtesy light bulb is contained in a plastic housing. Use a screwdriver to pry the housing out of the panel for access to the bulb (photo).

Rear end

Tail and back-up lights
13   On hatchback models, remove the interior panel to gain access to the tail and back-up lights. Remove the four plastic wing nuts and detach the tail light assembly. Turn the bulb socket assembly to remove it, then push the bulb in and turn it to replace it (photos).
14   The tail light bulbs on sedan models can be replaced after removing the three wing nuts retaining the lamp housing and detaching the housing. Remove the license plate for access to the back-up light bulb. Detach the bezel and socket and remove the bulb.

Side marker lights
15   The side marker light bulb on hatchback models can be replaced after removing the two plastic screws retaining the speaker cover trim panel in the rear compartment. Pull back the carpet and swing the speaker cover and speaker into the compartment and disconnect the wires. The bulb is accessible through the speaker hole.

License plate light
16   Access to the license plate light is gained by removing the two screws and the light assembly. Turn and pull the bulb to remove it.

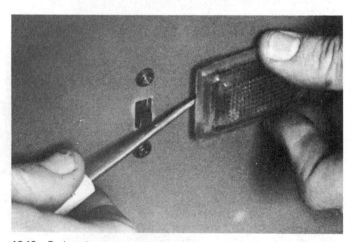

10.12   Prying the rear compartment courtesy light housing out of the trim panel

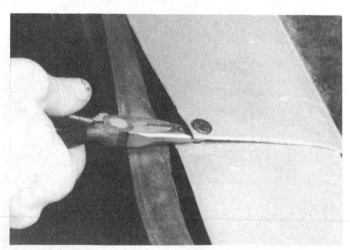

10.13a   Use needle-nose pliers to remove the trim panel retainers to gain access to the tail light housing

10.13b   After turning the socket it can be lifted out and the bulb removed by pushing in and turning (arrows)

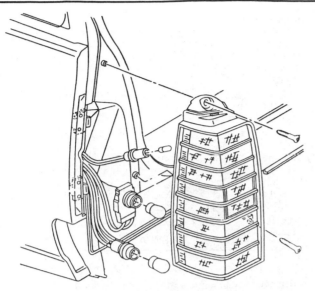

Fig. 10.4 Details of station wagon taillight bulb replacement (Sec 10)

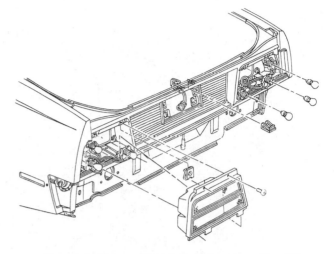

Fig. 10.5 Sedan taillight bulb replacement (Sec 10)

11 Radio and speakers — removal and installation

Radio

1   Remove the instrument panel trim plate (Section 15).
2   Remove the radio retaining bolts (photo).
3   Pull the radio out enough for access to the antenna wire.
4   Use a screwdriver to raise the retainer and disconnect the antenna wire (photo).
5   Unplug the wiring connectors from the radio by depressing the tabs (photo).
6   Separate the radio from the dash.
7   Installation is the reverse of removal.

Speakers

Front

8   Remove the two speaker grille attaching screws, disconnect the clips and separate the grille from the instrument panel.
9   Remove the two screws attaching the speaker to the instrument panel and lift the speaker enough to disconnect the wiring.
10 Remove the speaker.
11 Installation is the reverse of removal.

11.2   Radio retaining bolt locations (arrows)

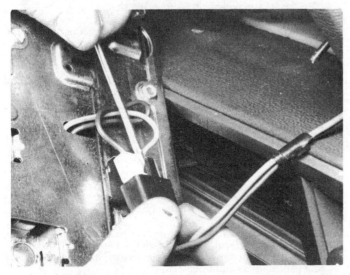

11.4   Insert a screwdriver into the antenna connector to release the retainer

11.5   Press the tabs in the direction shown (arrow) to unplug the radio connector

10

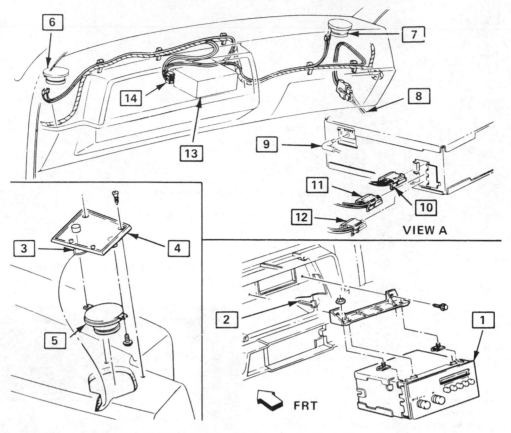

Fig. 10.6 Details of radio and front speaker installation (Sec 11)

1 Radio
2 The screw on the side of the radio
   fits in this location
3 Retainer
4 Grille
5 Speaker

6 Front speaker assembly
7 Rear speaker assembly
8 Rear speaker wire
9 Antenna lead

10 Rear speaker lead
11 Front speaker lead
12 Instrument panel electrical harness
13 Receiver assembly
14 Electrical harness connector

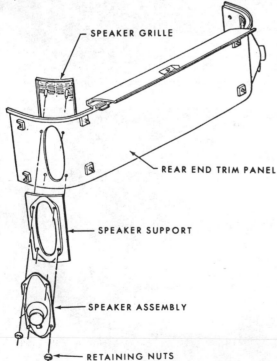

**Fig. 10.7 Hatchback rear speaker installation details
(Sec 11)**

Rear

12 On hatchback models, remove the two plastic retaining screws
and detach the speaker cover trim panel.
13 Pull the carpet back enough for clearance and swing the speaker
and cover assembly into the rear compartment.
14 Disconnect the wires and remove the speaker.
15 Installation is the reverse of removal.
16 On sedan models, the speakers are accessible after opening the
trunk. Refer to the accompanying illustration for removal and installation procedures.

12   Radio antenna — removal and installation

Standard

1   The antenna mast can be removed by loosening the retaining nut
and unscrewing the antenna as shown in the accompanying illustration.
2   The antenna body and cable assembly can be removed after the
mast by unbolting it from the fender.
3   Installation is the reverse of removal, taking care to locate the studs
securely in the fender.

Power

4   Turn the steering wheel to the far left position.
5   Disconnect the negative cable from the battery.
6   Remove the right inner fender splash shield, which is held in place
by four plastic studs and three screws.
7   Remove the screw retaining the antenna mast trim guide to the
fender.

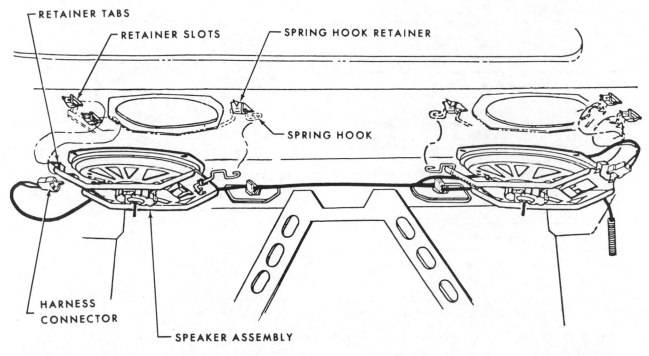

Fig. 10.8 Sedan rear speaker installation details (Sec 11)

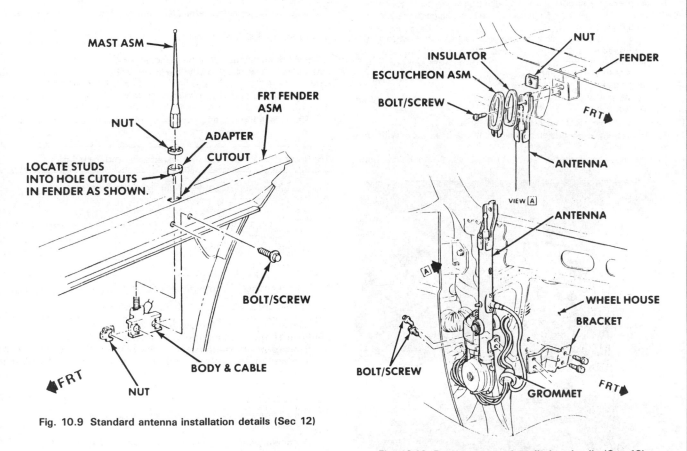

Fig. 10.9 Standard antenna installation details (Sec 12)

Fig. 10.10 Power antenna installation details (Sec 12)

10

8   Disconnect the antenna lead and motor wires.
9   Remove the two bolts from the lower antenna assembly bracket.
10 Carefully pull the antenna and wiring assembly down through the wheel opening and remove it.
11 Installation is the reverse of removal.

13   Speedometer — removal and installation

1   Disconnect the negative cable from the battery.
2   Remove the instrument panel cluster housing (Section 15).
3   Remove the instrument panel mask.
4   Remove the retaining screws and separate the speedometer assembly from the cluster.
5   Installation is the reverse of removal. If the vehicle speed sensor (VSS) has been removed with the speedometer, it must be reinstalled for proper operation of the lock-up torque converter.

14   Speedometer cable — replacement

1   Disconnect the cable from the negative battery terminal.
2   Remove the steering column trim plate.
3   Remove the instrument cluster retaining screws.
4   Pull the cluster out carefully so as not to disconnect the cluster wiring until there is enough clearance to reach the speedometer retaining collar.
5   Press the clip directly back toward the cluster to disconnect it (photo).
6   Disconnect the cable at the transaxle or cruise control transducer.
7   Slide the old cable out of the upper end of the casing, or, if broken, from both ends of the casing.
8   If the speedometer operation has been noisy, but the speedometer cable appears to be in good condition, take a short piece of speedometer cable with a tip to fit the speedometer and insert it in the speedometer socket. Spin the piece of cable between your fingers. If binding is noted, the speedometer is faulty and should be replaced with a new one.
9   Inspect the speedometer cable casing for sharp bends or cracks, especially at the transaxle end. If cracks are noted, replace the casing with a new one.
10 When installing the cable, perform the following operations to ensure quiet operation:
11 Wipe the cable clean with a lint-free cloth.
12 Flush the bore of the casing with solvent and blow it dry with compressed air.
13 Place some speedometer cable lubricant in the palm of one hand.

14.5   The speedometer cable can be disconnected after depressing the release clip (arrow)

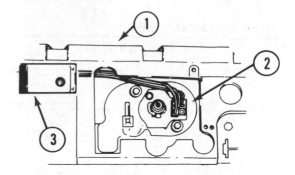

Fig. 10.11 Vehicle speed sensor installation details (Sec 13)

1   Instrument cluster   3   VSS assembly
2   Speedometer

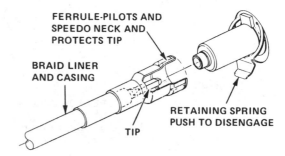

Fig. 10.12 Speedometer cable connection (Sec 13 and 14)

14 Feed the cable through the lubricant and into the casing until lubricant has been applied to the lower two-thirds of the cable. Do not overlubricate.
15 Seat the upper cable tip in the speedometer and snap the retainer onto the housing.
16 The remaining installation steps are the reverse of removal.

15   Instrument panel cluster — removal and installation

1   Disconnect the negative cable from the battery.
2   Remove the cluster retaining screws.
3   Disconnect the speedometer cable (Section 14).
4   Pull the cluster out, disconnect the wiring and remove it from the instrument panel.
5   Installation is the reverse of removal.

16   Cluster panel instruments (except speedometer) — removal and installation

1   Disconnect the negative cable from the battery.
2   Remove the instrument panel cluster (Section 15).
3   Remove the cluster mask.
4   Remove the retaining bolts and lift the instruments from the cluster.
5   Installation is the reverse of removal.

17   Headlight switch — removal and installation

1   Disconnect the negative cable from the battery.
2   Remove the left side instrument panel trim panel.
3   Remove the retaining screws and separate the switch from the instrument panel.
4   Installation is the reverse of removal, taking care not to press on the switch buttons when placing the switch in position.

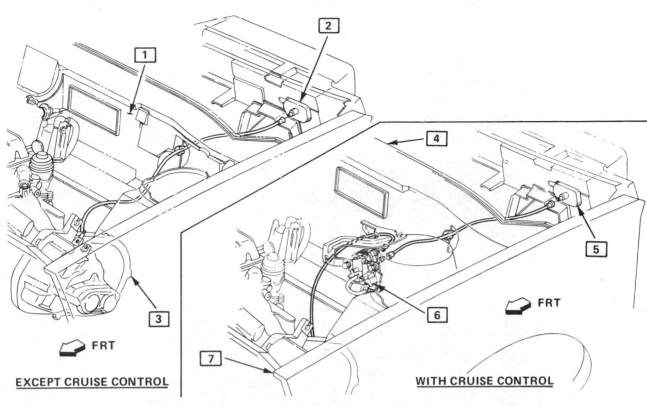

EXCEPT CRUISE CONTROL

WITH CRUISE CONTROL

Fig. 10.13 Speedometer cable routing details (Sec 14 and 24)

1 Dash panel	3 Transaxle	5 Cluster assembly
2 Cluster assembly	4 Dash panel	6 Cruise control transducer

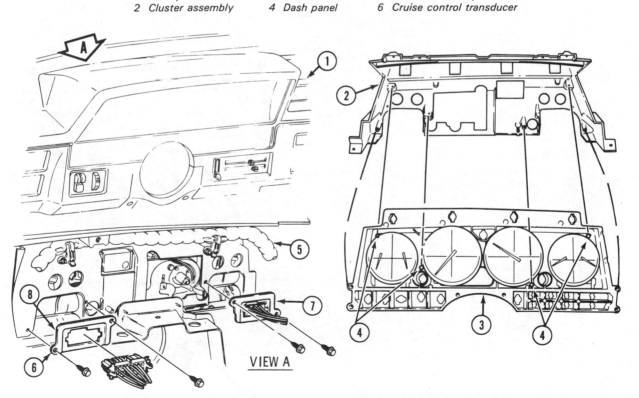

VIEW A

10

Fig. 10.14 Instrument cluster housing details (Sec 13 through 16)

1 Instrument panel	4 Screw	6 Retainer
2 Cluster carrier	5 Instrument panel electrical harness	7 Right side cluster electrical lead
3 Cluster housing		8 Left side cluster electrical lead

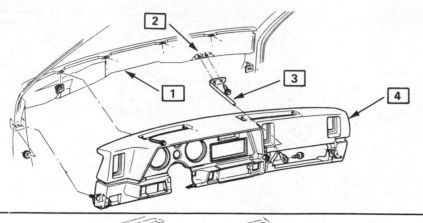

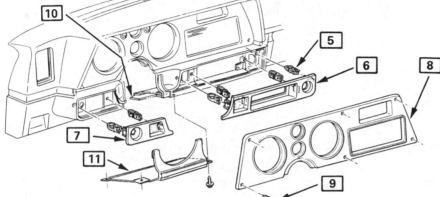

Fig. 10.15 Instrument panel
and trim plate installation
details (Sec 15 through 18)

1 Dash panel
2 Weld nuts
3 Center reinforcement
4 Pad assembly
5 Snap-in clips
6 Right side lower trim plate
7 Left side lower trim plate
8 Instrument panel trim plate
9 Torx head screw
10 Sound deadener panel
11 Steering column trim cover

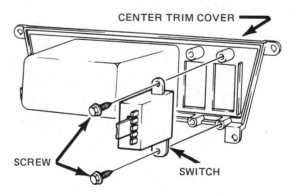

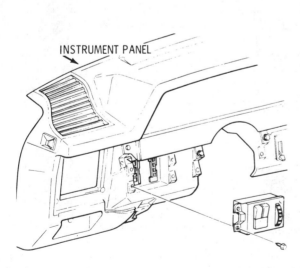

Fig. 10.16 Headlight switch installation details (Sec 17)

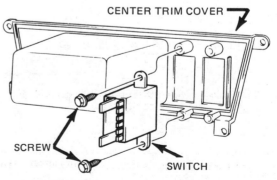

Fig. 10.17 Rear window defogger (top) and wiper/washer
switch installation details (Sec 18)

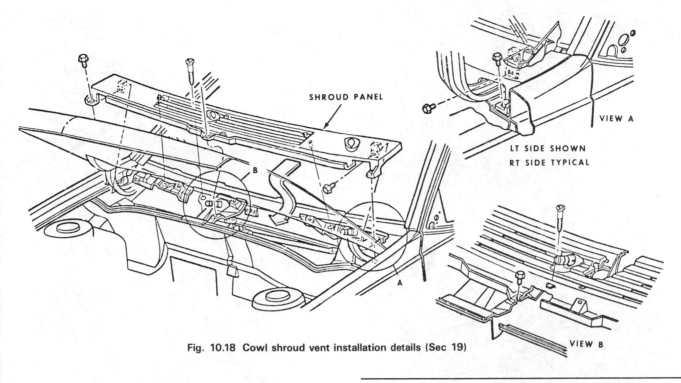

Fig. 10.18 Cowl shroud vent installation details (Sec 19)

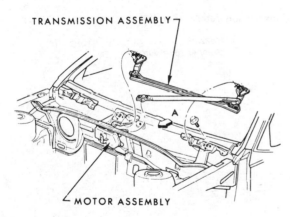

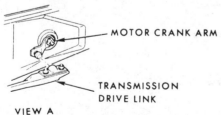

VIEW A

Fig. 10.19 Details of windshield wiper transmission arm assembly installation (Sec 19)

18 Rear window washer/wiper and defogger switches — removal and installation

1   Disconnect the negative cable from the battery.
2   Remove the right side instrument panel trim cover.
·3   Remove the retaining screws and lift the appropriate switch off the trim cover.
4   Installation is the reverse of removal.

19 Windshield wiper transmission arm assembly — removal and installation

1   Remove the cowl shroud vent grille.
2   Loosen, but do not remove, the nuts attaching the drive link to the crank arm.
3   Disengage the drive link from the crank arm.
4   Remove the screws attaching the transmission to the cowl panel and lift the arm assembly from the vehicle.
5   Installation is the reverse of removal.

20 Wiper motor — removal and installation

Windshield wiper
1   Disconnect the negative cable from the battery.
2   Unplug the electrical connector (photo).
3   Disconnect the wiper arm from the back of the motor (photo).
4   Remove the bolts and lift the motor from the firewall.
5   Place the motor in position and install the retaining bolts.
6   Connect the wiper arm to the motor.
7   Plug in the electrical connector.

Rear wiper
8   Refer to the accompanying illustrations for hatchback and station wagon rear wiper motor removal and installation procedures.

10

21 Wiper arm — removal and installation

1   The wiper arm must be pried off the serrated shaft and is best removed with a windshield wiper removal tool, which is available at most auto parts stores. The tool is also used for installing the wiper arm.
2   Mark the position of the wiper blade on the windshield and/or the shaft so it can be installed in its original position.
3   With the wiper arm reinstalled, check the parked position of the blade.
4   The windshield wiper blade in the parked position must be aligned with the top of the blackout strip at the bottom of the glass on the passenger's side.
5   Refer to the accompanying illustration for the proper wiper pattern and blade position on vehicles with rear wipers.

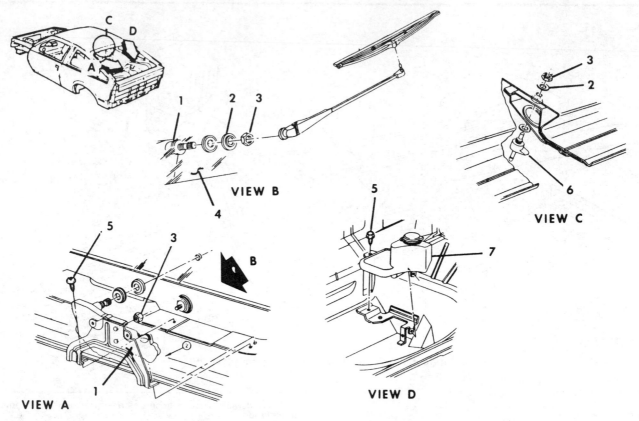

Fig. 10.20 Typical hatchback rear wiper installation details (Sec 20)

1 Motor	4 Glass	6 Nozzle
2 Washer	5 Screw	7 Washer reservoir
3 Nut		

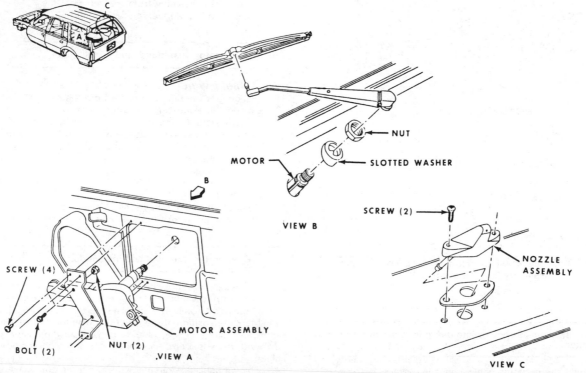

Fig. 10.21 Typical station wagon rear wiper installation details (Sec 20)

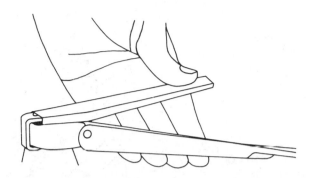

Fig. 10.22 The wiper arm is easily removed with a wiper arm removal tool (Sec 21)

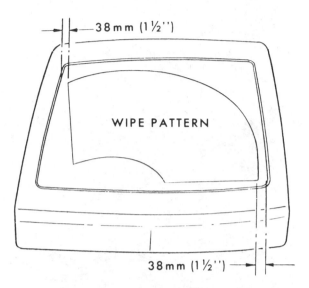

Fig. 10.23 Rear window wiper pattern and blade position diagram (Sec 21)

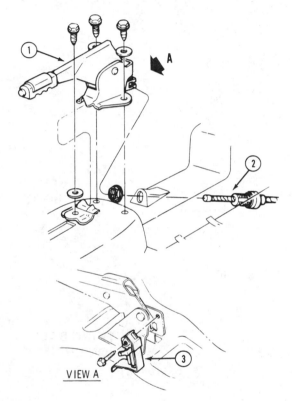

Fig. 10.24 Parking brake switch installation details (Sec 22)

1 Lever assembly   3 Parking brake switch
2 Cable

22 Parking brake switch — replacement

1   Remove the console cover (Chapter 12).
2   Unplug the electrical connector from the switch.
3   Remove the screw retaining the switch to the parking brake and remove the switch.
4   Installation is the reverse of removal.

23 Cruise control — general information and servicing

The cruise control with resume system is an option which maintains a desired vehicle speed under normal driving conditions. The system also has the capability of resuming a preset speed upon driver demand after the system has been disengaged. This is accomplished by moving a slide on the cruise control lever handle to the Resume position. Steep grades, up or down, may cause variations in the selected speed, which is considered normal.

The main components of the cruise control system are a transducer assembly, a resume solenoid valve, a vacuum servo with linkage, an engagement switch button and an On/Off/Resume switch on the turn signal lever, and vacuum and electric release switches attached to the brake pedal (automatic) or clutch pedal (manual).

Because of the variations in installations, it is not possible to include all the service procedures in this manual. However, those elements of the system most often requiring service and/or adjustment are covered.

If the servo unit requires replacement and/or adjustment, refer to the appropriate diagram and instructions accompanying this Section for your vehicle.

1   The transducer is calibrated during production, making overhaul operations impractical. A defective transducer must be replaced with a new one. However, one adjustment is possible. If there is a difference between the engagement speed selected and the actual cruising speed, proceed as follows:
2   Check all hoses for kinks and cracks. If there is still a difference between the engagement and cruising speeds, proceed to the next step.
3   If the cruising speed is lower than the engagement speed, loosen the orifice tube locknut and turn the tube out.
4   If the cruising speed is higher than the engagement speed, loosen the orifice tube locknut and turn the tube in.
5   Each 90-degree (1/4-turn) rotation will alter the engagement/cruising speed one (1) mph.
6   Tighten the locknut after adjustment has been made and check the system operation at 55 mph.
7   To remove, install and adjust the brake and clutch release switches and valves, refer to the accompanying illustration.
8   To remove the cruise control switch, vacuum valve assembly/TCC switch (automatic transmission) or vacuum release valve (manual transmission), pull the component from the bracket under the dash, then disconnect the wiring and/or vacuum connector and discard the faulty component and the retainer.
9   Install a new retainer in the bracket.
10 With the brake or clutch pedal depressed, install the new component in the retainer and make sure it is seated. Note that audible clicks can be heard as the component is pressed into the retainer.
11 Pull the brake or clutch pedal all the way up against the stop until the clicks can no longer be heard.
12 Release the clutch or brake pedal, then repeat the procedure to ensure that no more clicks can be heard. The component is now properly seated and adjusted.
13 Reconnect the wiring and/or vacuum connectors.
14 Other servicing of the cruise control system components should be done by your dealer.

10

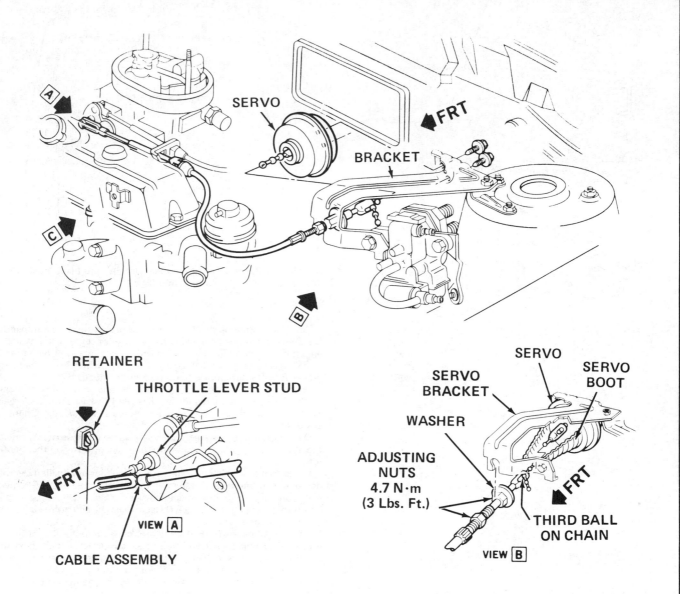

SERVO

FRT

SERVO

BRACKET

RETAINER

THROTTLE LEVER STUD

SERVO
BRACKET

SERVO
BOOT

WASHER

ADJUSTING
NUTS
4.7 N·m
(3 Lbs. Ft.)

THIRD BALL
ON CHAIN

FRT

FRT

VIEW A

CABLE ASSEMBLY

VIEW B

CABLE ADJUSTMENT

1. Cable must be installed and retained on the throttle lever stud.
2. Install cable to the servo bracket.
3. Using the third ball of the servo chain, install chain on cable.
4. With throttle completely closed (ignition off), rotate adjusting nuts until chain is almost tight (some slack).
5. Tighten nuts to specified torque.
6. Position servo boot over cable washer.

Fig. 10.25 Cruise control servo mounting and adjustment details (OHV engine with TBI) (Sec 23)

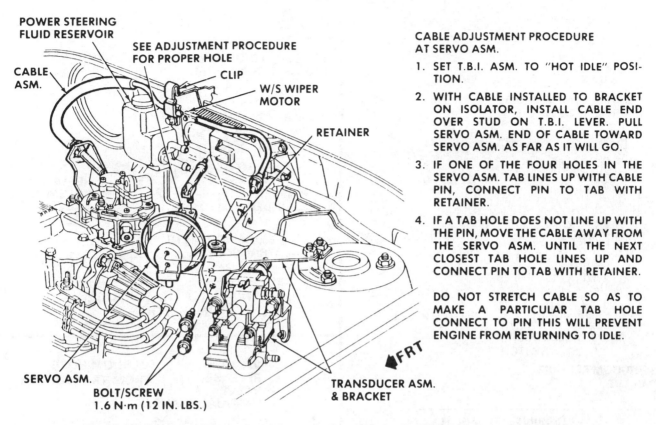

CABLE ADJUSTMENT PROCEDURE
AT SERVO ASM.

1. SET T.B.I. ASM. TO "HOT IDLE" POSITION.

2. WITH CABLE INSTALLED TO BRACKET ON ISOLATOR, INSTALL CABLE END OVER STUD ON T.B.I. LEVER. PULL SERVO ASM. END OF CABLE TOWARD SERVO ASM. AS FAR AS IT WILL GO.

3. IF ONE OF THE FOUR HOLES IN THE SERVO ASM. TAB LINES UP WITH CABLE PIN, CONNECT PIN TO TAB WITH RETAINER.

4. IF A TAB HOLE DOES NOT LINE UP WITH THE PIN, MOVE THE CABLE AWAY FROM THE SERVO ASM. UNTIL THE NEXT CLOSEST TAB HOLE LINES UP AND CONNECT PIN TO TAB WITH RETAINER.

DO NOT STRETCH CABLE SO AS TO MAKE A PARTICULAR TAB HOLE CONNECT TO PIN THIS WILL PREVENT ENGINE FROM RETURNING TO IDLE.

Fig. 10.26 Cruise control servo mounting and adjustment details (OHC engine with TBI) (Sec 23)

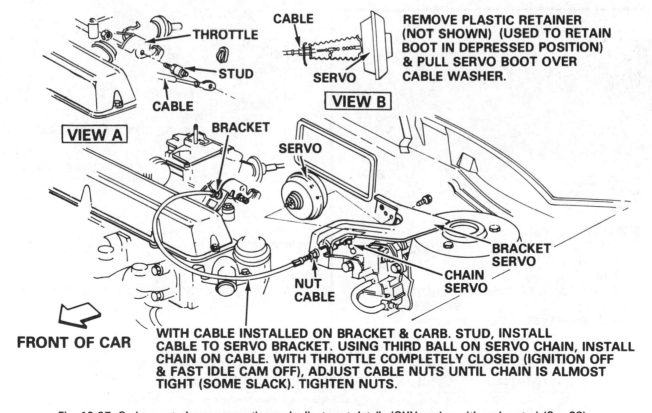

REMOVE PLASTIC RETAINER (NOT SHOWN) (USED TO RETAIN BOOT IN DEPRESSED POSITION) & PULL SERVO BOOT OVER CABLE WASHER.

WITH CABLE INSTALLED ON BRACKET & CARB. STUD, INSTALL CABLE TO SERVO BRACKET. USING THIRD BALL ON SERVO CHAIN, INSTALL CHAIN ON CABLE. WITH THROTTLE COMPLETELY CLOSED (IGNITION OFF & FAST IDLE CAM OFF), ADJUST CABLE NUTS UNTIL CHAIN IS ALMOST TIGHT (SOME SLACK). TIGHTEN NUTS.

Fig. 10.27 Cruise control servo mounting and adjustment details (OHV engine with carburetor) (Sec 23)

10

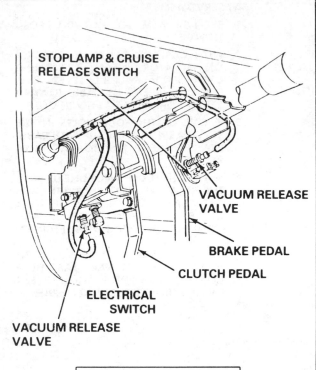

STOPLAMP & CRUISE
RELEASE SWITCH

VACUUM RELEASE
VALVE

BRAKE PEDAL

CLUTCH PEDAL

ELECTRICAL
SWITCH

VACUUM RELEASE
VALVE

**CONNECTIONS TO
RELEASE SWITCHES**

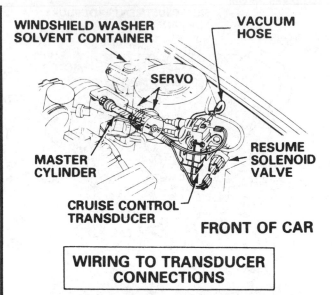

WINDSHIELD WASHER
SOLVENT CONTAINER

VACUUM
HOSE

SERVO

MASTER
CYLINDER

RESUME
SOLENOID
VALVE

CRUISE CONTROL
TRANSDUCER

FRONT OF CAR

**WIRING TO TRANSDUCER
CONNECTIONS**

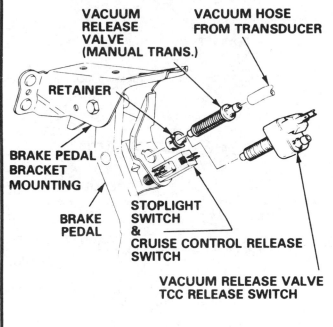

VACUUM
RELEASE
VALVE
(MANUAL TRANS.)

VACUUM HOSE
FROM TRANSDUCER

RETAINER

BRAKE PEDAL
BRACKET
MOUNTING

BRAKE
PEDAL

STOPLIGHT
SWITCH
&
CRUISE CONTROL RELEASE
SWITCH

VACUUM RELEASE VALVE
TCC RELEASE SWITCH

**VACUUM/ELECTRICAL
RELEASE SWITCHES**

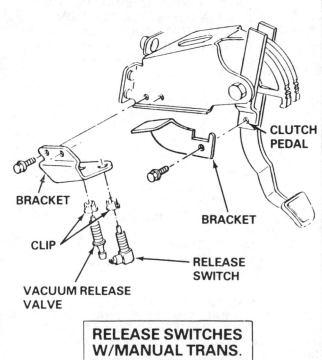

CLUTCH
PEDAL

BRACKET

BRACKET

CLIP

RELEASE
SWITCH

VACUUM RELEASE
VALVE

**RELEASE SWITCHES
W/MANUAL TRANS.**

Fig. 10.28 Cruise control brake and clutch release switch and valve connection details (Sec 23)

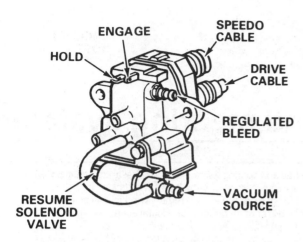

Fig. 10.29 Cruise control transducer assembly details (Sec 23)

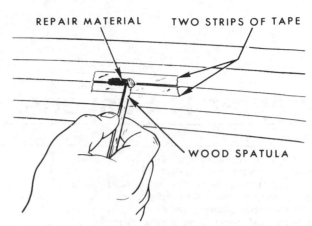

Fig. 10.30 Applying repair material to a broken rear window defogger grid (Sec 24)

24 Rear defogger (electric grid type) — check and repair

1 This option consists of a rear window with a number of horizontal elements, which were baked into the surface during the glass-forming operation.
2 Small breaks in the element can be successfully repaired without removing the rear window.
3 To test the grids for proper operation, start the engine and turn on the system.
4 Ground one lead of a test light and carefully touch the other lead to each element line.
5 The brilliance of the test light should increase as the lead is moved across the element from right to left. If the test light glows brightly at both ends of the lines, check for a loose ground wire. All of the lines should be checked in at least two places.
6 To repair a break in a line, it is recommended that a repair kit specifically for this purpose be purchased from a GM dealer. Included in the repair kit will be a decal, a container of silver plastic and hardener, a mixing stick and instructions.
7 To repair a break, first turn off the system and allow it to de-

energize for a few minutes.
8 Lightly buff the element area with fine steel wool and then clean it thoroughly with alcohol.
9 Use the decal supplied in the repair kit, or apply strips of electrician's tape above and below the area to be repaired. The space between the pieces of tape should be the same width as the existing lines. This can be checked from outside the vehicle. Press the tape tightly against the glass to prevent seepage.
10 Mix the hardener and silver plastic thoroughly.
11 Using the wood spatula, apply the silver plastic mixture between the pieces of tape, overlapping the undamaged area slightly on either end.
12 Carefully remove the decal or tape and apply a constant stream of hot air directly to the repaired area. A heat gun set at 500 to 700 degrees Fahrenheit is recommended. Hold the gun about one inch from the glass for one to two minutes.
13 If the new element appears off color, tincture of iodine can be used to clean the repair and bring it back to the proper color. This mixture should not remain on the repair for more than 30 seconds.
14 Although the defogger is now fully operational, the repaired area should not be disturbed for at least 24 hours.

WIRING DIAGRAMS BEGIN ON PAGE 244

10

Chapter 11 Suspension and steering systems

Contents

Specifications

Front wheel alignment

Camber (degrees)	+0.70 degrees ±0.50 degrees
Toe-in (degrees per wheel)	-0.13 degrees ±0.10 degrees

Torque specifications

	Ft-lbs
Steering	
Adjuster plug locknut	50
Coupling-to-column pinch bolt	30
Coupling-to-stub shaft pinch bolt	29
Inner tie rod bolts	65
Tie rod pinch bolts	25
Rack and pinion mounting clamp nuts	28
Tie rod end-to-strut	35
Power steering pump	
Pump-to-bracket bolts	23
Line fittings	20
Steering wheel and column	
Steering wheel-to-shaft nut	30
Steering column-to-intermediate shaft	35
Steering column cover-to-housing screws	8
Front suspension	
Balljoint-to-knuckle nut	55
Lower control arm pivot bolts	67
Strut damper-to-steering knuckle bolt	140
Strut damper-to-chassis	20
Suspension support-to-chassis bolts	63
Front hub nut	185
Front hub and bearing assembly – to – steering knuckle bolts .	70
Brake caliper-to-knuckle bolts	21 to 35
Rear suspension	
Shock absorber	
Upper end	13
Lower end	35
Stabilizer bar-to-chassis	10
Stabilizer bar-to-suspension arm	13
Control arm-to-body bracket	68
Rear wheel spindle nuts	37

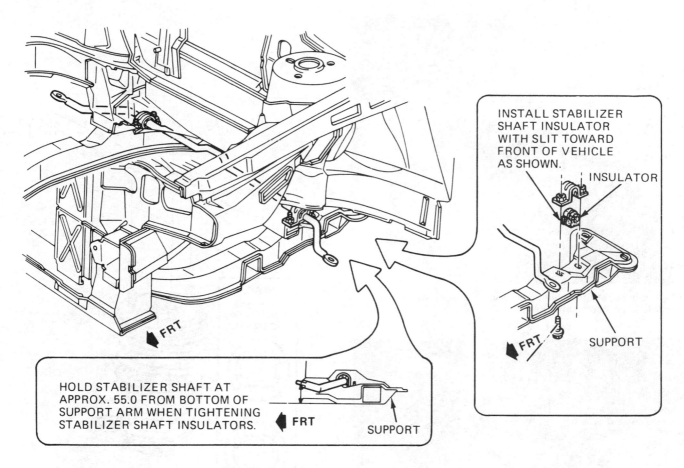

Fig. 11.1 Details of stabilizer bar installation (Sec 2)

INSTALL STABILIZER SHAFT INSULATOR WITH SLIT TOWARD FRONT OF VEHICLE AS SHOWN.

INSULATOR

FRT

SUPPORT

HOLD STABILIZER SHAFT AT APPROX. 55.0 FROM BOTTOM OF SUPPORT ARM WHEN TIGHTENING STABILIZER SHAFT INSULATORS.

FRT

SUPPORT

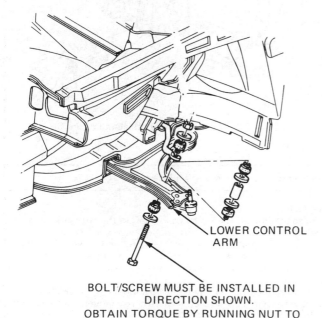

LOWER CONTROL ARM

BOLT/SCREW MUST BE INSTALLED IN DIRECTION SHOWN.
OBTAIN TORQUE BY RUNNING NUT TO UNTHREADED PORTION OF BOLT/SCREW.

Fig. 11.2 Details of stabilizer bar-to-lower control arm installation (Sec 2)

1 Front suspension — general information

The front suspension is of the MacPherson strut type. This design features a strut damper combining a shock absorber and spring into one unit, which is mounted to the chassis at the upper end and the steering knuckle at the lower end. The strut damper pivots for steering at the upper end on a sealed bearing and at the lower end on the knuckle ballstud. The ballstud is riveted to the lower control arm, which pivots at it's inner end on the chassis. A stabilizer bar is mounted to the chassis and the lower control arms.

2 Front stabilizer bar — removal and installation

Removal
1   Raise the front of the vehicle and support it securely on jackstands so that the lower control arms hang free.
2   Remove the left front wheel.
3   Disconnect the stabilizer bar at the lower control arms.
4   Remove the rear support clamp bolts and loosen the front bolts sufficiently to allow removal of the stabilizer bar from the vehicle.

Installation
5   Install the stabilizer bar with the split in the insulator facing forward, as shown in the accompanying illustration.
6   Install the bolts loosely and center the bar from side to side before tightening.
7   The bar must be held so that the ends are the specified distance from the insulator bolts, as shown in the illustration.
8   The remainder of installation is the reverse of removal.

11

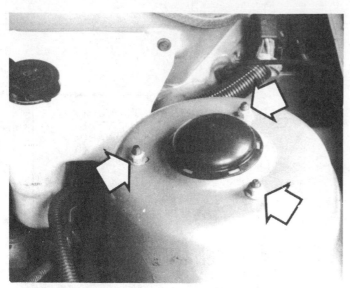

3.1   The upper strut-to-body nuts (arrows) are accessible from the engine compartment

3.6   Loosen the steering knuckle nuts until they are flush with the ends of the bolts (arrows)

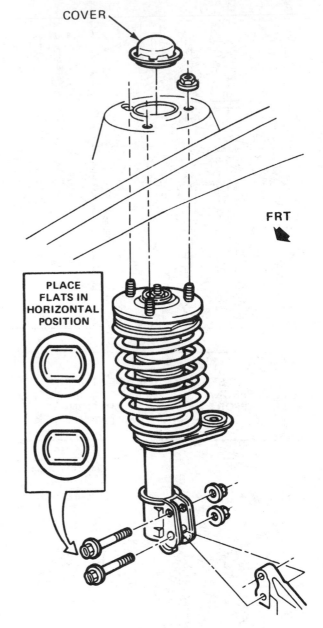

Fig. 11.3 Details of front strut installation (Sec 3)

---

3   Strut damper assembly — removal and installation

Caution: *Whenever the front suspension is disconnected use care to avoid damaging the driveaxle CV joint boots.*

1   In the engine compartment, remove the upper strut-to-body nuts (photo).
2   Raise the front of the vehicle, support it securely on jackstands and allow the suspension to hang free.
3   Remove the wheel(s).
4   Disconnect the tie rod from the strut.
5   Remove the brake caliper and support it out of the way with a piece of wire to prevent damage to the brake hose when the strut is removed.
6   Loosen the strut-to-knuckle bolts until they are flush with the end of the nut (photo). Drive the bolts, which are splined, out of the knuckle, using a brass hammer. Remove the nuts, extract the bolts, lower the assembly and remove the strut damper assembly from the vehicle.
7   Installation is the reverse of removal, making sure to tighten the nuts and bolts to the specified torque. The flats of the strut-to-knuckle bolts must be horizontal after tightening.

4   Balljoints — checking and replacement

Checking
1   Raise the front of the vehicle and support the chassis securely on jackstands.
2   Grasp the top and bottom of the wheel and move it in and out. If there is any horizontal movement of the steering knuckle in relation to the lower control arm, the balljoint is worn and should be replaced with a new one.
3   To check the ballstud when it is disconnected, grasp it and try to move it or twist it in the socket. If there is any movement, replace the balljoint.

Replacement
4   With the vehicle raised and securely supported, remove the front wheel.
5   The balljoint is riveted to the lower control arm, so first determine if there is a countersunk pilot hole in the center of the rivets. If there is not, carefully mark the rivet centers with a suitable punch.

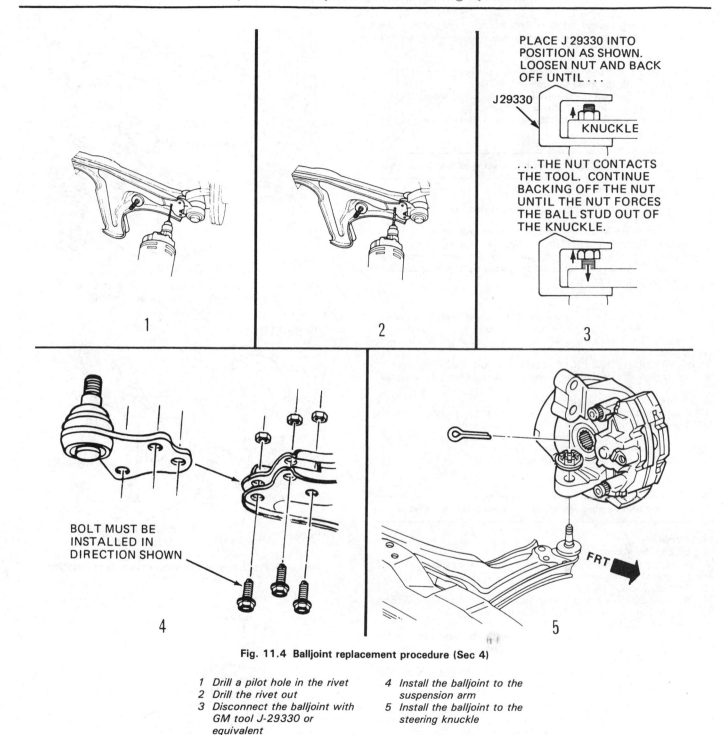

PLACE J 29330 INTO POSITION AS SHOWN. LOOSEN NUT AND BACK OFF UNTIL . . .

J29330

KNUCKLE

. . . THE NUT CONTACTS THE TOOL. CONTINUE BACKING OFF THE NUT UNTIL THE NUT FORCES THE BALL STUD OUT OF THE KNUCKLE.

BOLT MUST BE INSTALLED IN DIRECTION SHOWN

FRT

Fig. 11.4 Balljoint replacement procedure (Sec 4)

1 *Drill a pilot hole in the rivet*
2 *Drill the rivet out*
3 *Disconnect the balljoint with GM tool J-29330 or equivalent*

4 *Install the balljoint to the suspension arm*
5 *Install the balljoint to the steering knuckle*

6   Drill a pilot hole in the rivets with a 1/8-inch drill and then drill the rivet out with a 1/2-inch drill as shown in the accompanying illustration.
7   Disconnect the balljoint from the lower control arm using a suitable tool, such as GM tool J-29330, as shown in the illustration.
8   Disconnect the stabilizer bar from the lower control arm (Section 2).
9   Remove the balljoint from the vehicle.
10   Place the new balljoint in position and install the nuts and bolts as shown in the illustration, tightening to the specified torque.
11   Install the balljoint to the steering knuckle, tightening the nut to the specified torque and using a new cotter pin.
12   After installation, have the front end alignment checked by a dealer or a properly equipped shop.

5   Lower control arms — removal and installation

Removal
1   Raise the front of the vehicle, support it securely on jackstands and remove the front wheel(s).
2   Disconnect the stabilizer bar at the lower control arm.
3   Remove the steering knuckle from the balljoint (Section 4).
4   Remove the pivot bolts and remove the lower control arm from the vehicle
5   If the bushings located in the inner pivots of the lower control arm are cracked or worn they should be replaced with new ones. Because

11

of the special tools required, take the entire lower control arm assembly to a dealer or a properly equipped shop to have the bushings replaced.

Installation

6   Place the control arm in position, install the pivot bolts and nuts and tighten to the specified torque.
7   Connect the balljoint to the steering knuckle, install the nut, tighten to the specified torque and install a new cotter pin.
8   Connect the stabilizer bar, install the wheel(s) and lower the vehicle.

6   Front suspension support assembly — removal and installation

Removal

1   Raise the front of the vehicle, support it securely on jackstands and remove the left front wheel.
2   Remove the lower control arm inner pivot bolts.
3   Support the lower control arm, steering knuckle and strut damper assembly with a jack and move it away from the support assembly.
4   Remove the front suspension support assembly attaching bolts and lower the assembly from the vehicle.

Installation

5   Raise the support assembly into position and loosely install the center bolt (A in the accompanying illustration).
6   Loosely install the tie bar bolt (B in the illustration) into the outboard hole.
7   Install both rear bolts (C) and tighten to the specified torque.
8   Install the bolt into the center hole (D) and tighten to the specified torque.
9   Tighten bolt A to the specified torque.
10   Install the bolt into hole E and tighten to the specified torque.
11   Tighten the bolt in hole B to the specified torque.
12   Move the lower control arm back into position, install the pivot bolts and tighten to the specified torque.
13   Install the wheel and lower the vehicle.

7   Front hub and bearing assembly — removal and installation

Removal

1   Loosen the hub nut.
2   Raise the front of vehicle, support it securely on jackstands and remove the front wheel(s).
3   Remove the hub nut.
4   Remove the front brake caliper and hang it out of the way with a piece of wire so the brake hose won't be damaged.
5   Remove the brake rotor.
6   Remove the three bolts attaching the hub and bearing assembly to the steering knuckle.
7   Remove the shield.
8   If the bearing assembly is to be reinstalled, mark the location of the attaching bolt and corresponding hole for installation to the same position.
9   Use a suitable tool, such as GM J-28733, to press the hub and bearing assembly off the driveaxle. Be sure to support the driveaxle CV joint after it has been separated from the hub.
10   Remove the hub and bearing assembly.

Installation

11   Inspect the bearing and steering knuckle mating surfaces for corrosion, nicks or burrs.
12   Clean the contact surfaces as necessary and apply a thin coat of chassis or wheel bearing grease to the knuckle seal and bore. If a new bearing is being installed, install a new steering knuckle seal, using a suitable size socket to press it squarely into place.
13   Install the bearing attaching nuts and bolts, tightening to the specified torque.
14   Insert the driveaxle into the hub and install the hub nut. Tighten the nut to approximately 75 ft-lbs to seat the bearing assembly.
15   Install the brake rotor and caliper.
16   Install the wheel and lower the vehicle.
17   Tighten the hub nut to the specified torque.

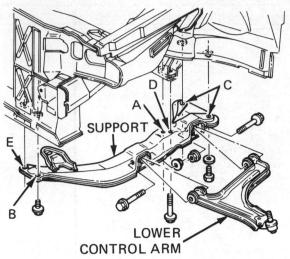

Fig. 11.5 Details of the suspension support assembly installation (refer to text) (Sec 5 and 6)

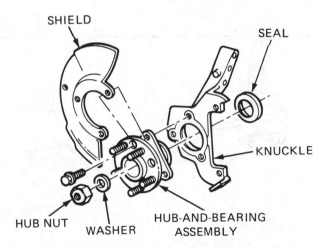

Fig. 11.6 Front hub and bearing assembly installation details (Sec 7)

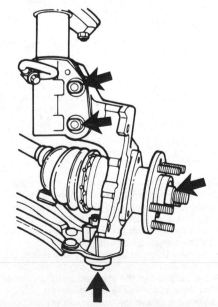

Fig. 11.7 Steering knuckle connecting bolts (arrows) (Sec 8)

8   Steering knuckle — removal and installation

Removal

1   Raise the front of the vehicle and support it securely on jackstands.
2   Remove the front wheel.
3   Loosen the front hub nut. This can be accomplished by inserting a screwdriver or similar tool through the caliper into the brake disc cooling vanes to lock the disc (photo).
4   Remove the brake caliper and rotor (Section 7).
5   Disconnect the driveaxle from the hub (Section 7).
6   Disconnect the lower balljoint (Section 4).
7   Remove the strut-to-knuckle bolts (Section 3) and lift the steering knuckle from the vehicle.

Installation

8   Place the steering knuckle in position and install the attaching bolts finger tight.
9   Connect the knuckle to the balljoint and install the nut, tightening to the specified torque and using a new cotter pin.
10   Tighten the strut-to-knuckle bolts to the specified torque.
11   Connect the driveaxle and install the hub nut.
12   Install the brake rotor and caliper.
13   Install the front wheel, lower the vehicle and tighten the hub nut to the specified torque

8.2   A screwdriver (arrow) inserted through the caliper will lock the brake disc so the hub nut can be broken loose

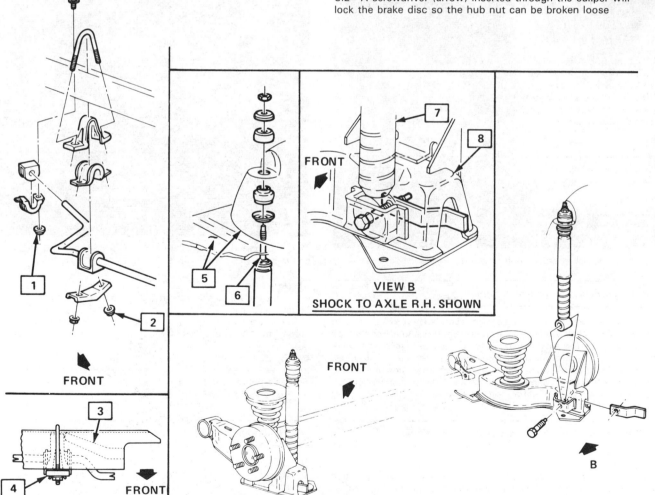

Fig. 11.8 Details of the rear axle and stabilizer bar installation (Sec 9, 10 and 12)

1   Stabilizer bar insulator nut
2   Stabilizer bar U-bolt nut
3   Brace
4   The spacer must contact the brace during installation
5   Underbody
6   Shock absorber stud
7   Shock absorber
8   Axle assembly

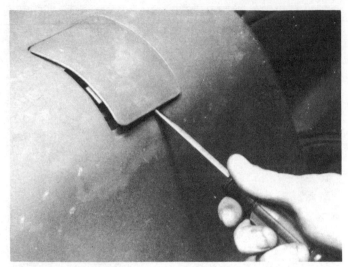

10.1A   Use a screwdriver to pry off the shock absorber access trim cover

10.1B   Hold the shock absorber shaft with the smaller wrench while removing the retaining nut

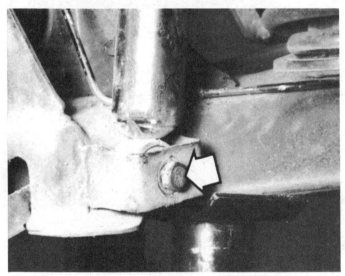

10.3   Lower shock absorber bolt location

11.7   Support the control arm as shown with a wood block and raise it into place with a jack to install the spring

9   Rear suspension — general information

The rear suspension is of the semi-independent type. This design features trailing arms which pivot from the chassis and are connected by a cross beam. The arms are supported by coil springs and separate shock absorbers, and some models are equipped with a stabilizer bar. The rear hub and brake assemblies are bolted to the ends of the trailing arms. The hub and bearing are non-serviceable and must be replaced with a new assembly should a fault develop.

10   Rear shock absorbers — removal and installation

Removal
1   Open the trunk or hatch, remove any trim which would interfere with access and remove the cover and upper shock absorber nut. If both shock absorbers are to be replaced, complete one replacement procedure before starting the other to avoid damage to the brake lines and hoses (photos).
2   Raise the vehicle and support it securely on jackstands. If the vehicle is being raised by the chassis, support the rear axle with a jack or jackstands.
3   Remove the lower shock absorber attaching bolt and remove the shock absorber from the vehicle (photo).

Installation
4   Place the shock absorber in position on the axle and install the bolt finger tight.
5   Lower the vehicle or raise the axle sufficiently to feed the upper stud of the shock absorber through the body opening and install the nut loosely.
6   Tighten the lower shock absorber bolt to the specified torque.
7   Remove the axle support, lower the vehicle weight onto the suspension and tighten the upper nut to the specified torque.
8   Replace the cover and trim.

11   Rear springs and insulators — removal and installation

Removal
1   Raise the vehicle by the chassis and support it securely on jackstands.
2   Support the rear control arms securely on jacks.
3   Remove the rear wheels.
4   Disconnect the brake line brackets by removing the retaining screws.
5   Remove the lower shock absorber attaching bolts.
6   Lower the rear axle with the jacks until the spring and insulator assemblies can be removed. Keep the springs separate so they are reinstalled in their original locations.

Fig. 11.9 Details of rear spring installation (Sec 11 and 13)

1 Center brake pipe	5 Spring insulator	9 Maximum clearance of 0.594 in
2 Brake hose	6 Spring	(15 mm)
3 Brake pipe bracket	7 Compression bumper	10 Spring
4 Chassis underbody	8 Axle assembly	11 Spring stop

Installation

7 With the help of an assistant, place the springs in position and slowly raise the control arms with the jacks, guiding the springs into place. The jacks must be placed under the control arms below the shock absorber mount to obtain the leverage needed to raise the arms evenly (photo).

8 Install the shock absorber bolts and tighten to the specified torque.

9 Connect the brake line brackets, install the wheels and lower the vehicle.

---

12 Rear stabilizer bar — removal and installation

Removal

1 Raise the rear of the vehicle, support it on jackstands and remove the rear wheels.

2 Remove the retaining nuts from the U-bolts and remove the stabilizer bar assembly from the vehicle.

Installation

3 Install the U-bolts, upper clamp, spacer and insulator on the axle and install the stabilizer bar with the lower clamp nuts finger tight, referring to the accompanying illustration.

4 Connect the stabilizer bar to the control arms, install the retaining nuts and tighten to the specified torque.

5 Tighten the stabilizer bar-to-axle U-bolt nuts to the specified torque.

6 Install the wheels and lower the vehicle.

---

13 Rear axle assembly — removal and installation

Removal

1 Raise the rear of the vehicle, support it securely on jackstands and remove the rear wheels.

2 Support the control arms with jacks or jackstands.

3 Remove the stabilizer bar (if equipped) (Section 12).

4 Disconnect the shock absorber lower ends from the control arms (Section 10).

5 Disconnect the parking brake cable.

6 Disconnect and plug the brake line at the axle assembly bracket.

7 Remove the rear springs and insulators (Section 11).

8 Remove the bolts attaching the control arms to the chassis and lower the axle from the vehicle.

Installation

9 Install the stabilizer bar to the axle.

10 Raise the axle into position with a jack.

11 Install the control arm-to-chassis bolts but do not tighten at this time.

12 Connect the brake line and parking brake cable.

13 Install the spring and insulator assemblies and tighten the shock absorber nuts to the specified torque.

14 Install the wheels, connect the parking brake cable to the guide hook and adjust the parking brake (Chapter 9).

15 Bleed the brake system (Chapter 9).

16 Lower the vehicle weight onto the suspension and tighten the control arm-to-chassis bolts to the specified torque.

---

14 Rear hub and bearings — removal and installation

1 Raise the rear of the vehicle and support it securely on jackstands.

2 Remove the brake assembly (Chapter 9).

3 Remove the four retaining nuts. The bolts have Torx heads and a special tool to hold the heads of the bolts will be necessary. Alternatively, locking pliers can be used to hold the bolts while the nuts are removed (photo).

14.3 If a Torx bit is not available, the hub nuts can be locked with suitable locking pliers

11

4   After removing the last bolt, be prepared to support the weight of hub and bearing assembly and lower it from the vehicle.

Installation
5   Place the hub and bearing assembly in position on the axle and install the bolts and nuts, tightening to the specified torque.
6   Install the brake assembly.

15 Steering system — general information

All models use rack and pinion steering. The components which make up the system are the steering wheel, steering column, intermediate shaft, rack and pinion assembly, tie rods and steering arms on the shock strut. In addition, the power steering system uses a belt-driven pump to provide hydraulic pressure.

The motion of turning the steering wheel is transferred through the column and intermediate shaft to the pinion shaft in the rack and pinion assembly. Teeth on the pinion shaft are meshed with teeth on the rack, so when the shaft is turned, the rack is moved left or right in the housing. Attached to the middle of the rack are tie rods which, in turn, are attached to steering arms on the shock struts. The shock struts pivot on bearings at the top and balljoints at the bottom. The left and right movement of the rack is the direct force which turns the wheels. On power steering models hydraulic pressure assists this function.

The steering column is of the collapsible, energy-absorbing type, designed to compress in the event of a front end collision to minimize injury to the driver. The column also houses the ignition switch lock, key warning buzzer, turn signal controls, headlight dimmer control and windshield wiper controls. The ignition and steering wheel can both be locked while the car is parked to inhibit theft.

Due to the column's collapsible design, it is important that only the specified fasteners, tightened to the specified torque, be used.

Because the disassembly of the steering column is more often performed to repair a switch or other electrical part than correct a steering fault, the steering column disassembly and reassembly procedure is included in Chapter 10.

16 Tie rod — removal and installation

Removal
1   Raise the front of the vehicle, support it securely on jackstands and remove the front wheels.
2   Bend back the lock plate tabs and remove the inner tie rod bolt.
3   Remove the tie rod-to-steering arm cotter pin and nut.
4   Disconnect the tie rod from the steering arm with a suitable tool (photo).
5   Remove the tie rod by withdrawing it through the wheel opening.

Installation
6   Place the tie rod in position and connect the ends to the steering arm and inner bolt.
7   Tighten the inner bolt to the specified torque and bend the lock tabs.
8   Tighten the tie rod-to-steering arm nut to the specified torque and install a cotter pin.
9   Install the wheels and lower the vehicle.
10   Have the front end alignment checked by a dealer or properly equipped shop.

17 Steering wheel — removal and installation

Removal
1   Disconnect the battery negative cable.
2   Remove the horn pad.
3   Mark the relative position of the steering wheel and shaft for installation in the same position (photo).
4   Remove the retaining nut.
5   Use a suitable puller to remove the steering wheel from the shaft (photo).

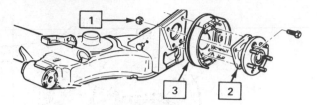

Fig. 11.10 Rear hub and bearing assembly installation details (Sec 14)

  1 Retaining nut
  2 Hub and bearing assembly
  3 Brake assembly

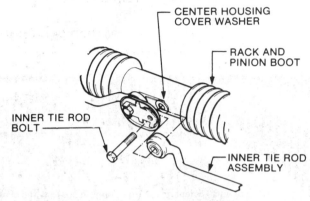

Fig. 11.11 Tie rod bolt installation details (Sec 16)

16.4   After removing the nut, use a ball joint removal tool to apply pressure to the joint and tap on the arm with a brass hammer to dislodge it

Installation
6   Place the steering wheel in position, aligning the marks made during removal.
7   Install the nut and tighten to the specified torque.
8   Install the horn pad and connect the battery negative cable.

18 Power steering system — general information

The power steering system operates in essentially the same way as the manual system, except that the power rack and pinion system uses

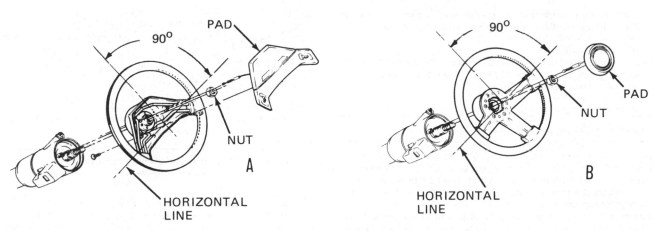

Fig. 11.12 Details of steering wheel installation (Sec 17)

A Standard wheel   *B Sport wheel*

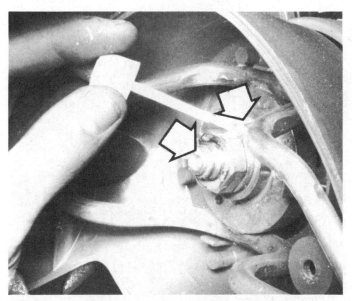

17.3 Use white paint to mark the position of the hub and shaft (arrows)

17.5 Draw the steering wheel off the shaft with a puller tool. Do not strike the end of the tool to dislodge the wheel as this will damage the shaft.

hydraulic pressure to boost the manual steering forces. A rotary control valve in the rack and pinion assembly directs hydraulic fluid from the power steering pump to either side of the integral rack piston, which is attached to the rack. Depending on which side of the piston this hydraulic pressure is applied to, the rack will be forced either left or right, which moves the tie rod and steering arms.

Hydraulic pressure is provided by a vane-type constant displacement pump with a remote reservoir. The pump is turned by an engine driven drivebelt.

If the power steering system loses it's hydraulic pressure it will still function manually, though with increased effort.

5   Bleed the system by turning the wheels from side to side without hitting the stops. This will work the air out of the system. Be careful that the reservoir does not run empty of fluid. Fluid with air in it will be light tan in appearance.
6   When the air is worked out of the system, return the wheels to the straight-ahead position and leave the vehicle running for several more minutes before shutting it off.
7   Road test the vehicle to be sure the steering system is functioning normally and is free from noise.
8   Recheck the fluid level to be sure it is up to the specified mark while the engine is at normal operating temperature. Add more fluid if necessary.

19 Bleeding the power steering system

1   Following any operation in which the power steering lines have been disconnected, the power steering system must bled of air to obtain proper steering performance.
2   If the fluid reservoir is be filled from empty, the pressure line must be disconnected at the pump. Fill the reservoir until the fluid begins running out at the pressure line fitting and connect the line.
3   Fill the reservoir to the specified level.
4   Start the engine and allow it to run at a fast idle. Recheck the fluid level and add more if necessary to reach the specified level on the dipstick.

20 Steering gear — removal and installation

Removal
1   In the passenger compartment, pull the seal assembly down from the a steering column and remove the flexible coupling upper pinch bolt (photo).
2   In the engine compartment, remove the air cleaner assembly and windshield washer reservoir.
3   Raise the front of the vehicle, support it securely on jackstands and remove the left front wheel.
4   Disconnect the tie rods from the strut steering arms (Section 16).

11

5   Remove the right side mounting nuts and clamp. It may be necessary to lift up the tie rod for clearance.
6   Remove the left side mounting nuts and clamp.
7   Pull the steering column coupling into the engine compartment sufficiently to allow removal of the flexible coupling lower pinch bolt (photo).
8   Separate the coupling and remove the dash seal from the from the steering rack assembly.
9   On power steering models, disconnect and plug the fluid lines.
9   Remove the left inner fender splash shield.
10 Turn the left steering knuckle and hub to the full right position and withdraw the steering gear assembly through the access hole (photo).

Installation

11 Insert the steering gear into position and install the splash shield.
12 Place the steering gear in position and install the dash seal.
13 Spread the flexible coupling clamp areas slightly with the blade of a screwdriver prior to installation. Check the steering gear clamp studs to make sure they were not loosened during the removal procedure. If the studs are backed out, reinstall them and use nuts to retain them.
14 With the help of an assistant in the passenger compartment, guide the flexible coupling onto the stub shaft and steering column and in-

stall the pinch bolts, tightening to the specified torque.
15 Install the left side and right side mounting clamps with the nuts finger tight, making sure the clamps are installed in the proper direction (photo).
16 Tighten the clamp nuts to the specified torque.
17 Connect the tie rod to the struts.
18 Install the wheel and lower the vehicle.
19 Install the air cleaner assembly and windshield washer reservoir.
20 Have the front end alignment checked by a dealer or properly equipped shop.

21 Power steering pump — removal and installation

Removal

1   Disconnect the battery negative cable.
2   Remove the air cleaner assembly.
3   Disconnect the pressure line from the pump and remove the clip which secures the line.
4   Loosen the adjustment and pivot bolts and remove the drivebelt.
5   Remove the pump-to-bracket bolts and lift the pump from the engine.

20.1   With the seal assembly pulled back the steering column pinch bolt (arrow) is accessible

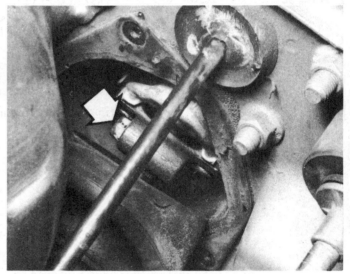

20.7   Lower steering column coupling pinch bolt location (arrow)

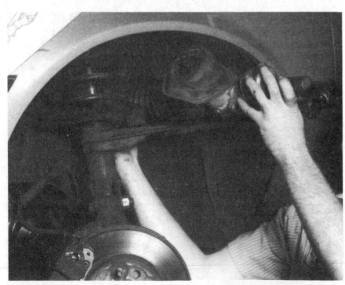

20.10   With the steering turned to the full right position, the steering gear can be lifted through the access hole and removed from the vehicle

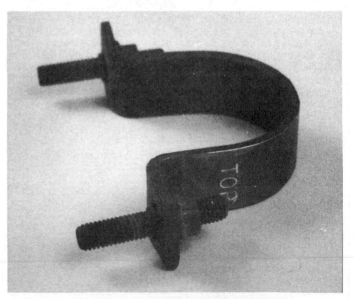

20.15   The mounting clamps must be installed with the TOP markings up

Installation

6   Place the pump in position on the bracket and install the retaining bolts, tightening to the specified torque.
7   Fasten the pressure line to the pump with the clip but do not connect it.
8   Connect the reservoir-to-pump hose.

9   Add the specified power steering fluid to the reservoir until the fluid can be seen at the pressure line port.
10   Connect the pressure line and secure the clip.
11   Install and adjust the drivebelt.
12   Install the air cleaner and connect the battery negative cable.
13   Bleed the system (Section 19).

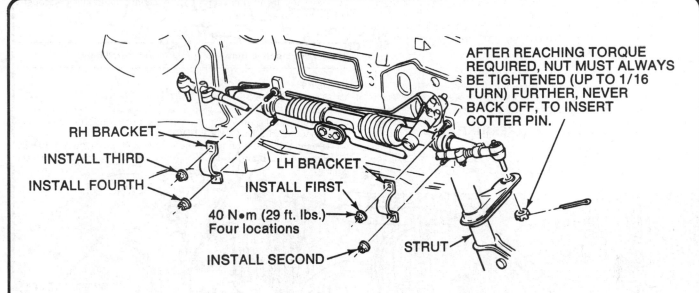

Fig. 11.13 Details of steering gear installation (Sec 20)

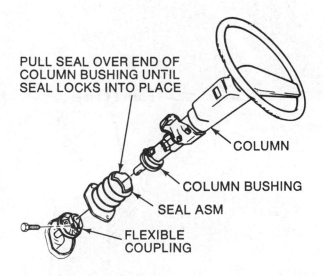

Fig. 11.14 Details of the steering column-to-steering gear installation (Sec 20)

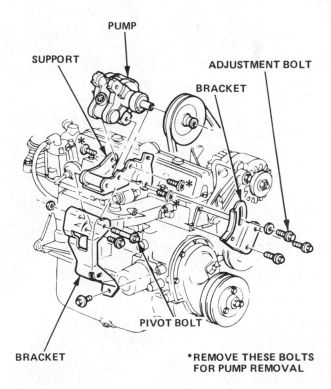

Fig. 11.15 Typical power steering pump installation (Sec 21)

11

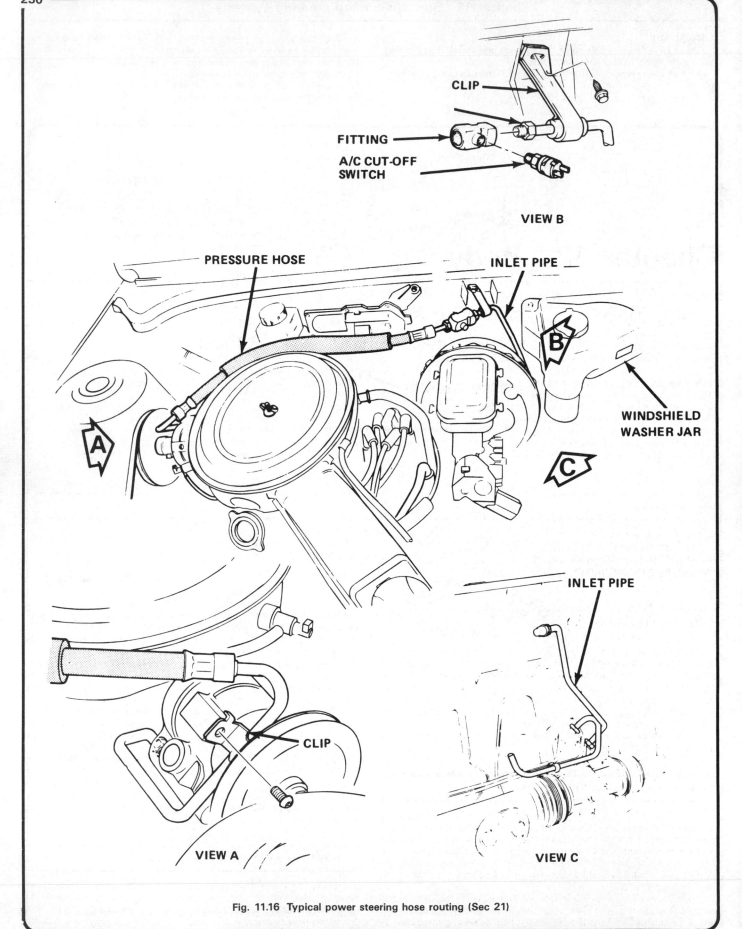

CLIP

FITTING

A/C CUT-OFF
SWITCH

VIEW B

PRESSURE HOSE

INLET PIPE

A

B

C

WINDSHIELD
WASHER JAR

INLET PIPE

CLIP

VIEW A

VIEW C

Fig. 11.16 Typical power steering hose routing (Sec 21)

Chapter 12   Body

Contents

Specifications

Torque specifications	Ft-lbs
Hatch retaining bolts	15 to 20
Door lock assembly screws	7 to 8
Exterior mirror retaining nuts	6

1   General information

These vehicles are of unitized construction. The body is designed to provide vehicle rigidity so that a separate frame is not necessary. Front and rear frame side rails, integral with the body, support the front end sheet metal, front and rear suspension systems and other mechanical components. With this type of construction it is very important that, in the event of collision damage, the underbody be thoroughly checked by a facility with the proper equipment.

Component replacement and repairs possible for the home mechanic are included in this chapter.

2   Body — maintenance

1   The condition of your vehicle's body is very important, because it is on this that the second-hand value will mainly depend. It is much more difficult to repair a neglected or damaged body than it is to repair mechanical components. The hidden areas of the body, such as the fender wells, the frame, and the engine compartment, are equally important, although obviously do not require as frequent attention as the rest of the body.

2   Once a year, or every 12 000 miles, it is a good idea to have the underside of the body and the frame steam cleaned. All traces of dirt and oil will be removed and the underside can then be inspected carefully for rust, damaged brake lines, frayed electrical wiring, damaged cables, and other problems. The front suspension components should be greased after completion of the cleaning and inspection.

3   At the same time, clean the engine and the engine compartment, using either a steam cleaner or a water soluble degreaser.

4   The fender wells should be given particular attention, as undercoating can peel away and stones and dirt thrown up by the tires can cause the paint to chip and flake, allowing rust to set in. If rust is found, clean down to the bare metal and apply an anti-rust paint.

5   The body should be washed once a week (or when dirty). Wet the vehicle thoroughly to soften the dirt, then wash it down with a soft sponge and plenty of clean soapy water. If the surplus dirt is not washed off very carefully it will, in time, wear down the paint.

6   Spots of tar or asphalt coating thrown up from the road should be removed with a cloth soaked in solvent.

7   Once every six months give the body and chrome trim a thorough wax job. If a chrome cleaner is used to remove rust from any of the vehicle's plated parts, remember that the cleaner also removes part of the chrome, so use it sparingly.

3   Upholstery and carpets — maintenance

1   Every three months remove the carpets or mats and clean the interior of the vehicle (more frequently if necessary). Vacuum the upholstery and carpets to remove loose dirt and dust.

2   If the upholstery is soiled, apply upholstery cleaner with a damp sponge and wipe it off with a clean, dry cloth.

12

4   Vinyl trim — maintenance

Vinyl trim should not be cleaned with detergents, caustic soaps or petroleum-based cleaners. Plain soap and water or a mild vinyl cleaner is best for stains. Test a small area for color fastness. Bubbles under the vinyl can be corrected by piercing them with a pin and then working the air out.

5   Hinges and locks — maintenance

Every 3000 miles or three months, the door, hood and rear hatch hinges should be lubricated with a few drops of oil and the locks treated with dry graphite lubricant. The door and rear hatch striker plates should also be given a thin coat of grease to reduce wear and ensure free movement.

6   Body repair — minor damage

See photo sequence

Repair of minor scratches

If the scratch is very superficial and does not penetrate to the metal of the body, repair is simple. Lightly rub the scratched area with a fine rubbing compound to remove loose paint and built-up wax. Rinse the area with clean water.

Apply touch-up paint to the scratch, using a small brush. Continue to apply thin layers of paint until the surface of the paint in the scratch is level with the surrounding paint. Allow the new paint at least two weeks to harden, then blend it into the surrounding paint by rubbing with a very fine rubbing compound. Finally, apply a coat of wax to the scratch area.

If the scratch has penetrated the paint and exposed the metal of the body, causing the metal to rust, a different repair technique is required. Remove all loose rust from the bottom of the scratch with a pocket knife, then apply rust-inhibiting paint to prevent the formation of rust in the future. Using a rubber or nylon applicator, coat the scratched area with glaze-type filler. If required, the filler can be mixed with thinner to provide a very thin paste, which is ideal for filling narrow scratches. Before the glaze filler in the scratch hardens, wrap a piece of smooth cotton cloth around the tip of a finger. Dip the cloth in thinner and then quickly wipe it along the surface of the scratch. This will ensure that the surface of the filler is slightly hollow. The scratch can now be painted over as described earlier in this section.

Repair of dents

When repairing dents, the first job is to pull the dent out until the affected area is as close as possible to its original shape. There is no point in trying to restore the original shape completely, as the metal in the damaged area will have stretched on impact and cannot be restored to its original contours. It is better to bring the level of the dent up to a point which is about 1/8-inch below the level of the surrounding metal. In cases where the dent is very shallow it is not worth trying to pull it out at all.

If the back side of the dent is accessible, it can be hammered out gently from behind using a soft-faced hammer. While doing this, hold a block of wood firmly against the opposite side of the metal to absorb the hammer blows and prevent the metal from being stretched.

If the dent is in a section of the body which has double layers, or some other factor that makes it inaccessible from behind, a different technique is required. Drill several small holes through the metal inside the damaged area, particularly in the deeper sections. Screw long, self-tapping screws into the holes just enough for them to get a good grip in the metal. Now the dent can be pulled out by pulling on the protruding heads of the screws with locking pliers.

The next stage of repair is the removal of paint from the damaged area and from an inch or so of the surrounding metal. This is easily done with a wire brush or sanding disk in a drill motor, although it can be done just as effectively by hand with sandpaper. To complete the preparation for filling, score the surface of the bare metal with a screwdriver or the tang of a file (or drill small holes in the affected area). This will provide a very good grip for the filler material. To complete the repair, see the Section on filling and painting.

Repair of rust holes or gashes

Remove all paint from the affected area and from an inch or so of the surrounding metal, using a sanding disk or wire brush mounted in a drill motor. If these are not available, a few sheets of sandpaper will do the job just as effectively. With the paint removed you will be able to determine the severity of the corrosion and decide whether to replace the whole panel, if possible, or repair the affected area. New body panels are not as expensive as most people think and it is often quicker to install a new panel than to repair large areas of rust.

Remove all trim pieces from the affected area (except those which will act as a guide to the original shape of the damaged body, i.e. headlight shells, etc.). Using metal snips or a hacksaw blade, remove all loose metal and any other metal that is badly affected by rust. Hammer the edges of the hole in to create a slight depression for the filler material.

Wire brush the affected area to remove the powdery rust from the surface of the metal. If the back of the rusted area is accessible, treat it with rust-inhibiting paint.

Before filling is done, block the hole in some way. This can be done with sheet metal riveted or screwed into place, or by stuffing the hole with wire mesh.

Once the hole is blocked off, the affected area can be filled and painted (see the following sub-section on filling and painting).

Filling and painting

Many types of body fillers are available, but generally speaking, body repair kits which contain filler paste and a tube of resin hardener are best for this type of repair work. A wide, flexible plastic or nylon applicator will be necessary for imparting a smooth and contoured finish to the surface of the filler material.

Mix up a small amount of filler on a clean piece of wood or cardboard (use the hardener sparingly). Follow the manufacturer's instructions on the package, otherwise the filler will set incorrectly.

Using the applicator, apply the filler paste to the prepared area. Draw the applicator across the surface of the filler to achieve the desired contour and to level the filler surface. As soon as a contour that approximates the original is achieved, stop working the paste. If you continue, the paste will begin to stick to the applicator. Continue to add thin layers of filler paste at 20 minute intervals until the level of the filler is just above the surrounding metal.

Once the filler has hardened, the excess can be removed with a body file. From then on, progressively finer grades of sandpaper should be used, starting with a 180-grit paper and finishing with 600-grit wet-or-dry paper. Always wrap the sandpaper around a flat rubber or wooden block, otherwise the surface of the filler will not be completely flat. During the sanding of the filler surface, the wet-or-dry paper should be periodically rinsed in water. This will ensure that a very smooth finish is produced in the final stage.

At this point the repair area should be surrounded by a ring of bare metal, which in turn should be encircled by the finely feathered edge of good paint. Rinse the repair area with clean water until all of the dust produced by the sanding operation is gone.

Spray the entire area with a light coat of primer. This will reveal any imperfections in the surface of the filler. Repair the imperfections with fresh filler paste or glaze filler and once more smooth the surface with sandpaper. Repeat this spray-and-repair procedure until you are satisfied that the surface of the filler and the feathered edge of the paint are perfect. Rinse the area with clean water and allow it to dry completely.

The repair area is now ready for painting. Spray painting must be carried out in a warm, dry, windless and dust-free atmosphere. These conditions can be created if you have access to a large indoor work area, but if you are forced to work in the open, you will have to pick the day very carefully. If you are working indoors, dousing the floor in the work area with water will help settle the dust which would otherwise be in the air. If the repair area is confined to one body panel, mask off the surrounding panels. This will help minimize the effects of a slight mismatch in paint color. Trim pieces such as chrome strips, door handles, etc., will also need to be masked off or removed. Use masking tape and several thicknesses of newspaper for the masking operations.

Before spraying, shake the paint can thoroughly, then spray a test area until the spray painting technique is mastered. Cover the repair area with a thick coat of primer. The thickness should be built up using several thin layers of primer rather than one thick one. Using 600-grit wet-or-dry sandpaper, rub down the surface of the primer until it is very smooth. While doing this, the work area should be thoroughly rinsed with water and the wet-or-dry sandpaper periodically rinsed as well. Allow the primer to dry before spraying additional coats.

Spray on the top coat, again building up the thickness by using several thin layers of paint. Begin spraying in the center of the repair area and then, using a circular motion, work out until the whole repair area and about two inches of the surrounding original paint is covered. Remove all masking material 10 to 15 minutes after spraying on the final coat of paint. Allow the new paint at least two weeks to harden, then use a very fine rubbing compound to blend the edges of the new paint into the existing paint. Finally, apply a coat of wax.

7 Body repair — major damage

1   Major damage must be repaired by an auto body shop specifically equipped to perform unibody repairs. These shops have available the specialized equipment required to do the job properly.

2   If the damage is extensive, the underbody must be checked for proper alignment or the vehicle's handling characteristics may be adversely affected and other components may wear at an accelerated rate.

3   Due to the fact that all of the major body components (hood, fenders, etc.) are separate and replaceable units, any seriously damaged components should be replaced rather than repaired.

Sometimes these components can be found in a wrecking yard that specializes in used vehicle components (often at considerable savings over the cost of new parts).

8 Hood — removal and installation

1   Raise the hood.

2   Place protective pads along the edges of the engine compartment to prevent damage to the painted surfaces.

3   Scribe or paint lines around the mounting brackets so the hood can be installed in the same position (photo).

4   Apply white paint around the bracket-to-hood bolts so they can be aligned quickly and accurately during installation.

5   With an assistant supporting the weight, remove the bracket bolts and detach the hood from the vehicle.

6   Installation is the reverse of removal. Be sure to align the brackets and bolts with the marks made prior to removal.

9 Hood latch release cable — replacement

1   Working in the engine compartment, disconnect the release cable from the latch mechanism (photo).

2   Disconnect the cable from the retaining bracket with pliers (photo).

3   Working in the passenger compartment, remove the cable handle (photo).

4   Using needle-nose or snap-ring pliers, remove the cable retainer from the dash (photo).

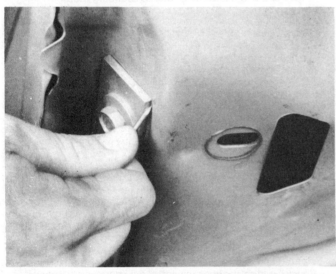

8.3   A nail can be used to scribe around the hood mounting bracket

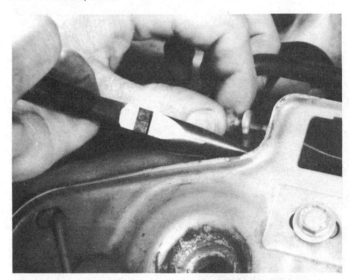

9.1   Disconnect the latch release cable while holding the bracket with needle-nose pliers

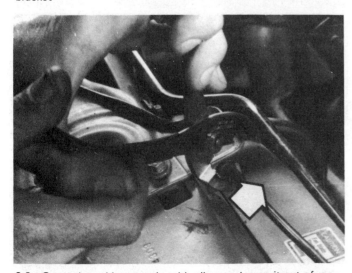

9.2   Grasp the cable securely with pliers and snap it out of the bracket in the direction shown by the arrow

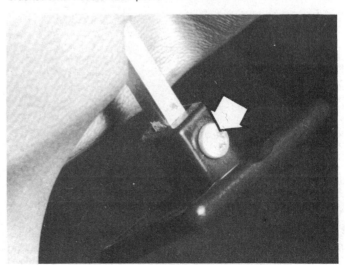

9.3   The parking brake cable handle is retained by a Torx head screw (arrow)

12

These photos illustrate a method of repairing simple dents. They are intended to supplement *Body repair - minor damage* in this Chapter and should not be used as the sole instructions for body repair on these vehicles.

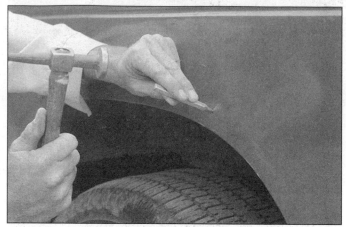

1 If you can't access the backside of the body panel to hammer out the dent, pull it out with a slide-hammer-type dent puller. In the deepest portion of the dent or along the crease line, drill or punch hole(s) at least one inch apart . . .

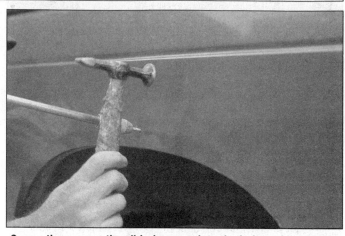

2 . . . then screw the slide-hammer into the hole and operate it. Tap with a hammer near the edge of the dent to help 'pop' the metal back to its original shape. When you're finished, the dent area should be close to its original contour and about 1/8-inch below the surface of the surrounding metal

3 Using coarse-grit sandpaper, remove the paint down to the bare metal. Hand sanding works fine, but the disc sander shown here makes the job faster. Use finer (about 320-grit) sandpaper to feather-edge the paint at least one inch around the dent area

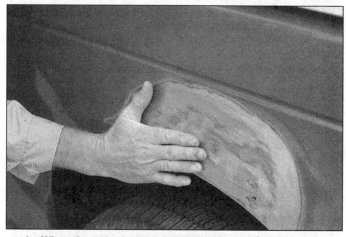

4 When the paint is removed, touch will probably be more helpful than sight for telling if the metal is straight. Hammer down the high spots or raise the low spots as necessary. Clean the repair area with wax/silicone remover

5 Following label instructions, mix up a batch of plastic filler and hardener. The ratio of filler to hardener is critical, and, if you mix it incorrectly, it will either not cure properly or cure too quickly (you won't have time to file and sand it into shape)

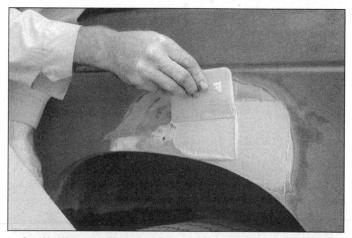

6 Working quickly so the filler doesn't harden, use a plastic applicator to press the body filler firmly into the metal, assuring it bonds completely. Work the filler until it matches the original contour and is slightly above the surrounding metal

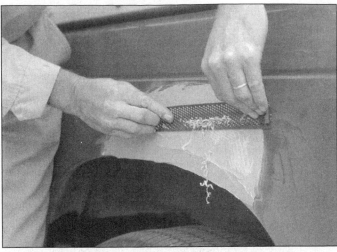

7   Let the filler harden until you can just dent it with your fingernail. Use a body file or Surform tool (shown here) to rough-shape the filler

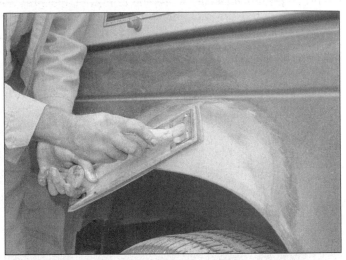

8   Use coarse-grit sandpaper and a sanding board or block to work the filler down until it's smooth and even. Work down to finer grits of sandpaper - always using a board or block - ending up with 360 or 400 grit

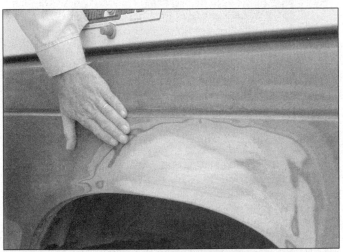

9   You shouldn't be able to feel any ridge at the transition from the filler to the bare metal or from the bare metal to the old paint. As soon as the repair is flat and uniform, remove the dust and mask off the adjacent panels or trim pieces

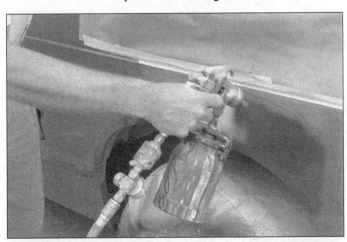

10   Apply several layers of primer to the area. Don't spray the primer on too heavy, so it sags or runs, and make sure each coat is dry before you spray on the next one. A professional-type spray gun is being used here, but aerosol spray primer is available inexpensively from auto parts stores

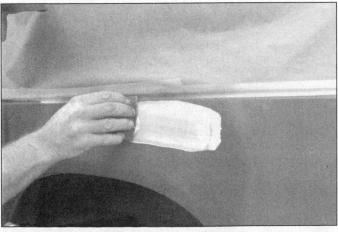

11   The primer will help reveal imperfections or scratches. Fill these with glazing compound. Follow the label instructions and sand it with 360 or 400-grit sandpaper until it's smooth. Repeat the glazing, sanding and respraying until the primer reveals a perfectly smooth surface

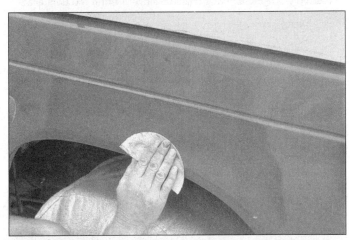

12   Finish sand the primer with very fine sandpaper (400 or 600-grit) to remove the primer overspray. Clean the area with water and allow it to dry. Use a tack rag to remove any dust, then apply the finish coat. Don't attempt to rub out or wax the repair area until the paint has dried completely (at least two weeks)

9.4   Snap-ring pliers are used to remove the cable retainer

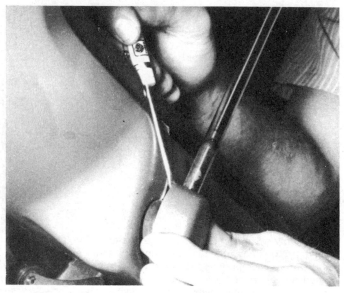

10.2a   Pry the damper strut trim cover off with a screwdriver

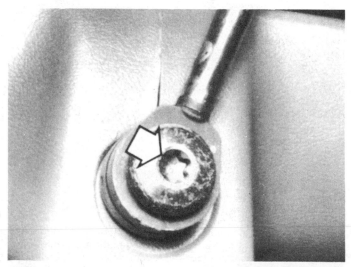

10.2b   The lower damper strut mount is retained by a Torx-head screw (arrow)

5   Connect string or thin wire to the end of the cable and remove it by pulling it through into the passenger compartment.
6   Installation is the reverse of removal (connect the string or wire to the new cable and pull it into position).

10   Rear hatch damper — removal and installation

1   Support the hatch in the fully open position.
2   On hatchback models, disconnect both ends of the dampers and remove them (photos).
3   On station wagon models, use a blade-type screwdriver to remove the clips from the ends and remove the damper as shown in the accompanying illustration.
4   Installation is the reverse of removal (be sure to replace the damper with one having the same color coded lettering).

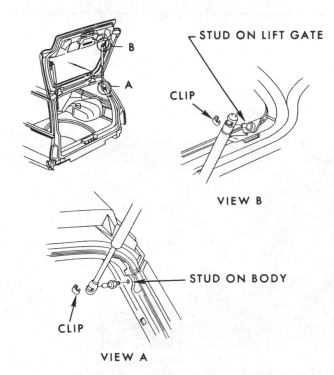

Fig. 12.1 Details of station wagon hatch damper strut installation (Sec 10)

10.2c   Use a screwdriver to pry off the upper strut retainer

11 Rear hatch — removal, installation and adjustment

Removal

1 Open the rear hatch and support it with a prop.
2 Place protective pads along the edges of the hatch opening to prevent damage to the painted surfaces while work is being performed.
3 On hatchback models, remove the trim panel covering the hatch-to-body bolts.
4 On all models, remove the damper struts (Section 10).
5 Disconnect any wiring harnesses which would interfere with hatch removal.
6 On hatchback models, remove the nuts from the hinge retaining bolts and lift the hatch from the vehicle with the help of an assistant.
7 On station wagon models, place a 3/16-inch metal rod on the pointed end of the hinge pin. Strike the rod sharply with a hammer to shear off the retaining clip tabs and drive the pin out of the hinge. With the help of an assistant, lift the hatch from the vehicle.

Installation

8 Installation is the reverse of removal except that on station wagon models, new retaining clips must be installed with their tabs toward the heads of the pins before the pins are driven into place.

Adjustment

9 The rear hatch on hatchback models can be adjusted, but the station wagon hatch cannot.
10 The hatch attachment bolt holes are oversize. With the hatch propped open, the dampers disconnected and the bolts loose, the hatch fore-and-aft and side-to-side position can be adjusted.
11 Hatch height may be adjusted by adding or subtracting the number of shims at the hinge-to-body locations. Height adjustment can also be made at the rubber bumpers on the lower panel.

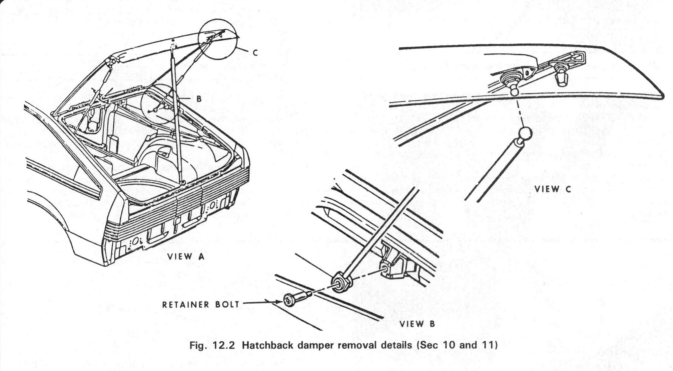

Fig. 12.2 Hatchback damper removal details (Sec 10 and 11)

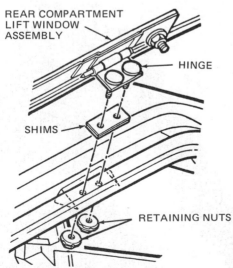

Fig. 12.3 Hatchback rear hatch hinge-to-body installation details (Sec 11)

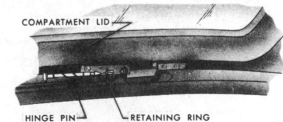
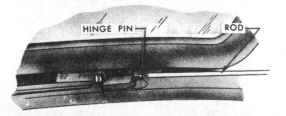

Fig. 12.4 Details of station wagon hatch hinge (Sec 11)

12

12.2 Disconnect the lock knob by prying it loose from the locking rod with a small screwdriver inserted behind the leading edge

13.6 Pry the trim panel loose by disengaging the retainers one at a time with a putty knife, screwdriver or pry bar

12 Door lock knob — removal and installation

1   Remove the control handle bezel screws to gain access to the back side of the lock knob.
2   Insert a small blade-type screwdriver behind the leading end of the lock knob and pry it away from the locking rod, located behind the knob (photo).
3   Once the end of the rod is free from the knob, slide the knob forward and remove it.
4   To install the knob, place the bezel in position with the lock rod through the hole and insert the small end of the knob to the rear, into place, until the end of the rod engages the depression in the front end of the knob.

13 Door trim panel — removal and installation

1   Remove all of the trim panel retaining screws.
2   Remove the inside door locking knob (Section 12).
3   On models with remote control mirrors, remove the escutcheon and disengage the control cable end from the escutcheon.
4   On power window-equipped models, disconnect the wiring harness from the switch assembly.
5   Remove the window regulator crank handle (Section 14).
6   Pry the trim panel loose by working around the outer edge with a large screwdriver or putty knife to disengage the plastic retainers. These retainers fit very tightly and care must be taken not to destroy them during removal (photo).

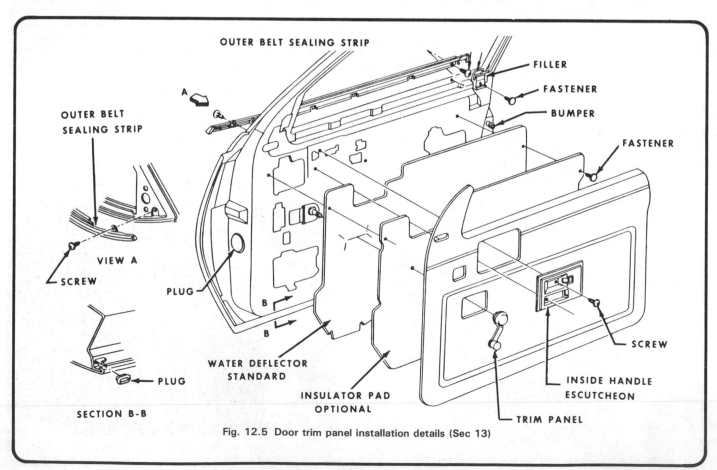

Fig. 12.5 Door trim panel installation details (Sec 13)

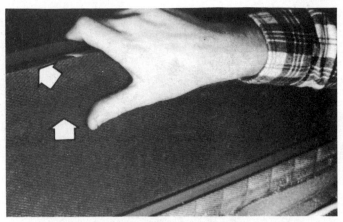

13.8 Disengage the panel by lifting it up and out (arrows)

7 On models with courtesy lights in the door panels, disconnect the wiring harness.
8 Remove the panel by pushing up and out to disengage it from the top of the door (photo).
9 Carefully peel back the water deflector for access to the inner door panel.
10 Installation is the reverse of removal, noting the following:
11 Before attaching the trim panel to the door, make sure that all the

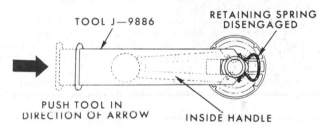

Fig. 12.6 Removing the window regulator handle spring clip with the special tool (Sec 14)

TOOL J—9886
RETAINING SPRING DISENGAGED
PUSH TOOL IN DIRECTION OF ARROW
INSIDE HANDLE

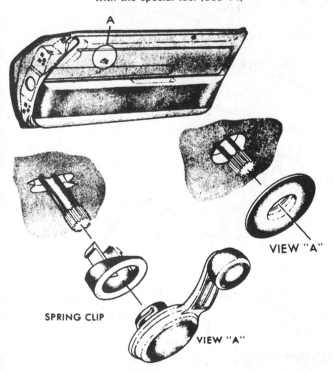

A

VIEW "A"

SPRING CLIP

VIEW "A"

Fig. 12.7 Window regulator handle components (Sec 14)

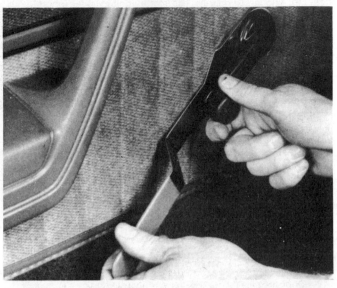

14.2 Using a special tool to remove the window regulator handle spring clip

plastic trim retainers are undamaged and installed tightly in the panel.
12 If the retainer is to be replaced with a new one, start the retainer flange into the cutout attachment hole in the trim panel, then rotate the retainer until the flange is fully engaged.
13 When attaching the door trim panel to the door, locate the top of the panel over the upper flange of the inner door panel and press down on the trim panel to engage the upper retaining clips.
14 Position the trim panel on the inner door panel so that the panel retainers are aligned with the holes in the door panel and tap the retainers into the holes with the palm of your hand or a rubber mallet.

14 Door window regulator handle — removal and installation

1 Push the trim panel away from the handle to expose the spring clip.
2 Insert two small screwdrivers or a special forked tool (available at auto parts stores) between the handle and the plastic washer and push the spring clip off the shaft (photo).
3 To install, replace the spring clip and press the handle into place.

15 Door lock cylinder — removal and installation

1 Raise the window, remove the trim panel and peel back the water

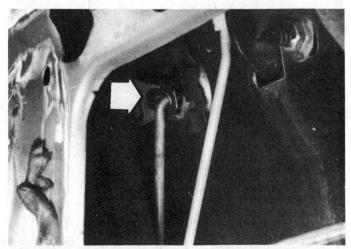

15.1 The door lock cylinder retaining clip (arrow) is accessible after removing the door panel

12

deflector enough to gain access to the lock cylinder (photo).
2   Disconnect the lock cylinder actuating rod from the cylinder.
3   Use a screwdriver to slide the lock cylinder retainer forward until
it is disengaged and the lock cylinder can be removed.
4   Installation is the reverse of removal (make sure the gasket is correctly installed).

16   Door lock assembly — removal and installation

1   Remove the door trim panel and peel back the water deflector for
access to the locking rods.
2   Disconnect the inside locking rod, the inside handle and lock
cylinder locking rods.
3   Remove the retaining screws, lower the lock assembly and
disengage the outside handle from the rod. Remove the assembly from
the door.
4   After attaching the spring clips to the lock assembly, installation
is the reverse of removal. Tighten the retaining screws to the specified
torque.

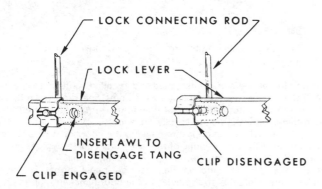

Fig. 12.8 Door locking rod connection details
(Sec 15 through 17)

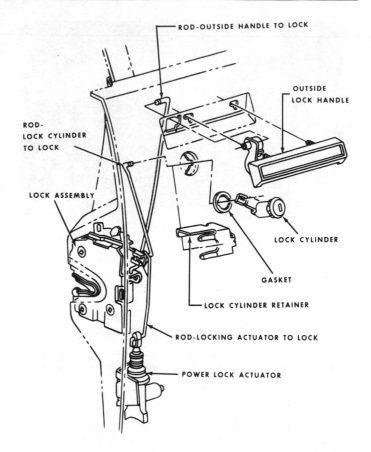

Fig. 12.9 Typical door lock mechanism component layout
(Sec 15 and 16)

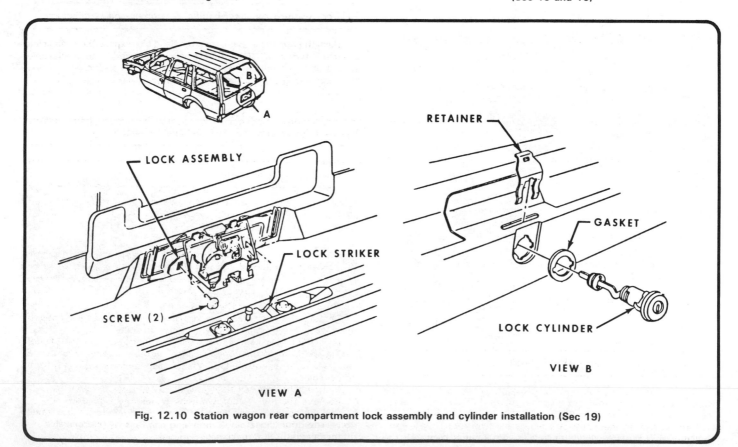

Fig. 12.10 Station wagon rear compartment lock assembly and cylinder installation (Sec 19)

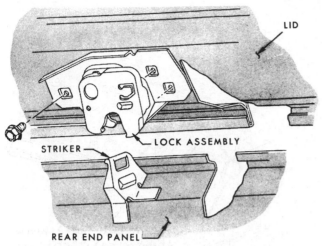

Fig. 12.11 Typical rear lock assembly installation (Sec 19)

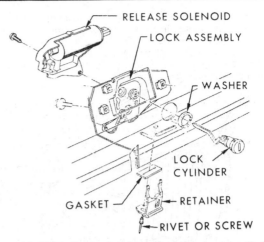

Fig. 12.12 Typical solenoid-equipped lock and cylinder assembly installation details (Sec 19)

17   Door outside handle — removal and installation

1   With the window in the full up position, remove the door trim panel and peel the water deflector back to expose the access hole.
2   Disengage the locking rod from the outside handle.
3   Remove the two nuts from the handle studs.
4   Remove the handle by sliding it forward while rotating it up to disengage it from the nut holes.
5   Installation is the reverse of removal.

18   Door window glass replacement

Due to the requirements for special handling techniques, window glass should be replaced by a dealer or auto glass shop.

19   Rear compartment lid lock cylinder — removal and installation

1   Open the rear compartment and remove the lock cylinder emblem (if equipped).
2   Remove the lock cylinder retaining screw. If retained by a rivet, carefully drill the rivet out using a 5/32-inch drill bit, taking care not to enlarge the hole.
3   Pull the retainer away to release the cylinder and then remove the cylinder from the vehicle.
4   Installation is the reverse of removal, making sure that the lock cylinder shaft engages with the lock and the gasket mates with the outer panel to form a watertight seal. A self-tapping screw can be used in place of a rivet to secure the retainer.

20   Rear compartment lid lock assembly — removal and installation

1   Open the compartment lid.
2   Remove the lock assembly attaching bolts and detach the assembly from the vehicle.
3   On models equipped with electric release units, it will first be necessary to unplug the electrical connector. Unbolt and remove the electric release unit.
4   Installation is the reverse of removal.

21   Exterior mirror — removal and installation

1   Remove the trim panel or bezel. On some models it may be necessary to remove the door trim panel and peel the water deflector back for access to the retaining nuts.
2   Remove the retaining nuts and separate the mirror from the vehicle. On remote control mirrors, detach the cable clip and remove the

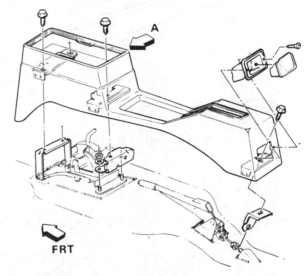

Fig. 12.14 Typical console installation details (Sec 23)

mirror and cable as an assembly.
3   Installation is the reverse of removal (make sure the mirror gasket is properly aligned).

22   Fixed glass replacement

Due to the requirements for special handling techniques, the fixed glass such as the windshield, rear and side glass should be replaced by a dealer or auto glass shop.

23   Console — removal and installation

1   Disconnect the negative cable from the battery.
2   Remove the front and rear ash trays.
3   Remove the two retaining screws in the bottom of the front ash tray well with a special Torx-type screwdriver.
4   Loosen the Allen head screw in the shift knob and remove the knob.
5   Tilt the front of the console cover and boot assembly and slide it forward to disengage the tabs, then detach the cover assembly from the console.
6   Remove the rear ash tray retainer cavity (two screws).
7   Remove the four hold-down bolts retaining the console.
8   Pull the parking brake lever up about three-quarters of its travel and remove the console by lifting and sliding it simultaneously.
9   Installation is the reverse of removal.

12

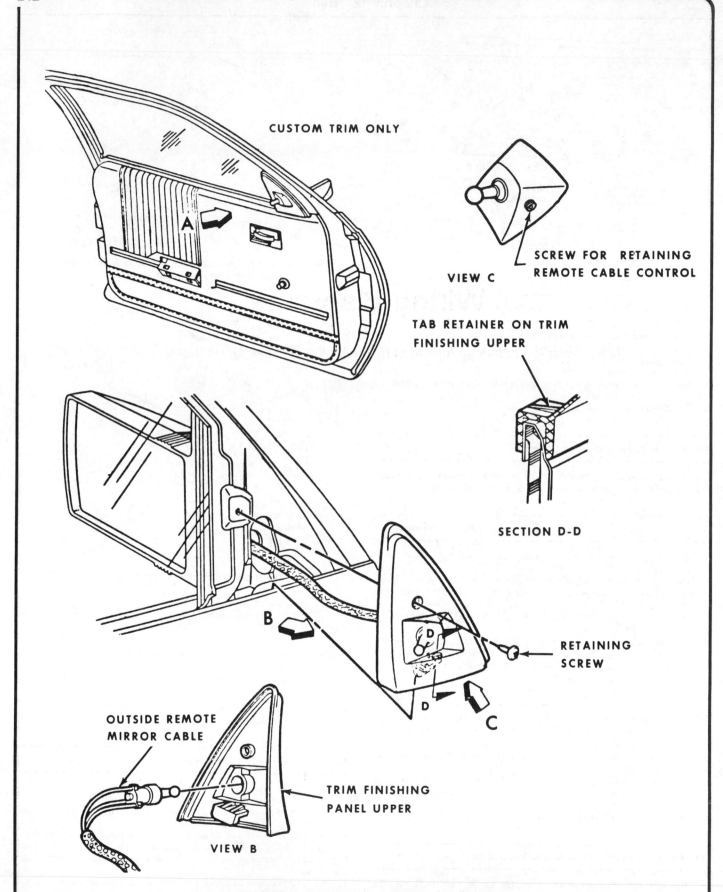

CUSTOM TRIM ONLY

VIEW C

SCREW FOR RETAINING REMOTE CABLE CONTROL

TAB RETAINER ON TRIM FINISHING UPPER

SECTION D-D

RETAINING SCREW

OUTSIDE REMOTE MIRROR CABLE

TRIM FINISHING PANEL UPPER

VIEW B

Fig. 12.13 Typical exterior mirror installation details (Sec 21)

Wiring diagrams

Note: *Refer to Chapter 13 for wiring diagrams for 1985 and later models*

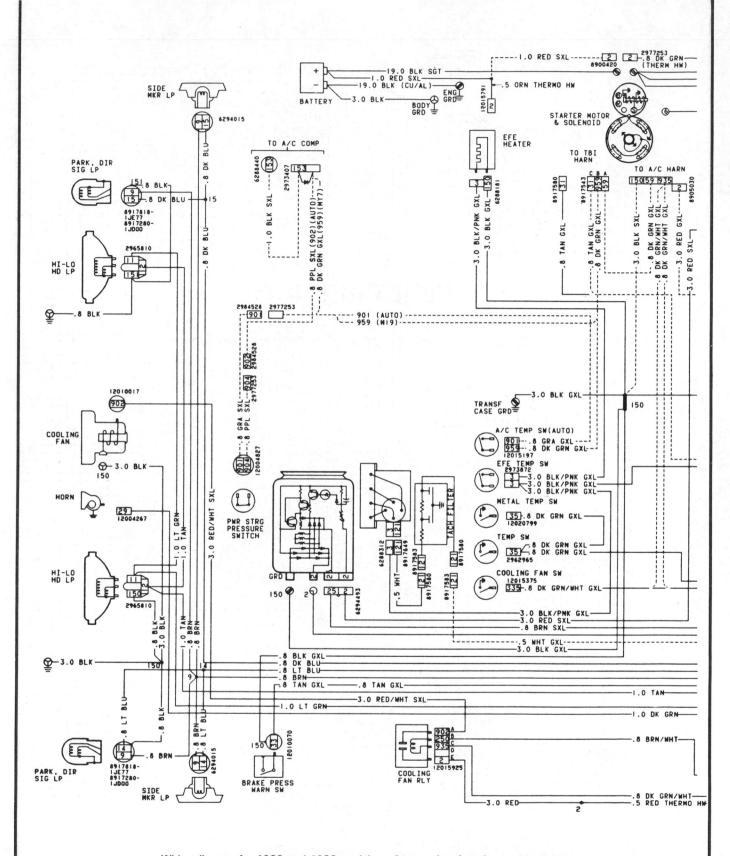

Wiring diagram for 1982 and 1983 models — front end and engine compartment

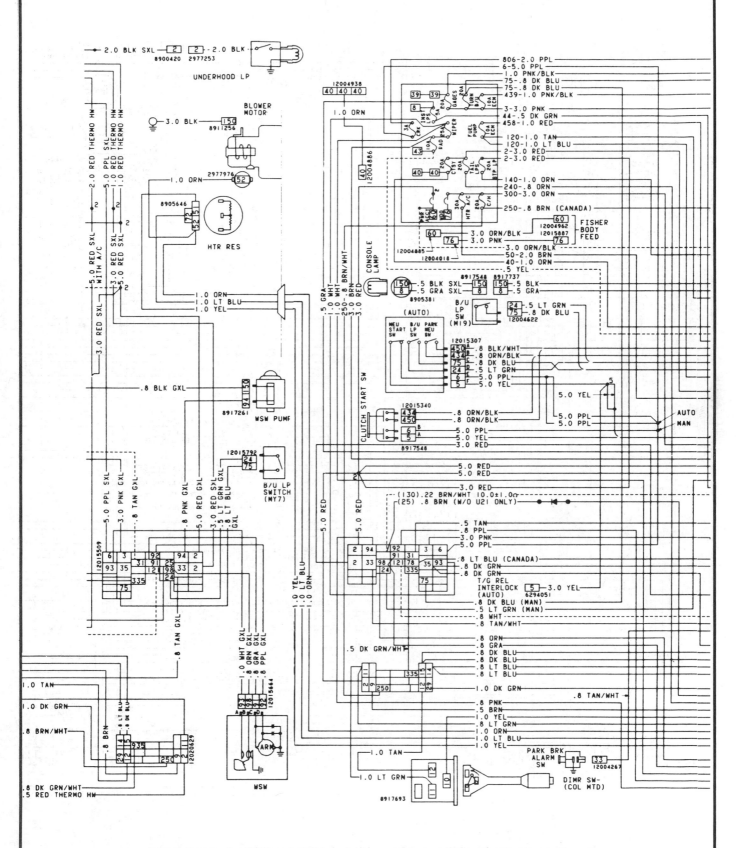

Wiring diagram for 1982 and 1983 models — engine compartment and instrument panel

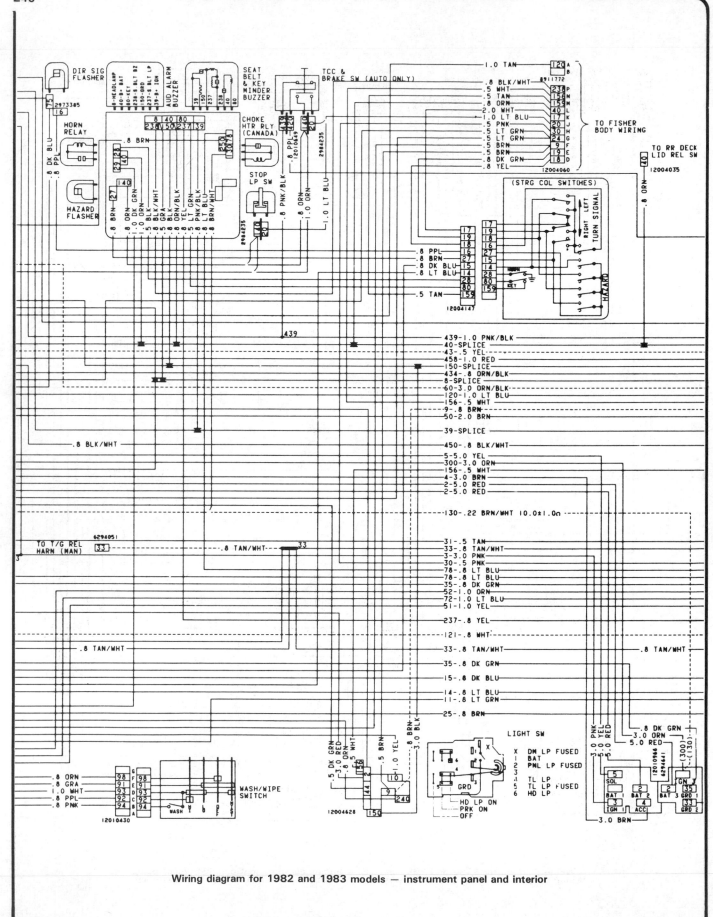

Wiring diagram for 1982 and 1983 models — instrument panel and interior

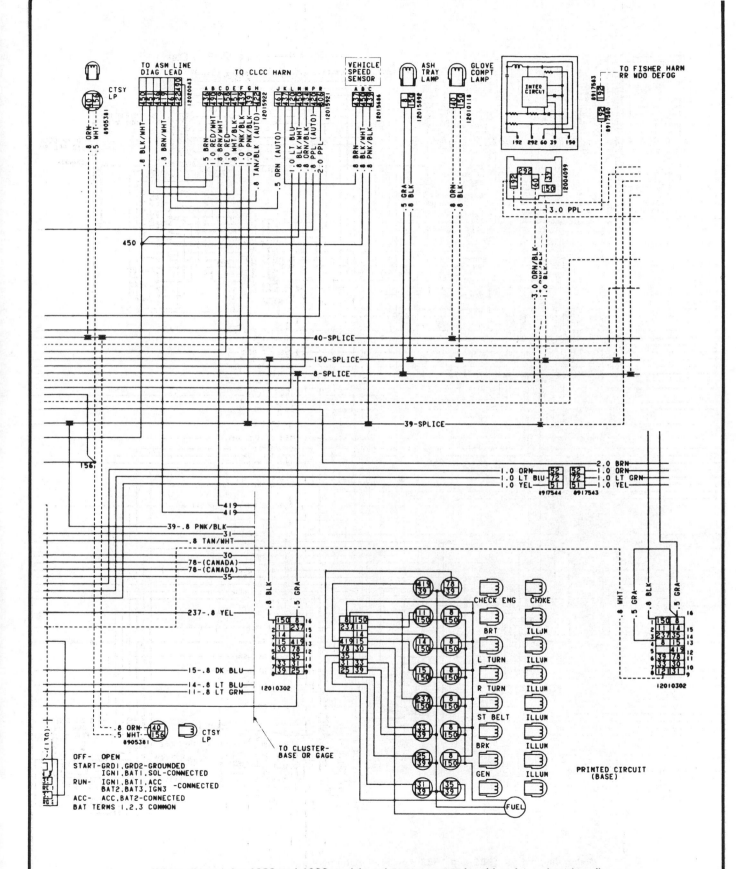

Wiring diagram for 1982 and 1983 models — instrument panel and interior — (continued)

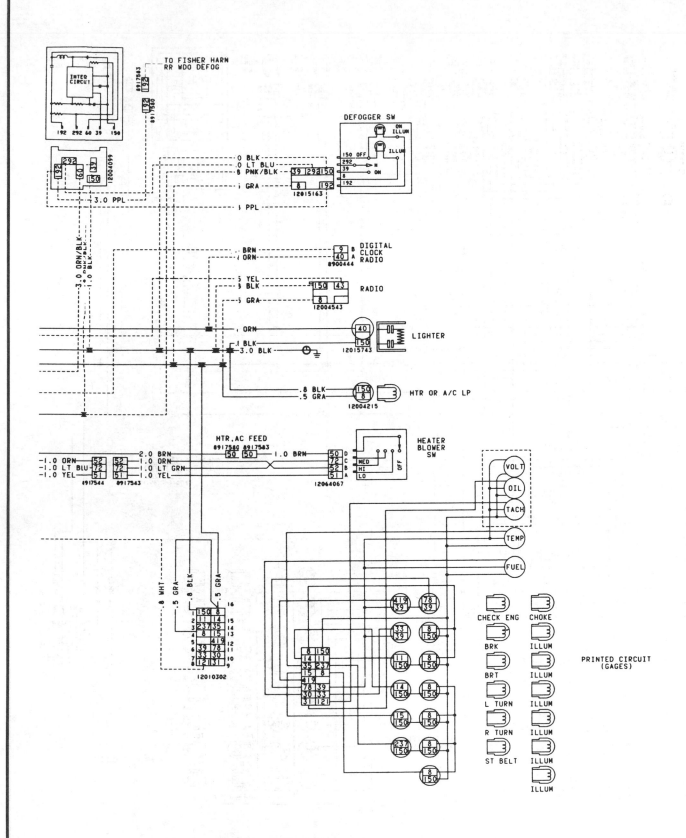

Wiring diagram for 1982 and 1983 models — instrument panel and interior (continued)

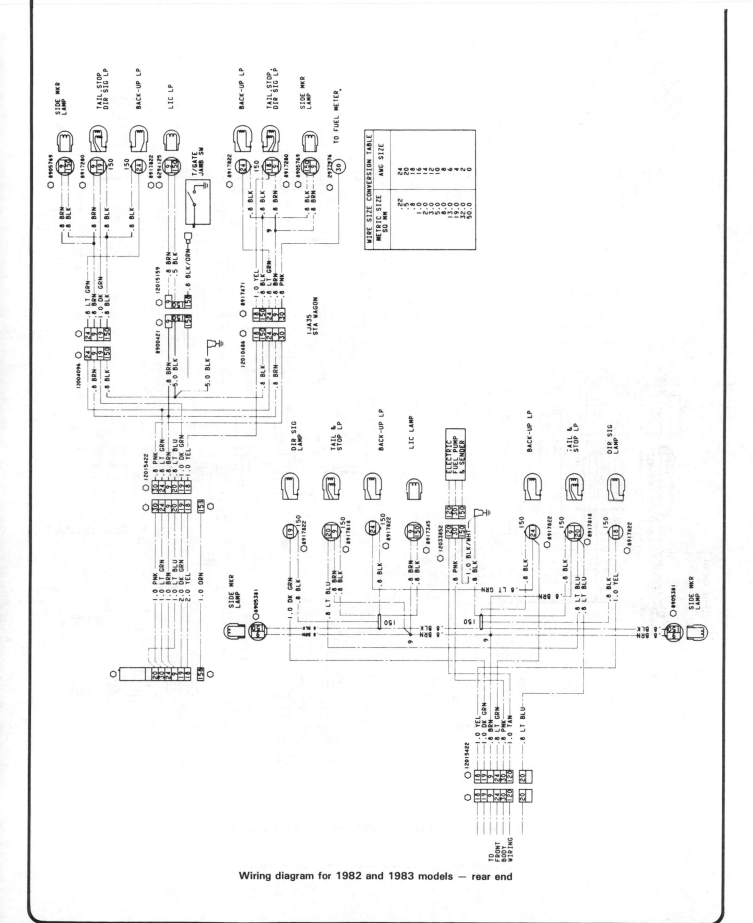

Wiring diagram for 1982 and 1983 models — rear end

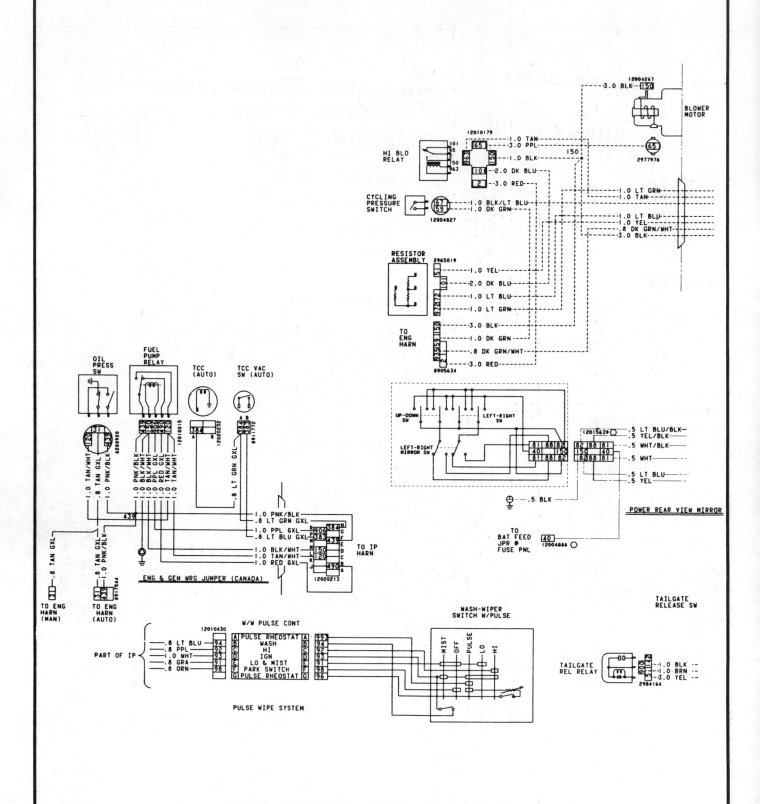

Wiring diagram for 1982 and 1983 models — optional circuits

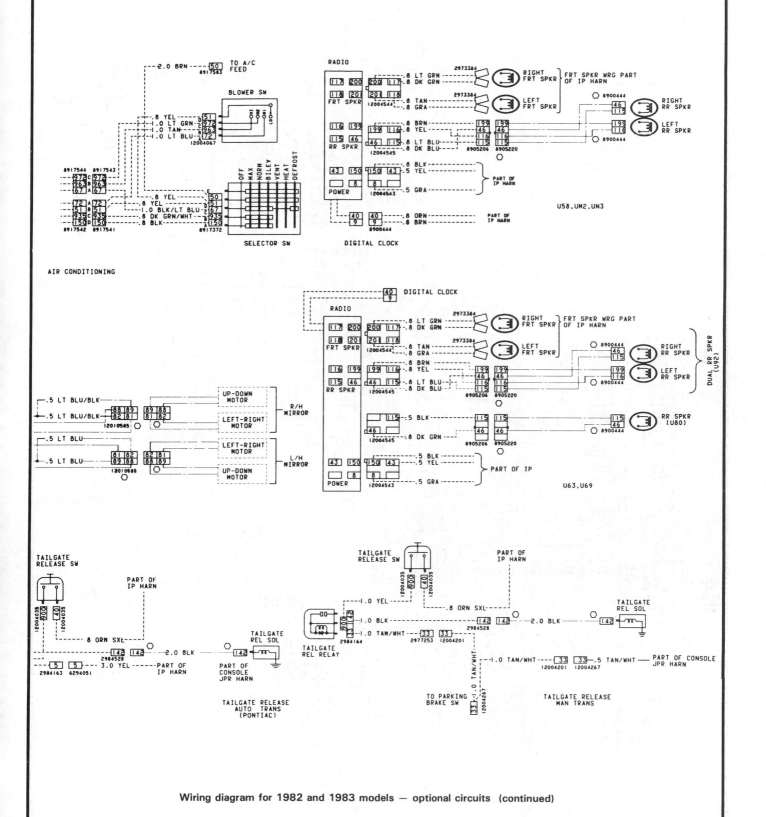

Wiring diagram for 1982 and 1983 models — optional circuits (continued)

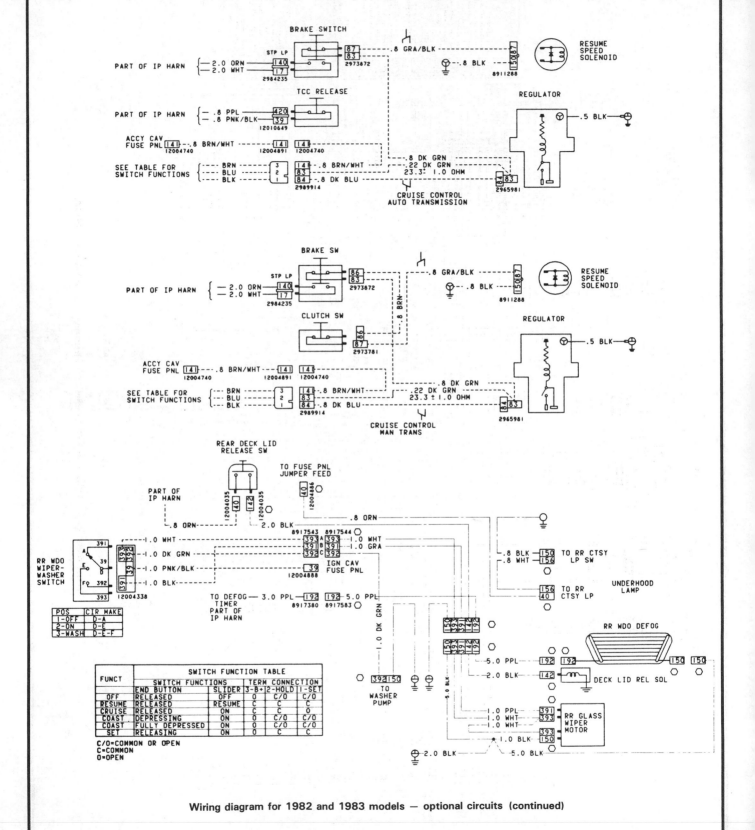

Wiring diagram for 1982 and 1983 models — optional circuits (continued)

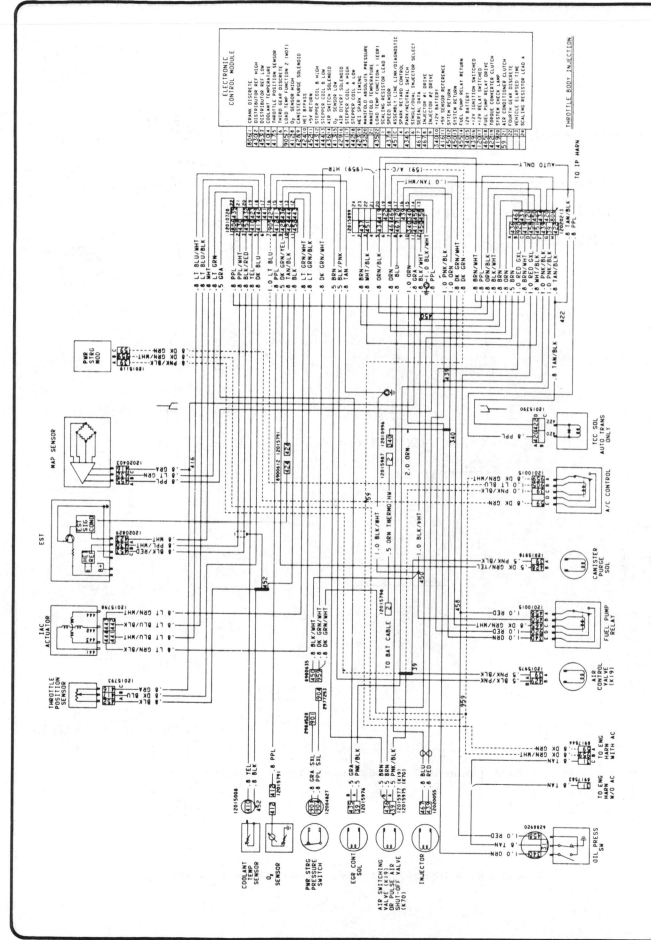

Wiring diagram for 1982 and 1983 models — Electronic Control Module (ECM)

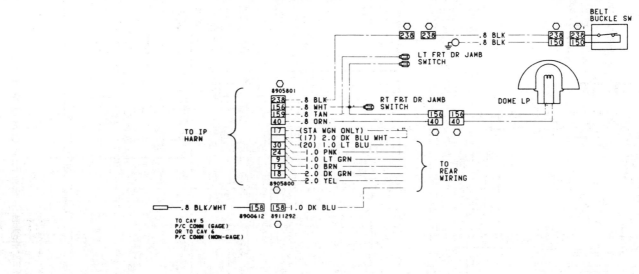

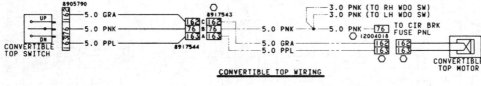

CONVERTIBLE TOP WIRING

Wiring diagram for 1982 and 1983 models — convertible top wiring

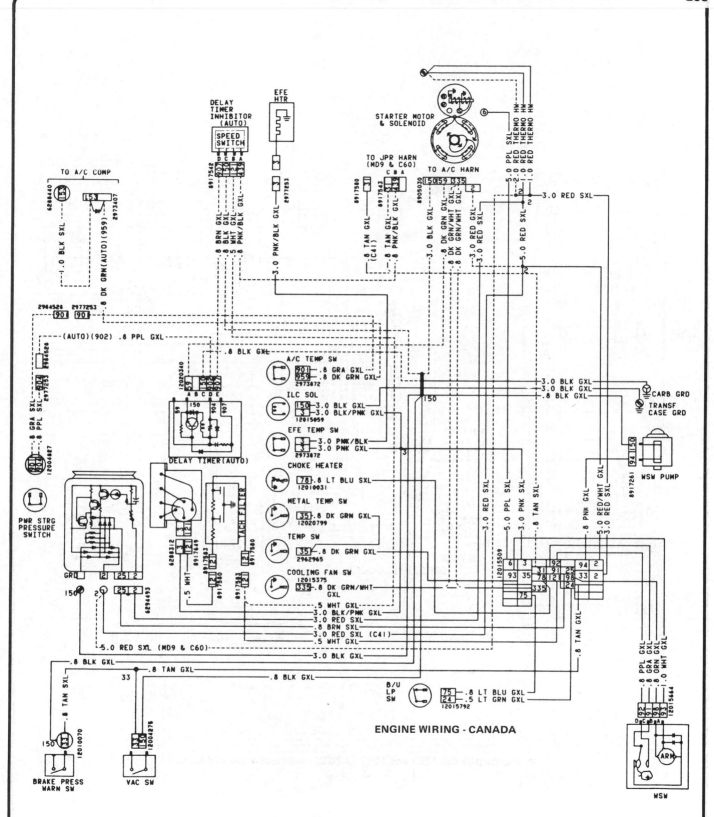

ENGINE WIRING - CANADA

Wiring diagram for 1982 and 1983 models — Canadian model engine wiring

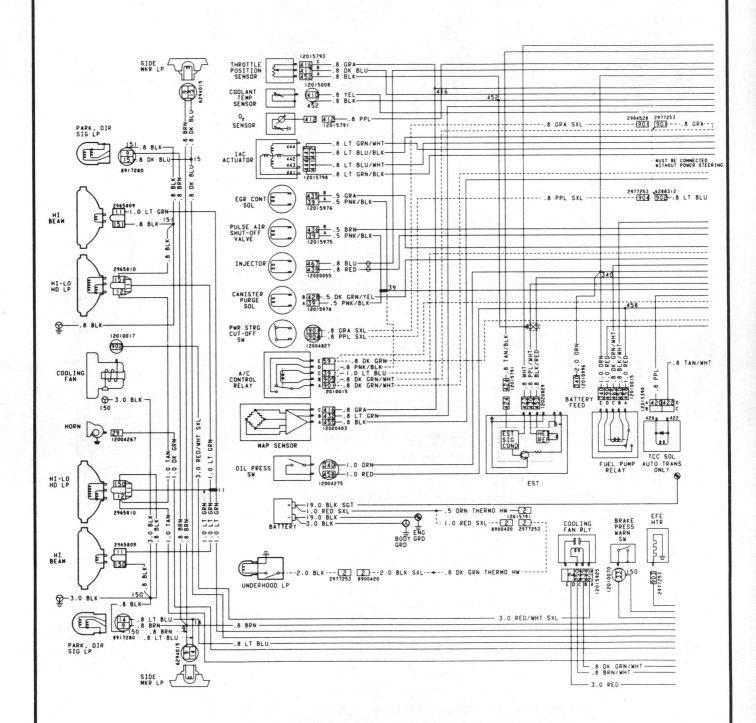

Wiring diagram for 1984 models — front end and engine compartment

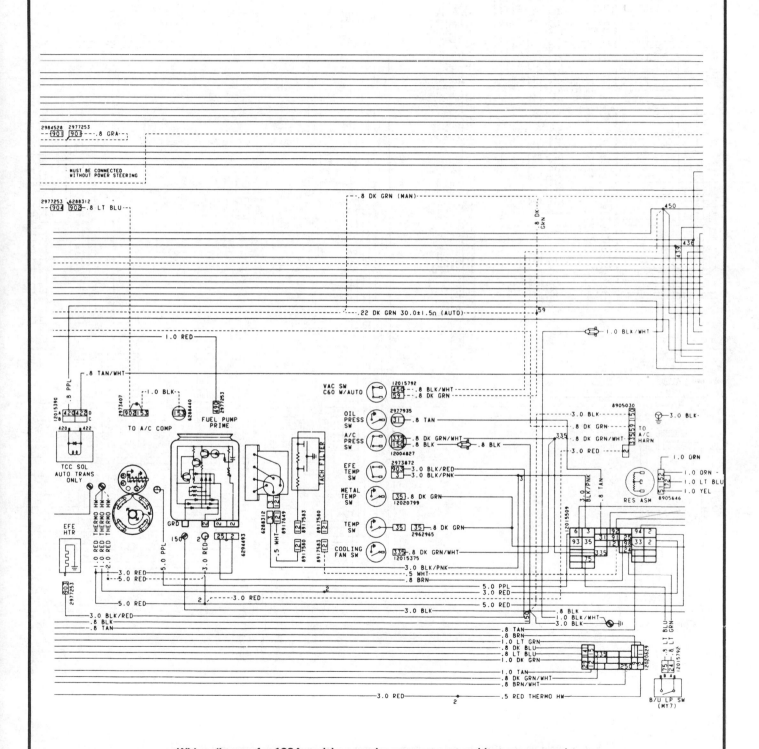

Wiring diagram for 1984 models — engine compartment and instrument panel

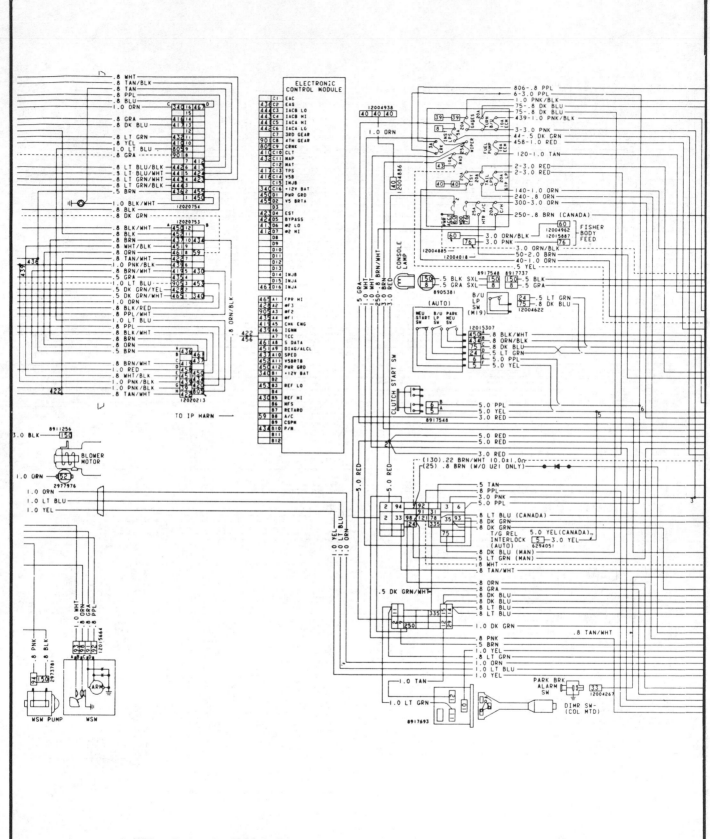

Wiring diagram for 1984 models — engine compartment and instrument panel (continued)

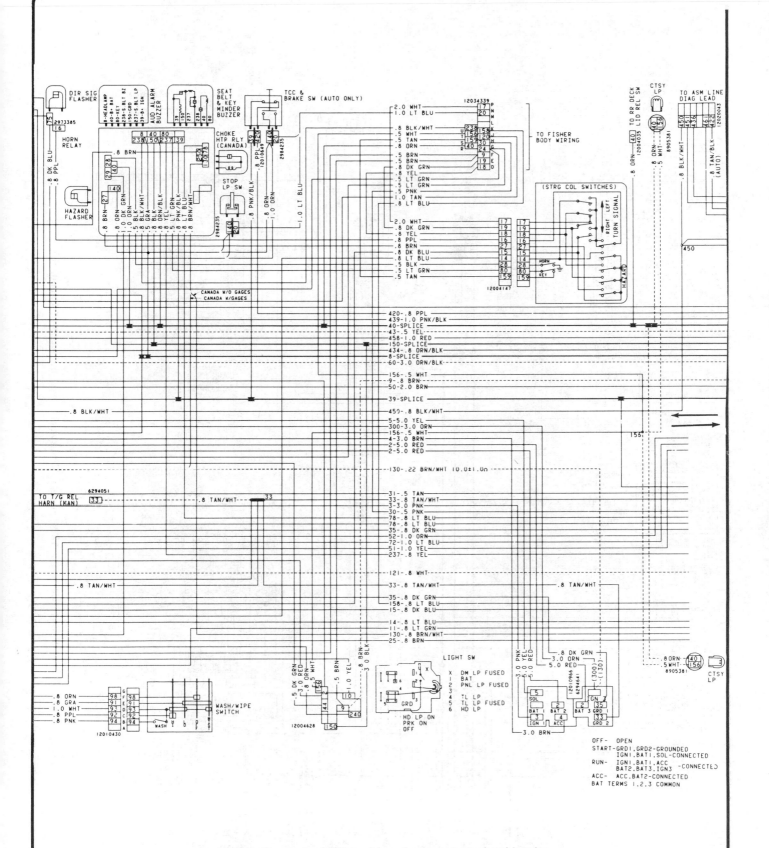

Wiring diagram for 1984 models — instrument panel and interior

Wiring diagram for 1984 models — instrument panel and interior (continued)

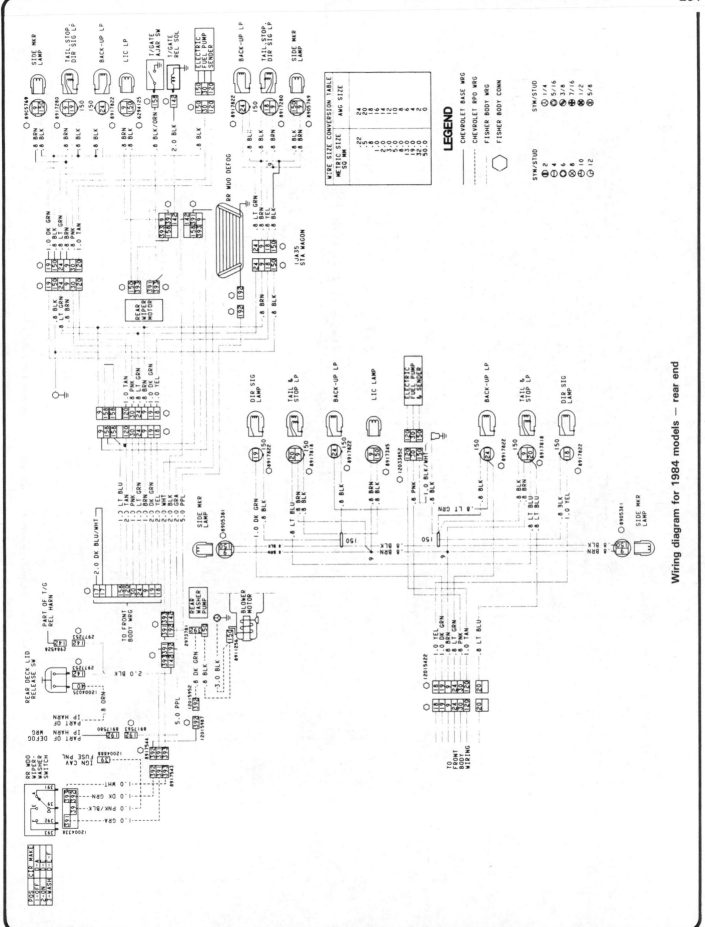

Wiring diagram for 1984 models — rear end

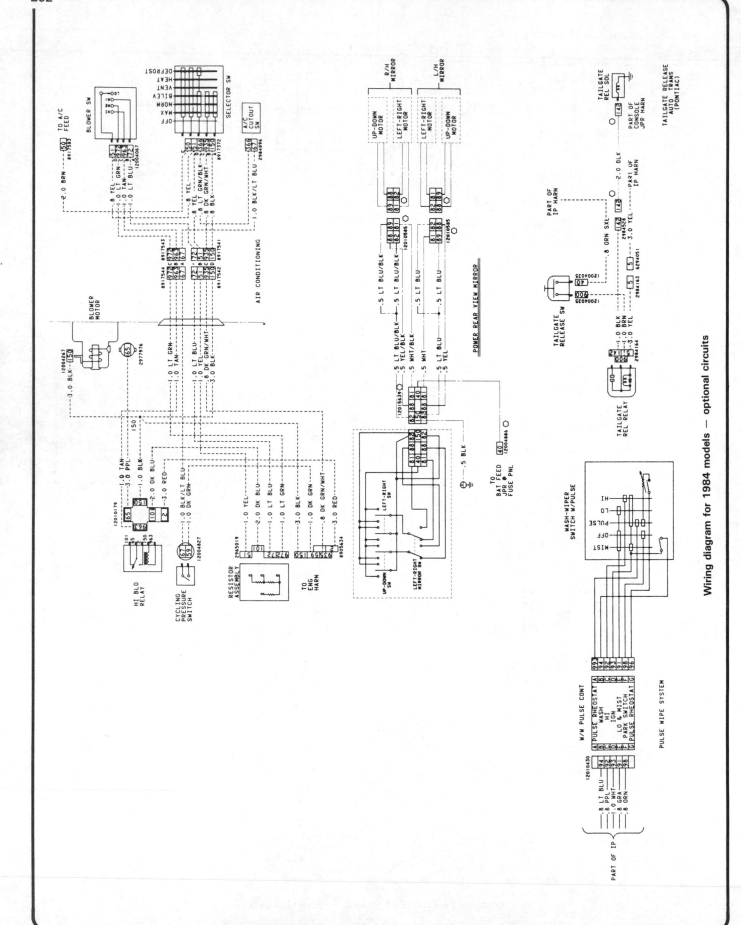

Wiring diagram for 1984 models — optional circuits

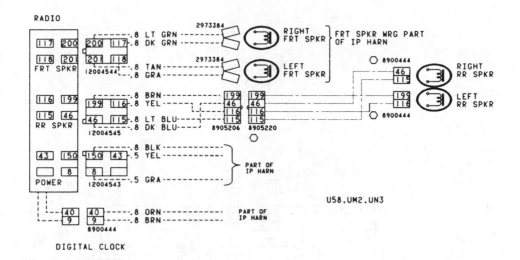

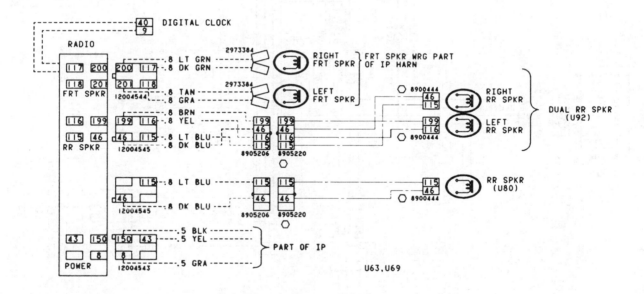

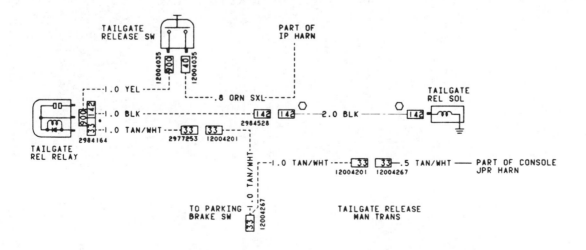

Wiring diagram for 1984 models — optional circuits

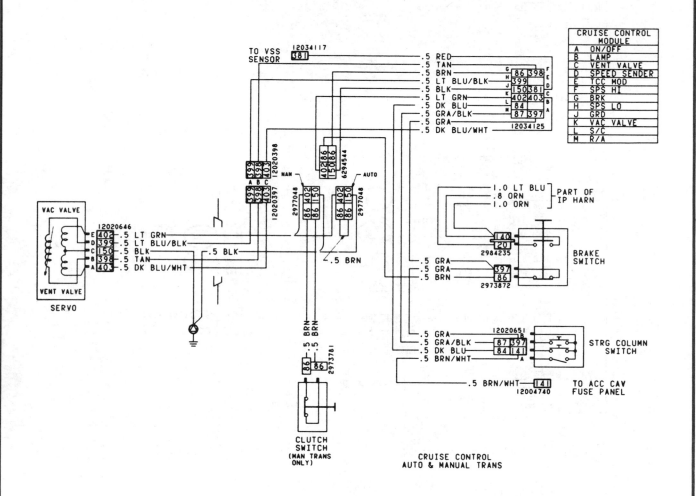

Wiring diagram for 1984 models — cruise control

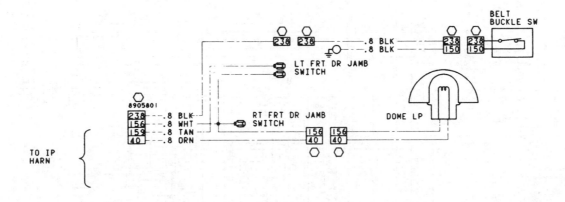

BELT
BUCKLE SW

238 238 .8 BLK 238 238
.8 BLK 150 150

LT FRT DR JAMB
SWITCH

8905801
238 .8 BLK
156 .8 WHT
159 .8 TAN   RT FRT DR JAMB
40 .8 ORN   SWITCH

DOME LP

156 156
40 40

TO IP
HARN

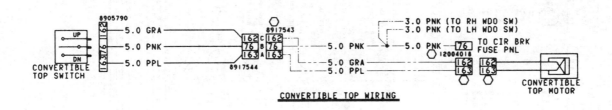

8905790
162
6376 5.0 GRA
5.0 PNK
5.0 PPL

UP
DN

CONVERTIBLE
TOP SWITCH

8917543
162 C 162
76 B 76
163 A 163

8917544

3.0 PNK (TO RH WDO SW)
3.0 PNK (TO LH WDO SW)

5.0 PNK   5.0 PNK   76   TO CIR BRK
12004018   FUSE PNL

5.0 GRA   162   162
5.0 PPL   163   163

CONVERTIBLE
TOP MOTOR

CONVERTIBLE TOP WIRING

Wiring diagram for 1984 models — convertible top wiring

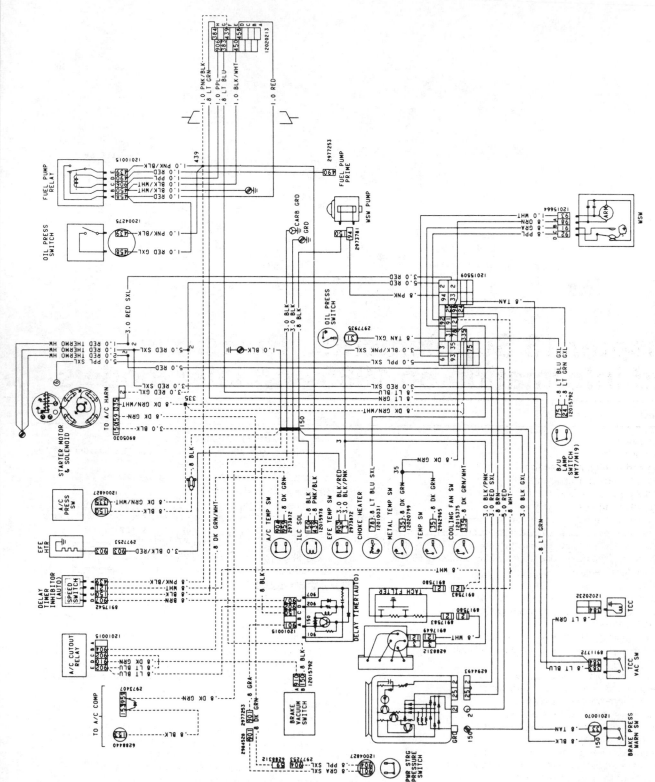

Wiring diagram for 1984 models — Canadian model engine wiring

Chapter 13 Supplement: Revisions and information on 1985 and later models

Contents

13

1   Introduction

This supplement contains specifications and service procedure changes that apply to General Motors J-cars manufactured from 1985 on. Also included is information related to previous models which was not available at the time of original publication of this manual.

Where no differences (or very minor differences) exist between 1984 models and later models, no information is given; the original material included in Chapters 1 through 12, pertaining to 1984 models, should be used.

Before beginning any service or repair procedure, check this supplement for new specifications and procedure changes. Note the supplementary information and be sure to include it while following the original procedures in Chapters 1 through 12.

2   Specifications

Note: *The following specifications are revisions of or supplementary to those listed at the beginning of each Chapter of this manual. The original specifications also apply to later models unless alternative figures are included here.*

Tune-up and routine maintenance
Note: *Due to the numerous options and variations, these figures are approximate – refer to an owner's manual for exact capacities.*

Cooling system capacity
  OHC engines .... 8 qts
  Four-cylinder OHV engines
    2.0L .... 9.7 qts
    2.2L
      1985 through 1990 .... 8.5 qts
      1991 .... 11.7 qts
      1992 .... 9.2 qts
  V6 engines
    1985 through 1990 .... 11 qts
    1991 .... 14.2 qts
    1992 .... 13.1 qts
Engine oil viscosily (turbo models only) .... 10W30 year-round
Manual transaxle (Isuzu 5-speed)
  Oil type .... No. 12345349 or equivalent
  Oil capacity .... 2 qts

2.0L four-cylinder (L4) OHC engine
Note: *All specifications for the 2.0L OHC engine not listed here are the same as the specifications for the 1.8L OHC engine listed in Chapter 2, Parts B and C.*

Bore .... 3.386 in (86 mm)
Stroke .... 3.386 in (86 mm)
Cylinder bore diameter .... 3.385 to 3.387 in (85.979 to 86.025 mm)
Piston-to-bore clearance
  non-turbo .... 0.0004 to 0.0012 in (0.01 to 0.03 mm)
  turbo .... 0.0012 to 0.0020 in (0.03 to 0.05 mm)
Piston ring end gap
  top end second (1988 on) .... 0.0012 to 0.0020 in (0.03 to 0.05 mm)
  oil control (1987 on) .... 0.16 to 0.55 in (0.40 to 1.40 mm)

Torque specifications   **Ft-lbs** (unless otherwise indicated)
Camshaft carrier cover bolts
  1987 and 1988 .... 72 in-lbs
  1989 on .... 80 in-lbs
Crankshaft sprocket bolt
  1987 .... 107 plus 45-degrees rotation
  1988 .... 96 plus 45-degrees rotation
  1989 on 114
Crankshaft pulley-to-sprocket bolts
  1987 and 1988 20
  1989 on 13
Connecting rod cap nuts* .... 26 plus 40 to 45-degrees rotation
Main bearing cap bolts* .... 44 plus 40 to 50-degrees rotation
Intake manifold nuts
  non-turbo 16
  turbo 18
Timing belt rear cover bolts
  1987 and 1988 5
  1989 on .... 89 in-lbs
Timing belt front cover bolts (1989 on) .... 89 in-lbs

Torque specifications (continued)

	Ft-lbs (unless otherwise indicated)
Exhaust manifold-to-cylinder head	
1987 and 1988	16
1989 on	115 in-lbs
Oil pan bolts (with thread locking compound)	44 in-lbs
Oil drain plug	33
Flywheel/driveplate-to-crankshaft bolts	
1987	48 plus 30-degrees rotation
1988 on	63
Clutch pressure plate-to-flywheel bolts	
1987	15
1988 on	22

When working on 1989 and later models, install NEW bolts

2.0L four-cylinder (L4) OHV engine

Torque specifications (continued)

	Ft-lbs
Cylinder head bolts (use new tightening sequence included here for all 1987 and later model engines)	
long	73 to 83
short	62 to 70
Intake manifold nuts (1987 on)	15 to 22

Cylinder head bolt tightening sequence for all 1987 and later model OHV four-cylinder engines

1   Intake side bolts   2   Exhaust side bolts

2.2L four-cylinder (L4) OHV engine

Note: *All specifications for the 2.2L OHV engine not listed here are the same as the specifications for the 2.0L OHV engine listed in Chapter 2, Parts A and C.*

Displacement	134 cu in
RPO	LM3
Valve stem-to-guide clearance (1990 on)	
intake	0.0006 to 0.0017 In (0.015 to 0.042 mm)
exhaust	0.0012 to 0.0024 in (0.030 to 0.060 mm)
Valve spring free length	2.06 in (52.3 mm)
Valve spring pressure and length (intake and exhaust)	
valve closed	
1990 and 1991	100 to 110 lbs at 1.613 in
1992	79 to 85 lbs at 1.64 in
valve open	
1990 and 1991	208 to 222 lbs at 1.22 in
1992	225 to 233 lbs at 1.25 in
Crankshaft	
main journal diameter (all)	2.4945 to 2.4954 in (63.360 to 63.384 mm)
main bearing oil clearance (all)	0.0006 to 0.0019 in (0.015 to 0.047 mm)
Cylinder bore	
diameter	3.5036 to 3.5043 in (88.991 to 89.009 mm)
out-of-round limit	0.0005 in (0.013 mm)
Piston-to-bore clearance	0.0007 to 0.0017 in (0.015 to 0.045 mm)
Oil end ring gap	0.010 to 0.050 in (0.25 to 1.27 mm)
Compression ring side clearance	0.0019 to 0.00267 in (0.05 to 0.07 mm)
Oil ring side clearance	0.0019 to 0.0082 in (0.05 to 0.21 mm)

Torque specifications

	Ft-lbs (unless otherwise indicated)
Camshaft thrust plate bolts	106 in-lbs
Cylinder head coolant outlet bolts	97 in-lbs
Crankshaft pulley-to-hub bolts	37
Crankshaft hub (center) bolt	
1990 and earlier	85
1991 on	77
Cylinder head bolts (follow sequence shown above)	
1987 through 1990	
step 1	41
step 2	Turn an additional 45-degrees (1/8 turn)
step 3	Turn an additional 45-degrees (1/8 turn)
step 4	
long bolts (intake side)	Turn an additional 20-degrees
short bolts (exhaust side)	Turn an additional 10-degrees

13

2.2L four-cylinder (L4) OHV engine (continued)

Torque specifications	Ft-lbs (unless otherwise indicated)
1991 and later	
step 1	
long bolts (intake side)	46
short bolts (exhaust side)	43
step 2	Turn all bolts an additional 90-degrees (1/4 turn)
Engine mounts	
front engine mount bolt	50
lower engine mount nut	18
engine mount-to-frame bolts	45
rear engine mount bolt	
1991	51
1992	40
Exhaust manifold	
nuts	115 in-lbs
studs	89 in-lbs
Flywheel-to-crankshaft bolts	
automatic	
1990 and 1991	70
1992	75
manual	75
Intake manifold nuts	
1990 and 1991	18
1992	30
Main bearing cap bolts	70
Connecting rod cap nuts	38
Oil pan bolts/nuts	
1990	89 in-lbs
1991 on	71 in-lbs
Oil pump	
drive assembly bolt	18
mounting bolts	32
Pressure plate-to-flywheel bolts	15
Rocker arm cover bolts	89 in-lbs
Rocker arm nuts	22
Timing chain	
cover bolts	97 in-lbs
tensioner bolts	18
Serpentine drivebelt tensioner bolt	37
Spark plugs	11

V6 engine

General

Type	60 degree V6
Displacement	
2.8 liter	173 cu in
3.1 liter	192 cu in
RPO number	
2.8 liter	LB6
3.1 liter	LHO
Cylinder numbers (left-to-right)	
firewall side	1–3–5
radiator side	2–4–6
Firing order	1-2-3-4-5-6
Oil pressure	15 psi @ 1100 rpm

CYLINDER NUMBERS

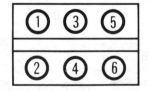

Cylinders

Diameter	
2.8 liter	3.503 to 3.506 in (88.992 to 89.070 mm)
3.1 liter	3.5046 to 3.5053 in (89.016 to 89.034 mm)
Out-of-round	0.0005 in (0.013 mm) maximum
Taper	0.0005 in (0.013 mm) maximum

Pistons

Piston-to-bore clearance	
through 1987	0.0020 to 0.0028 in (0.051 to 0.071 mm)
1988 on	0.00093 to 0.00222 in (0.0235 to 0.0565 mm)

Piston rings
  side clearance
    compression
      through 1987 .... 0.001 to 0.003 in (0.025 to 0.076 mm.
      1988 on .... 0.002 to 0.0035 in (0.05 to 0.09 mm)
    oil control (all) .... 0.008 in (0.20 mm)
  gap
    compression
      top (all) .... 0.010 to 0.020 in (0.25 to 0.50 mm)
      second
        1985 through 1989 .... 0.010 to 0.020 in (0.25 to 0.50 mm)
        1990 (3.1 liter) .... 0.020 to 0.028 in (0.50 to 0.71 mm)
    oil control
      through 1987 .... 0.020 to 0.055 in (0.51 to 1.40 mm)
      1988 on .... 0.010 to 0.030 in (0.25 to 0.75 mm)
Piston pin
  diameter .... 0.9052 to 0.9056 in (22.992 to 23.0022 mm)
  clearance
    through 1987 .... 0.00025 to 0.00036 in (0.0063 to 0.0091 mm)
    1988 on .... 0.0004 to 0.0008 in (0.0096 to 0.0215 mm)
  press fit in rod .... 0.00078 to 0.0021 in (0.020 to 0.0515 mm) interference fit

Crankshaft

Main journals
  diameter .... 2.6473 to 2.6483 in (67.241 to 67.265 mm)
  taper .... 0.0002 in (0.005 mm) maximum
  out-of-round .... 0.0002 in (0.005 mm) maximum
Main bearing oil clearance
  thrust bearing only
    1985 through 1987 .... 0.0021 to 0.0033 in (0.054 to 0.084 mm)
    1988 .... 0.0012 to 0.0027 in (0.032 to 0.069 mm)
    1989 .... 0.0016 to 0.0027 in (0.042 to 0.069 mm)
    1990 (3.1 liter) .... 0.0012 to 0.0030 in (0.032 to 0.077 mm)
  all others
    1985 through 1987 .... 0.0016 to 0.0032 in (0.041 to 0.081 mm)
    1988 and 1989 .... 0.0012 to 0.0027 in (0.032 to 0.069 mm)
    1990 (3.1 liter) .... 0.0012 to 0.0030 in (0.032 to 0.077 mm)
End play .... 0.0024 to 0.0083 in (0.06 to 0.21 mm)
Connecting rod journals
  diameter .... 1.9994 to 1.9983 in (50.784 to 50.756 mm)
  taper .... 0.0002 in (0.005 mm) maximum
  out-of-round .... 0.0002 in (0.005 mm) maximum
Connecting rod bearing oil clearance
  1985 and 1986 .... 0.0014 to 0.0037 in (0.035 to 0.095 mm)
  1987 .... 0.0013 to 0.0026 in (0.03 to 0.066 mm)
  1988 .... 0.0013 to 0.0031 in (0.032 to 0.079 mm)
  1989 .... 0.0014 to 0.0036 in (0.038 to 0.093 mm)
  1990 (3.1 liter) .... 0.0011 to 0.0034 in (0.028 to 0.086 mm)
Connecting rod side play
  through 1987 .... 0.006 to 0.017 in (0.152 to 0.432 mm)
  1980 on .... 0.014 to 0.027 in (0.36 to 0.68 mm)

Camshaft

Lobe lift
  intake .... 0.2626 in (6.67 mm)
  exhaust .... 0.2732 in (6.94 mm)
Journal
  diameter .... 1.8678 to 1.8815 in (47.44 to 47.79 mm)
  oil clearance .... 0.001 to 0.004 in (0.025 to 0.101 mm)

Valves

Valve face angle 45-degrees
Valve seat angle 46-degrees
Seat runout .... 0.001 in (0.025 mm) maximum
Seat width
  intake .... 0.061 to 0.073 in (1.55 to 1.85 mm)
  exhaust .... 0.067 to 0.079 in (1.70 to 2.0 mm)
Stem-to-guide clearance .... 0.001 to 0.0027 in (0.025 to 0.068 mm)
Valve springs
  free length .... 1.91 in (48.5 mm)
  load closed .... 90 lbs @ 1.701 in (400 N @ 43 mm)
  load open .... 215 lbs @ 1.291 in (956 N @ 33 mm)
  installed height .... 1.5748 in (40 mm)

13

V6 engine (continued)

Torque specifications   **Ft-lbs**

Camshaft sprocket bolts	15 to 26
Camshaft rear cover bolts	6 to 9
Torsional damper bolts	67 to 85
Oil pump bolts	20 to 31
Exhaust manifold bolts	15 to 23
Water pump bolts	6 to 9
Thermostat housing bolts	15 to 23
Front cover (see illustration 13.17)	
bolts labelled 3	13 to 26
bolts labelled 4	20 to 35
Head bolts	
step 1	33
step 2	Turn an additional 90-degrees (1/4-turn)
Intake manifold bolts	25
Timing chain damper bolts	14 to 19
Rocker arm cover bolts	6 to 9
Rocker arm nuts (MPFI engines)	15 to 20
Spark plugs	10 to 25
Oil pan	
1986 through 1989 bolts	
8 mm	15 to 23
6 mm	6 to 9
1990	
rear two corner bolts	18
remainder of bolts and nuts	13
studs	89 in-lbs
1991 on	
rear two corner bolts	18
remainder of bolts and nuts	71 in-lbs
studs	71 in-lbs
Main bearing cap bolts	63 to 83
Connecting rod cap nuts	39

Fuel system

TBI pintle valve extension	1.125 in (28 mm) maximum

Torque specifications   **Ft-lbs** (unless otherwise indicated)

2.0L four-cylinder and V6 engines	
Throttle body-to-intake manifold nuts	12
TBI air cleaner stud	12
Plenum bolts	16
Fuel rail bolts	19
1992 2.2L four-cylinder engine	
Pressure regulator fuel return pipe screw	22 in-lbs
Idle air control valve screw	27 in-lbs
Upper manifold stud/nut	22
EGR control solenoid bolt	17
MAP sensor screws	17

Turbocharger (1990 on)

Torque specifications   **Ft-lbs** (unless otherwise indicated)

Exhaust pipe-to-elbow	26
Exhaust manifold	106 in-lbs
Coolant feed and return lines	159 in-lbs

Engine electrical system

Torque specifications   **Ft-lbs**

Direct ignition system assembly-to-block bolts	20

Manual transaxle

Isuzu 5-speed

Torque specifications   **Ft-lbs**

Reverse shift bracket bolts	13
Transaxle case-to-clutch housing bolts	28

Manual transaxle

Isuzu 5-speed (continued)

Torque specifications	Ft-lbs
Reverse idler shaft bolt	28
Detent spring retaining bolts	18
Input/output shaft retaining nuts	94
Control box-to-case bolts	13
Rear cover bolts	13
Pressure plate-to-flywheel bolts (1988 on)	22

1992 V6 engine

Torque specifications	Ft-lbs (unless otherwise indicated)
Transaxle-to-engine bolts	55
Flywheel inspection cover bolts	89 in-lbs
Transaxle strut bracket bolt	40
Upper transaxle mount and bracket	
Bolt	41
Nut	24

Clutch

Torque specifications	Ft-lbs
Clutch release lever (Isuzu 5-speed)	36
Pressure plate-to-flywheel bolts (1988 on)	22

Brakes

Torque specifications	Ft-lbs
Proportioner valve caps	20
Master cylinder mounting nuts	20

Chassis electrical system

Bulb application	Type
Headlight	
Low beam	9006
High beam	9005
Front park and turn signal	2057NA
Front side marker	194
Reading light	90
Courtesy light	168
Tail, stop and turn signal	T24
Rear side marker	T24
Backup light	899

---

3   Tune-up and routine maintenance

Drivebelt check and replacement

1   Later models are equipped with a single "serpentine" drivebelt, which powers all engine accessories. This style belt requires no adjustment: it is handled by a spring-loaded tensioner pulley.

2   The belt should be inspected regularly for missing ribs and frayed plies. Cracks in the belt ribs do not necessarily indicate a faulty or damaged belt, since they do not impair belt performance.

3   To replace the belt, insert a half-inch drive breaker bar (some models require a 15mm socket) into the tensioner and rotate the pulley counterclockwise, releasing belt tension.

4   Remove the drivebelt from the pulleys, noting how it's routed.

5   Install the new belt, starting with the bottom pulleys, then release the tensioner. Make sure the belt is properly centered on each pulley.

Automatic transaxle fluid change

The automatic transaxle fluid change procedure is identical to the that described in Chapter 1 except for the application of a thread locking compound to one bolt.

Apply a thread-locking compound to the bolt in the arrowed hole to reduce the potential of a fluid leak at this location.

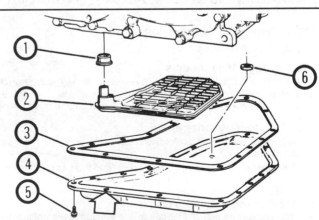

13.1   Automatic transaxle filter installation details – apply a thread-locking compound to the bolt in the hole with the arrow to prevent a possible fluid leak

1	Seal	3	Pan gasket	5	Bolt
2	Filter	4	Pan	6	Magnet

13

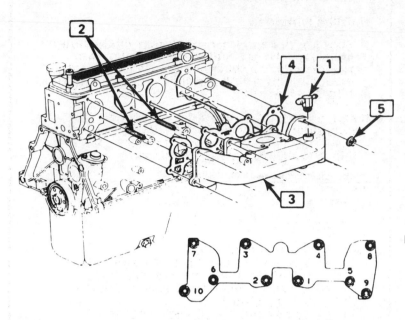

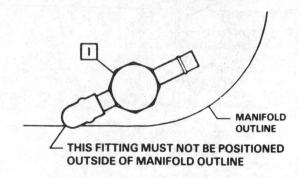

THIS FITTING MUST NOT BE POSITIONED OUTSIDE OF MANIFOLD OUTLINE

Fig. 13.2   Intake manifold nut tightening sequence – 1987 through 1991 model four-cylinder OHV engine

1	Fitting	4	Gasket
2	Stud	5	Nut
3	Manifold		

4   Four-cylinder engines

General information

Beginning with the 1985 model year, the 1.8 liter overhead valve (OHV) engine was discontinued. In 1987, the 1.8 liter overhead cam engine was enlarged to 2.0 liters through changes in the bore and stroke of the engine. In 1990, the 2.0 liter OHV engine was enlarged to 2.2 liters. Other than the changes included here in Chapter 13, all specifications and service procedures in Chapter 2, Part B, can be used.

Rocker arm cover – removal and installation (OHV engine only)

The 1987 and later model 2.0/2.2 liter four-cylinder OHV engine has some external changes. The rocker arm cover has been modified for improved sealing and the cylinder head has been changed accordingly.

Intake manifold – removal and installation (OHV engine only)

1987 through 1991 models

On 1987 through 1991 models, the intake (and exhaust) manifolds have been reconfigured and the intake manifold mounting nut tightening sequence is provided to prevent warpage due to improper tightening.

1992 2.2L four-cylinder engines

Note: *In 1992, the intake manifold was changed to accept the new fuel-injection system.*

1   Disconnect the negative battery cable from the battery.
2   Relieve the fuel system pressure (Section 7).
3   Remove the air intake duct.
4   Drain the coolant (refer to Chapter 1).
5   Tag and disconnect any electrical and vacuum lines which interfere with manifold removal.
6   Disconnect the throttle linkage.
7   Remove the power steering pump (if equipped) and lay it aside in an upright position.
8   Remove the MAP sensor and the EGR solenoid valve.
9   Remove the upper intake manifold assembly (Section 7).
10   Remove the EGR valve injector.

11   Remove the fuel injector retainer bracket, regulator, injectors and fuel lines (Section 7). Plug fuel lines to prevent entry of foreign matter.
12   Remove the nut securing the transaxle fill tube (automatic transaxle).
13   Disconnect the accelerator and TV cables and cable bracket (see Chapters 4 and 7B).
14   Raise the vehicle and support it securely on jackstands.
15   Remove lower six nuts on the manifold.
16   Lower the vehicle.
17   Remove the manifold upper nuts.
18   Separate the manifold and gasket from the engine. Scrape away all traces of gasket material from the intake manifold gasket mating surface.
19   Installation is the reverse of removal. Be sure to use a new gasket. Tighten the nuts in the sequence shown to the torque listed in this Chapter's Specifications.

Crankshaft – installation and main bearing oil clearance check (OHC engine only)

An engine bearing selection chart is included to assist in determining the correct main bearings to use in later model 2.0/2.2 liter four-cylinder OHC engines.

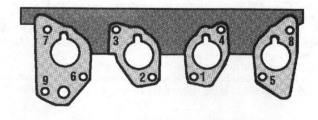

13.3   Intake manifold nut tightening sequence – 1992 model four-cylinder 2.2L OHV engine

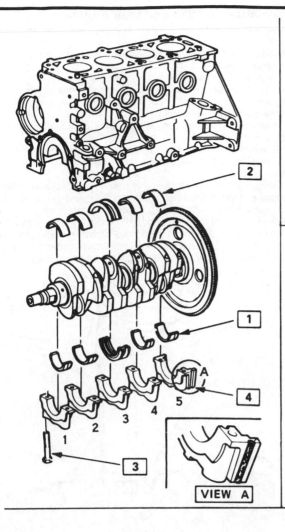

1—LOWER BEARINGS

2—UPPER BEARINGS

3—WITH BOLTS FINGER TIGHT, THRUST CRANKSHAFT REARWARD TO SET AND ALIGN BEARING CAPS. THEN THRUST CRANKSHAFT FORWARD TO ALIGN REAR FACE OF GUIDE BEARING. TORQUE ALL BOLTS TO SPECIFICATION.

4—FILL BEARING CAP NUMBER 5 HOLES WITH SEALING COMPOUND ON BOTH SIDES, UNTIL SEALER RUNS OUT THROUGH THE BEARING CAP BASE AT THE INTERSECTION WITH THE BLOCK.

PROCEDURE:

I. DETERMINE BLOCK SIZE
   a. STANDARD MARKED "O" ON PAN RAIL
   b. OVERSIZE MARKED "1" ON PAN RAIL
II. DETERMINE CRANKSHAFT SIZE (BY COLOR CODE—SEE CHART)
III. SELECT BEARING SIZE FROM COLUMN DIRECTLY TO RIGHT OF CRANKSHAFT COLOR CODE.
IV. ORDER BEARINGS BY COLOR CODE SPECIFIED
V. USE PLAST—GAGE METHOS TO DETERMINE BEARING CLEARANCE.

BEARING SELECTION CHART
STANDARD SIZE CRANKSHAFT

CYLINDER BLOCK IDENTIFICATION	CRANKSHAFT IDENTIFICATION	BEARING UPPER (BLOCK)	BEARING LOWER (CAP)
0—STANDARD	BROWN	BROWN	BROWN
	GREEN	BROWN	GREEN
1—OVERSIZE	GREEN	GREEN	GREEN
	BROWN	GREEN	BROWN

UNDERSIZE (.010) CRANKSHAFT

0—STANDARD	BROWN/BLUE	BROWN/BLUE	BROWN/BLUE
	GREEN/BLUE	BROWN/BLUE	GREEN/BLUE
1—OVERSIZE	BROWN/BLUE	GREEN/BLUE	BROWN/BLUE
	GREEN/BLUE	GREEN/BLUE	GREEN/BLUE

Fig. 13.4   OHC four-cylinder engine main bearing selection chart – engine with color-coded bearings

13

5   V6 engine

Rocker arm covers — removal and installation

Rear (firewall) side

1   Remove any air cleaner components which would interfere with rocker arm cover removal.

2   Disconnect the cable from the negative battery terminal.

3   Remove the spark plug wire cover and breather tube.

4   Disconnect all wires that would interfere with removal of the rocker arm cover. Tag them as they are disconnected.

5   Remove the heater hose at the filler neck.

6   Remove the rocker arm cover bolts.

7   Detach the rocker arm cover. **Note:** *If the cover sticks to the cylinder head, use your hand or a rubber hammer to bump the end of the cover, dislodging it.*

8   Before reinstalling the cover, clean all dirt, oil and old gasket material from the sealing surfaces of the cover and cylinder head with a scraper and degreaser.

9   Install a new gasket in the rocker arm cover groove and apply RTV sealant to the notches in the head (one in each end).

10   Place the rocker arm cover on the cylinder head and install the mounting bolts. Tighten the bolts a little at a time until the specified torque is reached.

11   Complete the installation by reversing the removal procedure.

Front (radiator) side

12   Remove any air cleaner components which would interfere with rocker arm cover removal.

13   Disconnect the cable from the negative battery terminal.

14   Disconnect the brake booster vacuum line.

15   Remove the cable bracket at the plenum.

16   Remove the vacuum line bracket at the cable bracket.

17   Remove the lines at the alternator brace stud.

18   Remove the rear alternator brace.

19   Remove the serpentine drivebelt.

20   Remove the PCV valve.

21   Loosen the alternator bracket.

22   Remove the rocker arm cover bolts.

23   Remove the spark plug wires.

24   Detach the rocker arm cover. **Note:** *If the cover sticks to the cylinder head, use your hand or a rubber hammer to bump the end of the cover, dislodging it.*

25   Before reinstalling the cover, clean all dirt, oil and old gasket material from the sealing surfaces of the cover and cylinder head with a scraper and degreaser.

26   Install a new gasket in the rocker cover groove and apply RTV sealant to the notches in the head.

27   Place the rocker arm cover on the cylinder head and install the mounting bolts. Tighten the bolts a little at a time until the specified torque is reached.

28   Complete the installation by reversing the removal procedure.

Valve train components — replacement (cylinder head installed)

29   Remove the rocker arm covers.

30   If only the pushrod is to be replaced, loosen the rocker nut enough to allow the rocker arm to be rotated away from the pushrod. Pull the pushrod out of the hole in the cylinder head.

31   If the rocker arm is to be removed, remove the rocker arm nut and pivot and lift off the rocker arm.

32   If the valve spring is to be removed, remove the spark plug from the affected cylinder.

33   There are two methods that will hold the valve in place while the valve spring is removed. If you have access to compressed air, install an air hose adapter in the spark plug hole. This adapter is available at most parts stores. When air pressure is applied to the adapter, the valves will be held in place by the pressure.

34   If you do not have access to compressed air, bring the piston of the affected cylinder to just before top dead center (TDC) on the compression stroke. Feed a long piece of 1/4-inch nylon cord in through the spark plug hole until it fills the combustion chamber. Be sure to leave the end of the cord hanging out of the spark plug hole so it can

be removed easily. Rotate the crankshaft in the normal direction of rotation until slight resistance is felt.

35   Reinstall the rocker arm nut (without the rocker arm).

36   Insert the slotted end of a valve spring compression tool under the nut and compress the spring just enough to remove the spring keepers, then release the pressure on the tool.

37   Remove the retainer (cap), shield, O-ring seal, spring, spring damper and valve stem oil seal.

38   The rocker arm studs may be replaced by removing the damaged one and replacing it with a new one. Be sure to reinstall the pushrod guide under the stud nut.

39   Installation of the valve train components is the reverse of the removal procedure. Always use new valve stem oil seals whenever the spring keepers have been disturbed. Before installing the rocker arms, coat the bearing surfaces of the arms and pivots with moly-base grease or engine assembly lube. On fuel-injected engines, tighten the rocker arm nuts to the torque listed in this Chapter's Specifications. On carbureted engines, adjust the valve lash using the procedures starting with Step 86.

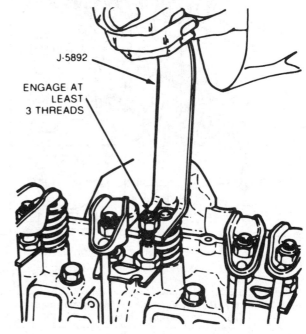

Fig. 13.5   With the valve spring tool locked under the rocker arm stud nut, depress the valve spring and remove the keepers

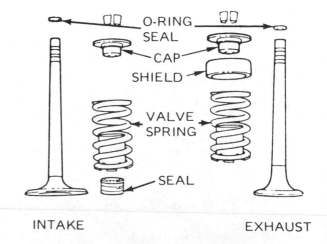

Fig. 13.6   V6 engine valve and spring assembly

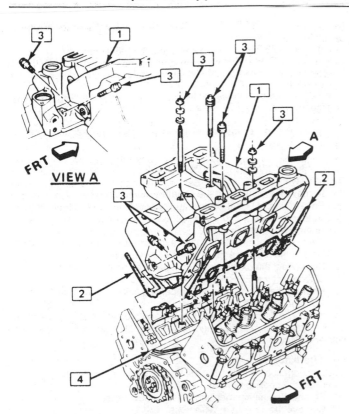

Fig. 13.7 Intake manifold assembly – exploded view

> 1 Intake manifold   3 25 Ft-lbs. (33 Nm)
> 2 Gasket   4 Sealant

Intake manifold — removal and installation

40 Remove the fuel injection components as described in Section 6 of this Chapter.
41 Disconnect the cable from the negative terminal of the battery.
42 Remove the throttle and TV cable bracket from the plenum.
43 Remove the EGR valve from the plenum.
44 Remove the plenum.
45 Remove the serpentine drivebelt.
46 Unbolt the power steering pump and suspend it to one side, out of the way.
47 Unbolt the alternator and suspend it to one side, out of the way.
48 Remove the rocker arm covers.
49 Drain the cooling system.
50 Disconnect the spark plug wires at the spark plugs.
51 Remove the upper radiator hose from the thermostat housing.
52 Disconnect the heater hose at the manifold.
53 Remove the coolant bypass hose from the filler neck and the head.
54 Remove the coolant sensor and oil pressure sending unit switch wires.
55 Remove the coolant sensor.
56 Remove the pushrods.
57 Remove the manifold mounting bolts.
58 Separate the manifold from the engine with a pry bar (do not pry between the mating surfaces) or by tapping the manifold with a hammer and wooden block to loosen it.
59 Before installing the manifold, place clean, lint-free rags in the engine cavity and clean the engine block, cylinder head and manifold gasket surfaces. All gasket material and sealant must be removed prior to installation. Remove all dirt and gasket remnants from the engine cavity.
60 Clean the gasket sealing surfaces with degreaser, then apply a 3/16-inch (5 mm) diameter bead of RTV-type sealant to each manifold ridge.
61 Install the new intake gaskets on the cylinder heads. Notice that the gaskets are marked *Right* and *Left*. Be sure to use the correct gasket on each cylinder head.

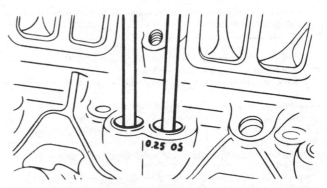

Fig. 13.8 Some engines are equipped with oversize valve lifters, as is indicated by the 0.25 OS mark on the lifter boss

62 Hold the gaskets in place by extending the bead of RTV sealant 1/4-inch onto the gasket ends.
63 Carefully lower the intake manifold into position, making sure that you do not disturb the gaskets.
64 Install the intake manifold mounting bolts and tighten them a little at a time until they are all at the specified torque.
65 Install the remaining components in the reverse order of removal.
66 Fill the radiator with coolant, start the engine and check for leaks.

Hydraulic lifters — removal, inspection and installation

Note: *Some engines are equipped with both standard and 0.010-inch (0.25 mm) oversize valve lifters. Where oversize lifters are used the block in the valve galley will be marked with a daub of white paint and 0.25 OS will be stamped on the lifter boss.*

67 A noisy hydraulic lifter can be isolated while the engine is idling. Place a length of hose or tubing near the position of each valve while listening at the other end of the tube. Another method is to remove the rocker arm cover and, with the engine idling, place a finger on each of the valve spring retainers, one at a time. If a valve lifter is defective, it will be evident from the shock felt at the retainer as the valve seats.
68 Assuming that adjustment is correct, the most likely cause of a noisy valve lifter is a piece of dirt trapped between the plunger and the lifter body.
69 Remove the rocker arm covers.
70 Remove the intake manifold.
71 Loosen the rocker arm nut and rotate the rocker arm away from the pushrod.
72 Remove the pushrod.
73 To remove the lifter, a special hydraulic lifter removal tool should be used, or a scribe can be positioned at the top of the lifter and used to force the lifter up. Do not use pliers or other tools on the outside of the lifter body, as they will damage the finished surface and render the lifter useless.
74 The lifters should be kept in order for reinstallation in their original positions.
75 To dismantle a valve lifter, hold the plunger down with a pushrod and extract the retainer ring with a small screwdriver.
76 Remove the pushrod seat and metering valve.
77 Remove the plunger, ball check valve and plunger spring. The ball check valve and spring are removed by prying them out with a small screwdriver.

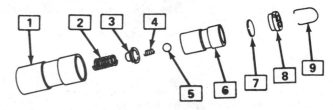

Fig. 13.9 Valve lifter assembly – exploded view

> 1 Lifter body   4 Ball check spring   7 Oil metering valve
> 2 Plunger spring   5 Ball check valve   8 Pushrod seat
> 3 Ball check retainer 6 Plunger   9 Retainer ring

13

78 Clean the lifter components with solvent and dry them with compressed air. Examine the internal components for wear and check the ball carefully for flat spots.

79 If the lifters are worn they must be replaced with new ones and the camshaft must be replaced as well. If the lifters were contaminated with dirt they can be cleaned and reinstalled.

80 Place the ball check valve on the small hole in the bottom of the plunger.

81 Insert the ball check valve spring into the seat in the retainer and place the retainer over the ball so that the spring rests on the ball. Using a small screwdriver, carefully press the retainer into position in the plunger.

82 Place the plunger spring over the ball retainer, invert the lifter body and slide it over the spring and plunger. Make sure the oil holes in the body and plunger line up.

83 Fill the assembly with engine oil. Place the metering valve and pushrod seat in position, press down on the seat with a pushrod and install the retainer spring.

84 When installing the lifters, make sure they are replaced in their original bores. Coat them with moly-base grease or engine assembly lube.

85 The remaining installation steps are the reverse of removal. If you're working on a fuel-injected engine, tighten the rocker arm nuts to the torque listed in this Chapter's Specifications. If you're working on a carbureted model, adjust the valve lash (see Step 86).

Valve lash – adjustment (Carbureted models)

86 Disconnect the cable from the negative battery terminal.

87 Remove the rocker arm covers.

88 Rotate the crankshaft until the number one piston is at top dead center (TDC) on the compression stroke. To make sure that you do not mix up the TDC positions of the number one and four pistons, check the position of the rotor in the distributor to see which terminal it is pointing at. Another method is to place your fingers on the number one cylinder rocker arms as the timing marks line up at the crankshaft pulley. If the rocker arms are not moving, the number one piston is at TDC on the compression stroke. If they move as the timing marks line up, the number four piston is at TDC on a compression stroke.

89 Back off the rocker arm nut until play is felt at the pushrod, then turn it back in until all play is removed. This can be determined by rotating the pushrod while tightening the nut. Just when drag is felt at the pushrod, all

lash has been removed. Turn the nut an additional 3/4 turns to center the plunger in the lifter.

90 Adjust the number one, five and six cylinder intake valves and the number one, two and three cylinder exhaust valves, with the crankshaft in this position, using the method just described.

91 Rotate the crankshaft one complete turn, until the number four piston is at TDC on the compression stroke, and adjust the number two, three and four cylinder intake valves and the number four, five and six cylinder exhaust valves.

92 Install the rocker arm covers and reconnect the negative battery cable.

Exhaust manifolds – removal and installation

Rear (firewall) side

93 Remove the cable from the negative battery terminal.

94 Raise the front of the vehicle and support it securely on jackstands. Block the rear wheels to keep the vehicle from rolling.

95 Remove the heat shield.

96 Remove the bolts attaching the exhaust pipe to the crossover pipe.

97 Detach the crossover pipe from the exhaust manifolds.

98 Disconnect the oxygen sensor pigtail electrical connector.

99 Disconnect the EGR pipe.

100 Remove the exhaust manifold mounting bolts and separate the manifold from the engine.

101 Installation is the reverse of the removal procedure. Before installing the manifold, be sure to thoroughly clean the mating surfaces on the manifold and cylinder head.

Front (radiator) side

102 Disconnect the cable from the negative battery terminal.

103 Drain the cooling system.

104 Remove the air cleaner and mass air flow sensor.

105 Remove the coolant bypass hose.

106 Remove the heat shields.

107 Disconnect the crossover pipe from the front manifold.

108 Remove the bolts and separate the exhaust manifold from the engine.

109 Installation is the reverse of the removal procedure. Be sure to thoroughly clean the cylinder head and manifold surfaces before installing the manifold.

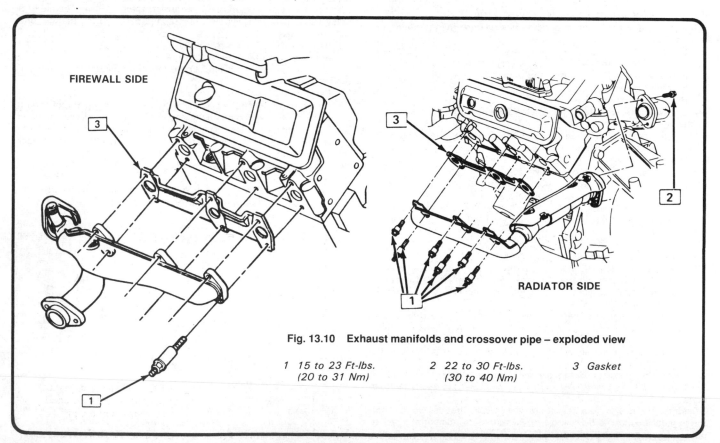

Fig. 13.10   Exhaust manifolds and crossover pipe – exploded view

| 1 15 to 23 Ft-lbs. (20 to 31 Nm) | 2 22 to 30 Ft-lbs. (30 to 40 Nm) | 3 Gasket |

Cylinder heads – removal and installation

Front (radiator) side

110 Raise the vehicle and place it securely on jackstands.
111 Locate the engine block drain plugs, remove them and drain the coolant.
112 Remove the jackstands and lower the vehicle.
113 Remove the rocker arm cover.
114 Remove the intake manifold.
115 Disconnect the exhaust crossover pipe from the rear manifold.
116 Remove the alternator and bracket.
117 Remove the oil dipstick tube assembly from the side of the engine.
118 Loosen the rocker arm nuts enough to allow removal of the pushrods, then remove the pushrods.
119 Remove the head bolts.
120 Detach the cylinder head and the exhaust manifold/crossover pipe assembly.
121 If a new cylinder head is being installed, transfer the various components, such as the manifold, brackets and coolant temperature sensor, from the old head. Before installing the new head, the gasket surfaces of both the head and the engine block must be clean and free of nicks and scratches. Also, the threads in the block and on the head bolts must be completely clean, as any dirt or sealant in the threads will affect bolt torque.
122 Place the gasket in position over the locating dowels with the note *This Side Up* visible.
123 Position the cylinder head over the gasket.
124 Coat the cylinder head bolts with RTV sealant and install them.
125 Tighten the bolts in the proper sequence to the specified torque.
126 Install the pushrods, making sure the lower ends are in the lifter seats. Place the rocker arm ends over the pushrods and loosely install the rocker arm nuts.
127 The remaining installation steps are the reverse of removal. If you're working on a fuel-injected engine, tighten the rocker arm nuts to the torque listed in this Chapter's Specifications. If you're working on a carbureted model, adjust the valve lash (see Step 86).

Rear (firewall) side

128 Raise the vehicle and place it securely on jackstands.
129 Locate the engine block drain plugs and drain the coolant from the block.
130 Disconnect the exhaust crossover pipe from the exhaust manifold.
131 Remove the jackstands and lower the vehicle.
132 Remove the rocker arm covers.
133 Remove the intake manifold.
134 Loosen the rocker arm nuts sufficiently to allow removal of the pushrods, then remove the pushrods.
135 Remove the head bolts.
136 Detach the cylinder head.
137 Before installing the head, the gasket surfaces of both the head and the engine block must be clean and free of nicks and scratches. Also, the threads in the block and on the head bolts must be completely clean, as any dirt or sealant in the threads will affect bolt torque.
138 Place the gasket in position over the locating dowels with the note *This Side Up* visible.
139 Position the cylinder head over the gasket.
140 Coat the cylinder head bolts with RTV sealant and install them.
141 Tighten the bolts in the proper sequence to the specified torque.
142 Install the pushrods, making sure the lower ends are in the lifter seats. Place the rocker arm ends over the pushrods and loosely install the rocker arm nuts.
143 The remaining installation steps are the reverse of removal. If you're working on a fuel-injected engine, tighten the rocker arm nuts to the torque listed in this Chapter's Specifications. If you're working on a carbureted model, adjust the valve lash (see Step 86).

Oil pan – removal and installation

144 Disconnect the cable from the negative battery terminal.
145 Raise the vehicle and support it on jackstands.
146 Drain the engine oil.
147 If equipped with an automatic transmission, remove the converter shroud.
148 If equipped with a manual transmission, remove the flywheel cover.
149 Remove the starter.
150 Remove the oil pan bolts. Note the four studs and nuts used and their locations.
151 Remove the oil pan.
152 Before installing the pan, make sure that the sealing surfaces on the pan, block and front cover are clean and free of oil. If the old pan is being reinstalled, make sure that all sealant has been removed from the pan sealing flange and from the blind attaching holes.

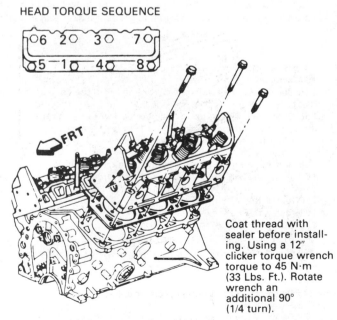

HEAD TORQUE SEQUENCE

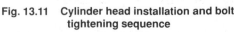

Coat thread with sealer before installing. Using a 12" clicker torque wrench torque to 45 N·m (33 Lbs. Ft.). Rotate wrench an additional 90° (1/4 turn).

Fig. 13.11   Cylinder head installation and bolt tightening sequence

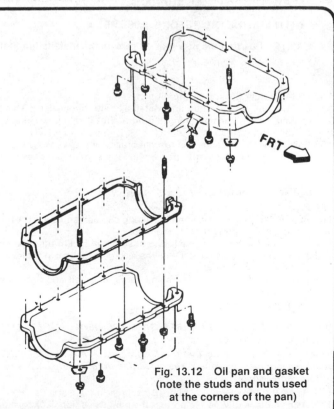

Fig. 13.12   Oil pan and gasket (note the studs and nuts used at the corners of the pan)

13

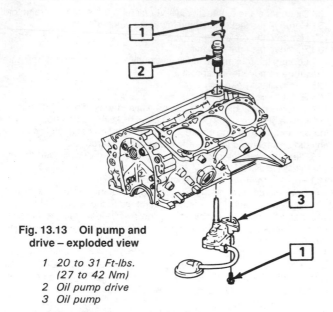

Fig. 13.13   Oil pump and drive – exploded view

1   20 to 31 Ft-lbs.
    (27 to 42 Nm)
2   Oil pump drive
3   Oil pump

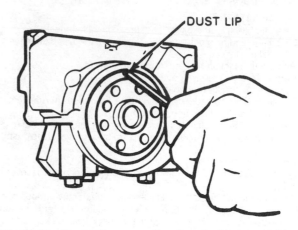

Fig. 13.14   Pry out the rear main oil seal with a screwdriver, being careful not to scratch the crankshaft

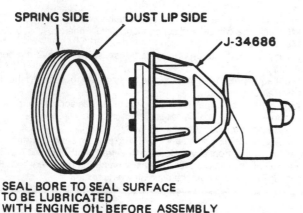

SEAL BORE TO SEAL SURFACE
TO BE LUBRICATED
WITH ENGINE OIL BEFORE ASSEMBLY

Fig. 13.15   Position the new rear oil seal on the installation tool

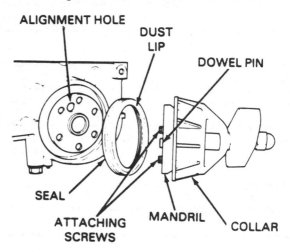

Fig. 13.16   Match the tool dowel pin to the dowel pin hole in the crankshaft, bolt the tool down and press the new seal into place

153 Install a new gasket on the oil pan.
154 Lift the pan into position and install all bolts finger tight. There is no specific order for tightening the bolts, but it is a good idea to tighten the stud nuts first.
155 Follow the removal steps in reverse order. Fill the crankcase with the correct grade and quantity of oil, start the engine and check for leaks.

Oil pump — removal and installation

156 Remove the oil pan.
157 Remove the pump-to-rear main bearing cap bolt and separate the pump and extension shaft from the engine.
158 To install the pump, move it into position and align the top end of the hexagonal extension shaft with the hexagonal socket in the lower end of the drive gear shaft.
159 Install the oil pump-to-rear main bearing cap bolt and tighten it to the specified torque.
160 Reinstall the oil pan.

*Rear main bearing oil seal — replacement
(engine in vehicle)*

Note: *A special tool is required for this procedure. It is available from your dealer or may, in some cases, be rented from an auto parts store or tool rental shop.*

161 Raise the vehicle and support it securely on jackstands.
162 Using a block of wood to protect the pan, use a floor jack to support the engine.

163 Remove the transaxle.
164 Remove the flywheel.
165 Using a screwdriver, pry the oil seal from the back of the block. Use care not to scratch the crankshaft with the screwdriver.
166 Coat the inside edge of the new seal with engine oil and install the seal over the installation tool (GM no. J-34686).
167 Align the installation tool dowel pin with the dowel pin hole in the crankshaft flange.
168 Bolt the installation tool to the crankshaft flange.
169 Turn the installation tool T-handle to force the seal into the block until the tool mandril is pressed tight against the rear face of the block.
170 Install the flywheel.
171 Install the transaxle.
172 Start the engine and check for oil leaks.

Torsional damper — removal and installation

173 Disconnect the negative cable at the battery.
174 Remove the serpentine drivebelt.
175 Raise the vehicle and support it securely on jackstands.
176 Remove the right inner fender splash shield for access.
177 Remove the damper retaining bolt.
178 Attach a puller to the damper. Draw the damper off the crankshaft, being careful not to drop it as it breaks free. A common gear puller should not be used to draw the damper off, as it may separate the outer portion of the damper from the hub. Use only a puller which bolts to the hub.
179 Before installing the damper, coat the front cover seal contact

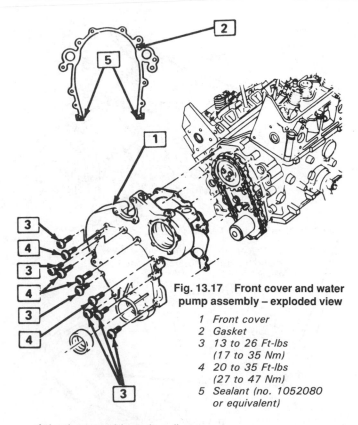

Fig. 13.17 Front cover and water pump assembly – exploded view

1 Front cover
2 Gasket
3 13 to 26 Ft-lbs
(17 to 35 Nm)
4 20 to 35 Ft-lbs
(27 to 47 Nm)
5 Sealant (no. 1052080 or equivalent)

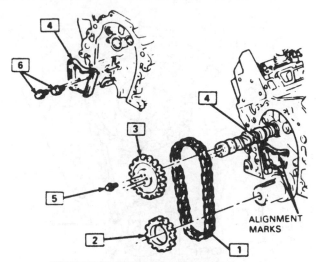

ALIGNMENT MARKS

NOTE—ALIGN TIMING MARKS ON CAM & CRANK SPROCKETS USING ALIGNMENT MARKS ON DAMPER STAMPING OR CAST ALIGNMENT MARKS ON CYL & CASE.

Fig. 13.18 Timing chain and sprocket assembly – exploded view

1 Timing chain
2 Crank sprocket
3 Camshaft sprocket
4 Damper
5 15 to 20 Ft-lbs.
(20 to 27 Nm)
6 14 to 19 Ft-lbs.
(18 to 25 Nm)

area of the damper with engine oil.

180 Apply RTV sealant to the crankshaft keyway and key.

181 Place the damper in position over the key on the crankshaft. Make sure the damper keyway lines up with the key.

182 Using a damper installation tool (GM no. J-29113 or equivalent), push the damper onto the crankshaft. The special tool distributes the pressure evenly around the hub.

183 Remove the installation tool and install the damper retaining bolt. Tighten the bolt to the specified torque.

184 Follow the removal procedure in the reverse order for the remaining components.

Crankcase front cover — removal and installation

Removal

185 Disconnect the negative cable from the battery.

186 Drain the cooling system.

187 Remove the serpentine drivebelt.

188 Remove the drivebelt tensioner.

189 Unbolt the alternator and carefully hang it out of the way.

190 Remove the alternator bracket.

191 Unbolt the power steering pump and carefully hang it out of the way.

192 Remove the drivebelt idler (if equipped).

193 Raise the vehicle and support it securely on jackstands.

194 Remove the right fender inner splash shield.

195 Remove the flywheel cover.

196 Remove the torsional damper.

197 Remove the starter.

198 Remove the oil pan.

199 Lower the vehicle.

200 Remove the radiator hose from the water pump.

201 Remove the heater hose from the cooling system filler pipe.

202 Remove the coolant bypass and overflow hoses.

203 Remove the water pump pulley.

204 Remove the spark plug wire shield where it attaches to the water pump.

205 Remove the canister purge hose.

206 Remove the front cover bolts and detach the front cover.

Installation

207 Clean all old gasket material and sealant from the sealing surfaces of the front cover and the block.

208 Install a new gasket on the front cover.

209 Apply a small amount of RTV sealant to the lower corners of the front cover where it contacts the oil pan.

210 Install the front cover on the engine.

211 Raise the vehicle and support it on jackstands.

212 The remainder of the installation is the reverse of the removal procedure.

213 Fill the cooling system, start the engine and check for oil and coolant leaks.

Front cover oil seal — replacement

With front cover installed on engine

214 With the torsional damper removed, pry the old seal out of the crankcase front cover with a large screwdriver. Be careful not to damage the surface of the crankshaft.

215 Place the new seal in position with the open end of the seal (seal lip) toward the inside of the cover.

216 Drive the seal into the cover until it is seated. GM tool no. J-35468 is available for this purpose. These tools are designed to exert even pressure around the entire circumference of the seal as it is driven into place. A section of large diameter pipe or a large socket can also be used.

217 Be careful not to distort the front cover.

With front cover removed from engine

218 This method is preferred, as the cover can be supported while the old seal is removed and the new one is installed.

219 Remove the crankcase front cover.

220 Using a large screwdriver, pry the old seal out of the front cover. Alternatively, support the cover and drive the seal out from the rear. Be careful not to damage the cover.

221 With the front of the cover facing up, place the new seal in position with the open end of the seal toward the inside of the cover.

222 Using a wooden block and hammer, drive the new seal into the cover until it is completely seated.

223 Reinstall the front cover.

Timing chain and sprockets — inspection, removal and installation

224 Disconnect the cable from the negative battery terminal.

225 Remove the torsional damper.

226 Remove the crankcase front cover.

227 Before removing the chain and sprockets, visually inspect the teeth

13

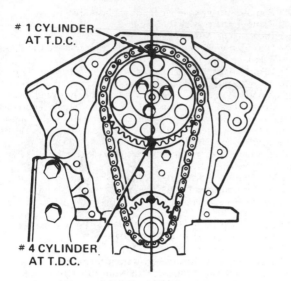

Fig. 13.19   Make sure the timing marks are properly aligned before removing or installing the timing chain

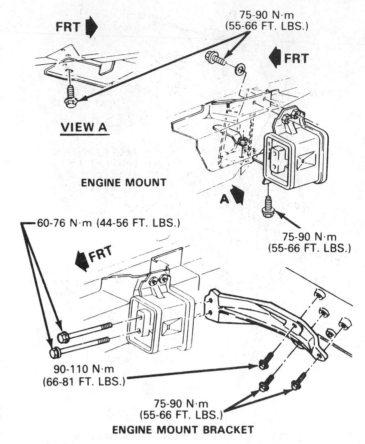

Fig. 13.20   Front engine mount – exploded view

on the sprockets for signs of wear and check the chain for looseness. Check the condition of the timing chain tensioners.

228 If either or both sprockets show any signs of wear (edges on the teeth of the camshaft sprocket not square, bright or blue areas on the teeth of either sprocket, chipping, pitting, etc.), they should be replaced with new ones. Wear in these areas is very common.

229 If the timing chain has not recently been replaced, or if the engine has over 25,000 miles on it, the chain is almost certainly in need of replacement. Failure to replace a worn timing chain may result in erratic engine performance, loss of power and lowered gas mileage.

230 If any one component requires replacement, all related components should be replaced as well.

231 Turn the engine over until the marks on the camshaft and crankshaft are in exact alignment. At this point the number one and four pistons will be at top dead center with the number four piston in the firing position (verify by checking the position of the rotor in the distributor). **Note:** *Do not attempt to remove either sprocket or the timing chain until this is done and do not turn the crankshaft or camshaft after the sprockets and chain are removed.*

232 Remove the camshaft sprocket retaining bolt and lift the camshaft sprocket and timing chain off the front of the engine. It may be necessary to tap the lower edge of the sprocket with a soft-face hammer to dislodge it.

233 If it is necessary to remove the crankshaft sprocket, it can be withdrawn from the crankshaft with a puller.

234 Push the crankshaft sprocket onto the nose of the crankshaft, aligning it with the key, until it seats against the shoulder.

235 Lubricate the thrust (rear) surface of the camshaft sprocket with moly-base grease or engine assembly lube. Install the timing chain over the camshaft sprocket with slack in the chain hanging down over the crankshaft sprocket.

236 With the timing marks aligned, slip the chain over the crankshaft sprocket and then draw the camshaft sprocket into place with the retaining bolt. **Note:** *Do not hammer or attempt to drive the camshaft sprocket into place, as it could dislodge the Welch plug at the rear of the engine.*

237 With the chain and both sprockets in place, check again to ensure that the timing marks on the two sprockets are properly aligned. If not, remove the timing chain and cam sprocket, turn the camshaft enough to change the chain position on the crankshaft sprocket one tooth, reinstall the chain and camshaft sprocket and check the timing mark alignment. Repeat as necessary until the marks are in alignment.

238 Lubricate the chain with engine oil and install the remaining components in the reverse order of removal.

Camshaft — removal and installation

239 Remove the engine from the vehicle.
240 Remove the valve lifters.

241 Remove the crankcase front cover.
242 Remove the timing chain and sprocket.
243 Install a long bolt in the camshaft bolt hole to be used as a handle and support for the camshaft.
244 Carefully draw the camshaft out of the engine block. Do this very slowly to avoid damage to the camshaft bearings as the lobes pass over the bearing surfaces. Always support the camshaft with one hand near the engine block.
245 Prior to installing the camshaft, coat each of the lobes and journals with engine assembly lube or moly-base grease.
246 Slide the camshaft into the engine block, again taking care not to damage the bearings.
247 Install the camshaft sprocket and timing chain.
248 Install the remaining components in the reverse order of removal.
249 Adjust the valve lash.

Powertrain mounts — replacement (engine in vehicle)

250 If the mounts have become hard, split or separated from the metal backing, they must be replaced. This operation may be carried out with the engine/transaxle still in the vehicle.

Engine mount
251 Disconnect the negative cable from the battery.
252 Remove the engine mount-to-body bracket bolts.
253 Remove the upper engine mount-to-engine bracket nuts and remove the mount.
254 Raise the vehicle and support it securely on jackstands.
255 Using a block of wood to protect the pan, support the engine with a floor jack.
256 Remove the inner fender shield.
257 Remove the lower engine mount-to-engine bracket bolt and remove the mount.
258 All engine mounting bolts should be coated with thread locking compound before installation, then tightened to the specified torque.
259 Installation is the reverse of the removal procedure.

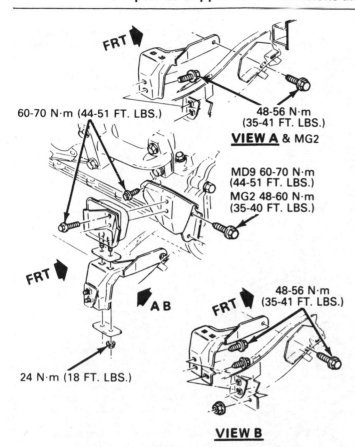

60-70 N·m (44-51 FT. LBS.)

48-56 N·m (35-41 FT. LBS.)

VIEW A & MG2

MD9 60-70 N·m (44-51 FT. LBS.)
MG2 48-60 N·m (35-40 FT. LBS.)

FRT

A B

FRT

48-56 N·m (35-41 FT. LBS.)

24 N·m (18 FT. LBS.)

VIEW B

Fig. 13.21   Rear engine mount – exploded view

Rear mount
260 Disconnect the negative cable from the battery.
261 Raise the vehicle and support it securely on jackstands.
262 Using a block of wood to protect the pan, support the engine with a floor jack.
263 Remove the engine mount-to-frame bracket nuts.
264 Remove the engine mount-to-engine bracket bolts and remove the mount.
265 All engine mounting bolts and nuts should be coated with thread locking compound before installation, then tightened to the specified torque.

Engine — removal and installation

Note: *A special support fixture, General Motors tool no. J-28467, is necessary to hold the engine during the removal procedure. This tool can often be rented from tool rental yards for a reasonable fee.*

Removal
266 Disconnect the cable from the negative battery terminal.
267 Remove the air cleaner, air inlet hose and the mass air flow sensor.
268 Drain the cooling system.
269 Remove the exhaust manifolds and crossover pipe assembly.
270 Remove the serpentine drivebelt.
271 Remove the power steering pump, without disconnecting the hoses, and hang the pump out of the way.
272 Remove the radiator hoses.
273 Disconnect the throttle and TV cables from the throttle valve bracket on the plenum.
274 Remove the alternator mounting bolts and hang the alternator to one side without disconnecting the wiring.
275 Disconnect the main engine wiring harness.
276 Remove the coolant bypass and overflow hoses.
277 Remove the canister purge hose from the canister.
278 Disconnect all engine vacuum hoses. Label them to simplify reinstallation.
279 Use General Motors tool no. J-28467 (or the equivalent) to support the engine.
280 Raise the vehicle and support it securely on jackstands.

281 Remove the right inner fender splash shield.
282 Remove the torsional damper.
283 Remove the flywheel cover.
284 Unplug the electrical connectors, then remove the starter from the engine.
285 Disconnect the wires from the oil pressure sending unit.
286 Remove the air conditioning compressor and bracket and hang the compressor out of the way without disconnecting any of the air conditioning hoses. **Warning:** *The air conditioning system is under high pressure, and air conditioning lines should not be disconnected unless the system has been depressurized by a dealer service department or air conditioning specialist.*
287 If equipped with an automatic transaxle, remove the flywheel-to-torque converter bolts.
288 Remove the front and rear engine mount bolts.
289 Remove the front and rear engine mount brackets.
290 On vehicles equipped with a manual transaxle, remove the intermediate shaft bracket-to-engine bolts.
291 Disconnect the shift cable bracket at the transaxle.
292 Remove the lower bellhousing bolts.
293 Remove the jackstands and lower the vehicle.
294 Disconnect the heater hoses from the engine.
295 Hook up the engine hoist, lift the engine slightly, then disconnect the engine support tool.
296 Use a floor jack to support the transaxle.
297 Remove the upper bellhousing bolts.
298 Remove the transaxle mount bracket.
299 Lift the engine out of the vehicle.

Installation
300 Lower the engine into the vehicle.
301 Install the engine support tool.
302 Install the upper bellhousing bolts.
303 Install the transaxle mount bracket and remove the jack from under the transaxle.
304 Connect the heater hoses to the engine.
305 Raise the vehicle and support it securely on jackstands.
306 Install the front and rear engine mount brackets.
307 On vehicles equipped with a manual transaxle, attach the intermediate shaft bracket to the engine.
308 Install the engine mount bolts and tighten them to the specified torque.
309 Install the lower bellhousing bolts.
310 Attach the shift cable bracket to the transaxle.
311 On vehicles equipped with an automatic transaxle, install the flywheel-to-torque converter bolts.
312 Install the air conditioning compressor and bracket.
313 Connect the wires to the oil pressure sending unit.
314 Install the starter and connect the starter wires.
315 Install the flywheel cover.
316 Install the torsional damper.
317 Install the right inner fender splash shield.
318 Remove the jackstands and lower the vehicle.
319 Connect all previously removed vacuum lines and electrical connectors.
320 Connect the canister purge hose to the canister. ·
321 Connect the coolant bypass and overflow hoses to the engine.
322 Connect the fuel lines.
323 Install the alternator.
324 Connect the throttle and TV cables to the plenum bracket.
325 Install the radiator hoses and the serpentine drivebelt.
326 Install the exhaust manifolds and the crossover pipe assembly.
327 Install the mass air flow sensor and the air cleaner.
328 Fill the cooling system.
329 Connect the negative cable to the battery.
330 Check the oil level, start the engine and check for fuel, oil and coolant leaks.

---

6   General engine overhaul procedures

Crankshaft — installation and main bearing oil clearance check

1   Upper and lower main bearing inserts may be different. Be sure to check for oil hole alignment between the bearing and the block bearing saddle when installing the bearings.

13

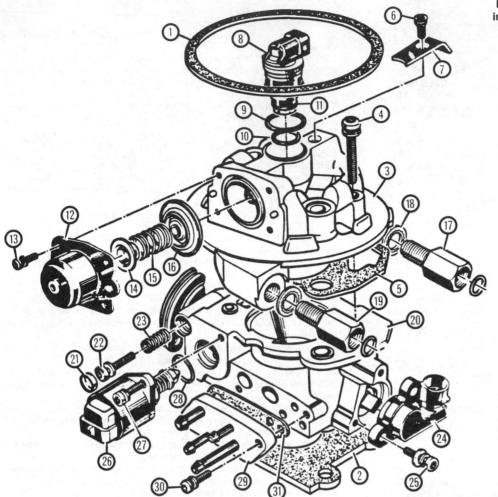

Fig. 13.22   Model 700 throttle body injector components – exploded view

1   Air filter gasket
2   Flange gasket
3   Fuel meter assembly
4   Fuel meter body attaching screw and washer assembly
5   Fuel meter body-to-throttle body gasket
6   Injector retainer screw
7   Injector retainer
8   Fuel injector
9   Upper fuel injector O-ring
10 Lower fuel injector O-ring
11 Injector filter
12 Pressure regulator cover
13 Pressure regulator attaching screw
14 Spring seat
15 Pressure regulator spring
16 Pressure regulator diaphragm
17 Fuel inlet nut
18 Fuel inlet nut seal
19 Fuel outlet nut
20 Throttle body assembly
21 Idle stop screw plug
22 Idle stop screw and washer assembly
23 Idle stop screw spring
24 Throttle Position Sensor (TPS)
25 TPS attaching screw and washer assembly
26 Idle Air Control Valve (IACV)
27 IACV attaching screw
28 IACV O-ring
29 Tube manifold assembly
30 Manifold attaching screw
31 Tube manifold gasket

2   In order to prevent damage to the main bearing caps and the block, the main bearing caps should be tapped into the recesses in the block with a brass or lead hammer *before* installing the main bearing cap bolts. **Caution:** *Do not use the bolts to pull the main bearing caps into place, as damage to the block and cap can occur.*

---

7   Fuel and exhaust systems

Warning: *Gasoline is extremely flammable, so extra precautions must be taken when working on any part of the fuel system. Do not smoke or allow open flames or bare light bulbs near the work area. Also, do not work in a garage if a natural gas-type appliance with a pilot light is present.*

Model 700 throttle body injection (2.0L four-cylinder engines)

1   Late model vehicles with the 2.0L four-cylinder engine are equipped with Model 700 throttle body fuel injection. **Caution:** *Many parts, including the fuel injectors, are externally identical to parts from the earlier throttle body injection unit and could be installed in the Model 700 unit. However, only parts specifically calibrated for the Model 700 unit will function properly and care should be taken to ensure that only the correct parts are installed during repair or overhaul.*

Fuel pressure relief
2   Before servicing any portion of the fuel system which would require that fuel lines be disconnected, the pressure in the fuel system must be relieved. **Warning:** *Pressure can remain in the fuel system even after the engine has been shut off for an extended period of time.*
3   Locate the fuel pump fuse in the fuse block and remove it.
4   Start the engine and allow it to run until it dies from lack of fuel.

5   Turn the engine over with the starter for three to five seconds to remove all pressure from the lines.
6   Be sure to replace the fuel pump fuse after servicing the fuel system.

Fuel injector replacement
7   Relieve the fuel pressure
8   Remove the air cleaner assembly.
9   Disconnect the electrical connector to the fuel injector.
10   Remove the injector retaining screw and retainer.
11   Using one screwdriver shank as a fulcrum, use a second screwdriver to pry under the ridge *opposite* the fuel injector electrical terminal. Pry the injector out of the fuel meter assembly housing.

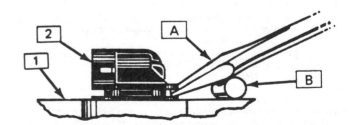

Fig. 13.23   Use one screwdriver shank as a fulcrum and another screwdriver to pry the fuel injector out of the fuel meter assembly

1   Fuel meter assembly   A   Screwdriver
2   Fuel injector   B   Fulcrum

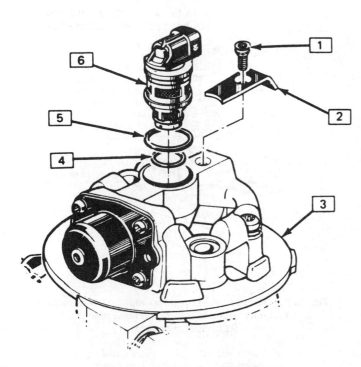

Fig. 13.24   Fuel injector – exploded view

1 Screw   4 Lower O-ring
2 Retainer   5 Upper O-ring
3 Fuel meter assembly 6 Injector

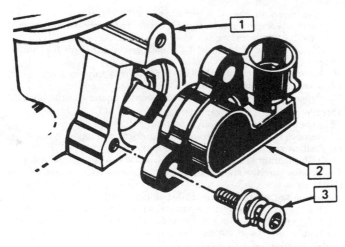

Fig.   13.26   Use thread locking compound on the screws when installing the new throttle position sensor

1 Throttle body assembly   3 Screw assembly
2 Throttle position sensor

12 Remove the upper and lower O-rings from the fuel injector and the injector cavity in the fuel meter assembly and discard them.

13 **Caution:** *Be sure to replace the injector with one having the same part number. Injectors from other models will fit in the Model 700 TBI, but will not function properly due to different flow rate calibration.*

14 Lubricate the new upper and lower O-rings with automatic transmission fluid and install them on the injector. Make sure the upper O-ring seats in the groove and that the lower O-ring is flush against the injector filter.

15 Install the fuel injector in the fuel meter assembly housing. **Note:** *The electrical terminal end of the injector should be pointing towards*

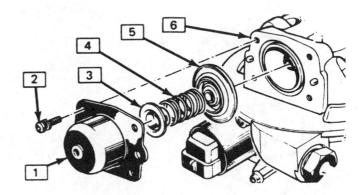

Fig. 13.25   Fuel pressure regulator – exploded view

1 Pressure regulator cover   4 Spring
2 Screw   5 Diaphragm
3 Spring seat   6 Fuel meter assembly

the cut out for the wire grommet in the fuel meter assembly.

16 Install the injector retainer. Use thread locking compound on the retaining screw.

17 Connect the electrical connector to the fuel injector.

18 Replace the air cleaner.

19 Turn the ignition switch on without starting the engine and check for fuel leaks.

Pressure regulator replacement

20 **Caution:** *Whenever the pressure regulator cover is removed, the diaphragm assembly must be replaced with a new one to prevent fuel leaks.*

21 Relieve the fuel pressure.

22 Remove the air cleaner.

23 While holding the pressure regulator against the fuel meter assembly housing, remove the four retaining screws. **Warning:** *The pressure regulator cover holds a large spring under heavy compression. Use caution when removing it to prevent personal injury.*

24 Remove the pressure regulator cover, spring seat and spring.

25 Remove the pressure regulator diaphragm assembly.

26 Installation is the reverse of the removal procedure.

27 Use thread locking compound on the pressure regulator cover retaining screws.

28 Turn the ignition switch on without starting the engine and check for fuel leaks.

Throttle position sensor replacement

29 Disconnect the negative cable from the battery.

30 Remove the air cleaner and gasket.

31 Remove the rear alternator bracket and metal PCV tube.

32 Remove the two screws and separate the throttle position sensor from the throttle body.

33 With the throttle closed, install the new throttle position sensor on the throttle shaft and rotate it counterclockwise until the holes in the TPS line up with the holes in the throttle body housing.

34 Using thread locking compound, install the two mounting screws.

35 The remainder of installation is the reverse of the removal procedure.

Idle air control valve replacement

36 **Caution:** *Although earlier units will fit on the Model 700 throttle body, only the flange mounted, dual taper idle air control valve with 10 mm pintle should be used.*

37 Remove the air cleaner.

38 Disconnect the idle air control valve electrical connector.

39 Remove the screws and separate the idle air control valve from the throttle body.

40 Remove the idle air control valve O-ring and discard it. Always use a new O-ring when reinstalling the idle air control valve.

41 Clean the sealing surface on the throttle body to ensure proper O-ring sealing.

42 Measure the distance between the tip of the pintle and the flange

13

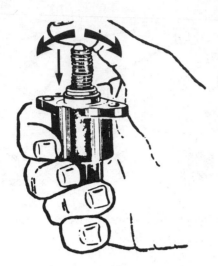

Fig. 13.27   Press down on the pintle while rocking it from side-to-side to depress it sufficiently for installation

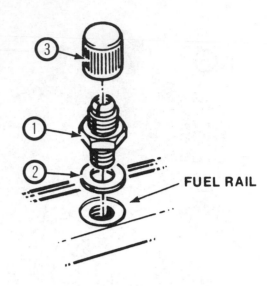

Fig. 13.28   The fuel pressure connector on the radiator side fuel rail is used to relieve the fuel pressure (V6 port fuel injection)

1	Fuel pressure connector	2	Seal
		3	Cap

mounting surface. If the distance is greater than 1-1/8 inches (28 mm) it must be reduced before installation.

43 Exert firm pressure combined with slight side-to-side movement to retract the pintle.

44 Lubricate the new O-ring with automatic transmission fluid and install it on the idle air control valve.

45 Install the idle air control valve on the throttle body, using thread locking compound on the screws.

46 Install the electrical connector.

47 Install the air cleaner.

48 Start the engine and allow it to reach normal operating temperature. Drive the vehicle at approximately 30 mph (48 kph), at which speed the ECM will automatically set the idle air control valve pintle to the correct position.

Throttle body assembly removal and installation

49 Relieve the fuel pressure.

50 Remove the air cleaner assembly.

51 Disconnect the electrical connectors to the idle air control valve, throttle position sensor and fuel injector.

52 Remove the wire grommet from the throttle body.

53 Disconnect the throttle linkage return spring, throttle cable and TV cable (if equipped).

54 Disconnect all vacuum hoses, identifying them with tape for proper reinstallation.

55 Disconnect the fuel inlet and outlet line nuts.

56 Remove the fuel line nut O-rings and discard them.

57 Remove the throttle body-to-intake manifold nuts.

58 Remove the air cleaner stud from the throttle body and separate the throttle body from the intake manifold.

59 Installation is the reverse of the removal procedure. Be sure to install a new throttle body-to-intake manifold gasket and tighten the mounting nuts and air cleaner stud to the specified torque.

60 Turn the ignition switch on without starting the engine and check for fuel leaks.

Port fuel injection (V6 engines)

61 A port fuel injection system, with individual injectors for each cylinder, is used on late model V6 engines.

Fuel pressure relief

62 Removing the fuel pump fuse from the fuse panel will not allow relief of the fuel pressure in the system, since the oil pressure switch can turn the fuel pump on even if the fuse is removed.

63 A fuel pressure connector is located on the front (radiator side) fuel rail. Wrap a towel or shop rags around the connector, remove the cap and quickly place a hose over the fitting to route the fuel into a metal container.

Throttle body removal and installation

64 Remove the negative cable from the battery.

65 Remove the air inlet duct.

66 Disconnect the electrical connectors to the idle air control valve and throttle position sensor.

67 Disconnect the two coolant hoses to the throttle body.

68 Label all vacuum lines to the throttle body to simplify installation, then remove the lines.

69 Disconnect the throttle and TV (if equipped) cables from the throttle body.

70 Remove the mounting bolts and lift off the throttle body.

71 Installation is the reverse of the removal procedure.

72 Replace any coolant lost during removal of the throttle body.

Throttle position sensor replacement

73 Remove the throttle body assembly.

74 Remove the mounting screws and retainers and separate the throttle position sensor from the throttle body.

75 With the throttle completely closed, install the throttle position sensor, making sure the lever lines up with the drive lever on the throttle shaft.

76 Install the screws and retainers finger tight.

77 Adjustment of the throttle position sensor requires a ''scan'' tool. Drive the vehicle to a General Motors dealer or a shop equipped with the scan tool to have the throttle position sensor adjusted properly.

Idle air control valve replacement

78 Remove the electrical connector from the idle air control valve.

79 Remove the idle air control valve screws and separate the valve from the throttle body.

80 Clean the sealing surfaces on the throttle body.

81 **Caution:** *The port fuel injection throttle body uses a 12 mm diameter dual taper pintle idle air control valve. Make sure you have the correct idle air control valve for this application.*

82 Measure the distance between the tip of the pintle and the flange mounting surface. If the distance is greater than 1-1/8 inches (28 mm), it must be reduced to prevent damage to the valve when it is installed.

83 Exert firm pressure on the pintle valve combined with slight side-to-side movement to retract the pintle.

84 Install the idle air control valve on the throttle body.

85 Attach the electrical connector to the idle air control valve.

86 Start the engine, then turn the ignition switch to Off. When the switch is turned to Off the ECM will automatically set the idle air control valve pintle to the proper position.

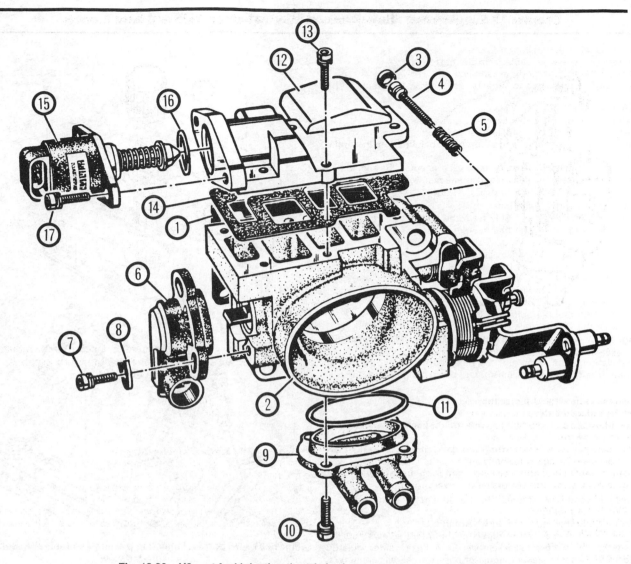

Fig. 13.29 V6 port fuel injection throttle body components – exploded view

1 Flange gasket
2 Throttle body assembly
3 Idle stop screw plug
4 Idle stop screw
5 Idle stop screw
   assembly spring
6 Throttle Position
   Sensor (TPS)
7 TPS attaching
   screw

8 TPS attaching
   screw retainer
9 Coolant cavity cover
10 Coolant cover attaching
   screw
11 Coolant cover-to-throttle body
   O-ring
12 Idle air/vacuum signal housing
   assembly

13 Idle air/vacuum signal
   assembly screw
14 Idle air/vacuum signal
   assembly gasket
15 Idle air control (IAC)
   valve assembly
16 Idle air control valve O-ring
17 Idle air control valve attaching
   screw

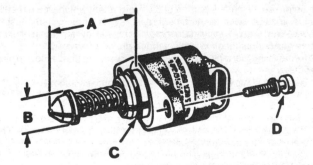

Fig. 13.30 The idle air control valve distance "A" must be as specified before installation

A Distance of pintle extension
B Diameter of pintle
C IACV O-ring
D IACV attaching screw

13

Plenum removal and installation

87 Remove the negative cable from the battery.
88 Remove the throttle body assembly.
89 Label any vacuum lines to simplify reassembly, then remove the lines.
90 Remove the EGR valve-to-plenum nuts.
91 Remove the throttle cable bracket bolts.
92 Remove the ignition wire plastic shield bolts.
93 Remove the plenum bolts and separate the plenum from the intake manifold.
94 Installation is the reverse of the removal procedure. Be sure to use new gaskets between the plenum and intake manifold and tighten the plenum bolts to the specified torque.

Fuel rail removal and installation

95 Disconnect the negative cable from the battery.
96 Relief the pressure in the fuel system.
97 Remove the plenum.
98 Remove the fuel line bracket bolt.
99 Disconnect the fuel lines from the fuel rail.
100 Remove the fuel line O-rings.
101 Remove the vacuum line from the pressure regulator.
102 Disconnect the fuel injector electrical connectors.
103 Remove the fuel rail bolts and lift off the fuel rails.
104 Remove the O-ring seals from the base of each injector.
105 Install new O-rings on the base of each injector and lubricate them with engine oil.
106 Installation is the reverse of the removal procedure. Be sure to install new O-rings on the fuel lines before connecting them to the fuel rail.

Fuel injector removal and installation

107 Remove the fuel rails.
108 Spread the open end of the fuel injector retainer clips slightly and remove the clips from the fuel rail.
109 Remove the fuel injectors from the fuel rail.
110 Remove the O-rings from both ends of the injectors.
111 Install new O-rings and lubricate them with engine oil.
112 Installation is the reverse of the removal procedure.

Fuel pressure regulator removal and installation

113 Remove the fuel rails.
114 Remove the fuel inlet and outlet fittings.
115 Remove the fuel pressure regulator mounting screws and the
116 Separate the two fuel rail assemblies from the pressure regulator.
117 Remove the fuel pressure regulator base-to-fuel rail connectors.
118 Remove the O-rings from the fuel rail connectors.
119 Install new O-rings and lubricate them with engine oil.
120 Installation is the reverse of the removal procedure.

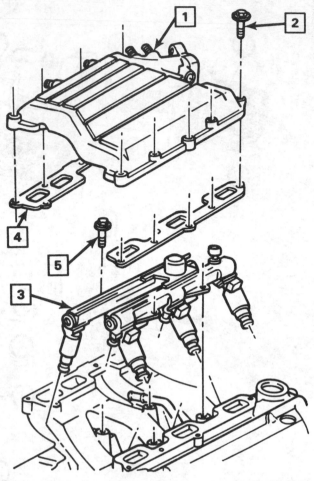

Fig. 13.31   V6 port fuel injection plenum and fuel rail assembly –
exploded view

1 Plenum	4 Gasket
2 Bolt (9)	5 Bolt (4)
3 Fuel rail	

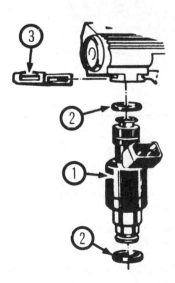

Fig. 13.32   V6 fuel injector and retaining clip – exploded view

1 Fuel injector assembly	3 Injector retainer clip
2 O-ring	

Port fuel injection (1992 2.2L four-cylinder engines)

Warning: *Gasoline is extremely flammable, so extra precautions must be taken when working on any part of the fuel system. DO NOT smoke or allow open flames or bare light bulbs near the work area. Also, don't work in a garage where a natural gas appliance such as a water heater or clothes dryer is present.*

Fuel pressure relief

121 Before servicing any portion of the fuel system which would require that fuel lines be disconnected, the pressure in the fuel system must be relieved. **Warning:** *Pressure can remain in the fuel system even after the engine has been shut off for an extended period of time.*
122 Remove the fuel tank cap to relieve tank pressure (leave the cap off at this time).
123 Raise the vehicle and support it securely on jackstands.
124 Disconnect the fuel pump electrical connector.
125 Lower the vehicle.
126 Start the engine and allow it to run until it stalls from lack of fuel.
127 Turn the engine over with the starter for three to five seconds to remove all pressure from the lines.
128 Disconnect the negative battery cable from the battery.
129 Install the cap onto the fuel tank.
130 Be sure to reconnect the electrical connector back onto the fuel pump after servicing the fuel system. Also reconnect the negative battery cable.

Fuel injector replacement

131 Relieve the fuel pressure.

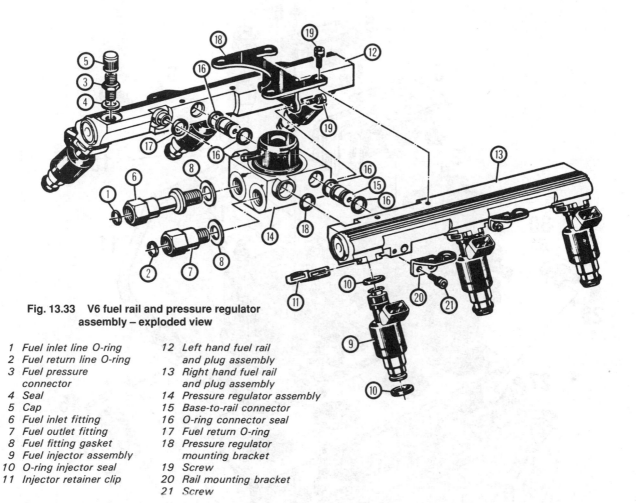

Fig. 13.33 V6 fuel rail and pressure regulator assembly – exploded view

1 Fuel inlet line O-ring	12 Left hand fuel rail
2 Fuel return line O-ring	and plug assembly
3 Fuel pressure	13 Right hand fuel rail
connector	and plug assembly
4 Seal	14 Pressure regulator assembly
5 Cap	15 Base-to-rail connector
6 Fuel inlet fitting	16 O-ring connector seal
7 Fuel outlet fitting	17 Fuel return O-ring
8 Fuel fitting gasket	18 Pressure regulator
9 Fuel injector assembly	mounting bracket
10 O-ring injector seal	19 Screw
11 Injector retainer clip	20 Rail mounting bracket
	21 Screw

132 Remove the upper intake manifold (see below).

133 Remove the fuel return line retaining bracket nut. Move the return line away from the fuel pressure regulator.

134 Remove the pressure regulator assembly. **Caution:** *Do not attempt to remove the bracket without first removing the fuel pressure regulator.*

135 **Caution:** *To prevent damage to the injector retaining bracket and/or injectors, do not try to remove the injectors by lifting up the injector retaining bracket while the injectors are still installed in the bracket slots.*

136 Remove the injector retaining bracket screws.

137 Remove the retaining bracket. Carefully slide the bracket off to clear the injector slots and regulator.

138 Disconnect the electrical connector from the fuel injector(s).

139 Remove the fuel injector(s). Remove the upper large O-ring seal and lower small O-ring seal; discard both seals. **Caution:** *Be sure to remove the lower small O-ring from the lower manifold if it did not come out with the injector. Failure to do so and installing a new injector with a new lower O-ring in place will prevent the injector from sealing properly during installation and could cause a fuel leak.*

140 Cover the injector opening in the lower intake manifold to prevent the entry of foreign matter.

141 **Caution:** *Be sure to replace the injector with one having the exact same part number. Each injector is calibrated for a specific fuel flow rate.*

142 Apply clean engine oil to the new O-rings and install them onto the fuel injector(s). **Note:** *If reinstalling the existing fuel injector(s), install two new O-ring seals.*

143 Install the injector into the lower intake manifold. **Note:** *Install the injector(s) with the electrical connector facing in.*

144 Install the bracket so the injector retaining slots and regulator are aligned with the bracket slots.

145 Install the retainer bracket screws. Use thread locking compound on the retaining screws.

146 Connect the electrical connector to the injector(s). Connect the electrical connector to the fuel pump and also connect the negative battery terminal.

147 Turn the ignition switch ON for two seconds, then turn it OFF for ten seconds. Again turn it to the ON position without starting the engine and check for fuel leaks. The remainder of installation is the reverse of removal.

Pressure regulator replacement

148 Relive the fuel pressure.

149 Disconnect the negative battery cable from the battery.

150 Disconnect the vacuum hose from the top of the regulator.

151 Remove the fuel return line clamp.

152 Remove the fuel return line from the regulator. Discard the O-ring seal.

153 Remove the regulator bracket mounting screw.

154 Remove the regulator from the lower intake manifold. Discard the O-ring seal.

155 Installation is the reverse of the removal procedure.

156 Apply clean engine oil to the new O-ring. Install the bracket mounting screw. Use thread locking compound on the retaining screws. Tighten the fuel return pipe to the torque listed in this Chapter's Specifications.

Throttle position sensor replacement

157 Disconnect the electrical connector from the throttle position sensor.

158 Remove the throttle position sensor mounting screw.

159 Remove the throttle position sensor from the upper intake manifold.

160 With the throttle valve in the closed position, position the throttle position sensor onto the throttle shaft and push the sensor into the upper intake manifold.

161 Align the screw mounting hole and install the screw. Use thread locking compound on the retaining screw and tighten the screw to the torque listed in this Chapter's Specifications.

13

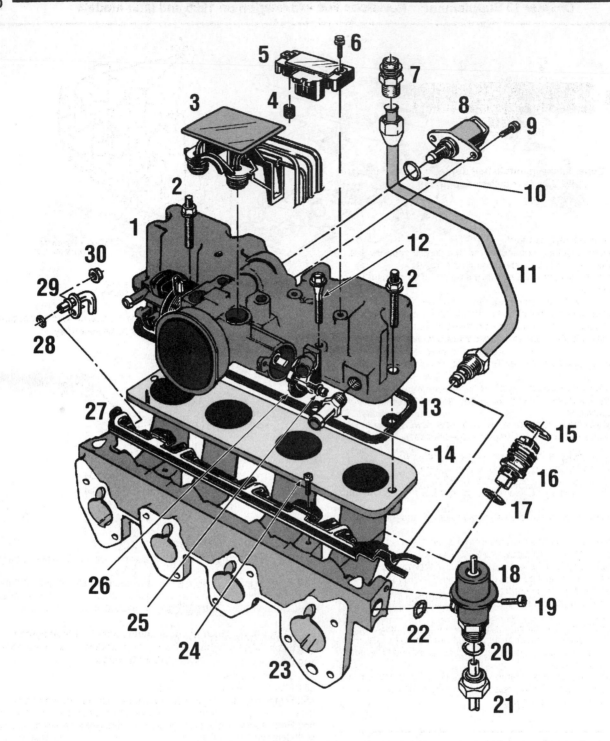

13.34 Upper and lower intake manifold assemblies – exploded view (1992 2.2L four-cylinder engines)

1	Upper manifold assembly	9	IAC valve attaching screw	20	Fuel return line O-ring seal
2	Stud	10	IAC valve O-ring	21	Fuel injector return line pipe assembly
3	Harness assembly – EGR	11	EGR transport tube assembly	22	Fuel pressure regulator
	valve and fuel pressure	12	Upper manifold bolt		O-ring seal
	regulator vacuum	13	Upper manifold gasket	23	Lower manifold assembly
4	MAP sensor seal	14	Power brake fitting assembly	24	Injector retainer attaching screw
5	Manifold absolute pressure	15	Injector upper large O-ring seal	25	TPS attaching screw
	(MAP) sensor	16	Bottom feed port (BFP)	26	Throttle position sensor (TPS)
6	MAP sensor attaching bolt		injector assembly	27	Injector retainer
7	Fitting and washer assembly	17	Injector lower small O-ring seal	28	Fuel feed line O-ring seal
8	Idle air control (IAC)	18	Pressure regulator assembly	29	Fuel injector fuel feed pipe assembly
	valve assembly	19	Pressure regulator attaching screw	30	Fuel feed line nut assembly

13.35   Upper intake manifold bolt tightening sequence (1992 2.2L four-cylinder engines)

Idle air control valve replacement
162 Disconnect the electrical connector from the idle air control valve.
163 Remove the idle air control valve mounting screws.
164 Remove the idle air control valve from the upper intake manifold. Discard the O-ring seal.
165 If installing a new idle air control valve measure the distance between the tip of the valve pintle and the mounting flange (dimension A). If dimension "A" is greater than 28 mm, use finger pressure and carefully and slowly push the pintle into the body to the specified dimension (see figure 13.30).
166 Apply clean engine oil to the new O-ring and install it onto the idle air control valve.
167 **Caution:** *Be sure to replace the idle air control valve with one having the exact same part number. The pintle shape and diameter are designed for a specific application.*
168 Use thread locking compound on the retaining screws and tighten the screws to the torque listed in this Chapter's Specifications.

Upper intake manifold assembly removal and installation
169 Disconnect the negative battery cable from the battery.
170 Remove the air duct from the upper manifold air inlet.
171 Remove the accelerator cable splash shield from the accelerator cable bracket.
172 Disconnect the accelerator, cruise (if so equipped) and transmission control cables.
173 Remove the vacuum hose harness from the top of the air inlet.
174 Disconnect the PCV and the power brake vacuum hoses from the fittings on the upper manifold. Move the hoses out of the way.
175 Disconnect the electrical connectors from the MAP sensor, throttle position sensor and the idle air control valve.
176 Remove the stud/nuts attaching the upper manifold to the lower manifold.
177 Move the EGR and injector wiring harness out of the way.
178 Separate the upper manifold and gasket from the lower manifold. Scrape away all traces of gasket material from the upper and lower manifold gasket mating surfaces.
179 Installation is the reverse of removal. Be sure to use a new gasket. Tighten the stud/nuts to the torque listed in this Chapter's Specifications. Use the tightening sequence shown.

---

8   Engine electrical systems

General information
Ignition system
Late model engines are equipped with a new ignition system which eliminates the conventional distributor and coil arrangement. Instead, a crankshaft sensor handles most of the distributor functions, while an ignition module and multiple coils provide the spark to the spark plugs.

Spark distribution is by the "waste spark" method, with opposite paired cylinders (1-4 and 2-3 on four-cylinder engines; 1-4, 3-6 and 2-5 on V6 engines) receiving a spark at the same time, even though one piston is in firing position on the compression stroke, while the other is coming up on the exhaust stroke. No timing adjustments are possible with this system.
Charging system
Later models are equipped with a CS type alternator, which can be identified by the rivets used to hold the alternator halves together. CS alter-

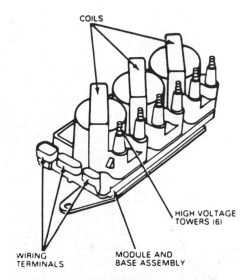

Fig. 13.36   V6 direct ignition system assembly, including coils, ignition module and base assembly

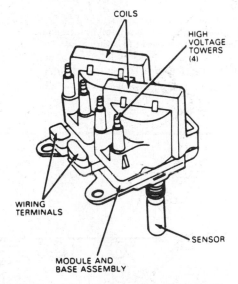

Fig. 13.37   Four-cylinder engine direct ignition system assembly, including coils, ignition module, base assembly and crankshaft sensor

nators are rebuildable if the rivets are drilled out, but we don't recommend it. For all intents and purposes, CS alternators should be considered non-serviceable and, if defective, should be exchanged for a new or factory-rebuilt unit.

CS alternators also have no test hole (see Chapter 5, Section 15). Proper testing requires special equipment and should be done by a dealer service department or a repair shop.

Direct ignition system assembly – removal and installation
1   Disconnect the negative cable from the battery.
2   Remove the electrical connectors to the ignition module.
3   Note the relationship of the spark plug wires to the ignition coils, marking them with tape if necessary, then disconnect the spark plug wires.
4   Remove the bolts holding the coil assembly to the block and detach the coil assembly.
5   Install the coil assembly on the block and tighten the bolts to the specified torque.
6   The remainder of the installation is the reverse of the removal procedure.

13

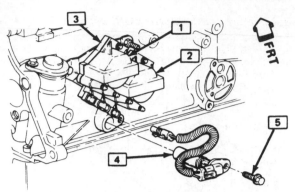

Fig. 13.38   Four-cylinder engine direct ignition system crankshaft sensor

1 2–3 coil	4 Crank sensor assembly
2 1–4 coil	5 Bolt
3 Module	

Crankshaft sensor – removal and installation

7   Disconnect the sensor harness from the ignition module.

8   Remove the bolt holding the sensor in the block, then remove the sensor.

9   Inspect the sensor O-ring for damage and replace it if necessary. Lubricate the new O-ring with engine oil before installation.

10   Installation is the reverse of the removal procedure.

Ignition coils – removal and installation

11   Remove the coil retaining screws from the ignition module and detach the coils.

12   Installation is the reverse of the removal procedure.

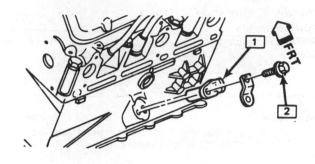

Fig. 13.39   V6 engine direct ignition system crankshaft sensor

1   Crankshaft sensor   2   Bolt

Ignition module – removal and installation

13   Disconnect the negative cable at the battery.

14   Remove the direct ignition system assembly from the engine block.

15   Remove the ignition coils from the assembly.

16   Remove the ignition module from the assembly plate.

17   Installation is the reverse of the removal procedure.

---

9   Emissions control systems

General information

Note that emission control component location diagrams for later model vehicles are included in this Chapter.

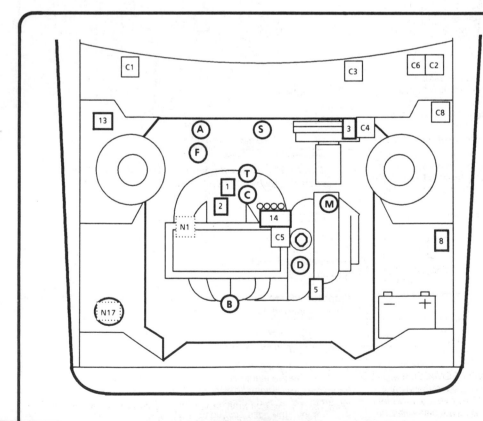

COMPUTER HARNESS

C1   Electronic Control Module (ECM)
C2   ALDL Diagnostic Connector
C3   "Service Engine Soon" light
C4   ECM Power Fuse
C5   ECM Harness Grounds
C6   Fuse Panel
C8   Fuel Pump Test Connector

CONTROLLED DEVICES

1   Fuel Injector Solenoid
2   Idle Air Control Valve
3   Fuel Pump Relay
5   TCC Solenoid Connector
8   Cooling Fan Relay
13   A/C Compressor Relay
14   Direct Ignition System Assembly

INFORMATION SENSORS

A   Manifold Pressure (MAP)
B   Exhaust Oxygen
C   Throttle Position
D   Coolant Temperature
F   Vehicle Speed
M   P/N Switch
S   P/S Pressure Switch
T   MAT Sensor

NOT ECM CONNECTED

N1   Crankcase Vent Valve (PCV)
N17   Fuel Vapor Canister

 Exhaust Gas Recirculation valve

Fig. 13.40   Typical later model four-cylinder engine emission control component locations

Computer Command Control System (CCCS) trouble codes

Additional trouble codes for later models are included in this Chapter.

Exhaust Gas Recirculation (EGR) system

All 1990 and later models are equipped with a Digital EGR Valve, which controls EGR flow electronically (through the ECM), rather than directly by intake manifold vacuum. The procedures outlined in Chapter 6 do not apply to the Digital EGR Valve. A new trouble code will reveal EGR valve problems.

Trouble code		Circuit or system	Probable cause
23	(2 flashes, pause, 3 flashes)	Manifold air temperature/low temperature	Faulty manifold air temperature sensor or connection (the sensor is located in the air cleaner assembly)
25	(2 flashes, pause, 5 flashes)	Manifold air temperature/high temperature	See code 23 above
32	(3 flashes, pause, 2 flashes)	Digital EGR valve	Digital EGR valve or connections
35	(3 flashes, pause, 5 flashes)	Idle speed – error	Faulty IAC valve or connections
53	(5 flashes, pause, 3 flashes)	Over-voltage	Check alternator output voltage
54	(5 flashes, pause, 4 flashes)	Low voltage in fuel pump circuit	Trace and repair fuel pump circuit wiring harness
61	(6 flashes, pause, 1 flash)	Oxygen sensor faulty signal	Replace sensor
62	(6 flashes, pause, 2 flashes)	Transaxle gear switch signal circuits (3.1 LV6)	Transaxle gear switch or connections
66	(6 flashes, pause, 6 flashes)	A/C pressure sensor circuit	Sensor, harness or connections

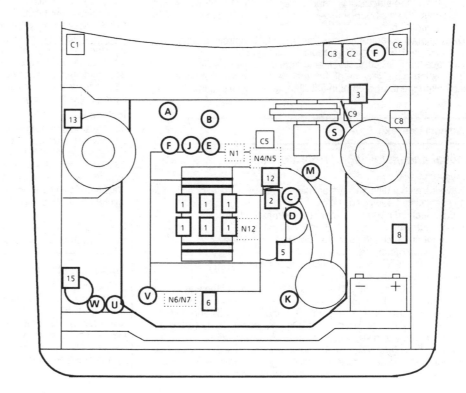

COMPUTER HARNESS
C1 Electronic Control Module (ECM)
C2 ALDL diagnostic connector
C3 "SERVICE ENGINE SOON" light
C5 ECM harness ground
C6 Fuse panel
C8 Fuel pump test connector
C9 Fuel pump / ECM fuse

CONTROLLED DEVICES
1 Fuel injector
2 Idle air control motor
3 Fuel pump relay
5 Trans. Converter Clutch connector
6 Direct Ignition System (DIS)
8 Engine fan relay
12 Exh. Gas Recirc. valve
13 A/C compressor relay
15 Fuel vapor canister solenoid

INFORMATION SENSORS
A Manifold Pressure (MAP)
B Exhaust oxygen
C Throttle position
D Coolant temperature
E Crank Shaft Sensor
F Vehicle speed
J Knock (ESC)
K MAT
M P/N switch
S P/S pressure switch
U A/C pressure fan switch
V A/C Low Press. switch (mounted in compressor)
W A/C Hi Press. cut-out sw.

NOT ECM CONNECTED
N1 Crankcase vent valve (PCV)
N4 Engine temp. switch (telltale)
N5 Engine temp. sensor (gage)
N6 Oil press. switch (telltale)
N7 Oil press. sensor (gage)
N12 Fuel pressure connector

Fig. 13.41 Typical later model V6 engine emission control component locations

13

Fig. 13.42 Hydraulic clutch system

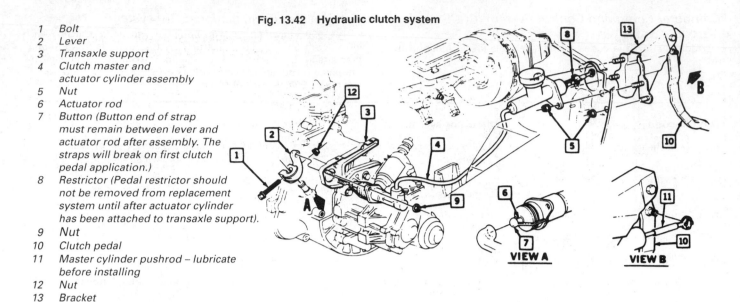

1   Bolt
2   Lever
3   Transaxle support
4   Clutch master and
      actuator cylinder assembly
5   Nut
6   Actuator rod
7   Button (Button end of strap
      must remain between lever and
      actuator rod after assembly. The
      straps will break on first clutch
      pedal application.)
8   Restrictor (Pedal restrictor should
      not be removed from replacement
      system until after actuator cylinder
      has been attached to transaxle support).
9   Nut
10   Clutch pedal
11   Master cylinder pushrod – lubricate
      before installing
12   Nut
13   Bracket

EGR control solenoid (1992 2.2L four-cylinder engines) – removal and installation

1   Disconnect the negative battery cable from the battery.
2   Remove the MAP sensor.
3   Disconnect the electrical connector from the EGR control solenoid, which is secured to the upper intake manifold by one of the manifold bolts next to the throttle body.
4   Disconnect the vacuum hoses from the EGR control solenoid.
5   Remove the EGR control solenoid attaching bolt.
6   Remove the EGR control solenoid from the upper manifold.
7   Installation is the reverse of the removal procedure. Tighten the attaching bolt to the torque listed in this Chapter's Specifications.

10   Manual transaxle

Removal and installation (1992 V6 models)

Removal

1   Have the air conditioning system discharged by a dealer or air conditioning specialist (if equipped).
2   Disconnect the negative battery cable from the battery.
3   Remove the left sound insulator.
4   Disconnect the clutch pushrod from the clutch pedal.
5   Remove the battery (see Chapter 5).
6   Remove the air cleaner assembly and bracket.
7   Remove the exhaust crossover pipe.
8   Remove the clutch slave cylinder and move it out of the way.
9   Disconnect the shift cables.
10   Remove the transaxle-to-engine upper mounting bolts and nuts.
11   Raise the vehicle to provide sufficient clearance for lowering the transaxle assembly and support it securely on jackstands.
12   Support the engine weight with a suitable lifting device. Alternatively, a jack under the engine can be used, although this must be placed in a position where it won't affect access while working underneath. **Caution:** If a jack must be placed under the engine oil pan, place a block of wood between the jack head and the engine oil pan to prevent damage to the oil pan.
13   Remove the transaxle upper mount and bracket.
14   Drain the transaxle lubricant (see Chapter 1).
15   Remove both front wheels.
16   Remove the driveaxle nut from each side.
17   Remove the balljoint nut from each side.
18   Remove both stabilizer bar links (Chapter 11).
19   Remove the driveaxle from each side (Chapter 8).
20   Remove the driveaxle intermediate shaft and housing.

21   Remove the air conditioner evaporator-to-accumulator line (if equipped).
22   Disconnect the vehicle speed sensor and backup light switch electrical connectors.
23   Remove the left inner splash shield.
24   Remove the transaxle strut bracket from the transaxle.
25   Remove the stabilizer bar left side U-bolt.
26   Remove the left suspension support attaching bolt (Chapter 11).
27   Remove the flywheel inspection cover.
28   Remove the shift linkage bracket.
29   Tag and remove all vacuum lines.
30   Disconnect the ground wires from the lower bellhousing bolts.
31   Remove the transaxle-to-engine lower mounting bolts.
32   Slide the transaxle away from the engine until it is clear and then lower it from the vehicle. Inspect the clutch components (Chapter 8).

Installation

33   Raise the transaxle into position.
34   Install the transaxle-to-engine lower mounting bolts, tightening them to the torque listed in this Chapter's Specifications.
35   The remainder of installation is the reverse of removal. Refill the transaxle with the specified lubricant, adjust the shift linkage (Chapter 7A) and have the air conditioning system purged and charged by the shop that discharged it (if equipped).

11   Clutch and driveaxles

Hydraulic clutch release system – general information

The hydraulic clutch release system consists of a master cylinder and fluid reservoir, a slave cylinder (actuator) and a hydraulic pressure line between the two. The system is serviced as a unit; the individual components are not available separately. Other than replacing the complete system, bleeding the system to remove air is the only service procedure that may be necessary (due to insufficient fluid level or any time after the hydraulic system has been opened).

Hydraulic clutch release system – removal and installation

Note: On vehicles with a V6 engine, the MAF sensor and air intake duct assembly must be removed to gain access to the clutch components. First, remove the battery and left fender brace. Next, disconnect the MAT sensor lead at the air cleaner. Disconnect the MAF sensor lead as well. Remove the clamps for the air intake duct. Remove the MAF sensor mounting bolt and the air cleaner bracket bolts (at the battery tray). Lift out the components as an assembly. Remove the windshield washer reservoir. If the vehicle has cruise control, remove the mounting bracket nuts from the strut tower.

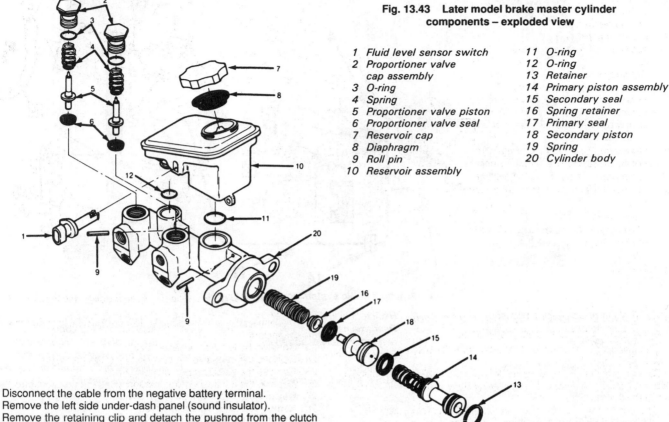

Fig. 13.43   Later model brake master cylinder components – exploded view

1 Fluid level sensor switch	11 O-ring
2 Proportioner valve cap assembly	12 O-ring
	13 Retainer
3 O-ring	14 Primary piston assembly
4 Spring	15 Secondary seal
5 Proportioner valve piston	16 Spring retainer
6 Proportioner valve seal	17 Primary seal
7 Reservoir cap	18 Secondary piston
8 Diaphragm	19 Spring
9 Roll pin	20 Cylinder body
10 Reservoir assembly	

1   Disconnect the cable from the negative battery terminal.
2   Remove the left side under-dash panel (sound insulator).
3   Remove the retaining clip and detach the pushrod from the clutch pedal.
4   Remove the master cylinder mounting nuts. Disconnect the remote reservoir (If equipped).
5   Remove the slave cylinder mounting nuts and detach the master cylinder, slave cylinder and hydraulic line.
6   Install the new slave cylinder in the support bracket and insert the pushrod into the cup on the clutch release lever. **Note:** *Do not remove the plastic strap that holds the pushrod in the retracted position. It will break the first time the clutch pedal is depressed.*
7   Mount the clutch master cylinder on the firewall and install the nuts.
8   Remove the pedal restrictor from the master cylinder pushrod. Coat the inside of the pushrod bushing with multi-purpose grease, connect the pushrod to the clutch pedal and install the retaining clip. If the vehicle is equipped with cruise control, check to see that the disengage switch on the clutch pedal bracket is in contact with the clutch pedal with the pedal at rest. If it is not, adjust it accordingly.
9   Pump the clutch pedal several times to break the slave cylinder retaining strap. Leave the remaining plastic button under the pushrod in place.
10   Reconnect the negative battery cable. On vehicles with a V6 engine, reinstall the components removed to get at the clutch components. **Note:** *If the vehicle has cruise control, the switch at the clutch pedal bracket must be adjusted.*

Hydraulic clutch release system – bleeding

11   If it becomes necessary to bleed the clutch hydraulic system, clean and remove the reservoir cap and fill the fluid reservoir to the top with the recommended fluid. Open the bleed screw on the slave (actuator) cylinder body and allow the fluid to drip into a container. When it is apparent there are no more bubbles at the bleed screw opening and a steady stream of fluid is flowing out, close the bleed screw. The system should now be free of air.
12   To confirm this, start the engine, depress the clutch pedal and shift into Reverse. There should be no grinding sounds as the gears mesh. If the gears do grind, the system still contains air and the bleeding operation should be repeated.

---

12   Brakes

General information

A new master cylinder is installed on late model vehicles. It utilizes a diagonally split system, with one front and the diagonally opposite rear brake being served by the primary piston, and the opposite front and rear brakes served by the secondary piston.

Fluid level sensor switch – removal and installation

1   Disconnect the electrical connector from the fluid level sensor switch.
2   Compress the switch locking tabs at the inboard side of the master cylinder and remove the switch.
3   To reinstall, push the switch into the master cylinder body until the locking tabs snap into place.
4   Reattach the electrical connector.

Master cylinder – removal and installation

5   Disconnect the electrical connector from the fluid level sensor.
6   Remove the tube nuts and hydraulic lines from the master cylinder and plug the lines to prevent fluid loss and contamination.
7   Remove the nuts attaching the master cylinder to the power brake booster and detach the master cylinder.
8   Place the master cylinder over the power brake booster studs and tighten the nuts to the specified torque.
9   Attach the hydraulic lines to the master cylinder.
10   Connect the fluid level sensor electrical connector.
11   Fill the master cylinder to the proper level with fresh brake fluid. The proper level is between the minimum and maximum level indicators in the reservoir opening.
12   Bleed the brake system.

Reservoir – removal and installation

13   Remove the master cylinder from the vehicle.

13

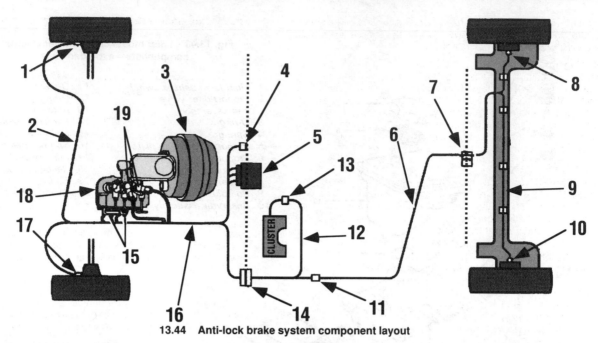

13.44   Anti-lock brake system component layout

1	Right front wheel speed sensor	8	Right rear wheel speed sensor	14	Bulkhead connector
2	Engine harness sensor branch	9	Rear axle harness	15	ABS motor/EMB connector
3	Master cylinder	10	Left rear wheel speed sensor	16	Engine harness sensor branch
4	ABS relay	11	Body connector	17	Left front wheel speed sensor
5	Electronic brake control module	12	I/P harness	18	ABS hydraulic modulator assembly
6	Body extension harness	13	ABS warning lamp driver module	19	Isolation solenoids
7	Rear body pass-through connector				

14   Clamp the master cylinder flange in a vise.

15   Use a 1/8-inch pin punch to drive out the roll pins.

16   Remove the reservoir by pulling it straight up away from the master cylinder body.

17   Remove the O-rings from the grooves in the reservoir.

18   Installation is the reverse of the removal procedure.

Proportioner valve – removal and installation

19   Remove the master cylinder from the vehicle.

20   Remove the reservoir.

21   Remove the proportioner valve cap assemblies.

22   Remove the O-rings and springs.

23   Use needle-nose pliers to remove the proportioner valve pistons, using care not to scratch the piston stems.

24   Remove the proportioner valve seals from the pistons.

25   Lubricate the new O-rings and proportioner valve seals with silicone grease. When installing the valve seals, make sure the seal lips point UP, towards the cap.

26   Installation is the reverse of the removal procedure. Tighten the proportioner valve caps to the specified torque.

Master cylinder – overhaul

27   Remove the master cylinder from the vehicle.

28   Remove the reservoir cap and diaphragm and empty the brake fluid from the reservoir.

29   Remove the reservoir.

30   Remove the fluid level sensor switch.

31   Remove the proportioner valve assemblies.

32   Depress the primary piston and remove the retainer.

33   Plug all the outlet ports except the upper outlet port at the blind end of the master cylinder and apply low pressure compressed air to the upper outlet port to force out the primary and secondary piston assemblies, spring and spring retainer.

34   Remove the seals and spring retainer from the secondary piston.

35   Clean the parts with denatured alcohol, new brake fluid or brake system solvent. **Warning:** *Do not, under any circumstances, clean brake parts with petroleum-based solvents or gasoline.* Inspect the master cylinder bore for scratches and corrosion. If found, the master cylinder must be replaced. The bore cannot be reconditioned by honing.

36   Install the seals and spring retainer on the secondary piston and lubricate the seals with clean brake fluid.

37   Install the secondary piston assembly in the master cylinder.

38   Lubricate the primary piston assembly with clean brake fluid and install the piston assembly in the master cylinder.

39   Depress the primary piston and install the retainer.

40   The remainder of reassembly is the reverse of the disassembly procedure.

41   Bleed the brake system after the master cylinder is reinstalled.

Anti-lock brake system (ABS) – general information (1992 models)

Some 1992 models are equipped with a anti-lock brake system to maintain vehicle steerability, directional stability and optimum deceleration under severe braking conditions and on most road surfaces. It does so by monitoring the rotational speed of the front and rear wheels and controls the brake line hydraulic pressure to all four wheels during braking.

Components

Hydraulic brake modulator

The modulator is attached to the side of the brake master cylinder and controls pressure generated by the brake master cylinder. It proportions this pressure to each wheel based on the input from the control module.

Wheel speed sensors

A speed sensor and a toothed ring are installed at each wheel. The sensor generates electrical signals, indicating wheel rotational speed, and sends these signals to the control module.

Electronic Brake Control Module (EBCM)

The control module is located under the dash panel. The function of the control module is to accept and process information received from the wheel speed sensors and send electrical signals to the modulator on the master cylinder. This controls hydraulic line pressure to all four wheels to prevent wheel lock-up. The control module also constantly monitors the ABS system, even under driving conditions, to find faults within the system.

When the control module finds a fault, a diagnostic code will be stored in the control unit which, when retrieved by a dealer service technician, will indicate the problem area or component.

ABS warning light (amber)

The electronic control unit constantly monitors itself and all other ABS components. If there is a problem in any portion of the system, but does not affect the ABS braking ability, the ABS warning light will flash on and off, signaling the driver there is a problem and that repairs should be made as soon as possible. If the ABS light comes on steadily, not flashing, there is a serious problem in the system and there is NO anti-lock braking available. If this occurs, repairs should be made immediately.

Diagnosis and repair

If the ABS LIGHT comes on and flashes or stays on while the vehicle is in operation, the ABS system requires attention. Although troubleshooting the ABS system is beyond the scope of the home mechanic, the home mechanic can perform a few preliminary checks before taking the vehicle to a dealer service department for diagnosis.

  a) Check the hydraulic brake fluid level in the master cylinder reservoir, adding fluid if necessary (Chapter 1).
  b) Check that the electronic brake control module unit electrical connector is securely connected and is free of corrosion.
  c) Check the electrical connectors at each speed sensor, modulator and all connection locations. Make sure each electrical connector is securely connected and is free of corrosion.
  d) Check the system electrical fuses, replacing them if necessary.
If the above preliminary check do not rectify the problem, the vehicle should be diagnosed by a dealer service department. Due to the rather complex nature of this system and the high operating pressures involved, all actual repair work must be done by a dealer service department.

---

13   Chassis electrical system

Composite headlights – removal and installation

1   Composite headlights are used beginning on 1987 vehicles. Since they have halogen bulbs, the replacement procedure is different than the one for sealed-beam units.
2   Disconnect the negative battery cable from the battery, then detach the wire harness connector and bulb assembly from the headlight assembly by turning the connector counterclockwise until it stops and pulling it straight out. **Caution:** *Touch the bulb only at the base – don't touch the glass!*
3   Remove the bulb from the connector after prying back the lock tab.
4   Installation is the reverse of removal. Remember, don't touch the bulb glass with your hands. It must be kept clean and free of dirt, grease and oil.

Wiring diagrams

Note that wiring diagrams for later models have been included at the end of this Chapter. Due to space limitations, we are not able to provide every diagram for each model; however, a representative sampling is included.

13

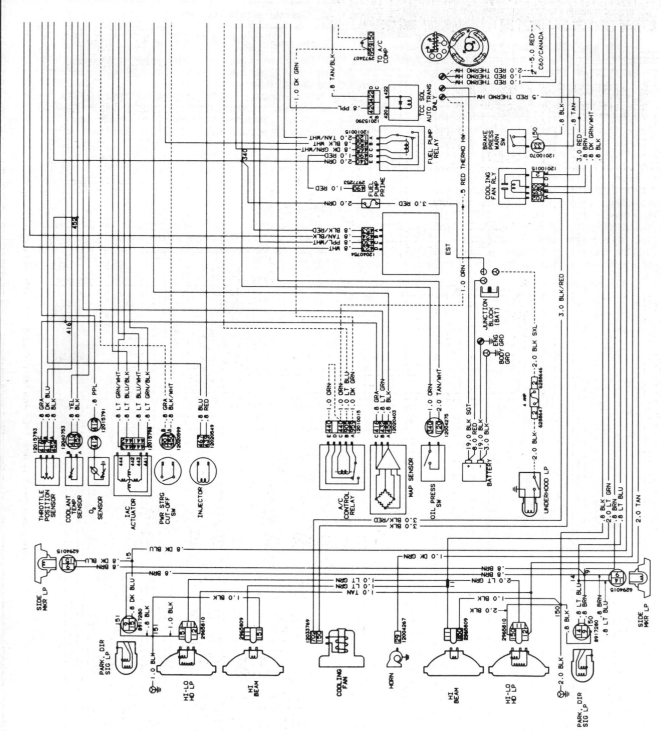

Wiring diagram – typical 1985 and later front end

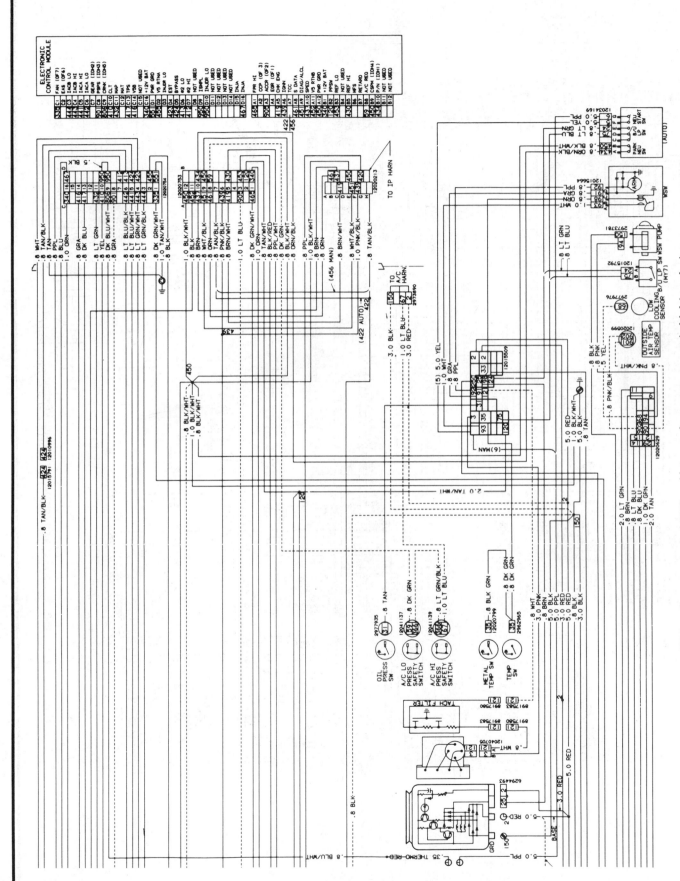

Wiring diagram – typical 1985 and later engine compartment (with L4 engine)

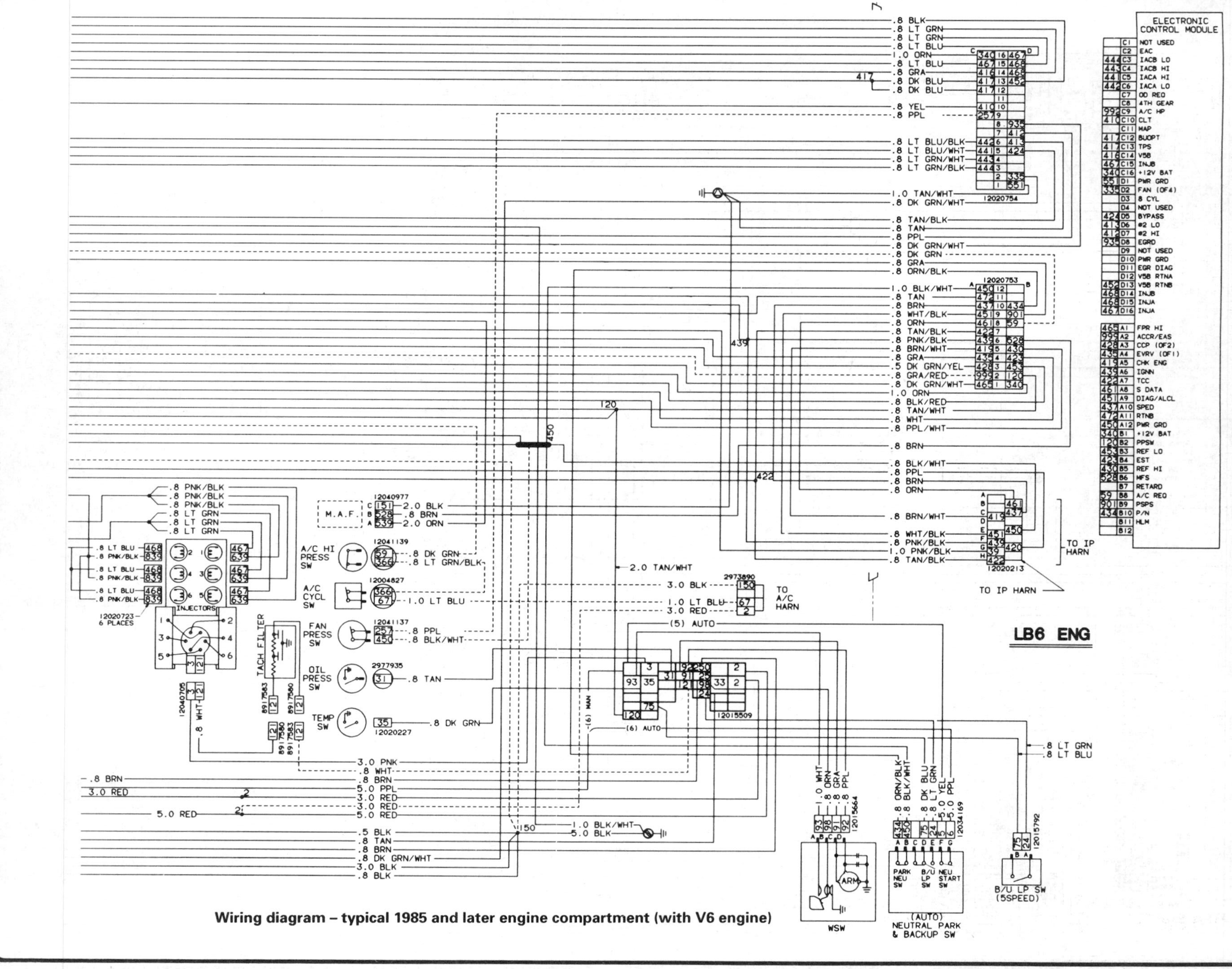

Wiring diagram – typical 1985 and later engine compartment (with V6 engine)

LB6 ENG

ELECTRONIC CONTROL MODULE

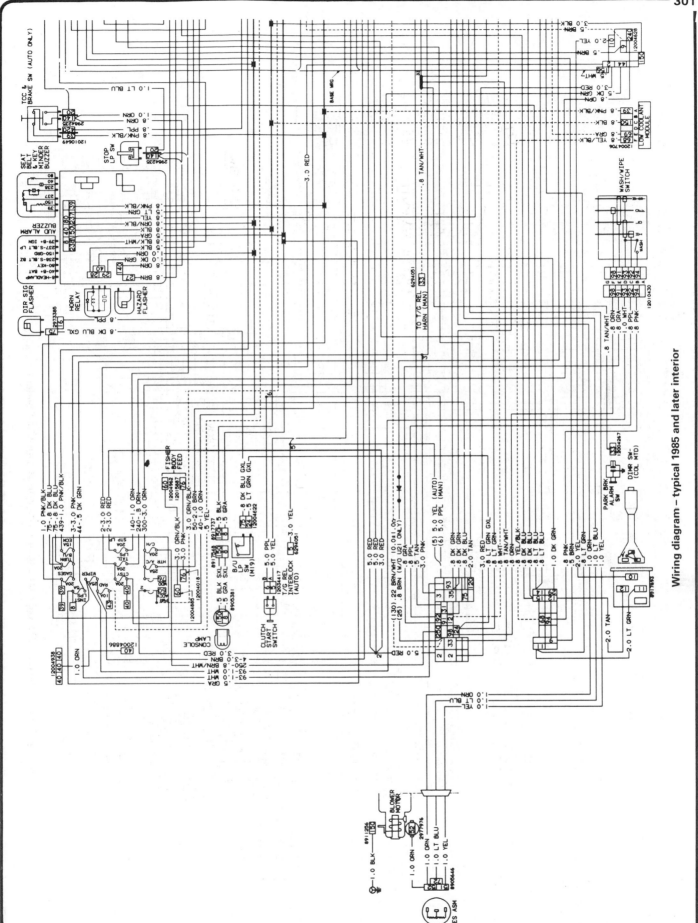

Wiring diagram – typical 1985 and later interior

13

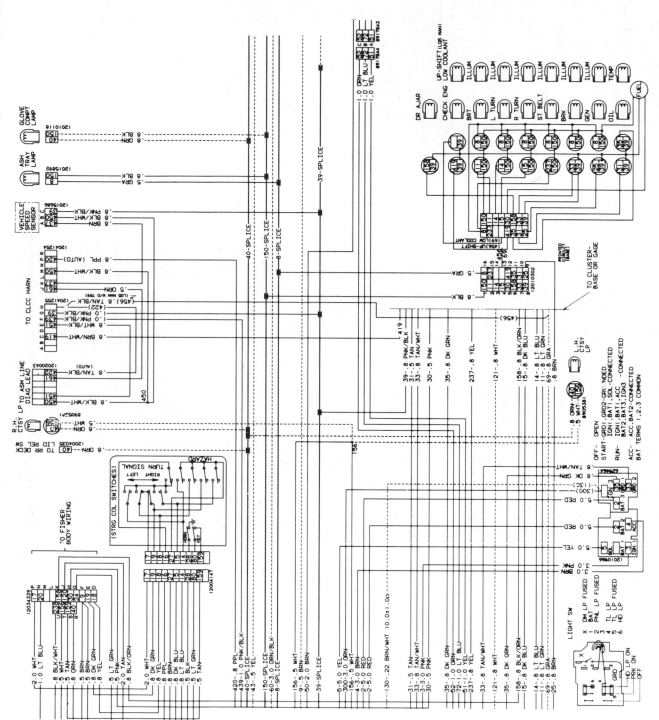

Wiring diagram – typical 1985 and later interior (continued)

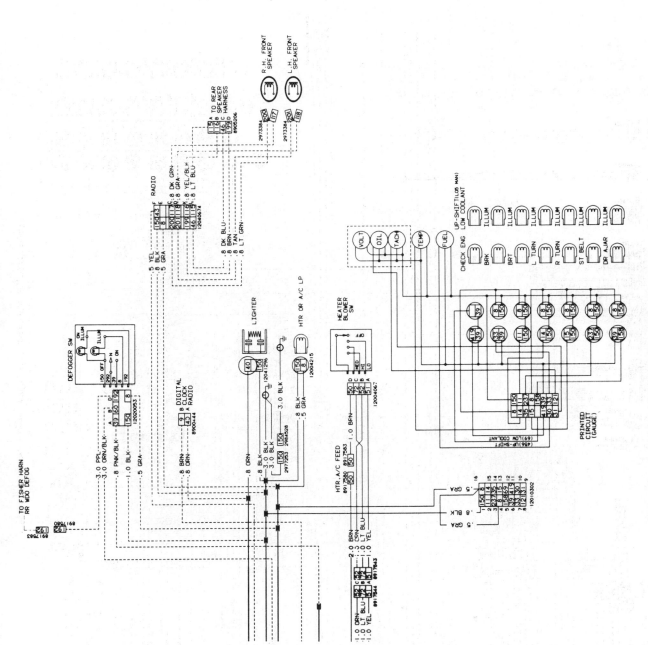

Wiring diagram – typical 1985 and later interior (continued)

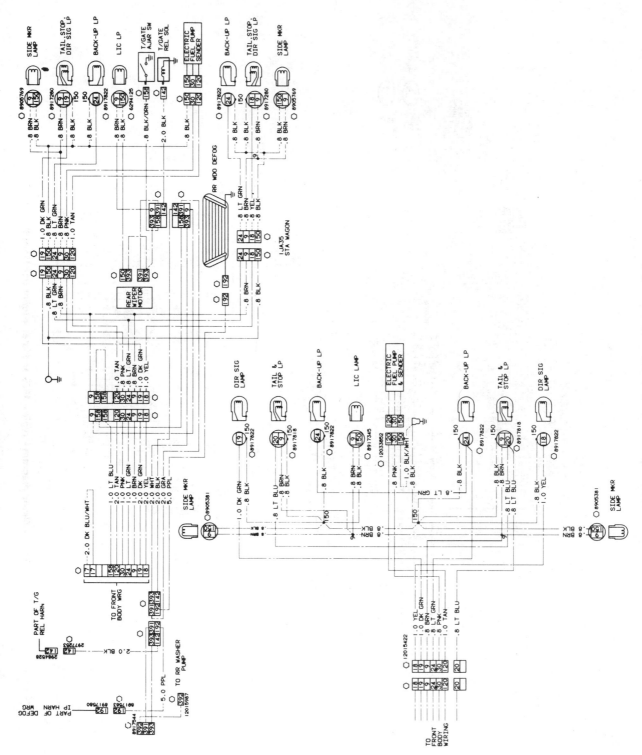

Wiring diagram – typical 1985 and later rear lights

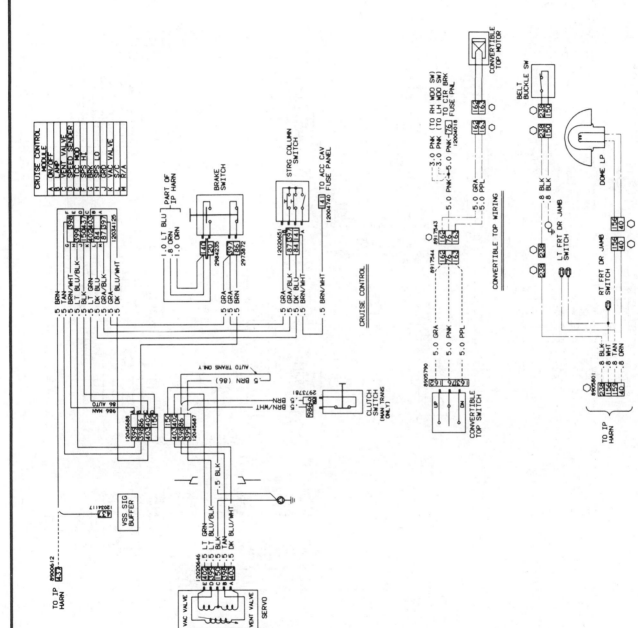

Wiring diagram – typical 1985 and later cruise control and convertible top

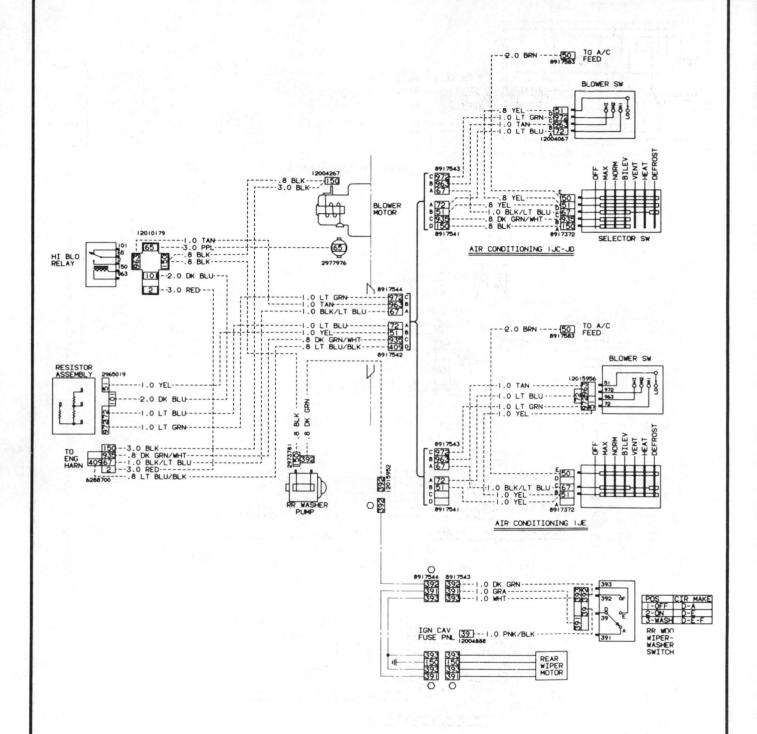

Wiring diagram – typical 1985 and later air conditioning

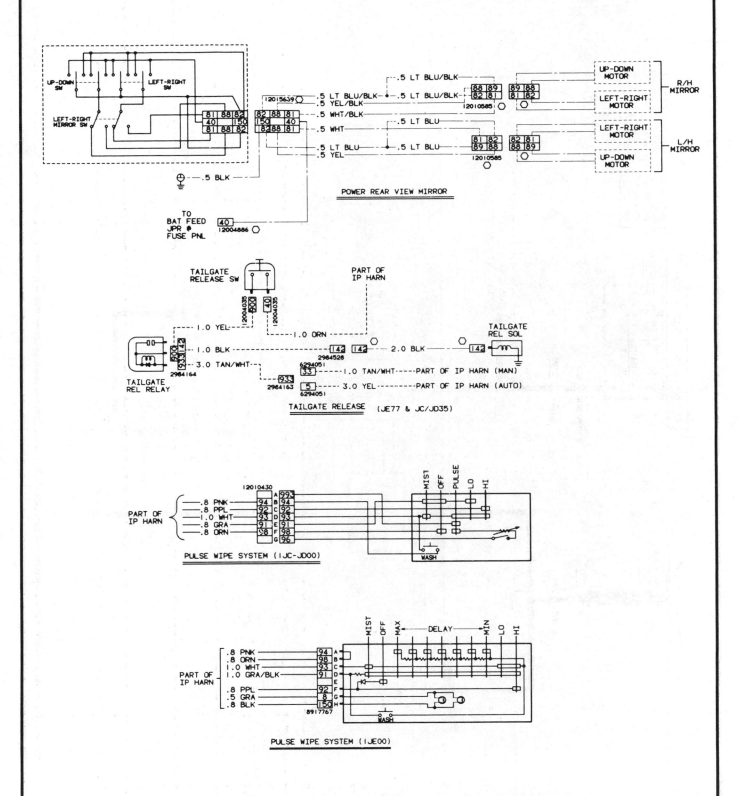

Wiring diagram – typical 1985 and later power mirror, tailgate release and pulse wiper

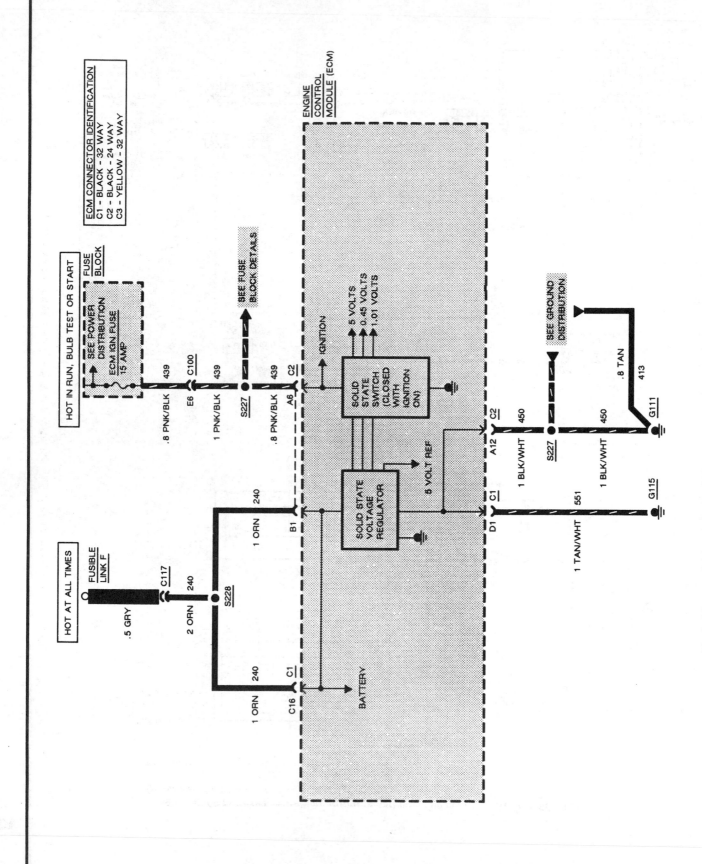

Typical late model four-cylinder OHV engine fuel-injection system wiring diagram (1 of 7)

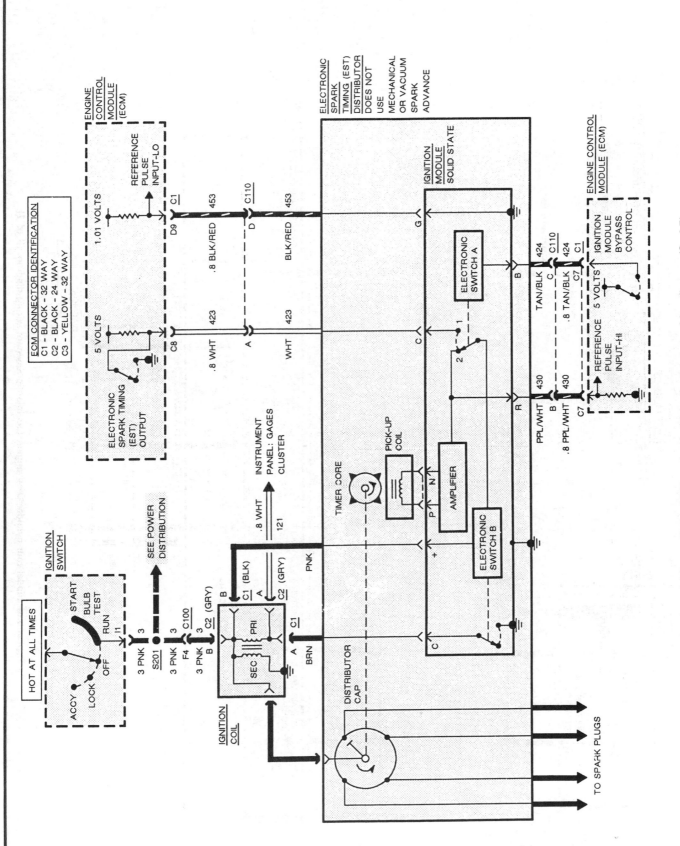

Typical late model four-cylinder OHV engine fuel-injection system wiring diagram (2 of 7)

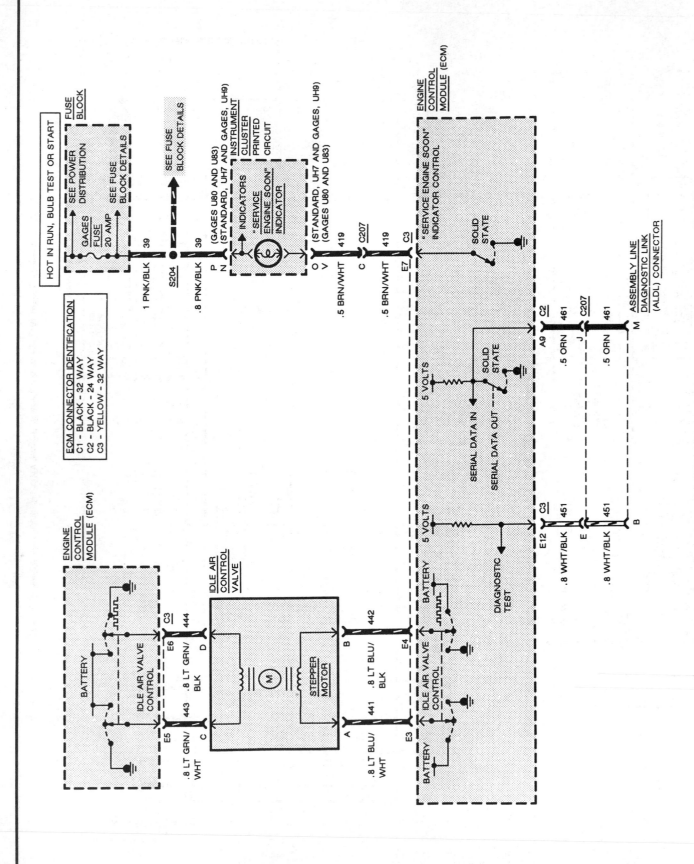

Typical late model four-cylinder OHV engine fuel-injection system wiring diagram (3 of 7)

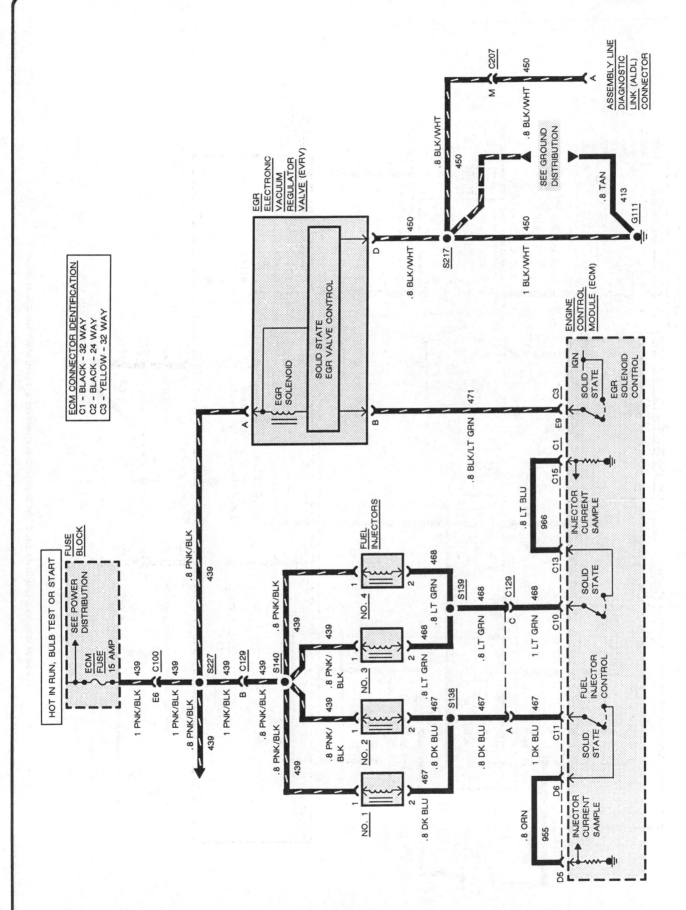

Typical late model four-cylinder OHV engine fuel-injection system wiring diagram (4 of 7)

13

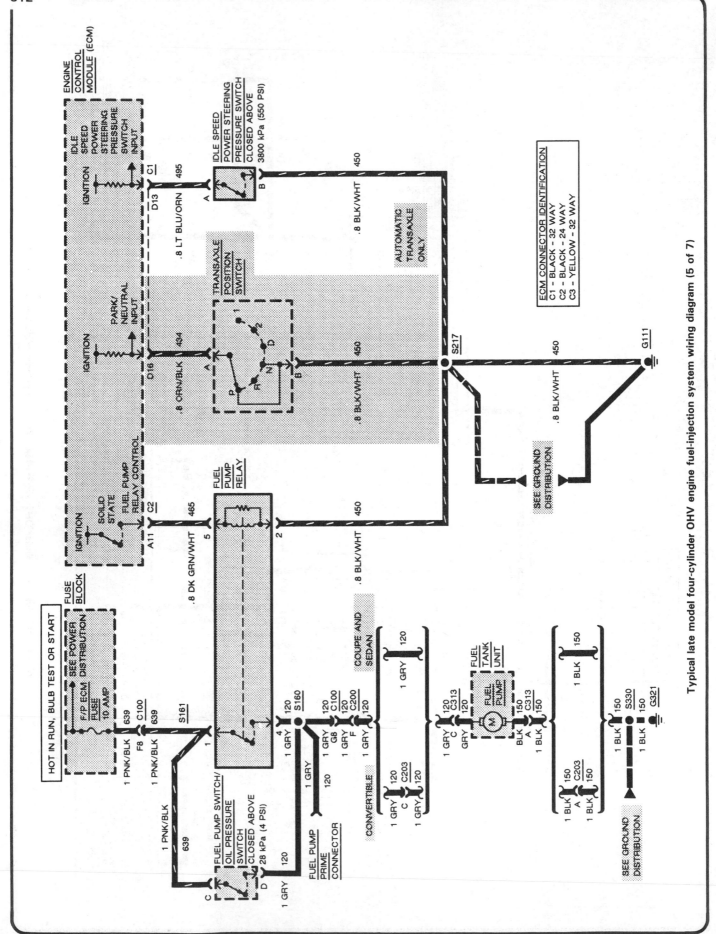

Typical late model four-cylinder OHV engine fuel-injection system wiring diagram (5 of 7)

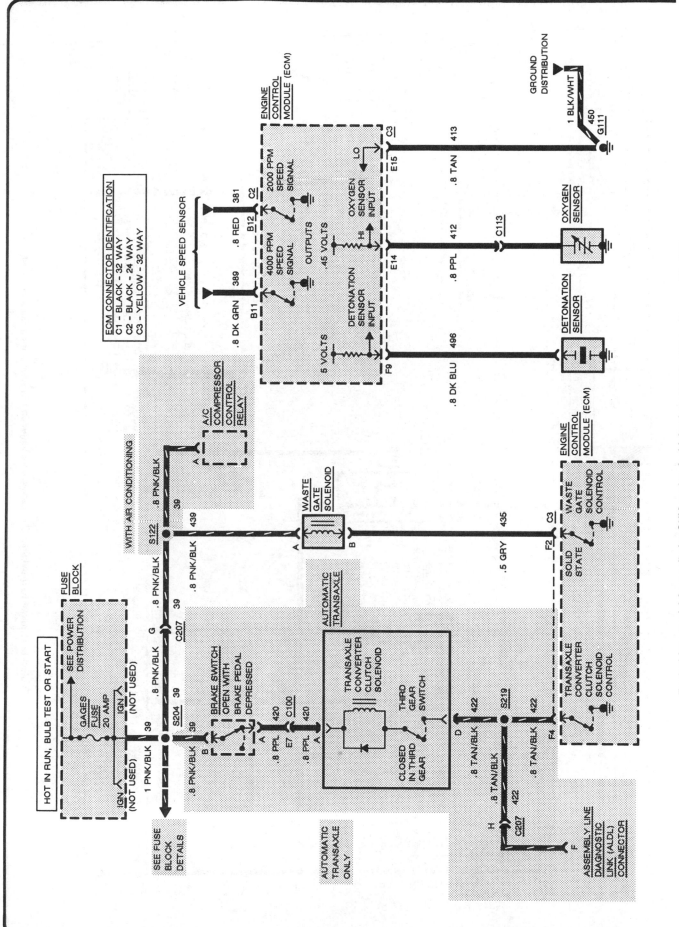

Typical late model four-cylinder OHV engine fuel-injection system wiring diagram (6 of 7)

13

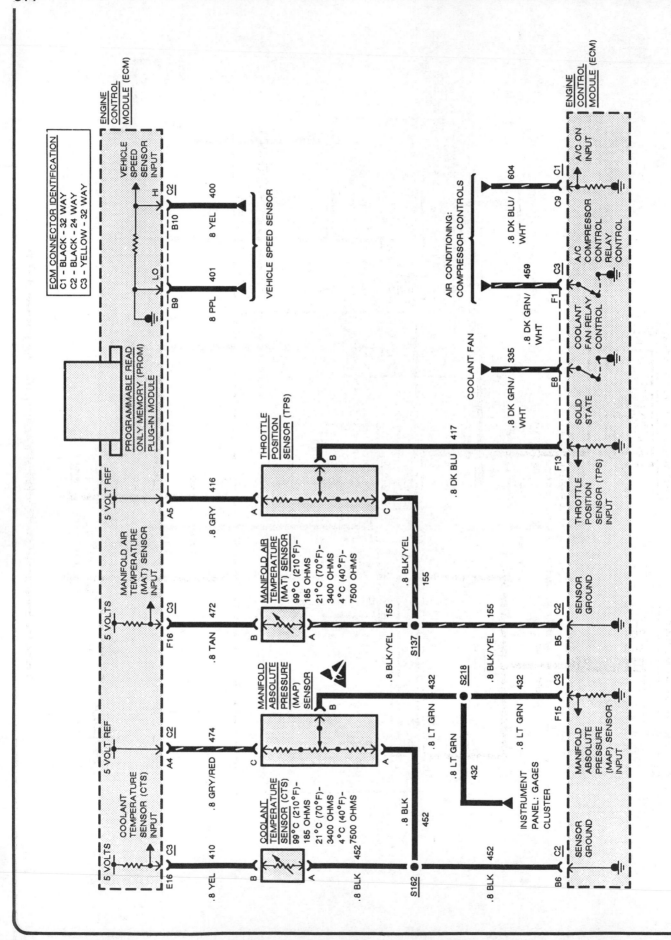

Typical late model four-cylinder OHV engine fuel-injection system wiring diagram (7 of 7)

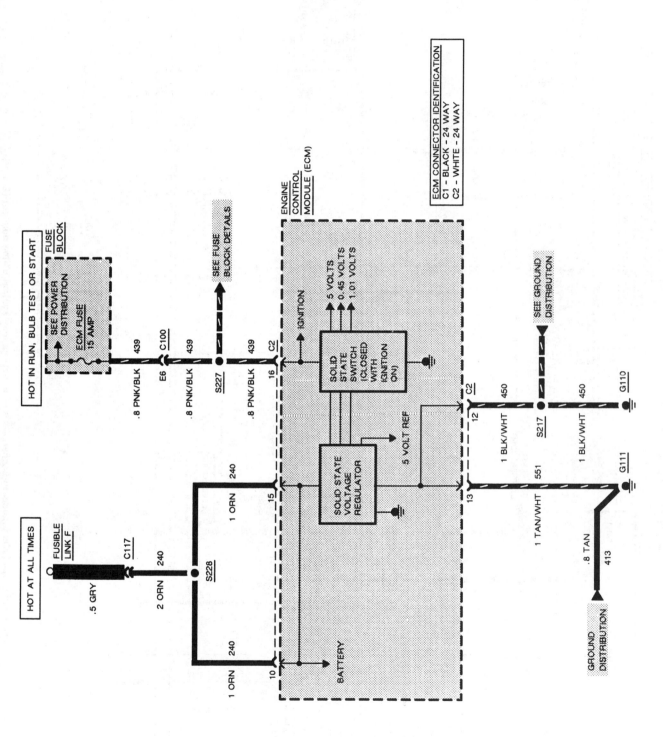

Typical late model turbocharged engine fuel-injection system wiring diagram (1 of 7)

ECM CONNECTOR IDENTIFICATION
C1 - BLACK - 24 WAY
C2 - WHITE - 24 WAY

HOT IN RUN, BULB TEST OR START

FUSE BLOCK

SEE POWER DISTRIBUTION

ECM FUSE 15 AMP

SEE FUSE BLOCK DETAILS

ENGINE CONTROL MODULE (ECM)

IGNITION

5 VOLTS
0.45 VOLTS
1.01 VOLTS

SOLID STATE SWITCH (CLOSED WITH IGNITION ON)

SOLID STATE VOLTAGE REGULATOR

.5 VOLT REF

SEE GROUND DISTRIBUTION

BATTERY

HOT AT ALL TIMES

FUSIBLE LINK F

C117

S228

.5 GRY

2 ORN   240

1 ORN   240

1 ORN   240

10

15

.8 PNK/BLK   439

.8 PNK/BLK   439

.8 PNK/BLK   439

E6   C100   S227   C2   16

C2   12   450   S217   450   G110

13   1 BLK/WHT   1 BLK/WHT   G111

551   1 TAN/WHT

.8 TAN   413

GROUND DISTRIBUTION

13

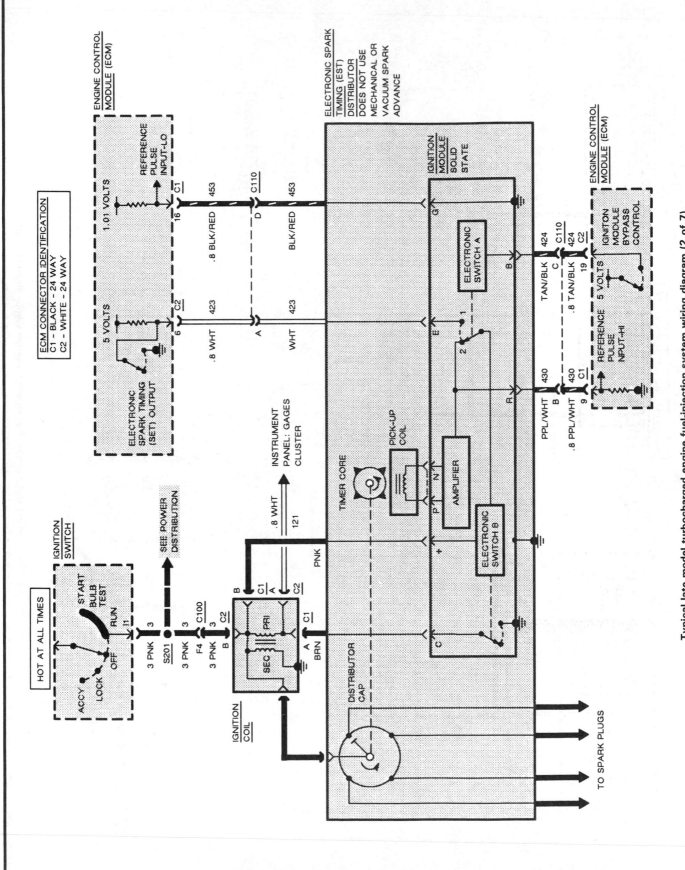

Typical late model turbocharged engine fuel-injection system wiring diagram (2 of 7)

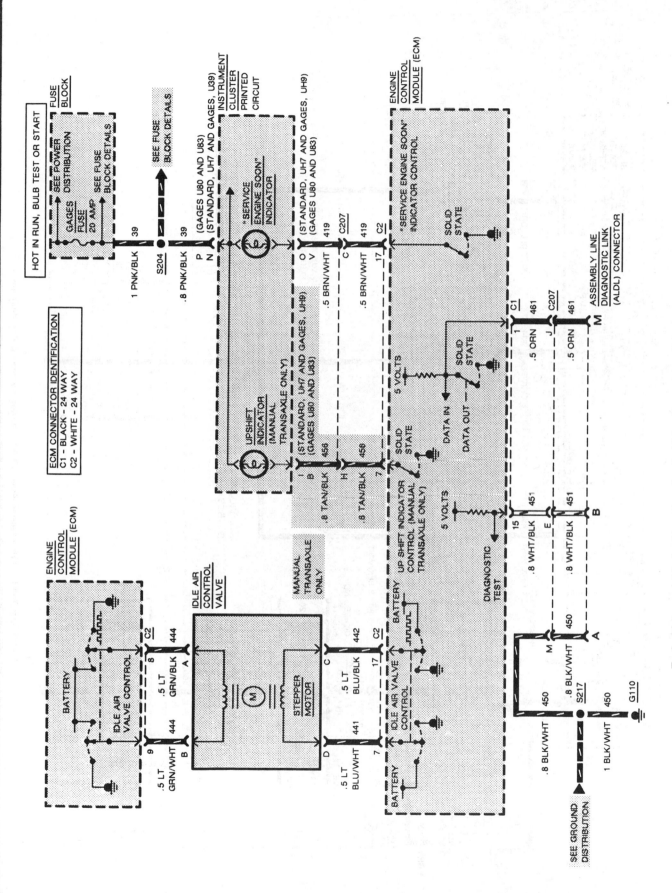

Typical late model turbocharged engine fuel-injection system wiring diagram (3 of 7)

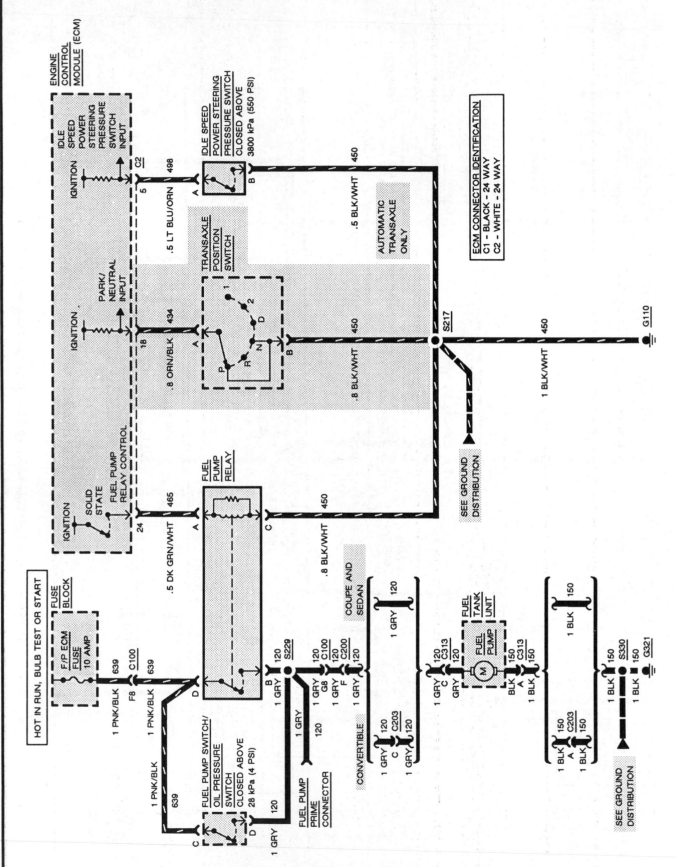

Typical late model turbocharged engine fuel-injection system wiring diagram (4 of 7)

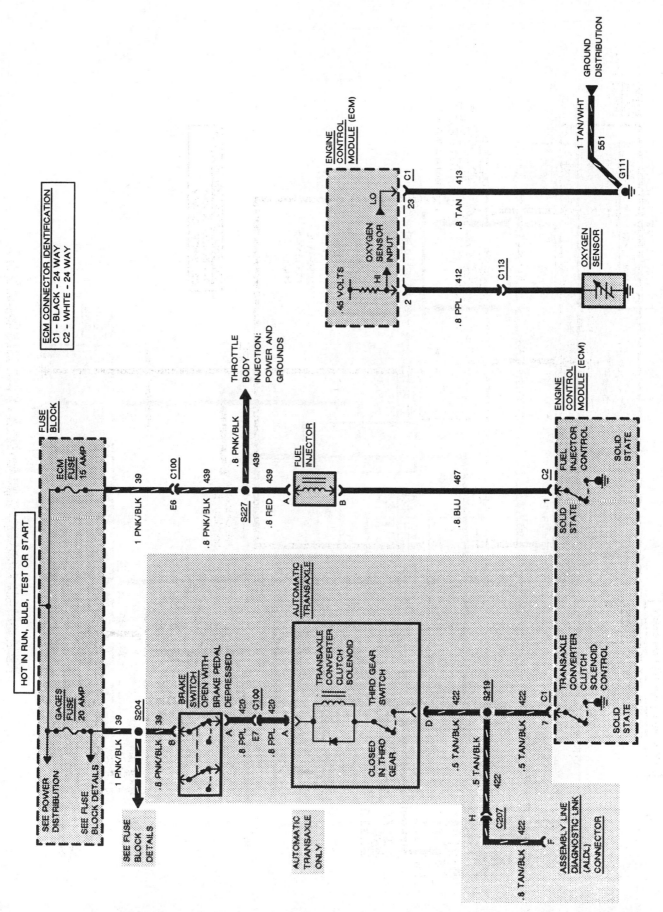

Typical late model turbocharged engine fuel-injection system wiring diagram (5 of 7)

13

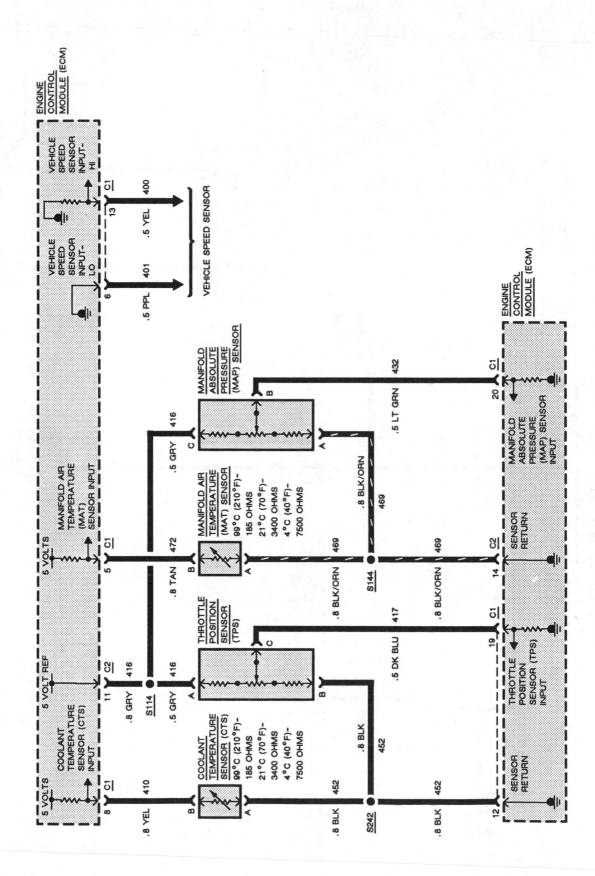

Typical late model turbocharged engine fuel-injection system wiring diagram (6 of 7)

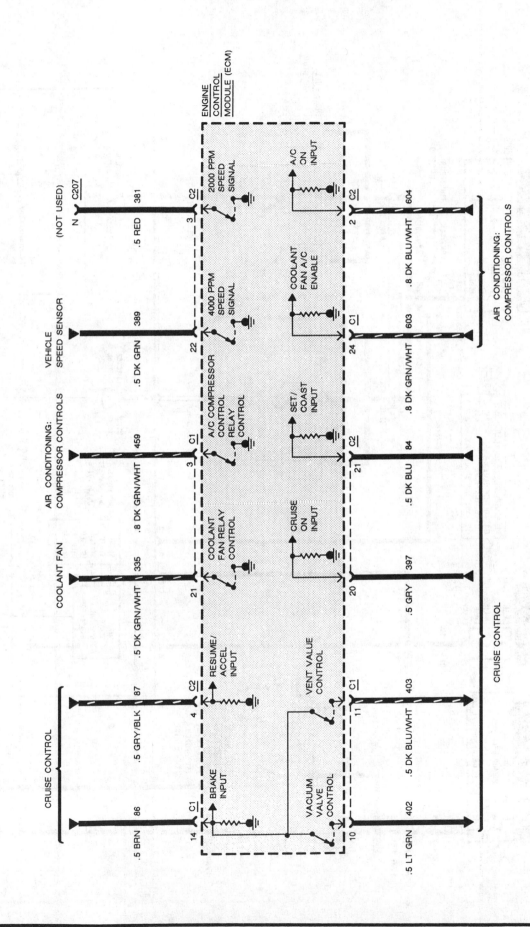

Typical late model turbocharged engine fuel-injection system wiring diagram (7 of 7)

13

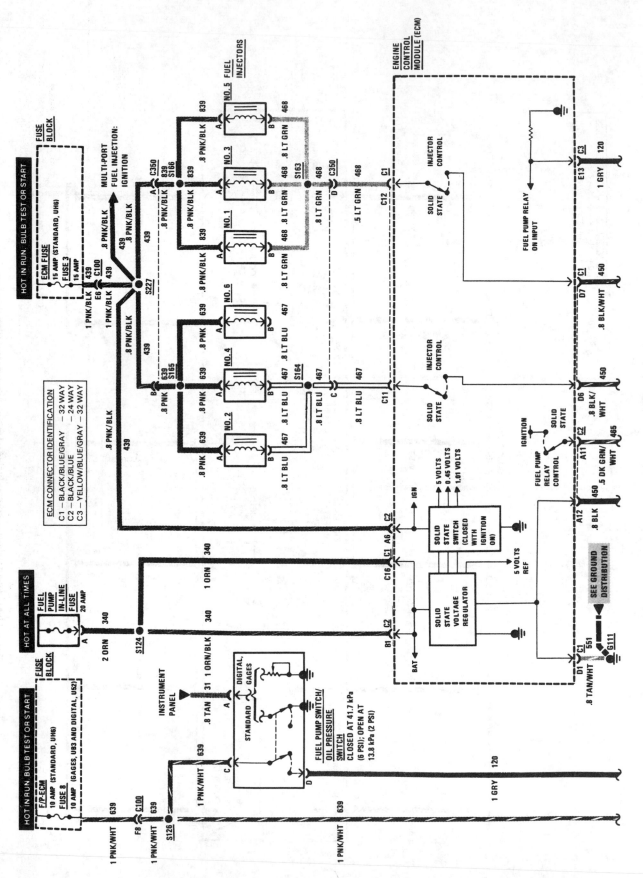

Typical late model V6 engine fuel-injection system wiring diagram (1 of 7)

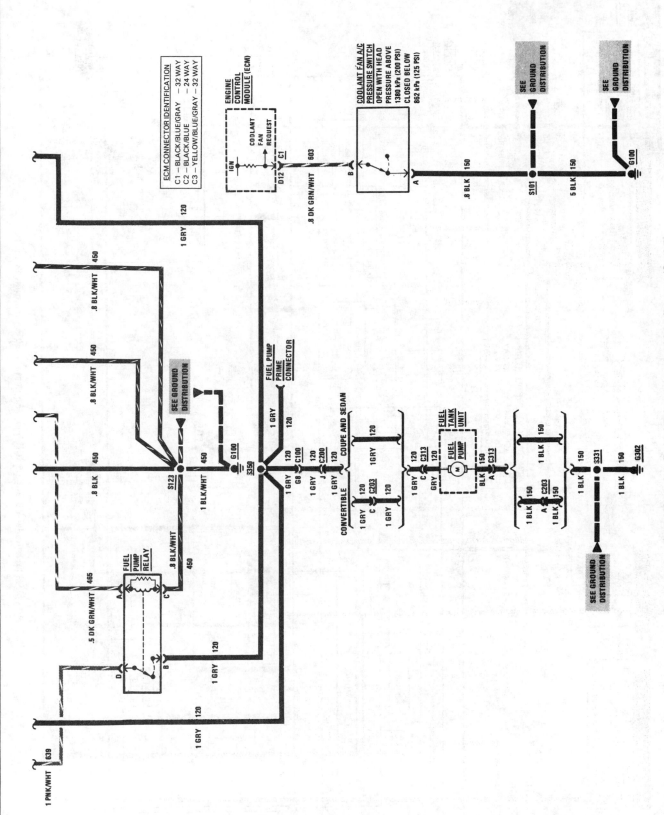

Typical late model V6 engine fuel-injection system wiring diagram (2 of 7)

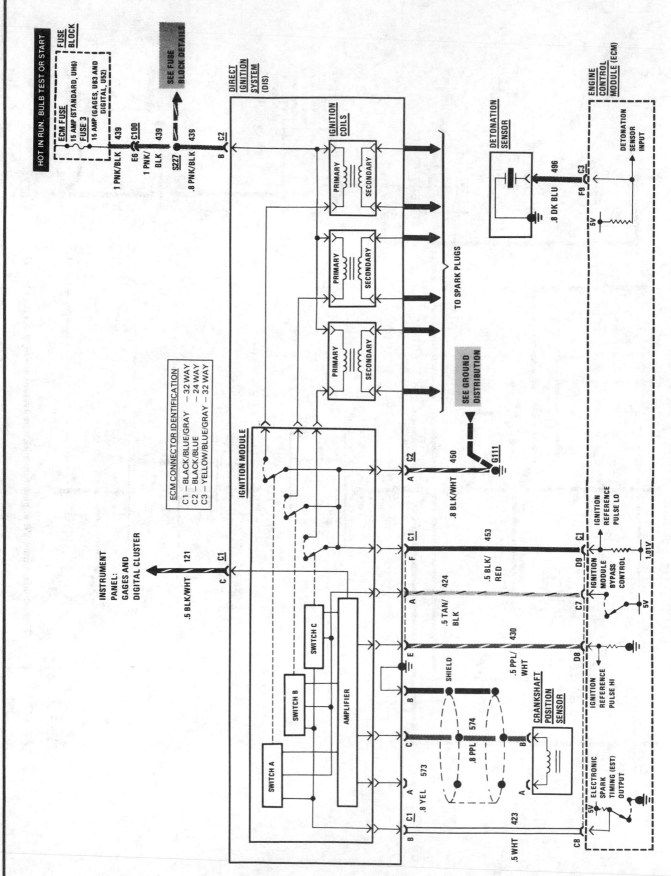

Typical late model V6 engine fuel-injection system wiring diagram (3 of 7)

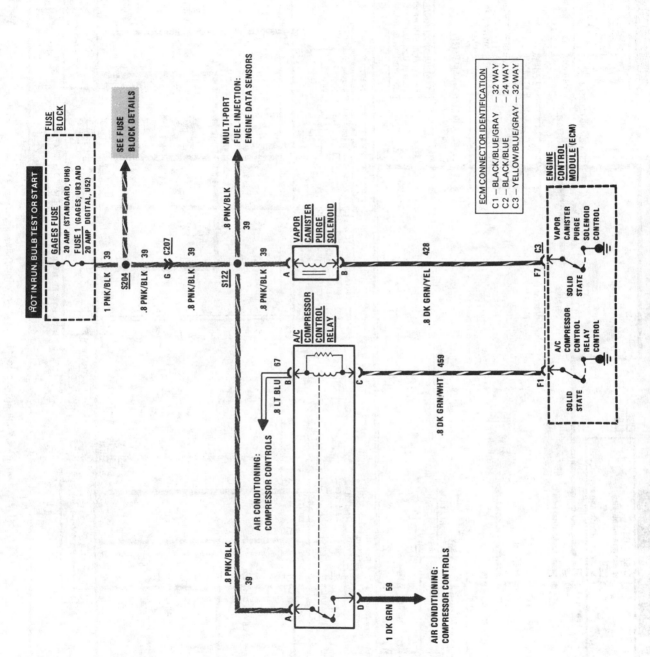

Typical late model V6 engine fuel-injection system wiring diagram (4 of 7)

13

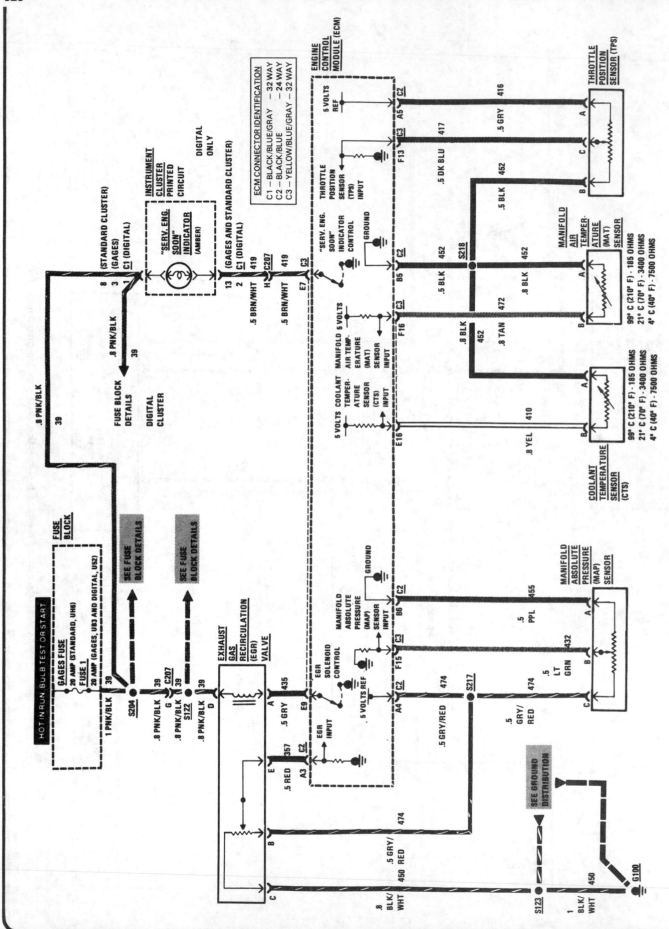

Typical late model V6 engine fuel-injection system wiring diagram (5 of 7)

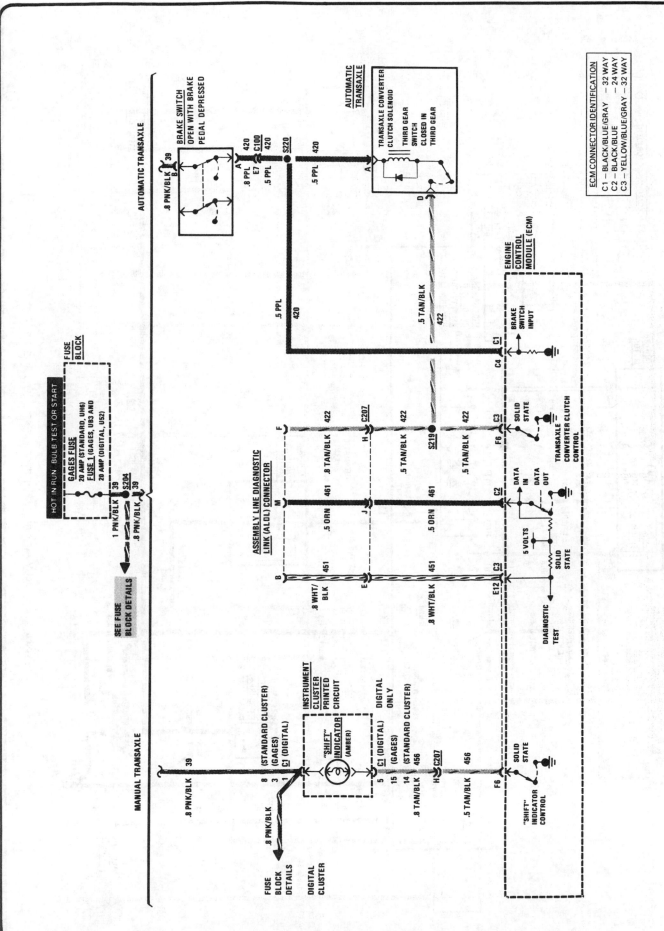

Typical late model V6 engine fuel-injection system wiring diagram (6 of 7)

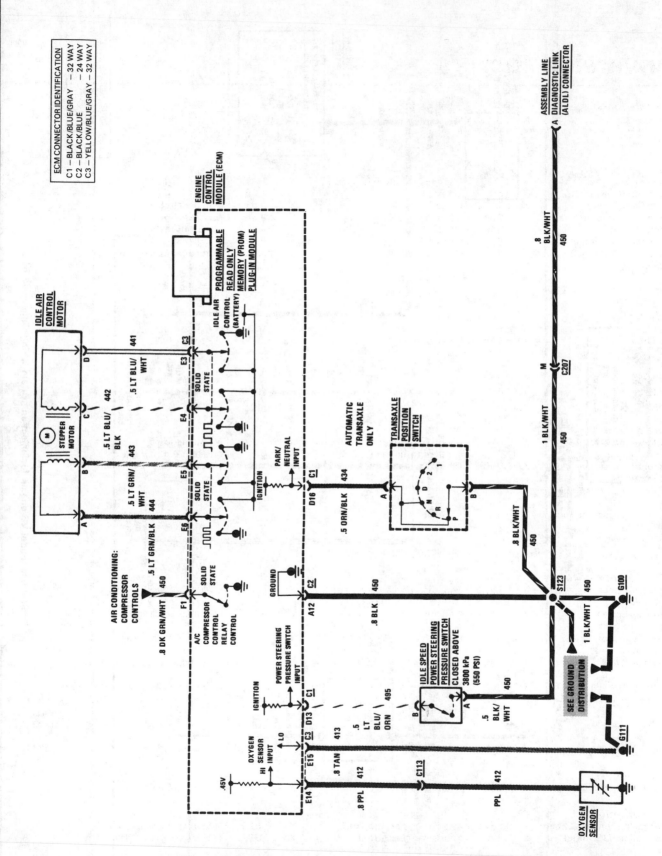

Typical late model V6 engine fuel-injection system wiring diagram (7 of 7)

Conversion factors

Length (distance)
Inches (in)	X 25.4	= Millimetres (mm)	X 0.0394	= Inches (in)
Feet (ft)	X 0.305	= Metres (m)	X 3.281	= Feet (ft)
Miles	X 1.609	= Kilometres (km)	X 0.621	= Miles

Volume (capacity)
Cubic inches (cu in; in^3)	X 16.387	= Cubic centimetres (cc; cm^3)	X 0.061	= Cubic inches (cu in; in^3)
Imperial pints (Imp pt)	X 0.568	= Litres (l)	X 1.76	= Imperial pints (Imp pt)
Imperial quarts (Imp qt)	X 1.137	= Litres (l)	X 0.88	= Imperial quarts (Imp qt)
Imperial quarts (Imp qt)	X 1.201	= US quarts (US qt)	X 0.833	= Imperial quarts (Imp qt)
US quarts (US qt)	X 0.946	= Litres (l)	X 1.057	= US quarts (US qt)
Imperial gallons (Imp gal)	X 4.546	= Litres (l)	X 0.22	= Imperial gallons (Imp gal)
Imperial gallons (Imp gal)	X 1.201	= US gallons (US gal)	X 0.833	= Imperial gallons (Imp gal)
US gallons (US gal)	X 3.785	= Litres (l)	X 0.264	= US gallons (US gal)

Mass (weight)
Ounces (oz)	X 28.35	= Grams (g)	X 0.035	= Ounces (oz)
Pounds (lb)	X 0.454	= Kilograms (kg)	X 2.205	= Pounds (lb)

Force
Ounces-force (ozf; oz)	X 0.278	= Newtons (N)	X 3.6	= Ounces-force (ozf; oz)
Pounds-force (lbf; lb)	X 4.448	= Newtons (N)	X 0.225	= Pounds-force (lbf; lb)
Newtons (N)	X 0.1	= Kilograms-force (kgf; kg)	X 9.81	= Newtons (N)

Pressure
Pounds-force per square inch (psi; lbf/in^2; lb/in^2)	X 0.070	= Kilograms-force per square centimetre (kgf/cm^2; kg/cm^2)	X 14.223	= Pounds-force per square inch (psi; lbf/in^2; lb/in^2)
Pounds-force per square inch (psi; lbf/in^2; lb/in^2)	X 0.068	= Atmospheres (atm)	X 14.696	= Pounds-force per square inch (psi; lbf/in^2; lb/in^2)
Pounds-force per square inch (psi; lbf/in^2; lb/in^2)	X 0.069	= Bars	X 14.5	= Pounds-force per square inch (psi; lbf/in^2; lb/in^2)
Pounds-force per square inch (psi; lbf/in^2; lb/in^2)	X 6.895	= Kilopascals (kPa)	X 0.145	= Pounds-force per square inch (psi; lbf/in^2; lb/in^2)
Kilopascals (kPa)	X 0.01	= Kilograms-force per square centimetre (kgf/cm^2; kg/cm^2)	X 98.1	= Kilopascals (kPa)

Torque (moment of force)
Pounds-force inches (lbf in; lb in)	X 1.152	= Kilograms-force centimetre (kgf cm; kg cm)	X 0.868	= Pounds-force inches (lbf in; lb in)
Pounds-force inches (lbf in; lb in)	X 0.113	= Newton metres (Nm)	X 8.85	= Pounds-force inches (lbf in; lb in)
Pounds-force inches (lbf in; lb in)	X 0.083	= Pounds-force feet (lbf ft; lb ft)	X 12	= Pounds-force inches (lbf in; lb in)
Pounds-force feet (lbf ft; lb ft)	X 0.138	= Kilograms-force metres (kgf m; kg m)	X 7.233	= Pounds-force feet (lbf ft; lb ft)
Pounds-force feet (lbf ft; lb ft)	X 1.356	= Newton metres (Nm)	X 0.738	= Pounds-force feet (lbf ft; lb ft)
Newton metres (Nm)	X 0.102	= Kilograms-force metres (kgf m; kg m)	X 9.804	= Newton metres (Nm)

Power
Horsepower (hp)	X 745.7	= Watts (W)	X 0.0013	= Horsepower (hp)

Velocity (speed)
Miles per hour (miles/hr; mph)	X 1.609	= Kilometres per hour (km/hr; kph)	X 0.621	= Miles per hour (miles/hr; mph)

Fuel consumption*
Miles per gallon, Imperial (mpg)	X 0.354	= Kilometres per litre (km/l)	X 2.825	= Miles per gallon, Imperial (mpg)
Miles per gallon, US (mpg)	X 0.425	= Kilometres per litre (km/l)	X 2.352	= Miles per gallon, US (mpg)

Temperature
Degrees Fahrenheit = (°C x 1.8) + 32   Degrees Celsius (Degrees Centigrade; °C) = (°F - 32) x 0.56

*It is common practice to convert from miles per gallon (mpg) to litres/100 kilometres (l/100km),
where mpg (Imperial) x l/100 km = 282 and mpg (US) x l/100 km = 235

Index

HAYNES AUTOMOTIVE MANUALS

NOTE: New manuals are added to this list on a periodic basis. If you do not see a listing for your vehicle, consult your local Haynes dealer for the latest product information.

ACURA

*1776   **Integra & Legend** all models '86 thru '90

AMC

     Jeep CJ - see JEEP (412)
694   **Mid-size models,** Concord, Hornet, Gremlin & Spirit '70 thru '83
934   **(Renault) Alliance & Encore** all models '83 thru '87

AUDI

615   **4000** all models '80 thru '87
428   **5000** all models '77 thru '83
1117   **5000** all models '84 thru '88

AUSTIN

     Healey Sprite - see MG Midget Roadster (265)

BMW

*2020   **3/5 Series** not including diesel or all-wheel drive models '82 thru '92
276   **320i** all 4 cyl models '75 thru '83
632   **528i & 530i** all models '75 thru '80
240   **1500 thru 2002** all models except Turbo '59 thru '77
348   **2500, 2800, 3.0 & Bavaria** all models '69 thru '76

BUICK

     Century (front wheel drive) - see GENERAL MOTORS (829)
*1627   **Buick, Oldsmobile & Pontiac Full-size (Front wheel drive)** all models '85 thru '93
     Buick Electra, LeSabre and Park Avenue; **Oldsmobile** Delta 88 Royale, Ninety Eight and Regency; **Pontiac** Bonneville
1551   **Buick Oldsmobile & Pontiac Full-size (Rear wheel drive)**
     Buick Estate '70 thru '90, Electra '70 thru '84, LeSabre '70 thru '85, Limited '74 thru '79
     Oldsmobile Custom Cruiser '70 thru '90, Delta 88 '70 thru '85, Ninety-eight '70 thru '84
     Pontiac Bonneville '70 thru '81, Catalina '70 thru '81, Grandville '70 thru '75, Parisienne '83 thru '86
627   **Mid-size Regal & Century** all rear-drive models with V6, V8 and Turbo '74 thru '87
     Regal - see GENERAL MOTORS (1671)
     Skyhawk - see GENERAL MOTORS (766)
552   **Skylark** all X-car models '80 thru '85
     Skylark '86 on - see GENERAL MOTORS (1420)
     Somerset - see GENERAL MOTORS (1420)

CADILLAC

*751   **Cadillac Rear Wheel Drive** all gasoline models '70 thru '92
     Cimarron - see GENERAL MOTORS (766)

CAPRI

296   **2000 MK I Coupe** all models '71 thru '75
     Mercury Capri - see FORD Mustang (654)

CHEVROLET

*1477   **Astro & GMC Safari Mini-vans** '85 thru '93
554   **Camaro V8** all models '70 thru '81
866   **Camaro** all models '82 thru '92
     Cavalier - see GENERAL MOTORS (766)
     Celebrity - see GENERAL MOTORS (829)
625   **Chevelle, Malibu & El Camino** all V6 & V8 models '69 thru '87
449   **Chevette & Pontiac T1000** '76 thru '87
550   **Citation** all models '80 thru '85

---

*1628   **Corsica/Beretta** all models '87 thru '92
274   **Corvette** all V8 models '68 thru '82
*1336   **Corvette** all models '84 thru '91
1762   **Chevrolet Engine Overhaul Manual**
704   **Full-size Sedans** Caprice, Impala, Biscayne, Bel Air & Wagons '69 thru '90
     Lumina - see GENERAL MOTORS (1671)
     Lumina APV - see GENERAL MOTORS (2035)
319   **Luv Pick-up** all 2WD & 4WD '72 thru '82
626   **Monte Carlo** all models '70 thru '88
241   **Nova** all V8 models '69 thru '79
*1642   **Nova and Geo Prizm** all front wheel drive models, '85 thru '92
420   **Pick-ups '67 thru '87** - Chevrolet & GMC, all V8 & in-line 6 cyl, 2WD & 4WD '67 thru '87; Suburbans, Blazers & Jimmys '67 thru '91
*1664   **Pick-ups '88 thru '93** - Chevrolet & GMC, all full-size (C and K) models, '88 thru '93
*831   **S-10 & GMC S-15 Pick-ups** all models '82 thru '92
*1727   **Sprint & Geo Metro** '85 thru '91
*345   **Vans - Chevrolet & GMC,** V8 & in-line 6 cylinder models '68 thru '92

CHRYSLER

*2058   **Full-size Front-Wheel Drive** '88 thru '93
     K-Cars - see DODGE Aries (723)
     Laser - see DODGE Daytona (1140)
*1337   **Chrysler & Plymouth Mid-size** front wheel drive '82 thru '93

DATSUN

402   **200SX** all models '77 thru '79
647   **200SX** all models '80 thru '83
228   **B - 210** all models '73 thru '78
525   **210** all models '78 thru '82
206   **240Z, 260Z & 280Z** Coupe '70 thru '78
563   **280ZX** Coupe & 2+2 '79 thru '83
     300ZX - see NISSAN (1137)
679   **310** all models '78 thru '82
123   **510 & PL521 Pick-up** '68 thru '73
430   **510** all models '78 thru '81
372   **610** all models '72 thru '76
277   **620 Series Pick-up** all models '73 thru '79
     720 Series Pick-up - see NISSAN (771)
376   **810/Maxima** all gasoline models, '77 thru '84
368   **F10** all models '76 thru '79
     Pulsar - see NISSAN (876)
     Sentra - see NISSAN (982)
     Stanza - see NISSAN (981)

DODGE

     400 & 600 - see CHRYSLER Mid-size (1337)
*723   **Aries & Plymouth Reliant** '81 thru '89
*1231   **Caravan & Plymouth Voyager Mini-Vans** all models '84 thru '93
699   **Challenger & Plymouth Saporro** all models '78 thru '83
     Challenger '67-'76 - see DODGE Dart (234)
236   **Colt** all models '71 thru '77
610   **Colt & Plymouth Champ (front wheel drive)** all models '78 thru '87
*1668   **Dakota Pick-ups** all models '87 thru '93
234   **Dart, Challenger/Plymouth Barracuda & Valiant** 6 cyl models '67 thru '76
*1140   **Daytona & Chrysler Laser** '84 thru '89
*545   **Omni & Plymouth Horizon** '78 thru '90
*912   **Pick-ups** all full-size models '74 thru '91
*556   **Ram 50/D50 Pick-ups & Raider and Plymouth Arrow Pick-ups** '79 thru '93
*1726   **Shadow & Plymouth Sundance** '87 thru '93
*1779   **Spirit & Plymouth Acclaim** '89 thru '92
*349   **Vans - Dodge & Plymouth** V8 & 6 cyl models '71 thru '91

EAGLE

     Talon - see Mitsubishi Eclipse (2097)

FIAT

094   **124 Sport Coupe & Spider** '68 thru '78
273   **X1/9** all models '74 thru '80

FORD

*1476   **Aerostar Mini-vans** all models '86 thru '92
788   **Bronco and Pick-ups** '73 thru '79
*880   **Bronco and Pick-ups** '80 thru '91
268   **Courier Pick-up** all models '72 thru '82
1763   **Ford Engine Overhaul Manual**
789   **Escort/Mercury Lynx** all models '81 thru '90
*2046   **Escort/Mercury Tracer** '91 thru '93
*2021   **Explorer & Mazda Navajo** '91 thru '92
560   **Fairmont & Mercury Zephyr** '78 thru '83
334   **Fiesta** all models '77 thru '80
754   **Ford & Mercury Full-size,** Ford LTD & Mercury Marquis ('75 thru '82); Ford Custom 500,Country Squire, Crown Victoria & Mercury Colony Park ('75 thru '87); Ford LTD Crown Victoria & Mercury Gran Marquis ('83 thru '87)
359   **Granada & Mercury Monarch** all in-line, 6 cyl & V8 models '75 thru '80
773   **Ford & Mercury Mid-size,** Ford Thunderbird & Mercury Cougar ('75 thru '82); Ford LTD & Mercury Marquis ('83 thru '86); Ford Torino,Gran Torino, Elite, Ranchero pick-up, LTD II, Mercury Montego, Comet, XR-7 & Lincoln Versailles ('75 thru '86)
*654   **Mustang & Mercury Capri** all models including Turbo. Mustang, '79 thru '92; Capri, '79 thru '86
357   **Mustang V8** all models '64-1/2 thru '73
231   **Mustang II** 4 cyl, V6 & V8 models '74 thru '78
649   **Pinto & Mercury Bobcat** '75 thru '80
1670   **Probe** all models '89 thru '92
*1026   **Ranger/Bronco II** gasoline models '83 thru '93
*1421   **Taurus & Mercury Sable** '86 thru '92
*1418   **Tempo & Mercury Topaz** all gasoline models '84 thru '93
1338   **Thunderbird/Mercury Cougar** '83 thru '88
*1725   **Thunderbird/Mercury Cougar** '89 and '90
*344   **Vans** all V8 Econoline models '69 thru '91

GENERAL MOTORS

*829   **Buick Century, Chevrolet Celebrity, Oldsmobile Cutlass Ciera & Pontiac 6000** all models '82 thru '93
*766   **Buick Skyhawk, Cadillac Cimarron, Chevrolet Cavalier, Oldsmobile Firenza & Pontiac J-2000 & Sunbird** all models '82 thru '92
1420   **Buick Skylark & Somerset, Oldsmobile Calais, Pontiac Grand Am** all models '85 thru '91
*1671   **Buick Regal, Chevrolet Lumina, Oldsmobile Cutlass Supreme & Pontiac Grand Prix** all front wheel drive models '88 thru '90
*2035   **Chevrolet Lumina APV, Oldsmobile Silhouette & Pontiac Trans Sport** all models '90 thru '92

GEO

     Metro - see CHEVROLET Sprint (1727)
     Prizm - see CHEVROLET Nova (1642)
*2039   **Storm** all models '90 thru '93
     Tracker - see SUZUKI Samurai (1626)

GMC

     Safari - see CHEVROLET ASTRO (1477)
     Vans & Pick-ups - see CHEVROLET (420, 831, 345, 1664)

(Continued on other side)

Haynes North America, Inc., 861 Lawrence Drive, Newbury Park, CA 91320 • (805) 498-6703

HAYNES AUTOMOTIVE MANUALS

NOTE: New manuals are added to this list on a periodic basis. If you do not see a listing for your vehicle, consult your local Haynes dealer for the latest product information.

HONDA

351	**Accord CVCC** all models '76 thru '83
1221	**Accord** all models '84 thru '89
2067	**Accord** all models '90 thru '93
160	**Civic 1200** all models '73 thru '79
633	**Civic 1300 & 1500 CVCC** '80 thru '83
297	**Civic 1500 CVCC** all models '75 thru '79
1227	**Civic** all models '84 thru '91
*601	**Prelude CVCC** all models '79 thru '89

HYUNDAI

*1552	**Excel** all models '86 thru '93

ISUZU

*1641	**Trooper & Pick-up,** all gasoline models Pick-up, '81 thru '93; Trooper, '84 thru '91

JAGUAR

*242	**XJ6** all 6 cyl models '68 thru '86
*478	**XJ12 & XJS** all 12 cyl models '72 thru '85

JEEP

*1553	**Cherokee, Comanche & Wagoneer Limited** all models '84 thru '93
412	**CJ** all models '49 thru '86
*1777	**Wrangler** all models '87 thru '92

LADA

*413	**1200, 1300. 1500 & 1600** all models including Riva '74 thru '91

MAZDA

648	**626 Sedan & Coupe (rear wheel drive)** all models '79 thru '82
*1082	**626 & MX-6 (front wheel drive)** all models '83 thru '91
267	**B Series Pick-ups** '72 thru '93
370	**GLC Hatchback (rear wheel drive)** all models '77 thru '83
757	**GLC (front wheel drive)** '81 thru '85
*2047	**MPV** all models '89 thru '93
460	**RX-7** all models '79 thru '85
*1419	**RX-7** all models '86 thru '91

MERCEDES-BENZ

*1643	**190 Series** all four-cylinder gasoline models, '84 thru '88
346	**230, 250 & 280** Sedan, Coupe & Roadster all 6 cyl sohc models '68 thru '72
983	**280 123 Series** gasoline models '77 thru '81
698	**350 & 450** Sedan, Coupe & Roadster all models '71 thru '80
697	**Diesel 123 Series** 200D, 220D, 240D, 240TD, 300D, 300CD, 300TD, 4- & 5-cyl incl. Turbo '76 thru '85

MERCURY

See FORD Listing

MG

111	**MGB** Roadster & GT Coupe all models '62 thru '80
265	**MG Midget & Austin Healey Sprite** Roadster '58 thru '80

MITSUBISHI

*1669	**Cordia, Tredia, Galant, Precis & Mirage** '83 thru '93
*2022	**Pick-up & Montero** '83 thru '93
*2097	**Eclipse, Eagle Talon & Plymouth Laser** '90 thru '94

MORRIS

074	**(Austin) Marina 1.8** all models '71 thru '78
024	**Minor 1000** sedan & wagon '56 thru '71

NISSAN

1137	**300ZX** all models including Turbo '84 thru '89
*1341	**Maxima** all models '85 thru '91
*771	**Pick-ups/Pathfinder** gas models '80 thru '93
876	**Pulsar** all models '83 thru '86
*982	**Sentra** all models '82 thru '90
*981	**Stanza** all models '82 thru '90

OLDSMOBILE

	Bravada - see CHEVROLET S-10 (831)
	Calais - see GENERAL MOTORS (1420)
	Custom Cruiser - see BUICK Full-size RWD (1551)
*658	**Cutlass** all standard gasoline V6 & V8 models '74 thru '88
	Cutlass Ciera - see GENERAL MOTORS (829)
	Cutlass Supreme - see GM (1671)
	Delta 88 - see BUICK Full-size RWD (1551)
	Delta 88 Brougham - see BUICK Full-size FWD (1551), RWD (1627)
	Delta 88 Royale - see BUICK Full-size RWD (1551)
	Firenza - see GENERAL MOTORS (766)
	Ninety-eight Regency - see BUICK Full-size RWD (1551), FWD (1627)
	Ninety-eight Regency Brougham - see BUICK Full-size RWD (1551)
	Omega - see PONTIAC Phoenix (551)
	Silhouette - see GENERAL MOTORS (2035)

PEUGEOT

663	**504** all diesel models '74 thru '83

PLYMOUTH

	Laser - see MITSUBISHI Eclipse (2097)
	For other PLYMOUTH titles, see DODGE listing.

PONTIAC

	T1000 - see CHEVROLET Chevette (449)
	J-2000 - see GENERAL MOTORS (766)
	6000 - see GENERAL MOTORS (829)
	Bonneville - see Buick Full-size FWD (1627), RWD (1551)
	Bonneville Brougham - see Buick Full-size (1551)
	Catalina - see Buick Full-size (1551)
1232	**Fiero** all models '84 thru '88
555	**Firebird** V8 models except Turbo '70 thru '81
867	**Firebird** all models '82 thru '92
	Full-size Rear Wheel Drive - see BUICK Oldsmobile, Pontiac Full-size RWD (1551)
	Full-size Front Wheel Drive - see BUICK Oldsmobile, Pontiac Full-size FWD (1627)
	Grand Am - see GENERAL MOTORS (1420)
	Grand Prix - see GENERAL MOTORS (1671)
	Grandville - see BUICK Full-size (1551)
	Parisienne - see BUICK Full-size (1551)
551	**Phoenix & Oldsmobile Omega** all X-car models '80 thru '84
	Sunbird - see GENERAL MOTORS (766)
	Trans Sport - see GENERAL MOTORS (2035)

PORSCHE

*264	**911** all Coupe & Targa models except Turbo & Carrera 4 '65 thru '89
239	**914** all 4 cyl models '69 thru '76
397	**924** all models including Turbo '76 thru '82
*1027	**944** all models including Turbo '83 thru '89

RENAULT

141	**5 Le Car** all models '76 thru '83
079	**8 & 10** 58.4 cu in engines '62 thru '72
097	**12 Saloon & Estate** 1289 cc engine '70 thru '80
768	**15 & 17** all models '73 thru '79
081	**16** 89.7 cu in & 95.5 cu in engines '65 thru '72
	Alliance & Encore - see AMC (934)

SAAB

247	**99** all models including Turbo '69 thru '80
*980	**900** all models including Turbo '79 thru '88

SUBARU

237	**1100, 1300, 1400 & 1600** '71 thru '79
*681	**1600 & 1800** 2WD & 4WD '80 thru '89

SUZUKI

*1626	**Samurai/Sidekick and Geo Tracker** all models '86 thru '93

TOYOTA

1023	**Camry** all models '83 thru '91
150	**Carina** Sedan all models '71 thru '74
935	**Celica Rear Wheel Drive** '71 thru '85
*2038	**Celica Front Wheel Drive** '86 thru '92
1139	**Celica Supra** all models '79 thru '92
361	**Corolla** all models '75 thru '79
961	**Corolla** all rear wheel drive models '80 thru '87
*1025	**Corolla** all front wheel drive models '84 thru '92
636	**Corolla Tercel** all models '80 thru '82
360	**Corona** all models '74 thru '82
532	**Cressida** all models '78 thru '82
313	**Land Cruiser** all models '68 thru '82
200	**MK II** all 6 cyl models '72 thru '76
*1339	**MR2** all models '85 thru '87
304	**Pick-up** all models '69 thru '78
*656	**Pick-up** all models '79 thru '92
*2048	**Previa** all models '91 thru '93

TRIUMPH

112	**GT6 & Vitesse** all models '62 thru '74
113	**Spitfire** all models '62 thru '81
322	**TR7** all models '75 thru '81

VW

159	**Beetle & Karmann Ghia** all models '54 thru '79
238	**Dasher** all gasoline models '74 thru '81
*884	**Rabbit, Jetta, Scirocco, & Pick-up** gas models '74 thru '91 & Convertible '80 thru '92
451	**Rabbit, Jetta & Pick-up** all diesel models '77 thru '84
082	**Transporter 1600** all models '68 thru '79
226	**Transporter 1700, 1800 & 2000** all models '72 thru '79
084	**Type 3 1500 & 1600** all models '63 thru '73
1029	**Vanagon** all air-cooled models '80 thru '83

VOLVO

203	**120, 130 Series & 1800 Sports** '61 thru '73
129	**140 Series** all models '66 thru '74
*270	**240 Series** all models '74 thru '90
400	**260 Series** all models '75 thru '82
*1550	**740 & 760 Series** all models '82 thru '88

SPECIAL MANUALS

1479	**Automotive Body Repair & Painting Manual**
1654	**Automotive Electrical Manual**
1667	**Automotive Emissions Control Manual**
1480	**Automotive Heating & Air Conditioning Manual**
1762	**Chevrolet Engine Overhaul Manual**
1736	**GM and Ford Diesel Engine Repair Manual**
1763	**Ford Engine Overhaul Manual**
482	**Fuel Injection Manual**
2069	**Holley Carburetor Manual**
1666	**Small Engine Repair Manual**
299	**SU Carburetors** thru '88
393	**Weber Carburetors** thru '79
300	**Zenith/Stromberg CD Carburetors** thru '76

*Listings shown with an asterisk (*) indicate model coverage as of this printing. These titles will be periodically updated to include later model years - consult your Haynes dealer for more information.

Over 100 Haynes motorcycle manuals also available

5-94

Haynes North America, Inc., 861 Lawrence Drive, Newbury Park, CA 91320 • (805) 498-6703